COGNITIVE SCIENCE
Third Edition

SAGE | 50 YEARS

COGNITIVE SCIENCE

An Introduction to the Study of Mind

Third Edition

Jay Friedenberg
Manhattan College

Gordon Silverman
Manhattan College

Los Angeles | London | New Delhi
Singapore | Washington DC

Los Angeles | London | New Delhi
Singapore | Washington DC

FOR INFORMATION:

SAGE Publications, Inc.
2455 Teller Road
Thousand Oaks, California 91320
E-mail: order@sagepub.com

SAGE Publications Ltd.
1 Oliver's Yard
55 City Road
London EC1Y 1SP
United Kingdom

SAGE Publications India Pvt. Ltd.
B 1/I 1 Mohan Cooperative Industrial Area
Mathura Road, New Delhi 110 044
India

SAGE Publications Asia-Pacific Pte. Ltd.
3 Church Street
#10-04 Samsung Hub
Singapore 049483

Acquisitions Editor: Reid Hester
Editorial Assistant: Morgan McCardell
eLearning Editor: Robert Higgins
Production Editor: Kelly DeRosa
Copy Editor: QuADS Prepress (P) Ltd.
Typesetter: C&M Digitals (P) Ltd.
Proofreader: Susan Schon
Indexer: Jean Casalegno
Cover Designer: Michael Dubowe
Marketing Manager: Shari Countryman

Printed in the United States of America

Library of Congress Cataloging-in-Publication Data

Friedenberg, Jay.

Cognitive science: an introduction to the study of mind / Jay Friedenberg, Manhattan College, Gordon Silverman, Manhattan College. — Third Edition.

pages cm
Revised edition of the authors' Cognitive science, 2012.
Includes bibliographical references and index.

ISBN 978-1-4833-4741-7 (pbk. : alk. paper)

1. Cognitive science. I. Silverman, Gordon. II. Title.

BF311.F743 2015
153—dc23   2015015153

This book is printed on acid-free paper.

SUSTAINABLE FORESTRY INITIATIVE
Certified Chain of Custody
Promoting Sustainable Forestry
www.sfiprogram.org
SFI-01268
SFI label applies to text stock

16 17 18 19 10 9 8 7 6 5 4 3 2

CONTENTS

DETAILED CONTENTS

PREFACE

One of the most challenging mysteries remaining to science is the human mind. The brain that forms the basis of mind is the most complex object in the universe. It is made up of billions of cells sending signals back and forth to each other over many more billions of connections. How can we make sense of all this? Recent years have seen great strides in our understanding, and this has been due in part to developments in technology. In this book, we provide an up-to-date introduction to the study of mind, examining it from an interdisciplinary perspective. We attempt to understand the mind from the perspective of different fields. Among these are philosophy, psychology, neuroscience, networks, evolution, emotional and social cognition, linguistics, artificial intelligence, and robotics. Beyond this, we make attempts to bridge some of these fields, showing what research at the intersection of these disciplines is like. Each chapter in this text is devoted to a particular disciplinary approach and examines the methodologies, theories, and empirical findings unique to each. Come with us as we explore the next great frontier—our inner world.

WHAT'S NEW IN THIS EDITION

New content has been added throughout. The topic of empirical philosophy is introduced in Chapter 1 as an expanded section on formal systems, the physical symbol system hypothesis, and the symbol grounding problem. In Chapter 4, there is greater discussion on theories of pattern recognition and depth perception. One of the latest methods in neuroscience, the measuring and stimulation of individual neurons by light (optogenetics) is detailed in Chapter 6. In Chapter 8, the authors discuss the concept of neural markers for intelligence in animals and humans, what are called spindle neurons, as well as the idea of anthropodenial when observing animal behavior. Chapter 9 on language has an entirely new section on domain-specific versus domain-general mechanisms in language acquisition. New artificial intelligence programs with world knowledge and conversational skill are outlined in this chapter as well. Chapter 10 on emotions has substantially new information added on basic emotions and on the relationship between emotions, evolutionary processes, and psychological disorders. Chapter 12 includes substantially new information on cognitive computing and ongoing research related to fabrication of the neocortex. Chapter 13 introduces advanced robotic concepts and applications as well as thought control of bionic limbs. Finally, in Chapter 14, there is discussion of the "WEIRD" model of cross-cultural testing. Other new features and benefits include in-depth topics now inserted into the body of the text where they expand and apply general principles and added discussion that integrates the various perspectives in cognitive science more tightly. Chapter introductions better preview what is to come to help students organize information. There are also new figures and tables that help summarize and differentiate important definitions.

BEYOND THE BOOK

The text comes with many ancillary materials. A password-protected Instructor's Resource Site (http://study.sagepub.com/friedenberg3e) contains PowerPoint lectures, a test bank, and other pedagogical material. A Student Study Site is also available online at http://study.sagepub.com/friedenberg3e. It contains electronic flash cards of glossary terms, practice quizzes that allow students to assess their level of understanding, and various web links to explore selected topics in greater depth.

ACKNOWLEDGMENTS

We would like to acknowledge the efforts of our editors at SAGE for their assistance and the following reviewers:

Emanuel J. Mason, Professor, Northeastern University
R. I. Arriaga, Georgia Institute of Technology
Michael J. Tetzlaff, University of Maryland, College Park
Robin Andreasen, University of Delaware
Karl Haberlandt, Trinity College
Marc Pomplun, University of Massachusetts at Boston

A Matrix for Exploring Cognitive Science Across Disciplines

Chapter No.	Name/Title	Chapter Summary	Primary Topic/ Issues	Secondary Topic/Issues	Methodologies	Major Figures	Evaluation
1	Introduction	An introduction to cognitive science and summary overview of different perspectives	• Interdisciplinary study • Representation and computation • Interdisciplinary perspective • Categories of mental representation	• Concepts • Propositions • Production rules • Declarative and procedural knowledge • Analogies	No methodologies discussed	• Thagard • Harnish • Pylyshyn • Marr	Cognitive science is unique in that it binds together different perspectives and methodologies in the study of mind
2	The Philosophical Approach	The search for wisdom and knowledge; frames broad questions about mind	• The mind–body problem • Functionalism • Knowledge acquisition • Consciousness	• Monism • Dualism • Nature–nurture debate • Reductionism • Emergence	• Deductive and inductive reasoning	• Aristotle • Plato • Berkeley • Democritus • Descartes • Ryle • Clark • Hume • Locke • Chalmers • Nagel • Jackson • Searle • Churchland • Dennett	Provides a broad perspective; asks fundamental questions; not an empirical approach
3	The Psychological Approach	The scientific study of mind and behavior	• The scientific method • Voluntarism • Structuralism • Functionalism • Gestalt psychology • Psychoanalytic psychology • Behaviorism	• Theory and hypothesis • Independent and dependent variables • Experimental and control groups • Stream of consciousness • Levels of consciousness	• Scientific method • Introspection • Phenomenology	• Wundt • Titchener • James • Wertheimer • Koffka • Kohler • Freud • Watson • Pavlov • Skinner	Multiple theoretical positions; first systematic and scientific study of mental phenomena; problems with introspection and phenomenology
4	The Cognitive Approach I	The information-processing view of mind; use of a computer as a metaphor for mind; use of process models and assumption of modularity	• Information-processing perspective • Modularity • Pattern recognition • Attention	• Template matching • Feature detection • Computational vision • Feature integration theory • Models of attention	• Experimentation • Modeling	• Neisser • Fodor • Selfridge • Norman • Marr • Treisman • Broadbent • Deutch • Posner • Snyder • Kahneman • Biederman	Fruitful synergistic use of experimentation and model building

Chapter No.	Name/Title	Chapter Summary	Primary Topic/Issues	Secondary Topic/Issues	Methodologies	Major Figures	Evaluation
5	The Cognitive Approach II	The information-processing view of mind; use of a computer as a metaphor for mind; use of process models and assumption of modularity (Same as Cognitive Approach I chapter)	• Memory • Models of memory • Visual imagery • Problem solving	• Memory types: sensory, working, and long-term • The modal, ACT*, and working memory models • The Kosslyn-Schwartz theory of visual imagery • Heuristics • Means-ends analysis • The GPS and SOAR models	• Experimentation • Modeling • Same as Cognitive Approach I chapter	• Sperling • Baddeley • Atkinson • Shiffrin • Anderson • Kosslyn • Block • Newell • Simon • Sternberg	Common set of assumptions underlying information processing and modularity; concepts of representation and computation need to be reconciled with connectionism
6	The Neuroscience Approach	The study of nervous system anatomy and physiology that underlies and gives rise to cognitive function	• Neuroscience methodology • Neuron anatomy and physiology • Brain anatomy • Neuroscience of visual object recognition, attention, memory, executive function, and problem solving	• The split brain • Dorsal and ventral pathways • Agnosias • Plasticity • Hippocampal function • Action schemas and scripts • Metacognition • Binding and neural synchrony	• Case studies • Lesion studies • Cell recording techniques • EEG, ERP, CAT, PET, and fMRI • MEG and TMS	• Sperry • Sacks • Humphreys • Posner • Lashley • Hebb • Shallice • Engel • Singer	The marriage of cognitive and neuroscience perspectives in cognitive neuroscience is a good integrative approach; specification of biological structures and processes of cognitive abilities
7	The Network Approach	View of mind as an interconnected set of nodes or web; processing consists of the spread of activation through the web	• Serial and parallel processing • Artificial neural networks • Semantic networks • Network science	• Perceptrons • Back propagation • Stability and plasticity • Catastrophic interference • Spreading activation • Retrieval cues • Priming • Propositional networks • Small-world networks	• Software simulations of artificial neural networks • Comparison of results with theory and empirical data	• McCulloch • Pitts • Hopfield • Kohonen • Grossberg • Collins • Quillian • Rumelhart • McClelland • Watts • Strogatz • Buchanan	Significant advantages to using networks for understanding learning and knowledge representation; challenges in building networks that rival the brain

(Continued)

(Continued)

Chapter No.	Name/Title	Chapter Summary	Primary Topic/Issues	Secondary Topic/Issues	Methodologies	Major Figures	Evaluation
8	The Evolutionary Approach	Mind as the adapted product of selection forces	• Natural selection • Evolved psychological mechanisms • Comparative cognition • Evolution and cognitive processes • Behavioral economics • Artificial life	• General purpose versus domain-specific view of mind • Wason selection task • Heuristics and fallacies • Exaptation, molecular drive, and spandrels	• Experimentation • Cross-species comparison	• Darwin • Buss • Cosmides • Tooby • Edelman	Powerful theoretical framework, but not all mental processes may be adaptive; good integration with neuroscience; domain-specific processing view clashes with general-purpose processor view
9	The Linguistic Approach	The multidisciplinary study of language	• The nature of language • Primate language use • Language acquisition • Language deprivation • Linguistic relativity hypothesis • Grammar • The Wernicke-Geschwind model • Natural language processing	• Phonology and morphology • Syntax and semantics • Animal language studies • Critical period • Second-language acquisition • Phrase structure, transformational and universal grammar • Aphasias • Speech recognition • Pragmatic analysis	• Case studies • Developmental studies • Experimentation	• Gardner • Premack • Savage-Rumbaugh • Sapir • Whorf • Chomsky • Broca • Wernicke	Multiple perspectives and techniques brought to bear on the complex cognitive topic of language; advances in computer-based language comprehension
10	The Emotional Approach	Emotions and moods influence all major cognitive processes and should be incorporated into cognitive theories and models of mind	• Emergence synthesis approach • Flashbulb and autobiographical memory • Mood-congruent and mood-dependent memory • Role of synapses in emotional processing • Affective computing	• Evolutionary accounts of psychological disorders • Analytical rumination hypothesis • The feel-good, do-good phenomenon • CogAff architecture • Social robots	• Experimentation • The Iowa Gambling Task	• Damasio • Fox • Minsky • Solomon	Need for an understanding of information flow and neural circuits that underlie emotions and how these impact thought; more work needed on how cognitions affect emotions

Chapter No.	Name/Title	Chapter Summary	Primary Topic/Issues	Secondary Topic/Issues	Methodologies	Major Figures	Evaluation
11	The Social Approach	Thinking about people is different from thinking about objects; social cognitive neuroscience is a good example of the interdisciplinary approach	• Mirror neurons • Theory of mind • Attitudes • Cognitive dissonance • Impressions • Attributions • Stereotyping • Prejudice	• Anterior and posterior attention systems • Autism • Prisoner's dilemma	• Brain imaging • The ultimatum game • Social dilemmas	• Fiske • Ochsner and Lieberman • Rizzolatti • Siegal and Varley • Frith • Schacter	Automatic versus effortful processing is a common theme; the historical focus on the individual is too narrow, cognitive science must embrace the social environment
12	The Artificial Intelligence Approach	Defining the concept of artificial intelligence; machine representation of cognitive function	• Historical perspective • Influence of Turing • Predictive architectures • Artificial general intelligence • Agent-based architectures: Multiagent systems	• Universal computation • Chatbots • Evolutionary computing	• Cognitive models • Turing Test	• Turing • Minsky • Kurzweil • Craik • Hawkins • Russell • Norvig • McCarthy • Goertzel	New computational technologies may lead to the densities required to achieve the requirements needed to implement an intelligence that is beyond the human level; a fundamental dilemma persists: "Brains must have programs yet at the same time must not be programmed."
13	Intelligent Agents and Robots	The intelligent agent (IA) paradigm; applying the principles to the design of IAs; cognitive models of IAs; robotic embodiments; biological and social influences on robots	• Importance of biology • Embodiment and situational aspects of IA (structure) • Expert systems • Building a brain • Robotic architectures	• Hierarchical, reactive, hybrid robotic architectures • Emotion in IAs	• Cognitive modeling • Simulation	• Turing • Minsky • Brooks • Russell • Norvig • Breazeal • Arkin	In some activities, machines already outperform humans; a great many problems need to be addressed in the future: perception, finely honed reasoning, and manipulative capabilities of adult humans; the more we try to replicate human intelligence, the more we may learn to appreciate and understand humans

(Continued)

(Continued)

Chapter No.	Name/Title	Chapter Summary	Primary Topic/Issues	Secondary Topic/Issues	Methodologies	Major Figures	Evaluation
14	Conclusion	An evaluation of the cognitive science approach	• Cognitive science needs to do a better job explaining physical environments, individual and cultural differences, and consciousness • The dynamical systems approach	• Predictability • Randomness • Constructivism	• Nonlinear modeling • Use of state space, trajectories, and attractors to describe cognitive phenomena	• Guastello • Gibson • Dreyfus • Brooks • Wilson • Spivey	Benefits of cognitive science are many and widespread throughout engineering, medicine, education, and other fields; lack of a single unified theory

ABOUT THE AUTHORS

Jay Friedenberg is Professor of the Psychology Department at Manhattan College, where he directs the Cognitive Science Program. He is interested in both vision and the philosophy of mind. He teaches courses in physiological psychology, cognition and learning, sensation and perception, and artificial intelligence and robotics. He has published several articles on visual estimation of center of mass. His current research projects focus on the aesthetics of geometrical shapes. He has published books on artificial intelligence, dynamical systems theory, and psychology. He is a member of the International Association of Empirical Aesthetics, the Eastern Psychological Association, the Vision Science Society, the Psychonomic Society, and Phi Beta Kappa. He obtained his PhD in cognitive psychology in 1995 at the University of Virginia.

Gordon Silverman is Professor Emeritus of Electrical and Computer Engineering at Manhattan College. His professional career spans more than 55 years of corporate, teaching, consulting, and research experience, during which he has developed a range of scientific instruments, particularly for use in physiological psychology research environments. He is the holder of eight patents, some related to behavior modification. The author of more than 20 journal articles and books, he has also served on the faculties of The Rockefeller University and Fairleigh Dickinson University. His current research interests include telemedicine, rehabilitation medicine, artificial intelligence, and biomedical instrumentation and modeling. He holds engineering degrees from Columbia University and received a PhD in system science from New York University Polytechnic School of Engineering in 1972.

1

INTRODUCTION

Exploring Inner Space

The sciences have developed in an order the reverse of what might have been expected. What was most remote from ourselves was first brought under the domain of law, and then, gradually, what was nearer: first the heavens, next the earth, then animal and vegetable life, then the human body, and last of all (as yet very imperfectly) the human mind.

—Bertrand Russell, 1935

A BRAVE NEW WORLD

We are in the midst of a revolution. For centuries, science has made great strides in our understanding of the external observable world. Physics revealed the motion of the planets, chemistry discovered the fundamental elements of matter, and biology has told us how to understand and treat disease. But during much of this time, there were still many unanswered questions about something perhaps even more important to us—the human mind.

What makes mind so difficult to study is that, unlike the phenomena described above, it is not something we can easily observe, measure, or manipulate. In addition, the mind is the most complex entity in the known universe. To give you a sense of this complexity, consider the following. The human brain is estimated to contain 10 billion to 100 billion individual nerve cells or neurons. Each of these neurons can have as many as 10,000 connections to other neurons. This vast web is the basis of mind and gives rise to all the equally amazing and difficult-to-understand mental phenomena, such as perception, memory, and language.

The past several decades have seen the introduction of new technologies and methodologies for studying this intriguing organ. We have learned more about the mind in the past half-century than in all the time that came before that. This period of rapid discovery has coincided with an increase in the number of different disciplines—many of them entirely new—that study mind. Since then, a coordinated effort among the practitioners of these disciplines has come to pass. This interdisciplinary approach has since become known as cognitive science. Unlike the science that came before, which was focused on the world of external, observable phenomena, or "outer space," this new endeavor now turns its full attention to the discovery of our fascinating mental world, or "inner space."

WHAT IS COGNITIVE SCIENCE?

Cognitive science can be roughly summed up as the scientific interdisciplinary study of the mind. Its primary methodology is the scientific method—although, as we will see, many other methodologies also contribute. A hallmark of cognitive science is its interdisciplinary approach. It results from the efforts of researchers working in a wide array of fields. These include philosophy, psychology, linguistics, artificial intelligence (AI), robotics, and neuroscience. Each field brings with it a unique set of tools and perspectives. One major goal of this book is to show that when it comes to studying something as complex as the mind, no single perspective is adequate. Instead, intercommunication and cooperation among the practitioners of these disciplines tell us much more.

The term *cognitive science* refers not so much to the sum of all these disciplines but to their intersection or converging work on specific problems. In this sense, cognitive science is not a unified field of study like each of the disciplines themselves but, rather, a collaborative effort among researchers working in the various fields. The glue that holds cognitive science together is the topic of mind and, for the most part, the use of scientific methods. In the concluding chapter, we talk more about the issue of how unified cognitive science really is.

To understand what cognitive science is all about, we need to know what its theoretical perspective on the mind is. This perspective centers on the idea of computation, which may alternatively be called information processing. Cognitive scientists view the mind as an information processor. Information processors must both represent and transform information. That is, a mind, according to this perspective, must incorporate some form of mental representation and processes that act on and manipulate that information. We will discuss these two ideas in greater detail later in this chapter.

Cognitive science is often credited with being influenced by the rise of the computer. Computers are, of course, information processors. Think for a minute about a personal computer. It performs a variety of information-processing tasks. Information gets into the computer via input devices, such as a keyboard or modem. That information can then be stored on the computer—for example, on a hard drive or other disk. The information can then be processed using software, such as a text editor. The results of this processing may next serve as output, either to a monitor or to a printer. In like fashion, we may think of people performing similar tasks. Information is "input" into our minds through perception—what we see or hear. It is stored in our memories and processed in the form of thought. Our thoughts can then serve as the basis of "outputs," such as language or physical behavior.

Of course, this analogy between the human mind and computers is highly abstract. The actual physical way in which data are stored on a computer bears little resemblance to human memory formation. But both systems are characterized by computation. In fact, it is not going too far to say that cognitive scientists view the mind as a machine or mechanism whose workings they are trying to understand.

REPRESENTATION

As mentioned before, representation is fundamental to cognitive science. But what is a representation? Briefly stated, a representation is something that stands for something else. Before listing the characteristics of a representation, it is helpful to describe briefly four categories of representation. A concept stands for a single entity or group of entities. Single words are good examples of concepts. The word *apple* denotes the concept of that particular type of fruit. Propositions are statements about the world and can be illustrated with sentences. The sentence "Mary has black hair" is a proposition that is itself made up of concepts. Rules are yet another form of representation that can specify the relationships between propositions. For example, the rule "If it is raining, I will bring my umbrella" makes the second proposition contingent on the first. There are also analog representations. An analogy helps us make comparisons between two similar situations. We will discuss all four of these representations in greater detail in the "Interdisciplinary Crossroads" section at the end of this chapter.

There are four crucial aspects of any representation (Hartshorne, Weiss, & Burks, 1931–1958). First, a "representation bearer" such as a human or a computer must realize a representation. Second, a representation must have content—meaning it stands for one or more objects. The thing or things in the external world that a representation stands for are called referents. A representation must also be "grounded." That is, there must be some way in which the representation and its referent come to be related. Fourth, a representation must be interpretable by some interpreter, either the representation bearer or somebody else. These and other characteristics of representations are discussed next.

The fact that a representation stands for something else means it is symbolic. We are all familiar with symbols. We know, for instance, that the dollar symbol ($) is used to stand for money. The symbol itself is not the money but, instead, is a surrogate that refers to its referent, which is actual money. In the case of mental representation, we say that there is some symbolic entity "in the head" that stands for real money. Figure 1.1 shows a visual representation of money. Mental representations can stand for many different types of things and are by no means limited to simple conceptual ideas such as "money." Research

Figure 1.1 Different aspects of the symbolic representation of money.

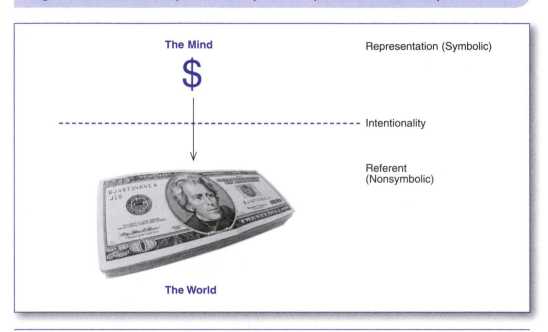

The Mind — Representation (Symbolic)

$

Intentionality

Referent (Nonsymbolic)

The World

Source: PhotoObjects.net/Thinkstock.

suggests that there are more complex mental representations that can stand for rules—for example, knowing how to drive a car and analogies, which may enable us to solve certain problems or notice similarities (Thagard, 2000).

Human mental representations, especially linguistic ones, are said to be **semantic**, which is to say that they have meaning. Exactly what constitutes meaning and how a representation can come to be meaningful are topics of debate. According to one view, a representation's meaning is derived from the relationship between the representation and what it is about. The term that describes this relation is **intentionality**. Intentionality means "directed on an object." Mental states and events are intentional. They refer to some actual thing or things in the world. If you think about your brother, then the thought of your brother is directed toward him—not toward your sister, a cloud, or some other object.

An important characteristic of intentionality has to do with the relationship between inputs and outputs to the world. An intentional representation must be triggered by its referent or things related to it. Consequently, activation of a representation (i.e., thinking about it) should cause behaviors or actions that are somehow related to the referent. For example, if your friend Sally told you about a cruise she took around the Caribbean last December, an image of a cruise ship would probably pop to mind. This might then cause you to ask her if the food onboard was good. Sally's mention of the cruise was the stimulus input that activated the internal representation of the ship in your mind. Once it was activated, it caused the behavior of asking about the food. This relation between inputs and outputs is known as an **appropriate causal relation**.

Symbols can be assembled into what are called physical symbol systems, or more simply as formal systems. In a **formal system**, symbols are combined into expressions. These expressions can then be manipulated using processes. The result of a process can be a new expression. For example, in formal logic, symbols can be words like "all" or "mammals" and expressions could be statements like "all mammals nurse their young." The processes would be the rules of deduction that allow us to derive true concluding expressions from known expressions. In this instance, we could start off with the two expressions "all mammals nurse their young," "whales nurse their young," therefore "whales are mammals." More on this below where we discuss propositions and syllogisms.

According to the **physical symbol system hypothesis (PSSH)**, a formal system can allow for intelligence (Newell & Simon, 1976). Since we as humans appear to have representational and computational capacity being able to use things that stand for things, we seem to be intelligent. Beyond this, we could also infer that machines are intelligent, since they too have this capacity, although of course, this is debated.

There are several critiques that have been leveled against the PSSH (Nilsson, 2007). First, it is argued that the symbols computers use have no meaning or semantic quality. To be meaningful, symbols have to be connected to the environment in some way. People and perhaps animals seem to have meaning because we have bodies and can perceive things and act on them. This "grounds" the symbols and imbues them with semantic quality. Since machines are not embodied, they cannot acquire meaning. This issue is known as **the symbol grounding problem** and is in effect a re-expression of the concept of intentionality.

A counterargument to this is that computer systems do have the capability to **designate**. An expression can designate an object if it can affect the object itself or behave in ways that depend on the object. One could argue that a robot capable of perceiving an object like a coffee mug and able to pick it up could develop semantics toward it in the same way that a person might. Ergo, the robot could be intelligent. Also, there are examples of AI programs like expert systems that have no sensor or effector capability yet are able to produce intelligent and useful results. Some expert systems, like MYCIN, are able to more accurately diagnose certain medical disorders than are members of the Stanford University medical school (Cawsey, 1998). They can do this despite being able to see or act in the world.

Types of Representation

The history of research in cognition suggests that there are numerous forms of mental representation. Paul Thagard (2000), in *Mind: Introduction to Cognitive Science*, propose four: concepts, propositions, rules, and analogies. Although some of these have already been alluded to and are described elsewhere in the book, they are central to many ideas in cognitive science. It is, therefore, useful to sketch out some of their major characteristics here.

A **concept** is perhaps the most basic form of mental representation. A concept is an idea that represents things we have grouped together. The concept "chair" does not refer to a specific chair, such as the one you are sitting in now, but it is more general than that. It refers to all possible chairs no matter what their colors, sizes, and shapes. Concepts need not refer to concrete items. They can stand for abstract ideas—for example, "justice" or "love." Concepts can be related to one another in complex ways. They can be related in a hierarchical fashion, where a concept at one level of organization stands for all members of the class just below it. "Golden retrievers" belongs to the category of "dogs," which in turn belongs to the category of "animals." We discuss a hierarchical model of concept representation in the network approach chapter. The question of whether concepts are innate or learned is discussed in the philosophical approach chapter.

A **proposition** is a statement or assertion typically posed in the form of a simple sentence. An essential feature of a proposition is that it can be proved true or false. For instance, the statement "The moon is made out of cheese" is grammatically correct and may represent a belief that some people hold, but it is a false statement. We can apply the rules of formal logic to propositions to determine the validity of those propositions. One logical inference is called a syllogism. A syllogism consists of three propositions. The first two are premises and the last is a conclusion. Take the following syllogism:

All men like football.

John is a man.

John likes football.

Obviously, the conclusion can be wrong if either of the two premises is wrong. If it is not true that all men like football, then it might not be true that John likes football, even if he is a man. If John is not a man, then he may or may not like football, assuming all men like it. Syllogistic reasoning of this sort is the same as deductive reasoning mentioned earlier.

You may have noticed that propositions are representations that incorporate concepts. The proposition "All men like football" incorporates the concepts "men" and "football." Propositions are more sophisticated representations than concepts because they express relationships—sometimes very complex ones—between concepts. The rules of logic are best thought of as computational processes that can be applied to propositions to determine their validity. However, logical relations between propositions may themselves be considered a separate type of representation. The evolutionary approach chapter provides an interesting account of why logical reasoning, which is difficult for many people, is easier under certain circumstances.

Logic is not the only system for performing operations on propositions. Rules do this as well. A **production rule** is a conditional statement of the following form: "If x, then y," where x and y are propositions. The "if" part of the rule is called the condition; the "then" part is called the action. If the proposition that is contained in the condition (x) is true, then the action that is specified by the second proposition (y) should be carried out, according to the rule. The following rules help us drive our cars:

If the light is red, then step on the brakes.

If the light is green, then step on the accelerator.

Notice that, in the first rule, the two propositions are "the light is red" and "step on the brakes." We can also form more complex rules by linking propositions with "and" and "or" statements:

If the light is red or the light is yellow, then step on the brakes.

If the light is green and nobody is in the crosswalk, then step on the accelerator.

The *or* that links the two propositions in the first part of the rule specifies that if either proposition is true, the action should be carried out. If an *and* links these two propositions, the rule specifies that both must be true before the action can occur.

Rules bring up the question of what knowledge really is. We usually think of knowledge as factual. Indeed, a proposition such as "Candy is sweet," if validated, does provide factual information. The proposition is then an example of declarative knowledge. **Declarative knowledge** is used to represent facts. It tells us what is and is demonstrated by verbal communication. **Procedural knowledge**, on the other hand, represents skill. It tells us how to do something and is demonstrated by action. If we say that World War II was fought during the period 1939 to 1945, we have demonstrated a fact learned in history class. If we ski down a snowy mountain slope in the winter, we have demonstrated that we possess a specific skill. It is, therefore, very important that information-processing systems have some way of representing actions if they are to help an organism or machine perform those actions. Rules are one way of representing procedural knowledge. We discuss two cognitive, rule-based systems—the atomic components of thought and SOAR (state, operator, and result) models—in the cognitive approach chapters.

Another specific type of mental representation is the **analogy**—although, as is pointed out below, the analogy can also be classified as a form of reasoning. Thinking analogically involves applying one's familiarity with an old situation to a new situation. Suppose you had never ridden on a train before but had taken buses numerous times. You could use your understanding of bus riding to figure out how to take a ride on a train. Applying knowledge that you already possess and that is relevant to both scenarios would enable you to accomplish this. Based on prior experience, you would already know that you have to first determine the schedule, perhaps decide between express and local service, purchase a ticket, wait in line, board, stow your luggage, find a seat, and so on.

Analogies are a useful form of representation because they allow us to generalize our learning. Not every situation in life is entirely new. We can apply what we already have learned to similar situations without having to figure out everything all over again. Several models of analogical reasoning have been proposed (Forbus, Gentner, & Law, 1995; Holyoak & Thagard, 1995).

COMPUTATION

As mentioned earlier, representations are only the first key component of the cognitive science view of mental processes. Representations by themselves are of little use unless something can be done with them. Having the concept of money doesn't do much for us unless we know how to calculate a tip or can give back the correct amount of change to someone. In the cognitive science view, the mind performs computations on representations. It is, therefore, important to understand how and why these mental mechanisms operate.

What sorts of mental operations does the mind perform? If we wanted to get details about it, the list would be endless. Take the example of mathematical ability. If there were a separate mental operation for each step in a mathematical process, we could say the mind adds, subtracts, divides, and so on. Likewise, with language, we could say that there are separate mental operations for making a noun plural, putting a verb into past tense, and so on. It is better, then, to think of mental operations as falling into broad categories. These categories can be defined by the type of operation that is performed or by the type of information acted on. An incomplete list of these operations would include sensation, perception, attention, memory, language, mathematical reasoning, logical reasoning, decision making, and problem solving. Many of these categories may incorporate virtually identical or similar subprocesses—for example, scanning, matching, sorting, and retrieving. Figure 1.2 shows the kinds of mental processes that may be involved in solving a simple addition problem.

The Tri-Level Hypothesis

Any given information process can be described at several different levels. According to the tri-level hypothesis, mental or artificial information-processing events can be evaluated on at least three different levels (Marr, 1982). The highest or most abstract level of analysis is the computational level. At this level, one is concerned with two tasks. The first is a clear specification of what the problem is. Taking the problem as it may originally have been posed, in a vague manner perhaps, and breaking it down into its main constituents or parts

Figure 1.2 Some of the computational steps involved in solving an addition problem.

$$\begin{array}{r} 36 \\ + 47 \\ \hline 83 \end{array}$$

Computational Steps

1. 6 + 7 = 13   Add right column
2. 3   Store three
3. 1   Carry one
4. 3 + 4 = 7   Add left column
5. 7 + 1 = 8   Add one
6. 8   Store eight
7. 83   Record result

can bring about this clarity. It means describing the problem in a precise way such that the problem can be investigated using formal methods. It is like asking, What exactly is this problem? What does this problem entail? The second task one encounters at the computational level concerns the purpose or reason for the process. The second task consists of asking, Why is this process here in the first place? Inherent in this analysis is adaptiveness—the idea that human mental processes are learned or have evolved to enable the human organism to solve a problem it faces. This is the primary explanatory perspective used in the evolutionary approach. We describe a number of cognitive processes and the putative reasons for their evolution in the evolution chapter.

Stepping down one level of abstraction, we can next inquire about the way in which an information process is carried out. To do this, we need an **algorithm**, a formal **procedure** or system that acts on informational representations. It is important to note that algorithms can be carried out regardless of a representation's meaning; algorithms act on the form, not the meaning, of the symbols they transform. One way to think of algorithms is that they are "actions" used to manipulate and change representations. Algorithms are formal, meaning they are well defined. We know exactly what occurs at each step of an algorithm and how a particular step changes the information being acted on. A mathematical formula is a good example of an algorithm. A formula specifies how the data are to be transformed, what the steps are, and what the order of steps is. This type of description is put together at the **algorithmic level**, sometimes also called the programming level. It is equivalent to asking, What information-processing steps are being used to solve the problem? To draw an analogy with computers, the algorithmic level is like software because software contains instructions for the processing of data.

The most specific and concrete type of description is formulated at the **implementational level**. Here we ask, What is the information processor made of? What types of physical or material changes underlie changes in the processing of the information? This level is sometimes referred to as the hardware level, since in computer parlance, the hardware is the physical "stuff" the computer is made of. This would include its various parts—a monitor, hard drive, keyboard, and mouse. At a smaller scale, computer hardware consists of circuits and even the flow of electrons through the circuits. The hardware in human or animal cognition is the brain and, on a smaller scale, the neurons and activities of those neurons.

At this point, one might wonder, Why do we even need an algorithmic or formal level of analysis? Why not just map the physical processes at the implementational level onto a computational description of the problem or, alternatively, onto the behaviors or actions of the organism or device? This seems simpler, and we need not resort to the idea of information and representation. The reason is that the algorithmic level tells us how a particular system performs a computation. Not all computational systems solve a problem in the same way. Computers and humans can both perform addition but do so in drastically different fashions. This is true at the implementational level, obviously, but understanding the difference formally tells us much about alternative problem-solving approaches. It also gives us insights into how these systems might compute solutions to other novel problems that we might not understand.

This partitioning of the analysis of information-processing events into three levels has been criticized as being fundamentally simplistic since each level can, in turn, be further subdivided into levels (Churchland, Koch, & Sejnowski, 1990). Figure 1.3 depicts one possible organization of the many structural levels of analysis in the nervous system. Starting at the top, we might consider the brain as one organizational unit, brain regions as corresponding to another organizational unit one step down in spatial scale, then neural networks, individual neurons, and so on. Similarly, we could divide algorithmic steps into different substeps and problems into subproblems. To compound all this, it is not entirely clear how to map one level of analysis onto another. We may be able to specify clearly how an algorithm executes but be at a loss to say exactly where or how this is achieved with respect to the nervous system.

Differing Views of Representation and Computation

Before finishing our discussion of computation, it is important to differentiate between several different conceptions of what it is. So far, we have been talking about computation as being based on the formal systems notion. In this view, a computer is a **formal symbol manipulator**. Let's break this definition down into its component parts. A system is formal if it is syntactic or rule governed. In general, we use the word **syntax** to refer to the set of rules that govern any symbol system. The rules of language and mathematics are formal

Figure 1.3 Structural levels of analysis in the nervous system.

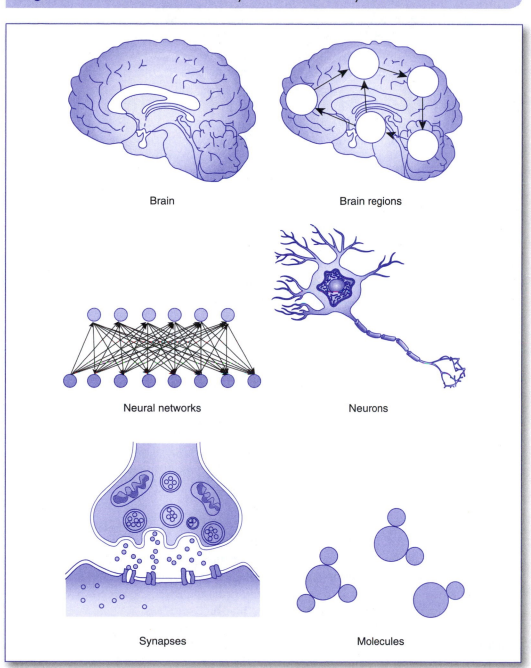

Brain

Brain regions

Neural networks

Neurons

Synapses

Molecules

systems because they specify which types of allowable changes can be made to symbols. Formal systems also operate on representations independent of the content of those representations. In other words, a process can be applied to a symbol regardless of its meaning or semantic content. A symbol, as we have already indicated, is a form of representation and can assume a wide variety of forms. Manipulation here implies that computation is an active, embodied process that takes place over time. That is, manipulations are actions, they occur physically in some type of computing device, and they take some time to occur (i.e., they don't happen instantaneously).

But this is not the only conception of what computation is. The connectionist or network approach to computation differs from the classical formal systems approach of cognitive science in several ways. In the classical view, knowledge is represented locally—in the form of symbols. In the connectionist view, knowledge is represented as a pattern of activation or weights that is distributed throughout a network and so is more global than a single symbol. Processing style is also different in this approach. The classical view has processing occurring in discrete serial stages, whereas in connectionism, processing occurs in parallel through the simultaneous activation of many nodes or elements in the network. Some cognitive scientists downplay these differences, arguing that information processing occurs in both systems and that the tri-level hypothesis can be applied equally to both (Dawson, 1998). We further compare and contrast the classical and connectionist views at the beginning of the network approach chapter.

What happens to representations once they get established? In some versions of the symbolic and connectionist approaches, representations remain forever fixed and unchanging. For example, when you learned about the concept of a car, a particular symbol standing for "car" was formed. The physical form of this symbol could then be matched against perceptual inputs to allow you to recognize a car when you see one or used in thought processes to enable you to reason about cars when you need to. Such processes can be simplified if the symbol stays the same over time. This, in fact, is exactly how a computer deals with representation. Each of the numbers or letters of the alphabet has a unique and unchanging ASCII (American Standard Code for Information Interchange) code. Similarly, in artificial neural network simulations of mind, the networks are flexible and plastic during learning, but once learning is complete, they must remain the same. If not, the representations will be rewritten when new things are learned.

A more realistic view of representation comes from the **dynamical perspective** in psychology (Friedenberg, 2009). According to this view, the mind is constantly changing as it adapts to new information. A representation formed when we first learn a concept is altered each time we think about that concept or experience information that is in some way related to it. For example, let's say a child sees a car for the first time and it is red. The child may then think that all cars are red. The next time he or she sees a car, it is blue. The child's concept would then be changed to accommodate the new color. Even after we are very familiar with a concept, the context in which we experience it is always different. You may hear a friend discussing how fast one type of car is, or you may find yourself driving a car you have never driven before. In each of these cases, the internal representation is modified to account for the new experience. So it is unlikely that biological representations of the sort we see in humans will ever stay the same. We talk more about the dynamical systems approach and how it can unify differing perspectives on representation and computation in the concluding chapter.

Computation as conceptualized in cognitive science is believed to be neural and multicellular. In other words, it is the result of the flow of an electrical signal across neuron cell membranes. Bray (2011), however, argues for an alternate form of computation, one that occurs within a cell rather than between them. He believes that single-celled organisms, such as amoebas, need to compute in order to carry out their complex behavioral repertoire of hunting, fleeing, and responding to environmental cues. To do this, they have evolved a molecular form of representation, where protein molecules can stand for referents and chemical processes that act on these molecules are the equivalent of symbolic transformations. Bray believes that individual cells even contain molecular circuits that are capable of performing the logical operations that are the basis of complex information processing. This new paradigm is not without its critics. For one, the machinery of molecular computation may not be capable of duplicating the complex sorts of computing we see in brains. Also, computation of this sort may be possible only in motile single-celled organisms that need to move and so face greater adaptive challenges. If this were the case, then neurons in brains may not be able to perform such feats.

THE INTERDISCIPLINARY PERSPECTIVE

There is an old fable about five blind men who stumble on an elephant (see Figure 1.4). Not knowing what it is, they start to feel the animal. One man feels only the elephant's tusk and thinks he is feeling a giant carrot. A second man feels the ears and believes that the object is a big fan. The third feels the trunk and proclaims that it is a pestle, while a fourth touching only the leg believes that it is a mortar. The fifth man, touching the tail, has yet another opinion: He believes it to be a rope. Obviously, all five men are wrong in their conclusions because each has examined only one aspect of the elephant. If the five men had gotten together and shared their findings, they may easily have pieced together what kind of creature it was. This story serves as a nice metaphor for cognitive science. We can think of the elephant as the mind and the blind men as researchers in different disciplines in cognitive science. Each individual discipline may make great strides in understanding its particular subject matter but, if it cannot compare its results to those of other related disciplines, may miss out on understanding the real nature of what is being investigated.

The key, then, to figuring out something as mysterious and complex as mind is communication and cooperation among disciplines. This is what is meant when one talks about cognitive science—not the sum of each of the disciplines or approaches but, rather, their

Figure 1.4 If you were the blind man, would you know it is an elephant?

interaction. Recent years have seen an increase in this cooperation. A number of major universities have established interdisciplinary cognitive science centers, where researchers in such diverse areas as philosophy, neuroscience, and cognitive psychology are encouraged to work together on common problems. Each area can then contribute its unique strength to the phenomenon under study. The philosophers can pose broad questions and hypotheses, the neuroscientists can measure physiological performance and brain activity, while the cognitive psychologists can design and carry out experiments. The consequent exchange of results and ideas then leads to fruitful synergies between these disciplines, accelerating progress with respect to finding solutions to the problem and yielding insights into other research questions.

We have alluded to some of the different approaches in cognitive science. Because this book is about explaining each approach and its major theoretical contributions, it is worth describing each now in terms of its perspective, history, and methodology. In the following sections, we will also provide a brief preview of the issues addressed by each approach.

The Philosophical Approach

Philosophy is the oldest of all the disciplines in cognitive science. It traces its roots back to the ancient Greeks. Philosophers have been active throughout much of recorded human history, attempting to formulate and answer basic questions about the universe. This approach is free to study virtually any sort of important question on virtually any subject, ranging from the nature of existence to the acquisition of knowledge to politics, ethics, and beauty. Philosophers of mind narrow their focus to specific problems concerning the nature and characteristics of mind. They might ask questions such as, What is mind? How do we come to know things? How is mental knowledge organized?

The primary method of philosophical inquiry is reasoning, both deductive and inductive. **Deductive reasoning** involves the application of the rules of logic to statements about the world. Given an initial set of statements assumed to be true, philosophers can derive other statements that logically must be correct. For example, if the statement "College students study 3 hours every night" is true and the statement "Mary is a college student" is true, we can conclude that "Mary will study 3 hours every night." Philosophers also engage in **inductive reasoning**. They make observations about specific instances in the world, notice commonalities among them, and draw conclusions. An example of inductive reasoning would be the following: "Whiskers the cat has four legs," "Scruffy the cat has four legs," and, therefore, "All cats have four legs." However, philosophers do not use a systematic form of induction known as the scientific method. That is employed within the other cognitive science disciplines.

In Chapter 2, we summarize several of the fundamental issues facing the philosophers of mind. With respect to the mind–body problem, philosophers wrangle over what exactly a mind is. Is the mind something physical like a rock or a chair, or is it nonphysical? Can minds exist only in brains, or can they emerge from the operation of other complex entities, such as computers? The knowledge acquisition problem deals with how we come to know things. Is knowledge a product of one's genetic endowment, or does it arise through one's interaction with the environment? How much does each of these factors contribute to any given mental ability? We also look into one of the most fascinating and enigmatic mysteries of mind—that of consciousness. In this case, we can ask, What is consciousness? Are we really conscious at all?

Interdisciplinary Crossroads: Science and Philosophy

Philosophers have often been accused of doing "armchair" philosophy, meaning they do nothing but sit back in comfortable chairs and reflect about the world. The critique is that they ignore empirical evidence, information based on observation of the world, usually under controlled circumstances as is the case in the sciences. This may be changing, however, with the development of a new trend known as experimental philosophy.

Experimental philosophy utilizes empirical methods, typically in the form of surveys that assess people's understanding of constructed scenarios, to help answer philosophical questions. Followers of the movement call themselves "X-Philes" and have even adopted a burning armchair and accompanying song as their motto, a video of which is viewable on YouTube.

One of the more prominent X-Philers, Joshua Knobe (2003), presented participants with a hypothetical situation. In the situation, a vice president of a company approaches the chairman of the board and asks about starting a new program. The program will increase profits, but it will also harm the environment. In one version of the survey, the chairman responds that he or she doesn't care at all about harming the environment but just wants to make as much profit as possible and so wants to begin the new program.

When participants were asked whether the chairman harmed the environment intentionally, 82% responded "yes." In a different version of the scenario, everything was identical except that "harming" was now replaced with "helping." The program had the side effect of helping the environment but the chairman again stated that he or she didn't care at all about helping the environment and wanted to go ahead with it. This time when asked if the chairman intentionally helped the environment, only 23% responded "yes."

Logically, there should be no difference in perceived intentionality between both conditions. In each case, there was a desire to make profit and a failure to care one way or the other about the environment. But clearly, the way we see intentionality involves moral evaluations, the way people judge what is good or bad. This conclusion, what is now called the "Knobe effect" could not necessarily have been determined a priori using pure reasoning. The term a priori relates to what can be known through an understanding of how certain things work rather than by observation.

Experimental philosophy has addressed a wide variety of issues. These include cultural differences in how people know or merely believe (Weinberg, Nichols, & Stich, 2001), whether a person can be morally responsible if his or her actions are determined (Nichols & Knobe, 2007), the ways in which people understand consciousness (Huebner, 2010) and even, how philosophical intuitions are related to personality traits (Feltz & Cokely, 2009).

Of course, this new field has been critiqued. Much of experimental philosophy has looked at intuitions, and Williamson (2008) argues that philosophical evidence should not just rely on people's intuitions. Another obvious issue is that experimental philosophy is not philosophy at all, but science. In other words, if it is adopting the use of survey methodology, statistics, and so on, then it really becomes psychology or a branch of the social sciences rather than philosophy. Researchers have noted that some of the science is sloppy, using low and unrepresentative sample sizes.

The Psychological Approach

Compared with philosophy, psychology is a relatively young discipline. It can be considered old though, particularly when compared with some of the more recent newcomers to the cognitive science scene—for example, AI and robotics. Psychology as a science arose in the late 19th century and was the first discipline in which the scientific method was applied exclusively to the study of mental phenomena. Early psychologists established experimental laboratories that would enable them to catalog mental ideas and investigate various mental capacities, such as vision and memory. Psychologists apply the scientific method to both mind and behavior. That is, they attempt to understand not just internal mental phenomena, such as thoughts, but also the external behaviors that these internal phenomena can give rise to.

The scientific method is a way of getting hold of valid knowledge about the world. One starts with a hypothesis or idea about how the world works and then designs an experiment to see if the hypothesis has validity. In an experiment, one essentially makes observations under a set of controlled conditions. The resulting data then either support or fail to support the hypothesis. This procedure, employed within psychology, and cognitive science in general, is described more fully at the start of Chapter 3.

The field of psychology is broad and encompasses many subdisciplines, each one having its unique theoretical orientations. Each discipline has a different take on what mind is. The earliest psychologists—that is, the voluntarists and structuralists—viewed the mind as a kind of test tube in which chemical reactions between mental elements took place. In contrast, functionalism viewed mind not according to its constituent parts but, rather, according to what its operations were—what it could do. The Gestaltists again went back to a vision of mind as composed of parts but emphasized that it was the combination and interaction of the parts, which gave rise to new wholes, that was important. Psychoanalytic psychology conceives of mind as a collection of differing and competing minds, while behaviorism sees it as something that maps stimuli onto behaviors.

The Cognitive Approach

Starting in the 1960s, a new form of psychology arrived on the scene. Known as cognitive psychology, it came into being, in part, as a backlash against the behaviorist movement and its profound emphasis on behavior. Cognitive psychologists placed renewed emphasis on the study of internal mental operations. They adopted the computer as a metaphor for mind and described mental functioning in terms of representation and computation. They believed that the mind, like a computer, could be understood in terms of information processing.

The cognitive approach was also better able to explain phenomena such as language acquisition for which behaviorists did not have good accounts. At around the same time, new technologies that allowed better measurement of mental activity were being developed. This promoted a movement away from the behaviorist's emphasis on external observable behaviors and toward the cognitive scientist's emphasis on internal functions, as these could, for the first time, be observed with reasonable precision.

Inherent in the cognitive approach is the idea of modularity. Modules are functionally independent units that receive inputs from other modules, perform a specific processing task, and pass the results of their computation onto yet additional modules. The influence of the modular approach can be seen in the use of process models or flow diagrams. These depict a given mental activity via the use of boxes and arrows, where boxes depict modules and arrows the flow of information among them. The techniques used in this approach are the experimental method and computational modeling. Computational modeling involves carrying out a formal (typically software-based) implementation of a proposed cognitive process. Researchers can run the modeling process so as to simulate how the process might operate in a human mind. They can then alter various parameters of the model or change its structure in an effort to achieve results as close as possible to those obtained in human experiments. This use of modeling and comparison with experimental data is a unique characteristic of cognitive psychology and is also used in the AI and artificial network approaches.

Cognitive psychologists have studied a wide variety of mental processes, including pattern recognition, attention, memory, imagery, and problem solving. Theoretical accounts and processing models for each of these are given in Chapters 4 and 5. Language is within the purview of cognitive psychology, but because the approach to language is also multidisciplinary, we describe it separately in Chapter 9.

The Neuroscience Approach

Brain anatomy and physiology have been studied for quite some time. It is only recently, however, that we have seen tremendous advances in our understanding of the brain, especially in terms of how neuronal processes can account for cognitive phenomena. The study of the brain and endocrine system and how these account for mental states and behavior is called neuroscience. The attempt to explain cognitive processes in terms of underlying brain mechanisms is known as cognitive neuroscience.

Neuroscience, first and foremost, provides a description of mental events at the implementational level. It attempts to describe the biological "hardware" on which mental "software" supposedly runs. However, as discussed above, there are many levels of scale when it comes to describing the brain, and it is not always clear which level provides the best explanation for any given cognitive process. Neuroscientists, however, investigate at each of these levels. They study the cell biology of individual neurons and of neuron-to-neuron synaptic transmission, the patterns of activity in local cell populations, and the interrelations of larger brain areas.

A reason for many of the recent developments in neuroscience is, again, the development of new technologies. Neuroscientists employ a wide variety of methods to measure the performance of the brain at work. These include positron emission tomography, computerized axial tomography, and **magnetic resonance imaging**. Studies that use these procedures have participants perform a cognitive task, and the brain activity that is concurrent with the performance of the task is recorded. For example, a participant may be asked to form a visual image of a word that appears on a computer screen. The researchers can then determine which parts of the brain became active during imagery and in what order. Neuroscientists use other techniques as well. They study brain-damaged patients and the effects of lesions in laboratory animals, and they use single- and multiple-cell recording techniques.

The Network Approach

The network approach is at least partially derived from neuroscience. In this perspective, mind is seen as a collection of computing units. These units are connected to one another and mutually influence one another's activity via their connections, although each of the units is believed to perform a relatively simple computation—for example, a neuron can either "fire" by initiating an action potential or not "fire" and fail to initiate an action potential. In these networks, the connectivity of the units can give rise to representational and computational complexity.

Chapter 7, which outlines the network approach, has two parts. The first involves the construction of artificial neural networks. Most artificial neural networks are computer software simulations that have been designed to mimic the way actual brain networks operate. They attempt to simulate the functioning of neural cell populations. Artificial neural networks that can perform arithmetic, learn concepts, and read out loud now exist. A wide variety of network architectures has developed over the past 30 years.

The second part of the network chapter is more theoretical and focuses on knowledge representation—on how meaningful information may be mentally coded and processed. In semantic networks, nodes standing for concepts are connected to one another in such a way that activation of one node causes activation of other related nodes. Semantic networks have been constructed to explain how conceptual information in memory is organized and recalled. They are often used to predict and explain data obtained from experiments with human participants in cognitive psychology.

In the chapter on networks, we will finish off with a discussion of network science. This is a new interdisciplinary field, much like cognitive science. However, in this field, researchers focus on the structure and function of networks. The term *networks* is meant in a very broad sense here to include not just artificial or natural neural networks but telephone and wireless networks, electrical power networks, and social networks. Surprisingly, we will see that there are commonalities among these different networks and that they share some organizational and operational features. We will examine these features and apply them particularly to the brain and psychology.

The Evolutionary Approach

The theory of natural selection proposed by Charles Darwin in 1859 revolutionized our way of thinking about biology. Natural selection holds that adaptive features enable the animals that possess them to survive and pass these features on to future generations. The environment, in this view, is seen as selecting from among a variety of traits those that serve a functional purpose.

The evolutionary approach can be considered in a quite general way and used to explain phenomena outside biology. The field of evolutionary psychology applies selection theory to account for human mental processes. It attempts to elucidate the selection forces that acted on our ancestors and how those forces gave rise to the cognitive structures we now possess. Evolutionary psychologists also adopt a modular approach to mind. In this case, the modules correspond with "favored" cognitive capacities that were used by ancestors successful at solving certain problems. Evolutionary theories have been proposed to account for experimental results across a wide range of capacities, from categorization to memory to logical and probabilistic reasoning, language, and cognitive differences between the sexes. They also have been proposed to account for how we reason about money—a new field of study known as behavioral economics.

Also in this chapter, we examine comparative cognition. This is the study of animal intelligence. We look at the cognitive capacities of a number of different species and discuss some of the problems that arise in comparing animals with one another and with humans.

The Linguistic Approach

Linguistics is an area that focuses exclusively on the domain of language. It is concerned with all questions concerning language ability, such as What is language? How do we acquire language? What parts of the brain underlie language use? As we have seen, language is a topic studied within other disciplines—for example, cognitive psychology and neuroscience. Because so many different researchers in different disciplines have taken on the problem of language, we consider it here as a separate discipline, united more by topic than by perspective or methodology.

Part of the difficulty in studying language is the fact that language itself is so complex. Much research has been devoted to understanding its nature. This work looks at the properties all languages share, the elements of language, and how those elements are used during communication. Other foci of linguistic investigation center on primate language use, language acquisition, deficits in language acquisition caused by early sensory deprivation or brain damage, the relationship between language and thought, and the development of speech recognition systems.

Linguistics, perhaps more than any other perspective discussed here, adopts a very eclectic methodological approach. Language researchers employ experiments and computer models, study brain-damaged patients, track how language ability changes during development, and compare diverse languages.

The Emotion Approach

As you may have surmised, humans don't just think—we also feel. Our conscious experience consists of emotions, such as happiness, sadness, and anger. Recent work in cognitive psychology and other fields has produced a wealth of data on emotions and how they influence thoughts. In Chapter 10, we start out by examining what emotions are and how they differ from feelings and moods. We examine several different theories of emotion and describe how they influence perception, attention, memory, and decision making. Following this, we look at the neuroscience underlying emotions and the role that evolutionary forces played in their formation. AI investigators have formulated models of how computers can "compute" and display emotional behavior. There are even robots capable of interacting with people in an emotionally meaningful way.

The Social Approach

Cognition happens inside individuals, but those individuals are strongly influenced by their social environment. The field of social cognition explores how people make sense of both themselves and others. We will see that thinking about people often differs from thinking about objects and that different parts of our brains are used when thinking socially. Neuroscience has revealed that in laboratory animals there are specialized cells, called mirror neurons, that are active both when an animal performs some action and when it watches another animal or person perform that same action. Later in Chapter 11, we introduce the concept of a theory of mind. This is an ability to understand and appreciate other people's states of mind. This capacity may be lacking in people suffering from autism. We conclude by summarizing work on specific social cognitive phenomena: attitudes, impressions, attributions, stereotypes, and prejudice.

The Artificial Intelligence Approach

Researchers have been building devices that attempt to mimic human and animal function for many centuries. But it is only in the past few decades that computer scientists have seriously attempted to build devices that mimic complex thought processes. This area is now known as artificial intelligence. Researchers in AI are concerned with getting computers to perform tasks that have heretofore required human intelligence. As such, they construct programs to do the sorts of things that require complex reasoning on our part. AI programs have been developed that can diagnose medical disorders, use language, and play chess.

AI also gives us insights into the function of human mental operations. Designing a computer program that can visually recognize an object often proves useful in understanding how we may perform the same task ourselves. An even more exciting outcome of AI research is that someday we may be able to create an artificial person who will possess all or many of the features that we consider uniquely human, such as consciousness, the ability to make decisions, and so on (Friedenberg, 2008).

The methods employed in the AI perspective include the development and testing of computer algorithms, their comparison with empirical data or performance standards, and their subsequent modification. Researchers have employed a wide range of approaches. An early attempt at getting computers to reason involved the application of logical rules to propositional statements. Later, other techniques were used. Chapters 12 and 13 give detailed descriptions of these techniques.

The Robotics Approach

Finally, we consider robotics. Robotics may be considered a familial relation to AI and has appeared on the scene as a formal discipline only recently. Whereas AI workers build devices that "think," robotics researchers build machines that must also "act." Investigators in this field build autonomous or semiautonomous mechanical devices that have been designed to perform a physical task in a real-world environment. Examples of things that robots can do presently include navigating around a cluttered room, welding or manipulating parts on an assembly line, and defusing bombs.

The robotics approach has much to contribute to cognitive science and to theories of mind. Robots, like people and animals, must demonstrate successful goal-oriented behaviors under complex, changing, and uncertain environmental conditions. Robotics, therefore, helps us think about the kinds of minds that underlie and produce such behaviors.

In Chapter 13, we outline different paradigms in robotics. Some of these approaches differ radically from one another. The hierarchical paradigm offers a "top-down" perspective, according to which a robot is programmed with knowledge about the world. The robot then uses this model or internal representation to guide its actions. The reactive paradigm, on the other hand, is "bottom up." Robots that use this architecture respond in a simple way to environmental stimuli: They react reflexively to a stimulus input, and there is little in the way of intervening knowledge.

Integrating Approaches

Many of the approaches we have just listed inform one another. For instance, the fields of AI and robotics are in some cases inseparable. AI programmers often write computer programs that serve as the "brains" of robots, telling them what to do and providing them with instructions on how to perform various tasks like object recognition and manipulation. In recent years, the cognitive and neuroscience approaches have come closer together, with cognitive psychologists providing information-processing models of specific brain processes. For example, we have seen cognitive models of hippocampal function that specify how this brain region stores memories based on our understanding of the neural substrates. In an even more interdisciplinary leap, we have seen the new area of social cognitive neuroscience in which social contexts are attached to cognitive-neural models. These are discussed in Chapter 11. In the concluding chapter (Chapter 14), we provide a more comprehensive summary of the ways in which these different approaches are and can be integrated.

SUMMING UP: A REVIEW OF CHAPTER 1

1. Cognitive science is the scientific interdisciplinary study of mind and sees contributions from multiple fields, including philosophy and its newest offshoot, experimental philosophy, psychology, cognitive psychology, neuroscience, the connectionist or network approach, evolution, linguistics, the scientific study of emotions and social behavior, AI, robotics, and more.

2. Mind can be considered an information processor. At least some mental operations bear similarity to the way information is processed in a computer.

3. Information processing requires that some aspect of the world be represented and then operated on or computed. A representation is symbolic if it stands for something else. The thing a symbol stands for in the world is called its referent. The fact that symbols are "about" these things is called intentionality.

4. A formal system is made of symbols—collections of symbols that form expressions and processes that act on those expressions to form new expressions. Formal logic is an example of a formal system.

5. According to the physical symbol system hypothesis, formal systems can be said to be intelligent implying that computers may be intelligent. A problem for this is the symbol grounding problem, which states that symbols in people are grounded because we have bodies, can perceive objects, and can act on them.

6. Examples of representations are concepts, propositions, rules, and analogies. Representations are realized by an information bearer, have content, are grounded, and need to be interpreted.

7. Computations are processes that act on or transform representations. According to the tri-level hypothesis, there seem to be at least three levels of computation: computational, algorithmic, and implementational.

8. There are several different schools of thought that differ in the way they view representation and computation. In the classical cognitive science view, representations are fixed symbols and information processing is serial. In the connectionist view, representations are distributed and processing is parallel. According to the dynamical view, representations are constantly changing, being altered with each new experience.

EXPLORE MORE

Log on to the student study site at http://study.sagepub.com/friedenberg3e for electronic flash cards, review quizzes, and a list of web resources to aid you in further exploring the field of cognitive science.

SUGGESTED READINGS

Friedenberg, J. (2009). *Dynamical psychology: Complexity, self-organization, and mind*. Charlotte, NC: Emergent.

Harnish, R. M. (2002). *Minds, brains, computers: An introduction to the foundations of cognitive science*. Malden, MA: Blackwell.

Sobel, C. P. (2001). *The cognitive sciences: An interdisciplinary approach*. Mountain View, CA: Mayfield.

Stainton, R. J. (2006). *Contemporary debates in cognitive science*. Malden, MA: Blackwell.

2

THE PHILOSOPHICAL APPROACH

Enduring Questions

"What is Matter?—Never mind."
"What is Mind?—No matter."

—Anonymous, 1855

WHAT IS PHILOSOPHY?

Philosophy in its broadest sense is the search for wisdom and knowledge. It is the first approach we will tackle in our voyage through the different disciplines of cognitive science. There are good reasons for beginning here. Philosophy plays a vital participatory role in cognitive science. It does this not by generating results, since it is a theoretical rather than experimental discipline, but by "defining problems, criticizing models, and suggesting areas for future research" (Garfield, 1995, p. 374). More than any other discipline in cognitive science, philosophy is not limited by its subject matter or a particular theoretical stance. It is, therefore, free to evaluate and contribute to the remaining disciplines in a way the others cannot. This approach is also the oldest of the different approaches, tracing its origins back to the ancient Greeks. It is, thus, fitting that we begin our tour here.

The translation of the word *philosophy* yields "love of wisdom," indicating the philosopher's concern with knowledge and understanding the universe. Philosophy as a formal discipline studies a wide range of topics. In fact, there is no topic that is not fair game for a philosopher; he or she may examine politics, ethics, esthetics, and other subjects. We concern ourselves here with two branches of philosophy. Metaphysics examines the nature of reality. The mind–body problem is a metaphysical one at heart because it seeks to understand whether the mental world is part of the physical material world. Epistemology is the study of knowledge and asks questions such as What is knowledge? How is knowledge represented in the mind? How do we come to acquire knowledge?

CHAPTER OVERVIEW

In this chapter, we survey philosophic thoughts that center on a couple of vexing issues, which can be summed up in terms of "this" versus "that." Such terminology suggests that the debates that have arisen from these issues have polarized the arguments and that there are only two possible answers to a problem. We will see that this is actually not the case and that there are multiple ways to conceptualize the issues. These issues are the mind–body and nature–nurture debates. In addition, we discuss the question of consciousness and its relation to cognitive science.

This chapter is motivated by great questions in the philosophy of mind. In the first section on the mind–body problem, we ask a very fundamental question: What is mind? Is it something that is physical or not? Is a body necessary to have a mind? These questions are primarily metaphysical in nature. In the second section on functionalism, we get more specific. If a mind is physical, then what sort of substrate can it be based on? Can a mind only be based on brains or can minds emerge from other things like computers? In the third section, we address the issue of knowledge. How does information get into our "heads"? Are we born knowing certain things or is information primarily learned? These are epistemological questions, since they concern information. In the fourth, and final, section we look at perhaps the most contentious and debated issue in the modern philosophy of mind—consciousness. Here we will address questions like What is consciousness? Can it exist in creatures? What exactly is happening in our brains when we have a particular conscious state?

THE MIND–BODY PROBLEM: WHAT IS MIND?

The mind–body problem addresses how psychological or mental properties are related to physical properties. The debate stems from a fundamental conception about what the mind is. On the one hand, we have the brain that is material and physical. It is made up of substances that we can measure and understand. The mind could be thought of in the same way, as simply a physical thing. On the other hand, there are those who argue that the mind is something more. They say we can't equate our subjective conscious experiences, such as beliefs, desires, and thoughts, with something as mundane as the brain. They say that the mind is nonphysical and consists of something resembling a soul or spirit. The mind as a nonphysical entity inhabiting the brain or some other physical entity is sometimes called "the ghost in the machine."

The first question of the mind–body problem is metaphysical and refers to the nature of what mind is. Is the mind physical or something else? A second and more specific question concerns the relationship between these two things. If we assume that there are two such entities, then what is the causal relationship between them? Does the mind control the body, or does the body control the mind? There are many theories supporting the directions this control takes. Some theories argue that only one exerts control; others state that they both control each other; additional theories state that the two work in parallel but that neither has any causal influence.

Our discussion in this section is structured around basic conceptions of the nature of mind. According to **monism**, there is only one kind of state or substance in the universe. The ancient Greek philosopher Aristotle (384–322 BCE) was a monist (see Figure 2.1). He

Figure 2.1 A bust of the early Greek philosopher Aristotle. He believed that there was no substantial difference between mind and matter.

characterized the difference between mind and body as the difference between form and matter. One way to think of his notion is to consider a lump of clay. It is made up of physical matter, and we can think of it as corresponding to the brain. We can shape the clay with our hands into different forms—for example, we can roll it into a ball or flatten it into a pancake. The shapes the clay can assume, Aristotle implied, are like the different thoughts the mind can take on when it undergoes different patterns of activity. These shapes are just different physical states and do not constitute any nonphysical or spiritual substance.

In **dualism**, one believes that both mental and physical substances are possible. Plato, another Greek philosopher (427–347 BCE), was a dualist. Plato was Aristotle's teacher, but the two held quite different views. Plato believed that the mind and the body exist in two separate worlds. Knowledge of the mind, he thought, exists in an ideal world of forms, which is immaterial, nonextended, and eternal. The body instead resides in a world that is material, extended, and perishable. There are crucial differences between the objects of one world and those of the other. Mental ideas such as "circle" that reside in the ideal world of forms are perfect, and according to Plato, the circles of this world are always perfectly round. Concrete examples of circles that we find in the real world are always imperfect. If we examine an actual circle, at some level of magnification, the circle's edge will lose its roundness.

A possible way out of the mind–body problem is to rely on behaviors as indicators of mental states. Behaviors such as talking, running, and laughing are external and more easily measured than brain activity. According to **philosophical behaviorism**, mental states are dispositions or tendencies to behave in certain ways under certain circumstances. Happiness, for instance, can be thought of as the tendency to smile or laugh. There is support for this idea in that there are strong connections between mental states and behavior. Many people do smile when they are happy or cry when they are sad. However, we cannot conclusively prove any causal link between the two. A "tough guy" or stoic might not cry when sad for fear of being perceived as weak. Alternatively, somebody might exhibit nervous laughter before going on stage, in which case anxiety and not happiness is causing the laughter. For these reasons, we cannot consistently rely on behaviors as indicators of mental states. Please note that philosophical behaviorism is not the same as psychological behaviorism, discussed in Chapter 3. The psychological version focuses on the laws that govern the relationship between stimuli and responses and how we can shape responses by manipulating stimuli such as rewards and punishments. Psychological behaviorism ignores mental states altogether.

MONISM

If we are monists, we are left with two fundamental choices. Either the universe is mental or it is physical. It is difficult to take the first argument, called **idealism**, seriously—although it cannot be falsified. Imagine that everything you know isn't real but is simply an illusion of reality. The world you perceive and understand exists only "in your head"— although, in this universe, you don't have a real head, so we can say this only colloquially. A supreme being such as God could be responsible for this. Alternately, it could be that aliens have taken our brains and are feeding them information in such a way as to make us think that we live in the world we do. This is known informally as the "brain in a vat argument." In either case, we could never get outside our own conscious experience to prove what reality is really like.

On the flip side of our metaphysical coin is **physicalism**, or materialism. The origins of this view go back to the Greek philosopher Democritus (ca. 460–370 BCE), who believed that all things were composed of atoms. The attributes and behaviors of the atoms, he said, can explain the differences between things. Physicalists are also monistic and believe that the universe is composed of a single substance. However, they regard this substance as physical and material rather than spiritual or ethereal. Physicalism is, thus, the doctrine that everything that exists is physical. The operations of the mind are seen here simply as the operations of the brain.

We can consider identity theory to be a form of physicalism. According to **identity theory**, the mind *is* the brain. Specifically, mental states are physical states of the brain. Just as salt is the same as its chemical structure of sodium chloride, in this perspective, we say that being happy is identical to a particular type of brain activity. In fact, for every type of what we think are mental states, there is a type of brain state. These physical brain states cannot be discovered through simple observation or an examination of the linguistic meaning of the terms. They can be understood only through proper scientific analysis.

Anyone who believes in identity theory will be left with more terminology than is needed. On the one hand, we have the common everyday subjective terms we all use to refer to mental states. These are words such as "feeling good" that we use to denote our subjective experiences. On the other hand, we have objective scientific phrases such as "activation of dopaminergic neurons in the meso-cortico-limbic system" to describe the brain states for these terms. Because the scientific descriptions are more accurate and better reflect what is actually going on, it makes sense to abandon our mental terms and rely solely on the scientific terminology. In effect, this is what **eliminativism** is about. Eliminativists reject not only the terminology but also the mental states they supposedly describe. They don't believe in mental states at all. Only physical brain states are acknowledged as existing.

Theories of mind that use subjective terms such as those mentioned above and that use commonsense or intuitive reasoning are collectively referred to as **folk psychology**. Here is an example of a folk psychology theory: cookies taste good. Robert likes to feel good. If Robert walks by the cookie store on his way home from school, he will buy and then eat some cookies. Folk psychology helps us understand and predict the behavior of people around us. In this sense, it is very useful. However, folk psychology is far removed from rigorous scientific explanations that are tested using experimental methods.

Churchland (1981) argues that folk psychology has outlived its usefulness and that we should supplant it with neuroscience. He argues that folk psychology has not yielded any new insights into human behavior. It fails to inform us on a wide range of issues such as mental illness, creativity, and memory. Unlike valid scientific theories that tend to support one another, no folk psychology theories support one another or support scientific theories. Folk psychology, however, may still prove its worth in that it may serve as a basis for generating scientifically testable hypotheses. This would work only if the translation between the ill-defined subjective notions could be translated effectively into well-defined hypotheses capable of validation.

Evaluating the Monist Perspective

Monist views have one clear advantage: They are simpler than dualist accounts. Rather than partitioning the universe into two types of things, they allow for only a single self-consistent universe. This follows the principle of Occam's razor, which states that all things being equal, the simplest explanation is usually the correct one. As mentioned above, idealism does not really qualify as a legitimate theory because it cannot be proved true or false. As a result, it doesn't serve as a legitimate subject of scientific scrutiny. On the other hand, there is abundant evidence in favor of physicalism. Indeed, most of the experimental results in this book support the notion of the brain as being the mechanism of mind. For example, deficit studies that look at behavior following brain damage show that when particular parts of the brain are damaged, very specific types of deficits follow. This suggests that those areas are where the so-called mental phenomena take place.

Physicalism, however, also has its share of critics. Some allow that physical processes can determine mental ones but deny that they can explain them. So, they might argue, changes in the brain may very well correlate with and produce fear, but they do not explain different kinds of fear, how a person becomes fearful, and so on. These critics acknowledge that the world is physical but indicate that there is no physical explanation for many phenomena. In these cases, they believe, it is perhaps better to explain using mental terms.

One argument that can be directed at identity theory goes by the name of **multiple realization**. Simply put, any given mental state, such as pain, can be instantiated or realized differently in different creatures. Pain in humans may be identical to activity in c-fibers, pain in squid may be identical to activity in d-fibers, while pain in aliens may be identical to activity in e-fibers (Ravenscroft, 2005). Furthermore, it is quite likely that differences exist not only between species but also between individuals within a given species. You and I may both feel pain when there is activity in c-fibers, but the particular pattern of activity in those fibers and in other areas of the brain could produce radically different mental perceptions of pain in each of us. Identity theory must, therefore, account for all the subtle mental differences that can exist between individuals.

DUALISM

Now that we have reviewed the various forms of monism, let us turn our attention to its logical alternative. Dualists believe both mental and physical realms are possible but differ in the way they think these two interact. **Classical dualism** originated with the French philosopher René Descartes (1596–1650). Descartes was a revolutionary philosopher for his time and introduced theories on many of the ideas that underlie cognitive science. He believed in a one-way causal link, with the mind controlling the body, but not vice versa. Descartes thought the mind exerted its control on the body through the pineal gland, perhaps because it is one of the few anatomical structures not duplicated on either side of the brain (see Figure 2.2). In this view, the mind is like a puppet master, the body is like a

Figure 2.2 Descartes believed the pineal gland to be the location where the mind influenced the body. This belief was itself influenced by the fact that the pineal gland is located in the center of the brain.

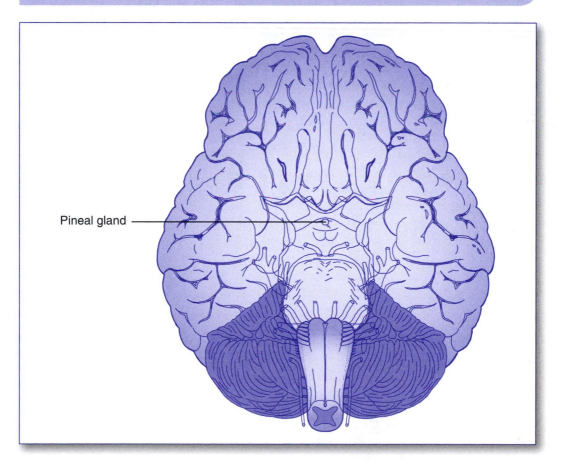

Pineal gland

puppet, and the pineal gland is like the puppet strings by which the former controls the latter. Classical dualism conforms to most people's commonsense notion of the mind–brain relationship, which is that our thoughts control our actions. For instance, when we feel hungry, we get up and eat a snack. It certainly seems as though the feeling of hunger comes first and causes the action of getting up to eat.

Substance Dualism

Descartes's views conform to what we now more commonly call **substance dualism,** where mind and body are composed of completely different substances. By *substance*, we mean the actual "stuff" that makes them up. In this view, there are two sorts of stuff: mental substances and physical substances. The physical substances can be the atoms, molecules, and cells of the natural world as we know it. It isn't clear what the basic elements or building blocks of mental substance might be.

There is a logical argument in favor of substance dualism that takes the form of several propositions. It goes as follows: Minds can do X. No physical object can do X. Therefore, minds are not physical objects. X can be any mental ability that has not been fully realized in some alternate physical form. Candidates include language, reason, and consciousness. The problem with this argument is that many of the abilities that we thought were exclusively human have now been replicated in machine form. Artificial intelligence (AI) is now capable of pattern recognition, language comprehension and production, and even artistic creativity (Friedenberg, 2008).

The arguments against substance dualism are stronger. One early attack came from Princess Elizabeth of Bohemia (1618–1680). She pointed out to Descartes that if mind and body are of two different substances, then they should not be able to causally interact. Saying they interact at the pineal gland specifies the location at which this might occur but not how. Descartes was unable to come up with a successful reply.

There are at least two other arguments against dualism that involve explanatory power. First, biology can give us a very good account of mental states. If we can explain these states completely in terms of neurons, action potentials, and synapses, then there is no need to even provide a nonphysical account. Second, substance dualism does not give us any kind of alternate explanation. What are mental things made of? How do these things interact or operate? These questions are left unanswered.

Property Dualism

There is another type of dualism that may overcome these difficulties. According to **property dualism,** the mind and the body can be of the same stuff but have different properties.

By *properties*, we mean characteristics or features. To illustrate, a golf ball and a tennis ball are both made of atoms, yet they differ in their properties. A golf ball is smaller, white, and dimpled. A tennis ball is larger, green, and fuzzy.

A property dualist believes that mental states are nonphysical properties of the brain. He or she would say that the brain has certain properties, such as being gray and wrinkled, weighing a certain number of pounds, and so on. But then he or she would also say that the brain gives rise to another set of properties, such as seeing red, being in pain, and feeling happy, that are wholly different from any of the currently understood properties of the brain.

Very little is gained in the dualist switch from substance to property. Nonphysicality still fails to provide an explanation for mental states, whether those are characterized as features or not. Again we can ask, How do physical brain processes give rise to mental features? We are still left with better and more complete physical accounts of mentality. So we can level the same arguments we have used against substance dualism to property dualism.

Evaluating the Dualist Perspective

One critique of dualism comes from the philosopher Gilbert Ryle. Ryle's (1949) argument centers on our conceptualization of mind and its relation to the body. He believes that the mind is not any particular component of the brain but, rather, all the parts working together as a coordinated, organized whole. He illustrates with a story: Imagine a visitor from a foreign country arriving at a large university. He is shown around the campus, and the various parts of the school are pointed out to him, including the dormitories, departments, and lawns. The visitor, who has never seen any of this before, is puzzled. He says, "Well, I've seen all this, but I haven't yet seen the university." We would have to explain to him that the university is not any of the individual sites he has viewed but all the sites together and the interconnections among them (see Figure 2.3). Ryle thinks philosophers fall into the same trap as the visitor, mistaking the part or parts for the whole. He argues that the mind belongs in a conceptual category different from that of the body, just as the university is in a category different from those of the things that make it up.

Andy Clark (2001) summarizes several other critiques of dualism. These would apply to Descartes's conception as well as other perspectives. Clark says that dualism is uninformative and tells us what the mind isn't rather than what it is. If the mind isn't the brain and isn't physical, then what is it? Dualists are remarkably silent on this matter, often conceding that it is something nonphysical that we can't understand yet. As a theory, dualism also is inelegant because it postulates two worlds that must be coordinated. An explanation that does not violate the principle of Occam's razor would involve a single type of world, not requiring coordination.

Figure 2.3 Where is the university?

Source: Courtesy of Peter Finger Photography 2003.

There are further problems with dualism. One has to do with the dependence of the mental on the physical. Factors that affect the brain, such as head trauma or drug use, have direct and dramatic mental effects. We can see that damage to a certain part of the brain—say, from a motorcycle accident—results in specific forms of mental disruption—for example, language deficits. Taking a drug such as marijuana, which alters brain chemistry, results in altered mental states. In addition, the evolutionary approach shows us that there is a general positive correlation between brain size and intelligence across species, with larger brain sizes linked to increased cognitive capacity. It is obvious from these observations that the mental is integrated with the physical, that the mind depends on the brain.

Some dualists, in response to attacks on their positions, have stated that the mind exhibits extraordinary abilities and that it is or will be impossible for a physical system to duplicate such abilities. For instance, how can a physical system, be it a brain or a computer, write a novel or negotiate a peace treaty? The truth is that as our technological sophistication increases, many of these abilities are becoming better understood and implemented computationally. There are now computers that can beat the best chess champions and successfully diagnose medical disorders. These are capacities once thought to be the exclusive domain of humans.

Dualists and other philosophers also argue that our subjective experiences—things such as thoughts, beliefs, and desires—are not equivalent to physical brain states. They base this conclusion primarily on introspection. When we examine what is inside our heads, they say, these subjective experiences seem to be something more than just physical. The problem with this argument is that introspection is a weak form of evidence and can be wrong (as are many of our ideas). What is required is objective proof that such experiential states are not physical.

FUNCTIONALISM: ARE MINDS LIMITED TO BRAINS?

The most influential philosophical theory of mind in cognitive science is functionalism. For this reason, we will discuss it in considerably more detail than any of the theories already discussed. To get an idea of what functionalism is about, we need to make a distinction between two ways of classifying things. **Physical kinds** are identified by their material composition only. In this view, jellyfish and carpets are different because they are made up of fundamentally different physical substances. **Functional kinds**, however, are distinguished by their actions or tendencies. Here, we could say that all automobiles fall under the same functional category because they do the same things—namely, transport goods and people—even though they may be made up of different elements.

So far so good, but things get interesting when we extend these ways of classifying to the idea of mind. If we think of mind as a physical kind, then minds must be the same things as brains, since, as far as we know, minds cannot exist apart from physical brains. To many, this seems too exclusive. It is possible, they argue, that computers might develop minds and that there might be alien species with minds (see Figure 2.4). Neither computers nor aliens need have brains in the sense that we know them. It is more fruitful, they say, to identify minds as functional kinds and, thus, to define them by the sorts of processes they carry out rather than the stuff they're made of. According to **functionalism**, mental states are not just physical states but also the functioning or operation of those physical states. According to this view, a mind could conceivably be implemented in any physical system, artificial or natural, capable of supporting the appropriate computation.

Functionalism has several significant implications (Garfield, 1995). One is that the same mental state could be realized in quite different ways in two separate physical systems. This can be illustrated with computing devices. Two such different devices, say a desktop computer and a palm-sized personal data assistant, can both compute the same result, such as displaying a page of text, but in different ways. The same might also be true for human

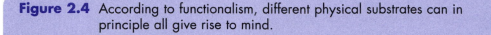

Figure 2.4 According to functionalism, different physical substrates can in principle all give rise to mind.

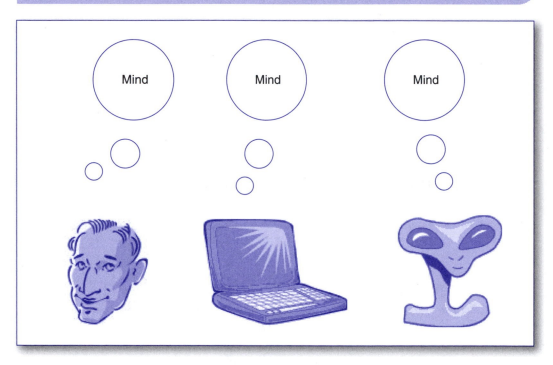

computation. If we examined the brains of two people thinking exactly the same thought, we would in all likelihood not find exactly the same processes at work. This is the idea of multiple realization that we first introduced when discussing identity theory.

There are several schools of thought in functionalism, ranging from conservative views that advocate direct connections between physical and computational states to more liberal ones that emphasize computation over physicality. The liberal schools give two reasons for their stance. They say that for both computers and thinking organisms, the number of possible computational states always exceeds the number of possible physical states. Take, for example, all the different possible beliefs one could hold concerning politics, the environment, one's friends, and so on. Mathematically, the number of such beliefs is infinite (Garfield, 1995). The number of possible physical states the brain can assume, though, is finite. A computational level of description, thus, becomes a richer and more diverse way of describing the mind and should be the preferred level. Second, liberal functionalists argue that psychological states such as beliefs are defined more by their relations to other such states, to inputs from the environment, and to behaviors than by their relations to physical states. A belief such as "patriotism" usually manifests itself in other beliefs—for example, in flag waving. It will elicit predictable reactions to environmental stimuli—for example, feeling upset when one's country has been criticized—and will produce external behaviors such as marching or protesting.

To summarize, functionalism implies that mental states might not be reduced to any particular physical state. This argument does not require us to be dualists. It is not saying that mental states don't conform to physical ones, only that there may be a wide variety of possible physical states capable of producing any given mental state. One last point of clarification needs to be made. As was the case with behaviorism, functionalism takes on two slightly different sorts of meaning within the philosophy of mind and psychology communities. Whereas the philosophical conception stresses multiple realizability, the psychological conception stresses the functions themselves. We elaborate more on this latter definition in the next chapter.

Evaluating the Functionalist Perspective

Although functionalism has been the dominant view in cognitive science since the 1970s, it is not without its deficiencies (Maloney, 1999). Remember that a tenet of functionalism is that minds that are not based on brains can exist. They can exist in objects such as computers as long as the physical substrates of those objects allow for the relevant computations. Critics have argued that, although it is possible that minds can exist in the absence of brains, this does not make it plausible. There is no current empirical evidence to justify this claim. We have yet to see something mental in the absence of a brain. Also, some have argued that the failure to identify mind with a physical kind can itself be considered a reason to do away with the concept of mind—rather than give it special status as a functional kind.

An additional problem with functionalism is that it cannot account for the felt or experienced character of mental states—a phenomenon known as **qualia** (quale, singular). Examples of qualia include the subjective experience of what it is like to feel hungry, to be angry, or to see the color red. It would seem that these kinds of experiences cannot be replicated as purely functional processes. A machine could be programmed to "see" the color red, even mimicking the same human functional process, but this machine could not have the same experience of what it is like to see red that a person has.

What is more, two individuals having the same conscious experience often do not experience it subjectively in the same way. A number of experiments have shown this to be the case with color perception. Participants looking at the same color will describe it differently (Chapanis, 1965). If asked to point out on a color spectrum what pure green looks like, one person may select a yellow-green, another a blue-green. This is the case even though the functional operations of their respective brains as they view the color are approximately equivalent. In this case, the neurophysiological operations behind color perception tend to be the same across individuals.

THE KNOWLEDGE ACQUISITION PROBLEM: HOW DO WE ACQUIRE KNOWLEDGE?

A fundamental question asked by even the earliest of philosophers was, How do we acquire knowledge? Clearly, you are not born knowing everything—otherwise, you would not need to go to school and wouldn't be reading this book. But are we born knowing anything at all? Is the mind completely blank, or do we start with some rudimentary understanding of the world? One way to frame these questions is within the **nature–nurture debate**. This debate centers on the relative contributions of biology and experience in determining any particular capacity. The term *nature*, in this context, refers to traits that are genetically or biologically determined. These are coded for in our genes and so are "hardwired," meaning they are present at birth or appear at a specific time during development. The term *nurture* refers to traits that are learned through experience and interaction with the environment. We will examine theories of knowledge acquisition that argue for the greater influence of one or the other.

According to **nativism**, a significant body of knowledge is innate or "built into" an organism. In this sense, nativism is a theory of knowledge that favors nature over nurture. Plato was the first to outline a nativist theory of knowledge. He thought learning was a matter of recollecting what is already known—these concepts existing in the ideal world of forms and being part of our immortal souls. **Rationalism** must be subtly distinguished from nativism. Descartes was the progenitor of this perspective. Rationalists also believe in the existence of innate ideas. These basic concepts include ideas such as "God" and "triangle." However, they additionally emphasize the existence of innate reasoning powers. These include certain logical propositions, such as knowing that something cannot exist and *not* exist at the same time. We can use these a priori rational powers to form new ideas that are not given to us innately. Descartes would agree that we are not born with the idea of "table" but can acquire it given our innate ability to perceive and think about objects.

Empiricism alternatively sees knowledge as acquired through experience: it favors nurture over nature. In this view, knowledge gets into the head through interaction with an environment, meaning it is learned. The senses provide the primary channels via which knowledge of the world is born. Our knowledge of the concept "lemon" in this account begins with looking at a lemon, touching it, and tasting it. The British philosopher John Locke (1632–1704) is credited as the founder of the empiricist movement. He used the phrase *tabula rasa*, which literally translates as "blank slate." Locke believed that we are born as blank slates, lacking any knowledge, and that over time experience puts writing on the slate, filling it up.

Locke had a more fully developed theory of learning. He differentiated between simple ideas and complex ideas. **Simple ideas** are derived through sensory input or simple processes of reflection. They are received passively by the mind and cannot be reduced to simpler ideas. Looking at a cherry would generate the simple idea of "red." Tasting a cherry would produce the simple idea of "sweet." **Complex ideas** are formed from the active mental combination of simple ideas. They are created through reflection only and can be reduced to parts, their component simple ideas. The idea of "cherry" would result from the associative combination of such simple ideas as "red," "sweet," and other commonly occurring sensations derived from one's experiencing cherries. This cluster of simple ideas is naturally associated because each time we experience a cherry, it comes to mind. For this reason, Locke and others who have proposed similar notions are sometimes known as the associationists.

Evaluating the Knowledge Acquisition Debate

One might be tempted to immediately dismiss the doctrine of innate ideas put forth by the nativists and rationalists. After all, it seems absurd that we should be born knowing factual information such as the content of the Gettysburg Address. But the scope of knowledge is broader than this. Think back to the previous chapter, in which we defined declarative knowledge for facts and procedural knowledge for skills. There is quite a bit of research supporting the notion that some forms of procedural knowledge are innate. Newborn infants, for instance, come into this world with a variety of different skills. These skills are universal across the human species and manifest themselves so soon after birth that they couldn't possibly have been learned. Therefore, they qualify as examples of innate knowledge. Let us examine a few of these.

All infants demonstrate a set of **reflexes.** These reflexes include the grasping reflex, in which the fingers tighten around a touch to the palm, and the rooting reflex, in which the infant turns his or her head and begins sucking an object placed near the mouth. Reflexes serve a clear adaptive function. Grasping and sucking, along with behaviors generated by other early reflexes, are important for survival. The physiology behind reflexes is simple and fairly well understood. A stimulus triggers one or more sensory neurons that then activate intermediary neurons. These in turn activate motor neurons, causing the resulting behavior. It is easy to see how such a simple mechanism could be hardwired at birth to enable the infant to respond effectively to its environment. Figure 2.5 shows the anatomy of a spinal reflex.

Figure 2.5 The neural connections in a spinal reflex. A reflex is an example of innate procedural knowledge.

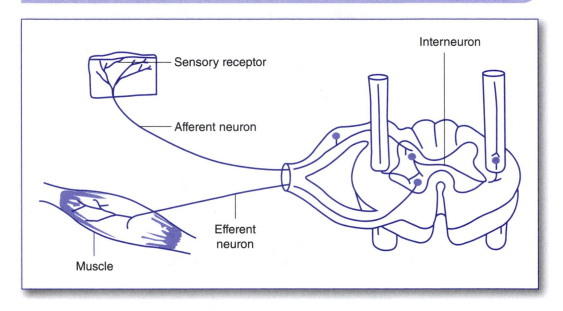

Smell preference is another example of innate behavior. Steiner (1979) found that newborns tend to agree with adults in terms of which odors they consider pleasant or unpleasant. He found that odors such as strawberry and banana elicited agreeable facial expressions from young infants—for example, smiling. Unpleasant odors, such as fish and rotten eggs, elicited expressions of disgust. As is the case with reflexes, these smell preferences have survival value. Babies who find the smell of fruit attractive will eat the fruit and thereby gain nutrients; those who are repulsed by spoiled or unpalatable food will reject the food and avoid getting sick. The neural mechanisms behind such preferences are probably not too complex either. They need to involve little more than a mapping between the odor and the emotional response.

Given the above examples, we see that it is not so far-fetched for us to be born with procedural knowledge. This knowledge is in the form of simple neural circuits that map stimulus inputs to appropriate behavioral outputs. This knowledge can even be represented using the conditional rules we talked about in Chapter 1. A coding of a smell preference might look something like this: "If *smell is fish*, then *disgust*." The odor, if it satisfies the first part of the conditional, would then trigger the response in the second part.

But how did these circuits get there in the first place? The early nativists and rationalists either did not specify the source of innate knowledge or attributed it to God. Evolutionary psychology offers us another explanation. It attributes such capacities to generations of selection pressures acting on a species. These pressures promote the development of adaptive (survival-related) cognitive abilities. Evolutionary psychologists can be considered modern-day nativists. See the evolutionary approach chapter for more on their views.

The phrasing of the nature–nurture debate as allowing for only a single alternative, either one or the other, is misleading. Although some traits may indeed be entirely the product of nature or of nurture, there is a large middle ground consisting of traits or cognitive abilities that can result from the complex interaction of the two. In these cases, nature may set constraints or limits on environmental influence. Take memory, for example. Tsien, Huerta, and Tonegawa (1996) engineered a mutation in a gene that affects a particular type of receptor in the hippocampus, a brain area responsible for the learning of new information. Rats with the mutation did poorly in a memory task as compared with normal rats in a control group. Tang et al. (1999) did something even more remarkable. Through genetic manipulation, they increased production of a particular subunit in the hippocampal receptor. This change increased the receptor's effectiveness. Rats with this "enhanced" version of the gene outperformed rats with normal receptors on a spatial memory test.

This research is exciting because it shows that memory in these animals is at least partially under genetic control. However, it is also well documented that human memory capability can be improved through organization and the use of memory strategies (Roediger, 1980). The way in which these genetic and environmental factors interact to determine memory in any given individual is complex. It could be that any amount of organization could produce no more than a small increase in memory performance if the aforementioned gene were lacking. Alternatively, those with the enhanced version of the gene who also employ memory strategies could perhaps acquire "supermemories" and then no longer need to employ memory strategies in order to remember effectively.

THE MYSTERY OF CONSCIOUSNESS: WHAT IS CONSCIOUSNESS AND HOW DOES IT OPERATE?

Consciousness is a complex concept and has no single agreed-on definition. In its broadest sense, we can think of it as the subjective quality of experience (Chalmers, 1996). It may be thought of as our individual subjective awareness of mental states. These states include sensation, perception, visual images, conscious thought processes, emotions, and sense of self, just to name a few. But these states assume that a person is in a normal, awake, and alert frame of mind. The issue becomes more complex when we think of other types of consciousness—for example, being unconscious, asleep, in a drug-induced state, hypnotized, or meditating. There are clinical cases representing other states of consciousness as well. In dissociative identity disorder, a person can alternate between separate personalities. Each personality can possess unique skills and may or may not be aware of the others. In split-brain patients, one half of the brain can possess an awareness of an object that the other half does not possess. For simplicity, we do not consider these alternate states of mind.

An interesting aspect of consciousness is whether it is unitary or divided. Subjectively, our consciousness seems to be unitary. That is, one recognizes himself or herself to be one person, experiencing things in the present moment. When one studies the brain, though, one finds that there is no single place or even time where consciousness seems to happen. Instead, the brain in action is a case of activity going on all over the place. Furthermore, the brain may even be processing different aspects of a single experience at different times. How can we reconcile this objective evidence with our subjective experience? See the "Interdisciplinary Crossroads" section for one theory on this apparent contradiction.

Chalmers (1996) makes a distinction between phenomenal and psychological concepts of mind. The **phenomenal concept of mind** is essentially the idea of mind as a conscious experience. Mental states in this view need to be explained in terms of how they feel. The **psychological concept of mind** sees mental states only in terms of how they cause and explain behavior. Here, mind is characterized by what it does—how it feels is irrelevant. Philosophers have concerned themselves primarily with the former, psychologists and cognitive scientists with the latter. To make this distinction clear, imagine biting into a candy bar. A phenomenal investigation would attempt to explain why you experience the mental states of "sweetness" or "chocolate" and why you might perceive them differently than does somebody else. A psychological investigation would concern itself with the neural circuits that become activated during the taste, how they might be represented computationally, and how this explains when you might stop eating. In this section, we concern ourselves with the phenomenal concept of mind and its relation to consciousness, since the psychological view is in most cases the topic of the remainder of this book.

Chalmers (1996) also differentiates between what he calls the easy and hard problems of consciousness. **Easy problems of consciousness** are those that can be solved by cognitive science and explained in terms of computational or neural mechanisms. His examples include the ability to discriminate, categorize, and react to environmental stimuli; the focus of attention; and the difference between wakefulness and sleep. Obviously, these correspond to the psychological concept of mind. The **hard problems of consciousness** are those involving subjective experience. Here we would need to explain why we have a visual or auditory experience when we look at or listen to something. In this case, we are now talking about the phenomenal concept of mind. Whereas science can give us answers to the easy problems, it may not be possible to provide answers to the hard ones. The fact that subjective human experience may not be fully explained by an objective account using physical and mechanical processes is known as the **explanatory gap** (Levine, 1983).

The What-It's-Like Argument

Nagel (1974) says that there is "something that it is like" to have a conscious mental state. When you bite into a candy bar, you have a subjective conscious experience of tasting it. The candy bar, of course, has no such experience. There is nothing that "it is like" for the candy bar being bitten. This is one way of describing consciousness—that organisms that possess it can be described as having some sort of experience. Things incapable of supporting consciousness cannot.

But what is this experience like? Nagel (1974) asks us to imagine what it must be like for a bat to navigate by echolocation. In echolocation, the bat emits high-pitched sounds. The sound waves bounce off an object in the animal's path, and the animal uses the reflection time as a measure of the object's distance (see Figure 2.6). We could conceivably build a machine that could compute echolocation the same way a bat does. It might even perform as successfully as the bat. But this would not tell us what it is like for the bat to

Figure 2.6 What is it like to be a bat?

experience the world in the way it does. We have seen this argument before in our evaluation of functionalism. There, we said that a functional description of a cognitive process does not account for the qualia, or subjective experience, of the process.

The problem here is that science can provide only an objective account of a phenomenon, and consciousness is an inherently subjective state. As organisms capable of supporting consciousness, we can introspect and analyze what it is like to have or to experience a mental state. Unfortunately for cognitive science, this is not what is needed. Cognitive science must, instead, have a scientific and objective account of what consciousness is. Frank Jackson (1982) aptly illustrates the difference between objective and subjective accounts of a conscious experience. He asks us to think about a neuroscientist named Mary who is well trained in the physical mechanisms underlying color vision. She understands everything there is to know about how the eye and brain process color information. Mary, however, is colorblind. Imagine now that we take away her colorblindness and allow her to look at a tomato. Interesting questions arise. Does Mary learn anything new by this experience? Does the scientific community gain anything by Mary's (or anybody else's) description of what it is like to see red? Jackson argues that we do gain something and that science needs to explain this new information.

In contrast to this position, some state that subjective knowledge is not factual knowledge at all and, therefore, does not constitute any kind of an explanation. Personally knowing what it is like to taste a candy bar or to see red is not the same thing as objectively and factually knowing it. Adopting this position, we as investigators would be forced to ignore introspection and any other form of subjective description. Our focus would be on only legitimate objective techniques for studying the mind, such as experimentation and brain imaging.

Mind as an Emergent Property

Consciousness is a "hot" topic in contemporary cognitive science. In the past 15 or so years, there have been renewed interdisciplinary efforts to understand it. A number of well-known authors have published books for academic and layperson audiences that outline their definitions and views on the subject. These authors' theories are too numerous to mention here. We instead describe one popular theory in this section and a more detailed description of another in the "Interdisciplinary Crossroads" part of the chapter. Before we begin this, however, we must articulate two different conceptions of how complex systems such as the brain might work.

Reductionism is the belief that everything about a whole can be explained entirely by understanding its parts. If this were true, we could say that phenomenon X is "nothing more than" phenomenon Y. X is, therefore, reduced to Y. If we were to let X be understanding the brain and Y be the functioning of neurons, then we could completely understand brains by completely understanding neurons. Were it so easy. There are very few cases of successful reduction in the sciences. Thermodynamics has not been reduced to statistical mechanics, nor has chemistry been reduced to quantum mechanics. In part, this is because it is not enough to understand the parts; one must also understand how they interact or relate to one another.

In emergence, the features of a whole are not completely independent of the parts that make them up. They are said to go beyond the features of those parts or emerge from them. Holland (1998) lists several characteristics of emergence. Emergent systems are made up of interacting parts. The function of these systems is rule governed. The rules stay the same even though the parts change over time. This constant dynamic gives rise to novelty and unpredictability. It is difficult or impossible to anticipate what such systems will do, even if some or all of the rules that govern their operation are known. A problem with the emergent account is that it doesn't constitute an explanation. All it says is that the behavior of the whole is more than the sum of its parts. What is needed is a causal or scientific explanation of how part interactions give rise to emergent features.

John Searle (1992) uses the concept of emergence in his book *The Rediscovery of the Mind*. He argues that consciousness is an emergent property of the brain. An emergent property of a system, as we have mentioned, is realized through the interaction of the system's parts. Searle says if we have a given emergent system, S, made up of elements a, b, c, and so on, then the features of S may not be the same as the features of a, b, c, and so on. This is because the features of S arise from the causal interactions of the parts. Water, for example, has the features or properties of liquidity and transparency. The H_2O molecules that make it up do not share these properties. The causal interactions of these molecules give rise to these properties. In the same way, Searle says, consciousness is a property of the brain but not of its parts. If we take neurons to be the relative parts, then they have their own properties, such as being able to communicate with one another via electrical signals. These properties that are inherent in the way the neurons interact give rise to consciousness, but the properties of individual neurons need not be those of a conscious mind.

Searle is very careful to point out that he is not a reductionist. He does not believe consciousness is reducible to its parts. In reductionism, explanation goes downward and a phenomenon is directly explainable in terms of what is happening at a smaller scale. In emergence, explanation goes upward. The smaller now gives rise to the larger. The large-scale phenomena are more than just what is happening in and around the parts and cannot be explained solely by an account of what the parts are doing. This idea is similar to the concept of a gestalt in perception. Gestalts are discussed in the next chapter ("The Psychological Approach").

Searle seeks to avoid the monism–dualism dichotomy of the mind–body problem. He does this by talking about consciousness as a property rather than a substance. He likens consciousness to an emergent characteristic of what brains do in the same way that digestion is what stomachs do or photosynthesis is what plants do. He sees consciousness as a natural process and a by-product of the brain's nature. However, he does classify conscious mental states as separate from physical ones. He states that they constitute a unique and novel category of phenomena, with an independent reality and a distinct metaphysical status.

Evaluating the Emergent View of Mind

As appealing as this formulation is, it still leaves us with some vexing questions. The reformulation of consciousness as a property, and a nonphysical one at that, still begs the question: What is a property? If a property is not physical, then of what substance is it? Although attempting to avoid the mind–body debate, Searle seemingly ends up as a property dualist. Restating consciousness as a nonmaterial property of a material brain doesn't get us any further toward understanding what this type of property is. Also, it is not clear how emergence happens—that is, we do not yet have an understanding of the relationship between microscopic and macroscopic properties. In the case of water, we can say its properties have something to do with the three-dimensional shape of the H_2O molecules and other conditions, such as the surrounding temperature. For consciousness and the brain, this relationship between the microscopic and the macroscopic is far more ambiguous.

Searle's reason for believing in a nonmaterial consciousness is based on his conception of the difference between physical and mental things. For physical things, we can make a distinction between appearance and reality. A piece of wood may subjectively appear a certain way to us—as brown, as having a certain length and weight, and so on. These characteristics can also be measured objectively; we can put the wood on a scale to determine its weight, use a ruler to determine its length, and a wavelength detector to measure its color. For mental things, this distinction between the subjective and the objective goes away. Regarding mental experience, Searle believes that appearance is the same as reality and that our subjective introspections are objectively correct. But if this were true, we would have to trust our intuitions about the mental world as metaphysically special and nonmaterial.

In opposition, Paul Churchland (1995) points out that this reliance on the infallibility of introspection is an outdated notion. He notes that introspection often does not give us direct and accurate knowledge of the mental. Our inner assessments of mental states can be quite often, and notoriously, wrong. It is commonplace for us to err in judging our thoughts, feelings, and desires. Many of the early psychologists relied on introspection as a means to study the mind. The next chapter provides a more elaborate discussion of the problems they encountered.

Consciousness: One or Many?

In his book *Consciousness Explained*, Dennett (1991) outlines an interesting theory on the nature of consciousness. He begins by refuting the classical view of consciousness.

The classical view, promoted by Descartes, posits a single point in the brain where all information funnels in. This area is a supposed center of consciousness, where we experience the world or the contents of our thoughts in a coherent, unified way. Dennett calls this center the "Cartesian theater." It is as though our consciousness is the result of a projector displaying information on a movie screen. The individual sitting in the theater watching the screen then has a single conscious experience of what is playing. Figure 2.7 gives a representation of the Cartesian theater.

There are a number of problems with the Cartesian theater. To start, linked modes of information do not arrive within the brain simultaneously. Light from an event precedes the arrival of sound. The sight of a fireworks display reaches the mind prior to the sound of the explosion, yet we experience the two in unison. This suggests that our consciousness is constructed; the visual experience is kept in check or delayed until arrival of the sound, at which point the two are integrated into a unified percept of the fireworks. This example and others imply that consciousness does not occur in real time—but (in many instances) several fractions of a second or so after an event. Our experience of consciousness as direct and immediate seems to be an illusion.

Another problem with the Cartesian theater is that anatomically it is difficult to find a brain region that links incoming sensory inputs and outgoing motor outputs. There is no **central processing unit (CPU)** in the brain as there is in a computer. The task of a computer's CPU is to schedule and coordinate ongoing activity. Furthermore, the Cartesian theater analogy requires an observer in the audience watching the screen. This observer is the subjective self who experiences the screen's contents. But how is this person inside

Figure 2.7 The Cartesian theater explanation of consciousness.

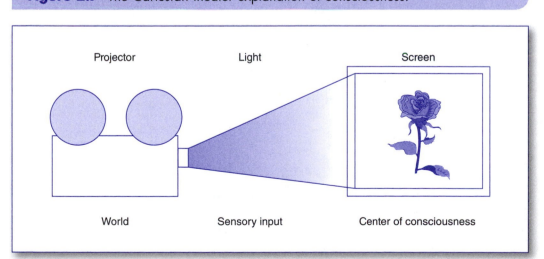

one's head interpreting the image and having the conscious experience? To explain this, we need to posit another mechanism or theater inside this person's head with another even smaller person and so on, ad infinitum. This is known as the homunculus problem in psychology and philosophy. **Homunculus** translated means "little man." An effective theory of consciousness must avoid the logical conundrum of homunculi nested inside each other.

Dennett replaces this problematic formulation with a multiple drafts model of consciousness (see Figure 2.8). In this model, mental activity occurs in parallel. Rather than projecting to a single location for processing in unison, different ongoing streams of information are processed at different times. Each of these streams can correspond to different sensory inputs or thoughts. Processing or editing of the streams can occur, which may change their content. Editing can consist of subtractions, additions, and changes to the information. Awareness of a stream's content can happen before or after editing takes place. To illustrate, take our fireworks example. One mental stream would contain the visual experience of the fireworks, while another would contain its auditory representation. The visual stream would undergo editing in the form of a delay to synchronize it with the auditory stream. Then the information from both streams could be tapped to produce awareness.

There is abundant evidence in support of the multiple drafts model. Take, for instance, the organization of the visual system. It adopts a "divide-and-conquer" strategy. The visual system carves up different aspects of an object during pattern recognition. These aspects

Figure 2.8 Dennett's multiple drafts model of consciousness.

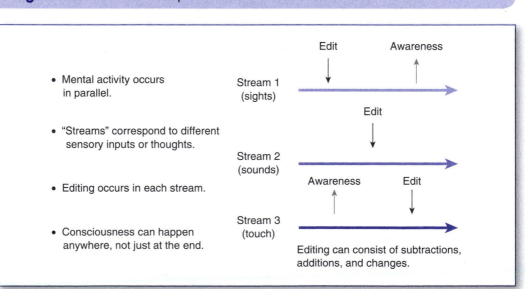

are each processed separately in different parts of the brain by anatomically distinct pathways. This information is later combined to yield a unitary percept, but we are not aware that the information has been separated and then united.

A famous experiment by Loftus and Palmer (1974) also provides support for Dennett's idea. In this study, participants viewed a film of a car crash. Afterward, they were asked to estimate the speeds of the cars. The crucial manipulation was in how the question was asked. Some were asked how fast the cars were going when they "bumped" into each other. Others were asked how fast they were going when they "smashed" into each other. As you might predict, those who were queried with a mild descriptor such as "bumped" estimated that the cars were moving more slowly. Those queried with a more severe descriptor such as "smashed" estimated the speeds as considerably higher. These results suggest that our memories of an event are not perfectly preserved "snapshots" of what happened but are actively edited over time. The posing of a question and other subsequent experiences after the event can cause the memory to be edited and changed.

Dennett's theory also allows for different levels of awareness. Some information that is part of a stream may be available to conscious awareness and could be verbally described by the individual experiencing it. Other data streams we may be only vaguely aware of, but they can persist and influence additional mental processes. Yet other information may simply fade into the background. We may never be aware of this information. These three levels of awareness are comparable to Freud's conscious, preconscious, and subconscious aspects of mind, discussed in the next chapter.

In summary, Dennett's theory is more logically coherent and captures some of the empirical evidence on conscious experience. It suggests that there is no central place where consciousness happens but that multiple mental events occur in parallel. These events may be edited and changed in such a way that consciousness need not take place in real time. We may or may not be aware of these events.

Consciousness and Neuroscience

What does the brain have to do with consciousness? Is there some part of the brain or some particular pattern of neural activity that gives rise to consciousness? What is the neural correlate of conscious experience? Although philosophers have been debating the relation between the brain and mental phenomena for millennia, recent advances in neuroscience have yielded more specific insights into these questions. Let's examine some of them here.

In general, the neuroscience view is that consciousness results from the coordinated activity of a population of neurons in the brain. Popper and Eccles (1981) see consciousness as an emergent property of a large number of interacting neurons. A different idea is that there are neurons specifically devoted to producing consciousness. Crick and Koch

(1995) believe that these are located throughout the cortex and in other areas associated with the cortex. Activity in at least some subset of these neurons produces conscious experience. They believe that these neurons are special and that they differ from other neurons in terms of their structure and function. A similar but slightly different conception is that any cortical neuron may contribute to a conscious experience; however, different groups of cortical neurons mediate different types of conscious experience.

If there were special consciousness neurons, where might they be located? It has been proposed that one area is the intralaminar nuclei of the thalamus (Purpura & Schiff, 1997). The thalamus is a relay center for incoming sensory information. It sends information from each of the different sensory modalities, such as vision, audition, touch, and taste, to specialized areas of the cortex devoted to processing the information. Lesions of or damage to this brain region results in coma and loss of consciousness. It may be that these thalamic neurons, because they have widespread projections to many cortical areas, serve to activate or arouse other cortical neurons. Specific activity in different cortical regions may then account for specific forms of consciousness. For example, activation or arousal in the occipital visual regions may correspond to visual awareness, while activation of the somatosensory cortex may produce awareness of different parts of the body.

Churchland (1995) formulates a neurocomputational theory of consciousness that focuses on connections between the intralaminar nuclei of the thalamus and disparate cortical areas. The circuit consists of ascending projections from the thalamus to the cortex, as well as descending pathways from the cortex to the thalamus. Figure 2.9 shows the anatomical layout of this area. These pathways are recurrent, meaning that a signal can be sent back and forth inside it. In this case, information coming into the thalamus can be passed to the cortex, while the cortex can also pass information back to the thalamus. Recurrence is an important network property because it allows for feedback and learning. Recurrent activity in a network may sustain information over time and be the basis for conscious mental awareness. Recurrent artificial neural networks and their properties are described in Chapter 7 ("The Network Approach").

Churchland believes that the characteristics of this network can account for a number of different features of consciousness. One such feature is the capacity of consciousness to hold information over time—the equivalent of a short-term memory in which we are aware of the current moment in relation to the past. This is in keeping with the network's recurrent nature, since information can be held over time as it is cycled back and forth. Churchland also shows that this network can maintain activity in the absence of sensory inputs—for example, when we are daydreaming or thinking with our eyes shut. It can additionally explain why we lose consciousness during sleep, why it reappears during dreaming, and a host of other such features.

Churchland is quick to acknowledge, however, that it is the dynamical properties of this recurrent network and not its particular neural locus that make consciousness possible. He admits that a consciousness circuit may exist in places that have been suggested by other

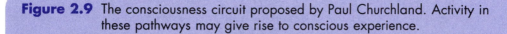

Figure 2.9 The consciousness circuit proposed by Paul Churchland. Activity in these pathways may give rise to conscious experience.

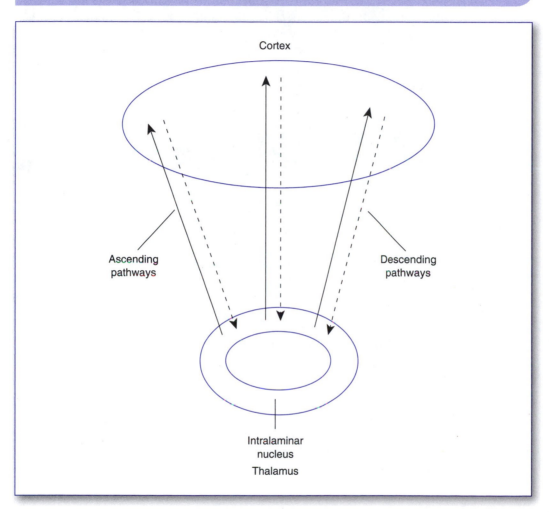

researchers. One such area is within the right parietal lobe (Damasio, 1994). The neuroscientist Rodolfo Llinas (2002) has suggested that consciousness may arise within the layers of the primary sensory cortex itself. He has written a comprehensive book that lays out his views.

Koch (2004) has also adopted a neurobiological approach to consciousness. He defines the **neural correlates of consciousness (NCC)** as the minimal set of neural events and structures sufficient for a specific conscious experience. Since the entire brain appears to be sufficient for consciousness, the term *minimal* in the above definition is used because we would like to know what specific brain areas or activity is necessary. There should be as many distinct NCC as there are different types of conscious experience. For instance, one pattern of activity may underlie the taste of chocolate, another the feel of wind on your face, and yet another the feeling of jealousy. If we change this pattern of activity, there should be a corresponding change in the subjective experience, and if we suppress it, the associated experience should disappear. Furthermore, it should be possible to induce a particular experience artificially by creating an NCC through electrode or some other form of stimulation.

Interdisciplinary Crossroads: Philosophy, Neuroscience, and Binocular Rivalry

Imagine an experiment where you are asked to put on glasses with one red lens and one blue lens. On a screen in front of you, there is a pattern consisting of vertical red bars crossed by horizontal blue bars. The glasses present a different image to each eye: One sees the red stripes, the other the blue stripes. Under normal circumstances, the information from both eyes is fused to form a single unitary sense of the world with depth. Under these new circumstances, though, the two eyes compete for conscious awareness. You might first see the horizontal blue bars for a few seconds; then there would be a shift, and for the next few seconds, you would perceive the vertical red bars. This phenomenon, where each perception alternately vies for visual consciousness, is called **binocular rivalry** (Alais & Blake, 2005).

Now in this study, we ask you to push two buttons, each corresponding to one of the possible percepts. You are instructed to push the left button when you see the vertical red bars and the right button for the competing perception. While this is happening, the researchers are measuring your brain activity using an imaging technique known as magnetoencephalography. In this procedure, a helmet containing a number of sensors that detect very small magnetic fields induced by neural activity is placed over your head. This allows the investigators to see which parts of your brain are active during the experience. In this way, they can determine the neural correlates of these conscious experiences.

The results from this work show a particular pattern of neural action when participants reported not being consciously aware of the images. This pattern is characterized by widespread action in the visual areas of the occipital lobes as well as in the frontal lobes that underlie more high-level cognitive processing. This pattern, however, changed dramatically once an observer reported seeing one of the two possible sets of bars. Awareness of the pattern produced an increase of 40% to 80% neural responding. There was much reentrant activity in this state, with looping feedback found between different brain regions. But perhaps what is most interesting is that in these studies no two observers had the same pattern, even when they reported seeing the same thing. These sorts of individual differences pose a problem for cognitive science because they imply that the brain does not always rely on the same areas to produce a given function. Fortunately, brain imaging does show some localization of function across individuals, as well as variability.

In another similar study, participants were presented a picture of a house to one eye and a picture of a face to the other eye (Tong, Nakayama, Vaughn, & Kanwisher, 1998). When the observers reported seeing a house, functional magnetic resonance imaging showed bilateral activation in the parahippocampal place area (PPA) and less activity in the fusiform face area (FFA). When they perceived the face, this pattern of activity was reversed, with greater activation in the FFA and less in the PPA. The FFA, as we will describe in more detail in the neuroscience chapter, is that portion of the temporal lobe that responds selectively to facial stimuli.

Experiments such as these can tell us what parts of the brain or what patterns of brain activity underlie conscious experience. Ultimately, the use of such imaging techniques may be able to give us a complete picture of brain action for any given conscious experience in any individual. This will certainly tell us a lot about the brain, but it falls short of explaining the subjective nature of conscious experience. That is because, in the end, we will be left with an objective description of an inherently subjective phenomenon. In fact, that is all that science as an objective method can provide. At that point, we will either need to be content with our physicalist account of consciousness at the neural level or continue our investigation further by looking for more physical correlates at different levels, such as the synaptic or molecular.

Consciousness and Artificial Intelligence

Researchers in AI design algorithms to perform real-world computational tasks such as language comprehension and problem solving. Many of these algorithms can be judged as successful from a behavioral standpoint because they adequately perform their tasks, some under a variety of different conditions. If we define thought as computation in some physical substrate, as functionalists do, then we can also, without much risk, say that the execution of these programs is equivalent to "thinking." But does this correspond to consciousness? This is a much riskier proposition, since, as we have seen, consciousness implies more than computation. It seems to involve subjective experience and perhaps other things. In this section, we address the question of whether a machine can be conscious. This is perhaps the most interesting philosophical issue in AI today.

There are a variety of different perspectives on whether or not a machine can become conscious (Freedman, 1994). These may be generally classified into two categories. The **strong AI** view asserts that consciousness can arise from a purely physical process.

Followers of this perspective believe that, eventually, as we create machines with greater complexity and computational power, we will see consciousness emerge in them. Proponents of **weak AI** claim that consciousness is itself either not a physical process, and so can never be reproduced, or a physical process but such a complex one that we will never be able to duplicate it artificially.

Let us examine the arguments both for and against strong AI. Daniel Dennett (1998) raises several points in its defense. He mentions that many phenomena that used to have mystical and supernatural explanations now have scientific ones. Consciousness should be no different, he argues. Some have claimed that consciousness may be possible only in an organic brain. Dennett concedes that this may be true but notes that science has already been able to mechanically reproduce small-scale biochemical processes. An alternate counterargument is that consciousness is simply too complex to be artificially replicated. In response to this, Dennett says that consciousness of a more basic form may not require a sophisticated artificial substrate. Dennett ends by noting that any conscious machine will probably have to develop this capacity through an extended learning process, just as humans do. From a practical standpoint, this is not a barrier, since a number of machines that learn from experience have been designed.

Perhaps the most persuasive and well-known argument against the strong AI position is the **Chinese room scenario** (Searle, 1980). In this hypothetical situation, a man is in a room by himself. Outside the room is a person who asks a question in Chinese. This question is converted into written Chinese symbols on paper. The man in the room understands no Chinese whatsoever but has a book of rules that tells him how to relate the Chinese symbols that make up the question into a set of symbols constituting a response (see Figure 2.10). These written symbols are then converted back into a spoken reply. For example, if the outside person utters, "How are you?" in Chinese, the man in the room may, using the rule book, counter with, "I'm doing fine!" To an outside observer, it would seem as if the person in the room understands Chinese. After all, he has a reply to any question that is given. But Searle's point is that the man knows no Chinese. He is only following a prescribed set of rules that maps one set of symbols onto another. This is a rote execution of an algorithm, and according to Searle, it is all a machine can do. Therefore, he says, machines can never "understand," "know," or "be aware of" the information they process. They cannot be conscious of what they do. Consciousness of the human sort requires something more than just following an algorithm. To Searle, these extra ingredients are intentionality and meaning—aspects of mental representation discussed in the introductory chapter.

Boden (1990) raises a number of objections to the Chinese room argument. First, the terms *understanding* and *intentionality* are not well defined. Understanding could be operationally defined as being able to respond successfully when asked, rather than as entailing some inherent meaning on the part of the person. Second, a person who remained for some time in the Chinese room or even a machine in the room, if of sufficient complexity and if

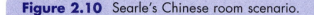

Figure 2.10 Searle's Chinese room scenario.

left there long enough, might eventually achieve some level of understanding. Either might eventually notice that certain combinations of characters always go together and from this learn the basic elements of syntax. Finally, Boden mentions that one could take this argument to its extreme by building a robot that, following rules, is indistinguishable from a human, yet one would have intentionality and the other would not.

OVERALL EVALUATION OF THE PHILOSOPHICAL APPROACH

One of the main advantages of the philosophical approach is that it allows us to ask much broader questions than those of other disciplines. A cognitive psychologist studying memory for nouns might wonder why concrete nouns are recalled better than abstract ones. This psychologist is constrained into formulating specific questions and hypotheses by the narrow focus of the research. This very focus, of course, is an advantage since it allows the researcher to examine and understand a natural phenomenon in depth. A philosopher examining the results of this same research is free to inquire about the nature of concreteness or what it means that something is abstract. He or she could also inquire as to how concrete or abstract stimuli are processed in other cognitive systems, such as attention and language. Of course, he or she is free to ask even more fundamental questions such as, Why do we have memory? What purpose does memory serve? What would a person be like without a memory? Philosophy, thus, shows us the "bigger picture." It gives us key insights into the relationships between different areas of study—within and between disciplines—and, therefore, plays a very important role in the interdisciplinary endeavor of cognitive science.

Keep in mind that philosophy is a nonempirical approach. It does not utilize the scientific method. Concepts in philosophy are validated through logical reasoning and argument rather than by systematic observation and experimentation. For this reason, the conclusions reached in philosophy are speculative and theoretical until tested. Philosophy is better suited to the asking of important questions—how, what, and why we should study something—than to providing definitive answers. These answers come from the scientific disciplines. It is, therefore, important that a good two-way working relationship exists between philosophers and these science-based approaches.

Summing Up: A Review of Chapter 2

1. Philosophy plays a key role in cognitive science by asking critical questions.

2. According to the mind–body problem, it is not known whether mental states are physical states. Two approaches to this are (1) monism, which argues that mind and body are unitary, and (2) dualism, which states that mind and body are separate.

3. There are two versions of monism: (1) idealism, where the universe is nonphysical, and (2) physicalism, where it is. Identity theorists hold that the mind is the brain, while eliminativists wish to do away completely with the concept of mind as well as with any folk psychology or commonsense explanations of the mind.

4. There are also two schools of dualism. Substance dualism holds that mind and body are composed of different substances. Property dualism holds that mental states are nonphysical features of physical bodies.

5. Functionalists believe that mental states are equivalent to the functioning or operation of physical states. It may be that different material substrates can give rise to mental states.

6. The knowledge acquisition problem is about how mental capacities are acquired. Nativists believe that we are born with knowledge. Empiricists believe that we attain knowledge through learning and experience.

7. Consciousness is the subjective quality of experience. The easy problem of consciousness is explaining qualia (subjective experience) in computational or neural terms. The hard problem is explaining how we have such experiences at all.

8. Mind may be an emergent property of a physical brain. That is, it may not be fully explained by an understanding of its component parts.

9. The neurobiological approach to consciousness tries to discover the neural states corresponding to different types of consciousness experience, known as the neural correlates of consciousness.

10. The strong AI view is that it may be possible some day to engineer a complex system that is conscious. In contrast, the weak AI view advocates that consciousness is either nonphysical or that it is physical but too difficult to engineer.

Explore More

Log on to the student study site at **http://study.sagepub.com/friedenberg3e** for electronic flash cards, review quizzes, and a list of web resources to aid you in further exploring the field of cognitive science.

Suggested Readings

Bechtel, W. (1988). *Philosophy of mind: An overview for cognitive science.* Hillsdale, NJ: Erlbaum.

Blackmore, S. (2012). *Consciousness: An introduction.* Oxford, England: Oxford University Press.

Chalmers, D. (1996). *The conscious mind.* Oxford, England: Oxford University Press.

Churchland, P. M. (1986). *Neurophilosophy: Toward a unified science of the mind-brain.* Cambridge: MIT Press.

Churchland, P. M. (1995). *The engine of reason, the seat of the soul: A philosophical journey into the brain.* Cambridge: MIT Press.

Clark, A. (2001). *Mindware: An introduction to the philosophy of cognitive science.* New York, NY: Oxford University Press.

Dennett, D. C. (1991). *Consciousness explained.* Boston, MA: Little, Brown.

Pinker, S. (2002). *The blank slate: The modern denial of human nature.* New York, NY: Viking Press.

Searle, J. R. (1992). *The rediscovery of the mind.* Cambridge: MIT Press.

3

The Psychological Approach

A Profusion of Theories

Mind, n. A mysterious form of matter secreted by the brain. Its chief activity consists in the endeavor to ascertain its own nature, the futility of the attempt being due to the fact that it has nothing but itself to know itself with.

—Ambrose Bierce, 1911

WHAT IS PSYCHOLOGY?

This chapter highlights a number of different perspectives adopted within the discipline of psychology, primarily during the 20th century. Each has a relatively unique answer to the question, What is mind? But first, we need to ask ourselves another question: What is **psychology**? As a discipline, it is best defined as the scientific study of mind and behavior. Psychology uses the scientific method as a means of gaining valid knowledge. Its focus of study includes internal mental events, such as perception, reasoning, language, and visual imagery. However, it also studies behaviors, which are external events. Behaviors include things such as walking, talking, and running. This distinction between mind and behavior makes its appearance in the fundamental questions that this approach attempts to answer. These questions include, What are the contents of the mind? How do these contents interact with one another? How does the mind explain what we do?

The different movements in psychology described in this chapter have focused on different themes. Many of the movements, including voluntarism and structuralism, were concerned with cataloging the "stuff" inside our heads. That is, they tried to list the basic elements of the mind and delineate how they interact to form other elements. We see this question of mental content taken up later by other approaches. Cognitive psychologists, who studied memory later on, tried to describe concepts that exist in our memories and how these concepts are related to one another. They formulated the idea of a mental lexicon or dictionary as a way of explaining how concepts exist in memory. In the network approach, we see that semantic networks were created explicitly to describe the location and arrangement of concepts.

A second major theme that emerges in the history of psychology is centered on operations—that is, what the mind does rather than what it contains. We see the issue of operations being addressed first by the functionalists. Functionalism veered away from a listing of the mind's supposed "parts" and studied the ways in which the mind performs various mental actions. The psychoanalytic psychologists, such as Freud, were also operational in their approach. Their focus was on how mental structures such as the id and the ego dynamically interrelate. Gestalt psychology focused on a specific aspect of mental operations—namely, how mental parts form wholes. The Gestalt psychologists wanted to know how the mind creates larger order structures during perception and problem solving. This theme of mental operations occurs repeatedly in other areas of cognitive science too. Cognitive psychologists would later form elaborate models of mental processes to explain perception, memory, and attention. In neuroscience, brain scans would reveal the neural sequences of events that underlie mental tasks. Connectionists would devise neural networks with specific patterns of operation to simulate mental function, and in the domain of artificial intelligence, computers would be programmed with complex sets of rules to mimic the kinds of things the brain can do.

Interestingly, in the behaviorist movement, we see a counterreaction to the whole concept of studying the mind. Behaviorists viewed the mind as something that passively mapped aspects of the environment onto an organism's response. It was the environment and not the mind, they believed, that controlled a person's actions. The study of behavior and its relation to the environment appears again in cognitive science in the field of robotics. A challenging goal in this field is to get a machine to perform some task successfully in a real-world environment. To do so requires an understanding of how variable stimulus inputs can map onto a robot's possible responses.

A number of commonalities run through the different movements in psychology. Many were influenced by developments in other branches of the sciences. Particularly influential were chemistry and physics. Voluntarism and structuralism both adopted fundamental ideas from chemistry and embraced the idea that the mind, like the physical world, is made up of basic elements that combine into larger wholes. Similarly, the Gestalt psychologists adopted the idea of field theory from physics and employed the notions of fields, particles, and forces in their descriptions of mental phenomena. In addition, many movements in psychology arose as counterreactions to existing movements or as a means to address problems raised by prior movements. Both functionalism and Gestalt psychology, for instance, arose in opposition to structuralism.

PSYCHOLOGY AND THE SCIENTIFIC METHOD

Before describing the foremost theories of each movement, we need to digress and examine how psychology goes about its business. Early psychologists relied on techniques such as introspection and phenomenology. Modern psychologists employ a wider variety of methods. They administer questionnaires and surveys, analyze case studies of single individuals, and record behavior in the wild through naturalistic observation. A number of modern-day psychologists also cross over into other disciplines such as neuroscience or artificial intelligence and, thus, employ the methodologies of these approaches as well. Many of these techniques are characterized by the principles of science.

The scientific endeavor in general is characterized by the hypothetic-deductive approach. In this approach, a hypothetical conjecture about the way the world works is tested deductively. The testing is accomplished by carefully observing the way the world works under controlled conditions. If the observation supports our conjecture, we can elaborate and expand on it. If it doesn't, we must change it to account for what has been observed. The testing, as we alluded to in the previous paragraph, can assume a variety of forms. In neuroscience, it can be the observation of brain-damaged patients or the scanning of brain activity. In artificial intelligence or cognitive psychology, it may involve constructing a computer simulation. The scientific method, in which an experiment is conducted to test a hypothesis, is perhaps the most widely used method in all of psychology and cognitive science. For this reason, we will look into it now.

The **scientific method** uses an experiment that is designed to test a **hypothesis**—a specific statement about the world. For example, one could hypothesize that a participant's memory for a list of words will be worse when the participant is listening to music while studying them. The validity of a hypothesis is based on the outcome of an experiment. The results of an experiment can either support or fail to support a given hypothesis. Hypothesis testing helps researchers construct a **theory**—a more general understanding of the world that organizes a set of facts and aids us in understanding how the world works.

Any experiment involves the use of independent and dependent variables. An experimenter manipulates an **independent variable** to see if it will produce a change. Going along with our previous example, a researcher might vary the presence of music in a memory experiment. In the music condition, participants memorize a list of 30 words while listening to music being played in the background. In the no-music condition, a different group of participants must memorize the same 30 words without any music playing. The **dependent variable** is what is measured or observed by the experimenter to see if a change of some kind has occurred. Such a change may be thought of as the effect or the thing that happened as a result of the independent variable. In this instance, the independent variable would be music and the dependent variable might be the average number of words successfully recalled.

Generally, experiments consist of a minimum of two conditions. The **experimental group** receives the independent variable, while the **control group** does not. In our hypothetical example, the music condition would correspond to the experimental group and the no-music condition to the control group. Assuming that everything else that makes up the two conditions is held constant by the researchers, any difference between the two sets of results must be attributed to the manipulation. If we find that average word recall is higher in the no-music condition than in the music condition, then we could conclude that background music interferes with memorizing words. As stated above, this would support our hypothesis. This in turn would help us build a more general theory. The type of theory that might take shape from this and other similar experiments might be that memory processes require attention and that if attention is removed by a distractor task while memorizing, performance will suffer. The steps in this process are shown graphically in Figure 3.1. It should be noted that, historically, psychology has employed other techniques too. Among these are introspection and phenomenology, which will be defined later.

MENTAL ATOMS, MENTAL MOLECULES, AND A PERIODIC TABLE OF THE MIND: THE VOLUNTARIST MOVEMENT

Duane Schultz and Sydney Ellen Schultz (1987), in *A History of Modern Psychology*, give a good overview and critique of the various theoretical movements in the history of psychology. These movements include voluntarism, structuralism, functionalism, behaviorism, Gestalt psychology, and the psychodynamic view. They all preceded the cognitive revolution, which we will discuss in the next chapter. We refer our readers to their text for a more detailed discussion of the history and ideas behind these movements.

We will begin our discussion of psychology with voluntarism. The **voluntarism** movement viewed the mind as consisting of elements but stressed that these elements were assembled into higher level cognitive components through the power of the will. It was the will, or voluntary effort of the mind, that was seen as the force behind the creation of more complex mental elements. The German physiologist and psychologist Wilhelm Wundt (1832–1920) was the founder of voluntarism (see Figure 3.2). Another scientific field, chemistry, had a significant influence on voluntarism. During Wundt's time, chemists were attempting to describe the material world in terms of its basic components and how they combine. The Russian chemist Dimitri Mendeleev developed the periodic table of chemical elements during this time. The idea behind this table was that the entire physical universe consisted of atoms—characterized by different properties—and that atoms could, under certain conditions, combine to create more complex, higher order molecules. Wundt may also have been attempting to create a periodic table of mental elements and to specify how these elements combine (Marx & Hillix, 1979).

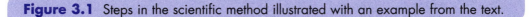

Figure 3.1 Steps in the scientific method illustrated with an example from the text.

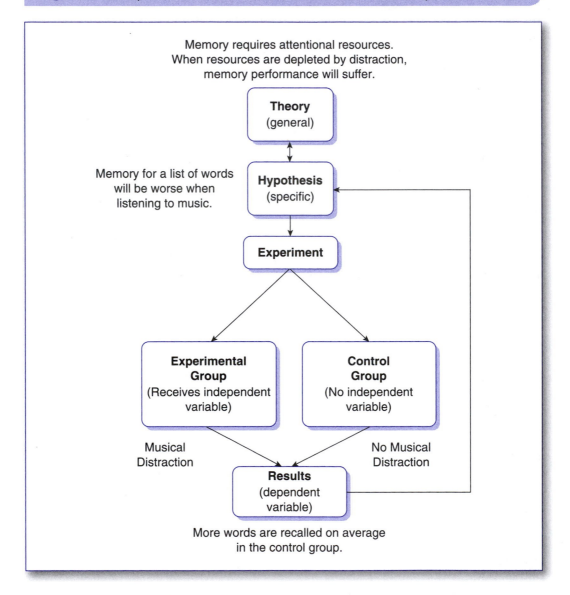

Wundt's method was **introspection**, or internal perception. *Introspection* literally means "inward looking." Just as one can look out at the external world to see various objects, such as a chair or table, Wundt believed that one could also look inward to experience and describe mental objects. He presented the students in his lab with various stimuli, such as colored shapes, and asked them to introspect. The students then recorded their subjective

Figure 3.2 Wilhelm Wundt established the first experimental psychology laboratory in Leipzig, Germany, in 1879.

Source: Hulton Archive/Stringer/Getty Images.

experiences about the stimuli. Although various forms of introspection had been used by philosophers for centuries, Wundt attempted to systematize and objectify the technique. He had his students put themselves in a ready state of attention prior to their introspecting and repeat their observations several times as he varied specific physical aspects of the stimulus, such as size and duration of the exposure. This kind of methodological exactness exemplifies the influence of the scientific method.

Wundt believed that psychology should study consciousness; however, he distinguished between two types of conscious experience. **Immediate experience** is our direct awareness of something. For example, if we see a rose, our perception of the rose as red is immediate. It is the redness that we experience directly while we are looking at it. If someone then asked us what we were looking at and we responded, "A red rose," then that thought would be a mediate experience (it was a thought about the rose). **Mediate experiences** are those that come from mental reflection about an object. Wundt emphasized the study of immediate experiences. He believed that they are the best way to describe the basic elements of the mind since they are "untainted" by elaborate thought processes.

Wundt went on to develop a **tridimensional theory of feeling,** according to which all feelings can be characterized by three dimensions: (1) pleasure or displeasure, (2) tension or relaxation, and (3) excitement or depression. Wundt would play a metronome, a device that produces audible clicks at different time intervals. As he varied the rate of the metronome, he discovered that some rhythms were more pleasant than others. He also reported a feeling of tension that accompanied his waiting for a click, followed by a feeling of satisfaction after the click occurred. Finally, he noted feeling excited when the tempo of clicks was increased and calm when they were played at a slower rate. Based on these introspective observations, he believed that any feeling could be characterized by pleasure or displeasure, tension or relaxation, and excitement or depression.

Although voluntarism attempted to describe and classify the basic elements of the mind, it also needed to account for the fact that we perceive unitary wholes rather than collections of individual elements. For instance, when looking at a face, we see a face in its entirety, not just a collection of its different parts: two eyes, a nose, and a mouth. To account for this, Wundt postulated the principle of **creative synthesis**, also called the law of psychic resultants. According to this principle, the mind actively organizes disparate elements together such that the resulting whole contains new properties. These new properties cannot be explained by the characteristics of the individual elements themselves. A similar phenomenon is seen in chemistry. Here, characteristics of individual atoms—for example, hydrogen and oxygen—are insufficient to specify the characteristics of the water molecules that form when they combine. Water has unique properties that cannot be understood simply by analyzing it down to its component parts.

To Wundt, creative synthesis was an active process in which the mind took hold of elements and forcefully combined them. This contrasts with the earlier views of the empiricists and associationists, who saw mental combination as a passive and mechanical effect. They argued that mental wholes were created through automatic processes of association and that these processes did not require the active participation of the mind deemed necessary by Wundt. This topic of the relationship between parts and wholes does not end here. The Gestalt psychologists would have much to say on this issue several years later.

Evaluating the Voluntarist Approach

The voluntarist approach was beneficial because it was the first scientific attempt at studying the mind. The establishment of a laboratory, the application of experimental methods, and the formulation of the clearly defined goals of listing elements and describing their combinations are all strengths of this movement. However, many of the criticisms that have been leveled at voluntarism also center on the elements of its methodology—introspection in particular. Critics have pointed to a number of flaws in introspection. First, a mental experience may change over time. A person's experience of red may undergo alteration after several seconds have elapsed—the experience perhaps becoming less vivid. Also, it may be impossible to separate immediate and mediate experiences because the act of introspecting could itself change an experience. According to this idea, the simple reporting of red, even as a sensation, involves reflective and perhaps other thought processes that alter the true experience of red. And there was the issue of individual differences. Some observers in Wundt's lab experienced the same stimulus in different ways, which suggested that people's expectations or learning experiences could change their perceptions. Finally, Wundt was never able to compile a short list of fundamental mental elements comparable to the list of elements that had been compiled in physical chemistry. The list of elements derived from his students' introspections with respect to their immediate, sensory-type experiences was growing far longer than what a simple periodic table would accommodate.

STRUCTURALISM: WHAT THE MIND IS

Structuralism shares a number of ideas with its predecessor, voluntarism. The subject matter of psychology was again conscious experience, and the method was a modified version of introspection with an emphasis on the scientific method. There were, however, major theoretical differences between the two schools. The structuralist view of the mind held, once again, that the mind was a passive agent, with mental elements combining according to mechanistic laws. Structuralism, per its name, focuses on mental elements; that is, the structure of the mind is to be understood in terms of basic elements and their combination—suggesting once again the analogy to chemistry. Its progenitor was the U.S. psychologist Edward Bradfort Titchener (1867–1927).

Titchener cautioned against making the stimulus error, which is to say, confusing our true experience of an object with a description of the object based on language and past experience. When one looks at a banana, the true experience would be that it is yellow and curved—not the recognizing of it as a banana or a type of fruit. This distinction parallels Wundt's differentiation between immediate and mediate experience. Titchener, in addition, broke away from Wundtian-style introspection. He believed that only well-trained observers could introspect accurately and not make the stimulus error.

According to Titchener, psychology had three goals: (1) to describe consciousness in terms of its simplest and most basic components, (2) to discover the laws by which these elements or components associate, and (3) to understand the relation between the elements and their physiological conditions. The initial aim was, as with voluntarism, to come up with a set of fundamental mental units. Titchener believed that a mental element was fundamental when it remained constant over numerous introspective trials. So if multiple introspective observers all consistently experienced an object in the same way, then this experience qualified as a true element.

The combination of elements, in Titchener's scheme, was not affected through active mental processes, as Wundt believed. Instead, Titchener saw the mind as a passive mechanism or substrate within which elements combined according to set laws. In chemistry, a **reagent** is a substance added to a mixture to produce a particular chemical reaction. Reagents are used to quantify these reactions and their chemical products. In a similar fashion, structuralists believed the mind to be a reagent, a medium inside of which mental reactions and processes unfolded. Researchers of the day even went so far as to call their subjects reagents.

Like Wundt, Titchener listed his elements. He described a total of 44,000 sensation elements alone. Out of these, 32,820 were visual and 11,600 were auditory (Titchener, 1896). He thought that each of these elements was fundamental and indivisible and that each was capable of combining with others to form more complicated perceptions and ideas. Titchener believed that all sensations could be characterized by four attributes. **Quality** is what separates a sensation from any other sensation. The experience of heat, therefore, has a different quality than that of sound. **Intensity** refers to how strong a sensation is; for example, a noise can be loud or soft and a light can be bright or dim. **Duration** refers to how long a sensation persists, whether it is short-lived or longer lasting. Sensations are characterized also by **clearness**. Sensations that one pays attention to possess greater clarity. To these basic four attributes, Titchener later added **extensity**, the extent to which a sensation fills or occupies space. The sensation of pressure coming from a pencil tip that touches the skin has less extent than that coming from a chair bottom.

Evaluating the Structuralist Approach

Many of the advantages and disadvantages of the structuralist movement are identical to those of its ancestor, voluntarism. Structuralism further refined scientific methodological procedures and applied them to the study of psychological phenomena. It employed a variety of techniques, including measurement, observation, and experimentation. Introspection in a modified form would be put to use later in other areas of psychology, such as **psychophysics**—in which observers judge the relative intensity of stimuli—and clinical psychology—in which participants are asked to evaluate themselves along personality continua, such as those centering on anxiety or depression (Schultz & Schultz, 1987).

More elaborate critiques of introspectionism were now pointed at the structuralist school. Among these were that the process itself is subjective and unreliable; that training participants to introspect only biases their responding even more; and that some mental experiences, such as habits, happen without conscious awareness and so cannot be introspected about at all. The psychoanalytic school would expound considerably on this idea of an unconscious mind that is inaccessible to attention or awareness. In conclusion, structuralism was found to be too analytic and reductionistic. It was found to overemphasize the role of low-level mental elements and to ignore holistic perception and experience, once again opening the way for the Gestalt psychologists' concern with this issue.

FUNCTIONALISM: WHAT THE MIND DOES

In the scientific disciplines, a theoretical perspective that has been entrenched for many years is often quickly replaced with an alternative, sometimes completely contrary, perspective. This was certainly the case with functionalism's supplanting of structuralism. Rather than focusing on the contents of the mind, functionalism focused on what the mind could do. Its emphasis was on the mental processes or functions that operate on the elements, instead of the elements themselves. Harvey A. Carr (1873–1954), one of the later U.S. functionalists, summarizes the subject matter of functionalist psychology as follows:

> Psychology is primarily concerned with the study of mental activity. This term is the generic name for such activities as perception, memory, imagination, reasoning, feeling, judgment, and will. . . . Stated in comprehensive terms, we may say that mental activity is concerned with the acquisition, fixation, retention, organization, and evaluation of experiences and their subsequent utilization in the guidance of conduct. (Carr, 1925, p. 1)

The formal development of psychological functionalism in the United States is credited to John Dewey (1859–1952) and James Rowland Angell (1869–1949), as well as to Harvey A. Carr. However, it was William James (1842–1910) who was its pioneer and perhaps its most lucid expositor (see Figure 3.3). James is often considered the greatest American psychologist. James rebelled against the Wundtian and structuralist conception of experience as being made up of discrete elements and believed that such elements existed simply as a result of the attentive, introspective process. He thought that an individual erroneously created the notion of an element by attempting to "freeze" or stop a moment in the mind's ongoing activity. He stated that one person's subjective element in response to a perception, for instance, does not guarantee that the same element will exist in anyone else's mind who experiences the same perception—what he called the **psychologist's fallacy**.

James replaced the "mind-as-elements" notion with the idea of the mind as a **stream of consciousness**, suggesting that the mind was a process undergoing continuous flow

Figure 3.3 William James was one of the early American psychologists.

Source: FPG/Staff/Archive Photos/Getty Images.

or change. He likened thought to the water in a river that is always moving. He provided another analogy when, referring to mind, he declared, "Like a bird's life, it seems to be made of an alternation of flights and perchings" (James, 1890, p. 243). James termed the resting places or "perchings" of thought as *substantive*. **Substantive thought** occurs when the mind slows down, perhaps when focusing attention. James called the "flights" of the mind **transitive thought**. They correspond to a less focused, more associative form of thinking.

James Rowland Angell (1907) articulated the three major themes of functionalism. The first theme was the study of **mental operations**. By this, he meant that functionalism should investigate how a mental process operates, what it accomplishes, and under what conditions it occurs. Second, Angell believed that functionalism should study the **fundamental utilities of consciousness**. One ought to understand the role consciousness plays in the survival of the organism. This means asking questions such as Why are we conscious? Of what utility or usefulness is consciousness? How does consciousness help keep an organism alive? Third, functionalism should study **psychophysical relations**, the relations between the psychological mind and the physical body. The term also refers to the total relationship of the organism to the environment and to how the organism, both physically and mentally, may have adapted to the environment.

From these themes, it is clear that functionalism was strongly influenced by Darwin's theory of natural selection. Functionalism then sought to explain not just mental operations in and of themselves but also how the mind in general arose through evolutionary pressures to serve the organism. The idea of an organism–environment fit and how it may help explain a variety of different psychological characteristics was to be elaborated on more fully at a later date by evolutionary psychologists. Functionalism, thus, serves as the theoretical precursor to evolutionary psychology, discussed in greater detail later in this book.

Evaluating the Functionalist Approach

The functionalist movement broadened the field of what could acceptably be studied in psychology. Unconscious phenomena were fair game, as was the study of children, the mentally retarded, and the "insane." It allowed for a wider variety of methods, such as tests, questionnaires, and objective behavioral descriptions, and it permitted the continued use of introspectionism (Schultz & Schultz, 1987).

Criticisms of functionalism came, perhaps not surprisingly, from the structuralist camp. In 1913, C. A. Ruckmick, a student of Titchener's, accused the functionalist movement of failing to define the term *function*, having noted that functionalists used the term in two different ways. First, *function* was used to refer to an activity or process itself, such as perception or memory. Second, *function* was used to mean the utility or usefulness of an activity to the organism (Schultz & Schultz, 1987). Functionalists sometimes used these terms interchangeably, which occasionally invited confusion. Another reported fault of functionalism was that it was too applied and practical. Its adherents were accused of focusing excessively on the usefulness of functions. In contrast, the structuralists took a more basic scientific approach in their attempt to describe and elucidate the basic aspects of the mind. This debate over which is better—basic or applied research—is ongoing in psychology and other sciences.

THE WHOLE IS GREATER THAN THE SUM OF ITS PARTS: MENTAL PHYSICS AND THE GESTALT MOVEMENT

In the early part of the 20th century, another field of psychology arose. This field was called Gestalt psychology, and its three founders were all German. They were Max Wertheimer (1880–1943), Kurt Koffka (1886–1941), and Wolfgang Kohler (1887–1967). The Gestalt movement, like functionalism, was a counterreaction to structuralism and the atomism it entailed. The Gestalt psychologists even referred to structuralism as "brick-and-mortar psychology." They saw wholes as more than just the sum of their parts; such an integrated whole they called a **gestalt**. What characterizes the Gestalt approach is the importance of conscious wholes. The Gestalt psychologists believed that conscious wholes could not simply be reduced to a listing and description of their parts. The Gestalt psychologists also borrowed a metaphor from physics: They believed that mental parts combined into wholes in much the same way that physical particles organized when subjected to fields of force.

The contributions of Gestalt psychology were greatest in two areas: (1) perception and (2) learning. Gestalt psychology is phenomenological in method. **Phenomenology** refers to subjective experience rather than objective description. When studying perception, for example, the Gestaltists preferred to create stimulus patterns, show them to observers, and have the observers describe their subjective experiences. Phenomenological description differs from introspection in that it focuses on a person's immediate and subjective perception of an external stimulus. It does not require training or an intensive examination of one's internal state. The Gestalt psychologists were looser methodologically when studying learning as well. They preferred to observe human or animal subjects, finding solutions to problems rather than setting up rigorously controlled experimental conditions.

In vision, the relationship between parts and wholes is an important one. As mentioned earlier, when we look at an object, we tend to see the entire object rather than the parts of which it is composed. We tend to see a face, not an aggregate of eyes, nose, and mouth. We tend to see trees and not collections of leaves and branches. Max Wertheimer (1923) illustrates the problem this way: "I stand at the window and see a house, trees, sky. Theoretically I might say there were 327 brightnesses and nuances of color. Do I have 327? No. I have sky, house, and trees" (p. 301).

Wertheimer then went on to formulate the **principles of perceptual organization**. These are ways in which visual parts group to form objects. The principles demonstrate that the relationships between the parts are important in determining how these parts are assembled into wholes. According to the principle of **proximity**, parts that are close to one another in the visual field are perceived as a whole. Here, the physical distance between elements is a relationship independent of those elements but one that serves to group them together. According to the principle of **similarity**, parts that are similar in lightness,

Figure 3.4 Dot lattices and other figures that demonstrate several of the Gestalt principles of perceptual organization. In the lattice in (a), the organization is seen in terms of columns, not rows, because the dots in that orientation group by proximity. In (b), the organization is one of rows because the dots group by similarity of size. The inward-pointing pairs of parentheses and bracket-like figures in (c) form a coherent whole because of closure. The shapes in (d) are almost always perceived as a square overlapping a circle, rather than as a Pac-Man and a square, because a circle is simpler according to the law of pragnanz.

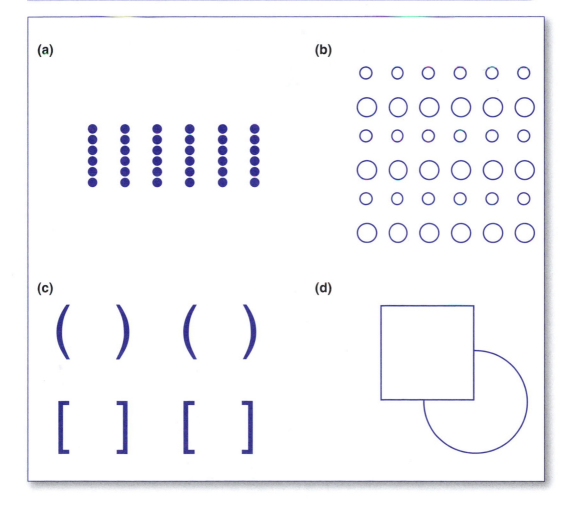

color, shape, or some other characteristic group together. The relationship here consists of the elements' shared properties. The principle of closure holds that the parts that form a complete or almost complete and enclosed object go together. Wertheimer also proposed the idea of pragnanz, or "good figure." According to pragnanz, parts that are simple will group together. Simple organizations are those that have fewer parts or are bilaterally symmetrical. Wertheimer created lattices, or matrices of regularly arranged parts, to demonstrate these principles. Several lattices and other Gestalt stimulus patterns are shown in Figure 3.4. It should be noted that these are only a few representative examples of grouping principles proposed by the Gestaltists. More recent perceptual investigators have suggested others.

Interdisciplinary Crossroads: Gestalt Phenomenology, Experimental Psychology, and Perceptual Grouping

As mentioned earlier, the Gestalt psychologists, such as Wertheimer, formulated the principles of perceptual grouping to explain how parts are grouped together to form wholes. This type of process is necessary for us to see objects rather than bits and pieces of the visual world. However, these principles as originally formulated are qualitative. They tell us why some things go together but don't tell us what the strength of grouping is. In addition, they don't tell us what grouping is like when two or more principles are at work. Remember also that these rules were created on the basis of phenomenological evidence where observers looked at patterns and verbally reported what they saw. Verification of these observations is needed using the scientific methods of modern-day experimental psychology.

Recent work has gone some way toward achieving these goals. Contemporary researchers have turned once again toward using dot lattice stimuli to estimate perceptual grouping. It turns out that there are a total of six different lattice types: (1) square, (2) rectangular, (3) centered rectangular, (4) rhombic, (5) oblique, and (5) hexagonal (Bravais,1949; Kubovy & Wagemans, 1995). Examples of each are shown in Figure 3.5. The distances between points in different directions can be varied, as can the similarity of the elements in relation to one another. For instance, we can make the dots in one direction closer to one another, causing them to group by proximity. At the same time, we can make the dots in that direction or in other competing directions more or less similar based on various types of similarity, such as color or luminance.

Using these stimuli, Kubovy and Wagemans (1995) obtained an attraction function that expresses the probability of grouping over distance. The function was an exponential decay, giving a quantitative measure of how grouping strength weakens with

Figure 3.5 Examples of the six different dot lattice types.

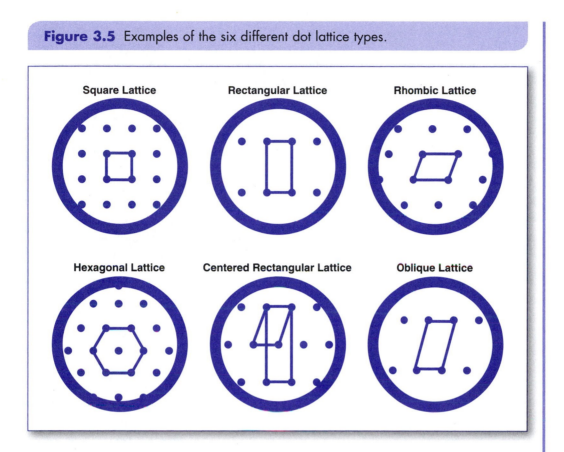

increased separation between dots. A later reanalysis of these data showed that this grouping relationship remained constant with changes in scale (size) or time (Kubovy & Holcombe, 1998). In another study, Lars and Kubovy (2006) employed lattices where one organization was linear (i.e., the dots in one direction formed a line), while the rest were curvilinear, forming curves. In the competition between these two types of organizations, the curved configuration was stronger. What can account for the saliency of curvature? The authors speculate that curved alignment of dots is less likely to have occurred by accident and, thus, more likely to be the result of a structured object than are straight lines. Curved lines are more prevalent in the natural world, so it is possible that our brains may have evolved or adapted to be more sensitive to the presence of curvature.

But what about other cases where two or more grouping principles are pitted against one another? A gestalt is often defined as a whole that is greater than the sum of its parts. This suggests that if two principles such as proximity and similarity both predict the same organization, their combined effect should be stronger than both of their individual strengths together. One might predict, for example, that their effects are multiplicative and equal to the multiplication of their separate forces. It turns out that this is not the case. Perceived grouping in dot lattices is actually additive (Kubovy & Van den Berg, 2008).

These studies show that it is possible to take an old approach and combine it successfully with a new one. Phenomenology as employed by the earlier Gestalt psychologists is qualitative and nonempirical. It is useful for demonstrating basic principles or forming hypotheses. But these ideas must be submitted to the rigor of modern experimental methods if we are to validate any of their assumptions. The newer research described here may be thought of as phenomenological psychophysics because it relies on subjective report while utilizing the methodology of psychophysics (Kubovy & Gepshtein, 2003). Psychophysics is the use of quantitative methods to measure relationships between stimuli, which are physical, and perception, which is psychological.

Wolfgang Kohler's greatest contribution was in the area of animal learning. Kohler (1927) studied chimpanzees on the island of Tenerife during World War I and described those studies in *The Mentality of Apes*. He would place a banana on a ceiling hook and observe how the chimps would use available materials to try to reach it. The chimps at first would use different approaches at random—trying to knock the banana down with a stick, for example. He then noticed that the chimps, with great suddenness, often after a period of inactivity, would solve the problem by stacking crates on top of each other and climbing that stack of crates to reach the prize (see Figure 3.6). Kohler termed this behavior **insight learning,** the ostensibly spontaneous understanding of relationships that produces a solution to a problem. He believed that this phenomenon was operational in humans as well. Because the solution is a holistic configuration and involves a set of interrelationships among component parts, it demonstrates again the Gestaltists' emphasis on mental wholes. These wholes can be perceptual, as is the case during the perception of an object, or conceptual, as is the case during learning. It should be stressed that these wholes in the Gestalt view consist not just of individual parts but, additionally, of the relationships between them.

According to Wallas (1926), insight learning happens in four stages. The first is **preparation** and consists of the acquisition of and understanding of the problem as well as preliminary attempts at solving it. The second stage is **incubation,** whereby the problem is put aside for a while. During this period, there are no conscious attempts at problem solving, but the unconscious mind may be attempting to find or may have found a solution. In the third stage, **illumination** occurs. It is a flash of insight, a sort of "Aha!" experience in which the solution comes suddenly to awareness. Finally, there is **verification,** in which the insight is confirmed and one checks to see that it yields a correct solution.

Figure 3.6 If you were the chimpanzee, how would you reach the bananas?

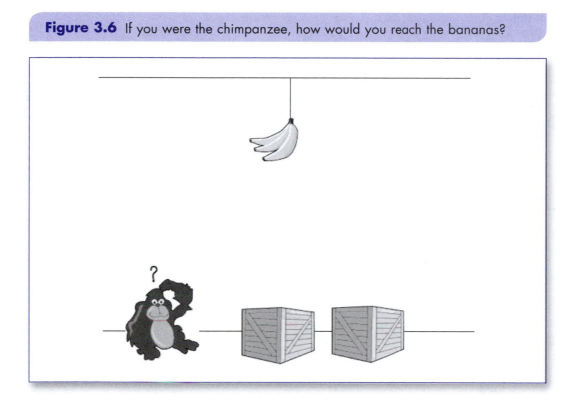

The Gestalt psychologists formulated a theory of how underlying brain mechanisms give rise to Gestalts. Wertheimer suggested that the cerebral cortex was a dynamic system, in which the elements in force at a given time interacted. Kohler (1920), in *Static and Stationary Physical Gestalts*, further proposed that cortical processes operate as do the fields of force that are studied in physics. Metal filings caught in an electromagnetic field generated by the poles of a magnet will organize themselves around the poles. These and related phenomena in physics are described by **field theory**. Similarly, it was believed that perceptual elements spontaneously organized themselves because they were caught in "mental force fields." In this mental equivalent of field theory, sensory impulses coming from a stimulus initiate neuronal activity. This electrochemical activity then produces a mental field that causes the perceptual grouping. Here again, we see the influence on psychology of another discipline in the natural sciences.

The Gestalt psychologists believed that there was a correspondence between the psychological or conscious experience on the one hand and the underlying brain experience on the other. This perspective is called isomorphism because the perception is identical (Greek: iso) in form or shape (Greek: morph) to the brain activity that gives rise to it. The mental representation of elements and the fields operating on them were thought to be quite similar to the conscious perception of the stimulus, in the same way that a map is similar to the geography it represents.

Evaluating the Gestalt Approach

Gestalt theory gave an interesting alternative formulation of the part–whole problem. It addressed the problem in a more detailed fashion than had the structuralists or voluntarists. It also spawned research traditions in perception and in learning and problem solving. However, critics soon pointed out a number of flaws. The Gestalt psychologists' methodology was the first aspect of Gestalt theory to receive harsh treatment. The phenomenological approach was labeled as "soft" and lacking in scientific rigor. Gestalt psychologists were accused also of being too theoretical and of failing to back up their assertions with empirically derived data. Much of their data, because these were not obtained within controlled experimental settings, were not amenable to statistical analysis. Their approach was, thus, critiqued as too qualitative and not quantitative enough in orientation. Field theory was additionally accused of being speculative and based on poorly defined physiological assumptions.

Some of the specific findings of the Gestalt researchers were also attacked. The principles of perceptual organization were said to be merely descriptive; they described how parts grouped but did not provide a real explanation. Field theory as an explication for grouping was seen as too vague as well as inadequate. Critics averred that the organizational laws seemed sufficient to describe grouping when one principle was at work but failed to make predictions about organization taking place under more complex real-world circumstances. Figure 3.7 shows three dots—A, B, and C. Dots A and B group by proximity, while dots B and C group by similarity. What is the resulting organization? A further criticism was that

Figure 3.7 The first two dots group by proximity. The second and third dots group by size similarity. The resulting perceptual organization cannot be predicted by the individual laws of organization alone.

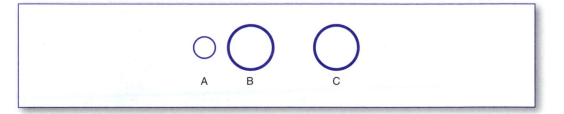

A   B   C

the concept of pragnanz was ill defined. Stimuli can be constructed where a more compli-cated, not simpler, organization is perceived. Gestalt findings in learning were also not immune to such evaluations. Kohler's idea of insight learning as something that happened quite rapidly was questioned. Later investigators found that insight learning in animals such as chimpanzees does not always occur suddenly and can depend on factors such as prior experience and learning (Windholz & Lamal, 1985).

MINI MINDS: MECHANISM AND PSYCHOANALYTIC PSYCHOLOGY

Psychoanalytic psychology as promulgated by Sigmund Freud (1856–1939) saw the mind as being made up of distinct components, or "miniature minds." Each of these minds com-petes with the others and vies for control of behavior. Psychoanalytic psychology posited not just one state of consciousness but three and emphasized the role of the unconscious mind, of which the individual has little awareness and over which he or she has little con-trol, in influencing thought and action. Freud also thought that sex, pleasure, aggression, and other primitive motivations and emotions were powerful influences on personality, as were early childhood experiences.

Freud proposed a three-tiered system of consciousness: (1) the **conscious** mind, which contains those thoughts and feelings of which we are aware and can directly access; (2) the **preconscious** mind—that is, those aspects of the mind that we can bring into awareness with effort; and (3) the **unconscious** mind, or the aspects of the mind of which we are completely unaware. An example of conscious content would be knowing the street address where one lives. Preconscious content requires some mental effort for one to be made aware of it. An example would be trying to recall and eventually recalling what one did on his or her birthday the past year. Unconscious content may never come into awareness, although one goal of psychoanalytic therapy is to try to allow this to happen. An example of unconscious content is memories of childhood abuse or other traumatic experiences from the early developmental years.

Freud described three other mental structures, each having a different operating principle. The **id** contains unconscious impulses and desires such as sex and hunger. It operates on the **pleasure principle** and attempts to attain gratification for its desires immediately. The **super-ego** is responsible for our ethical sense. It operates on the **idealistic principle** and motivates the individual to do what it considers morally sound or proper. The **ego** balances the com-peting demands of the id and superego. It operates on the **reality principle**, spurring one to act in a rational and pragmatic fashion.

A metaphor Freud proposed for thinking about these structures was an iceberg, depicted in Figure 3.8. He likened the conscious mind to the visible part of an iceberg above the waterline; thus, it is always visible. The preconscious mind is equivalent to the

Figure 3.8 Sigmund Freud's iceberg model of the mind.

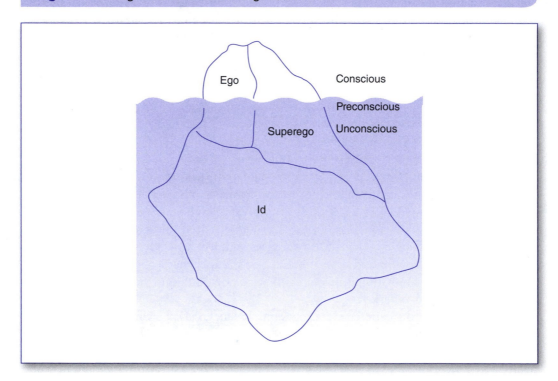

part of the iceberg near the waterline since it is sometimes submerged and unconscious but sometimes above the waterline and inside awareness. The largest part of the iceberg is then the unconscious, which is always submerged and hidden from view. The id lies completely in the unconscious, its large mass indicating its power. Both the ego and the superego occupy all three states of consciousness.

A crucial part of this perspective is the dynamic interplay between the id, ego, and superego. The id demands immediate satisfaction of its appetite for pleasure, while the superego in most cases advocates controlling or suppressing such urges in the name of decency. It then falls to the ego to attempt a rational and viable solution to the conflict. The ego is thus being barraged with the id's impulses and the superego's restraints. If it fails to satisfy either one, the result is anxiety. To shield itself against anxiety, Freud believed that the ego constructs **defense mechanisms**, which reduce or redirect anxiety in various ways. Examples of defense mechanisms include **repression**, the banishing of anxiety-arousing thoughts and feelings from consciousness, and **sublimation**, the transformation of unacceptable impulses into socially valued motivations. If a person lost memory of his or her being abused as a child, Freud would say that he or she repressed the memory because it was too painful. If instead that person channeled the anger he or she felt as a result of having been abused toward becoming successful in a career, he or she would be sublimating.

Mechanism and determinism are inherent in the psychodynamic view. One can envision Freud's model of the mind as an elaborate machine with different interacting parts. In his writings, he uses many terms drawn from mechanics, electrical circuitry, and hydraulics. Without too much imagination, it is possible to construct a Freudian hydraulic or "plumbing" model of the mind, with pumping stations connected by valves and tubes. Id impulses in this model could be represented as an increase in water pressure. Forces deriving from other components that release or redirect this pressure could counteract that increase. This view of the mind as a machine implies determinism as well. Freud thought that all mental events, including slips of the tongue and dreams, were determined and that nothing in human thought or behavior could occur by chance.

Evaluating the Psychoanalytic Approach

Many of the ideas in the psychoanalytic approach have permeated the wider culture. Freud drew our attention to important issues such as the unconscious and the influence of biological forces. The psychoanalytic approach served to stimulate further research in these areas and inspired several generations of clinical practice, but its lasting legacy may be in the strong counterarguments it elicited.

The neo-Freudians, although they accepted most of the substantive parts of Freud's theory, differed in several respects. They placed more emphasis on the role of the conscious mind and downplayed the importance of sex and aggression as all-powerful motivators. Modern psychological research suggests that Freud overestimated parental and early childhood influence and underestimated the importance of other social factors, such as peer influence (Frieze, Parsons, Johnson, Ruble, & Zellman, 1978). In addition, repression has been found to be a relatively rare mental response to psychological trauma. In fact, it is typically the case that horrible memories are remembered quite clearly (Loftus, 1995). The unconscious mind is now viewed not so much as a seething cauldron of primitive urges but as a reservoir of information processing that goes on without awareness (Greenwald, 1992).

Psychoanalytic psychology also has been critiqued for its scientific shortcomings. The theory is not based on objective observations. Its raw material comes from Freud's subjective notes about his patients, written several hours after therapy. Freud additionally offers few hypotheses that can be scientifically verified or rejected. Some have censured psychoanalytic descriptions as being incapable of being proved one way or another. For example, the presence of anxiety in an individual could indicate the fear of giving in to id impulses. The absence of such anxiety could indicate its repression. The perspective thus offers after-the-fact explanations for personality. It also fails to predict behavior or traits (Myers, 2001). One could in this framework explain why someone is angry but not anticipate accurately when he or she might get angry in the future.

MIND AS A BLACK BOX: THE BEHAVIORIST APPROACH

The weaknesses of the psychoanalytic position were the behaviorists' strengths. Instead of attempting to describe complex mental operations, the behaviorists, as their name implies, focused entirely on the study of behavior. In their view, the internal workings of the mind were simply too complex as well as incapable of being measured in an objective and scientific fashion. Behaviors, however—the actions that are produced by organisms, such as running, grasping, or bar pressing—are external, which makes them easily measurable and quantifiable. They are, thus, ideally suited for scientific study. Behaviorism was influenced by work in animal and comparative psychology. In these disciplines, there was a trend to discover which environmental conditions might cause animals to act in certain ways, as opposed to an emphasis on constructing elaborate mental models of how they might be thinking. Humans were de facto lumped into the same category as animals, making behaviorism a more general science and an extension of the more rigorous natural sciences.

The behaviorists clearly saw themselves as true scientists. Because the mind could not be studied scientifically during their time, they preferred not to study it at all! This did not mean that behaviorists, such as B. F. Skinner, denied the existence of the mind or that they thought that brains were unworthy of study. Rather, they believed that the scientific method could not be appropriately applied in this situation and so redirected their empirical investigations to something that was, namely, behaviors.

Behaviorism did, however, reject outright the study of consciousness through introspection, its adherents claiming that the goal of psychology was not to study consciousness at all but, instead, behaviors and the antecedent conditions that give rise to them. Figure 3.9 shows a version of the stimulus–response model that represents their position. In the model, a stimulus (S) in the environment impinges on an organism (O). The stimulus then causes the organism to produce a response (R). The most important class of stimuli that influence responses, according to behaviorists, is rewards and punishments. In this case, a stimulus might consist of a reward given to an organism—for example, a rat—which would then cause the rat to respond by continuing to press a bar. Notice that in this model, the mind, contained in the organism, is not depicted. It is treated as a "black box," meaning that it is unfathomable and unexplainable. The mind becomes simply an entity that serves to convert stimuli to responses.

Important figures associated with the movement were Edward Lee Thorndike (1874–1949), Ivan Pavlov (1849–1936), and Burrhus Frederick Skinner (1904–1990). Pavlov was a Russian physiologist who studied the dog's digestive system. In his lab, he noticed that

Figure 3.9 The behaviorist stimulus–response model of behavior. The mind of an organism (O) that emits a response (R) to a stimulus (S) in this view could not be well understood. The mind was treated as a "black box."

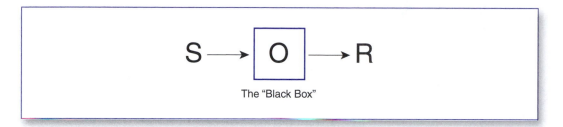

The "Black Box"

dogs would salivate not only when eating but also immediately before. This was true only for dogs that had been fed in the lab for some time. He assumed that, in addition to the food itself, any stimulus that was put forward repeatedly just before the food was presented would also be able to trigger salivation. To test this idea, Pavlov applied meat powder to the dogs' tongues. This caused them to salivate. Then, he sounded a tuning fork each time, just prior to administering the powder. He did this over several trials. Finally, he sounded the fork without presenting any powder and found that the dogs still salivated.

As a result of these experiments, Pavlov was inspired to propose several terms. The **unconditioned stimulus** is that which elicits a response all on its own. In this instance, it is the meat powder. An **unconditioned response** is a response elicited by an unconditioned stimulus—here, the salivation caused by the administration of the meat powder. A **conditioned stimulus** elicits a response only after it has been paired repeatedly with an unconditioned stimulus—here, the sound of the tuning fork. Last, a **conditioned response** is a response elicited by a conditioned stimulus—here, the salivation caused by the tuning fork. This form of learning came to be known as **classical conditioning**. Note that it pertains only to built-in reflexes and does not require any conscious thought on the part of the animal. The dog learns simply by associating the two stimuli.

Skinner was responsible for uncovering more about the nature of learning. Whereas classical conditioning works only with involuntary reflexive behaviors, such as the salivatory response, operant conditioning is pertinent to any voluntary motor act and is, thus, far more general. **Operant conditioning** is that type of learning in which a behavior is strengthened if it is followed by reinforcement and diminished if followed by punishment. A **reinforcement** is anything that increases the frequency of a response. Food is a good reinforcer for most animals. A child, if given a cookie for taking out the garbage, will be more likely to take out the garbage in the future. **Punishment**, on the other hand, is any consequence of a behavior that is apt to decrease the future incidence of that behavior. A painful stimulus such as electric shock can serve as an effective punishment. Lab rats repeatedly shocked for touching an object in their cage will soon cease to do so. Skinner was able to use various forms of reinforcement and punishment to control the behavior of animals such as rats and pigeons.

Evaluating the Behaviorist Approach

The strength of the behaviorist position is its adoption of a completely objective science of behavior. Behaviorists understood that mentalistic concepts were poorly defined and could be measured only via subjective methods such as introspection. They were very rigorous in their application of the scientific method to the study of psychological phenomena. As such, they were confident that their results yielded the most accurate and valid information. The testimony to behaviorism's success is that it was the dominant paradigm in research psychology for approximately 50 years. It didn't begin to decline until it was challenged by the rise of cognitive psychology in the 1960s. Some of the specific challenges posed by the cognitive movement will be discussed in the next chapter.

Behaviorism had allowed for the controlled and systematic study of behavior, but the behaviorists' abandonment of consciousness and mind was the movement's greatest weakness. During the behaviorists' reign, evidence came to light that animals do indeed have mental representations that affect how they learn. The work of Edward Chace Tolman (1886–1959), a behaviorist himself, challenged some of the assumptions of traditional behaviorist doctrine. Tolman allowed rats to explore a maze and, in some cases, transported them through the maze. In both scenarios, the rats were subsequently able to navigate the maze successfully, even though they had never been rewarded for doing so. Tolman suggested that the rats developed a cognitive map, or a mental representation of the maze, that enabled them to navigate the maze without conditioning. This shows that animals can acquire behaviors through experience, without being reinforced—a concept called latent learning.

Tolman believed in five initiating causes of behavior: (1) the environmental stimuli (S), (2) physiological drive (P), (3) heredity (H), (4) previous training (T), and (5) age (A). Behavior (B) can then be expressed as a function of these in a simple equation: $B = f_x (S, P, H, T, A)$. But between these initiating causes and the final behaviors exist what he called intervening variables. It is the intervening variables that are the determinants of behavior. They are the internal processes that connect the prior stimulus situation with the response. An example of an intervening variable is hunger. Although hunger cannot easily be observed, it can be related to other experimental variables that are readily observable, such as the amount of time that has elapsed since an animal last ate or how much food the animal consumes at the end of a period of not eating. Intervening variables were the behaviorists' attempt to objectify internal mental states. However, these states were acknowledged to exist only as they pertained to some external, easily measured variable, and in many cases, it was difficult to objectify them. Tolman himself later came to accept that a complete understanding of intervening variables was perhaps not possible.

OVERALL EVALUATION OF THE PSYCHOLOGICAL APPROACH

We have covered a plethora of theoretical positions in this chapter. There are several reasons for this. Psychology was the first discipline to systematically apply experimentation to the study of mind. It was, thus, a new discipline with many followers advocating many positions. Psychologists additionally had a very difficult task in front of them, which was to try to understand things that at the time could not be easily seen or measured. This lack of precision and early reliance on nonscientific methods such as introspection may have led to an overreliance on theory. Also, as was not the case in other disciplines, there was no overarching theory or framework for psychologists to work within. It would not be until the rise of the cognitive approach and the adoption of an information-processing perspective that some kind of unity would come to the field. We turn our attention to this cognitive approach in the next chapter.

SUMMING UP: A REVIEW OF CHAPTER 3

1. Psychology is the scientific study of mind and behavior. Throughout its relatively short history, this discipline has been characterized by the development of many competing theories of what the mind is.

2. In the scientific method, a hypothesis or conjecture about the world is tested using an experiment. In an experiment, an independent variable is manipulated and its effect on a dependent variable is measured. The results either support or fail to support the hypothesis. Over time, this process, when repeated, produces a theory—a more general understanding of how the world works.

3. The voluntarist movement marks the first time experimental methods were applied to mental phenomenon. Its progenitor, Wilhelm Wundt, also utilized introspection, or inward looking, as a means to catalog the elements of the mind.

4. The structuralists, led by Edward Titchener, had a research agenda similar to that of the voluntarists. They also attempted to catalog mental elements and believed that they interacted with one another in much the same way as chemical elements do.

5. William James is considered the founder of the functionalist movement in psychology. In this view, the mind is best understood as a flow or ongoing process.

6. Gestalt psychologists, such as Max Wertheimer, wanted to know how mental parts combined to form wholes. They postulated the laws of perceptual grouping, which describe how we see visual objects.

7. Sigmund Freud started psychoanalytic psychology. He believed that the mind as a whole consisted of multiple different and competing minds that were in constant conflict with one another.

8. Skinner was one of the most prominent members of the behaviorist movement. According to this perspective, an organism's behavior is understood by looking at the environmental stimuli that come before it or following it. Punishments and rewards were thought to play a prominent role in shaping behavior.

EXPLORE MORE

Log on to the student study site at http://study.sagepub.com/friedenberg3e for electronic flash cards, review quizzes, and a list of web resources to aid you in further exploring the field of cognitive science.

SUGGESTED READINGS

Freud, S. (1962). *The ego and the id*. New York, NY: W. W. Norton.

James, W. (1890). *The principles of psychology*. New York, NY: Dover.

Koffka, K. (1935). *Principles of Gestalt psychology*. New York, NY: Harcourt.

Kohler, W. (1927). *The mentality of apes*. Berlin, Germany: Royal Academy of Sciences.

Myers, D. G. (2001). *Psychology*. New York, NY: Worth.

Schultz, D. P., & Schultz, S. E. (1987). *A history of modern psychology* (4th ed.). Orlando, FL: Harcourt Brace Jovanovich.

Skinner, B. F. (1971). *Beyond freedom and dignity*. New York, NY: Alfred A. Knopf.

Watson, J. B. (1970). *Behaviorism*. New York, NY: W. W. Norton.

4

THE COGNITIVE APPROACH I

Vision, Pattern Recognition, and Attention

I sometimes worry about my short attention span, but not for very long.

—Strange de Jim, 1974

SOME HISTORY FIRST: THE RISE OF COGNITIVE PSYCHOLOGY

To understand the cognitive perspective, we need to backtrack to our prior discussion of behaviorism. You may recall from the previous chapter that for many decades, behaviorism was the dominant movement in psychology. Behaviorists avoided the study of mental phenomena because they believed that they were too difficult to define or measure. They stuck instead to external, observable behaviors, which were more amenable to scientific scrutiny.

Cognitive psychology can be seen as a backlash or counterrevolution to the behaviorist movement. This becomes evident when one examines the basic assumptions of the cognitive movement (Ashcraft, 2002). Whereas the behaviorists avoided studying the mental world, the cognitivists firmly acknowledged the existence of mental processes and focused their investigatory attentions on them. Whereas behaviorism saw the mind as a passive organ that operated according to the simple rules of conditioning, cognitive psychology saw the mind as active—selecting information from the environment, relating it to prior knowledge, and acting on the results of such processing.

In addition to this backlash against behaviorism, perhaps the most significant reason for the rise of cognitive psychology was the development of new technology. During the behaviorist era, there were no ways of "peering inside the head." That is, one could not directly measure mental processes. After the start of the cognitive movement, new technologies emerged that provided a more accurate picture of mental processes as they were occurring. The new devices included positron emission tomography, computerized axial tomography, and functional magnetic resonance imaging. These techniques are described further in the neuroscience chapter.

Another important technological innovation was the development of the personal computer. The introduction of the transistor brought down the size and the cost of computers, making them available to more people, both inside and outside academia. This spurred psychologists to begin thinking more about them. Psychologists realized that the mind, like a computer, could be viewed as a device that represented and transformed information. The mind-as-computer metaphor was born. Computers thus accelerated the adoption of the information-processing view, not only in psychology but also, more generally, in other cognitive science fields.

THE COGNITIVE APPROACH: MIND AS AN INFORMATION PROCESSOR

So now that we know how cognitive psychology came about, what exactly is it? **Cognitive psychology** is the study of knowledge representation and use in human beings. It is concerned with understanding how people represent, process, and store information. According to Ulric Neisser (1967), one of the early founders of the movement, *cognitive psychology* refers to all processes whereby "the sensory input is transformed, reduced, elaborated, stored, recovered, and used" (p. 4). The many verbs used in the preceding sentence give us a sense of the many possible information-processing activities of the human mind.

Cognitive psychology differs from other approaches in cognitive science in that its focus is on human information processing (as opposed to animal or machine modes of information processing). Like the practitioners of many other disciplines in psychology, cognitive psychologists adopt the scientific method as their primary tool of investigation. Researchers test hypotheses by analyzing data from controlled experiments. However, cognitive psychology also supplements experimentation with modeling and computer simulation. A specific information-processing model of a mental capacity can be run on a computer. The results can then be compared with data from human experiments. This is often a synergistic and iterative procedure. Parameters of the computer model can be refined so as to provide a better fit between the computer model and the empirical data. Aspects of the simulation can also yield insights that cause researchers to go back and design new experiments.

A defining characteristic of the cognitive approach is the way it represents human information processing. These processes are often conceptualized using a **process model**. In a diagram of a process model, boxes are used to designate each stage or step in an information-processing sequence. Arrows that point toward or away from the boxes represent the flow of information among the stages. Many of the figures in this chapter show a process model that depicts a particular theory of human computation. Feel free to examine a few of them now.

Process models, in the classical view of information processing, carry two assumptions. First, they are assumed to be sequential, meaning that information that lies within one stage is processed before it is output to the next. Information cannot be processed simultaneously in multiple stages. Second, excluding inputs and outputs, processing that occurs within one stage is independent of processing that occurs within other stages. These assumptions were later challenged by the connectionist view of information processing, which adopts a radically different architecture as the basis of cognition.

Process models are a very important part of the cognitive perspective. They are a powerful conceptual tool for understanding human information processing. In fact, the remainder of this chapter and the next are devoted to describing the major processing models that underlie various domains in cognition. These domains include perception, attention, memory, imagery, and problem solving. Humans can perform a wide range of cognitive processes, so many in fact that it is not possible to describe all of them in this book. In this chapter, we focus on visual pattern recognition and attention as these topics have been well investigated. We neither discuss other visual processes like color perception nor describe auditory perception. Similarly, in Chapter 5, we do not discuss reading or story comprehension. These are all very important, but entire courses can be devoted to each. In this and the next chapter, our goal is more limited: to demonstrate how major cognitive processes take place and how cognitive process models can account for them.

MODULARITY OF MIND

An assumption of many cognitive theories is **modularity of mind**. According to this idea, the mind is made up of innate, functionally independent modules. The boxes in the process models that are described throughout this chapter and in the next chapter can in many cases be viewed as modules. Because modularity of mind is such an important and pervasive assumption in the cognitive perspective, let's take some time now to examine it further.

Jerry Fodor (1983) is the outspoken proponent of the modular view. In his book *The Modularity of Mind*, he gives a general description of the role these putative structures play. In his view, information arriving from the outside environment passes first through a set of sensory transducers. These convert the information to a code that is suitable for processing by the modules, which are domain specific—that is, able to handle information of a specific type only. The modules then convert the results of their operations into a common code that can be interpreted by other nonmodular, domain-general processors.

In the same volume, Fodor (1983) lists the many characteristics of a module. Modules are hardwired, meaning that they cannot be constructed from more basic units. They are genetically determined, domain specific, fast, automatic, stimulus driven, and not subject to control by a central authority. Modules are mandatory: They are triggered into operation by the presence of the appropriate information. Fodor also states that modules are informationally encapsulated. By this he means that other mental processes can only have access to a module's output; they cannot influence or access its inner workings.

Evaluating the Modular Approach

Case studies of brain-damaged patients support the modular view. There are many case studies of patients who have suffered damage to a particular brain area as a result of a stroke or an accident. These patients then suffer very specific deficits. In an aphasic patient, damage to one part of the brain might hamper the patient's understanding or comprehending language, whereas damage to another region might cause difficulties in his or her speaking or in producing language. See the chapter on linguistics for more on these disorders. Similarly, there are patients with developmental genetic disorders in whom one language ability has been preserved while another has not. Individuals with Williams syndrome suffer grave deficits in visuospatial cognition but are relatively unaffected with respect to the processing of face-specific information (Bellugi, Wang, & Jernigan, 1994).

Skeptics counter these claims. They point out that in many brain-damaged patients, there is no clear-cut dissociation of one function from another (Tyler, 1992). Also, genetic disorders of the sort described above rarely evidence highly specialized deficits— usually, more general impairments are manifest (Bishop, 1997). Evidence from studies of early brain development additionally fails to support claims of modularity. Experiments that have utilized brain scanning techniques show that some language abilities are bilateralized—that is, located in both cortical hemispheres—early in development. Hemispheric specialization occurs later, which strongly suggests that these abilities cannot be genetically preprogrammed (Mills, Coffey-Corina, & Neville, 1993).

Current thinking is that the brain may contain a number of processing structures that are modular but that these may be a result of normal developmental processes. However, the view opposite that of modularity—that the brain is entirely domain general—does not appear to be tenable either. The task for future researchers in this area is to define which developmental factors shape the formation of modules and which cognitive functions are more general purpose and nonmodular in nature. The role that development and genes play in the creation of modules is discussed further in Chapter 8.

THEORIES OF VISION AND PATTERN RECOGNITION: HOW DO WE RECOGNIZE OBJECTS?

Perception is the process by which we gather information from the outside world via the senses and interpret that information. Most work in perception has focused first on vision and second on audition. Far less research attention has been given to the remaining senses. This bias is species-centric, as vision is our most sophisticated sense and the one we rely on most. Many of the major perceptual theories are, therefore, based on and framed exclusively in terms of visual processing. In this section, we will examine several broad theories of human vision, as we acknowledge that there is much theoretical work that remains to be done for the other senses.

One of the main functions of a visual system is the recognition of patterns. To demonstrate how important this is, imagine looking out at the world and not being able to recognize what you see. You would be able to navigate successfully—for example, you would be able to step out of the way of an oncoming car, but you would not recognize what just went by. You would be able to see your best friend but not know who he or she is. You would be able to see written words but not read them. **Pattern recognition** is the ability to identify objects in the environment. We seem to do it effortlessly. Yet as we will see, this process is actually quite complex and far from being entirely understood.

Template Matching Theory

Any description of a pattern recognition process must begin with the stimulus. The stimulus is the actual object in the external world that we are trying to recognize. Light striking the stimulus is reflected and projects an inverted image of the stimulus onto the retina. The retina is a layer of photoreceptor cells that lines the inside of the back portion of the eye. The retina performs some preliminary processing of the image, after which information about the stimulus is passed posteriorly along a set of pathways toward visual areas in the brain. It is in these areas where the bulk of pattern recognition and other perceptual processing takes place. Figure 4.1 shows an overview of these steps.

According to the template matching theory of pattern recognition, an image generated by an external stimulus is matched to an internal mental representation of the stimulus, called a **template**. The degree of overlap between the image and the template is then computed. This overlap is a measure of how similar the two are to each other. A high degree of overlap will produce recognition of the object. Note that both the perceptual image formed from the world object and the template drawn from memory are examples of visual representation. They represent the object but in different ways. The image is constructed from visual perceptual processes and is more of a tight visual replica of what is "out there," its purpose being to reproduce as carefully as possible its visual appearance. The template is an internally constructed representation drawn from information in long-term memory and is based on past experience. In the model, they differ from verbal symbolic representations of the sort found in linguistic processes. The computational processes in this model are the construction of the image and the template and the matching between them. Template construction would require search and retrieval of information from long-term memory storage. Matching would require some sort of "difference operator," a way of comparing the two to determine their differences.

Figure 4.1 Early steps in the recognition of a stimulus object.

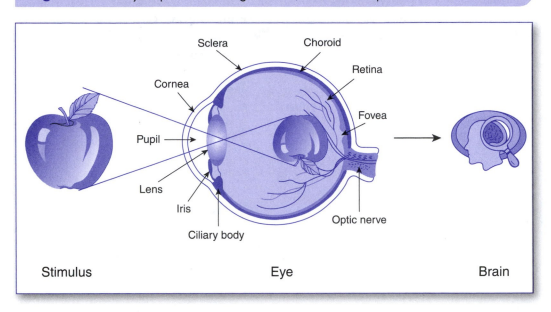

Stimulus   Eye   Brain

Evaluating Template Matching Theory

The problem with this approach is that there is a wide range of variation and possibility for any individual stimulus. Take the simple case of the letter *A*. It can vary in terms of its location in one's visual field, its size, shape, and orientation. For template matching to work, there must be a separate template for each of these possibilities. Imagine how many templates would be required for just one letter of the alphabet. We would need a template for an *A* that appears to the left or the right side of the visual field, other templates for big and small *A*s, others for *A*s written in script or appearing in different fonts, yet others for *A*s that are placed horizontally or upside down. The number of possible templates for an individual object multiplied by the number of possible objects one could recognize becomes so large that it would become impractical to store templates or to use them effectively in memory. Figure 4.2 shows the template matching process and some examples of the ways in which a stimulus can vary.

For this reason, template matching is quickly dismissed as a theory of the way in which humans recognize patterns. It is considered a "straw man" theory, in that it is insubstantial. As a theory, though, it helps us conceptualize what is required of and what gets in the way of a pattern recognition process. Several computer versions of template matching have been successfully implemented. One is designed to read checking account numbers off the bottoms of checks. In these cases, the procedure works because variability in the stimulus

Figure 4.2 The top panel provides various depictions of the letter *A*, all recognizable. The bottom panel shows the sequence of events in the template matching model.

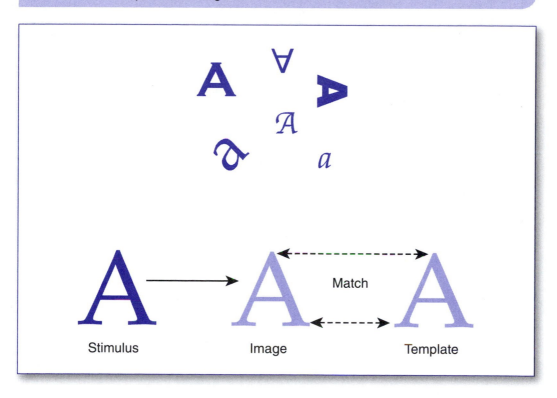

has been reduced. The sizes, styles, and numbers of the digits that must be matched are relatively unvarying. These systems would fail under real-world conditions, in which stimulus variability is much greater.

Feature Detection Theory

With feature detection models, an image of a stimulus, rather than being matched in its entirety to a template, is broken down into its component features. A feature is a part or a subset of an object. The idea is that each different combination of features uniquely specifies a different object. The upright letter *A* can be specified by the fact that it has a short horizontal line as one of its features and two longer diagonal lines as additional features. It can be distinguished from the upright letter *B*, which has a long vertical line and two short loops as features.

The best known feature detection model is called the **pandemonium model** (Lindsay & Norman, 1972; Selfridge, 1959). It gets its name from little mental "demons" that represent processing units. These demons "shout" during the recognition process (creating a pandemonium). Figure 4.3 depicts a representation of the model in terms of how it might be used to identify the letter *R*. First, the stimulus, a letter *R*, is presented. It is represented by an *image demon*, which preserves the overall appearance of the letter. In the next step, there are *feature demons*. There is one feature demon for each possible stimulus feature. A feature demon shouts if he sees his own feature in the image. The upright letter *R*, in this example, can be thought of as having a vertical line, a diagonal line, and a loop, and so has three feature demons. These feature demons would shout out in the presence of their own features. In the next step, there are *cognitive demons*, one for each possible letter. If they hear any of their corresponding features, they too will shout. The cognitive demon with the most features shouts the loudest. Finally, there is a *decision demon*. It listens to the cognitive demons. Whichever one shouts the loudest is chosen by the cognitive demon as the recognized letter.

Each of the demons in this model is a representation. However, given the advances in neuroscience, we have a better understanding of what they might be like. It is now known that simple features of the sort discussed here, like lines and angles, are coded for by neurons in area V1 of the visual cortex and that more complex features made up of their combinations are also represented neurally higher up in the visual processing stream. Neurons that respond to letters or other complex images like faces can be found in area IT of the temporal lobe. The more complex features are constructed through a process of convergence, whereby lower level features that make up their component parts send connections forward. This process is described in the network chapter and involves hierarchical organization. A summary of the process is outlined in Figure 7.13.

Evaluating Feature Detection Theory

The pandemonium model of pattern recognition represents a significant improvement over template matching. It doesn't require an extensive number of templates and will have only as many feature demons as there are features and as many cognitive demons as there are letters or other objects. The model can also explain the types of mistakes that people make during recognition. Often, an individual will confuse two visually presented letters that have features in common. Continuing with our example, a person might mistake the letter *R* for the letter *B* because both have a vertical line and a loop. The decision demon might accidentally choose the cognitive demon that represents the *B* because it will be shouting almost as loud as the *R* cognitive demon.

Another reason to like the pandemonium model comes from neurophysiology. Evidence from this field demonstrates that neurons in the visual system act as feature detectors. Single-cell recordings of neurons in the primary visual cortex of cats show that these cells respond selectively to different features, such as a line of a given length and orientation (Hubel & Wiesel, 1962).

Figure 4.3 The pandemonium model of pattern recognition. Different "demons" perform different steps in the recognition of the letter *R*.

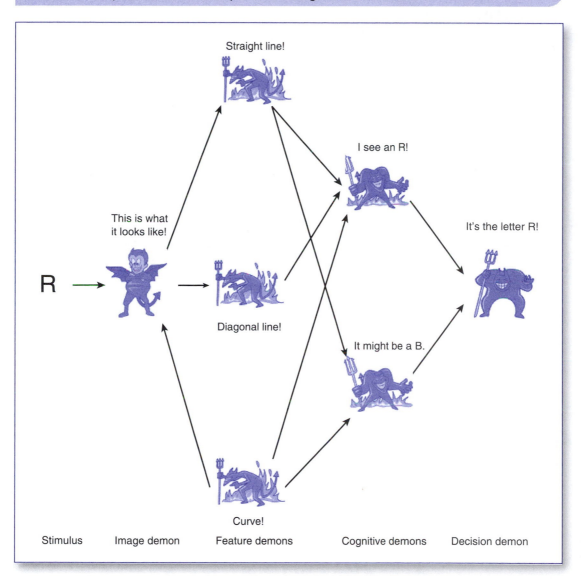

But feature detection models are not without their share of difficulties. For one thing, there is no good definition of what a feature is. For the letter *R*, the vertical and diagonal lines could together form the single feature of an angle, as opposed to their being separate features. Feature detection models are also bottom-up or **data-driven processes**. This means that they are driven entirely by the physical characteristics of the stimulus itself and fail to take into account the larger context or meaning. In real-world recognition scenarios, objects appear in varied contexts. The surrounding conditions often yield clues that can aid identification. In Figure 4.4, the central figure, when viewed alone, is ambiguous. The features alone are not enough to produce recognition. When this figure is grouped with surrounding figures—in this instance, letters or numbers—it takes on a new meaning: It appears either as a *B* or as a 13.

Additional evidence for the role of context in recognition comes from what is called the word superiority effect (Reicher, 1969). Here, the time it takes to recognize the letter *A* in CAT is shorter than the time it takes to recognize it alone or as part of a nonsense word. This suggests that the overall word is processed before any of the letters. Because the letter *A* appears in the word CAT, the presence of the entire word facilitates recognition of the individual letter. Both the example of the ambiguous figure given above and the word superiority effect are examples of top-down or **conceptually driven processes**, in which context and higher level knowledge aid recognition.

Recognition by Components Theory

Stimuli as they are represented on the retina are rarely viewed in the same way again. As we discussed in the template matching model, an object may appear in different locations, sizes, orientations, and shapes, to name just a few possible types of variation. Any pattern recognition mechanism must, therefore, produce a description of the object that is impervious to these kinds of changes. This is known as the **object constancy** problem in perception. Somehow, our visual system must extract from the stimulus input aspects that are invariant with respect to viewing angle, lighting, and so on. The template matching solution was to

Figure 4.4 Effects of context in perception. What is the central figure?

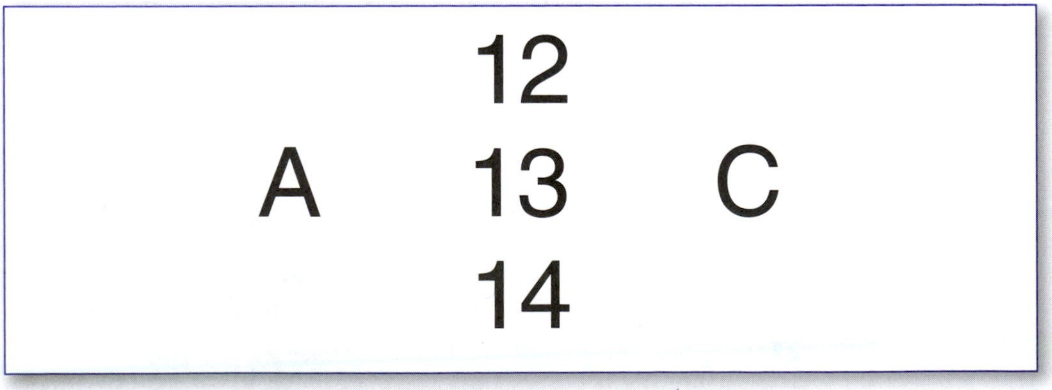

store multiple copies of the object. The feature detection solution was to extract certain invariant features—aspects of the object that remain constant.

The psychologist Irving Biederman (1987) also proposes a feature extraction account for the constancy problem; his approach is interesting because it specifies how object constancy may be achieved for three-dimensional (3-D) object representations. In his theory, features gathered from a stimulus are recombined to form an object representation. These features he calls **geons**. A geon has a basic volumetric shape—for example, a cube or a cylinder. Altogether, there are 36 of them. Figure 4.5 shows two examples of individual geons.

Geons are said to have three basic properties. The first is view invariance. This means that geons can be identified when viewed from many different perspectives. The second is discriminability: One can tell one geon apart from another no matter what the viewing angle. The fact that geons have these characteristics supports the notion that they may be used as features in human pattern recognition since they can account for the view-invariant aspect of object constancy.

The third property of geons is resistance to visual "noise." Geons can be perceived even when many of the contours that make them up are obscured. In one study, Biederman (1987) showed observers line drawings of objects that were masked by noise. The noise in this case was amorphous black regions resembling patches of spilled ink. In one condition,

Figure 4.5 Cubes and cylinders can be considered examples of geons. These can then be assembled to form more complex objects.

the noise covered the object contours in a way that preserved the geons. The noise for the most part in this condition covered single stretches of contour. In a second condition, the noise covered the contours such that the perception of the geons was disrupted. The noise here covered contour junctions, which are needed for the construction of the surface planes of 3-D shapes. Observers had no trouble recognizing the shapes in the first condition but had great difficulty doing so in the second. These results suggest that geons may help us recognize objects that have undergone occlusion, a partial covering up by other objects, since in the real world, occluding shapes rarely obscure junctions.

Geons are examples of very high-level representations. The visual input presented to the retina is 2-D, but as we are all aware, what we perceive is 3-D. The visual system uses cues in the environment to determine what objects and parts of objects are closer or farther. For instance, objects or parts that are larger are generally closer. It also uses the disparity or difference of view between the two eyes to tell us what is close or far. This sort of processing, known as **depth perception**, is a necessary part of geon formation. The advantage of a 3-D representation is obvious; it is a more accurate depiction of the object and allows us to manipulate and interact with it more successfully. The way in which individual geons may be assembled to form more complex objects is outlined below in David Marr's (1982) computation model of pattern recognition.

Evaluating Recognition by Components Theory

Biederman's recognition by components theory is supported because it can account for view invariance and occlusion. Another strength of the theory is the small basic feature set that consists of just 36 geons. In other pattern recognition theories, features are either unspecified or extremely numerous. Critics of the theory point out that broad classes of objects can be discriminated on the basis of geons but that fine-level object categories cannot. For example, geons can explain why we have no problem telling the difference between an airplane and an automobile, but they have difficulty in providing an explanation for how we can also tell apart objects that are much more similarly shaped, such as two similar bird species (Perrett & Oram, 1993). For these sorts of differences, we must rely on other features, such as the angle or taper of a part or perhaps color and texture.

Interdisciplinary Crossroads: Computational Vision and Pattern Recognition

In 1982, the renowned cognitive scientist David Marr wrote a book that described his influential theory of pattern recognition. He adopts a computational approach to vision. In this approach, the visual system is treated as a computer. The "computer" receives an image of an object and, after performing several algorithmic processing steps, accomplishes recognition of the object. Each major processing step produces a more fully articulated version of the object—what Marr calls "sketches."

Figure 4.6 Object representations in Marr's 3-D sketch.

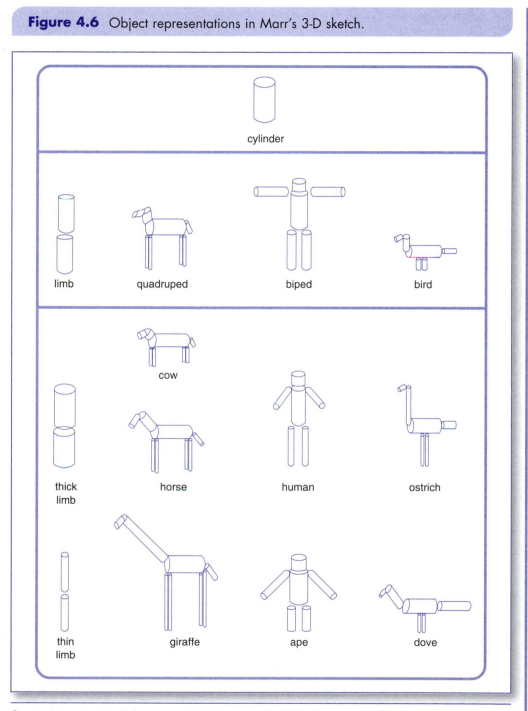

Source: Marr, D., & Nishihara, H.K. (1978). Representation and recognition of the spatial organization of three-dimensional shapes. *Proceedings of the Royal Society of London,* B200, pp. 269–294.

In the first stage, the image of an object is presented to the retina. This image is "analyzed" in terms of the intensity values, or areas of light and dark, that make up the image. Adjacent regions of sharp contrast in the image (that go from light to dark or vice versa) indicate the presence of edges and contours. The edges and contours in turn determine the basic features of the object. In his scheme, these features include line segments and circular shapes. The result is a **raw primal sketch** of the image.

The raw primal sketch then undergoes further processing. Features that are similar in size and orientation get grouped, in much the same way that parts are grouped into wholes according to the Gestalt principles discussed earlier. The groups of features are then processed again to produce a representation of the object that includes its surfaces and layout. Marr calls this the **2½-D sketch**.

This image is next transformed into a complete 3-D representation. In this **3-D sketch**, the axes of symmetry and elongation link the resultant object parts (see Figure 4.6). A symmetry axis is a line that divides an object into mirror image halves. An elongation axis is the line defining the direction along which the main bulk or mass of a shape is distributed. These axes serve to hierarchically organize the parts into a coherent, large-scale object that can be recognized. According to Marr, it is this final 3-D construct that we perceive and are consciously aware of.

In Marr's model, the 2½-D sketch contains a **viewer-centered description**. This is one that is particular to the viewer's point of view. Because the viewer's location, perspective, orientation, and so on are subject to change, object recognition under these conditions is difficult. But Marr's 3-D sketch has an **object-centered description**. The object's parts are described relative to one another and are linked on the basis of shared properties and axes. The relationships between parts, thus, remain intact across object transformations, solving the object constancy problem and enabling recognition under a broad variety of conditions.

Whereas the template matching model focuses on the form of representations in pattern recognition, Marr's model focuses on the computational steps or processes involved. Notice here that we get a detailed step-by-step description of what must transpire if an object is to be recognized. Each step is a computation—from the determination of intensity values, to edge extraction, to basic feature determination, to the grouping of features, to a sketch of surfaces and the overall layout, to the formation and linkage of 3-D object parts. This is an algorithmic approach, one that can be implemented both in a neural system like the brain or a computer software program.

Evaluating the Computational Approach to Vision

It is important to point out that Marr's theory is not a statement of how the visual system actually recognizes but how it might go about doing so. Although it is based on existing experimental and neurophysiological evidence, Marr's theory is more a specula-tion on the processes required of any pattern recognition mechanism, human or machine. We should also emphasize that Marr's theory involves feature detection, as the image is first broken down into component features that are then reassembled to form a complete, holistic object.

Feature Integration Theory

Another theory that entails feature extraction and recombination goes by the name of feature integration (Treisman & Gelade, 1980). This theory is unique because it brings to light the special role that attention plays in pattern recognition. It is based on a rather extensive set of cognitive psychology experiments, some of which we will describe below. Feature integration, like Marr's computational view, is also a stage theory. An object's basic features are identified by way of the image in the **preattentive stage**. These features can include color, motion, orientation, and curvature. Then, the features are combined during a **focused attention stage**. Following this, the object is recognized.

Let us examine more closely how features are identified and combined in these two stages. In a series of clever experiments, Treisman asked participants to identify a target item located in a visual field that was filled with nontarget items, or distractors (Treisman & Gelade, 1980). This task has since become known as **visual search**. With each trial, there is always one target, but the number of distractors can vary. For example, in one trial the target might be the single letter *T*, hidden among five *S*s. In another trial, the *T* might be hidden among 10 *S*s. In each trial, the time it takes for the participant to locate the target is recorded. A plot that shows the time needed to identify the target as a func-tion of the number of distractors is then made. Figure 4.7 shows a display and the plot of the search function.

For the sort of task described above—locating a *T* among *S*s—the search function is flat. The amount of time it takes to locate the target is small and constant, regardless of the number of distractors. Having 10 distractors does not make locating the target more difficult than having only 5. Participants in the experiment report that, under these circum-stances, the target seems to "pop out" at them, so the phenomenon has since been identified as perceptual **pop out**. Treisman argues that pop out is preattentive. A preatten-tive process is one that happens automatically and effortlessly. In vision, preattentive processes that are part of the processing of an image happen very quickly—usually within the first 100 milliseconds. The target item segregates out from the background of distrac-tors and draws attention to itself before participants even know what is happening. The participants have no voluntary control over the process and don't need to proactively search through the display to locate the target. Treisman calls this **parallel search** because the target seems to be scanned in parallel across all the display items at once. Parallel

Figure 4.7 Location of the target letter in the top panel is an instance of preattentive and parallel search. The target seems to "pop out" effortlessly. The bottom panel shows an idealized version of the flat search function for this type of task.

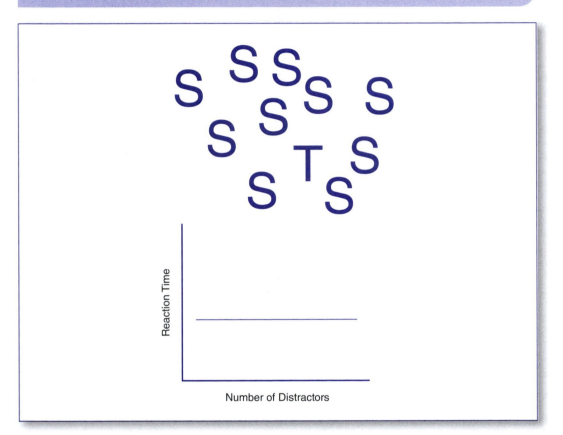

search is characterized by a flat search function. It occurs when the target differs from the distractors along a single perceptual dimension. In this example, the relevant dimension is curvature. The *T* is composed of straight lines, whereas the *S*s are curved. Pop out also happens when the target and the distractor differ in color, motion, or brightness, suggesting that these dimensions constitute a basic set of visual features.

Now imagine a second type of visual search (see Figure 4.8). This time, your job is to locate a blue *T*. It is hidden among red *T*s, and red and blue *S*s. The search function in this case shows a linear increase. The greater the number of distractors, the more time it takes to identify the target. This suggests that a very different type of search strategy will be

Figure 4.8 Location of the target letter in the top panel is difficult in this example of attentive and serial search. Attention must be paid to each item in the display. The search function for this task, an idealized version of which is shown in the bottom panel, is linear and increasing.

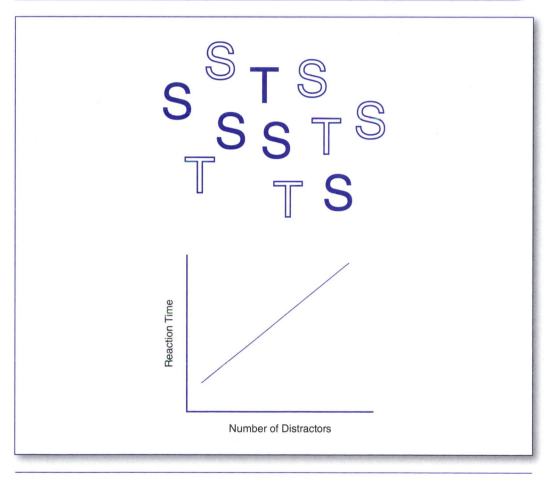

Source: Kahneman (1973).

needed. Participants in this instance report having to look at each item in the display, one after the other, until they find the target. For this reason, Treisman calls this **serial search**. Serial search is characterized by a linear increasing search function and appears to require focused, concentrated attention that is under voluntary control. Participants apparently need to match each item with respect to two dimensions. They must ask themselves if an item is blue and if it is shaped like a *T*. If the item fails to satisfy either of these conditions, the participants must then turn their attention to the next item and do the same thing, over and over, until the target is located. Serial search is necessary when the target differs from the distractors along two perceptual dimensions, such as shape and color. Treisman says that the job of voluntary attention, in this situation, is to "glue" together the different features. This attentional glue binds features together into coherent objects—a necessary step before recognition can take place.

So let's review what we know of Treisman's theory up to this point. In the preattentive stage, an object's features are identified. This process is fast, automatic, and effortless. In other words, it does not require attention and happens before attentional processes can even be brought to bear. A blue *T* in this stage is immediately broken down into its basic components of the color blue and its particular line segment orientation. In the subsequent focused attention stage, concentrated attention is required to glue these different features together in one place so that they form an object representation. The color and line segments are effectively linked together by attention in one location in the visual field. Only the combination of such features can tell us what an object really is and whether it differs from other objects with which it shares some of those features.

You may encounter a real-life example of visual search as you're about to leave the shopping mall. You look out into the parking lot to try to find your car, a red Honda Civic. If your car is the only red car or the only Civic of the same model as yours in the lot, it will pop out, and you will locate it immediately. If, however, there are other red cars and/ or other Civics of different colors, you will have to focus attention on each car in the lot before you will be able to locate yours.

Evaluating Feature Integration Theory

Feature integration theory has been widely accepted in the community of perceptual researchers. Investigators have conducted experiments that have generated numerous replications and extensions of its basic findings. An issue arising out of the theory, however, is exactly how and where in the visual system features get bound together. This is not a trivial problem, because, as we discuss elsewhere, the visual system uses a "divide-and-conquer" strategy. It breaks up an image into separate streams that correspond to object identity and location. Distinct parts of the brain process distinct aspects of a stimulus, such as its color, form, and motion. So if focused attention is the glue that binds such features, where does it all come together and how does the brain do it? This is referred to as the **binding problem** in vision. An intriguing solution to the binding problem is that neurons that represent separate features may synchronize their firing rates. This synchronization may then serve to link the features. Focused attention, perhaps mediated by other parts of the brain, could be the driving force behind this process.

THEORIES OF ATTENTION: HOW DO WE PAY ATTENTION?

We have already alluded to attention, having described the role it plays in the extraction and formation of features in pattern recognition. In this section, we will examine the nature of attention and describe several theories of how it is used in a wider cognitive context.

Attention is defined as concentrated mental activity. In general, we can think of attention as a form of mental activity or energy that is distributed among alternative information sources. Informational sources can be stimuli from the outside world or thoughts or other forms of internal mental content. When attention is allocated to one source, that source comes into conscious awareness, and the processing of that information is usually facilitated. From a cognitive perspective, attention can be considered as having two sets of opposing characteristics. It is selective but divisible, as well as shiftable but sustainable. Let's discuss each of these.

By **selective attention**, we mean that attention can be focused onto one source of information and away from another. For example, in class you can decide to listen to the sound of the instructor's voice or to some competing sound, such as the conversation of two students in the row behind you. At the same time, attention can be split or **divided** among several alternative information sources. You could, with some effort, listen to the voices of both the instructor and the students. In this situation, the ability to process information from the two sources would be significantly reduced. Generally, the greater the number of sources among which attention is divided, the lesser the attention to devote to any single source and the worse is the individual performance with respect to each.

Implicit in the notion of selectibility is **shiftability**. One can selectively attend to information source A while ignoring B, then switch back to B and ignore A. Or one could attend source A, then B, then C, and so on. The point is that attention can be repeatedly shifted among different sources. This shifting can be voluntary or involuntary. Distraction is an example of the involuntary shifting of attention to some irrelevant or undesirable piece of information. The converse of shifting is **sustainability**. Here, attention is focused exclusively on one source and sustained in this way over time. We can think of sustained attention as extended focus or concentration.

There are two general classes of theories that attempt to explain attention. **Bottleneck theories** describe why it is that of all the information presented to us, only a small portion actually gets through. These theories attempt to explain the apparent bottleneck effect or the narrowing down of the information that reaches conscious awareness. Bottleneck theories are inherently theories of selective attention because they describe how some information is selected for processing as the rest gets discarded. Broadbent's filter model, Treisman's attenuation model, the Deutsch-Norman memory selection model, and the multimode model are all bottleneck theories. **Capacity theories**, on the other hand, are essentially theories of divided attention. They conceptualize attention as a limited resource that must be spread around different informational sources. Kahneman's (1973) capacity model is an example of a capacity theory.

Broadbent's Filter Model

The British researcher Donald Broadbent did some of the earliest pioneering work in cognitive psychology. In his 1958 book, *Perception and Communication*, he proposed a theory to account for why we can't follow two streams of information coming in simultaneously via the two ears. Before we get to the details of his filter model, we need to describe some of the experimental evidence that led to it.

The dichotic listening task has been widely used to study selective attention. In this paradigm, a participant wearing headphones listens to two different messages being played, one over each ear. For instance, a male voice may be reciting a list of words into the left ear as a female voice recites a different list of words into the right ear. The participant's task is to pay attention to, or shadow, one of the voices and to ignore the other. The messages, or information sources, presented to the participant through both ears are in this context referred to as channels. Afterward, the participant is asked to recall what he or she has heard, for both the shadowed and unattended channels.

Early dichotic listening studies showed that participants were fairly accurate in recalling content from the shadowed ear but quite poor in recalling that coming from the unattended ear (Cherry, 1953). To Broadbent, this suggested the presence of a filter that could block out messages that were being relatively ignored, allowing only attended information to enter awareness. Figure 4.9 shows a diagram of Broadbent's filter model. Information from both channels first arrives in sensory memory. This is a place where incoming sensory information is briefly held before it is processed. Next, a filter is applied to this information. The filter selects certain portions of the information—that coming from the shadowed channel in this case—and allows it to pass through. Information coming from the unattended channel is blocked.

The selection in Broadbent's model is based on the physical characteristics of the stimulus, such as location (left or right ear), pitch, and loudness. This conclusion was based on the fact that one could shadow messages easily using these as criteria. In the next step, whatever information gets past the filter then undergoes pattern recognition. Following this step, information travels past any selection mechanism to a short-term memory store, where it is held for a longer period of time and made available for subsequent processing and response. Notice that selection in this model is performed entirely by the filter and not by any selection mechanism that comes later. We describe this selection mechanism only to show how this model compares with others. Broadbent's model is referred to as an early selection model because the filter screens out information before it can be recognized.

Figure 4.9 Information-processing models of selective attention. The solid arrows indicate information from the attended message. The dashed arrows indicate information from the unattended message.

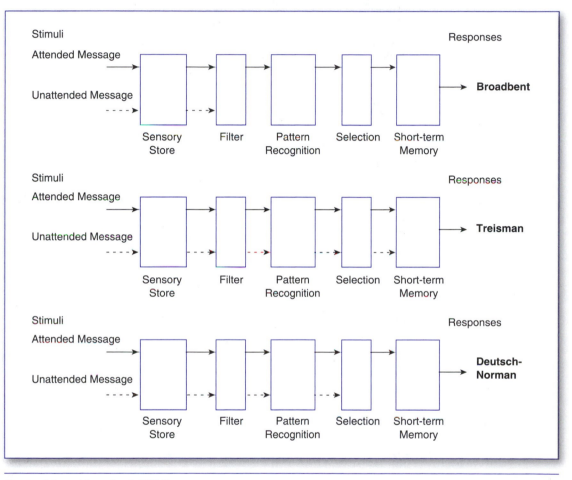

Source: Adapted from Reed (2000).

Evaluating the Filter Model

Almost from the get-go, it was realized that there were some problems with Broadbent's filter model of the theory. One problem is summed up in what is one of the better names for a psychological phenomenon, the so-called **cocktail party effect**. Imagine that you are attending a party and chatting with several people. Somebody across the room then mentions your name. To your surprise, you realize that you heard it, even though you were completely engrossed in the immediate conversation. Researchers have empirically validated this intuitive finding (Moray, 1959; Wood & Cowan, 1995). The observed cocktail party effect and other studies have demonstrated that some information gets through the unattended channel. The filter does not block words of great personal relevance, such as your name and words associated with danger—for example, *fire*. Broadbent's model has the filter completely blocking all information coming from the unattended channel. Clearly, his view requires some revision.

Treisman's Attenuation Model

Attenuation theory is similar to filter theory but with one exception (Treisman, 1964). Instead of completely blocking out the unattended message, the filter attenuates or weakens it. Message attenuation is like having water running through two faucets, where each of the faucets constitutes a different information channel. The faucet corresponding to the shadowed message would be open all the way, allowing water to pour through. The faucet corresponding to the unattended channel would be only partially open, allowing just a small amount of water through. The addition of Treisman's model to Figure 4.9 would have the unattended message passing through all the processing stages, but in a weakened form.

Treisman explains that different words have different chances of making it through the unattended channel, due to a threshold effect. A **threshold** is the minimum amount of activation required to produce conscious awareness of a stimulus. Stimuli with associated low thresholds easily make their way into awareness. Those with associated high thresholds do not. A word's meaning determines its threshold. Important words and those with personal relevance, such as your name, have a lower threshold for recognition and make it past the filter. Less important words—for example, *chair*—have higher thresholds and are filtered out.

The Deutsch-Norman Memory Selection Model

The cocktail party effect shows that meaning, or semantics, is another criterion according to which information is selected. This runs contrary to early filter models that posit physical characteristics such as loudness or pitch as the primary basis for selection. Deutsch and Deutsch (1963) and Norman (1968), therefore, proposed a second selection process, one that is based on semantic characteristics. This selection happens later in processing. Their model is an example of a **late selection model**. The first stages of processing in this model are the same as those of the other models. Information from the sensory store is filtered on the basis of physical characteristics and then recognized. However, before being passed into short-term memory, it goes through a secondary selection mechanism. This mechanism selects information on the basis of semantic characteristics or message content. The selected items end up in short-term memory and awareness. Those items not selected never reach an awareness. The Deutsch-Norman model shown in Figure 4.9 depicts information from two channels reaching the selection mechanism, which makes the choice as to which information gets through.

The Multimode Model of Attention

So where does selection take place? A more current view is that selection can occur early or late. Michael Posner and Charles Snyder (1975) advocate the idea of a "movable filter," one that can operate at various points in processing according to the observer's needs. Data from another study support what seemed to some to be the case all along, that selection can be based on physical or semantic properties (Johnston & Heinz, 1978). They found, however, that semantic selection imposes a greater cost—that is, it requires greater attentional resources than physical selection. The model that arises from the view that selection can be based on multiple modes—for example, the physical and the semantic—is called the **multimode model of attention**.

There is also neurophysiological evidence to support the multimode model. Hillyard, Hink, Schwent, and Picton (1973) used an event-related potential (ERP) technique to investigate when selection occurs. The ERP records brain electrical activity that happens in response to the presentation of a stimulus. According to their design, the researchers had participants attend to a stimulus—say, coming from the left ear—and compared the activity observed under that condition with observable activity related to an identical unattended target—say, coming from the right ear. They observed a very rapid change in electrical activity only 80 milliseconds after the stimulus was presented, which suggested that selection was happening early on in response to perceptual characteristics. However, other ERP studies showed a change in electrical activity that happened approximately 300 milliseconds after stimulus onset, which suggested a late selection based on task relevance and, perhaps, semantic features (Luck & Hillyard, 1994). To summarize, it appears that attentional selection is more flexible than was first assumed. It can happen early or late and can be based on more than just a single mode.

All three of the selective attention models discussed thus far are based on the same general information-processing mechanisms. They all involve the same stages of cognitive processing that occur in the same order. The messages are each represented in a sensory store, then filtered, recognized, selected, and represented again in short-term memory. Since they are assemblies of individual processes that interact, they are instances of a cognitive architecture like the SOAR model, defined and described in more detail in the following chapter.

Each of these stages by themselves consists of a complex set of computational processes that are not elaborated on here. The stages can be considered to be modules as each takes in information from a previous stage, performs a particular computation, and then passes the output of that computation on to the next stage. Note that the representations in these models are auditory, not visual, as the messages being processed are sounds rather than sights. As such, they will be generated by the auditory system and will have different properties than visual representations do.

Kahneman's Capacity Model of Attention

Capacity models describe attention as a resource. We can think of this resource as the amount of mental effort or energy required to perform a task. Like many other resources, attention exists in limited supply. At any given time, we have only so much of it that is available for use. Daniel Kahneman (1973), in his book *Attention and Effort*, outlined a detailed capacity model of attention. In it, he described the factors that affect available attentional capacity as well as the factors that determine how this capacity gets utilized. Because we are talking about the distribution of attention to different sources, capacity models are really models that describe the division, rather than the selection, of attention.

Figure 4.10 shows Kahneman's model. Let's walk our way through it. The rectangular box at the top represents the pool of available attention. A person's arousal level is one thing that can affect this capacity. **Arousal** refers to physiological activation and is reflected in values such as cardiac and respiratory rates. Moderate levels of arousal are assumed to produce the greatest amount of available capacity. This follows from the Yerkes-Dodson law, which states that there is an inverted U-shaped performance function for arousal (Yerkes & Dodson, 1908). Performance is poor for low and high levels of arousal, wherein individuals are presumably too tired or anxious, but it is optimal at intermediate levels.

Miscellaneous determinants of arousal include things such as the amount of sleep a person has had or the amount of food he or she has consumed. If a person has not slept well or has not eaten recently, arousal and, therefore, capacity are assumed to be low. Miscellaneous manifestations of arousal can include overt behaviors such as finger tapping or other nervous habits that result from excessive arousal. Notice, too, that the circle that depicts the evaluation of demands on capacity can itself affect capacity. If there is a greater demand for attention, there may be increased arousal. Knowing that you have a final examination early tomorrow morning might increase the attention you give to studying the night before.

Attentional capacity must now be allocated to the cognitive activities that need it. How is this determined? The ellipse in the center of Figure 4.10 represents the allocation policy. We can think of it as an executive or a decision maker who determines how much attention will be given to a variety of tasks. It is influenced by several factors. First among these

Figure 4.10 Kahneman's capacity model of attention.

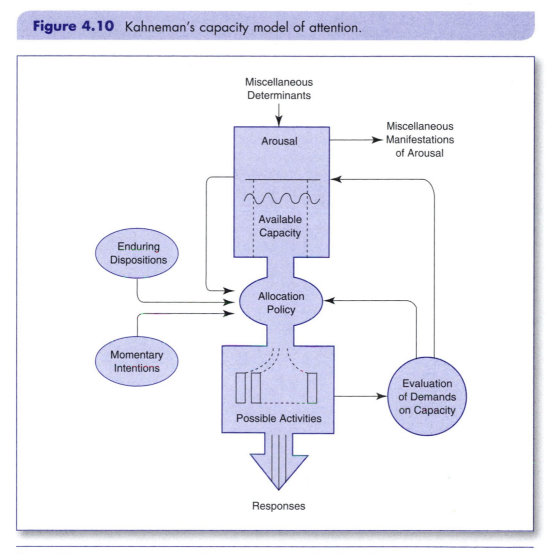

Source: Kahneman, D., *Attention and effort*, 1st edition, © 1973. Published by Pearson Education, Inc., Upper Saddle River, NJ.

are enduring dispositions. An **enduring disposition** is an automatic influence on where attention gets directed. A new event or a sudden movement is a thing that automatically draws attention. Momentary intentions also influence allocation. A **momentary intention** is a conscious decision to pay attention to something. Momentary intentions reflect our specific goals at a given moment in time. A mother driving a car might redirect her attention to her children fighting in the back seat, but she would quickly have to direct her attention back to her primary goal of driving. Notice that the evaluation of demands on capacity and the available capacity also have arrows pointing to allocation, indicating that they, too, exert an influence. The amount of available arousal and the urgency of a task both have an effect on the amount of attention that will go to a particular task.

The rectangular box at the bottom of Figure 4.10 contains a representation of possible activities. These are all the cognitive processes or tasks that need attention. The allocation policy that gives attention to them is flexible. For example, equal amounts of attention could be given to all the activities or all available attention could be given to just one activity. Those activities with the greatest demand will be given the most attention. In the driving example given above, the driver's attention was momentarily taken away from driving—the most demanding activity—and given to the children in the back seat and was then switched back again.

Evaluating the Capacity Model of Attention

Stephen Reed (2000), in his book *Cognition*, makes some summary comments on attentional theories. He notes that capacity models such as Kahneman's (1973) are not designed to replace selection models but, rather, to supplement them. Both types of models predict that it will be difficult for an individual to pay attention to two things at once (but for different reasons). According to selection theories, it is because a bottleneck develops, prohibiting the entry of two packages of information at the same time. According to capacity theories, it is because the demands of the two tasks exceed available capacity. Capacity models give us a good overview of the many influences and interdependencies that are involved in the allocating of attention. Selection models provide us with a better feel for the discrete stages of information flow during attentional processing.

EVALUATING THE MODEL-BUILDING APPROACH

Our discussion of perceptual and attentional theories so far has demonstrated several things. First, even within a discipline, there is no single widely agreed-on model that explains how a given cognitive process operates. In the case of pattern recognition, we summarized four major models of how it might take place. Second, although these models may vary widely, each model captures some unique aspect of the process better than the others. The feature detection model is better suited to explain errors in recognition, whereas the computational approach (discussed in the Interdisciplinary Crossroads section) can best account for object constancy. Third, and the most important, we learn more about a process by evaluating all the theories and comparing competing theories. The problems posed by the template matching model show that any model of pattern recognition must extract some invariant feature from the image. That is what is postulated in one form or another by the remaining theories. This cross-theory analysis may not tell us what the features actually are—we see that they differ slightly from model to model—but it does tell us that the process of feature extraction is a key element in the process.

Another major point worth mentioning here is that there is cross-fertilization between model formation and experimentation. In the case of attention, we have seen a constant tug and pull between the models and the experimental evidence. This dynamism led to the formation of better and more improved models. Broadbent's filter theory showed us the basics of how a selective attentional system might operate. Later research, however, proved that information could get through the unattended channel. This led to the formation of Treisman's attenuation model, which by itself could not adequately explain selection that is based on semantic characteristics. This, in turn, led to the development of the Deutsch-Norman memory selection model. The results of later experiments necessitated the introduction of multimode models and the idea of a movable filter. Drawing on this short history, it becomes obvious that we should not put too much faith in one model. Instead, we must realize that each model is a point along a developmental continuum, and we must also encourage researchers to modify their models based on current research.

SUMMING UP: A REVIEW OF CHAPTER 4

1. In the cognitive approach, the mind is viewed as a computer that represents and processes information.

2. A module is a functionally distinct information-processing component that receives, transforms, and transmits information to other modules.

3. Pattern recognition is the ability to identify objects in the environment. The major theories of visual pattern recognition are template matching, feature detection, recognition by components, feature integration, and computational.

4. In template matching, an image of a stimulus is matched to an internally generated representation. If the two match, then recognition occurs. The problem with this process is that it requires different templates for each of the many ways the stimulus can vary.

5. In the feature detection theory of pattern recognition, features such as oriented line segments are extracted from the stimulus input. The number and type of features present are used to diagnose object identity.

6. In feature integration theory, features are extracted preattentively and then combined in a focused attention stage. Preattentive processing is all that is required to locate a target that differs in one way from distractors. Focused attention is needed to locate a target that differs in more than one way from surrounding distractors.

7. Attention may be thought of as a concentrated mental activity that is allocated among alternative information sources. Attention can be selective or focused on one source. It can also be divided between sources or shifted among them.

8. Historically, there have been five major theories of attention. In the filter model, information from one source is allowed to enter conscious awareness. Information from other channels is blocked completely very early in processing. In the attenuation model, some filtered information gets through. In the Deutsch-Norman model, information can be filtered later on the basis of semantic content. The multimode model allows for both early selection based on stimulus features and later selection based on meaning.

9. In the capacity model, attention is viewed as a resource that can vary in terms of available capacity, how it is allocated, and how many available activities need it.

10. The computational theory of pattern recognition posits that an image is processed in a number of different stages. A raw primal sketch of the stimulus with light and dark values is generated first. Feature grouping, surface, and layout are processed next in a 2½-D sketch. Object parts are linked and organized in the final 3-D sketch.

EXPLORE MORE

Log on to the student study site at **http://study.sagepub.com/friedenberg3e** for electronic flash cards, review quizzes, and a list of web resources to aid you in further exploring the field of cognitive science.

SUGGESTED READINGS

Fodor, J. A. (1983). *The modularity of mind.* Cambridge: MIT Press.

Kahneman, D. (1973). *Attention and effort.* Englewood Cliffs, NJ: Prentice Hall.

Marr, D. (1982). *Vision.* San Francisco, CA: Freeman.

Pashler, H. (1998). *Attention.* Hove, England: Psychology Press.

Reisberg, D. (2001). *Cognition: Exploring the science of the mind* (2nd ed.). New York, NY: W. W. Norton

5

THE COGNITIVE APPROACH II

Memory, Imagery, and Problem Solving

It isn't so astonishing, the number of things that I can remember, as the number of things I can remember that aren't so.

—Mark Twain, 1912

TYPES OF MEMORY: HOW DO WE REMEMBER?

In this chapter, we continue our discussion of cognitive theories as we focus on three other prominent cognitive processes: memory, imagery, and problem solving. In the previous chapter, we looked at processes that may be considered "low level." That is because they focus on information coming in from the environment and how to pay attention to it. In the current chapter, we examine the so-called high-level processes because they focus on how information is represented and processed more internally with less reliance on the environment. We will describe the major theoretical approaches to each of these major processes as well as some of the classic experiments that led to their development. There has been an immense amount of research on these and other topics in cognitive psychology, and by necessity, we must leave out many interesting and important findings. As in previous chapters, we refer interested readers to the works in the "Suggested Readings" section if they wish to learn more of these findings.

Memory, very generally defined, is the capacity to retain information over time. Memory is, of course, very important to any information-processing system, animal, or machine, because it underlies the ability to learn. Any system incapable of learning from its mistakes would soon perish or become obsolete in a dynamic, real-world environment. Memory allows us to store our past experiences and draw on them. In this way, we can deal with new situations that bear similarity to older situations and not have to solve each new problem from scratch.

Any discussion of memory must begin with the notion that there is no single type of memory. Cognitive research in this area has led to a rather consistent finding: the existence of functionally distinct memory systems. Models of memory specify how these different memory systems interact. Before we can understand this interaction, we must lay out some of the characteristics of these individual memory systems. They include duration, which refers to how long information remains viable in a memory system; capacity, which refers to how much information the memory system can hold; and coding, which refers to the particular type of information the system contains. In the first part of this chapter, we will summarize these characteristics. Following this, we will describe formal memory models.

Sensory Memory

Sensory memory is a repository for incoming sensory information. Raw, unanalyzed data that are derived from the senses are held here very briefly. The purpose of sensory memory is to maintain the representation of a stimulus long enough for it to be recognized. Although you may have glanced at a visual scene for only 100 milliseconds, a representation of it is still preserved in sensory memory. This gives the information a chance to be operated on by selection and pattern recognition mechanisms.

There are different forms of sensory memory—one for each of the five senses. Each of these forms has different characteristics. Iconic memory is visual sensory memory. It holds a brief "snapshot" of what you have just looked at. Iconic memory has a very short duration; it lasts only about 250 to 300 milliseconds (Averbach & Sperling, 1961; Sperling, 1960). Echoic memory is an auditory sensory store. You can think of it as an "echo" of what you have just heard. It lasts considerably longer than iconic memory, on the order of several seconds or more (Darwin, Turvey, & Crowder, 1972). The coding or representation of information in sensory memory, thus, varies with the modality. Iconic memory stores visual representations; echoic memory stores auditory ones. More research needs to be done on sensory memory for the other senses, including olfactory (smell), gustatory (taste), and tactile (touch). In each case, we are dealing with a different type of representation, one corresponding to each modality. So we see that the issue of representation gets complicated; we can have multiple representations for each sensory modality.

George Sperling first began investigating iconic memory in the 1960s. He presented participants with a short display of English alphabet letters arranged in a four-column by three-row letter array. On a given trial, a display might look something like the following:

R G C P

L X N F

S B J Q

There were two conditions in this study (Sperling, 1963). In the **whole-report condition**, the participant's task was to remember as many of the letters as possible. Most participants recalled only four or five. Sperling had a hunch that they were actually remembering more than this. He suspected that the procedure was testing not for what is available in the icon (in this case, the entire display of letters) but for what we pay attention to or process after the fact. Four or five individual items might be what is remembered but not what is actually present in the icon. To investigate this, he developed a **partial-report condition**. Participants, immediately after being shown the letter display, heard one of three tones. A high-pitched tone cued the top row, indicating that the participants would be expected to report on that row; a medium-pitched tone prompted the middle row; and a low-pitched tone cued the bottom row. The results then showed that participants were able to recall all the letters, regardless of their location. This demonstrates that all the letters were stored and available in the icon, as the observers had no way of knowing which row was going to be cued.

We learn from this research that the capacity of the visual icon—how much it can hold—is at least 12 items. Subsequent research has shown that iconic memory can, in fact, hold much more than this. Its capacity is essentially unlimited. Everything that can be taken in during a glance—all the information in the visual field—can be stored there. But the integrity of this information is short-lived, not lasting more than one second. The image is clearly represented early on but then fades quite rapidly. The loss of information over time in memory is known as **decay**.

More recent research on iconic memory has revealed various factors that can influence performance. Becker, Pashler, and Anstis (2000) presented a visual array of items that could be followed by either a blank interstimulus interval (ISI) or an ISI with a cue providing the location of a changed item. Change detection performance was poor in the blank ISI condition but improved significantly in the cued condition. They hypothesize that the blank interval overwrites or erases the icon formed in response to the first array, whereas attention to the cue insulates the icon against overwriting. This erasing process is called **masking** and is manipulated as an independent variable in many different types of perceptual studies.

In another work, Thomas and Irwin (2006) presented observers with a letter array using the partial-report method. When participants were instructed to blink following the offset of the target array and the onset of the cue, they made more mislocation errors. They conclude that blinking interferes with the binding of object identity and object position in iconic memory and named this phenomenon *cognitive blink suppression*. Blinks were found to reduce neural activation in area VI (primary visual cortex), which may disturb formation of the icon.

What other brain areas might underlie iconic memory formation? Keysers, Xiao, Foldiak, and Perrett (2005) presented brief visual stimuli with and without interstimulus gaps to humans and monkeys. For an ISI of 93 milliseconds, they found continued neuronal activation in monkeys' temporal cortices as if the stimulus was still present on the screen. Ruff, Kristjansson, and Driver (2007) used six items in their displays, three in each hemifield (left or right visual field). Their auditory cues indicated which side of the display to report. In the precue condition, which measures selective spatial attention, the cue came before the array. In the postcue condition, measuring iconic memory, it came after. Using functional magnetic resonance imaging techniques, they found that both types of cues led to contralateral (opposite side) activation in the lateral occipital cortex. This suggests that read-off of iconic memory and spatial attention share some underlying neural mechanisms. They also found bilateral activation in the fronto-parietal network for each cue type. However, postcues triggered more activity in the right middle frontal gyrus.

Working Memory

Working memory is also sometimes known as short-term memory. Researchers sometimes use these terms interchangeably, as will we throughout this text. As the term *short-term memory* suggests, information is briefly stored there. However, the duration of items residing in working memory is, as we will see, much longer than that of items residing in sensory memory. Working memory retains less information; its capacity is unlike the unlimited capacity of the visual icon. Working memory is limited to storing just a small number of items. Whereas information in the different sensory stores is specific to modality, coding in working memory can be acoustic, semantic, or visual. We will have more to say about how the different types of codes are put to use when we discuss Alan Baddeley's model of working memory later in this chapter.

It is helpful to use the analogy of a workbench when thinking about working memory. A workbench is a space where one can construct something using parts and tools. For example, if one wanted to build a spice rack, he or she would need several pieces of wood, some nails, and varnish. In addition to these, he or she would need saws—to cut the wood to size, a hammer, and a paintbrush. With these items in hand, one could set about creating the final product. Working memory is the mental equivalent of this workbench. It is a place where data (the parts) can be temporarily stored so that they can be operated on by cognitive processes (the tools). In this sense, working memory is the site where conscious thinking takes place. It is here that you remember a phone number, figure out how to navigate your way around a new city, or solve an arithmetic problem.

In a classic study, Peterson and Peterson (1959) demonstrated the duration of items that reside in short-term memory. They presented participants with the items to be remembered. A tone was sounded following the presentation of the items. In separate trials, the tone was sounded at varying time intervals. Sometimes, it would go off immediately; during other trials, there would be a substantial delay. The participants were instructed to recall the items on the sounding of the tone. In this condition, all participants were able to remember the items correctly, no matter the length of the delay. In a second condition, presentation of a three-digit number followed presentation of the items. Participants were instructed to count backward in threes from this number. If the number was 796, they would have to count out 793, 790, 787, and so on. A tone was sounded, again at varying intervals, cueing recall of the items. At this point, the results were quite different. The ability to remember the items deteriorated rapidly as the period of delay increased. After an 18-second recall interval, the accuracy of recall had dropped to just 5%, meaning that participants could recall only 5% of the items correctly. Figure 5.1 shows idealized results for both conditions of such a study.

You may have guessed what's happening here. In the first condition, participants were able to rehearse the trigrams. **Rehearsal** is the mental repetition or mental "practicing" of some to-be-learned material. It is usually manifested as implicit speech, or "talking to oneself"—what you do when you need to remember somebody's phone number but can't write it down. Rehearsal refreshes items in short-term memory; it keeps them active and prevents them from decaying. In the second condition, participants were prevented from rehearsing because of the backward counting. Here, the items underwent decay. Using this

Figure 5.1 Idealized results of a memory study in which participants are asked to remember an item after a given recall interval. Having to count backward after presentation of the item interferes with rehearsal.

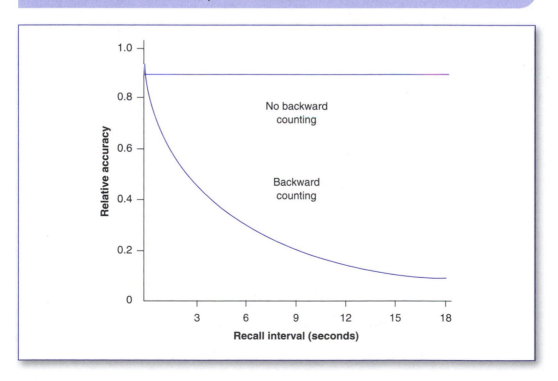

paradigm, Brown (1958) and Peterson and Peterson (1959) were able to determine that the duration of short-term memory was about 18 seconds. If you are interested in some of the other processes that can act on information in working memory, go to the next section, where you will see that—in addition to rehearsal—items can be scanned.

Our next discussion is of capacity. How much can working memory hold? It is easy to devise an experiment that tests this question. It would involve presenting participants with a series of lists, each containing a different number of items. For example, we could present a list of four digits, then a five-digit list, a six-digit list, and so on. If there were a limit to how many digits could be held in working memory, we would see a dramatic drop-off in retention as we arrived at that limit. Many early experiments of this sort demonstrated that this was the case. On average, individuals can retain about seven items, give or take two, commonly denoted as 7 ± 2. This limit has come to be called the "magical number seven" (Miller, 1956).

Therefore, short-term memory has a limited capacity. We can hold only about seven items in it at one time. But what exactly is an "item"? Is it a number? A letter? A word? To understand this, let's start with a demonstration. Glance quickly at the letters below and then close your eyes to see how many you can remember.

N   F   L   C   B   S   I   R   A   M   T   V

Did you have a hard time? If you weren't able to recall all the letters easily, take a closer look. You may at this point notice that the letters cluster in groups of three—each group is a popular acronym. "NFL" stands for National Football League, "CBS" for Columbia Broadcasting System, and so on. If you had noticed these groupings, it would have been easy for you to remember all the letters. This is because you would then be remembering only four groups of three letters and not 12 individual letters. A grouping of items into a single meaningful whole in short-term memory is known as **chunking**. We can increase the total amount of information that is contained in short-term memory by chunking: the bigger the chunk, the greater the capacity.

Let us turn now to the issue of coding. How is information coded or represented in working memory? Research in this area shows that information can be coded in a variety of formats. Conrad (1964) presented letter strings to participants and then asked them to perform immediate recall. He found that although the letters had been presented visually, the pattern of errors was based on the sounds of the letters. For example, participants would mistake an *A* for a *K* or an *E* for a *P*. This suggests that the letters were being converted to an **acoustic code**, one based on the sounds of the items.

Studies by Wickens (1972) and others have demonstrated the existence of an alternate code that is part of working memory. To make sense of their experiments, we must first differentiate between two types of interference. In **proactive interference**, information that is learned earlier interferes with information learned later. In **retroactive interference**, information that is learned later interferes with information learned earlier. The more closely related items are with respect to meaning, the greater this interference. Wickens presented words to subjects along the lines of the tasks that were given to participants in the Brown and Peterson experiments. He found that after they had studied words that belonged to a single category, there was proactive interference, which engendered a steady decline in recall over the first few trials. For example, the word *apple*, learned earlier, would interfere with recall of the word *orange*, learned later. But in a final trial, during which the semantic categories of the words the participants were asked to remember were sometimes switched—in one condition, from fruits to flowers—there was an increase in recall. In this instance, the word *apple*, learned earlier, would interfere less with the word *tulip*, as they belong to separate semantic categories. These results showed that the words were represented not acoustically but, instead, on the basis of their inherent meanings—the code was a **semantic code**.

Additional studies showed that information in working memory may be represented in yet a third way. A **visual code** is one that preserves spatial characteristics. In studies of the mental rotation of objects, participants were presented with a visual pattern and were asked to compare it with another that was either a different pattern or the same pattern rotated by a certain angle. The plot of reaction time in these studies showed that subjects apparently formed a visual representation of the pattern and rotated it mentally to enable them to perform the comparisons (Cooper & Shepard, 1973; Shepard & Metzler, 1971). The representation seems to be visual because the greater the angular difference between the two patterns being compared, the longer it takes to respond—exactly what one would expect if a real spatial object were rotated. We will describe these experiments and the controversy that surrounds them in greater detail later in this chapter.

Scanning Items in Working Memory

You go to the grocery store to buy some food for dinner. Because you need only a few items, you memorize the items rather than writing out a list. After buying rice and broccoli, you pause to consider what else it is you have to purchase. What mental process occurs when we perform this sort of task? The process in question is called "search," and it is one of the many operations carried out in working memory. In this section, we describe a classic experiment from cognitive psychology that suggests how such a mechanism might work. Please note that search in working memory is not the same process as the visual search we discussed in the previous chapter.

Search, in an abstract informational sense, involves looking for a target among a set of items. Each of the items must be represented mentally, as must the target. Then, a representation of the target must be compared against each of the represented items in the set in the expectation that a match will be made. But now a question arises. This search process can proceed in two ways. If it is a **serial memory search**, then comparisons take place one at a time, with a participant perhaps starting at the beginning of the list and proceeding through until the end. If this is the case, then search times should be long, as each comparison takes time. If it is a **parallel memory search,** then the target can be compared with all the items at once. Assuming this to be the case, search times should be short, as only one comparison is being made.

To find out whether the search was serial or parallel, Sternberg (1966) asked participants in his study to memorize a set of items, such as a series of digits. The size of the set varied between one and six digits—always below the 7 ± 2 limit. Sternberg then presented a target digit. The participants had to decide whether the target was a member of the memory set or not. For example, in one trial that used a set size of four, the participants might have had to memorize the digits 4, 9, 0, and 2. They were then given a target, the number 9. Following the presentation of the target, they were to respond as quickly as possible, pushing one button if the target was present in the set (a positive trial) and another if it was absent (a negative trial).

Reaction time (the time it took to push the buttons) was analyzed and plotted against set size for both positive and negative trials. Sternberg made two predictions. If the search was serial, he should obtain an increasing function with longer search times for larger set sizes. This follows, because if each comparison takes a given amount of time, a greater number of comparisons will require more time. If, on the other hand, the search was parallel, he should obtain a flat function over set size, indicating the shorter time it takes to compare the target with all items in the set at once.

Sternberg made yet another prediction. He speculated that the search, if it was serial, could be self-terminating or exhaustive. In a **self-terminating search,** the search process stops as soon as a positive match occurs. Because the target can be located anywhere in the set, the search times will be variable. Sometimes, if the target matches an item at the beginning of the list, the search will end quickly. On other occasions, when the target matches an item that is near the end of the list, it will take longer. This effect manifests itself as lesser slopes in the search function for positive trials, in which a target is present in the set, but as steeper slopes for negative trials, in which scanning must always continue to the end. In an **exhaustive search,** comparisons are made all the way to the end of the list, even if the target has already been located. In this situation, the slopes for positive and negative trials should be both steep and identical.

Data showed that the search was serial and exhaustive. The search function increased with set size and had a lowered slope for positive trials (see Figure 5.2). At first blush, this result seems counterintuitive and inefficient. Why should you continue looking for something you've already found? There are several possibilities. Exhaustive search could serve as a "double check," a way to ensure that the target isn't duplicated later in the list. Or it could be that once the search is initiated, it proceeds automatically and cannot be stopped. The latter possibility is interesting because it implies that the search is only partially under voluntary control. The central executive in the working memory model may issue a command to the articulatory loop to begin a search, but once this command is issued, it cannot be further regulated.

Figure 5.2 The results for the Sternberg experiment showed that search was serial and exhaustive. A Yes response in the plot indicates a positive trial in which the target was present. A No response in the plot means a negative trial in which the target was absent. The regression line equation is also shown.

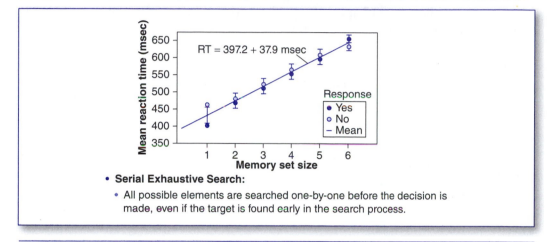

- **Serial Exhaustive Search:**
  - All possible elements are searched one-by-one before the decision is made, even if the target is found early in the search process.

Source: Sternberg, S. (1966). High-speed scanning in human memory. *Science, 153,* 652–654.

Long-Term Memory

Obviously, individuals are capable of remembering information for longer than just a few seconds. Many of us can recall quite vividly events from our childhoods or facts learned decades ago in school. We must, therefore, have another memory system, one that is capable of storing data for months or years.

It turns out, as is the case for memory in general, that long-term memory has several distinct types. **Procedural memory** holds procedural knowledge. It is memory for skill, is demonstrated by doing, and arises without conscious recall. Knowing how to ride a bicycle is a good example of this memory type. A person who knows how to ride a bike can demonstrate that he or she has this ability only by actually doing it. The subconscious nature of this memory becomes evident when we learn how to perform some skill—such as playing the piano—forget how, but then show improvement when we attempt to perform the action at a later date. Procedural memory also sometimes goes by the name of implicit memory.

Declarative memory contains declarative knowledge. It is memory for facts and events, is demonstrated by speaking, and arises with conscious recall. There are two types of declarative memory. Knowing that Thomas Jefferson wrote the Declaration of Independence is an example of the first type, called semantic memory. **Semantic memory**

is knowledge of facts and general knowledge of the sort learned in school. The second type is episodic memory. **Episodic memory** contains episodes or personally experienced events—for example, what you did on your last birthday. We are usually consciously aware of declarative information, which is sometimes referred to as explicit memory.

A study by Bahrick (1984) shows us how long information in semantic memory lasts. Bahrick studied a group of people who studied Spanish early in life, usually during the high school or college years. They were tested at various times throughout their lives with respect to how much they remembered from their Spanish classes. When recall for various types of information was plotted as a function of time, three distinct memory stages were discovered (see Figure 5.3). In the first stage, stretching from 3 to 6 years after the classes, there was an initial, rather dramatic, loss of information. In the second stage, stretching from 6 to up to 30 years after initial learning, there was no further loss—the amounts

Figure 5.3 Percentage of correct recall for Spanish learned in school, at different time periods after original learning.

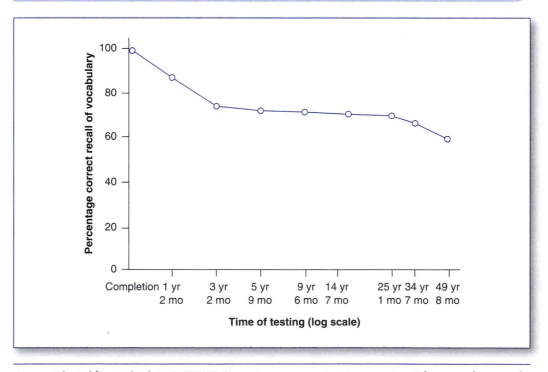

Source: Adapted from Bahrick, H. P. (1984). Semantic memory content in permastore: Fifty years of memory for Spanish learned in school. *Journal of Experimental Psychology: General, 113,* 1–29.

remembered stayed relatively constant. In the third stage, stretching from 30 to 35 years later, there was another loss of information, but only a slight one.

We can draw conclusions from each of the three stages. First, information in long-term storage, if not used or rehearsed, decays fairly rapidly over the first few years. Second, there is some residual amount of learned information that remains intact over a long period of time. Third, there appears to be a slight additional loss of information that occurs later in life. This loss could be due to the kind of general decline in cognitive function that accompanies aging. The basic shape of this memory function stayed the same regardless of the levels of training or the grades the participants had received. Better initial learning, as measured by these indices, resulted in an elevation of the function such that overall performance was better but the shape of the function remained unchanged.

Now back to capacity. How much can be retained in semantic long-term memory? It has been proposed that we remember virtually everything we've ever experienced in our entire lives but simply have difficulty recalling it. Therefore, although information may get into long-term memory and stay there without its being lost, our inability to remember it could be due to a failure in "getting it out." One researcher estimates that the average adult has about a billion bits of information in memory and a storage capacity that is perhaps one thousand to one million times greater than that (Landauer, 1986). However, we must be skeptical about such estimates, since the inability to recall an item in a memory test can be due to either retrieval failure or decay.

With respect to coding, the current belief is that information in long-term memory is represented in various formats. Implicit memories may be stored in the form of production rules—formalized if–then statements that match a sensory input to a motor output. The proposed neural locus for production rules is in the cerebellum, a part of the brain that mediates motor learning. Refer back to the introductory chapter for more on production rules. Explicit memories may be stored as networks of connected nodes, each node representing a fact or event that is linked to others. The distribution of these nodes is most likely throughout the entire cortex and other diffuse brain areas. See the network approach chapter for more on these networks.

MEMORY MODELS

We turn now to summarizing some of the most influential theories of information processing that attempt to describe memory. These theories specify interactions between all the different memory types we've seen so far. Alternatively, some of these theories describe the interactions between components of a single memory system. In each case, the interactions are conceptualized through the use of process models that show how information is transformed and shuttled back and forth among the successive stages of processing.

The Modal Model

The **modal memory model** was the first model to provide a general overview of how information is processed in each of the different memory types (Atkinson & Shiffrin, 1971). Figure 5.4 shows the stages of the modal model. To start, stimulus information from the outside world first enters sensory memory where, as we have seen, it is very briefly held. From there, the information is transferred to short-term or working memory, where a wide variety of computations can be performed. These include rehearsal and recoding. Following this, to-be-remembered information is passed to long-term memory. **Encoding** is the name

Figure 5.4 The Atkinson and Shiffrin (1971) modal memory model.

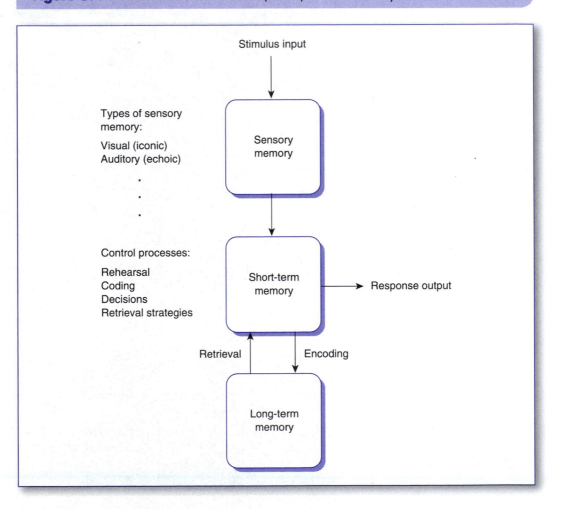

of the process by which information is taken into long-term memory and converted into a usable form. A related process, discussed at length in the neuroscience chapter, is consolidation. Consolidation is another process by which information is transferred from short- to long-term memory. Consolidation "strengthens" information so that it lasts longer.

Once in long-term memory, information may not be used immediately. We say that the information is in a state of storage. Stored information is represented but not available for immediate use. As alluded to above, this information may sit in limbo for a very long time. When information that resides within long-term memory is needed, a retrieval process takes place. Retrieval is the act of accessing needed data and making them available for use. In the modal model, retrieval is shown as the transfer of the information from long-term to working memory, where it can then be operated on.

Evaluating the Modal Model

The modal model provides us with a good summary of memory function and serves as a useful starting point. However, it was developed very early in the course of cognitive psychology and fails to specify many of the nuances of memory structure and function. Upgrading the model would require the postulation of additional memory subtypes and the insertion of a number of additional processing steps. For instance, inside the long-term memory box, we would need to designate distinctions for implicit and explicit memories. In addition, the modal model fails to acknowledge the large number of information-processing operations that can be performed in working memory. More recent models of working memory satisfy this and are discussed later in this chapter.

The ACT* Model

John Anderson (1983, 1990) proposes a global model of memory function that is similar to the modal model. Anderson's model is more than just a description of how memory works. It is considered a cognitive architecture—a concept we will discuss later. However, we talk about it here in the context of memory. The layout of his design, which he calls ACT* (read "act star," where ACT stands for *adaptive control of thought*), is shown in Figure 5.5. A revised version, ACT-R, also has been formulated (Anderson & Lebiere, 1998). Anderson's model has three components: (1) working memory, (2) declarative memory, and (3) production memory. Declarative memory is equivalent to explicit memory, and production memory is equivalent to implicit memory. The arrows in the figure indicate different kinds of processing that occur as information is exchanged between the memory systems.

Let's use two examples to illustrate how the model works. The first demonstrates the use of procedural knowledge. Imagine that you are driving your car and you see a stop light. The stimulus of the red light is encoded into working memory. From there, the

Figure 5.5 Anderson's (1983) ACT* model of memory.

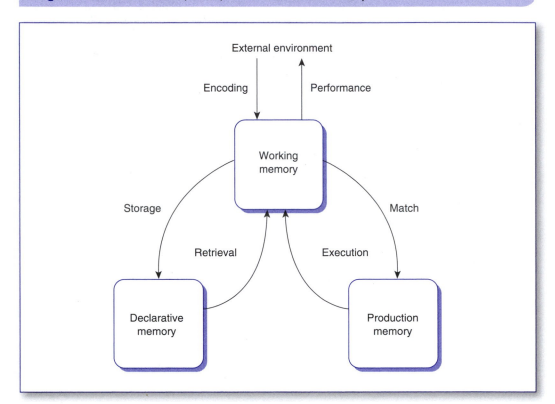

stimulus is weighed against a production rule in production memory. If there is a match, the corresponding command to step on the brakes is given. This command is passed back to working memory in the step labeled *execution*. The command is then translated into action in the process of performance. In the model, this encoding–match–execution performance loop is activated when one is carrying out any learned skill—whether driving, skiing, or playing the piano.

Now imagine that you are answering a factual multiple-choice question on a college exam. A representation of the question enters working memory and is transferred to declarative memory, where semantic knowledge that is related to the question is located. This transfer step is called storage. The question then activates the answer and it is retrieved back into working memory where it can be applied to the question. Once an appropriate response is selected, you can write in the answer, this action of writing being the performance. This encoding–storage–retrieval–performance loop is activated when one is using declarative knowledge.

Evaluating the ACT* Model

The strength of Anderson's model lies in its description of separate processing loops for implicit and explicit memories. Notice that there are no arrows that connect production memory and declarative memory. These are considered two entirely distinct and independent memory stores. They do not share information or communicate with each other. You should remember that conscious awareness accompanies explicit, but not implicit, memory. The absence of any information exchange between these two systems reflects this dichotomy.

Anderson postulates an additional component of this model that represents how propositional information in declarative memory is organized. This organization takes the form of a network in which nodes represent concepts and links represent the relationships between them. He also allows for different types of nodes that stand for specific examples of concepts we've encountered—for example, a specific person we know. In this way, the network can represent episodic as well as semantic information, both of which are part of declarative memory.

The Working Memory Model

Baddeley (1986, 1992) has formulated a detailed model for the components and processes of working memory. These are shown in Figure 5.6. In Baddeley's scheme, working memory is composed of three separate units. He calls the primary unit the **executive control system.** The job of this system is to initiate and control ongoing processes. Like the captain of a large ship, this system issues orders and directs subsidiary crews. Some of its activities are reasoning, language comprehension, information transfer to long-term memory via rehearsal and chunking, and information retrieval, also from long-term storage.

The second major component in Baddeley's model is the **articulatory loop,** sometimes called the phonological loop. This is the place where speech- and sound-related information is rehearsed. Information such as a telephone number that you want to remember and actively maintain for immediate recall is passed to the articulatory loop to refresh it. A third unit, called the **visuospatial sketchpad,** is specialized for the processing of visual information. It is here that visual imagery tasks such as mental rotation or visual search are performed. If you were to form an image of a cat with your eyes shut, the image would be represented in the visuospatial sketchpad.

Both the loop and the sketchpad are "slave systems" to the central executive. They carry out processes such as rehearsal and image formation. Other processes, such as reasoning and language, are the responsibility of the executive. Notice also that these two slave systems are domain specific: One is devoted to the processing of acoustic information only, the other to the processing of spatial information only. This means that each one operates on a different code—the loop on an acoustic code, the sketchpad on a visual code. Tests of

Figure 5.6 The different components of the working memory model.

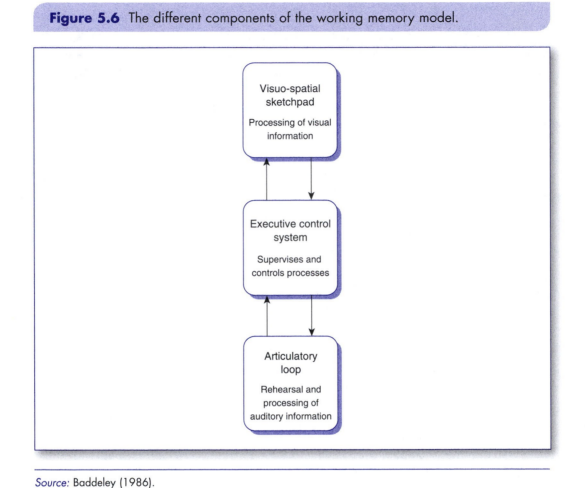

Source: Baddeley (1986).

working memory have shown that each slave system relies on its own pool of attentional resources (Baddeley & Hitch, 1974; Logie, Zucco, & Baddeley, 1990). If the tasks that one of these systems is performing are simple and don't require much in the way of attentional resources, then working memory performance is unchanged. If one of the systems is given a demanding task, though, it either fails to complete the task or draws on the attentional resources of the executive, which results in impaired working memory performance.

Evaluating the Working Memory Model

Baddeley's working memory model is in essence a reformulation of the traditional idea of short-term memory. This idea would have us believe that short-term memory is a relatively inactive location where information is either rehearsed or decays. Baddeley extended our concept of this memory system to encompass a self-regulating collection of processors that perform imagery, reasoning, and language tasks. Recent studies have shown that there are specific brain regions that correspond to the different components of the Baddeley model (Smith, 2000; Smith & Jonides, 1999). Verbal storage, rehearsal, and executive tasks were found to activate a number of regions in the parietal and frontal lobes of the left hemisphere. In contrast, visual processing activated regions in the occipital, parietal, and frontal lobes of the right hemisphere. Much work in the area of uncovering exactly which types of neural activity underlie the specific operations of working memory remains to be done. For example, we do not as of yet have a detailed and accurate neural processing model that can account for the performance of various mental arithmetic tasks, such as addition.

VISUAL IMAGERY: HOW DO WE IMAGINE?

How many windows are there in your living room? What is the shape of a German shepherd's ear? To answer these questions, you may have resorted to the use of visual images. A **visual image** is a mental representation of an object or a scene that preserves metric spatial information. Visual images are, therefore, isomorphic to their referents. They preserve spatial characteristics of the objects they represent. An example would include distance. If it takes longer to scan what is between two parts of a physical object because the distance between those parts is relatively greater, then it should also take longer to scan between those parts in the image representation.

Isomorphisms do not imply that images have the same physical properties as the objects themselves. An imagined banana is, of course, not really yellow or curved. But the representation of the banana in the image allows it to be treated as if it were a real banana. That is, it may be *mentally* picked up, peeled, or squashed. The image allows us to perform the same sorts of operations on the "banana" in our heads as we would on the actual banana with our hands. Although images in many ways seem to follow the same laws as real objects, they are by no means constrained by such laws. We could, if we wanted, imagine a flying banana or a banana singing the blues!

A defining hallmark of imagery is that, unlike perception, it is not driven by sensory input from the outside world. We can form a visual image of a car with our eyes completely shut. Imagery can be driven by information coming from memory, an internal information source. Having said this, though, numerous studies have shown that there are many similarities between perceptual processes and imagery. In particular, both processes seem to draw on the same underlying neural machinery. Farah (1988) showed that patients who had suffered damage to the visual cortex as the result of a stroke could no longer form visual images. Goldenberg, Podreka, Steiner, and Willmes (1989) showed that when participants are asked to answer questions that require the use of visual imagery, there is a greater increase in their vision-related brain activity, measured as increased blood flow to the visual cortex, than in participants who are given questions that do not require the use of imagery.

It is important to note that *imagery* in a more general sense refers to the mental representation of something and need not be restricted to the visual domain. It is possible to have auditory, or olfactory, images as well. For example, one can imagine the melody to the song "Yankee Doodle Dandy" or imagine the smell of a steak being grilled over an open fire. As was the case with perception, most of the research that has been conducted in this area—as well as theorizing on this subject—has focused on the visual, so we'll discuss only visual imagery here.

The Kosslyn and Schwartz Theory of Visual Imagery

In this section, we devote much of our attention to an early and influential theory of imagery (Kosslyn, 1980; Kosslyn & Schwartz, 1977). It is a functional theory, meaning that it describes what the brain does with images. It is also a general theory; it attempts to account for the diverse operations that are involved in image processing, as opposed to it being a specific theory that focuses only on one type of operation. Mental rotation, described in this section, would be an example of a more specific theory. The Kosslyn and Schwartz theory of visual imagery was elaborated in enough detail that it has been implemented as a computer program. In describing this theory, Kosslyn differentiates between the structures that are involved and the processes that act on them. In keeping with this, we will describe the structures first and the processes second.

Image Structures

Kosslyn posits two kinds of image structures. A **surface representation** is a quasi-pictorial representation that occurs in a spatial medium. It depicts an object or a scene and underlies our experience of imagery. But what is this medium? He describes the medium as a **visual buffer**. This buffer is a surface matrix that consists of an array of points, similar to what makes up an image on a TV screen. The visual buffer functions as coordinate space and has a limited extent and a specific shape. It also has a grain, or limited resolution (Kosslyn, 1975). The resolution is highest at the center and decreases toward the periphery (Finke & Kosslyn, 1980).

Representations in the buffer are short-lived. Much like an image on a computer or TV screen, a visual buffer representation fades away if it is not refreshed. If an object with many parts is imagined, the parts generated first may decay before those generated later. This can explain why images of objects that are part of complex scenes are more degraded than images of objects in simple contexts (Kosslyn, 1975).

According to the Kosslyn theory, certain characteristics of the surface image are unique to analog representations. The images exhibit features not present in propositional representations. To start, the size of the image, the shape of the image, its orientation, and the location of information in the image do not exist independently. When the value of one is specified, values of the others must also be specified. If we were imagining a fish in different ways—for example, as a big or a small fish, a fat or a thin fish, a right-side-up or an upside-down fish, or a fish to the left or to the right—then no part of the fish in the image is guaranteed to stay the same after the transformation. Images in this sense are holistic; a change in the image produces changes across its entire extent. In addition, any part or piece of an image is a representation of a part or a piece of the actual object being represented, the referent. The part of an image of a fish that corresponds to the fin would represent that fin on the real fish.

What about the content of such images? Images are about objects. They are viewer centered and represented according to the perspective of the observer who is viewing them. An image can represent an object directly, as a photograph does, or indirectly, as a diagram or schematic does. Content is determined not just by the image itself but also by how the image is interpreted. The meaning of an image, therefore, does not lie entirely within the image itself but also in how that image is processed by an interpretive device.

Deep representations constitute the second type of image structure. They consist of information in long-term memory that is used to generate the surface representations. Kosslyn describes two classes. **Literal encodings** contain lists of coordinates that detail the placement of points in the surface matrix such that the represented object is depicted. Some evidence suggests that they originate in the right hemisphere. **Propositional encodings** are abstract, language-like representations, similar to declarative statements. They contain information about an object's parts, the locations of these parts, and their sizes. They are believed to lie in the left hemisphere. It helps to think of these encodings in the following way: Imagine that you receive a chair that requires assembly from an office supply store. The chair would come with a list of parts, such as the base, legs, and back, as well as the various nuts and bolts needed to fasten the parts together. This list of parts corresponds to the propositional encodings. The chair would also come with a set of instructions specifying how to connect the parts. It would tell you which bolt to use to fasten Part A to Part B. This instruction list is analogous to the literal encodings.

Image Processes

We have already reviewed the empirical evidence that supports each of the three types of image processes. **Image generation** occurs when the encodings in long-term memory are used to form an image in the visual buffer. Kosslyn envisions this process as a set of distinct operations, each labeled with a distinct command in the computer simulation. A PICTURE command converts the information that has been received from the encodings, FIND locates the position for the placement of a new part, PUT adjusts the size of the imagined part, and IMAGE coordinates other commands and performs operations such as determining the appropriate level of detail.

One question concerning image generation is whether images are formed all at once or bit by bit. The evidence suggests that they are formed bit by bit (Kosslyn, 1980). Images that have more parts take longer to create. The same is true for images that have more detail. Data from another study show that people who are asked to create images have some control over how complete and detailed their images will be; depending on task demands and individual preferences, images can be sketchy or elaborate (Reisberg, Culver, Heuer, & Fischman, 1986). This result is in accord with the idea that images are formed gradually rather than all at once.

Image inspection occurs when we are asked some question about an image—for example, "Is a pig's tail lower than its snout?" Inspection is like looking at the image with the proverbial "mind's eye." It also consists of a number of distinct processes, each labeled with a different command in the computer simulation. RESOLUTION determines if the image is at the right scale and calls on ZOOM or PAN to expand or contract the image. SCAN, as its name suggests, scans between locations within the image.

An experiment by Kosslyn (1975) suggests that we can zoom in on or magnify images as part of the inspection process. He asked participants to imagine a large object next to a small one. For instance, subjects were asked to imagine an elephant standing next to a rabbit. They were then asked to respond to questions—for example, "Does the rabbit have a tail?" Kosslyn found that, under these conditions, participants took longer to respond to questions about the rabbit. His explanation was that the rabbit was relatively small in the image and, therefore, difficult to resolve. Kosslyn inferred that participants zoomed in on or magnified the part of the image in question to respond.

Another study, by Kosslyn, Ball, and Reiser (1978), showed that images may be scanned or "looked across" in the same way that real objects are. To get a sense of what participants were asked to do in this study, try the exercise depicted in Figure 5.7. The participants in the study were asked to memorize a map of a fictitious island. They were then instructed to form an image of the entire island and to focus on one of the objects on it. The name of a second object was announced, and participants were asked to scan their images by imagining a black speck moving in a straight line from the first object to the second. When the black speck arrived at the second object, participants pushed a button, stopping a timer. When reaction times were plotted as a function of map distance, a linear relationship was revealed. Participants took longer to respond when the distances between objects on the island were greater. From this result, it was inferred that images do preserve spatial extent. Figure 5.8 shows the pattern of the results that have been obtained in experiments like this one.

Figure 5.7 Study this picture of a bus for one minute. Then close your eyes and form a visual image of it, focusing on the back of the bus. Answer these two questions: Is the luggage compartment open? How many headlights are there? Which question took longer to answer? Why?

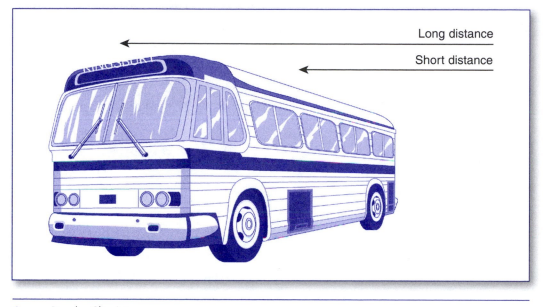

Long distance

Short distance

Source: Deneba Clip Art.

Image transformation refers to an operation performed on an image. Kosslyn describes two transformation modes—shift transformations and blink transformations. Most image transformations are shift transformations, in which the image is altered incrementally. These changes can be seen as continuous changes in which the image passes through intermediate stages along a trajectory of size, orientation, or location. Blink transformations, in contrast, alter the entire image at once and can be used to re-form a complete image after it has decayed in the buffer.

A classic experiment in cognitive psychology calls attention to an example of a shift transformation. Shepard and Metzler (1971) presented participants with drawings of pairs of three-dimensional objects (see Figure 5.9). Sometimes, the paired objects were different. But sometimes, they were the same, in which case the two objects were rotated versions of each other. The observers were asked to evaluate the pairs and to respond by pulling one lever with their right hand, if the objects were the same, and another lever with their left hand, if they were different. The response times were then plotted as a

Figure 5.8 Idealized results from a visual image study showing time needed to mentally scan from one point of an image to another as a function of the distance between objects.

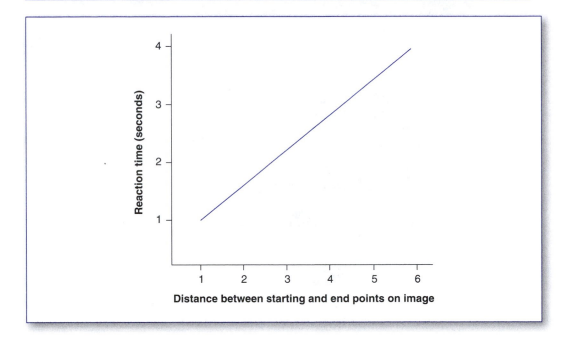

function of the angle of rotation (see Figure 5.10). The plot demonstrates that the greater the angular difference between the shapes, the longer it took to respond. Shepard and Metzler (1971) concluded that participants had formed a visual image of an object that was based on one of the objects in the drawings and then mentally rotated this image until it matched the other object.

Evaluating the Kosslyn and Schwartz Theory

Pylyshyn (1981) provides several critiques of the theory. He says that there are too many free parameters—that is, functions or assumptions that are uncontrolled and that can affect the results of any experiment designed to test the theory. For instance, Pylyshyn points out that the transformation processes that are hypothesized to act on an image are very flexible. This flexibility, rather than being a strength, leaves many questions unanswered—for example, "Under what circumstances will a given transformation process operate?" Pylyshyn would like to see a more detailed theory and a greater number of constraints put on its operation. He sees the theory as too open and as allowing for too many uncontrolled possibilities.

Figure 5.9 Stimuli from an early mental rotation experiment. Participants were asked to judge whether the two patterns were rotated versions of each other.

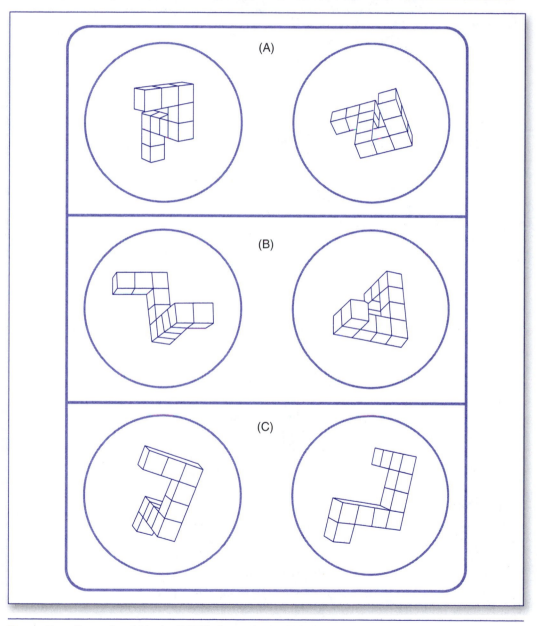

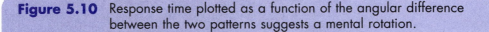

Figure 5.10 Response time plotted as a function of the angular difference between the two patterns suggests a mental rotation.

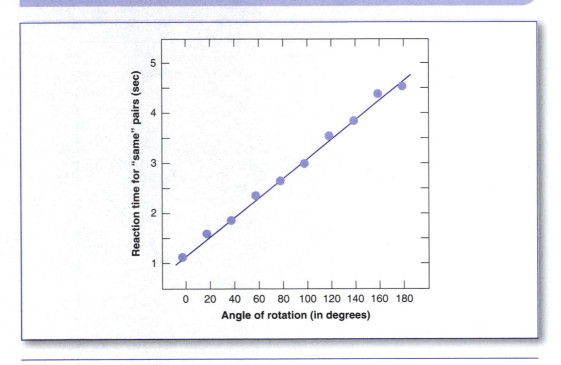

Source: From Shepard and Metzler (1971). Copyright © 1971 AAAS.

A second critique concerns **cognitive penetration**, in which one's knowledge, beliefs, goals, or other cognitive states alter performance of a mental task. Pylyshyn argues that mental imagery processing is biased by people's expectations. In Pylyshyn's view, our knowledge of what objects are like and the way they act in the world influences the way we process images of these objects. For example, if we think that an object is heavy, we may mentally rotate it more slowly. If this is the case and if imagery operations are cognitively penetrable, then they cannot be—as suggested by the theory—innate, universal, or automatic.

Pylyshyn also makes the argument that participants performing a mental rotation task may not be rotating at all. They may, in fact, be employing nonanalog or propositional means of carrying out image transformation. The data that appear to support image rotation are not reliable, according to Pylyshyn, and have been obtained because the task and the instructions led participants to re-create, as accurately as they could, the perceptual events that would have occurred if they had been observing an analog process. In other words, the observers are doing what the stimuli, task, and experimental situation seem to demand of them. This phenomenon is believed to be a potential source of error in many psychology experiments and goes by the name of **demand characteristics**.

Kosslyn counters these three arguments. He makes the distinction between parameters and free parameters, and he points out that his theory contains many of the former but not many of the latter. This theory, or any general theory that explains new cases, must include many parameters. Specific theories have fewer parameters but can explain only a limited number of cases. With regard to cognitive penetrability, Kosslyn admits that rotation and other image transformation processes ought to be cognitively penetrable; otherwise, the processes cannot be applied to solve problems or cannot be used in novel ways. Finally, Kosslyn points out several experiments in which task demands affected the results but argues that these studies in no way preclude the use of analog imagery processing.

PROBLEM SOLVING: HOW DO WE SOLVE PROBLEMS?

Problem solving is the transformation of a given situation into a desired situation or goal (Hayes, 1989). Problems are solved not only by people but also by computers. The former type of problem solving is within the purview of the cognitive approach and is studied by experimental psychologists. Researchers in artificial intelligence and robotics study machine problem solving. We will postpone a discussion of their perspective on problem solving until later in the book.

One approach to problem solving was the Gestalt perspective, described in Chapter 3. You may recall that the Gestalt psychologists focused on insight learning, in which a solution suddenly manifests itself, perhaps as a result of some amount of subconscious processing. In this section, we focus on an approach to problem solving that has been influenced by the discipline of artificial intelligence. The approach relies on the setting of subgoals and the testing of different possible solutions in the pursuit of a solution.

Anderson (1980) lists four characteristics of problem solving:

1. *Goal directedness:* Problem-solving behavior is directed toward the attainment of a **goal**, which is the desired end point or solution to the problem. If we were attempting to solve an arithmetic problem—say, 25 + 36, our goal would be to find the sum of these two numbers.

2. *Sequence of operations:* This problem-solving behavior involves a sequence of steps. To add 25 + 36, we can first add 20 + 30, to obtain 50. This would be Step 1. We would then add 5 + 6, to get 11, in Step 2. We would then add 50 + 11, to get 61, in Step 3, the last step.

3. *Cognitive operations:* This is the application of some process to the problem-solving situation that transforms the situation. Each permissible cognitive action that is applied in this way is called an **operator**. Operators in arithmetic include the addition of two numbers, the carrying of a remainder, or the retrieval of a number from memory.

4. *The setting of subgoals:* Each step in the problem-solving sequence produces a **subgoal**, an intermediate goal that is set along the way to an eventual solution of the problem. There is, thus, a hierarchical organization of goals in problem solving. The overall goal is broken down into subgoals. Each subgoal may in turn be broken down further, into additional subgoals. In our example, adding 20 + 30 yielded 50, in Step 1. This would generate the subgoal of adding 5 + 6, which produces the new subgoal of adding 50 + 11 in pursuit of the final goal, the total sum.

Problem space is a very important concept in problem solving. A **problem space** may be thought of as different situations or states that can exist in a problem. For any problem space, one can define three important states. The initial state is what the problem is like at the outset. The intermediate state is what results after some action is applied to the problem. The goal state is a desired situation and can include the final situation or con-figuration of the problem after a solution has been obtained. A problem space also includes the problem solver's knowledge at each step of the problem-solving sequence, knowledge that is applied at the step being negotiated, as well as knowledge that is in memory and could be applied. Problem spaces are usually represented in a diagram, called a solution tree, that shows all the possible steps that can be taken in pursuit of a solution (see Figure 5.11). The solution tree contains a series of branches. Each fork that has two or more branches represents the possibility of choosing one course of action over another.

Figure 5.11 A representation of a problem space showing the solution path.

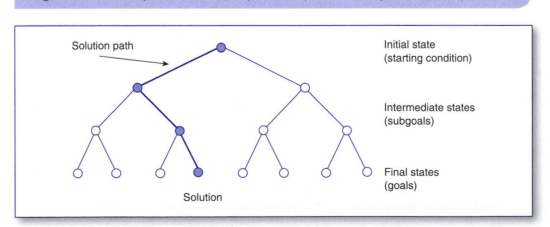

A given path can ultimately lead to a dead end in a nonsolution. The correct solution to a problem is a particular path or a set of paths if there is more than one procedure that produces a correct solution.

One approach to problem solving is to try all possible paths represented in the solution tree. This brute-force method is computationally intensive and time-consuming. As an example, the game of chess has been estimated to have 10^{20} states, or possible moves, a player can make. It is simply not possible to search through all these states to locate the right one. Current computers can search several billion states, still far fewer than the total number of states. Chess grandmasters usually don't consider more than 100, and an average player might consider only fewer than 100.

What is needed, then, is some guide to tell us which part of the space is likely to yield a correct answer. Heuristics serve this function. A **heuristic** is an informal "rule-of-thumb" method of problem solving that does not guarantee a solution but is faster and easier to use than a systematic search. Imagine that you have misplaced your keys somewhere in your apartment. You could engage in a systematic search and look everywhere for the keys: in each room, under the bed, on the shelves, behind the drawers, and so on. Alternatively, you could look first in those places where you usually put the keys down: in a desk drawer, on a tabletop near the door, or some other likely location. This heuristic would usually enable you to locate the keys more quickly and with less effort.

The most effectual heuristic in problem solving is the **means–ends analysis**. In this technique, the problem is solved via successive determinations of the difference between the existing state and the goal or subgoal state and then the identification of and utilization of an operator that reduces this difference. We all use means–ends problem solving in our everyday lives. If you wanted to get groceries for the week (the goal), you would need to first get to the supermarket (a subgoal). If you were at home, you would need to drive to the supermarket (an operator). If this were accomplished, the first subgoal would, therefore, have been attained, and the difference between the state of being at home and that of needing to get to the market would be reduced. Once you were at the market, you would set up another subgoal of getting the food, which would require a second operator: obtaining a shopping cart. This process would continue until the final goal had been reached.

The Tower of Hanoi problem has been studied quite thoroughly by investigators and serves as a good example of the application of the means–ends analysis. In this problem, there are three pegs, marked—from left to right—1, 2, and 3 (see Figure 5.12). Initially, there are three disks of different sizes—A, B, and C—that have been stacked on Peg 1—the largest disk at the bottom, the smallest on top. The goal is to get all three disks on Peg 3, stacked in exactly the same way. There are several constraints: You can move only one disk at a time and only to another peg. You can also place only a smaller disk on top of a larger one. Try to solve the Tower of Hanoi problem before reading on.

Figure 5.13 shows the seven-step solution. The first goal is to free up disk C, since it must always be at the bottom. Doing this entails setting the subgoal of getting disk B off

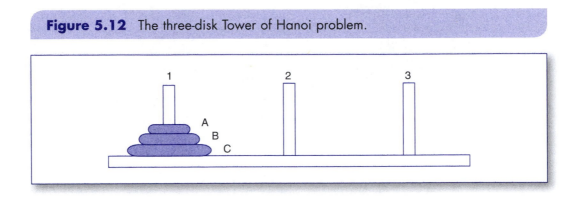

Figure 5.12 The three-disk Tower of Hanoi problem.

disk C. However, this necessitates the setting of another subgoal, getting A off B. The first move is, thus, to transfer A to Peg 3, which then allows us to move B to Peg 2. The next few moves are along these lines, with the generation of new subgoals and new operators for their attainment. We cannot move C to Peg 3 just yet, because A occupies that position. To remove A, we place it on top of B on Peg 2. This frees up Peg 3 so that we can now place C there. The remaining moves are straightforward. A goes to Peg 1, B goes to Peg 3, on top of C, and A can finally be placed atop B to complete the attainment of the goal.

The General Problem Solver Model

Alan Newell and Herb Simon were early pioneers in problem-solving research. They developed the first comprehensive computer simulation of human problem solving (Newell & Simon, 1972). Their program applied means–ends analysis to a wide range of problems, and thus, the program earned the name General Problem Solver (GPS). The GPS model serves as a useful analogy for how humans sometimes solve problems—by first representing the problem and the goal, then identifying the subgoals and operators that will produce that goal. The model suggests that humans and computers can both solve problems this way—by constructing "plans within plans" to effect a solution.

A key component of the model was its use of production rules. These rules were used to perform the operations that were required to bring about a solution. Ashcraft (2002) gives some examples of production rules for the Tower of Hanoi problem:

1. IF the destination peg is clear and the largest disk is free, THEN move the largest disk to the destination peg.

2. IF the largest disk is not free, THEN set up a subgoal that will free it.

3. IF the subgoal of freeing the largest disk has been set up and a smaller disk is on that disk, THEN move the smaller disk to the stack peg.

Figure 5.13 The seven-step solution to the three-disk Tower of Hanoi problem.

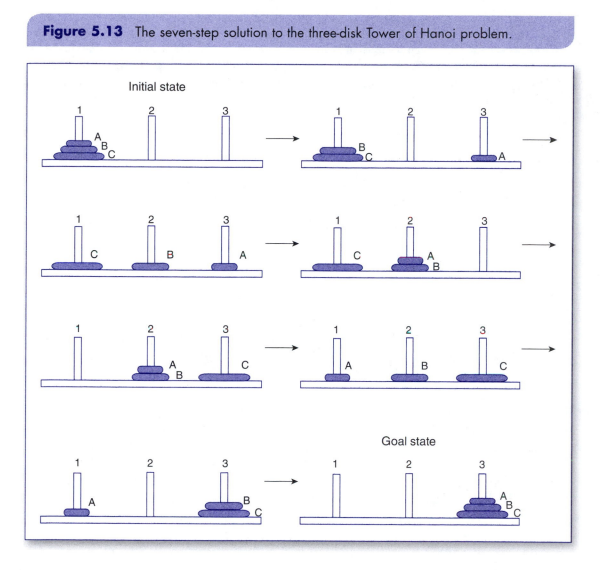

The GPS program has been applied to several well-known logic puzzles, including the Tower of Hanoi problem, the Missionary-Cannibal problem (described later in this chapter), the three coins puzzle, the water jug task, and more. The GPS program was able to solve each of these. In addition, Newell, Simon, and others have tested the model. In one study, they had participants talk out loud as they attempted to solve abstract logic problems (Newell & Simon, 1972). They found that there was a significant correspondence between the steps the participants reported using in their verbal protocols and the steps employed by GPS.

Evaluating the General Problem Solver Model

However, GPS has its limitations. In some cases, it diverges from the strategies human beings use to solve problems. With some problem solving, human beings are apt to use another heuristic, called the hill-climbing strategy. It involves taking actions that always bring one closer to the goal. To illustrate, if you were climbing a mountain and your goal was to get to the top, you would always choose a path that led upward. This strategy can sometimes fail, however—in this example, in the case of a path that goes downward and then back upward toward the summit. In the Missionary-Cannibal problem, there are three missionaries and three cannibals on one side of a river. The goal is to move all the missionaries to the opposite side by a boat, two at a time. If there are more cannibals than missionaries on one side, they get eaten. To solve the problem correctly, there is a necessary step where one must carry people who have been transported to the far side of a river back to the original side of the river. Because this step leads away from the final goal, which is to move everyone to the far side, persons attempting to solve the problem do not take the step and, therefore, fail to solve the problem. The GPS program doesn't have difficulty with this particular kind of pitfall but does sometimes fail to obtain a solution because it applies the means–ends heuristic too rigidly (Greeno, 1974).

Interdisciplinary Crossroads: Artificial Intelligence, Problem Solving, and the SOAR Model

SOAR—which historically stood for "state, operator, and result"—is a problem-solving model, but it is also a universal cognitive architecture, a system designed to account for a wide range of cognitive phenomena (Newell, 1991). **Cognitive architectures** specify the structure and function of many different cognitive systems and how the structure and function interact. Broadbent's (1958) early model of attention, the Atkinson and Shiffrin (1971) modal model of memory, and Anderson's (1983) ACT* memory model are all examples of cognitive architectures. These models can be applied within a specific domain—such as attention, memory, or problem solving—but they go beyond this, as they attempt to describe the basic principles of cognitive functioning.

As we will see, SOAR incorporates some of the elements found in GPS but is more general. Let's discuss its main features. SOAR represents all its tasks as problem spaces. Any problem is broken down into an initial state (the problem's initial starting point), a desired state (the goal or solution), and the current state (what the problem is like at any given moment). It can apply any one of a set of operators to the current state, thereby altering it to create a new state that is closer to that of the desired goal. SOAR was tested on block-world problems. A block-world problem consists of a set of blocks that has one configuration—a starting configuration—that must be rearranged so as to yield a desired end-state configuration (see Figure 5.14).

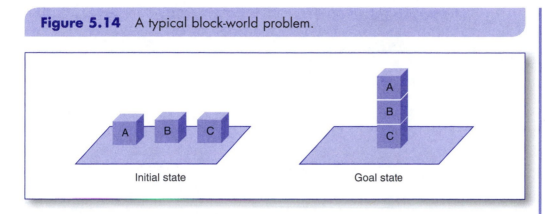

Figure 5.14 A typical block-world problem.

Initial state   Goal state

In SOAR, knowledge stored in long-term memory is used to select operators and guide movement through the problem space. The memory consists entirely of production rules that specify an action that is to be taken if a set of preconditions is met. Objects, such as blocks in the block-world problem or disks in the Tower of Hanoi problem, are represented by attributes and values. These are simple descriptive characteristics that can be used to define objects exclusively in the problem scenario.

SOAR goes through a decision cycle, where it accumulates evidence that has to do with the problem. Once this has taken place, a decision is executed. Examples of decisions that can be made are which problem space is to be used, which state is to be used within a given space, and which operator is needed to enable progression to the next state. One of the model's most interesting aspects is its capacity to develop preferences as it is accumulating evidence. These preferences are for actions that ought to be taken, given their likelihood of bringing about the goal. Based on these preferences, a given operator may be accepted, rejected, or considered as better, indifferent, or worse.

SOAR, like other computer programs, can follow a preprogrammed set of instructions for solving a problem. But, unlike these programs, it is also capable of generating new ways of approaching the problem. SOAR creates novel subgoals when it comes up against an impasse—a situation in which there is no option better than the rest. The setting of the new subgoal is based on knowledge stored in memory. This ability allows SOAR to adapt itself to the demands of a novel situation flexibly and dynamically.

Figure 5.15 gives an example of how SOAR would solve a simple block-world problem. The initial state has blocks A, B, and C arranged in a row on a table. The goal state is a reconfiguration of the blocks such that block A is on top of block B and block B is on top of block C. At the initial starting point, there are three permissible operators. A can go on top of C (A → C), B can go on top of C (B → C), or A can go on top of B (A → B). SOAR evaluates these three options by trying them out in an evaluation space. The A → C option produces a configuration that leads to an unacceptable solution, with B on top of A and

Figure 5.15 How SOAR might solve a block-world problem.

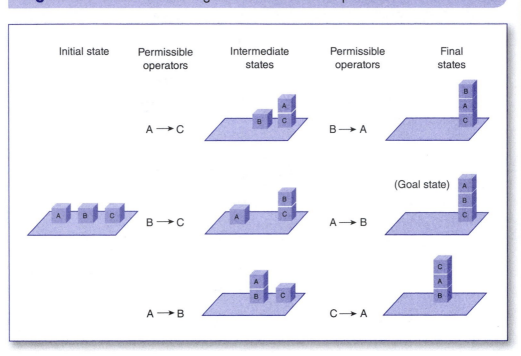

A on top of C. The A → B option also produces an unacceptable state, with C on top of A and A on top of B. SOAR then selects and implements the only remaining operator to produce a successful solution.

A final comment on the SOAR model concerns chunking, which in this context is comparable to the process of grouping items together in memory, discussed earlier. Chunking in this context corresponds to learning from experience. If SOAR has tested possible solutions and found a particular solution to a problem in the past, it stores this solution in a general form in its memory. When SOAR encounters a similar problem at a later date, it can then apply operators it has applied previously to reach a similar solution. SOAR, in effect, recognizes the problem as a combination of conditions that trigger the appropriate action. This grouping or chunking of the conditions into a single precondition for applying an operator gives the process its name.

Evaluating the SOAR Model

The SOAR program represents an ambitious attempt to develop a cognitive architecture that does more than solve problems. It was designed as a model for delving into the general principles that underlie learning, memory, problem solving, and the interactions among these systems. It has a good track record, having been applied to and having solved a variety of problems.

What's more, the incorporation of the chunking feature parallels the way human experts diagnose and solve problems. Chase and Simon (1973) presented pictures of a chess board whose pieces occupied random positions and pictures of a game in progress to two groups of participants—expert chess players and novice chess players. There was no difference between the recall of the novice players and that of the expert players when it came to remembering the pictures of the randomly placed chess pieces, but experts were better than novices when it came to remembering the game-in-progress pictures. This suggests that the experts were chunking information; they were organizing portions of the information into meaningful wholes. These wholes then guided the selection of the appropriate operator to be applied to the problem. For the expert chess players, seeing a particular configuration of pieces apparently triggered a memory of how that situation was dealt with in the past. Auto mechanics and physicians also chunk when they diagnose the cause of a mechanical breakdown or biological illness from a set of symptoms.

A critique of the model centers on the assumption that only production rules make up memory. Other architectures, notably ACT*, posit separate memory types with separate structures that code for declarative and procedural knowledge. The SOAR view of a single unitary type of memory simplifies the model but runs contrary to evidence that supports the existence of distinct memory systems.

OVERALL EVALUATION OF THE COGNITIVE APPROACH

The strengths of the cognitive approach are many. Unlike the disciplines that preceded it, cognitive psychology is governed by a set of common assumptions. These assumptions are that the mind represents and operates on information and that specific models of how the mind does these things can be formulated. Another advantage of the cognitive approach is that—rather than viewing the mind in a general, undifferentiated way, as some of the adherents of other approaches did—it compartmentalizes the mind into distinct processes. This carving up of the mind into modules makes research easier because it simplifies and delimits the range of a phenomenon under investigation. Although not all cognitive processes may actually be compartmentalized, this compartmentalization usually has proved to be a useful approach.

Another advantage of the cognitive approach, as discussed at the end of the previous chapter, is its use of model building. Models provide a concise way of formulating how a given mental process might operate. They are more precise than theories and can be tested using experimental data. The implementation of a theory as a model and the subsequent modification of the model on the basis of empirical findings is a fruitful method for uncovering more about a cognitive process.

Of course, like any other discipline, the cognitive approach has its limitations. It supports the traditional view of information processing, in which representations are symbolic and transformations are operations that are performed on the symbols. This needs to be reconciled with the network view—that information is coded in a distributed way and that transformations consist of activations of nodes in a network. Model builders in cognitive psychology also need to consider findings from neuroscience. Any model maker that attempts to provide an information-processing explanation of a brain function should map the different components of the relevant model onto the known anatomical and physiological evidence. This will help delineate and develop the model so that it reflects its biological implementation more accurately.

SUMMING UP: A REVIEW OF CHAPTER 5

1. Memory is the capacity to retain information over time. Without memory, a human, animal, or machine could not learn. There are three major types of memory: sensory, working, and long-term.

2. Sensory memory is where information from the senses is held very briefly so that it may be processed. There are as many different forms of sensory memory as there are sense modalities. However, we focus on the two most studied forms: iconic and echoic.

3. Iconic memory holds a brief visual representation of whatever it is you have just seen, whereas echoic memory holds a brief auditory representation of whatever you have just heard. Researchers test iconic memory by presenting a letter array and then cueing participants to a portion of the array to report what they see. The results show that capacity is unlimited; it can hold a representation of an entire scene but only for less than a second.

4. Working memory holds the contents of one's thoughts in immediate awareness to allow for reasoning and problem solving. It is capable of retaining only 7 ± 2 items on average for less than a minute without rehearsal. There are auditory, visual, and semantic codes.

5. There are several different types of long-term memory. Implicit memories hold procedural knowledge, which is a skill or action. This information is subconscious and is demonstrated by doing. Explicit memory is for declarative knowledge, which deals with facts (semantic) or events (episodic). This is demonstrated verbally and is a part of conscious awareness.

6. The earliest process model of memory is the modal model. It gives a very broad overview of the memory types and of the information flow between them. In particular, it outlines encoding, as the process by which information gets into the system; storage, for the preservation of information; and retrieval, whereby data may be called out of long-term storage for immediate use.

7. Anderson's ACT* model best shows the relationships between working and long-term memories. Baddeley's working memory model shows the sorts of interactions that take place between the components of working memory, which are the visuospatial sketchpad, the articulatory loop, and the executive control system.

8. According to Kosslyn, visual images preserve the same spatial characteristics as the real-world objects or scenes they depict. This means that it would take longer to scan across a visual image of a large object than to scan across a visual image of a comparatively short object.

9. Rotation is another transformation that could be applied to a visual image. Mental rotation studies show that it takes longer to match a figure against another the more one is rotated relative to the other.

10. Problem solving involves taking a given situation and transforming it into a desired situation or goal. Many of us will resort to using heuristics to solve problems. A heuristic is a "quick-and-dirty" solution that has worked in the past but may not guarantee a correct solution. Two early computer problem-solving models are GPS and SOAR.

EXPLORE MORE

Log on to the student study site at **http://study.sagepub.com/friedenberg3e** for electronic flash cards, review quizzes, and a list of web resources to aid you in further exploring the field of cognitive science.

SUGGESTED READINGS

Baddeley, A. D. (2007). *Working memory, thought, and action*. Oxford, England: Oxford University Press.

Baron, J. (2007). *Thinking and deciding*. Cambridge, England: Cambridge University Press.

Kosslyn, S. M., Thompson, W. L., & Ganis, G. (2006). *The case for mental imagery*. Oxford, England: Oxford University Press.

Newell, A. (1994). *Unified theories of cognition*. Cambridge, MA: Harvard University Press.

Radvansky, G. (2005). *Human memory*. Boston, MA: Allyn & Bacon.

6

THE NEUROSCIENCE APPROACH

Mind as Brain

Referring to the brain: "My second favorite organ!"

—Woody Allen, 1973

THE NEUROSCIENCE PERSPECTIVE

Neuroscience is the study of nervous system anatomy and physiology. It is concerned with both the structure as well as the function of the nervous system in humans and other animals. As such, neuroscience provides a body of knowledge that serves as a foundation for understanding how cognitive operations are carried out. It gives us a hardware or implementational level of description on which we can base an algorithmic and computational description. Neuroscience is invaluable in this regard because it constrains the sorts of models of brain function that can be formulated in the other approaches.

There has been a fairly recent trend in neuroscience toward the integration of biology with cognition. Out of this union, a new discipline has emerged, called cognitive neuroscience. The goal of this discipline is to explicate the structures and physiological processes that underlie specific cognitive functions. We adopt a cognitive neuroscience perspective in this chapter and focus on the cognitive operations that were surveyed in the two chapters on cognitive approach (Chapters 4 and 5). These cognitive operations are visual object recognition, attention, memory, and problem solving. This neuroscience perspective builds and expands on the information-processing models for these operations that were described previously. For neuroscientific accounts of visual imagery and language, please see the relevant sections in Chapters 5 and 9, respectively.

A fair amount of background knowledge is needed to interpret the findings of neuroscience studies. We will, therefore, provide general information on methodology, anatomy, physiology, and terminology prior to a discussion of the specific topic areas. Our present discussion begins with the tools used by neuroscientists and is followed by a discussion of the geography and function of neurons and of the overall brain. We will then address the neuroscience of cognitive functions and models of their operation.

METHODOLOGY IN NEUROSCIENCE

There are many procedures for collecting data in neuroscience. In this section, we group these procedures into three main categories. The first category of procedures involves the investigation of brain damage. In studies of humans, researchers—using the case study method—investigate the behavioral deficits of patients who have suffered damage to some part of the brain as a result of an accident. In animal lesion studies, this damage is deliberately induced. The second category of procedures involves the recording of brain activity in healthy subjects. The electrical action of individual neurons or small groups of neurons can be measured with cellular recording techniques that use an implanted electrode. Larger patterns of brain activity can be measured through the use of surface electrodes that have been implanted on the scalp or through the use of more sophisticated brain imaging devices. The third category involves direct stimulation of the brain itself.

Techniques for the Study of Brain Damage

It is, of course, unethical to damage a person's brain deliberately to look at the effects of brain damage. For this reason, researchers examine brain damage and its effects in people for whom the damage has come about as a result of an accident—what is called the **case study** method. There are different types of brain damage. In a patient who has had a stroke, a blood vessel servicing a part of the brain bursts, depriving blood supply to that part of the brain. Direct mechanical damage to the brain accompanies head trauma. This type of damage can be incurred in an automobile accident or a fall. Brain damage is also an end result of exposure to carbon monoxide gas. Usually in these cases, localized damage occurs and follow-up evaluations of affected persons can reveal exactly which areas were damaged. The resulting behavioral and cognitive deficits can then be mapped against the damaged areas. If, for example, the front part of the brain has suffered damage and the patient has subsequently had trouble making decisions, we can conclude that this part of the brain is implicated in the cognitive operation of planning.

A related method of study involves the deliberate destruction of brain areas in animals and the examination of the resulting behavioral deficits. A brain lesion is a wound in or injury to brain tissue. A study that uses this method is referred to as a **lesion study**. Lesions can be generated in several ways. Brain tissue can be drawn off by suction, destroyed by passing a high-frequency radio current through an electrode, or frozen by pumping a coolant through an implanted probe. With this last procedure, the tissue is preserved, and normal function returns as the affected area warms up. The motivation for using these procedures is the same as that for using the case study, and this type of study suffers from the same flaws that we outline below.

Evaluating Techniques for the Study of Brain Damage

There is logic behind case studies and lesion studies. If brain area X is damaged and a deficit is subsequently observed in behavior Y, researchers infer that area X plays some role in the control of behavior Y. This seems straightforward enough but is actually fraught with difficulties. Some have likened this kind of conjecture to removing part of a car engine to see how its removal affects the car's function. If we removed the carburetor or fuel injector, the engine wouldn't run because the spark plugs wouldn't receive any gasoline. However, the same would be true if we removed the gas tank. The point is that in a car, many of the systems are interdependent. Removing any of a number of different parts can produce the same symptom. Areas of the brain are also interdependent. The effects of damage to one area could have a variety of functional interpretations. That area could be entirely responsible for a cognitive ability or part of a collection of areas that mediate that ability. Alternatively, the area could be a center where information is processed or simply a region through which pathways that connect one center to another pass.

Traditional Brain Recording Methods

In **single-cell recording**, a very fine microelectrode is inserted into either a single neuron or the extracellular fluid adjacent to it. Changes in that cell's electrical conductivity or rate of firing can then be measured. In **multiple-unit recording**, a larger electrode is used to measure the collective electrical activity of a group of neurons. In a classic study, Hubel and Wiesel (1962) recorded activity in single cells of a cat's visual cortex. They discovered that some cells responded to lines of a specific orientation in the cat's visual field, implying that line orientation constitutes a basic visual feature of pattern recognition. Although cell recording can give us very detailed information about what one neuron or a relatively small number of neurons are doing, it fails to yield the "big picture." That is, it does not inform us about more global brain activity.

If one wants to investigate what the brain as a whole is up to, he or she can choose from a variety of other tools. The **electroencephalogram (EEG)** is a recording of the brain's gross electrical action. The procedure uses large electrodes that are taped to the scalp. The output of an EEG is in the form of wave patterns. This method has been used extensively in the measurement of brain activity during sleep. From research that has used this method, we have learned that the brain passes through several distinct sleep stages, each having its own pattern of wave activity.

The EEG can also be used to measure a subject's brain activity in response to his or her experience of a particular event. The resulting waves that are recorded are called **event-related potentials (ERPs)**. For instance, a researcher could sound a tone to a participant in a study and then record the subsequently occurring brain activity. This has been used in many studies to yield insights into the brain mechanisms that underlie perception and attention. A problem with the EEG is that it is a very crude measurement. It shows us activity only in relatively large brain areas, such as the different cortical lobes. Most researchers would like to have a more fine-grained temporal and spatial description of brain activity.

Modern Brain Imaging Methods

Modern technology has produced new **brain imaging** techniques that allow us to "peer inside" the head with greater accuracy than ever before. These techniques allow imagery of both brain structure and function. They allow us to see not only the static three-dimensional organization of brain areas but also the dynamic activities of these areas as they unfold in time.

Positron Emission Tomography

Positron emission tomography (PET) scan measures blood flow in the brain while a participant is carrying out a cognitive task. This is accomplished through the use of radioactive isotopes or tracers attached to carrier substances such as glucose or oxygen molecules. The molecules are injected into the participant's bloodstream, wherein they make their way to the brain. Brain areas that are more active during the execution of a task will show greater regional cerebral blood flow (rCBF) and, correspondingly, a greater concentration of the tracer molecules bearing the isotopes. The activity in these areas is measured using a detection device that counts the positron particles that are emitted by the isotopes. PET scans are especially useful for mapping those parts of the brain that are involved in specific cognitive operations, such as visual imagery, language, and memory.

PET scans have a fairly good spatial resolution, being able to monitor locational changes in brain activity to within just a few millimeters. PET scans lack some of the temporal resolution of other brain mapping techniques, however. They cannot show rapid changes in brain activity—those that occur over time periods that are on the order of milliseconds. The radioactive isotopes that are used are expensive, and their radioactivity is short-lived. There is also a small risk associated with the frequent introduction of radioactive compounds into the body.

Functional Magnetic Resonance Imaging

In most **functional magnetic resonance imaging (fMRI)** evaluations, a patient is placed inside a tube that contains a powerful magnet. Protons, which are subatomic particles present everywhere in the body, align themselves in the magnetic field in the same way iron filings organize themselves around a small magnet. A radio wave pulse is then applied to the brain or other part of the body undergoing the scan. The radio signals are bounced back and picked up by a detector unit. The reflected signals are then converted to video images showing dynamic changes in brain activity over time.

Like PET scans, fMRI scans detect alterations in local blood flow and oxygen level. Brain areas that show increases in these measures are those that have been activated during specific cognitive operations. So fMRI scans, like PET scans, are used to map out these active brain areas. fMRI scans provide better spatial resolution than PET scans, without any of the risks associated with the injection of radioactive isotopes. They are the current method of choice for investigation of brain function. Figure 6.1 depicts an MRI image showing a sagittal section of the brain.

Figure 6.1 Results of an MRI scan showing a sagittal section (top to bottom cut) of the human brain.

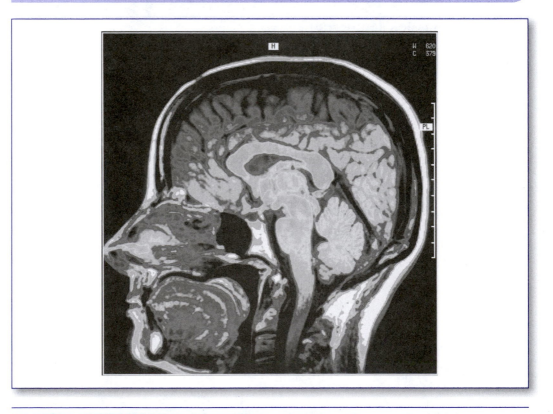

Source: Comstock/Thinkstock.

Magnetoencephalography

Small changes in magnetic fields occur when neurons fire. In a technique called **magnetoencephalography (MEG)**, these changes are measured to determine patterns of brain action (Schwartz, 1999). MEG has reasonably good spatial and temporal resolution. It can resolve neural activity in a region as small as a millimeter and over times as fast as several milliseconds. A patient first dons a helmet filled with an array of supercooled magnetic detectors. The individual then performs an experimental task while his or her magnetic activity is recorded. The resultant data can then be converted into a three-dimensional video depicting the precise locations and patterns of activation.

Knife-Edge Scanning Microscope

A recent development in brain imaging technology is the **knife-edge scanning microscope (KESM)**. This device consists of a diamond-tipped knife that slices through tissue. A white light source illuminates the strip of tissue as it comes off the blade, reflecting an image to a camera. The subsequent video is then processed by a computer system to provide a three-dimensional reconstruction accurate down to the cellular level (see Figure 6.2). The KESM is capable of digitizing the entire volume of a mouse brain (which is about a cubic centimeter) at a 300 nanometer resolution within 100 hours (McCormick & Mayerich, 2004). If machines like this were used to scan the human brain, we could record the location and connectivity of each neuron, providing a static but invaluable data set from which to extrapolate brain function.

Brain Stimulation Techniques

Electrode Stimulation

So far, we have examined procedures that measure brain damage or normal brain function. There is a third procedure that is neither as intrusive nor as passive. This method involves the actual activation of a specific brain area via electrical or magnetic stimulation. In **electrical stimulation,** an electrical current is passed through a bipolar electrode, which causes the neurons of a localized area of brain tissue to become active. The resulting behavioral effects are usually the opposite of those observed in the brain lesion technique. Lesions prevent neurons from firing, resulting in negative symptoms—the absence of some behavior governed by the affected region. Stimulation, on the other hand, encourages neuronal firing, resulting in positive symptoms—the facilitation of the behavior governed by the area. A difficulty with this procedure is that stimulation might induce supranormal activity, or an overactivation of the region and the areas associated with it. This would produce behaviors not associated with normal functioning.

Figure 6.2 A three-dimensional image of mouse brain neurons.

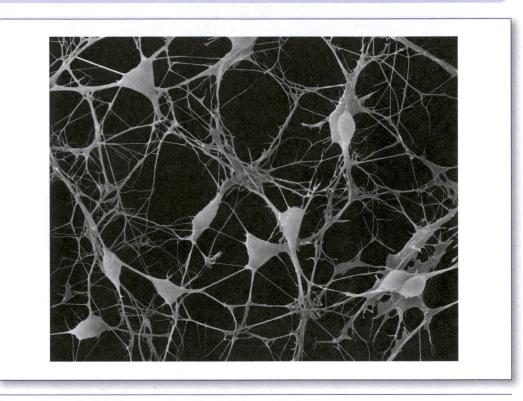

Source: ©Dennis Kunkel Microscopy, Inc./Visuals Unlimited/Corbis.

Transcranial Magnetic Stimulation

In **transcranial magnetic stimulation (TMS)**, a wire coil is placed on a person's head. An electrical current is passed through the coil, inducing a magnetic field. This field directly causes neurons to fire. If we place the field over different parts of the cortex, we can witness the functionality of these areas. Activation of the motor cortex causes movement of different body parts, such as the fingers (Pascual-Leone et al., 1998). If it is placed over the primary visual cortex, vision is temporarily suppressed (Walsh & Pascual-Leone, 2005). If TMS is applied over and over again for a period of time, it can be used to treat a variety of disorders, including depression (Schutter, 2008). This technique is called repetitive TMS, or rTMS.

Optogenetics

Optogenetics is an exciting new technology that allows researchers to control neurons using light (Deisseroth, 2010). It involves the use of genes that code for a category of proteins called opsins. Opsins embedded in a cell membrane regulate the flow of electrical charge across it. This in turn affects the way in which neurons signal, whether or how they transmit messages to other neurons around them. When opsin genes are inserted into neurons, the proteins are manufactured by the cell and incorporated into the membrane. However, these proteins are now light sensitive; they can be activated by particular wavelengths of light, such as blue or green.

This light sensitivity allows researchers incredibly accurate control over individual neuron behavior. They can be turned on or off, for instance, simply by shining pulses of light onto them. Moreover, this can be done at very rapid speeds, on the order of milliseconds. For example, "fast" channel rhodopsins have allowed the generation of action potentials at more than 200 times per second. Investigators have even been able to control different groups of cells at the same time, one group being stimulated by blue light and the other by yellow light.

The potential for the use of this technology is enormous. Recently developed fiber optic technology allows light to be delivered anywhere inside an animal's brain, and in conjunction with new optical recording techniques, neural tissue can be both stimulated and measured simultaneously without interference. This has been done even in moving animals and will allow us to infer with much greater precision the types of computations neural populations are performing. Rather than just trigger activity with a stimulus, we can now modify activity as it is happening. Other benefits include better understanding of and promising treatments for Parkinson's disorder, schizophrenia, and autism.

THE SMALL PICTURE: NEURON ANATOMY AND PHYSIOLOGY

Neurons are the microscopic basis of the brain. They are the individual functional units that perform computations. The purpose of a neuron is to conduct a message in the form of an electrical impulse. A neuron can be thought of as a link in a complex chain because it receives messages from other neurons and then "makes a decision" whether to send a message of its own. Figure 6.3 depicts the major structures of a typical neuron. Messages are received by the feathery projections known as **dendrites**. Dendrites form an extensive branching "tree," which connects the neuron to many other neurons. Any incoming messages picked up by the dendrites are then passed along to the cell body.

Received messages from other cells converge at the axon hillock, where the cell body meets the axon. Here, the neuron summates all the inputs it receives. The cell fires if the sum of these inputs exceeds the cell's **threshold of excitation**. This process represents a sufficient change in the neuron's resting electrical state. If the "decision" to fire is made, an electrical signal called an **action potential** is initiated. The action potential then propagates down the **axon**, a long tubular structure that projects outward from the cell body. The axon, which can extend for some distance, ends in a **terminal button**.

Figure 6.3 Anatomy of a neuron.

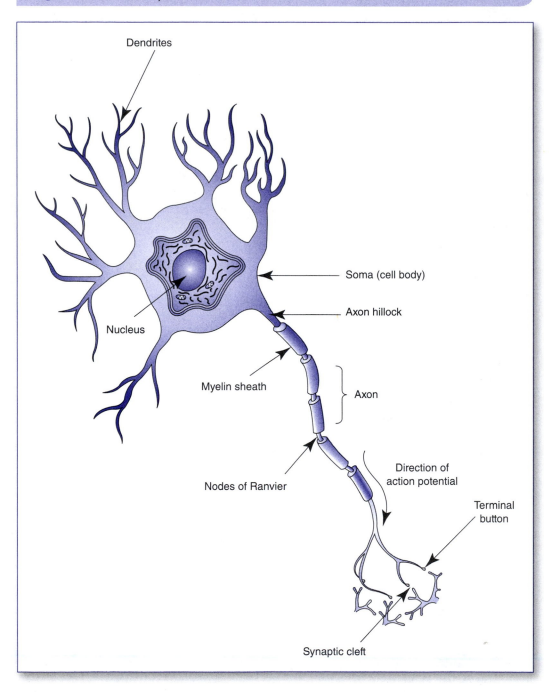

The terminal button does not have direct physical contact with the next cell. Instead, there is a gap between the two cells known as the **synaptic cleft** (see Figure 6.4). How, then, is a message passed from one cell to the next? The answer lies in molecules known as **neurotransmitters**. The job of these neurotransmitters is to complete the transmission of the signal across the synapse. When the action potential arrives at the terminal button, it triggers the release of neurotransmitter molecules into the synapse. The transmitters diffuse across the synaptic cleft and attach to receptor molecules located on the dendritic surface of the next cell. A neurotransmitter molecule fits into a cavity in the receptor molecule and activates it, in much the same way that a key fits into and opens a lock. These activated **receptors** then contribute to the formation of a new signal in the receiving cell. There are a large number of neurotransmitters in the human brain. Table 6.1 gives a summary overview of some of the major neurotransmitters, what functions they subsume, and their associated disorders.

Figure 6.4 Cross section of a synapse.

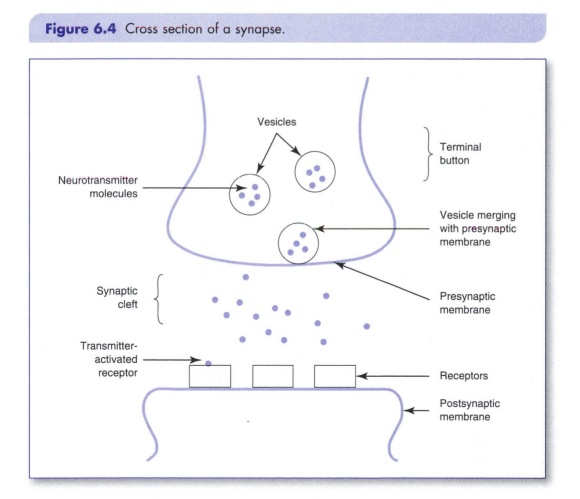

Table 6.1 Some of the major neurotransmitters, their functions, and associated disorders.

Neurotransmitter	Function	Disorder
Acetylcholine	Used to control muscles; also involved in learning	Alzheimer's disease
Dopamine	Brain reward system, control of movement	Schizophrenia, Parkinson's disease
Endorphins	Reduce pain, enhance reinforcement	Chronic pain
Gamma-aminobutyric acid (GABA)	Primary inhibitory transmitter	Anxiety, epilepsy
Glutamate	Primary excitatory transmitter, memory formation	Depression, schizophrenia
Norepinephrine	Arousal and attentiveness	Stress
Serotonin	Regulates mood and sleep	Depression, obsessive-compulsive disorder

THE BIG PICTURE: BRAIN ANATOMY

We now step back a bit and look at the brain from a broader perspective. The brain is a complex structure, with many areas and parts that are associated with particular functions. Rather than catalog all these, we will describe only the ones relevant to important cognitive processes. For those interested in delving deeper, a number of more comprehensive texts on this topic are listed in the "Suggested Readings" section.

Directions in the Nervous System

Our discussion of brain anatomy must begin with a discussion of the terms used to imply direction in the nervous system. Anatomists use a special set of terms when referring to these directions. With respect to the human brain, **dorsal** means "toward the top" and **ventral** means "toward the bottom." **Anterior** is used to signify regions that are toward the front of the brain, and **posterior** signifies those that are toward the back. Regions that are located toward the middle of the brain are **medial**, whereas those near the outside are **lateral** regions. Figure 6.5 illustrates the application of some of these terms to a view of the cortex.

Figure 6.5 Major lobes of the left hemisphere of the human cortex. Some common anatomical directions are also indicated.

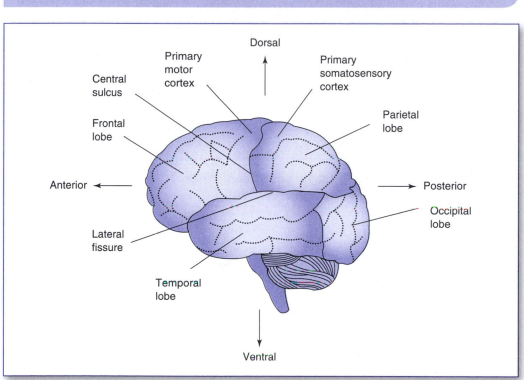

The Cortex

The cortex is the most recent part of our brain to evolve and is responsible for a number of higher order cognitive abilities. The cortex is naturally divided into two halves, or **cerebral hemispheres**. Each hemisphere is associated with a unique processing style (Sperry, 1985). The left hemisphere is the seat of more analytic, serial, and logical reasoning. The right hemisphere is the seat of more synthetic, parallel, and relational thought processes. Language function in most persons is localized to the left hemisphere, whereas spatial ability is usually concentrated in the right hemisphere. Information is transferred back and forth between the hemispheres via connecting fibers that are known, collectively, as the **corpus callosum**.

A **fissure** is a large cleft or separation between two areas of brain tissue, whereas a sulcus refers to a smaller such separation. A **sulcus** typically separates neighboring ridges or folds of tissue. A single ridge of this kind is known as a **gyrus**. At a smaller scale, brain tissue is made up of nuclei (singular: nucleus), which are collections of cell bodies and tracts. The tracts are collections of nerve cell axons.

Figure 6.5 is a view of the cortical regions of the left hemisphere. The first thing you may notice is that the cortex has several large regions, called lobes. The frontal lobe is located to the anterior and is bounded by the central sulcus and the lateral fissure. It contributes to problem solving and language production. The temporal lobe lies posterior to the lateral fissure. The temporal lobe mediates auditory processing, pattern recognition, and language comprehension. Just posterior to the central sulcus is the parietal lobe. It governs aspects of attention and spatial processing. The parietal lobe also plays a role in somatosensory processing. Finally, there is the occipital lobe, where visual information begins to undergo more extensive processing.

Two other cortical regions should be noted. Anterior to the central fissure is the precentral gyrus. It is the location of the primary motor cortex. It is a homunculus because it consists of a spatial representation or map of the body's parts. Electrical stimulation of the primary motor cortex at a specific point provokes muscular contraction at the site of the corresponding body part. The function of the primary motor cortex is to initiate behavior via the activation of different muscle groups. Just posterior to the primary motor cortex, on the postcentral sulcus, is the primary somatosensory cortex. It is also a homunculus. Electrical stimulation of any portion of the primary somatosensory cortex triggers the perception of a sensation coming from the corresponding part of the body. The primary somatosensory cortex processes sensory information arriving from the body surface.

The Split Brain

An important feature of the cortex is that information received from the right or left halves of the body is mapped onto the opposite, or contralateral, side of the brain. This means that a stimulus presented in the left visual field—basically everything to the left of your nose—is projected onto the right hemisphere, whereas a stimulus presented in the right visual field is projected onto the left hemisphere. Information presented to one side of the body is not processed on the same, or ipsilateral, side of the brain. This contralateral organization is the result of the crossing of fibers originating from sensory neurons that are located on one side of the body over to brain areas on the other side. The same holds true for motor control: The left hemisphere sends commands to the right side of the body, while the right hemisphere controls the left side.

A split-brain patient has had his or her corpus callosum surgically cut to prevent the spread of epileptic seizures. Experiments with these patients demonstrate just how specialized the two brain hemispheres are. In these studies, a patient is presented with either a word or a picture of an object that is presented to the left or right visual field. This presents the information about the object to either the right or the left hemisphere, respectively. The patient can identify the object either by naming it or by grasping the object the word represents from among a set of objects that are hidden from view. The word can be vocalized only if the information that has been presented to the patient reaches the left hemisphere, as the left hemisphere is specialized for language. Either hemisphere with information about the object can identify it through grasping because this response relies on tactile information alone.

Imagine that the word *spoon* is presented to a split-brain patient in his or her left visual field. The information projects to the right hemisphere. The patient, in all likelihood, cannot read the word because, in most persons, language ability is lateralized to the left hemisphere. He or she also cannot identify the object with his or her right hand because that is controlled by the left hemisphere, which has no knowledge of the spoon. The participant can, however, reach out and select a spoon with his or her left hand. Imagine another scenario. The word *spoon* is flashed in the right visual field and, so, projects to the left hemisphere. The participant can at this point say that it is a spoon, as well as grab a spoon with his or her right hand. Correspondingly, this patient would not be able to identify the spoon with the left hand.

THE NEUROSCIENCE OF VISUAL OBJECT RECOGNITION

You may recall the different models of pattern recognition we discussed in Chapter 4. These models were all ways of describing how we visually recognize objects. In this section, we examine several clinical disorders to see what they can tell us about the neurological basis of these recognition mechanisms. But first, we must introduce a basic principle of information processing in the visual system—the partitioning of visual input into separate streams.

The visual system, as we mentioned earlier, breaks objects down into their parts or features, with different areas of the brain handling them. Research has revealed two distinct anatomical pathways for the processing of visual information (Ungerleider & Mishkin, 1982). Visual inputs undergo preliminary processing in the primary visual cortex—located in the occipital lobes, at the back of the head. Following this, the information is divided and projects to two different parts of the brain. One stream, called the **dorsal visual pathway**, travels upward to the parietal lobe where information about motion and location is extracted. It is sometimes called the "where" pathway because of its representation of the spatial positions of objects. A second stream, the **ventral visual pathway**, carries data about color and form and travels downward to the temporal lobe. It is referred to as the "what" pathway because of its role in object identification. Figure 6.6 shows the locations of both.

Figure 6.6 The dorsal and ventral pathways of the monkey's visual system.

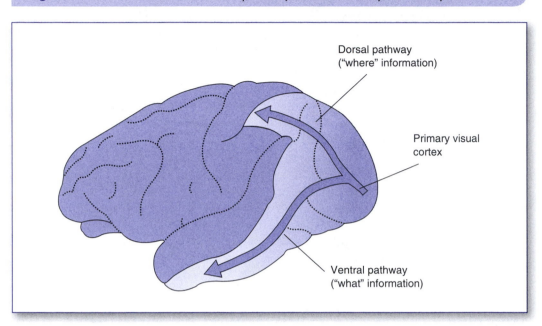

Visual Agnosias

Oliver Sacks is a neurologist who is also a gifted writer. In *The Man Who Mistook His Wife for a Hat*, he recounts the case histories of several patients with disorders so bizarre that they border on the fantastical (Sacks, 1998). Take, for example, the case of patient P., who is a music teacher. P.'s gaze is unusual; his eyes dart around as they take in Sacks's face, fixating on one feature and then another. P. is unable to recognize a rose and describes it as "a convoluted red form with a linear green attachment." During one interview with Sacks, P. took hold of his wife's head as he apparently tried to lift it and put it on his own head. Sacks writes, "He had . . . mistaken his wife for a hat!" Although it may seem improbable, such patients really do exist. They have a pattern recognition disorder called visual agnosia. What is wrong with these patients' brains? How can they make such errors? Let's take a look.

A visual agnosia is an inability to recognize a visual object (Farah, 1990). Visual agnosias are perceptual in nature and cannot be attributed to problems that have to do with memory. They are modality specific. In one case study, a woman who was not able to recognize a picture of a hammer was able to recognize an actual hammer through the use of another sense. She was able to pull a hammer out of a bag that was filled with objects. Furthermore, it seems that in patients with visual agnosias, most other visual system–processing abilities remain intact. These patients do not have difficulty detecting motion, interpreting location information, or recognizing other types of objects. Agnosias are associated with damage to the brain regions that process visual object information.

There are two broad categories of visual agnosia. Persons with **apperceptive agnosia** cannot assemble the parts or features of an object into a meaningful whole. Persons with **associative agnosia** perceive this whole but have difficulty assigning a name or label to it. The apperceptive form of the disorder seems to involve a disruption of the formation of an object representation and is, therefore, more perceptual, or "lower level," in nature. The associative form involves a disruption of the ability to categorize or identify objects and can be considered more cognitive, or "higher level," in nature.

Apperceptive Agnosia

In patients suffering from apperceptive agnosia, most of their basic visual functioning is intact. This includes the capacity to see details, discriminate between lights of different brightness, and perceive color. However, they have great difficulty naming, matching, copying, or telling the difference between simple visual forms. In one test, patients were asked to indicate which of four drawings of common objects matched a single target drawing. The apperceptive agnosic patient, Mr. S., was unable to do this. He matched a circle to a triangle and a paperclip to a key. Mr. S. was also incapable of copying letters of the alphabet. While attempting to copy a capital letter *X*, he drew two separated oblique lines.

So how can we explain this disorder? The current explanation is that apperceptive agnosics have suffered a disruption of their perceptual grouping mechanism. In the psychological approach chapter, we described grouping as the process of assembling basic perceptual features. These agnosics lack the ability to integrate the various features of an object, although they can perceive the individual features accurately. For example, an apperceptive agnosic patient might be able to recognize that a picture of a car has wheels, windows, and doors, but he or she may not be able to combine these parts into a complete percept of a car (see Figure 6.7). These individuals have sustained general damage to the occipital lobes and nearby areas. In these individuals, this kind of damage interferes with the combination or assembly of features into a unified object representation.

Another disorder that may be considered a type of apperceptive agnosia involves difficulty recognizing objects when they are viewed from unusual angles or are lit unevenly. This disorder sometimes goes by the name of **perceptual categorization deficit**. It often goes unnoticed, as patients who have the disorder usually have no problems performing other visual tasks. The existence of the disorder can be revealed under certain testing conditions, however. Affected persons are, for instance, not able to say that the object represented in a picture of an upright ladder is the same object as that represented in a picture of a ladder as viewed from below. Notice that this deficit constitutes a failure of

Figure 6.7 A patient with apperceptive agnosia can recognize the features of an object but, when asked to draw it, is unable to put the features together in the right way.

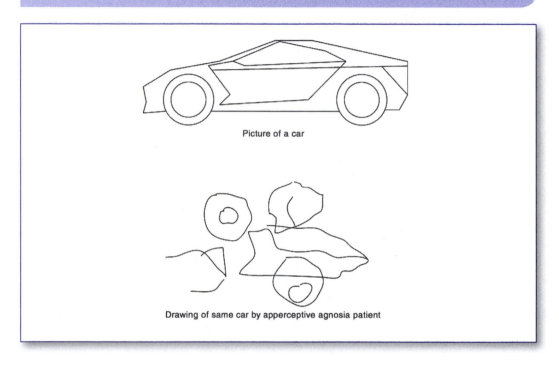

Picture of a car

Drawing of same car by apperceptive agnosia patient

object constancy as it is an inability to recognize an object after it has undergone a transformation, such as a change in perspective (see Figure 6.8). These patients have sustained damage to the right hemisphere, especially the right parietal lobe.

Associative Agnosia

Associative agnosias have three diagnostic criteria. First, affected persons have difficulties recognizing objects visually. Second, these patients can recognize objects using sensory modalities other than vision—for example, touch or sound. Third, they do have the ability to perceive objects holistically, at least in the operational sense of their being able to copy or match drawings of objects. It is with respect to this third criterion that associative agnosics differ from apperceptive agnosics, who cannot perform these tasks.

Individuals with this disorder demonstrate a behavioral anomaly. They can copy a drawing accurately, albeit quite slowly, but cannot name what it is they just copied. One patient, L. H., copied line drawings of a teabag, a diamond ring, and a pen rather precisely

Figure 6.8 Patients with visual agnosia can have difficulty recognizing an object when it is viewed from an unusual angle (foreshortened view) or from a perspective with few features visible (minimal feature view).

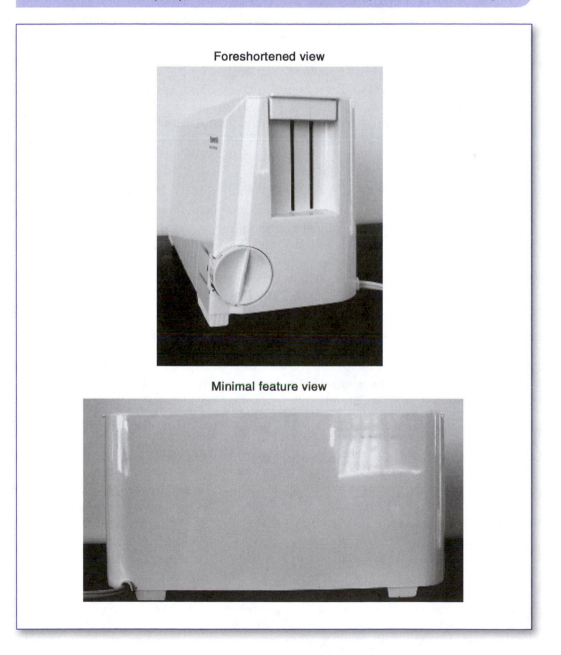

Foreshortened view

Minimal feature view

but could not supply the correct verbal label for any of the items (Levine & Calvanio, 1989). This implies that associative agnosics are able to perceive entire objects correctly. Their difficulty lies in coming up with a name for what they see.

Several theoretical explanations of this disorder have been proposed (Farah, 1990). Early explanations posited a disconnection between language areas that contain linguistic representations and visual areas. Under these theories, the two areas have remained intact; it is the connections between them that are damaged. This prevents them from matching visual inputs to verbal labels. Humphreys and Riddoch (1987) later elaborated on this idea. They believed that the deficit was due to damage to a system that contains stored visual object representations. More recent explanations use neural network pattern recognition architectures (Hinton, 1981). Damage to the connections that enable the formation of object representations can then account for the observed anomalous behaviors.

Face Perception

Prosopagnosia. **Prosopagnosia** is an inability to recognize faces, despite the capacity to recognize other types of visual stimuli and the presence of generally intact intellectual functioning. Prosopagnosia is considered a type of associative agnosia because in persons who have the disorder the ability to perceive faces is mostly intact. The difficulty lies in being able to identify the faces. Individuals with this disorder are sometimes unable to recognize close friends, family members, and, in some cases, even the reflection of their own face in the mirror (Burton, Young, Bruce, Johnston, & Ellis, 1991; Parkin, 1996). The faculty of discrimination is also impaired. Prosopagnosics have problems telling faces apart from one another.

Research with monkeys has uncovered the existence of cells that respond selectively to faces. The area that has been identified is in the inferotemporal (IT) cortex, part of the ventral pathway that is responsible for the recognition of forms (Desimone, Albright, Gross, & Bruce, 1984; Perrett, Rolls, & Caan, 1982). Bruce, Desimone, and Gross (1981) found that some IT neurons fired most rapidly when the animal was presented with the stimulus of a complete face, either that of a monkey or that of a human being. The neurons fired less rapidly when the monkeys were presented with images of incomplete faces—those that had one feature, such as the eyes, removed. A caricature of a face produced even slower responding. Wachsmuth, Oram, and Perrett (1994) also measured neural firing in IT area in monkeys. They discovered that there were cells that became active when the animal was shown a picture of a face or a face and a body. Response dropped significantly when the stimulus consisted of a picture of a body only, with the face covered.

Neural Coding. It is worth digressing for a moment to discuss the idea of neural coding. The research just described makes it seem possible that we have individual neurons that respond to individual faces—that there are single cells that fire only when the stimulus consists of a particular face. This type of representation is known as **specificity coding**. In specificity coding, a single cell fires in response to the presence of a particular face—say, your grandmother's—but not in response to any other face. Another cell would fire in response to your grandfather's face, but not to your grandmother's or anybody else's. Although specificity coding of this sort is possible, it is unlikely for two reasons (Goldstein, 2002). First, it is now known that cells that respond to one face often respond to others as well. Second, a tremendous number of cells would be required for the coding of all the faces we know, and of all the possible views and expressions of these faces.

A more likely explanation is **distributed coding**, in which a specific face is coded for by a specific pattern of activation among a group of cells. In this scheme, your grandmother's face might cause cell A to fire rapidly, cell B to fire slowly, and cell C to fire at a moderate rate. Your grandfather's face might induce a different pattern of activation among these same three cells. Distributed coding can efficiently represent a large number of faces or facial attributes and in a way that uses fewer neurons.

In human beings, "face cells" seem to be located in the **fusiform face area (FFA)**. Studies using fMRI show that pictures of faces activate this area, located in the fusiform gyrus of the human IT (Clark et al., 1996; Puce, Allison, Asgari, Gore, & McCarthy, 1995). This region appears to be dedicated to the processing of face information. That there should be a part of the brain devoted to faces is not surprising, considering the important role they play in social interaction. Evolutionary forces may have selected for a face-processing mechanism that differs functionally from how other objects are recognized, although there is an ongoing debate over whether faces constitute a special class of perceptual stimulus.

Interdisciplinary Crossroads: Perceptual Binding and Neural Synchrony

If you think back to Chapter 4 and the feature integration theory of pattern recognition, you will remember that serial search takes place when the target to be identified shares several properties with the distractors. The only way to locate it successfully is to focus attention on it to determine whether the particular shape and color at a given location match. Attention in this case was said to "glue" the different features together, cementing in place if you will the shape of a letter T and the color blue at a specific location in the visual field.

How does this happen? The parts of the brain that code for shape, color, and location are actually in different areas. Shape is processed by neurons in the IT cortex of the visual pathway in the temporal lobe, color is coded for by neurons in a location called V4 in the occipital lobe, and location is coded for in the parietal lobe, part of the dorsal processing stream. How does all this information come together to produce a unified perceptual object? This question of how to recombine the various features of an object is called the binding problem.

One group of researchers appears to have come up with a solution (Engel, König, Kreiter, Schillen, & Singer, 1992; Singer, 1996). They suggest that an object is represented by the joined and coordinated activity of a constellation of cells—a concept known as **neural synchrony**. Distinct cell subgroups of this constellation stand for individual features and may be separated by relatively large physical distances in the brain, but the dynamic activities of all of them serve to represent an entire object. The same group of neurons that code for a particular feature in one object can participate in different cell assemblies and, thus, stand for this same feature in other objects. For example, a network of cells representing the color red can participate in the assembly for a stop sign. These same cells can then participate in the assembly for a tomato.

A problem with the existence of functionally distinct cell populations in the brain is how they stand out amid all other ongoing activities. Singer (1999) proposes three solutions. First, other neurons not participating in the assembly can be inhibited. Second, the amplitude or strength of the cells in the assembly can be increased. Third, the cells in the assembly can synchronize their firing rates. This temporal synchrony means that all the participating neurons would fire at the same time. It is helpful to use an analogy here. Imagine a group of drummers in a band. If all the drummers banged out different rhythms, they wouldn't stand out much. But if the other musicians played more softly and the drummers played louder and, most important, began beating the same rhythm, we would hear the drums as a salient ensemble.

There are some problems with temporal synchrony (von der Malsburg, 1981; Singer et al., 1997). Not all cells coding for features fire at the same rate. To overcome these difficulties, it was postulated that single or partial discharge rates of neurons, rather than their entire pattern of activity, can be synchronized (Gray, König, Engel, & Singer, 1989; Singer & Gray, 1995). In this scheme, only one cell output or a small number of outputs that are part of a given sequence of outputs are timed to coincide with others. Returning to our musical example, it would be like having every fourth beat of one of the drummers coinciding with every fourth beat of the other drummers. Alternatively, two drummers could synchronize recurrent clusters of beats. This partial discharge synchrony would allow the drummers to play at different rates yet still coordinate their activity.

There is evidence to support the synchrony hypothesis. Engel et al. (1992) measured the electrical activity of spatially separated cells in the primary visual cortex. These cells respond individually to lines of a given orientation (Hubel, 1982; Hubel, Wiesel, & Stryker, 1978). In this case, both cells responded to vertical lines. When each cell was stimulated individually with a vertical line, the cells showed moderately correlated activity. But when a single prominent vertical line was used to stimulate both, they showed much stronger coordinated activity. They fired short-lived bursts of output at the same time, alternating with periods of lowered activity. These two cells firing out of synchrony suggest that they represent object parts. When they fire synchronously, they could then be part of a larger assembly that codes for the entire object. Neural synchrony could be the basis for more than just perceptual binding. It may explain memory formation and consciousness as well (Axmacher, Mormann, Fernandez, Elger, & Fell, 2006).

More recent research on this topic shows that the brain can synchronize far-flung activity in a much more flexible way than previously assumed. Guttman, Gilroy, and Blake (2007) differentiate between temporal synchrony and temporal structure. In the first case, neurons must be in phase with one another. The impulses or spikes representing action potentials have to occur at the same moment, either for the entire pattern or for subsets within the pattern. In the second case, there can be similar patterns of impulses over time in either location and these can be linked. Imagine that neurons in one brain area fire two bursts of high-frequency impulses followed by one burst of low-frequency impulses. In another area, this same pattern occurs but several seconds later. Even though the impulses don't happen at exactly the same time, their similar patterning or temporal structure can still serve as a basis for synchronization.

THE NEUROSCIENCE OF ATTENTION

Attention plays a key role in many different cognitive phenomena. This may explain why there are at least six distinct brain structures that underlie attentional effects (Posner & Peterson, 1990). We can think of these structures as being interconnected and as collectively forming an attentional neural network. Figure 6.9 shows their locations. These different areas work, sometimes in concert, to control attention.

We will describe the location and function of each of these structures in detail in the numbered list that follows, but first, let us give you a sense of how they work together. The **reticular activating system (RAS)** is responsible for our overall arousal level, the extent to which we will pay attention to anything. The thalamus regulates the amount of incoming sensory information that reaches the cortex for processing. A more refined processing of the information becomes possible once it reaches the cortex. This processing becomes the job of the parietal lobe, which allocates attentional resources to certain aspects of the information, such as an object's spatial location. Ultimately, the cingulate cortex initiates a response on the basis of what is attended.

The following structures are considered parts of the neural attention network:

1. The RAS, with cell bodies located in the hindbrain, consists of a network of about 100 nuclei. These nuclei have projections to diverse areas of the cortex. The function of this system is very basic: It controls the brain's overall arousal and alertness levels. Activation of the RAS is linked to the ability to sustain attention over time. Bilateral lesions to the RAS result in a comatose state in which patients are unresponsive to most stimuli.

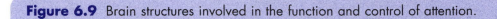

Figure 6.9 Brain structures involved in the function and control of attention.

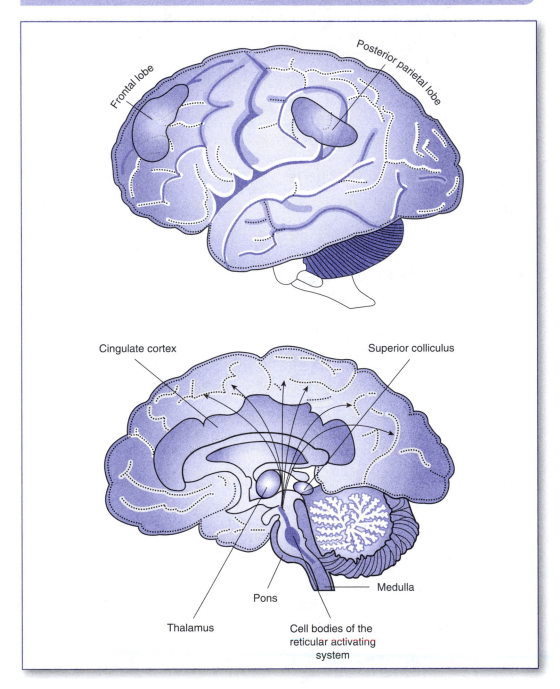

2. The **superior colliculus** is located in the midbrain. Its function seems to be the shifting of visual attention from one object or location in the visual field to another. Monkeys with superior colliculus lesions are unable to shift their gaze to a novel stimulus that appears suddenly in the peripheral visual field (Schiller, Sandell, & Maunsell, 1987). This type of deficit has also been observed in humans in whom there has been a degeneration of the colliculus (Rafal, Posner, Friedman, Inhoff, & Bernstein, 1988).

3. The **thalamus** is dorsal and anterior to the superior colliculus. It receives inputs from the RAS and forwards them to the cortex. It is a part of the general RAS arousal circuit. The thalamus also serves as a relay center. It forwards incoming sensory information to the different parts of the cortex specialized for processing them. It is believed that a particular nucleus within the thalamus is responsible for regulating those sensory messages. It serves as a filter or gatekeeper, determining how much information is allowed to continue to the cortex for further processing. A study that used PET observed a greater amount of thalamic activity in instances when a participant was asked to single out a target item from a collection of items, as compared with when the participant was asked to identify a target item that had been presented by itself (LaBerge & Buchsbaum, 1990).

4. The parietal lobe seems to service a broad variety of visual attention-related tasks. In monkeys, cells in the intraparietal sulcus of the parietal lobe are active when a particular spatial location is attended (Colby, Duhamel, & Goldberg, 1996). In human beings, the **intraparietal sulcus** is active in processing a combination of visual stimulus features, such as color and shape, which suggests that it is responsible for the binding together of features in visual search (Wojciulik & Kanwisher, 1999). The parietal lobe is also the site where attentional resources are allocated to different tasks (Coull & Nobre, 1998; Fink, Dolan, Halligan, Marshall, & Firth, 1997). Think back to Kahneman's capacity model of attention from Chapter 4. You may remember that there was a component of that model called the allocation policy. Its job is to distribute attentional resources among a range of possible activities. The parietal lobe appears to be the neural equivalent of that component.

5. The **cingulate cortex** is believed to be the site where a response is selected, especially in cases where the response entails the inhibition of an alternative response. An example of the selection of a response in the presence of competing inputs is the Stroop effect (Besner & Stolz, 1999). In this phenomenon, participants are asked to look at a word printed in a particular color. They then have to name the color or read the word. These two attributes can be congruent, as when the word red is presented in the color red. They can also be incongruent, as when the word red is presented in the color blue. In the congruent condition, observers react quickly because the two attributes prompt similar responses. In the incongruent condition, observers' reactions are slowed because one of the attributes elicits a response that must be ignored. Milham et al. (2001) found activation of the cingulate cortex when participants were responding to the incongruent condition of the Stroop task.

6. We already have introduced the frontal lobes. With respect to attention-related tasks, their job—like that of the parietal lobes—is quite varied. The frontal lobes play a role in the selection of motor responses, in goal-directed action, and in adherence to a task, among other things. The frontal lobes feature prominently in executive-function and problem-solving situations, so we reserve the greater part of our discussion of the frontal lobes for later.

Models of Attention

Banich (2004) outlines several types of attention models. We describe two of them here. In component process models, distinct brain areas each have a unique and nonredundant function. In distributed network models, the areas can be characterized as having some operational overlap.

A Component Process Model

Posner, Inhoff, Friedrich, and Cohen (1987) propose that each of the multiple brain areas responsible for the control of attention performs a distinct operation. Their model specifically describes the changes that occur in visual selective attention, where attention is shifted from one spatial location to another. They posit that cells of the parietal lobe are used to disengage attention or remove it from a specific location. The superior colliculus then moves attention to a new location. Finally, the thalamus engages the attention and focuses it on the new location.

The data that support this model come from an experimental paradigm in which participants are asked to focus on a central cross and are then cued to respond to a target, such as an asterisk, that can appear on either side (Posner, 1980). The target appears in one of two boxes to the left or to the right of the cross. There are two types of trials. On "valid" trials, the box that contains the target lights up. On "invalid" trials, the opposite box without the target lights up. For one of the conditions, the majority (80%) of the trials are valid while the remaining trials (20%) are not. Participants in this condition respond faster to valid trials because the cue is a reliable indicator of where the target will appear. In effect, they are able to move a visual "spotlight" of attention into the target location before it appears and respond to it more rapidly. On invalid trials, it takes longer, ostensibly because they move the attentional spotlight in the opposite direction and then must bring it back to the target location.

In a variation of the Posner visual selective attention paradigm, patients with damage to either the right or left parietal lobe had no difficulty responding when the cue and target appeared on the side contralateral to the damage. In these cases, the cue was valid, and the damaged parietal lobe that processed information coming from the opposite visual field did not have to disengage attention. But during invalid trials in which the cue appeared on the side ipsilateral to the lesion and the target appeared on the other side, response time was slow. In these cases, the parietal lobe of the damaged hemisphere did have to disengage attention (Posner, Walker, Friedrich, & Rafal, 1984).

Patients with collicular damage show delayed responses in valid trials. This suggests that they are slower to shift attention from the fixation cross to the cued target location, no matter which side of the cross it is on (Rafal et al., 1988). Individuals with sustained damage to the thalamus exhibit yet another result. They are slower to respond whenever the target appears on the side contralateral to the side of the thalamus that is damaged, whether the trial is valid or invalid. This implies that they cannot engage attention on the target.

Distributed Network Models

Mesulam (1981) proposes an alternative model for the neural machinery that controls attention. In this model, the separate neural structures are not specialized and functionally independent, as they are in the component process model. Instead, the functions of the different areas overlap to some degree. Each brain region performs a major operation that is attention related but can perform other attention-related functions as well. This redundancy in the network implies that any given area can suffer damage, while the system as a whole will maintain some of the functionality subsumed by the damaged region.

This model explains how attention is directed to areas outside the body and is derived from the deficits observed in specific types of brain damage in monkeys and humans. The model encompasses four brain areas, each playing a primary, but not exclusive, role in controlling an aspect of attention. First, the posterior parietal cortex provides a sensory map or representation of the space in which attention will be directed. Second, the cingulate gyrus in the limbic cortex plays a motivational role. It determines what should be paid attention to and what can be ignored. Third, the frontal cortex coordinates motor programs for attention-related actions. These actions include fixating on certain regions in the visual field, scanning across the visual field, or reaching out to grasp an object. Finally, reticular structures generate arousal and vigilance levels.

Let's give an example that will illustrate how all these areas might work together. Imagine that Susan is sitting at the breakfast table. She missed dinner the night before and so is quite hungry. Her posterior parietal cortex contains a sensory representation of the breakfast table that includes the locations of items such as a glass of orange juice and a bowl of cereal. Her cingulate cortex directs her attention to items and/or regions of significance. In this case, she would pay more attention to the orange juice than to the tablecloth. Her frontal cortex supervises motor actions, such as her reaching out to pick up the orange juice. Underlying all this are arousal levels that have been determined by her reticular system. If Susan had a good night's rest, her arousal and vigilance ought to be at high levels.

If multiple brain areas are responsible for our attention, then you might be wondering how these areas coordinate their activity. This might be achieved via a synchronization of nerve cell firing in each area. To learn more about how such synchronization might take place in perception, see the "Interdisciplinary Crossroads" section.

Disorders of Attention

Hemispatial Neglect

Neglect is the opposite of attention. It refers to information that we ignore or fail to pay attention to. Although we do notice a lot of what we perceive, just think of all that we miss. In the case of vision, we can usually see what we are looking at directly but not what is in the periphery. This is normal and doesn't usually impede everyday functioning. But certain types of brain damage can result in a profound loss of attention. In **hemispatial neglect**, there is a tendency to ignore one side of the body and its surroundings. These include visual, auditory, and touch information. This disorder occurs with damage to the superior temporal gyrus usually in the right hemisphere (Karnath, Ferber, & Himmelbach, 2001). This gyrus receives inputs from the auditory system and from the dorsal and ventral visual systems and has outputs to the basal ganglia, so symptoms of damage to this area include neglect for each of these senses as well as motor impairments.

Remarkably, patients with left hemispatial neglect can perceive only the right side of objects (Driver & Mattingley, 1998). When asked to recall what they've seen, they describe only the right side, and when asked to draw what they see, they copy only the right side (see Figure 6.10). However, they also have difficulty attending to two items that are presented at the same location. This is true visually when two objects are at the same location, but it is also true for audition. When two notes at different pitches are played at the same time, patients have difficulty telling which tone was played first (Cusack, Carlyon, & Robertson, 2000). With training, some of these deficits can be overcome. For example, patients can be cued in various ways to attend more to one side (Frassinetti, Pavani, & Làdavas, 2002). It is important to point out that neglect is an attention problem, not a perceptual one. These patients have intact sensory systems. They can see and hear perfectly well but are unable to allocate attention to the perceptual information.

Attention-Deficit Hyperactivity Disorder

Commonly known as ADHD, **attention-deficit hyperactivity disorder** is characterized by distractibility, impulsivity, mood swings, short temper, overreaction to small stressors, and difficulties in planning or carrying out plans (Wender, Wolf, & Wasserstein, 2001). This disorder has been estimated to afflict around 10% of children in the United States as

Figure 6.10 A patient with left hemispatial neglect, when asked to draw a picture of a ship, can reproduce only the right side.

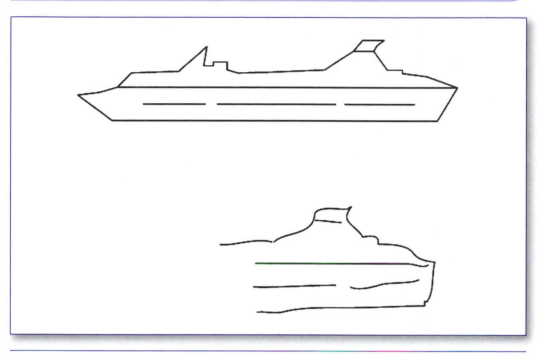

Source: Adapted from Shallice, 1982

well as a smaller percentage of adults. A complicating factor is that the disorder is difficult to diagnose. Some children may be misdiagnosed with ADHD. Likewise, some children with the disorder may be misdiagnosed as not having it and are considered to be on the high end of the normal spectrum for these symptoms.

There is clear evidence for a genetic basis to ADHD. It runs in families. The gene for one type of dopamine receptor is more common in some patients (Faraone, Doyle, Mick, & Biederman, 2001). They also have slightly smaller than normal brain volumes with smaller cerebellums and a smaller right prefrontal cortex (Giedd, Blumenthal, Molloy, & Castellanos, 2001; Ravizza & Ivry, 2001). However, these differences are small, and brain imaging cannot be used to make a diagnosis (Kalat, 2004). The current drug of choice for treating ADHD is a stimulant medication called Ritalin. In children, Ritalin increases the ability to concentrate, reduces impulsivity, and improves both school grades and social interaction (Elia, Ambrosini, & Rapoport, 1999). Similar results have been obtained with adults. Ritalin acts by boosting the action of the neurotransmitter dopamine.

THE NEUROSCIENCE OF MEMORY

Early research on memory asked a very basic question: Where in the brain are memories located? Karl Lashley (1950) was one of the first researchers who attempted to find out. He was searching for the **engram,** a physical change in a part of the brain that is associated with learning. His methodology was to train monkeys to perform different tasks. For example, he would teach his monkeys how to open a box with a latch in the expectation that the animals would form a memory of the task. He would then introduce lesions to parts of the brain to see if the memory of the task was destroyed in the process. Lashley's rationale was that if you destroy the part of the brain that contains the engram for the task, the monkey's memory of how to perform it will be lost. In one experiment, he destroyed larger and larger areas of cortex in a graded manner. He found that the greater the amount of tissue that had been destroyed, the greater was the amount of time needed to retrain the monkeys to perform the task. But in no case did the animals actually forget how to perform the task.

Lashley concluded that memories are not laid down in any one area of the brain but that all parts of the brain participate in memory storage—a principle referred to as **equipotentiality**. This principle has some interesting implications. It suggests that multiple copies of a single memory are stored throughout the brain and that multiple brain regions participate in memory formation. We now know that there is some truth to this. The distinct cortical areas that process information derived from a single sensory modality do contain very different representations. It is also the case that many brain areas are involved in memory. These areas include the hippocampus, the entorhinal cortex, the amygdala, the striatum, the left parietal cortex, and the prefrontal regions (see Figure 6.11). In this section, we will examine some of the more recent work on the neuroscience of memory. Our focus, as before, is to describe the different brain structures that underlie memory processes and to formulate models of how they work together to create memories.

Learning and Memory

Learning takes place when an event provokes a nervous system alteration that in turn provokes a change in an organism's behavior. It is this change in the nervous system that is a memory. From a neuroscience point of view, a memory is essentially the formation of a neural circuit—the forging of a pathway among neurons. The memory can then be considered to be the circuit itself. When the circuit is reactivated at some point in time after its establishment, the memory that corresponds to the circuit is experienced and informs the organism's behavior. In this way, nervous systems preserve the past and help organisms adapt to novel environments.

Learning at the cellular level requires **synaptic plasticity**, a capacity for change in the structure or biochemistry of a synapse. Donald Hebb (1949) was perhaps the first to

Figure 6.11 Brain areas that form part of the human memory system.

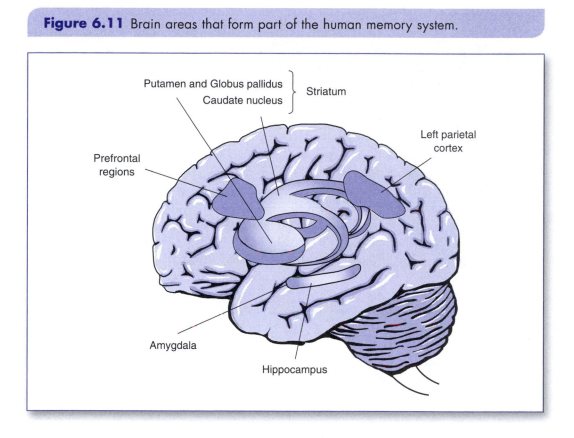

understand this and formulated what has become known as the **Hebb rule**. It states that if two connected neurons are active simultaneously, the synapse between them will become strengthened. Imagine two cells, A and B. An increase in the strength of their connection means that when cell A is active, it is now more likely to activate cell B. Cells A and B have now become linked together in a circuit: When A fires, B fires also.

The specific neural change that mediates this Hebbian form of learning is called **long-term potentiation (LTP)**. It is the enduring facilitation of synaptic transmission that occurs following activation of a synapse by intense high-frequency stimulation. Rapid repeated stimulation is the key to LTP. It induces changes such as an increase in the number of receptors (Tocco, Maren, Shors, Baudry, & Thompson, 1992), as well as other structural alterations that result in increased neurotransmitter release (Edwards, 1995). These changes strengthen the synapse, increasing its responsiveness to further stimulation. LTP occurs in parts of the brain where learning and the creation of new neural circuits are important. It has been most often studied in the cells of the hippocampal system, which we will now discuss.

The Hippocampal System

We begin our discussion of the hippocampus with a famous case study (Corkin, 1984). H. M. was a patient who suffered from **epilepsy**. This is a disorder in which neurons fire uncontrollably, producing muscle spasms and seizures. H. M. did not respond to anticonvulsant medication. To stop his seizures, surgeons took drastic measures. They removed portions of his medial temporal lobes, including the hippocampus. The surgery was successful in the sense that it put an end to his seizures, but it left him with a profound memory deficit. After the operation, H. M. lacked the ability to learn any new information. He could have a conversation with a friend, turn around to talk to someone else, and in just a minute or so completely forget that his friend was even there. The removal of the medial temporal lobe tissue disrupted the process by which information is transferred from working memory to long-term memory. This process is called **consolidation**.

Despite his memory deficit, many of H. M.'s other memory abilities were unaffected. His working memory and problem-solving capacity were intact. In fact, he enjoyed solving crossword puzzles—but he would sometimes solve the same puzzle several times, as he forgot that he had already completed it! The content of his long-term memory prior to the surgery was also unaffected. This was true for both declarative and procedural knowledge. He could remember the location of the house he lived in and could still perform the skills he had acquired prior to the surgery. The case of H. M. demonstrates that different memory functions are handled by different neural structures. Damage to one of those structures can selectively remove a component of memory ability. This is a theme that is repeated later in this section.

Hippocampal damage is associated with **anterograde amnesia**, an inability to retain new information following the traumatic incident that caused the damage. H. M. suffered from this type of amnesia, as he could not retain any new information after the surgery. As we will discuss shortly, it is the hippocampus and associated areas that are responsible for the consolidation of newly acquired information. Anterograde amnesia needs to be distinguished from **retrograde amnesia**, an inability to remember information acquired prior to the damage-inducing event. Retrograde amnesia is often caused by head injury, and in most cases, the loss extends only as far back as a week or so before the injury.

The job of the hippocampus is essentially to take information about "current events" that it has received from the cortex, process this information, and send it back out to the cortex, where it is stored in a more permanent state. Inputs from the cortical regions contain representations of episodes or events that the organism has just experienced. More specifically, we may think of the hippocampus as an integrator. If the job of the cortex is to "divide and conquer" sensory input into distinct processing streams, the job of the hippocampus is to "combine and reunite" them. The hippocampus weaves the disparate parts of an experience into a single unified memory. Let's use the example of a birthday party to illustrate this. The various parts of the cortex have divided your experience of the party into fragments. The visual system maintains an image of the presents; the auditory system, the sounds of your friends' singing; the gustatory system, representations of the taste of the cake; and so on. All these representations converge as inputs to the hippocampus, which combines them to form a whole memory of the birthday party.

Neural Substrates of Working Memory

In Chapter 5, we discussed the components of working memory. These are the articulatory loop, where operations on verbal representations are performed; the visuospatial sketch-pad, where visual information is processed; and the executive control system, which coordinates activities. Recent neuropsychological evidence confirms the existence of these structures as functionally distinct units and has pinpointed their locations in the brain.

Smith, Jonides, and Koeppe (1996), using PET in an experimental scenario, have discovered the existence of anatomically separate areas for storage and rehearsal of verbal information in working memory. They employed a design in which participants in one condition viewed a stream of letters and were asked to judge whether a given letter matched the one they had viewed two letters back in the sequence. This task requires both storage and rehearsal. The performance of these participants was compared with that of two control groups. Participants in the first control group were asked to search for a single target letter. This ostensibly requires storage only. Participants in the second control group viewed the letter stream and were asked to make only manual responses to the presentation of a letter as they rehearsed that letter until the next one appeared. This condition requires rehearsal only.

The PET images that were obtained under these study conditions were compared with each other using a subtraction technique. In this technique, the record of brain activity obtained in one condition is subtracted from that of another. According to this logic, if the "two-back" condition calls on storage and rehearsal and the "search" condition calls on storage, the subtraction of the latter from the former should identify the brain areas that are responsible for rehearsal. Similarly, the subtraction of the record of brain activity of the "manual" group from that of the two-back group should identify those brain areas that are involved in storage.

Using this type of analysis, the researchers found that activation of the left hemisphere's posterior parietal cortex corresponded to the storage of verbal material. Three other sites also turned up. All three were in the prefrontal cortex and corresponded to rehearsal for verbal materials. These sites were the inferior frontal gyrus (Broca's area), another region in the premotor cortex, and a region of the supplementary motor area. These areas are believed to generate a code for use in explicit speech, as we will discuss in the linguistics chapter. This code can be used to represent verbal materials for rehearsal and implicit speech as well. These two areas, the left hemisphere's posterior parietal cortex and prefrontal cortex, can be considered to form a portion of the articulatory loop that is part of Baddeley's (1986) model of working memory.

In a separate experiment, Smith et al. (1996) investigated the neural substrate of spatial working memory. Participants in this study were presented with letters that appeared at different positions around an imaginary circle. They were asked to judge whether a given letter appeared in the same position as that of a letter that had appeared three letters back in the series. The resulting PET analysis showed activation in the posterior parietal cortex, but this time in the right hemisphere. The researchers identified this region as the area where spatial information in working memory is stored. They noted that these data were in accord with those of other studies that have identified the same area as the site of storage of spatial information (Jonides et al., 1993; Petrides, Alivisatos, Meyer, & Evans, 1993).

Evidence from animal studies suggests a location for the rehearsal or maintenance of a spatial code in working memory. Goldman-Rakic (1993) tested monkeys by giving them a delayed-response task. In this procedure, a monkey is shown two locations, only one of which contains a food item. There is then a forced delay of several seconds, during which a barrier visually obscures the locations. The delay forces the monkey to maintain the spatial location of the food item in working memory. The barrier is then removed, and the monkey must choose the location that holds the food item to get the item as a reward. Monkeys whose dorsolateral prefrontal cortex has been lesioned cannot perform this task—implying that this region is the site for the maintenance of spatial information in the working memory system.

Studies with both animal and human subjects reveal a third working memory system for objects. This system codes and stores visual object representations. Whereas spatial working memory would code for the location of a letter in space—for example, whether it appears to the left or to the right—visual object memory would code for a visual representation or image of the letter itself, which would include attributes such as its shape and color. This differentiation reflects the existence of the dorsal "where" path for location and the ventral "what" path for identity, discussed earlier in this chapter. Data from Wilson, O'Scalaidhe, and Goldman-Rakic (1993) show that in monkeys, one brain region mediates object–shape memory and another mediates object–location memory. The principal sulcus is the area corresponding to spatial location; the inferior convexity corresponds to shape location. Both are located in the frontal area. In humans, distinct brain areas lateralized to either hemisphere carry out these functions. Occipital, parietal, and frontal sites in the right hemisphere are linked to spatial memory, whereas parietal and IT sites in the left hemisphere are linked to object memory (Smith et al., 1995; Smith & Jonides, 1994).

Evaluating the Neuroscience of Working Memory

Jonides and Smith (1997) make a few general conclusions concerning the neural architecture for working memory. They speculate that there may be a separate working memory system for each sensory modality—each having its own storage buffer and rehearsal capacity. The visual object memory system described above would service vision, another system would serve audition, yet another gustation, and so on. Verbal and spatial working memory, however, are modality independent. They can represent and rehearse information from any modality.

These investigators are also careful to point out that the various memory codes are in the service of other cognitive processes, and they give several examples (Jonides & Smith, 1997). One could use the spatial code to form a mental map of how to get somewhere and a visual code to mentally compare the shapes of two objects. What is lacking, they argue, is a more abstract conceptual code that could represent semantic items such as words. This type of code would allow for additional cognitive tasks such as language comprehension, problem solving, and deductive reasoning. There are hints in the literature of the existence of a semantic code of this nature. Future research would be needed to determine whether such a code would have its own attendant working memory structures for storage and rehearsal.

The studies of the neural basis of working memory that we have surveyed thus far have been very informative. They show us that there are, in fact, a large number of distinct working memory systems that correspond to different sensory modalities and various abstract characteristics. This work can help us reconceptualize Baddeley's (1986) model of working memory, which originally postulated the existence of verbal and visual components only. We could update this model by incorporating these additional working memory systems. You might recall that Baddeley's model also included an executive control system. This system is responsible for the control of various aspects of working memory function. Executive processes are also used in reasoning and problem solving. For this reason, we will talk about reasoning and problem solving in the section on executive function.

Neural Substrates of Long-Term Memories

We have already reviewed some aspects of long-term memory in our discussion of learning and the hippocampal system. Remember that when information first arrives at the brain, multiple areas of the cortex—each corresponding to a unique sensory modality—process it. These representations, however, are short-lived and would fade away quickly if it were not for the hippocampal system, whose job it is to integrate the disparate aspects of a memory experience and to return the consolidated memory to the cortex. So the cortex is the site where some of our long-term memories reside. But there are multiple forms of long-term memory. Procedural memories store procedural or skill knowledge and are demonstrated through action. Declarative memories store factual or event knowledge and are demonstrated through explanation. The two types of declarative memory are semantic memory for facts and episodic memory for events. See Chapter 5 for a more extensive treatment of these types.

Given this variety of types of long-term memory, what can we say about their neural bases? Are there different brain areas that mediate processing with respect to the different types of long-term memory? The answer is yes. Research in this area shows that they are governed by different brain regions.

Declarative memories rely on the cortex for storage and the hippocampal system for consolidation. But two separate aspects of this system mediate semantic and episodic information. This conclusion comes from an examination of case study data. Vargha-Khadem et al. (1997) reported on patients who sustained damage to only the hippocampus early in life. In these patients, there was no damage to the limbic cortex of the medial temporal lobe. The limbic cortex consists of the parahippocampal, entorhinal, and perirhinal cortices. These areas are considered part of the overall hippocampal system and mediate connections between it and the overall cortex. These patients could not recall anything that happened to them during the course of a day. If they went to a movie or visited a friend, they would have no memory of it. They did, however, have excellent memory for facts and did relatively well in school. This suggests that the hippocampus proper is responsible for the consolidation of episodic memory and that the limbic cortex mediates semantic memory. These researchers also concluded that if both the hippocampus and the limbic cortex were destroyed, all declarative memory ability would be lost. More research is needed to confirm these conclusions.

Learning in procedural memory corresponds to a change in the neural systems that underlie the acquisition of a given task. It is the motor regions that govern skill performance and procedural knowledge, not the widespread sensory cortical areas that hold declarative information. Also, procedural memory does not depend on the hippocampus for consolidation. The **basal ganglia** play a critical role in skill learning (Graybiel, Aosaki, Flaherty, & Kimura, 1994). This is a cluster of brain areas involved in voluntary motor responses. The basal ganglia consist of the striatum—which is made up of the caudate nucleus, putamen, and globus pallidus (see Figure 6.11). Changes to the motor cortex also have been documented as taking place during skill learning (Grafton et al., 1992; Grafton, Woods, & Tyszka, 1994). In one study, monkeys trained to pick up small objects using fine finger and hand movements evidenced increased representation of those body areas in the primary motor cortex (Nudo, Milliken, Jenkins, & Merzenich, 1996).

THE NEUROSCIENCE OF EXECUTIVE FUNCTION AND PROBLEM SOLVING

Executive function refers to cognitive operations such as planning, the sequencing of behavior, the flexible use of information, and goal attainment. Many of these same operations are called on in problem solving. As we saw in our examination of the cognitive approach, problem solving consists of trying to attain a final goal via the performance of a sequence of operations that leads to the attainment of individual subgoals. In this section, we discuss the neural basis of such problem-solving ability.

The hallmark of frontal lobe damage is a diminished capacity to perform goal-directed behaviors. Patients who have sustained this type of brain damage suffer from **executive dysfunction**, a disorder characterized by a broad array of deficits. Some of these patients have difficulties initiating actions or terminating them once initiated. For example, the patients may be listless, sitting around the house all day—but once they are engaged in some action, such as brushing their teeth, they may have difficulty stopping. This kind of behavioral deficit is referred to as **psychological inertia**. These patients sometimes appear to be impelled to perform actions that are "suggested" by the environment, such as picking up a pencil and writing with it as soon as they see it. This phenomenon in which a stimulus in the environment triggers an automatic behavior is called **environmental dependency syndrome**. Needless to say, these individuals have difficulty solving even simple problems.

Sequencing, that is, the sequential ordering of actions, is necessary in problem solving. Any strategy that is part of problem solving includes sequencing because multiple steps are part of the problem-solving process. The Tower of London problem is a tool that researchers have used to test this capacity (Shallice, 1982). Figure 6.12 shows several Tower of London configurations. There are three sticks of different heights. Three balls of different colors have holes through them and can be placed on the sticks. The leftmost stick is the tallest and can accommodate all three balls. The middle stick is intermediate in height and can accommodate two balls. The stick to the right is the shortest and can hold only a single ball. The solution to any of the Tower of London problems involves moving the balls that make up an initial starting configuration until they conform to a final target configuration, in the smallest number of moves possible.

Patients who have sustained frontal lobe damage, especially to the left frontal lobe, have great difficulty solving Tower of London problems. Shallice (1982) studied 61 patients with and without localized lesions of either frontal lobe. The patients were then given Tower of London problems. The number of problems the patients were able to solve in one minute was tallied. The results showed that the group with left anterior frontal lobe damage had scores that were significantly worse than those of the other groups. This area, thus, seems responsible for planning and sequencing of the type that is needed in Tower of London tasks.

In a more recent study, healthy individuals were asked to solve a computer version of the Tower of London task. rCBF in these individuals was measured (Morris, Ahmed, Syed, & Toone, 1993). rCBF is the amount of blood flowing to a particular area of the brain. The higher this measure, the more this brain region is working. Participants who performed the computer task showed increased levels of rCBF in the left prefrontal cortex. Those subjects who took more time to plan their moves and computed the solutions in fewer moves had even greater rCBF, suggesting that activity in this brain area is responsible for planning during problem solving.

Figure 6.12 The Tower of London task. Players must produce the goal position in as few moves as possible.

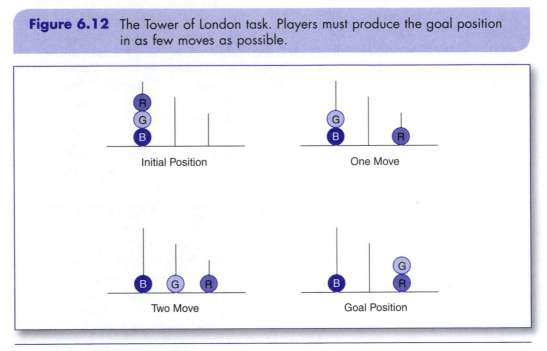

Initial Position

One Move

Two Move

Goal Position

Source: Adapted from Shallice (1982).

When we examine the insights that are to be gleaned from studies of frontal lobe damage, we see a good example of convergence between cognitive science approaches. In this case, the convergence is between neuroscience and studies of problem solving in the areas of cognition and artificial intelligence. Patients with frontal lobe damage clearly demonstrate deficits that have to do with directing themselves toward a goal or breaking down a problem into subgoals. They also have difficulty sequencing their actions appropriately. These components of problem solving are exactly what would be required in the solution of any problem and what computer programs such as General Problem Solver and SOAR do to solve problems. The fact that these ideas come up independently in different disciplines shows that they are fundamental to an understanding of problem solving.

Theories of Executive Function

In this section, we consider two theories of executive function. The theories are cognitive in nature but have specific neurological implications. Both are formulated to account for automatic versus controlled forms of attention. **Automatic attentional processes** do not require conscious control. They occur when one is experiencing familiar situations. Automatic responses are then triggered by environmental stimuli. Driving a car is an example of an automatic process. It can be carried out virtually without thinking while carrying on a conversation. **Controlled attentional processes**, on the other hand, require conscious control. They are operational when one responds to novel or difficult situations for which there is no prior learned reaction. In these instances, attention must be voluntarily directed. Problem solving calls for this type of processing.

Norman and Shallice (1980) proposed a model that relies on **action schemas**, structures that control automatic attentional processes. In this model, a schema can be triggered either by perceptual input or by the output of other schemas. An example of the former would be the image of your unmade bed in the morning. The sight of it could activate a bed-making schema. An action schema can be thought of as an if–then production rule where perceptual inputs serve as the preconditions necessary to trigger a context-specific action.

In a more general sense, a schema can be thought of as a stored framework or body of knowledge on the subject of some topic (Schank & Abelson, 1977). This type of schema is sometimes referred to as a **script**. The most often used example is a script for eating in a restaurant. It would consist of a sequence of events: being seated, getting menus, ordering, waiting, eating, paying the bill, and so on. Scripts can be used for solving problems because they specify goals and the sequences of actions needed to achieve them.

In the Norman and Shallice (1980) model, schemas can be activated independently of one another. This can pose a problem, since in everyday situations, usually just one action needs to be performed at any given time. The model specifies two ways in which a subset of appropriate schemas can become activated. The first is **contention scheduling** and is used to govern routine habitual performances as well as the performance of novel tasks. The second selection mechanism is the **supervisory attentional system (SAS)** and is used only for nonroutine actions.

In contention scheduling, each action schema is executed when the level of activation in one of its control units reaches a certain threshold. However, each schema has mutually inhibitory connections to others so that the more one schema is activated, the more it suppresses the activation of those it is connected to. This prevents the simultaneous activation of multiple schemas and ensures that the most appropriate one—the one receiving the greatest amount of activation—is triggered. Contention scheduling ensures that you don't do two things at once, such as trying to step on the accelerator and the brake while driving.

In the solving of problems that are related to new situations, existing schemas can fail or there may be no learned schema that can be applied. In these cases, the contention system needs to be supplemented with an alternate selection process. According to the model, this occurs as the additional activation of other schemas from the SAS. The SAS contains general programming or planning systems that are slower and more flexible than the fast, automatic, and unchanging schemas of contention scheduling. These schemas are designed to be more general purpose and applicable to a wide variety of problem types.

Therefore, one can think of the SAS as a higher level monitoring system, one that can apply general strategies to bear on a problem. The SAS can also suppress or turn off inappropriate schemas that might be triggered inadvertently. The failure to suppress these inappropriate schemas can result in "capture errors." Reason (1979) describes a person who, while walking across his back porch on the way to his car, began putting on his boots and jacket for working in the garden. Perhaps you can recall a similar situation from your own personal experience. Momentary lapses of attention seem to correspond to reduced activity or monitoring in the SAS.

So where in the brain are the different components of this model located? The left anterior frontal lobe is the probable location for the SAS. As mentioned above, lesions in this region are associated with difficulties in solving Tower of London problems. Damage to this region would explain the pattern of symptoms we see in executive dysfunction, where patients have trouble with problem solving but little difficulty performing well-learned tasks. This would also explain environmental dependency syndrome. Here, the contention scheduling system is clearly operating, as environmental stimuli automatically trigger their learned responses. These responses are out of place, however, as they cannot be overridden by the supervisory system. It could also be that schemas or some aspects of schematic knowledge may be stored in the frontal lobes. This makes sense, as disruptions to the frontal areas result in the failure to apply and use schemas and in a consequent deficit in problem-solving ability.

Stuss and Benson (1986) offer a second theory of executive function involving controlled and automatic attention. In their view, there is a three-tiered hierarchy of attentional systems. The automatic system that corresponds to the lowest level makes associations between sensory representations and is governed by posterior brain areas. The supervisory system corresponds to the middle level and runs executive processes and is used in problem solving. It resides in the frontal lobe. In addition, Stuss and Benson postulate a metacognitive system that corresponds to a third level. **Metacognition** refers to any process that monitors, regulates, or controls any aspect of cognition. Metacognitive regulation includes planning, resource allocation, checking, and error detection and correction (Brown, Bransford, Ferrara, & Campione, 1983). The prefrontal cortex is believed to be the site of the metacognitive system. In a problem-solving situation, metacognitive processing would evaluate whether a particular strategy is working and, if it decided that it was not working, would initiate consideration of another strategy. Individuals lacking metacognitive control would persist in their applications of inappropriate strategies, meaning that they would get stuck on one approach to a problem and fail to consider other options.

OVERALL EVALUATION OF THE NEUROSCIENCE APPROACH

Neuroscience provides us with a straightforward description of the brain that includes microscopic-level descriptions of individual neurons and larger scale descriptions of brain structures. Although we have not mentioned it, comparative neuroscience compares these structures across species to see how evolutionary pressures have changed them. In this sense, neuroscience and the evolutionary approach go very well together. For more on this, go to the section on comparative cognition in the evolutionary approach chapter.

Of course, physical structure cannot be divorced from function, so neuroscience also addresses physiology. But physiology is best described within some organizing framework. In recent years, that framework has become cognitive processes; so we see the birth of cognitive neuroscience that attempts to map cognitive function onto brain structure and function. Just as with the cognitive approach, the neuroscience researchers have produced various models. These neuroscience models differ from their counterparts in that they specify the locations in the brain where information is represented and processed. They also specify the pathways by which information is passed from one processing center to another. The integration of the two types of models is a fruitful procedure for future investigations.

SUMMING UP: A REVIEW OF CHAPTER 6

1. Neuroscientists study nervous system structure and function. Researchers in the field of cognitive neuroscience attempt to relate these findings to cognitive processes.

2. A number of different methods are used in neuroscience. Case studies of human patients and lesion studies with animals investigate the behavioral deficits that follow damage to neural tissue. Traditional brain recording techniques include single- and multiple-unit recording, in which the activity of single or multiple neurons is recorded. The EEG yields a global pattern of brain action. When these are taken in response to a stimulus, they are called event-related potentials. More modern brain imaging methods include PET, fMRI, MEG, and the KESM. Electrical and magnetic stimulation of brain tissue are also possible. One of the newest forms of brain stimulation is called optogenetics, which allows researchers to directly stimulate neurons using light pulses.

3. A neuron can be considered the functional unit of the brain, as it receives messages from other neurons and can also send messages. These messages are in the form of an action potential—an electrical signal that starts at the cell body, travels down the axon, and ends at the terminal button. The action potential triggers the release of neurotransmitter molecules that diffuse across the synaptic cleft, attach to receptors on the membrane surface of a receiving cell, and initiate postsynaptic potentials. These potentials are summated at the axon hillock and regulate the neuron's firing rate.

4. The cortex consists of four lobes. The frontal lobes govern motor behavior and problem solving. The temporal lobes are involved with hearing and speech comprehension.

The parietal lobes underlie somatosensory perception and attention, while the occipital lobes are responsible for initial processing of visual information.

5. There are two visual system–processing streams. (1) The dorsal pathway handles information regarding location and motion. (2) The ventral pathway is concerned with object recognition.

6. Visual deficits, or agnosias, result from brain damage to cortical recognition areas. In apperceptive agnosia, patients cannot assemble features together to create a whole object percept. In associative agnosia, patients can perceive an entire object but have difficulty naming or assigning a verbal label to it. Prosopagnosics cannot identify faces and suffer damage to the fusiform gyrus in the temporal lobe.

7. A number of different brain structures underlie attentional processing. These include the RAS, the superior colliculus, the thalamus, the intraparietal sulcus, the cingulate cortex, and the frontal lobes. In the component process model, these areas are functionally specialized but work together to govern attention. In the distributed network models, there is some functional overlap between the areas.

8. Brain damage to these regions can produce attention disorders. In hemispatial neglect, patients have difficulty attending the left side of objects because of damage to the right superior temporal gyrus. ADHD does not have clear-cut physical causes but is heritable. Symptoms include difficulty focusing, impulsiveness, short temper, and difficulties in following plans.

9. The engram is the physical location of a memory. In animal lesion studies, it has been difficult to locate the engram. Greater tissue damage is associated with greater memory loss, but there does not appear to be a single place in the brain where memories are deposited. Memory seems to be laid down in many different parts of the brain, a principle called equipotentiality.

10. Memory circuits in the brain are created by repeated high-frequency stimulation of synapses. This LTP strengthens these synapses so that they are more easily activated in the future.

11. The hippocampus is the site where information gets transferred from working to long-term memory, a process called consolidation. Damage to the hippocampus can result in anterograde amnesia, an inability to consolidate new information.

12. Brain imaging studies show that there are multiple sites in the brain for storage and rehearsal of visual and auditory information.

13. Declarative memories are stored in cortical regions. Episodic memory, in particular, seems to be consolidated by the hippocampus, whereas the limbic cortex mediates semantic memory. The basal ganglia are implicated in procedural knowledge and skill acquisition.

14. Executive dysfunction is a product of frontal lobe damage and is characterized by problems in initiating and terminating actions.

15. Research suggests that there are two separate executive systems. Action schemas are hypothesized to control automatic attention, while the SAS governs the performance of novel tasks that have not yet been automatized.

EXPLORE MORE

Log on to the student study site at **http://study.sagepub.com/friedenberg3e** for electronic flash cards, review quizzes, and a list of web resources to aid you in further exploring the field of cognitive science.

SUGGESTED READINGS

Banich, M. T. (2004). *Cognitive neuroscience and neuropsychology.* Boston, MA: Houghton Mifflin.

Boleyn-Fitzgerald, M. (2010). *Pictures of the mind: What the new neuroscience tells us about who we are.* Upper Saddle River, NJ: FT Press.

Eichenbaum, H. (2002). *The cognitive neuroscience of memory.* New York, NY: Oxford University Press.

Goldberg, E. (2002). *The executive brain: Frontal lobes and the civilized mind.* New York, NY: Oxford University Press.

Posner, M. I. (2004). *Cognitive neuroscience of attention.* New York, NY: Guilford Press.

7

THE NETWORK APPROACH

Mind as a Web

The more the mind receives, the more does it expand.

—Seneca the Younger, 5 BCE

THE NETWORK PERSPECTIVE

The network approach is influenced by the principles of operation and organization of real-world brains. All biological brains are made up of cells called neurons that are wired to one another in a complicated fashion. Activity in one neuron or a set of neurons in turn activates other neurons through these connections. It is this activity that underlies all mental operations—whether it be recognizing your cousin's face, calculating the tip on a restaurant bill, or deciding which law school to attend. **Connectionism** is a field of study in the network approach. Connectionists try to understand how the mind performs these kinds of operations via the construction of an **artificial neural network (ANN),** which is a computer simulation of how populations of actual neurons perform tasks. Semantic and propositional networks constitute another field of study under the network approach. They look at frameworks for how concepts and sentence-like representations might be implemented in networks. At the end of the chapter, we will examine an emerging discipline called network science that analyzes the structure and function of all networks.

The use of ANNs brings up a host of interesting issues in cognitive science. Perhaps the most interesting of these is the issue of knowledge representation. The dominant paradigm in cognitive science is the use of symbols to represent information. These symbols are then represented, stored, and operated on by cognitive or computer processes. In the case of ANNs, information is represented not in the form of a symbol but as a pattern of activation in the network. The classical symbol representational view and the connectionist view also differ in their functional architecture. Traditional notions in cognitive psychology and machine intelligence have processing occurring in stages, whereby information is pulled from one relatively large-scale system and fed to another. In the network approach, by contrast, processing events occur in parallel and are mediated by many small processing units.

In the second part of this chapter, we discuss knowledge representation in a new light. Most ANNs are capable of only limited representation—enough to enable the implementation of tasks such as pattern recognition and classification. These limited representations do not adequately reflect the complexity and the considerable interrelatedness of the human conceptual faculty. To accommodate this limitation, a different kind of network is needed, one that is capable of storing and using knowledge in the broadest sense. Semantic networks, therefore, model how information in a permanent memory store, such as human long-term memory, might be structured. They do this through their use of a rich set of interconnected concept and concept property nodes to represent information.

Whereas ANNs are computation dominant, semantic networks are representation dominant. Researchers in the first discipline are concerned with how to get a system to do something such as recognize a face, learn a language, or solve a math problem. The primary goal in this field is to achieve results: to take some information as input, perform a computational process on it, and produce an output that is judged as being correct. The focus is on functionality. Researchers in the second field are concerned with how information is ordered, how symbols and other types of representations are organized with respect to each other. The focus here is on structure, in particular, how information is stored in our long-term memories and how it is interrelated.

The third and final part of this chapter will look at an emerging paradigm in the sciences, one that is called network science. This field of study shows that networks are not just limited to the traditional fields of cognitive science. Surprisingly, very different networks have been found to act alike. It seems crazy, but the routes airlines fly, the ways by which diseases spread, and the way in which voice data are transmitted on cellular telephone systems all share similarities with the way information is processed in the brain. In this last section, we examine the way other networks operate, and show that these can inform human mental processes like the way the visual system assembles features or how we "brain storm" and think creatively. Network science also gives us new insights into classic issues in cognitive science, such as whether we have a single "self" or a unified center of mental control or are in fact made up of a collection of competing control centers, a topic we took up in the philosophy chapter.

ARTIFICIAL NEURAL NETWORKS

Traditional computers are **serial processors**. They perform one computation at a time. The result of a particular computing unit can then serve as the input to a second computation, whose new result serves as the starting point for yet another computation, and so on (see Figure 7.1).

Figure 7.1 The top panel represents a serial processing architecture. Boxes are processing units, and arrows are data. Each box performs a computation on the input it receives. The result of the computation is transmitted as an output to another processing unit. Unit B cannot start its computation until it receives its input from Unit A. The bottom panel shows a parallel processing architecture. Each processing unit can be connected to every other unit. Computation in the units occurs simultaneously.

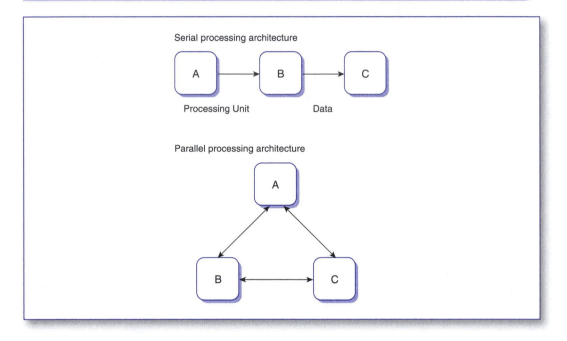

The brain, as well as ANNs, relies on a completely different processing strategy. Here, large numbers of computing units perform their calculations in parallel. One computing unit does not need to wait for another to finish its computation before it can begin its work. As shown in Figure 7.1, these units that operate in parallel are also not limited to receiving inputs from only a single unit: They can receive and process multiple inputs and transmit multiple outputs. This type of architecture is referred to as **parallel distributed processing (PDP)**.

Researchers in the field of artificial intelligence and, more generally, in computer science solve a particular problem by constructing an algorithm, or a procedure for solving it. Every detail and step of the procedure is planned or anticipated ahead of time. One conceptualizes the problem and its solution in terms of symbolic representations and transformations of these symbolic representations. This is referred to as the **knowledge-based approach** to problem solving, and it is used in many artificial intelligence approaches. In contrast, researchers using ANNs are more concerned with the overall behavior of a network. They leave the computational details to the network itself and don't pay much attention to symbolic representations or rules. This is known as the **behavior-based approach** to problem solving.

ANNs are pretty good at solving certain kinds of problems. Among them are problems of classification. These involve producing a learned label for a stimulus (pattern recognition) and assigning stimuli to categories (a form of concept formation). ANNs are also fairly adept at solving control problems—for example, the programming of the movements of a robot arm—and problems of constraint satisfaction—for example, the devising of airline schedules. In these situations, the data are often "noisy," the problem is usually ill defined, and the outcome may be unclear. There are, though, many scenarios in which the problem is well defined and the solution process is clearly understood. In these scenarios, a conventional rule-based system, such as the ones used in artificial intelligence, is preferred.

But let's get back to the issue of symbols. Why is it apparently *ok* for connectionists to ignore them? After all, it seems impossible that any kind of problem could be solved without concepts being represented in some fashion. The answer is that representations are inherent in ANNs but do not exist in them in the form of symbols. They exist in most networks as a pattern of activation among the network's elements. This is known as a **distributed representation**. To illustrate, the idea of "banana" in a connectionist model might be represented by the simultaneous activity of the different elements—or nodes A, B, and C—and the connections among them. However, having said this, some ANNs do represent concepts via activity in single nodes. In these networks, activity in node A alone would represent, let's say, "apple." This is a form of **local representation**. In either case, though, we need not employ the idea of a symbol, such as a letter, to stand for the concept. The concept is instead represented as the activity of the nodes or node. We have already discussed both types of these representations and how they might code for visual objects in the neuroscience chapter, where we referred to them as distributed coding and specificity coding.

One advantage of neural nets is that they are capable of learning. That is, they can adaptively change their responses over time as they are presented with new information. However, it should be noted that ANNs are not the only form of simulated cognition capable of learning. Learning is also evidenced in machines that use symbolic methods. The acquisition of new information or a new skill usually requires repetition. For example, a child learning the multiplication tables will repeat them over and over again to himself or herself. If he or she makes a mistake, he or she must correct himself or herself and then repeat the new information. Neural networks operate on these same principles. They learn over a series of trials to perform a task or to come up with an answer to a question. If they produce a wrong answer, the correct answer can be "shown" to them. This feedback is then used to adjust the performance of the network until it produces the correct answer.

CHARACTERISTICS OF ARTIFICIAL NEURAL NETWORKS

Real neural networks exist in the brain in the form of neurons and the connections between them. The artificial networks constructed by connectionists exist only as software simulations that are run on a computer. Each neuron, or basic computing unit in an artificial network, is represented as a **node**, and the connections between nodes are represented as **links**. A node, if it is stimulated, sends out a signal, represented as an activation value, which runs along the link that connects it to another node or nodes. A node follows a set of internal rules that "decide" if it is to fire. The simplest of these rules is this: The node fires if the input it receives exceeds a threshold value. If the input is greater than or equal to the threshold, it fires. If the input is less than the threshold, it does not.

Links in a neural network have **weights**, which specify the strength of the link. A weight can be positive, negative, or zero. The numeric value of a weight runs between −1.0 and 1.0: The higher the numeric value, the heavier the weight. The net output of a unit is its activation value multiplied by the weight of the relevant link. So, for example, a unit with an activation value of 1 passing along a link that has a weight of 0.5 will have a net output of 0.5. It will positively stimulate the node to which it is connected by a factor of 0.5. The greater the value of a node's net output in the positive direction, the more likely it is that the nodes it is connected to will fire.

A unit with an activation value of 1 passing along a link that has a weight of −0.5 would have a net output of −0.5, which would negatively stimulate whatever nodes it feeds to. The greater the value of a node's net output in the negative direction, the less likely it is that the nodes it is connected to will fire. A negative output, thus, serves the function of dampening or shutting down the activity of other nodes. This is similar to the role of inhibition in biological networks, whereby one neuron can "turn off" or slow down another. The output of any node that is part of a link that has a zero weighting is of course zero, meaning that there is no effect on any downstream nodes. If a node receives two or more outputs from other nodes, it takes these outputs and, in effect, summates them to determine whether it should fire. Figure 7.2 shows a simple neural network with activation values, weights, and net outputs.

Figure 7.2 A simple neural network. Activation values are shown inside each node. Weights are indicated on the links and net outputs at the endpoint of each connection. Node A has an activation value of 2 and a weight of 0.6. Its net output is, thus, 1.2. Node B's activation value is 1 and its weight is −0.3, yielding a net output of −0.3. These outputs are summated at node C so that it has an activation value of +0.9. The activation value of node C multiplied by its weight of 0.4 produces an output of +0.36.

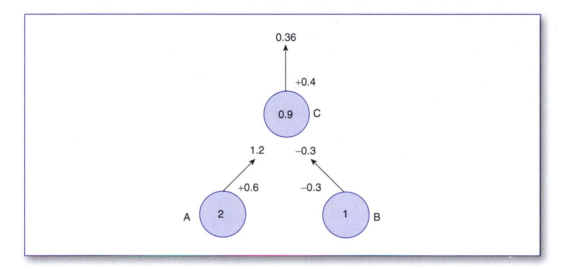

EARLY CONCEPTIONS OF NEURAL NETWORKS

In 1943, Warren McCulloch and Walter Pitts were the first researchers to propose how biological networks might function. They made a few simple assumptions about how neurons might operate. They assumed that each neuron had a binary output—that is, it could either send out a signal, corresponding to its being "on," or not send out a signal, corresponding to its being in an "off" state. Whether or not a neuron would fire was determined by a threshold value. The weights of the connections between neurons, in their model, were additionally assumed to be at a fixed value. Networks operating under these rules are capable of computing simple logical operations, such as *or, and,* and *not.* A neuron programmed to compute a *not* operation will fire if it receives activation at or above the threshold. It won't fire if it receives inhibitory input. Digital computers of the sort that sit on our desks perform calculations that are based on these simple logical functions. This means that a neural network capable of performing these calculations can in theory do anything a digital computer can.

Donald O. Hebb (1949) was the first person to propose how changes among neurons might explain learning. According to the Hebb rule, when one cell repeatedly activates another, the strength of the connection between the two cells is increased. In this fashion, pathways or circuits among neurons are formed. These circuits are believed to be the neural foundation of learning and memory. Imagine being at a party and trying to remember someone's name. How would you do it? Imagine that at the party you are trying to remember a phone number you had been given. If you could not write the number down, you would repeat it over and over again—a process called rehearsal. Each repetition would correspond to a new activation of the circuit, strengthening it further. The circuit itself, once strong enough, would represent the telephone number. Retrieval of the number at a later date would then be equivalent to a reactivation of the circuit.

Hebb (1949) defined two types of cell groupings. A **cell assembly** is a small group of neurons that repeatedly stimulate one another. A **phase sequence** is a group of connected cell assemblies that fire synchronously or nearly synchronously (see Figure 7.3). If a cell

Figure 7.3 A phase sequence consisting of cell assemblies.

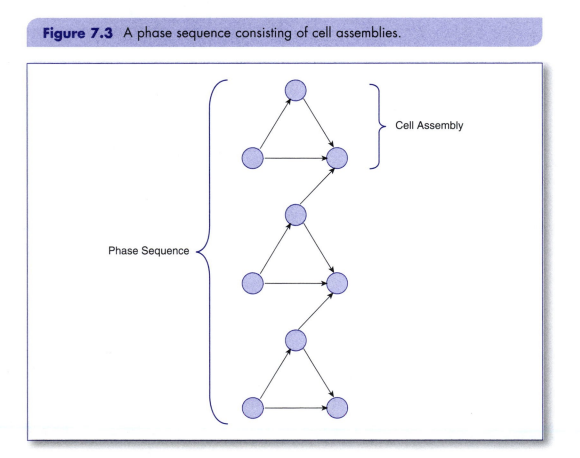

assembly coded for simple perceptual qualities, such as "red" or "round," then these qualities could become linked so as to form a phase sequence during learning and code for a higher order concept, such as "apple."

Beginning in the 1950s, research on neural nets focused less on logical operations and more on mimicking real biological functions. An artificial nervous system called the **perceptron** was introduced (Rosenblatt, 1958). Perceptrons are neural nets designed to detect and recognize patterned information about the world, store this information, and use it in some fashion. Perceptrons are also characterized by their ability to learn from experience: They can modify their connection strengths by comparing their actual output with a desired output called **the teacher**. The ANN networks discussed in subsequent parts of this chapter constitute different types of perceptrons.

The earliest perceptron was an artificial retina called the "Mark I" (Rosenblatt, 1958). This network could recognize simple visual patterns, such as vertical and horizontal lines. It was capable, with training, of producing a desired output for each different type of visual pattern. The first perceptrons were quite simple. Each contained a single layer of input units or an input and an output layer (see Figure 7.4). The limitations of these fledgling perceptrons soon become clear. A major flaw was their inability to distinguish among certain patterns (Minsky & Papert, 1969). This was in part due to their relatively weak computing power. A single layer or two layers and the connections between them do not provide for much in the way of complexity and flexibility. The solution, of course, was to build more complicated networks.

BACK PROPAGATION AND CONVERGENT DYNAMICS

In a three-layer network, the computing units or nodes are organized into three distinct groups. A representation of the stimulus is presented to the **input layer**. These units send signals to a **hidden layer**, which in turn feeds activation energy to an **output layer**. The output layer generates a representation of the response. Figure 7.5 depicts a three-layer

Figure 7.4 An example of an early perceptron with two layers. Notice that each input unit maps onto every output unit.

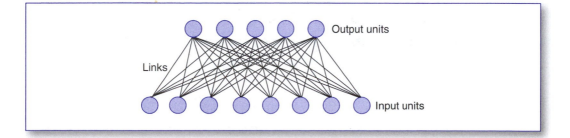

Figure 7.5 A three-layered neural network with input, hidden, and output units.

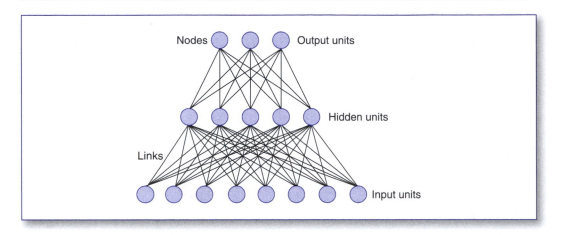

network. For a detailed description of a three-layer network that learns through back propagation, read about NETtalk, discussed later in this chapter.

Here's how a three-layer network designed to recognize letters works: The capital letter *A* activates the nodes in the input layer. These nodes send activation energy via links to the hidden layer. The nodes in the hidden layer send signals via their links to nodes in the output layer. The pattern of activation in the output layer is the network's initial response to the letter. This response is then compared with the target response, represented by the teacher. The difference between the actual and the desired outputs, the **error signal**, then feeds back to the output layer. The network uses the error signal to modify the weights of the links. Figure 7.6 shows these different steps that are part of the training of a three-layer perceptron. The modified weights allow the network (the next time it "sees" the letter *A*) to generate a response that is closer to the desired one. After repeated presentations of the stimulus in the presence of feedback, the network is able to produce the target response. It has, in effect, learned to recognize the letter. This kind of training based on error feed-back is called the **generalized delta rule** or the **back-propagation** learning model.

NETtalk: An Example of a Back-Propagation Artificial Neural Network

NETtalk is an ANN designed to read written English (Sejnowski & Rosenberg, 1986). It is presented with written letters of the alphabet. Its output is the correct pronunciation of the sounds represented by the letters, which is then fed to a speech synthesizer for the production of the sounds. Unlike programs that existed at the time it was developed,

Figure 7.6 Steps in the training of a three-layered network using the back-propagation learning model.

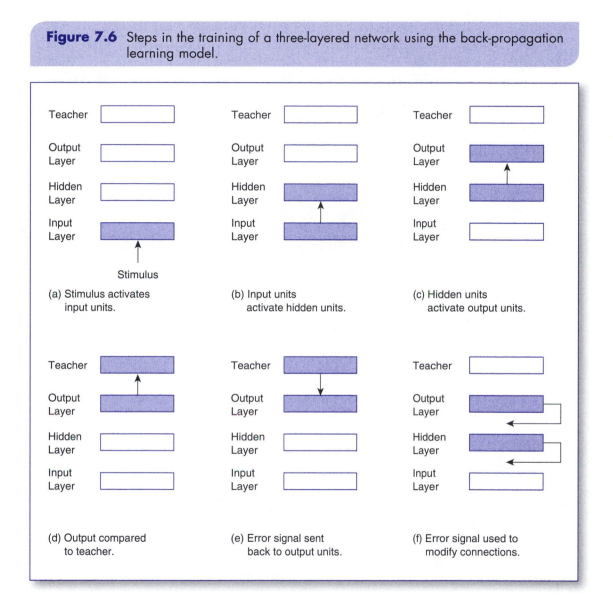

(a) Stimulus activates input units.

(b) Input units activate hidden units.

(c) Hidden units activate output units.

(d) Output compared to teacher.

(e) Error signal sent back to output units.

(f) Error signal used to modify connections.

NETtalk actually learned to make correct pronunciations after it had been supplied a given number of examples. Although the network could not understand what it was reading, it serves as a good demonstration of what networks of its kind are capable of and how they can serve as models of human learning.

The NETtalk system consists of three layers. The input layer has seven groups, each containing 29 individual units. The overall activity of these 29 units specifies one letter.

NETtalk, thus, processes seven letters at a time. It focuses, though, on the fourth and middle letters of these seven. It is these target letters that the network attempts to pronounce. The other surrounding letters serve as a context and to help disambiguate the correct pronunciation, due to the fact that in English the sound of any given letter depends heavily on the adjacent letters. Figure 7.7 shows a diagrammatic representation of the network.

The input units next connect to a hidden layer of 80 nodes, which effect a partial recoding of the input data. These in turn connect to 26 nodes in the output layer, whose pattern of activation represents the system's initial response to the letters. This response is, in effect, the network's first guess at pronouncing the target letter. The guessed pronunciation

Figure 7.7 A diagrammatic representation of the NETtalk network, capable of converting written English text into speech.

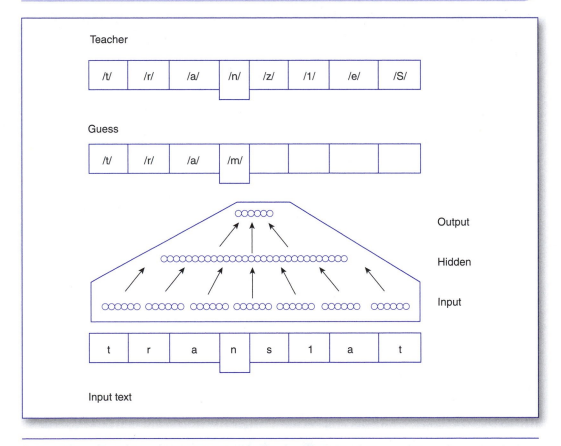

Source: Sejnowski and Rosenberg (1986). Reprinted with permission.

is then compared with the correct response, specified by a teacher. Weights are then adjusted using the back-propagation algorithm. Finally, the "window" or read head that viewed the seven letters at a time would move one letter to the right, to process the next letter in the text. The total number of weighted links that directly connect one node to another in NETtalk is 18,829, so this is a fairly large network by most standards.

How does NETtalk perform? After 50 passes through a sample text, which corresponded to about 250,000 letter-to-pronunciation pairings, it achieved a 95% accuracy rate. When the network was then tested on a new sample text without further training, it performed at 78% accuracy. This relatively impressive performance on the new text demonstrates the network's capacity for generalization; the network had extended its abilities to new words and letter combinations. NETtalk was also found to perform well after simulated damage. The simulated damage was in the form of changes made to the weights: Every weight was changed to a new random value that was within some prespecified range of the old value. When the randomized values were less than 65% of the average, performance was hardly affected—showing that the network is resistant to degradation.

EVALUATING THE CONNECTIONIST APPROACH

Advantages

The connectionist approach has many strengths. The most important one is the similarity between network models and real-life neural networks—what is termed **biological plausibility** (Stillings et al., 1995). This plausibility can be demonstrated in three fundamental ways. First, artificial networks share general structural and functional correlates with biological networks. Second, and as pointed out previously, artificial networks, like their biological cousins, are capable of learning. Third, artificial networks react to damage in the same way that human brains do. In this section, these advantages and other advantages of networks are discussed in depth.

Many of the elements of artificial networks have their counterparts in biological networks. The nodes are equivalent to neurons, whereas the links are analogous to axonal and dendritic connections. The functioning of constructed neural networks is also very biological. At a microscopic scale, the decision rules that specify when and how an individual node fires are based on neuron physiology. At a macroscopic scale, the parallel, distributed processing of connectionist networks is also found in the brain.

Learning in connectionist models takes place via the adjustment of the weights of the links between nodes. Work in neurophysiology shows that this process, at least in simulation, is not too far off from what happens in real brains. Recall from the preceding chapter our discussion of synaptic plasticity and how it is mediated by long-term potentiation. If two cells in a circuit are simultaneously active, the synapse between them is strengthened. This increase in synaptic strength corresponds to a numerical increase in the weight of a connection between nodes in an ANN.

A third argument in support of the biological plausibility of connectionist models is the way they respond to damage. Neural networks demonstrate **graceful degradation**. This is a gradual decrease in performance with increased damage to the network. In graceful degradation, small amounts of damage engender only small reductions in performance, whereas greater damage produces correspondingly larger deficits. Human patients who have sustained brain damage show evidence of the same phenomenon. Graceful degradation is a property of a parallel computing architecture. If some nodes are destroyed, others can "take over." In other words, the network can adapt to the damage by calling on its distributed function across the existing nodes and links. Of course, this advantage holds only for nets with distributed representations. Those networks with localized representations, such as the adaptive resonance theory network, are more subject to failure in the event of damage.

Connectionist networks display two other interesting "psychological" phenomena: (1) interference and (2) generalization (Green & Vervaeke, 1996). **Interference** refers to instances in which two sets of information that are similar in content interfere with each other. If a student were studying Spanish and Italian at the same time, he or she might forget words in one language that are similar in sound to words in the other language. Small networks trained to learn large numbers of patterns show signs of interference: They have difficulty distinguishing similar patterns. **Generalization** is represented by the ability to apply a learned rule to a novel situation. If one assumed that any animal that had wings was a bird and then saw an animal for the first time that also had wings and called it a bird, he or she would be generalizing. Rumelhart, McClelland, and PDP Research Group (1986) trained a network to learn the past tenses of verbs. The network learned to conjugate new verbs. It was able to produce *wept* for *weep* because it had been trained to associate *slept* with *sleep*. The network was capable of bona fide generalization.

Problems and Disadvantages

We have looked at the many advantages of the connectionist approach, but it is also limited, in a number of respects. What at first seems like its primary strength, biological plausibility, should also be viewed as problematic. If we make a more detailed comparison of ANNs and actual brains, we discover a number of significant differences. First, real neurons are massively parallel—they exchange signals with thousands of others. It is not yet possible to simulate parallel processing of this magnitude; such processing would simply require too many nodes and connections and too much processing power. It is likely that some of the emergent characteristics of the brain arise from massive parallelism. Until we are able to build ANNs of this complexity, we may not be able to understand these emergent characteristics.

Second, most networks, as stated earlier, show a **convergent dynamics** approach. The activity of such a network eventually dies down and reaches a stable state. This is not the case for brain activity. Real neural networks are oscillatory and chaotic—their states fluctuate over time and do not settle. Neural activity in the hypothalamus, for example, is oscillatory. Regarding this type of dynamic, it is a fascinating but difficult question to determine where in the network a representation exists. In convergent networks, the presentation of a stimulus pattern reliably elicits the trained response. This response is the network's distributed representation of the correct answer in the form of a pattern of activation among nodes. But in oscillatory and chaotic networks, there is no such representation. The network, because it is constantly changing, has not formed any specific pattern of activation that can be linked to a stimulus. Representations in these systems might correspond to more global characteristics, such as the frequency or phase of the network's activity.

Dawson (1998) points out an additional problem. He discusses Elman's (1990) recurrent-type network, which has difficulty analyzing inputs that are staggered in time. Dawson (1998) speculates that the problem lies either in the architecture of the network itself or in the learning rule. In the case of Elman's network, it turned out to be the latter, because in instances in which a new rule was implemented, the network was adequate for the task (Kremer, 1995). We see here another difficulty, which is that networks may have inadequate learning rules. The error correction procedures for adjusting weights that are currently in use represent only one of many possible ways of training a network. A subject for future research would be the exploration of alternate learning methodologies.

One specific problem that arises in network learning is the **stability–plasticity dilemma**. It states that a network should be plastic enough to store novel input patterns; at the same time, it should be stable enough to prevent previously encoded patterns from being erased (Grossberg, 1987). This apparent conflict is analogous to the phenomenon of psychological interference, discussed previously. The fact that ANNs show evidence of being caught in this dilemma is useful because it may offer some insights into human interference. But it becomes a real problem when one is attempting to implement artificial networks. **Catastrophic interference** occurs in instances in which a network has learned to recognize a set of patterns and then is called on to learn a new set (French, 2001). The learning of the new set modifies the weights of the network in such a way that the original set is forgotten. In other words, the newly learned patterns suddenly and completely ("catastrophically") erase the network's memory of the original patterns. A variety of solutions to the problem have been proposed, ranging from the introduction of "novelty vectors" to a reduction in the internal overlap of representations, to pretraining the network with random samples of patterns (French, 1992; Kortge, 1990; McRae & Hetherington, 1993).

We should discuss learning a bit further. In **supervised networks**, a "teacher" or a training pattern is necessary for the network to learn. But where does this teacher come from? Humans and other animals learn in many instances in which no right answer is provided, or in which the answer is less accurately provided (Barto, Sutton, & Anderson, 1983). Also, there is no evidence that biological networks feed an error signal back to "previous" units to modify connection strengths, as in the back-propagation model (Bechtel & Abrahamsen, 1991).

This is simply a convenient engineering solution to the problem but fails to address how an analogous process in actual brains might occur.

SEMANTIC NETWORKS: MEANING IN THE WEB

There is another class of network models that have many features in common with neural nets. Nodes, links, thresholds, and summation of inputs also characterize these networks. They are **semantic networks**. But in semantic networks, each node has a specific meaning. Semantic networks, therefore, employ the local representation of concepts. Semantic networks have been adopted primarily by cognitive psychologists as a way to explain the organization and retrieval of information in long-term memory. In this section, we will discuss the characteristics of such networks, drawing on experimental results from cognitive psychology.

One motivation for studying semantic networks centers on representational capacity. The distributed representations formed in convergent ANNs are very simple and fail to capture the richness of human conceptual capacity. Even if it turned out that humans store concepts as distributed patterns in a neural circuit, it would be unclear how this kind of storage might account for the complexity of our concepts. When we think of a concept such as "dog," we are doing much more than coming up with a label. Our concept of "dog" goes beyond pattern recognition to include semantic content—what dogs look like, what they do, what our own experience of dogs is, and so on—and is intimately tied up with other concepts we possess. Semantic networks allow us to represent and understand these more complex aspects of concepts.

Characteristics of Semantic Networks

In semantic network models, a node's activity can spread outward along links to activate other nodes. These nodes can then activate still others—a process called **spreading activation**. An assumption of some models is that activation energy decreases with increasing distance, since it is believed that the activation energy encounters resistance as it passes through succeeding links and nodes. This means that spreading activation may lose strength as it travels outward from its point of origin. Another characteristic of these networks is that the distance between two nodes is determined by their degree of relatedness. Concepts such as "automobile" and "truck" are semantically related and, hence, fairly close to each other, whereas concepts such as "automobile" and "flower" are less related and are farther apart. It is, therefore, easier to activate the "truck" node via the "automobile" node than it is to activate the "flower" node in this way.

Spreading activation is thought to underlie retrieval of information from long-term memory. For example, suppose a test question in history class asks for the names of major western European nations. While you were studying, you had memorized these nations in several ways:

on the basis of their geographic locations, whether they fought each other in wars, how related their languages are, and so on. You start by naming Germany, then Italy. At the end, you realize you've left out a country but can't think which it is. Finally, it comes to you. You remember that the country is France—because while you were studying, you realized that France and Germany fought each other during the two world wars. Although you were not able to retrieve France on the basis of the Mediterranean characteristics it shares with Italy, you were able to retrieve it on the basis of its historical relation with Germany. This underscores an important principle of effective studying: It is best to associate a concept with as many other related concepts as possible, to ensure a higher likelihood of retrieval. In this way, there exist a greater number of alternative pathways that lead to a given node. If one nodal connection fails to activate the target item, spreading activation will ensure that some other pathway does. These alternate associations that facilitate recall are also called **retrieval cues**. Figure 7.8 illustrates how a semantic network might represent knowledge of western European countries.

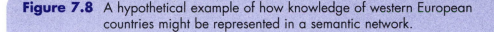

Figure 7.8 A hypothetical example of how knowledge of western European countries might be represented in a semantic network.

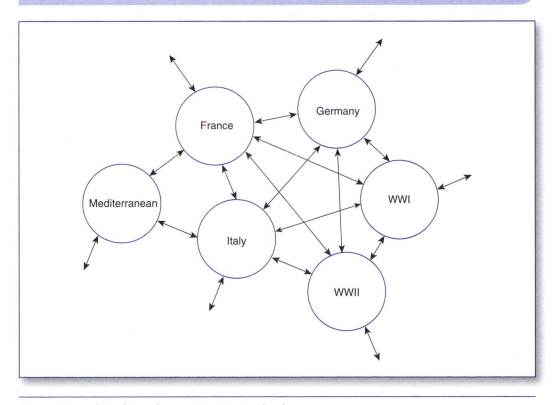

Source: Sejnowski and Rosenberg (1986). Reprinted with permission.

An important characteristic of semantic networks is **priming**. In priming, the processing of a stimulus is facilitated by the network's prior exposure to a related stimulus. A study by Meyer and Schvaneveldt (1971) demonstrates this phenomenon. The participants in their study were presented with pairs of letter strings. Each letter string was either an actual word or a nonsense word. Participants were asked to push a button when they encountered actual words. The button push recorded how long it took them to respond. If both words in a pair were meaningful and related, the participants were faster to respond correctly to the second word in the pair. So if the first word was *nurse* and the second *doctor*, responses were faster than if the first word was *nurse* and the second *butter*. The explanation goes as follows. The "nurse" node in long-term memory becomes activated first. Through spreading activation, it activates other, semantically related, nodes, such as "doctor." A short time later, when the participant's response to *doctor* is required, the response time is reduced because that node is already partially activated. This technique can be used to map out the structures of semantic networks. The larger the priming effect, the closer together the relevant nodes should be (McNamara, 1992).

A Hierarchical Semantic Network

A classic study by Collins and Quillian in 1969 suggests that semantic networks may have a **hierarchical organization**, with different levels representing concepts ranging from the most abstract down to the most concrete. They used a **sentence verification** task. Participants were asked to respond to individual sentences that appeared on a computer screen. If they judged a sentence to be true, they hit one button. If they judged it to be false, they hit another. Examples of true sentences were "A canary is a bird" and "A canary is an animal." Response times were recorded.

Collins and Quillian (1969) theorized that a correct response to one of these sentences required overlap of spreading activation. To know whether a canary is a bird would require the activation of both a "canary" node and a "bird" node. Recognition of both concepts would activate these nodes. Activation would then radiate outward through the network from each node until individual units' activations would mutually affect one another. When the activation of these two nodes overlaps, the participant knows that the two are related and can then confirm the sentence. If the nodes have a close semantic relation, they should be in proximity to each other in the network, and responses will be fast because spreading activation will have less distance to cover. If the nodes are less related, the distance between them will be greater and response times will be longer.

Based on the set of reaction times they obtained in the study, Collins and Quillian (1969) sketched out a hypothetical memory structure for knowledge of animals. This is shown in Figure 7.9. The hierarchical nature of the network is immediately clear. The concept "animals" and its properties—such as "eat food," "breathe," and "have skin"—are at the top of the hierarchy. Because the idea of animals is abstract and encompasses all known types of animals, *animals* constitute a **superordinate** category. At the next lower level, we have examples of classes of animals—such as "birds," "cats," and "dogs"—accompanied by nodes corresponding to their characteristics. For birds, these would be "can fly" and "lay eggs." Because these different classes of animal are at a moderate level of specificity, they are **ordinate** categories. At the bottom of the hierarchy are nodes that are even more concrete, corresponding to exact species of animals; these animal species are **subordinate** categories. Properties of these animal species are also at this same level. A node corresponding to "canary" would have links at the subordinate level connecting it to "can sing" and "is yellow."

Figure 7.9 The hierarchical semantic network proposed by Collins and Quillian.

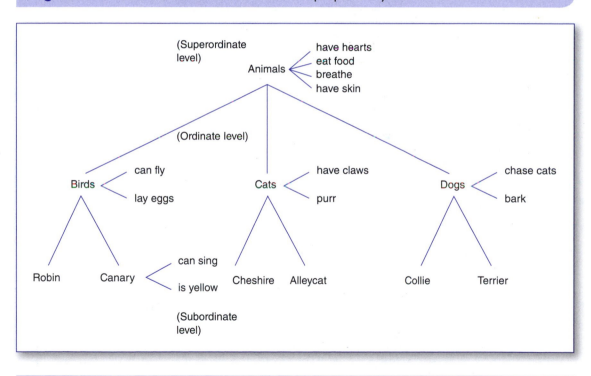

Source: Collins, A. M., & Quillian, M. R., Retrieval time from semantic memory in *Journal of Verbal Learning and Verbal Behavior, 8*, pp. 240–247, copyright © 1969, with permission from Elsevier.

Figure 7.10 depicts a graph of the reaction times that led to the models being proposed. Responses for which spreading activation occurs entirely within a level were quite fast. It took participants about 1,000 milliseconds, on average, to confirm that "A canary is a canary." In this instance, no effective spreading activation is required; the statement is self-referential, and only the canary node is active. To confirm "A canary is a bird" took slightly longer—about 1,200 milliseconds. Presumably, the longer time is owing to the fact that both the canary and the bird nodes must be activated and spreading activation must travel along a link, between the subordinate and ordinate levels. Verification of the statement "A canary is an animal" took even longer. In this instance, the canary and animal nodes are activated and spreading activation must travel along two links, from the subordinate level to the superordinate level.

Figure 7.10 A graph depicting the results of the Collins and Quillian experiment.

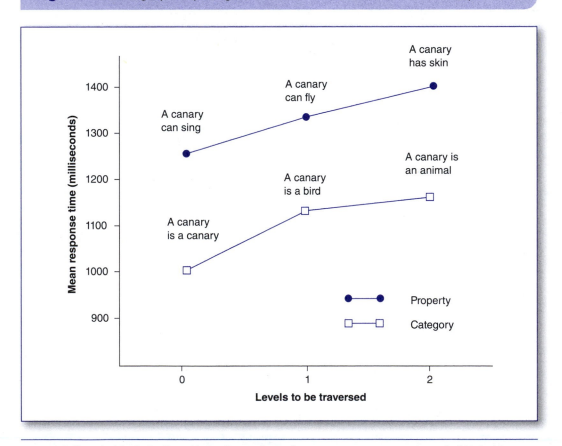

Source: Collins, A. M., & Quillian, M. R., Retrieval time from semantic memory in *Journal of Verbal Learning and Verbal Behavior, 8,* pp. 240–247, copyright © 1969, with permission from Elsevier.

Finally, you will notice that response times for property statements follow this same function. But the verification of these statements is apt to take even longer. Sentences like "A canary can sing" were quickly verified, because the "can sing" node that defines canary properties is at the same level as the "canary" node. Sentences like "A canary can fly" were verified less quickly, because the property node "can fly" is attached to the "bird" node at the ordinate level. In general, property statements take more time because activation must spread from property nodes to concept nodes—within a level, as well as between concept nodes that occupy different levels.

Evaluating the Hierarchical Model

The hierarchical model is intuitively appealing but fails to account for several findings (McCloskey & Glucksberg, 1978). Participants are faster to make the correct response to "A dog is an animal" than to "A dog is a mammal," even though "animal" is farther away from "dog" in a hierarchical scheme. Evidently, people tend to think of dogs more as animals than as mammals, even though "mammals" are a subset of animals and should have greater proximity to the concept of dog than does "animals." Also, the sentence "A robin is a bird" is responded to more quickly than "An ostrich is a bird," even though the two sentences are equivalent and ostriches and robins are both subordinate to the bird category. This suggests that some birds are more "typical" than others and that concepts may be represented by **prototypes** that represent generic or idealized versions of those concepts. If this were the case, then the network would need restructuring, and the "robin" node would have to be moved so that it was closer to "bird" than was the "ostrich" node. These results imply that the hierarchical organization of the sort seen in the Collins and Quillian model may be overly contrived and may represent only one of the ways in which we organize concepts.

A final criticism of the hierarchical model has to do with the principle of **cognitive economy**. This principle states that nodes should not have to be coded for more times than is necessary. Collins and Quillian (1969) attempted to preserve cognitive economy by placing property nodes only at their appropriate levels in the hierarchy. For instance, "can fly" is positioned as a property of birds only, even though it could be linked to the canary node and to nodes representing every other kind of bird as well. The advantage of cognitive economy is obvious. It eliminates redundancy and frees up resources in a memory system. But research has found no difference in the response times for the sentences "A bird has feathers" and "A canary has feathers." So the property "has feathers" seems to be attached to our concept of "canary" as well as to that of "birds." Like the network hierarchy, cognitive economy seems to work better in principle than in reality.

Propositional Semantic Networks

Semantic networks of the sort described above are fine for representing simple factual properties of objects in the world. They can represent a category relationship, which is depicted by an "**isa**" **link**. The connection between the "bird" and "animal" nodes would be this type of link, as "A bird *isa* animal." They can also represent a property-type relationship with a "**hasa**" **link**. The "bird" and "feathers" nodes would be connected by a "hasa" link, since "A bird *hasa* feathers." But how would we set up a network to stand for more complicated relationships among concepts? What would the network that could encompass the sentence "The dog chased the cat" look like?

The answer is a new class of network, designed to code for propositions. John Anderson has developed such a network as part of his ACT* model of cognition, which was discussed in the cognitive psychology chapter. ACT* is, thus, a **hybrid model**: It specifies how multiple memory systems interact and how explicit knowledge is represented. A proposition is the smallest unit of knowledge that can be verified—that is, proved to be either true or false. Propositional networks allow for a greater variety of relationships among concepts, including actions. Figure 7.11 shows a propositional network that might underlie someone's understanding of his or her friend Bob. Each ellipse denotes a proposition. The proposition is defined by the arrow links that radiate away from it and point to concepts.

Figure 7.11   An example of a propositional network (after Anderson & Lebiere, 1998).

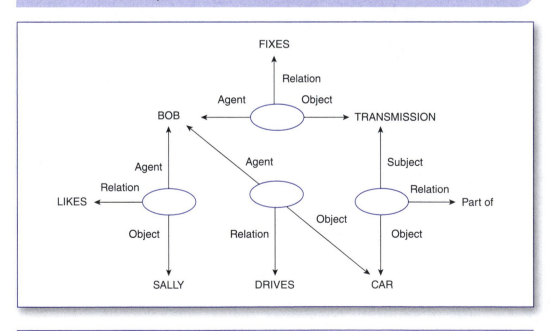

Source: Anderson and Lebiere (1998).

There are different links that stand for different parts of the proposition. An **agent link** specifies the subject of the proposition, the one performing some action. An **object link** denotes the object or thing to which the action is directed. The **relation link** characterizes the relation between the agent and the object. The proposition "Bob likes Sally" would, thus, have "Bob" as its agent, "Sally" as the object, and "likes" as the relation.

Anderson's ACT* model can also account for the specific memories each of us has as part of our experience, episodic knowledge, and traditional factual world knowledge. His model does this via its creation of two classes of nodes. A **type** node corresponds to an entire category. The node that corresponds to "dogs" in general is a type node. **Token** nodes correspond to specific instances or specific items within a category. The node that represents "Fido," where Fido is the name of your dog, is a token node. In this way, the network can code for general world knowledge as well as personal memories.

Evaluating Semantic Networks

Semantic network models can be implemented as computer simulations and then put to the test to see if they account for humanlike memory processes. This has been done, and although many of the simulations can reproduce aspects of performance in limited domains, there is no associative network that successfully simulates all of human memory.

A phenomenon that presents a challenge to these network models is called the **T.O.T. phenomenon,** the acronym standing for "tip of the tongue." Try to recall the name of the navigational device used by sailors that measures the positions of the stars. You may find yourself frustrated in trying to recall the word, as many people can come up with the first letter and the number of syllables but not the word itself (Brown, 1991). A person who gets stuck trying to remember the word is, in a manner of speaking, in the vicinity of the node or network that codes for the word because he or she has some knowledge of the word. He or she also presumably has activated nodes that are in proximity to that of the concept in question because he or she is devoting a great deal of time and effort to recalling the word. So why doesn't spreading activation activate the appropriate node? Semantic networks cannot easily explain these sorts of retrieval blocks. By the way, if you couldn't get it, the word is *sextant*.

The phenomenon opposite to the T.O.T. phenomenon is the situation in which we can successfully retrieve an item from memory despite the fact that there are no close connections between retrieval cues and the target. Reisberg (2001) gives a good example when he asks us to think of the node that represents "water." Because water is an eminently familiar concept, it has connections to many others. The water node, thus, ought to have multiple links that radiate outward toward other nodes—a high **degree of fan**. In contrast, the concept "xylophone" has a low degree of fan, at least for most people, as we don't often think about this musical instrument. Assuming that the water node has links to 100 other nodes—probably a conservative estimate—then spreading activation would, in just one step, activate all 100. Assuming that each of these 100 nodes is, in turn, connected to 100 other nodes, then 10,000 (100 × 100) nodes would be activated in a memory search after only two steps. The number of activated nodes increases tremendously with increasing numbers of steps. This process is inefficient from a computational standpoint. It is also counterintuitive. It certainly doesn't feel as though we think of a million or more things when we are trying to remember the capital of Texas.

A solution to the problem of excessive activation would be the implementation of an inhibitory network. Here, the links are inhibitory, so activation of a given node causes it to dampen the activity of its neighbors. In this model, the greater a node's activity, the more it will inhibit the nodes to which it is immediately linked. Nodes that receive several inputs are more highly activated and, thus, stand out in the crowd since they can suppress their neighbors more powerfully. Concepts with multiple inputs are probably the ones we are searching for because these input pathways are what are activated during the retrieval process. To go back to our earlier example, if we are trying to remember "France," this node ought to stand out among the others in an inhibitory network. This is because it is activated in two ways: (1) on the basis of the "commonly taught languages" path and (2) on the basis of the "fought with Germany" path. Inhibitory networks, thus, dampen activity in nodes that are unlikely candidates in a memory search and increase activity in nodes that are likely candidates.

One of the nice things about semantic networks is that the search for an item takes place automatically. All one needs to do is hear a question, and the answer seems to pop into one's head. The relative ease with which we recall, at least much of the time, is in accord with the idea of spreading activation. The question triggers nodes that are near the desired node; activation then spreads across the network until the target item is sufficiently activated. But, as we all know, recall is not always this easy. Sometimes, as in the T.O.T. phenomenon, we must expend effort trying to remember something. If somebody asked you what you did on your last birthday and it didn't immediately come to mind, you might engage in a **guided search**—one governed by intelligence and reasoning. You would think of your friends and members of your family who might have been at the party, what kinds of presents you received, and where the party was held. All these could serve as retrieval cues or associated nodes and, as such, are elements in the network. But they weren't triggered automatically. Instead, you had to willfully and deliberately reconstruct what happened on your last birthday, based on what you know of your past birthdays in general. This type of **reconstructive memory** is used quite often and has been shown to be influenced by environmental cues, such as how the question is phrased (Loftus, 1979). But the important point here is that reconstructive memory constitutes a separate process of retrieving items—one that does not rely on spreading activation and the inherent, automatic characteristics of the network.

NETWORK SCIENCE

Recent years have seen the development of a new area of study called **network science** (Watts, 2003). Scientists, mathematicians, and others in this area have begun to explore the way in which complex networks operate. A network in this view is considered as any collection of interconnected and interacting parts. Like cognitive science, which is made up of investigators from multiple disciplines, network science is also interdisciplinary. Investigators come from different areas such as mathematics, physics, finance, management, and sociology. This is because networks are everywhere, as electromagnetic fields, stock markets, companies, and societies.

Contemporary network scientists additionally consider networks as dynamical systems that are *doing* things. Power grids distribute power, companies manufacture products, and brains think. All these are networks in action. The structure of networks can also change over time. New links can form and new organizations emerge. The new science of networks investigates not just network structure but also its function. Researchers in this field are interested in the anatomy of networks, how they operate, and how these operations evolve and change.

Network scientists consider networks as abstract structures, and to some extent, they can disregard their specific context. Whether the network is a brain, a traffic system, or the Internet, in some sense, it doesn't matter. That is, because there are commonalities these networks share. In other words, all networks share some universal mechanisms of action. For instance, most known networks exhibit a critical point where activity propagates suddenly through the entire system. It seems amazing that cars on the road and employees in a company should act in the same way, but, because they are both elements in interconnected relationships, they can.

It is also important to note that although networks do share some characteristics, they don't act exactly the same. In some cases, the nature of the nodes that make up the network produce different behavior. A neuron in the brain acts differently from a consumer in a society. So we need to acknowledge that there are both universal and particular features to networks. In the following sections, we describe aspects of network science and how they apply to cognition. Friedenberg (2009) provides a more detailed treatment of these topics.

Centrality

One of the most important questions concerning networks is how activity in them is coordinated. A network might have one or perhaps several centers that perform this function. This is known as the issue of centrality. If there is a "leader" or part of the network that receives information, evaluates it, and issues commands, then centrality is accounted for. Many examples of such systems exist. Computers have a central processing unit, armies have generals, and political organizations can be run by a dictator. The more interesting case is how networks without any such center achieve this kind of coordinated action.

This question has particular relevance for the human mind. For many years, it was believed that the brain must have a central coordinating agency, a center where everything comes together. This was the notion of the Cartesian theater that we addressed in the philosophy chapter. This center begs the question though, because if we allow for a homunculus, then we must explain how it coordinates. If we cannot, we are stuck with the familiar infinite regress of little men inside little men.

When we introspect, it seems that we have a single unified self. This seems to run contrary to the known physical evidence that activity is occurring throughout many separated brain areas simultaneously. Some have suggested that consciousness must be the mechanism by which this distributed activity is unified into a single form of awareness. If we could figure out the centrality issue, we might also determine the answer to the mystery of consciousness. Candidate explanations for this include Dennett's (1991) multiple drafts model and the phenomenon of neural synchronization (Singer, 1996).

In some networks, coordinated global activity happens simply as a function of spreading activation that disperses throughout the system quickly but which can arise from any part of it. Take, for example, the clapping of an audience after a show. If one group of people starts clapping in synchrony, the sound gets louder than the clapping in their immediate surround. This causes the audience nearby to clap in synchrony with them, which raises the group's volume even more and perpetuates its spread until the entire audience is clapping at the same speed. What makes this interesting is that it can originate in any part of the audience. All that is required is a minimum number of initial starting clappers as a seed to start the propagation.

Hierarchical Networks and the Brain

Connections in **hierarchical networks** are organized into different levels. The number of nodes decreases as we travel upward, with each group of nodes converging onto another group above it with fewer elements. We already have seen hierarchical networks. Figures 7.4 and 7.5 are examples. Hierarchical organization is perhaps most evident in the visual system (Hubel & Wiesel, 1962). Here, neurons at the bottom of the hierarchy code for specific features, such as lines at a particular orientation and at a specific position in the visual field. Connections from these **simple cells** converge on neurons in the next layer up. These cells code for the combined input of the lower features that feed to them. If they received inputs from multiple adjacent vertical line detectors, they would in turn code for the sum of these representations, which would be a vertical line moving in a specific direction. These **complex cells** next converge to neurons at an even higher level that would again stand for their combined inputs. In this case, these new **hypercomplex cells** represent a right angle made of vertical and horizontal lines that are moving conjointly in the same direction (Figure 7.12).

If we extrapolate up the hierarchy, we end up with cells in the highest layers that code for large complex objects. These have been nicknamed "grandmother cells" because there may be some that fire only in response to the stimulus of your grandmother's face. So the visual system uses hierarchical networks to successively integrate features of the visual

Figure 7.12 Hierarchical organization in the visual system. Converging input from lower layers results in the coding of more complex objects.

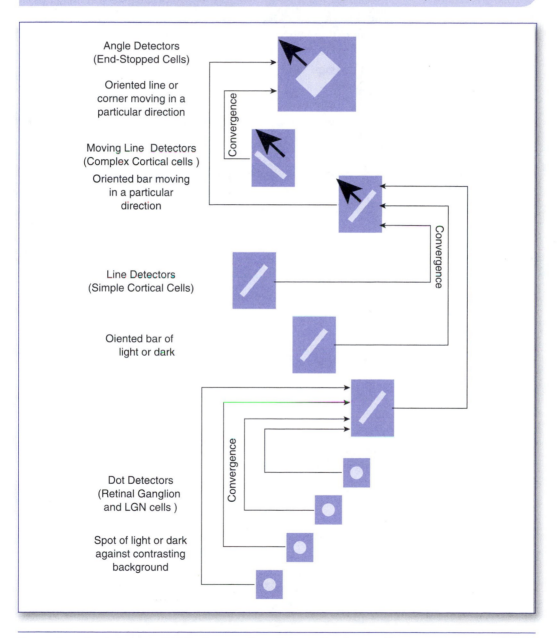

Angle Detectors
(End-Stopped Cells)

Oriented line or
corner moving in a
particular direction

Convergence

Moving Line Detectors
(Complex Cortical cells)

Oriented bar moving
in a particular
direction

Convergence

Line Detectors
(Simple Cortical Cells)

Oiented bar of
light or dark

Convergence

Dot Detectors
(Retinal Ganglion
and LGN cells)

Spot of light or dark
against contrasting
background

Source: From Friedenberg, J. (2009). *Dynamical psychology. Complexity, self-organization and mind.* ISCE Publishing.

field and build a percept. In effect, the hierarchy allows the visual system to employ a "divide-and-conquer" strategy where it breaks down the complex visual image into microscopic features and then assembles these features into parts and then wholes that can be recognized. Similar hierarchies may exist that allow concepts to be formed from component characteristics. This example illustrates an important feature of hierarchies. Traveling up through them allows for convergence and integration—that is, the putting of pieces together. Traveling downward through them allows for divergence and separation, a splitting apart or distribution of elements.

Communication between levels in hierarchies can also allow for the resolution of ambiguity in visual perception. Recall the word *superiority effect* discussed in the first cognitive chapter. In this effect, it is easier to determine the identity of a feature—say, the letter *I*—when it is presented as part of a meaningful word, such as "fit," than when it is presented by itself as an isolated letter. The surrounding letters in the word provide a context that helps disambiguate the central letter's identity. But this could happen only if information about the word, processed at a higher level, was compared against information about the letter, processed at a lower level. This shows that perception is not purely "bottom-up" or data driven, with only parts forming wholes. It must also be "top-down" and conceptually driven, with wholes helping form the developing percept. Information in the visual system, thus, appears to travel in two directions. It goes not only in a feed-forward direction from the eye to the brain but also in a feedback direction from higher brain centers to lower centers. Both are necessary parts of the pattern assembly process.

Small-World Networks: It's a Small World After All

A number of years ago, several undergraduate students at Albright College discovered an interesting fact. They realized that every American movie actor could be related to the actor Kevin Bacon in only four steps or less. The links are through actors who appeared in the same film together. The actor Will Smith, for example, was in the movie *Independence Day* (1996) with Harry Connick Jr., who was in the film *My Dog Skip* (2000) with Kevin Bacon. So in this case, only two steps separate each actor. This finding garnered widespread public attention on television and the Internet. One website, called the Oracle of Kevin Bacon, received 20,000 hits a day at its peak and was ranked as one of the top 10 websites of 1996.

This finding is real. It is true that any two American actors can be connected by a maximum of four links. In fact, the principle holds not just for film actors but also for most social relationship networks. The psychologist Stanley Milgram first noted this when he sent out 160 letters to people. The letters were addressed to a stockbroker. He asked these people to pass on the letter to someone who they thought would know the stockbroker. Surprisingly, a number of the letters did actually get through, most of them in about six steps (Milgram, 1967). This small-world network is actually far more general than even social relationships. It exists in the U.S. electrical power grid, in road and railway networks that are spread out across continents, and even in the nervous systems of many animals.

So we can define a **small-world network** as any network where one can get from any single point to any other point in only a small number of steps even though the total number of elements may be exceedingly large. How could the units of such networks be so easily connected when the networks themselves are so vast? After all, there are billions of web pages and billions of people on earth. It seems as though it would take a large number of connections to link any two elements together. There must be some intrinsic organization or structure to these networks that allows such ease of connectivity. We examine this issue next.

Ordered and Random Connections

The answer to this question has to do with network architecture. Watts and Strogatz (1998) simulated a variety of network types. At one end, they created a highly ordered network with only local connections. In this network, a node was connected only to other nodes in its immediate neighborhood. At the other end of the continuum, they had a completely random network where a node could be linked with any other node in the network with equal likelihood. **Random networks** of this sort contain an equal mix of link distances, both local and global.

Let's start with a network of 6 billion nodes and imagine them arranged in a circle (Strogatz, 2003). The population of the world was 6 billion several years ago, so we can imagine each node standing for an individual person and the links between nodes standing for a type of relationship. In the case of an **ordered network**, each node would be connected with 1,000 others—500 to the left and 500 to the right. Each connection can be represented as a line drawn between nodes that are themselves denoted as smaller circles (Figure 7.13). In this ordered network, it would take 3 million steps on average to link any one node to any other. The farthest connection is a node diametrically opposite its counterpart on the circle. To reach it would require hopping around the circle in steps of 500. It would thus take 3 billion divided by 500, or 6 million, steps to reach. Since the closest node is just one step away, the average number of steps separating any two nodes would be midway between 1 million and 6 million, a whopping 3 million.

Now, let's take the case of the completely random network. Here, it takes only four steps to get between any pair of nodes, on average. If every person knows 1,000 others and each of those knows 1,000 additional people, then there are 1 million people ($1,000^2$) within two steps of each other, 1 billion ($1,000^3$) within three, and 1 trillion ($1,000^4$) within four. So any two people in this system are separated only by between three and four degrees.

Figure 7.13 Ordered networks have only local connections to immediate neighbors. Random networks have more long-distance connections that allow messages to travel faster through the network.

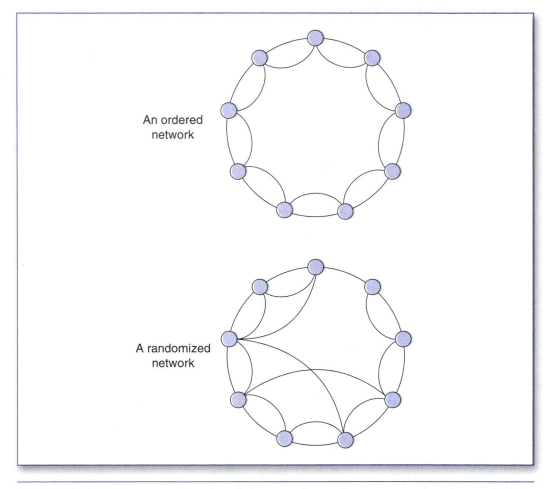

An ordered network

A randomized network

Source: Friedenberg, J. (2009). *Dynamical psychology. Complexity, self-organization and mind.* ISCE Publishing.

Egalitarians and Aristocrats

It turns out that there are at least two kinds of small-world networks. The first is of the type discovered by Watts and Strogatz, where a few random connections are thrown in among mostly local neighborhood links. Buchanan (2002) calls these **egalitarian networks** because the links are distributed more or less equally. But there is also what he

Figure 7.14 An example of a hub-based network where some nodes have many more connections than others. The three hubs are indicated by shading.

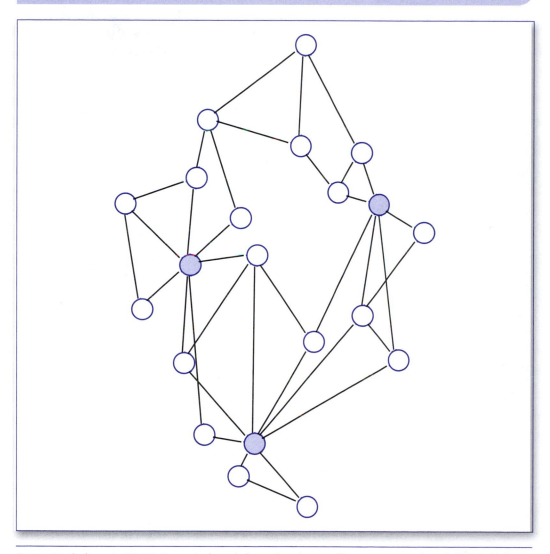

Source: Friedenberg, J. (2009). *Dynamical psychology. Complexity, self-organization and mind.* ISCE Publishing.

calls **aristocratic networks**. Here, the long-distance connections result from the presence of a small number of hubs. **Hubs** are nodes that have many more links than the rest of the network's nodes. There are numerous examples of hub-based aristocratic networks, both in the natural and technological realm. Examples include the Internet and the World

Wide Web, the spread of sexual disease among people, scientific papers linked by citations, and the probability of words occurring next to one another in English sentences.

The aristocratic organization seems to emerge through a very simple process, one that Buchanan (2002) calls "the rich getting richer" or, more properly, **preferential attachment**. When a network is created, there can be slight differences in the number of links each node has. Those with more links will gradually be linked to more often because they serve as good portals to gain access to large numbers of other nodes. If you created a website on the World Wide Web and wanted lots of people to access it, you would link to other popular sites such as Yahoo.com or Google.com, because you know that lots of other people are already visiting those pages. Hubs, therefore, turn the network into a small world, one where information flow between widespread points is facilitated. The fact that networks naturally and unintentionally develop hubs as they grow suggests that it is an emergent property, a solution nature has found to solving the problem of rapid and efficient communication.

The two types of small-world network both accomplish the same function but in different ways. As a result, they each have different weaknesses (Baran, 1964). Egalitarian nets are more robust to nonspecific damage. They can stand up better to the destruction of randomly selected nodes. As long as there are several long-distance connections intact, messages can get rerouted along them. Aristocratic nets are more sensitive to selective attack where the hubs are targeted and destroyed. Because the hubs carry most of the links, the destruction of only a few can shut down the entire network. The current Internet and World Wide Web are both aristocratic. This means that special attention should be given to securing those hubs and shielding them from attack. Figure 7.14 shows an example of a hub-based network.

Neuroscience and Networks

Let's now apply these ideas to cognitive science. One question we can ask is whether the brain is a small-world network. Scannell (1997) studied the cortex of cats and monkeys. He located 55 distinct cortical regions in the cat, each associated with a particular function. In macaque monkeys, there are 69 such regions. For both of these animals, about 400 to 500 links connect these areas. These links consist of not only single axons but also nerve fibers made up of numerous axons. Latora and Marchiori (2001) analyzed Scannell's data and determined that there are only between two and three steps separating neurons. They also found that these neurons were highly clustered, with many shared local connections.

So it appears that mammalian brains are small-world networks after all. This makes sense. If an animal is to respond rapidly to a stimulus—say, to the sight of a predator or prey—the information can't pass through too many synapses. Each synaptic link would add additional response time, slowing down the animal and putting it at risk.

Epilepsy is a brain disorder characterized by uncontrolled neuronal firing. Much like a forest fire that can start in one part of the forest and then spread, epileptic seizures can also multiply. Unfortunately, the brain's long-range connections allow a seizure in one part of the brain to easily spread to other areas. It is not uncommon for a seizure to expand from one hemisphere to another along the corpus callosum or from one cortical area in one hemisphere to another that is more distant but on the same side.

In an ischemic stroke, an object such as a blood clot blocks blood flow and kills neurons by denying them oxygen and nutrients. Depending on the location and extent of damage, several kinds of disorders can result. Many stroke patients, however, can recover all or most of their former ability through therapy. What is happening is that their brains are reconfiguring, in some cases forming new pathways that avoid or flow around the area of damage. The ability of the brain to recover from injury in this fashion is called **plasticity**. It is the dense weave of local connections that allows this reconfiguration to occur. If one node or set of nodes is knocked out by the stroke, the signal passing through there can reroute along alternate intact pathways. **Clustering** thus ensures that the brain doesn't fragment into isolated islands.

Small-World Networks and Synchrony

Elsewhere in this book, we discuss the importance of neural synchrony, which generally refers to correlated activity between neurons. It turns out that small-world networks seem to be necessary for **synchrony**. Kuramoto (1984) found that synchrony between coupled oscillators with distributed natural frequencies (each firing at a variety of different rates) failed to occur in ordered networks, where each oscillator was connected only to its immediate neighbors. But randomizing this network just a little bit produced global synchrony, where all the oscillators beat in unison (Strogatz, 2003). The explanation is intuitive: Just a few long-distance connections transmit timing information to more distant parts, allowing mutual influence to spread quickly. The fact that small-world networks and synchrony are both properties of brains is no accident. The former is a prerequisite for the latter.

Lago-Fernandez, Huerta, Corbacho, and Siguenza (2000) created a simulation of the olfactory antennal lobe in the locust. They connected the neurons in their model together in different ways and measured how the network responded to simulated olfactory input representing smells. When the network was ordered with only local connectivity, the simulated neurons synchronized but took a long time to do it. This sluggish response was ostensibly due to the time it took for the timing signals to propagate throughout the system. Next, they wired up the network at random. Now, the signal spread rapidly throughout the network, but synchrony didn't occur. The randomly wired networks apparently lacked sufficient order to allow the network to produce an organized response.

Finally, these researchers tried ordered networks with just a slight amount of randomization. Now, the system synchronized and did so quickly. But Lago-Fernandez et al. (2000) discovered another interesting finding in addition to this. In real-world locusts, some of the neurons either slow down or speed up compared with the group frequency. They speculate that this frequency distribution codes for odor intensity or for different types of odors. Only the small-world wiring pattern was able to replicate this effect.

Percolation

If we wish to better understand how information spreads in a network, we can look at the spread of disease. A disease starts off by infecting one or more individuals, who then come into contact with others. These new people become infected and infect yet additional people. A number of factors affect how far a disease will spread in a social network. The interconnectedness of the network is important, as is the susceptibility to infection. An elementary school teacher can contribute greatly to the spread of a disease because he or she comes into contact with many children, who may all be highly susceptible to infection. A loner who works at home most of the time, on the other hand, may not infect anyone at all.

A number of models have been proposed for how disease spreads. Here, we will discuss the percolation model. The term **percolation** refers to the propagation of a disease through a social network. We start with a large population of people connected by bonds along which the disease can spread. Each site is either susceptible or not according to an occupation probability. Each bond is either open or closed. Open bonds allow the disease to be transmitted. Closed bonds do not. A disease starts at a source and flows along any open bonds, traveling from one susceptible person to another. It stops when it fails to encounter any new open bonds. The portion of the network that becomes infected from a randomly chosen starting point is called a cluster. Once a disease gets into a cluster, it will infect all the bonds within it.

Obviously, when the occupation probability is high and most bonds are open, the disease will spread to fill up most of the network. In this case, we see a **percolating cluster**, a single giant group of susceptible sites, connected by open bonds, that occupies the majority of the network. If the occupation probability is low and/or most bonds are closed, the disease will be contained and a percolating cluster will not form. In this situation, the groups of diseased individuals will be small and scattered.

The presence of a percolating cluster determines whether an epidemic turns into a pandemic. If a disease originates in the percolating cluster, all individuals within it will ultimately be infected. Under these conditions, it spreads very rapidly and is difficult to contain. If the disease starts outside the percolating cluster, it will eventually die out after having infected only a proportionately small number of individuals.

Percolation and Psychology

The percolation model gives us a theoretical perspective with which to understand the spread of activation in neural networks. If sites are neurons and bonds are synaptic connections, then we can determine how easily messages between neurons will spread. Some brain areas may have the equivalent of a percolating cluster. Neural activity that makes contact with the cluster will diffuse throughout it unimpeded. There are several psychological conditions that suggest the presence of percolating clusters in the human brain. These are seizures encountered in epilepsy, disorganized thinking in schizophrenic patients, and divergent thinking. We will now describe each of these in turn.

There are many different types of epilepsy, but they are all characterized by seizures. A **seizure** is an uncontrolled surge of synchronous electrical activity in the brain. For causes that are not well-known, large populations of neurons in an epileptic's brain begin to fire simultaneously. In some cases, the seizure originates in one part of the brain, such as the temporal lobe or hippocampus, and spreads to other areas. Seizures result when there is too much activity in excitatory neurons and/or too little activity in inhibitory ones. Medications used to treat epilepsy work by decreasing activity in excitatory glutamate synapses. Others work by increasing the efficacy of inhibitory neurotransmitters such as GABA (gamma-aminobutyric acid). The neurons participating in a seizure are analogous to the sites in a percolating cluster. Once these sites are triggered, activation spreads rapidly through the entire cluster, much the same way a disease would spread throughout a population.

One of the symptoms of schizophrenia is **disorganized thinking**. It is characterized by a loose association between ideas and manifests itself in bizarre speech or "word salad." Susan Sheehan (1982) recorded what Maxine, a young female schizophrenic patient, said to herself one day:

> This morning, when I was at Hillside [Hospital], I was making a movie. I was surrounded by movie stars. The X-ray technician was Peter Lawford. The security guard was Don Knotts. That Indian doctor in Building 40 was Lou Costello. I'm Mary Poppins. Is this room painted blue to get me upset? My grandmother died four weeks after my eighteenth birthday. (p. 25)

The train of thought in disorganized thinking is illogical and jumps from one unrelated topic to another. It is as if the patient's brain state enters a neural percolating cluster that "takes over" his or her thought processes, causing them to leap along open bonds between disparate sites. Each topic that comes to mind in disorganized speech might then correspond to a localized area of neural tissue made up of a cluster of sites. The jumps in thought from one topic to the next seem to be the long-distance bonds linking these clusters together.

Creative individuals tend to score high on tests measuring **divergent thinking**. The goal of divergent thinking is to generate many different ideas about a topic in a short period of time. It typically occurs in a spontaneous, free-flowing manner, such that the ideas are generated in a random, unorganized fashion. One question measuring divergent thinking on a creativity test would be "How many uses can you find for a brick?" A highly creative person would produce more responses—such as "paperweight," "bookend," and so on— than a less creative individual. Creative people are usually also better at generating ideas during **free association**, which involves stating whatever thoughts come to mind.

Divergent thinking seems to be a milder version of disorganized thinking, since it is controlled and more focused. During divergent thinking or free association, a person is allowing neural activation to flow along without inhibition. Ideas within a mental percolating cluster that aren't normally linked or are only weakly linked may then become related. Attention seems to be implicated in both disorganized and divergent thinking. During normal thinking, we may consciously and voluntarily direct our flow of thought to stay on topic. When this attentional focus is released, it may become easier to enter a percolating cluster of ideas.

The Future of Network Science

Network science is a powerful framework that we can use to better study cognitive phenomena. Researchers in this approach have uncovered basic architectural and functional features that underlie many different systems—whether those are brains, transportation networks, or ecologies. The application of network principles to the study of the mind should yield some fascinating insights over the next few years.

But we still have a long way to go. Many current network models assume that all nodes in the network are identical. This is clearly not the case. In many systems, the functioning of nodes can differ dramatically. Surely not every individual in a society thinks or acts alike, and we may discover that not every neuron operates identically either. The same signal sent to two nodes will not always produce the same response if the nature of the nodes differs.

We know that the brain is hierarchical, with processes operating at many different scales, from the synaptic to the cortical. This could pose a problem for network theory, where much of the dynamics occurs at a single scale. One way of dealing with this is to model hierarchical network processes. We could, for instance, place little small-world architectures inside bigger ones. We could then vary the type of connectivity between these networks at different spatial scales. Alternatively, we could implement networks that operate at different time scales—some running slowly, others more quickly. The application of network science to cognitive science has just begun and promises a number of fruitful approaches to the study of mind.

OVERALL EVALUATION OF THE NETWORK APPROACH

The network approach in general has received its share of criticism. Attacks leveled against connectionism are that its architectures are too simple and that its learning rules are inadequate. Semantic and propositional networks have their own problems related to organization and the proper role of inhibition. Having said all this, the network approach is still a strong perspective, both in terms of its theoretical assumptions and methodology. Connectionist networks are good at simulating learning and have biological plausibility, at least in the gross sense of the term. Semantic and propositional networks probably come the closest to representing certain features of the way knowledge is represented in memory.

The network approach poses a number of challenges to the classic information-processing view. Several differences need to be reconciled. These have to do with the numbers and sizes of processing units, and include the argument of serial processing versus parallel processing, as well as the argument of knowledge-based versus behavior-based approaches. What is needed, then, is a way of integrating the opposing views. New computers with parallel processing architectures are being developed. These machines may yield new insights that will help bridge the gap between the classic and the connectionist perspectives. Another way to bridge this gap would be to have network researchers working with practitioners of other cognitive science disciplines in model building. Network models seem to constitute a "middle ground" between the actual biological structures studied in neuroscience and the more abstract representations of cognition and artificial intelligence. Cooperative model building between these disciplines might resolve some of the discrepancies.

Interdisciplinary Crossroads: Emotions and Networks

So far, we have been discussing how networks can serve to store cognitive representations such as concepts and propositions. Bower (1981) postulates that we can use networks to represent emotional states as well. For instance, we can take a mood such as "sadness" and assign it to a node in an associative network. When this node is activated, the person will then experience the corresponding mood. The sadness node through learning could have developed links not only to other mood nodes but also to nodes representing concepts and events. This would explain why a girl might feel sad when she thinks of an ex-boyfriend: The node standing for him was linked to the experience of being sad that happened during the breakup.

These "mixed" networks that combine emotional and cognitive representations can also explain why we might think of a concept when we are in a particular mood. In other words, the associative relation is a two-way street. Thinking of an ex-boyfriend might make a girl sad, but being sad might also make her think of her ex-boyfriend. This model can, therefore, predict the mood congruency effect where we are more likely to remember information that was learned in a particular mood if we try to recall it in that same mood later. We discuss this effect as well as other aspects of mood and memory in more depth in the emotional cognition chapter.

In Bower's (1981) model, there are six basic emotions, each with associated nodes that can be activated by various trigger factors. These factors become more developed over the course of the individual's life span. Presumably, some of these triggers are hardwired, as in the case of arachnophobia. They could also be acquired through experience, as when a person develops a learned association between a stimulus and a response. Figure 7.15 shows how a sadness node may be connected to others.

Figure 7.15 An example of an emotion network. An emotion node can have links to other emotion nodes as well as to nodes representing types of physiological arousal, facial expression or other behaviors, and stored memories of related events.

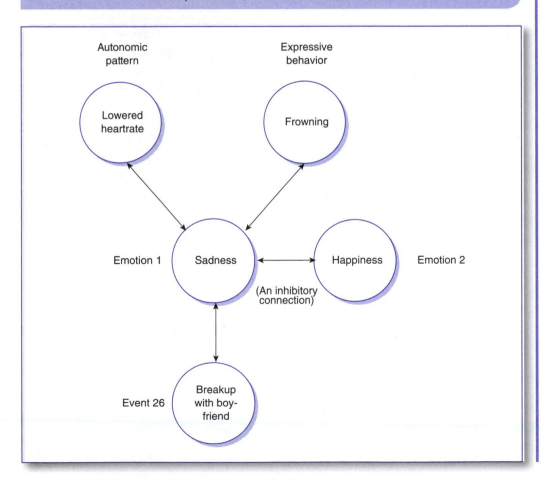

Notice that there is an inhibitory connection between it and the happiness node, as these are opposing emotions. The happier you are, the less sad you will feel—and vice versa. In addition, if happiness inhibits sadness, not only will you feel less sad, but you will also be less likely to recall sadness-related information.

Several criticisms have been leveled at this emotional network model. For starters, not all moods elicit mood congruency effects. Anxiety does not produce the effect, while depression does. Second, people often distract themselves to either prolong positive states or to avoid being in a depressive state (Rusting & Nolen-Hoeksema, 1998). For example, they can attend to mildly positive events, such as a comedy TV show, or actively think about uplifting events. Active distraction runs against the passive spreading activation that would induce same-mood cognitive biases. Rusting and DeHart (2000) induced a negative mood state in participants and then had them perform one

Figure 7.16 The Affect Infusion Model of emotion and cognition.

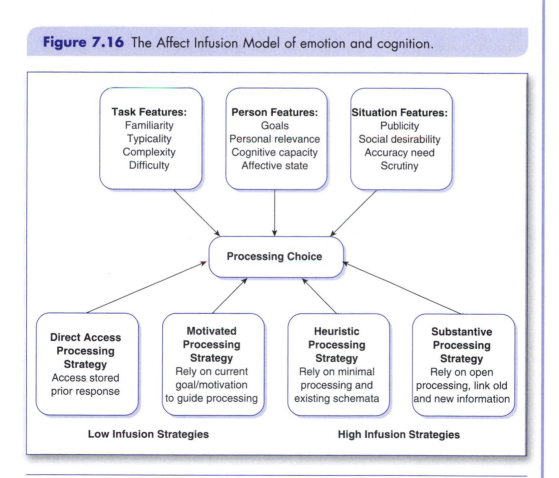

Source: Forgas (1995).

of three tasks followed by memory recall. They were to ruminate about the cause of the negative mood, think of distracting thoughts, or simply free associate on whatever thoughts passed through their mind. The results varied depending on the condition. Those who ruminated recalled more negative memories compared with the free-associating controls, and those who were distracted recalled more positive memories in comparison with the control group. The simple associative network cannot account for these results.

Forgas (1995) has developed the **Affect Infusion Model** to explain the conditions under which emotions and moods infuse (influence) cognitive processing. These are depicted in Figure 7.16. When the situation involves a heuristic processing strategy, where one relies on minimal processing and the use of existing schema, then emotions produce mood congruency effects. Under these conditions, there are no simple responses available and the task is simple, familiar, and not of personal relevance. Emotional infusion also occurs when a substantive processing strategy is used. In this case, an individual would rely on an open processing method that links old and new information. Under these conditions, the task is difficult, complex, or novel and there is no motivational goal.

However, there are also two situations in which emotions are unlikely to infuse cognition. The first of these is when we use a direct access processing strategy. This is one where we access stored prior responses, when the task is familiar and there are no cues for more elaborative processing. Emotion also plays little role when we engage in a motivated processing strategy. In this situation, we rely on current motivations to guide processing because there is a specific motivational objective and there is a very specific search for information in memory that is required.

SUMMING UP: A REVIEW OF CHAPTER 7

1. In serial processing, computation is performed one step at a time. Contemporary computers operate this way. The brain, however, computes in a massively parallel and distributed way, with different ongoing operations at any given time.

2. ANNs simulate the way real neurons compute. They consist of nodes connected by links. Links have associated weights that can be positive or negative. A node's output is determined by multiplying its activation value times its weight. Multiple outputs typically converge on a single node. If these values exceed a threshold, the receiving node "fires," producing its own activation.

3. The perceptron was one of the earliest ANNs. It could recognize simple visual patterns and was limited because it contained only two layers. More recent ANNs have

an input, a hidden, and an output layer and are capable of more complex computation. In back-propagation networks, the pattern of activation produced by a stimulus is matched to a known response. The difference between the two is fed back into the net so that it gradually becomes capable of recognizing and classifying a broad array of stimuli.

4. Convergent networks show a large amount of activity that gradually diminishes with time. Oscillatory nets show regular and periodic activity. Chaotic networks demonstrate a mixture of regular and nonperiodic action.

5. Connectionism is the approach that favors the use of network models to understand cognitive processes. The advantage to this approach is biological plausibility, learning, and resistance to damage. A disadvantage is that it omits some obvious features of real-world brains and can lose data when new information is acquired.

6. In semantic networks, nodes stand for concepts. Activation in these networks can explain a variety of results from memory experiments, including how long it takes to verify sentences.

7. Propositional networks are more complex and capable of representing propositional representations. They can code for linguistic relations such as category membership and property relationships.

8. Network science is a relatively new field of endeavor. Investigators in this discipline study the architecture and function of all networks that show some common features.

9. Small-world networks are those whose nodes are separated by at most a few links. There are a mixture of both local "neighborhood" links and more global long-distance links. Information in these nets can spread very rapidly. Mostly, highly connected hubs form the connections in hub-based or aristocratic networks. These are nodes with a large number of links.

10. Anatomical studies show that mammalian brains have a small-world organization. This helps explain a wide variety of brain behaviors such as epilepsy, plasticity, and synchrony.

11. Percolation is the process by which information propagates through a network. In the disease model of percolation, infection spreads through open bonds and susceptible nodes. A percolating cluster refers to that component of a network through which all the sites are infected. Examples of percolation in psychology include seizures, disorganized thinking, and divergent thinking.

EXPLORE MORE

Log on to the student study site at **http://study.sagepub.com/friedenberg3e** for electronic flash cards, review quizzes, and a list of web resources to aid you in further exploring the field of cognitive science.

SUGGESTED READINGS

Anderson, J. (2000). *Learning and memory: An integrated approach* (2nd ed.). New York, NY: Wiley.

Buchanan, M. (2002). *Small worlds and the groundbreaking theory of networks.* New York, NY: W. W. Norton.

Gurney, K. (1997). *An introduction to neural networks.* London, England: UCL Press.

Rumelhart, D. E., McClelland, J. L., & PDP Research Group. (Eds.). (1986). *Parallel distributed processing: Foundations* (Vol. 1). Cambridge: MIT Press.

Strogatz, S. (2003). *Sync: How order emerges from chaos in the universe, nature, and daily life.* New York, NY: Hyperion.

Watts, D. J. (2003). *Six degrees: The science of a connected age.* New York, NY: W. W. Norton.

8

THE EVOLUTIONARY APPROACH

Change Over Time

> *I have called this principle, by which each slight variation, if useful, is preserved, by the term of natural selection.*
>
> —Charles Darwin, 1859

THE EVOLUTIONARY VIEW

Cognition doesn't come out of "nowhere." Natural forces create it. Animal and human cognition are products of these forces. If we wish to understand cognitive ability, then we need to understand how they work. These forces go by the name of evolution, a process that involves adaptation to changing environments. Animals, including ourselves, have minds that allow us to think and survive in a given environmental situation or niche. We have evolved capacities that allow us to perceive, pay attention to, remember, and problem solve so that we can acquire food, avoid predators, and mate and reproduce. All of our cognitive abilities are a product of these earlier environments and have evolved in response to such physical and social demands.

In this chapter, we will examine the evolutionary approach and its relation to cognitive science from several perspectives. The first perspective is **comparative cognition**, where researchers examine the similarities and differences in cognitive ability between different animal species. In this section, we will see how different environments have shaped different cognitive skills in animals. Birds that need to store large numbers of nuts, for instance, have evolved large memory capacities to recall their location. Animals that don't have such needs may not develop such superb memories. So this section will show us how specific needs in particular environments give rise to particular forms of thought.

The second perspective, **evolutionary psychology (EP)**, is concerned with how the human mind came into existence. It attempts to describe the selection forces in our ancestral past that gave rise to our mental structures. Here, we will extend what we have learned in the comparative cognition section to people, showing which specific demands have driven different human cognitive skills. For example, we show that our ability to reason logically seems to fail when a problem is described in abstract terms, but it is quite robust when couched in terms of a social situation. Such results suggest that our reasoning capacity did not evolve in response to scoring higher on the SAT but in response to detecting cheaters in a group.

A field that is related to EP is **behavioral economics**. It focuses on how evolution shaped the way we make decisions involving money. Here, we apply evolutionary principles to the domain of economics. Humans are economic creatures. We have always lived in societies where we must produce, consume, and exchange goods and services. Living in these societies affects our reasoning with regard to money. Take, for instance, the situation where someone else is given money but only offers you a small amount. Most people under such circumstances refuse to accept it. This is an irrational decision as it is free money, but it makes sense in a society where people must share reciprocally to survive. The rejection is a statement of distrust and could get the greedy lender kicked out of his group for failure to cooperate. In conclusion, we will wrap up the chapter with a brief discussion of sex differences in cognition and how evolutionary forces might account for them.

Other cognitive science approaches, in addition to those just mentioned, have adopted and used evolutionary principles. In the psychology chapter, we saw the functionalists asking the same questions that evolutionary psychologists ask. These functionalists wondered why we have certain mental abilities, for what purpose a given ability exists, and how a specific mental ability may have arisen. Evolutionary principles are also used in contemporary robotics, in which generations of robots are bred to produce robot offspring that are best adapted to the tasks for which they've been designed.

A number of important themes are touched on in this chapter. Evolutionary psychologists argue that many of our cognitive mechanisms are innate. This argument echoes the nativist position that we are born with knowledge. Evolutionary psychologists also argue that the mind consists of a set of special-purpose devices or **evolved psychological mechanisms** that are activated only within specific environmental contexts. This runs counter to the tenet of artificial intelligence and cognition that states that the mind is a general-purpose computing device, capable of solving virtually all kinds of problems equally well.

A LITTLE BACKGROUND: NATURAL SELECTION AND GENETICS

Before delving specifically into the evolution of mental structures, it is helpful to review some basic concepts of biological evolution. The biologist Charles Darwin (Figure 8.1)—in his classic 1859 work, *On the Origin of Species*—outlines the basic principles of his **theory of natural selection**, which is a description of the process by which animal species change over time. Darwin noticed that animals vary (within a species as well as from species to species) in all sorts of ways—for example, they have longer or shorter legs, bigger or smaller ears, or different coloration. The fact that animals differ in their physical traits is known as **variation**. Second, parent organisms pass on some of their gene-based characteristics to their offspring. This process is called **inheritance**. A change in environmental conditions can make it more likely that animals with a specific trait will survive. Those without this trait could die. This process, whereby a particular attribute or attributes promote survival under altered conditions, is known as **selection**. The overall process by which animal species change in response to their environment is called **adaptation**.

Figure 8.1 The biologist Charles Darwin (1809–1882) proposed the theory of natural selection.

Source: Photos.com/Thinkstock.

Variation, inheritance, and selection are the vital ingredients of species change. Looking at the fossil record, we can see that there had been alterations in the foot structure of horse-like animals. Early progenitors of the horse had feet with several toes. Figure 8.2 shows that, over time, these toes became fused, and the hooves of modern-day horses came into being. Originally, the members of this progenitor species varied with respect to toe structure. Some animals had toes that were closer to each other and less distinct anatomically. These animals were perhaps better able to run in an emerging grassland environment, as their feet were likely to have given them better support and locomotive power on flat terrain. Presumably, these horses ran faster and so were able to escape predators more easily. They were more likely to survive and pass on their adaptive trait to future generations.

Natural selection is concerned with survival in the strictest sense—that is, whether an organism lives or dies. Animals that possess an adaptive trait are better equipped to deal with a changed or changing environment. They are better at escaping predators, locating food, and keeping warm or cool, and so they are likely to survive. **Sexual selection**, in contrast, refers to reproductive success—that is, the ability to attract a mate and, thereby, produce offspring. Some traits that are selected for naturally are not always selected for sexually. Females of some beetle species consider the presence of large horns on males of

Figure 8.2 Evidence from the fossil record showing the evolution of the hoof from a toed foot in horse species.

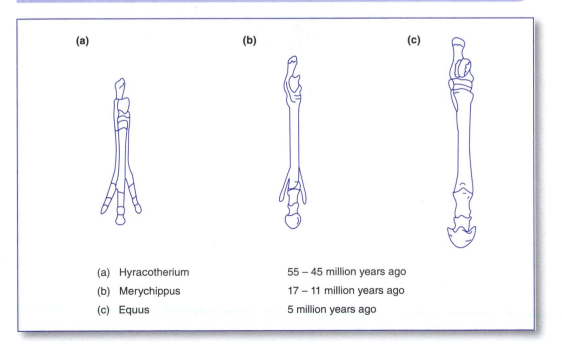

(a)   Hyracotherium   55 – 45 million years ago

(b)   Merychippus   17 – 11 million years ago

(c)   Equus   5 million years ago

the species to be attractive. The males with these large horns mate more often and pass this trait to future generations more often. However, very large horns are also an impediment to survival. If they are too big, the males cannot easily escape predators such as birds. In this case, the optimum horn size represents a compromise between natural and sexual selection trading off against each other.

COMPARATIVE COGNITION

In this section, we will discuss evolution in broad terms of how it has affected cognition in nonhuman animals of different species. This will serve as an introduction to thinking about the relationship between evolution and cognition and will set the groundwork for our later discussion, where we will focus on human cognition only.

Cognitive Adaptation in Animals

When looking at animals, we see that they are each adapted to a specific environment, what is called their **ecological niche**. Some birds migrate over vast distances and so need physical structures such as wings to enable them to fly, but they also need specific cognitive capacities that enable them to fly effectively. Studies show that carrier pigeons form an odor map of the environment that enables them to fly back more than 100 miles to a starting point after being released (Able, 1996; Wallraff, 1980). Pigeons may also be able to sense Earth's magnetic field to navigate, in effect using a built-in "compass" to steer them in the right direction (Wiltschko, 1996).

Some fish species, amphibians, and mammals have evolved the capacity to perceive electric fields. This sense enables them to detect prey that would normally be difficult to find using more typical senses, such as vision. Weak electric fields are given off by the muscles in an animal's body and can change when the animal moves, revealing its location. African fish have an organ in their tail that produces a weak electric field. Using this organ, the fish can send out an electrical signal that is then reflected back to the fish by objects in its immediate surroundings. Sensors on both sides of the fish's body pick up this electrical echo and allow it to estimate the distance of a prey it can eat (Von der Emde, Schwarz, Gomez, Budelli, & Grant, 1998).

Apes, monkeys, cats, dogs, and some birds can understand that an object once it disappears from view still exists. This ability is called **object permanence** and develops in human children at the age of 12 to 18 months (Piaget, 1938/1952). Object permanence is a primitive form of concept formation, because the animal must retain the idea that the object is still present in the absence of perceptual evidence. Gagnon and Dore (1994) found that dogs successfully look for a favorite toy that is hidden behind one of three boxes. In the natural world, having object permanence is crucial in locating animals that have disappeared behind obstacles such as rocks or trees. Even if a prey animal is not at the location where it disappeared, this is still a good starting point to continue the search.

Memory is a great adaptive capacity. It enables animals to remember where they have looked for something so that they don't have to expend valuable time and energy revisiting locations already searched. The Hawaiian nectar-feeding honeycreeper can remember which flowers it has collected nectar from and will avoid going back to those flowers if it has recently fed from them (Kamil, 1978). Memory also allows animals to recall where they have stored food. The Clark's nutcracker bird can store 33,000 pine nuts at 6,000 different sites during the summer and remember all these locations when it comes back to eat them in the winter and spring! Many different animals have both short-term and long-term memories and demonstrate some of the same memory phenomena that people do, including primacy and recency effects and proactive and retroactive interference (Bolhuis & van Kampen, 1988).

Animals are also able to reason and solve problems as people do. Remember from the psychology chapter that Kohler's chimps demonstrated insight learning. They were able after some time to realize that a box and a stick could be used together to get at food. Another reasoning skill is **transitive inference.** This is equivalent to deductive reasoning, which we previously introduced. In a transitive inference problem, an animal must realize that if A is bigger than B and B is bigger than C, then A must be bigger than C. McGonigle and Chalmers (1977) presented squirrel monkeys with paired colored food containers, only one of which contained a hidden peanut. If the red container contained the peanut in one trial and the green did not, on the next trial the green container would contain the peanut but the blue would not. Based on this training, the animals could eventually choose that the red container would have the peanut rather than the blue in a test trial.

Later research has shown that pigeons and rats can also solve transitive inference problems (Davis, 1992; von Fersen, Wynne, Delius, & Staddon, 1991). What is the evolutionary advantage of such a skill? According to Wynne (2001), it allows an animal to grasp rank orderings. This is particularly important in social animals with a hierarchical power structure. If chimp A is dominant over chimp B and chimp B is dominant over chimp C, one can infer that chimp A is dominant over chimp C without having to directly test this relationship, which could result in a fight and physical injury. Table 8.1 shows the cognitive skills of some other animal species and the adaptive selection pressures that gave rise to them.

In each of the cases outlined above, specific selection pressures have shaped particular cognitive skills. Note that these skills are often shared between members of different species. The key difference here is in the adaptive problem that needs to be solved, not the species in question. We would expect that all animals, regardless of their genetic and physical structure, might develop similar cognitive capacities to solve similar problems. However, this is not an ironclad rule, as it is also the case that species can develop different solutions to similar problems; witness the different ways in which a bird's and bee's wings operate. In concluding this section, we need to mention that we do not address animal linguistic abilities here because those will be covered in the next chapter on language.

Table 8.1 Cognitive skills for different animal species and the adaptive function they serve.

Species	Cognitive Skill	Behavior	Adaptive Function	Reference
Lions	Counting	The greater the number of lions in a pride that are roaring, the less likely another pride will approach.	To avoid potentially harmful interaction with other competing groups	McComb, Packer, and Pusey (1994)
New Caledonian crows	Tool use	They nibble strips off the stiff edges of leaves so that they can stick them into holes to extract insects.	To obtain food	Bluff, Weir, and Rutz (2007)
Baboons	Deception	Subordinate males groom females who are hidden behind rocks out of view from dominant males.	To gain access to females for sexual reproduction	Byrne (1995)
Chimpanzees	Self-concept	Chimps who have colored marks applied to their faces while anesthetized will touch these marks while looking in a mirror.	Possible basis for intentionality and theory of mind	Gallup, Anderson, and Shilito (2002)

Interdisciplinary Crossroads: Evolutionary Processes and Artificial Life

Artificial life (alife) is the study of human-made systems that have been designed to behave in ways that simulate the behavior of natural living systems (Langton, 1989). Alife researchers produce artificial "creatures" that inhabit virtual environments. They then study the behavior of these creatures and how they interact with one another and with aspects of their environments. What makes alife interesting and relevant to cognitive science is that although the rules that govern the creatures are often quite simple, the emergent behavior of these creatures is complex and can be considered intelligent.

We discuss alife in this chapter because these creatures learn and adapt via the use of evolutionary principles.

A good starting point for a discussion of alife is Animat (Wilson, 1985). Animat is a single animal that lives in a simple environment. Its world consists of a square computer screen taken up by food items, which Animat can eat, and trees, which are obstacles Animat must navigate around. Animat can sense its environment; it is aware of the objects that are in its immediate vicinity. It can also act on its environment by moving one step at a time in one of the eight directions that are specified by the points of a compass (N, NE, E, SE, etc.).

Animat is initially endowed with a set of rules that govern its performance. These rules are in the form of classifiers, templates that match an environmental condition that Animat is subject to at a given moment in relation to an action. Classifiers are really a modified version of if–then production rules. Each classifier has an associated strength or fitness. Classifiers with greater strength values are more likely to be utilized by Animat, as they promote Animat's survival. Animat's actions also have consequences. A good action is one that promotes its survival, such as its moving to a location where there is food. Good actions are rewarded by increases in the strengths of their classifiers. Neutral actions, ones that have no effect on the well-being of Animat, such as bumping into a tree, engender no change in classifier strength.

Animat is "born" with a collection of classifiers. These classifiers, along with their strength values, are randomly determined and, as such, give Animat no inherent advantage. These starting classifiers may be considered as equivalent to the genetic variation that exists among individuals or the members of a species and is shaped by selection forces. As Animat moves around its little world, classifiers are chosen and their strength values are altered on the basis of a system of reinforcement in such a way that survival-enhancing actions become more likely. However, this system alone is not enough to ensure Animat's survival. What Animat needs is a way of creating new classifiers that will better attune it to its world. This is where evolution comes in.

Wilson (1985) has equipped Animat with an evolutionary algorithm. Two classifiers that correspond to the same general type of action are selected. Individual components of these classifiers are then swapped. Segments of each classifier are randomly picked and exchanged and then used to create new classifier offspring. This is, of course, analogous to sexual reproduction in which genetic material from both parents is used to create children. Wilson, however, also allows for asexual reproduction. In this case, individual classifiers are cloned (reproduced in their entirety) to have random mutations.

The result of all this is that Animat's behavior becomes gradually more adaptive. Rather than modify the probabilities of its selections that represent its existing genetic endowment, it is able to generate entirely new actions, at least some of which will have beneficial results. It has been shown that these Animats, along with some more recent versions, learn quite rapidly. In one simulation, Animat was able to find food in only four steps compared with a chance-level performance in which it did the same in 41 steps.

Other alife programs demonstrate greater complexity. Ackley and Littman (1992) have created an entire population of creatures. Some are herbivores that eat plants, while others are carnivores that hunt and eat herbivores. Over time, the herbivores learned to "climb" trees to avoid predators, while the carnivores learned to cannibalize their fellow carnivores that died of starvation! Other emergent social behaviors of alife creatures include parasitism, symbiosis, and flocking.

Alife simulations show that evolution-based software entities interacting in a diversified environment are capable of complex behavior. If we define intelligence as one's ability to modify one's behavior in an advantageous way over time in the pursuit of goals, then Animat and other alife creatures may be labeled as intelligent. There is, however, no generally accepted definition of intelligence; therefore, the issue of whether such creatures possess it remains unresolved.

The field of alife is closely tied to the study of artificial intelligence. One of the key differences between the two fields is that alife attempts to model the behavior of the entire organism rather than the functioning of the mind or some specific mental process (Beer, 1990). Because the behavior of alife creatures is reactive, they lack an "understanding" of their world; they have no means of representing knowledge. Another criticism of alife has to do with the difference between simulation and realization. It is one thing to simulate life (some say) but another thing altogether to instantiate or create it in a true physical sense. Much of real life's complexity, exemplified by the ability to perceive and to move around, is given to alife creatures in the form of default abilities—in the absence of any real explanation as to how they may have arisen in these creatures.

Comparative Neuroscience

A common question that may come to mind when thinking about cognitive differences between species is brain size. One might expect that "smarter" animals have bigger brains, or brains that differ qualitatively from less intelligent species. Researchers first examined the size issue by ranking animals in terms of their brain size. When this is done, we find that elephants and whales have the largest overall brains, in excess of 5 kilograms. Intuitively, this doesn't seem right since humans are the most intelligent species and our brains are smaller than these animals. Larger animals generally have larger brains because they have a greater body size. What we need, then, is a measure that expresses brain size in proportion to body size.

This measure is called the **cephalization index** (expressed as the letter K). High K values indicate that an animal has a larger-than-average brain for its body size, while a low K value indicates the opposite. Now, we see that humans are at the top of the list with *K* values of 0.89. In second place are dolphins with a value of 0.64. Primates and whales come in third with values of 0.2 to 0.3, whereas other mammals fall below 0.2. This is depicted in Figure 8.3.

However, we need to interpret this index with caution (Kaas, 2000). Other factors not related to intelligence influence brain size. Birds, for example, have evolved compact brains because extra weight interferes with flying. Dolphins, on the other hand, may have exceptionally large brains because weight is generally not an issue in an aquatic environment. Another complication is that not all parts of brains are involved in cognition. The hindbrain in many animals does little more than regulate basic physiological functions, such as respiration, heart rate, digestion, and movement. So if we were to make our comparison

Figure 8.3 The cephalization index allows us to compare brain size relative to body size across different species.

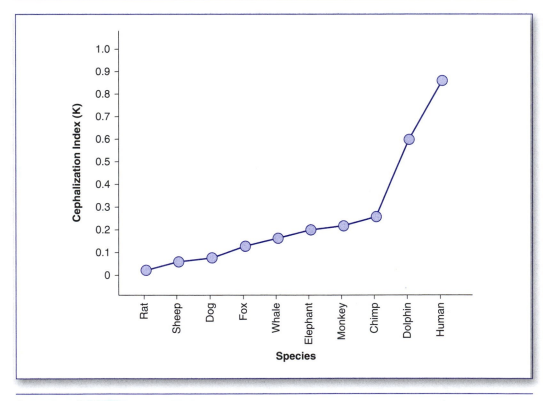

Source: Russell (1979).

correctly, we would need to express cephalization only in terms of the cognitive brain areas rather than the entire brain.

The brain structure that underlies most cognition is the neocortex. In humans, the neocortex constitutes 80% of total brain volume. For primates, this is 50%; in rodents, 30%; and for insectivores (mammals that eat insects), only 13%. However, even this measure has problems. To start, only mammals have a neocortex. Other species, such as birds, do

Figure 8.4 Brain size in several different animal species.

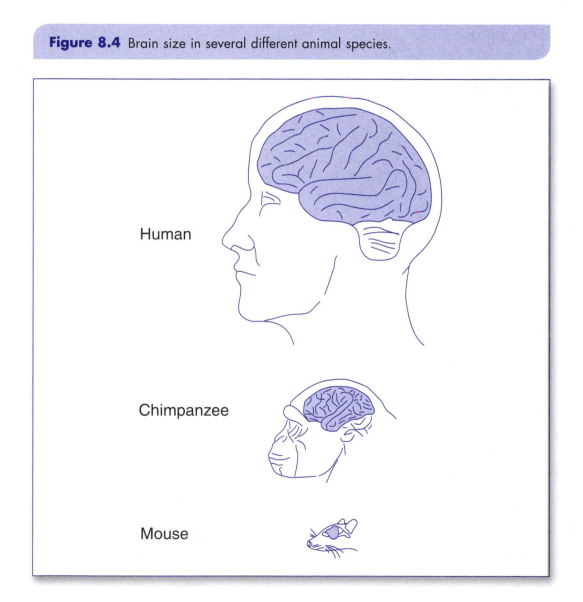

Human

Chimpanzee

Mouse

not possess one, so this prevents us from comparing neocortex size across all species. Figure 8.4 shows the brains of several different animals.

Another neural marker for intelligence may be **von Economo neurons**, also called spindle neurons. In humans and apes, these cells are found in the anterior cingulate cortex and the fronto insular cortex. In people alone, they are also located in the dorsolateral prefrontal cortex (Fajardo et al., 2008). They are also found in beluga, humpback, killer, and sperm whales; bottlenose dolphins; and elephants. They allow for the fast transmission of signals across larger distances as would be necessary in animals with larger brains. These cells in conjunction with a small world network architecture could promote rapid global information flow.

The location of von Economo cells in the cingulate cortex is no accident. The anterior cingulate cortex plays a vital role in higher cognitive function. It is involved in focused problem solving, the recognition of having made a mistake, and the initiation of correcting a mistake (Allman, Hakeem, Erwin, Nimchinsky, & Hof, 2001). Neurons in this region become active in experiments where participants must differentiate a correct response from conflicting cues and when there is a discrepancy between a desired state and a current state. It has been hypothesized to play a role in self-control and in the regulation of emotion and drive states, all signs of higher intelligence.

So what other measure can we use? One suggestion is the number of nerve cells. Unfortunately, the size and density of neurons in brains of different species differ. Some species, such as dolphins, have large cortical volumes but relatively few neurons. Other species, such as humans, have smaller volumes but more neurons. Although the comparison between dolphins and humans on this measure corresponds to actual intelligence differences, we cannot be sure that some other neuron property such as the number of dendritic connections is confounded with number. Future possibilities might include physiological function measures rather than anatomical differences. It would be interesting to see if intelligence correlates with plasticity—the ease with which synaptic connections are forged—or with complexity of neural circuits.

Evaluating the Comparative Approach

There are two methodological issues that plague the comparative approach (Wasserman & Zentall, 2006). Many of the studies investigating cross-species animal abilities have used different techniques. This makes them hard to compare, since any differences can be attributed to the different ways in which the experiments were conducted. A second problem is that some of the studies are done in artificial laboratory settings, while others are based on the naturalistic observation of animals in the wild. The laboratory studies can control for extraneous variables or alternate explanations of behavior but may be looking at actions the animals wouldn't normally engage in. The naturalistic observation studies yield natural behavior but have less control over other factors.

Perhaps one of the largest problems in this field is in how one attributes mental states to animals. People throughout history have had a tendency to attribute humanlike characteristics to animals, what is called **anthropomorphism**. Unfortunately, animal researchers are not immune to this tendency and can ascribe more advanced cognitive abilities to animals than the data actually warrant. However, we must also guard against **anthropodenial**, which is a blindness to the humanlike characteristics of animals, or the animallike characteristics of ourselves (De Waal, 1997a). According to this perspective, we are not so different from some animals, and it may be easiest and most accurate to describe their behavior in the same way that we would describe our own, in terms of internal intentions, desires, and beliefs.

Cheney and Seyfarth (1990) observed a low-ranking vervet monkey named Kitui utter a leopard alarm call whenever a new male tried to join his group. The addition of a new male would lower his status and introduce more competition for him for food and mates. The call caused all the monkeys to scatter into the trees and prevented the entry of the new male. At first blush, Kitui's action might make it seem as though he was capable of deceit and perhaps had a theory of mind, an understanding that the other members had beliefs. However, further study showed that he came down from the tree and uttered the cry again closer to the intruding male. By coming down from his hiding spot, Kitui would reveal to the others that he really didn't believe a leopard was there. This would negate any deceitful action and cause the other group members to suspect him. So it is unlikely, given this behavior, that he intended to deceive or had a developed theory of mind.

Other examples of overattributing cognition to animals come from studies of imitative behavior. One reason an animal might imitate another is because it understands that the other animal is performing an action to achieve a desired goal, such as acquiring food. The animal in question would then copy this action to obtain the desired goal for itself. Studies of potato washing in Japanese macaques and following behavior in ducks have instead shown that imitation can be a consequence of **stimulus enhancement**, where attention simply has been drawn to the location or the behavior and there is no inference of desired goals. Many other abilities ranging from concept formation to self-perception can also be accounted for by simpler explanations that don't require sophisticated thought processes.

EVOLUTIONARY PSYCHOLOGY

We humans don't look like much. We are thin skinned—and almost gawky looking when we stand upright. To a passing predator, we must seem like a particularly easy kill. We have no armor, fangs, or claws with which to defend ourselves, nor are we particularly strong or fast in comparison with other animals. So what has enabled humans to survive and thrive in a harsh world? The answer, in a word, is our minds. The species *Homo sapiens* has the most sophisticated mental faculties of any species on earth. Our capacities to think, to use language, and to solve problems outstrip those of any other animal. It is our minds that set us apart. An advanced mind allows for planning, communication, social cooperation, and the development of technology, which give us a tremendous competitive survival advantage.

But how did the human mind come into existence? What processes formed it? These are some of the questions asked by the evolutionary approach. In evolutionary theory, changes in an environment give rise to corresponding physical changes in an animal species that better enable it to survive. Giraffes, to use an often-cited example of adaptation, have developed longer necks over many generations to better enable them to get at treetop vegetation. Similarly, we can consider the mind to be such a body structure—comparable to the giraffe's neck—that has been shaped by evolutionary processes. EP not only attempts to describe these forces that are believed to have fashioned the human mind, but it is also concerned with understanding the mind's organization and function and how interaction with an environment produces observable behaviors.

Evolutionary psychologists face a fundamental problem. They need to understand the selection forces that gave rise to mental structures but cannot know precisely what these were because they correspond to events that were taking place far back in human prehistory. It is believed that the period of time during which many human psychological mechanisms evolved was the Pleistocene era, which began approximately 2 million years ago. This period is referred to as the **environment of evolutionary adaptation** (**EEA**; Bowlby, 1967). Because we cannot go back in time to study what occurred during this period, we must make inferences about the physical and social environment of that time based on evidence of various types. Buss (1999) describes the types of evidence used to test evolutionary hypotheses. These include archeological records, data from studying hunter-gatherer societies, systematic observation of human behavior, and self-reports in the form of interviews and questionnaires. EP also relies on a variety of methods for the testing of its hypotheses. Among these are comparisons across species, comparisons of males and females within a species, and experimentation (Buss, 1999). The evolutionary approach, thus, adopts a wide variety of methods rather than relying exclusively on the scientific method.

Evolved Psychological Mechanisms

Evolutionary biology focuses on all aspects of an animal's makeup. It is concerned with how selection forces came to shape the individual parts of an organism and how these parts became integrated. The scope of EP is narrower—it examines the impact that these forces had on psychological mechanisms only. Whereas evolutionary biology looks at organs and organ systems, EP looks primarily at a single organ—the brain. This perspective views the mind as a collection of psychological mechanisms that have evolved and attempts to describe how each came to be and how each operates.

The traditional view in cognitive psychology is that the mind is a **general-purpose processor**. This processor can be "fed" a problem in any format and can come up with a solution by applying a known set of rules. Modern computers operate in this way. The advantage of this process is that it can solve all problems of a given kind, assuming that the correct values of the problem's variables are mapped onto the algorithm designed to solve the problem correctly. The evolutionary perspective adopts a very different view. It argues that the mind is not general in any way but, instead, a set of many specific capacities. Each of these capacities is called an evolved psychological mechanism.

Cosmides and Tooby (1992) refer to the mind as a "Swiss army knife." In this analogy, each part of the knife unfolds to solve a different problem: the corkscrew takes out corks, the scissors cut paper, and so on. Likewise, each evolved psychological mechanism is assumed to have evolved in response to the need to solve a specific problem of adaptation and is activated by the contextual information of that problem alone. They are, thus, examples of modules we discussed previously. The general characteristics of modules are discussed in Chapter 4. Table 8.2 lists the six properties of evolved psychological mechanisms and illustrates them with an example.

Table 8.2 The six properties of an evolved psychological mechanism.

Property	Explanation	Example: Arachnophobia
1. Purpose	To solve a specific problem of survival or reproduction	Prevents being bitten by a poisonous spider
2. Perceptual focus	Mechanism triggered only by a visual image of a specific stimulus	Two body parts with eight legs
3. Communication	Input of mechanism informs the organism of the type of problem	Organism knows adaptive problem is one of death, not food selection or mating
4. Output	Input produces a behavioral output or response	Scream or swipe spider off body
5. Type of output	Can be physiological activity, input to another psychological mechanism, or a behavior	Heart acceleration and sweating, decision to swipe or run away, resulting behavior
6. Solution	Mechanism evolved to provide a solution to the problem	Removing spider from immediate vicinity reduces threat

Source: Buss (1999).

To sum up, EP views the mind not as a one-size-fits-all machine but as a collection of functionally distinct mechanisms. Evolutionary forces operating over vast periods of time created each of these mechanisms. Each evolved to solve a problem our ancestors faced during the EEA. It is important to keep this multiple-mechanism view in mind as we describe specific examples of cognitive processes. For every possible cognitive process, it is not the brain as a whole that is acting (according to this perspective) but a particular component of the brain. Thus, when we talk about the evolution of memory or logic, we are talking about specific mechanisms that may constitute only a part of the brain's memory or logic systems.

Evolution and Cognitive Processes

In the following sections, we will describe specific evolutionary hypotheses that pertain to several domains in cognition and the evidence that supports them (Gaulin & McBurney, 2001; Palmer & Palmer, 2002). These hypotheses concern cognitive processes only, which include categorization, memory, logical reasoning, judgment under uncertainty, and language. The motivation that underlies this research is the desire to arrive at an evolutionary account of how these cognitive processes arose. In other words, Why do we categorize and remember things the way we do? Why are we so poor at reasoning logically and making judgments under uncertain conditions? How is it that human beings alone of all the species on earth have developed such a complex linguistic ability?

Categorization

Research conducted by Eleanor Rosch (1973, 1975) shows that people form mental categories not in an "either–or" fashion but, rather, in a continuously graded way. Why should this be the case? Why do we not lump things together into one group on the basis of a single characteristic—for example, "red objects" or "curved objects"? The organization of concepts, it turns out, is governed by "fuzzy" categories, whereby a particular item can be more or less representative of the category. In this section, we will examine why humans form concepts in this way. Recall the finding—from the chapter on networks— that a bird such as a robin is thought of as being more representative or prototypical of the category of "birds" than another type of bird—for example, a penguin. This is because robins tend to come closer to our idea of what a bird is—something that is small, sings, flies, and so on. Robins are, thus, more typical of "birds" than are penguins, and participants in studies respond more quickly when they are asked to make judgments that have to do with robins—the so-called **typicality effect** (Rips, Shoben, & Smith, 1973; see Figure 8.5).

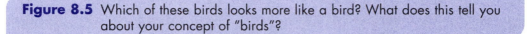

Figure 8.5 Which of these birds looks more like a bird? What does this tell you about your concept of "birds"?

Categories of the sort found in nature are almost always continuous: They contain items that span the entire spectrum of typicality—from being very representative and prototypical to being quite unrepresentative and perhaps easily mistaken for items that belong to another category. The categories that result from human categorization processes, therefore, mirror the distribution of natural objects in the world. This suggests an evolutionary process whereby we came to acquire concepts and a sense of their relatedness on the basis of how the items that these concepts represented were ordered in the natural environment. Further evidence in support of this notion comes from Boster and D'Andrade (1989). They found that professional ornithologists as well as those who had little experience and/or knowledge of birds all grouped stuffed bird specimens in similar ways. Their groupings demonstrated typicality and hierarchical effects reflective of what exists in nature.

What purpose do typicality-based categories serve? They must have provided us with some sort of selective advantage—otherwise, they would not have arisen. The advantage is this: If we know something about an item we have experienced, then it becomes possible to form judgments that have to do with related items (Rips, 1975). Imagine encountering for the first time a plant with four leaves and purple spots. After eating this plant, you become ill. Several months later, you stumble across a plant with three leaves and reddish-purple spots. Would you eat it? Probably not. There is a good chance that the two species of plant, because they are similar, share properties. Typicality categories, thus, allow us to capitalize on past experience. We generalize from what we know to what we don't know.

Memory

Other approaches in cognitive science tend to study basic memory processes. You will recall that cognitive psychologists are concerned with, among other things, how information is transferred from short-term to long-term memory. Neuroscience can identify the brain structures that underlie this transfer. Connectionists can then create artificial networks to model the process. EP, on the other hand, cares less about memory function per se and more about the purposes our memories serve. EP researchers want to know why our memories are the way they are. Specifically, they want to know how the demands of our ancestral environment have shaped memory and have made our memories operate the way they do. In this section, we will examine one aspect of memory—the relationship between the frequency of contact with an item in one's environment and recall.

Every day, we are bombarded with a tremendous amount of information. Only a small fraction of it is actually remembered. This is a good thing, as most of the information is trivial. For instance, can you remember the color of the shirt your best friend was wearing the previous Monday? It would make sense, then, for us to remember only the information that may be of some benefit to us and to forget that which doesn't benefit us. But what constitutes beneficial information? What things should we be better at remembering? An evolutionary account avers that information that we encounter more often should be better remembered. The more often we encounter an item, the greater its relevance to our daily life and our survival. And the less often we encounter an item, the lesser its relevance to our survival. Remembering your roommate's name is important—because he can help you in a variety of ways. You would also be likely to hear your roommate's name quite often, as you see him practically every day. Remembering the name of your niece who lives in another country is less important to you, as you are far removed from interacting with her on a daily basis. Correspondingly, you would very rarely hear her name, assuming that it is not the same as that of someone else you know better.

One way to test this hypothesis is to compare the frequency of our encounters with specific items with our ability to remember them. Clearly, this relationship will be positive: The more frequently we encounter items, the better our memory of them. In addition, the relationship is described by a power function. For our purposes, we need to know only that a power function is a specific kind of mathematical relationship. This specific relationship is represented when we plot on a graph our ability to remember items versus how often we encounter them.

Anderson and Schooler (1991) tested this relationship. They examined several real-world sources of information and determined for each type of information the function for the frequency of occurrence and recall. That is, they determined the mathematical relationship specifying how many times a piece of information occurred and how accurately it was remembered. They used newspaper headlines, utterances made by parents to their children, and names of the authors of e-mails that were received by one of the researchers over an approximate 4-year period. For all these sources, the probability that a particular utterance or word would crop up a second time was a decreasing function of the number of days since its previous appearance. For example, if the word *north* appeared in a newspaper headline yesterday, there would be a relatively good chance that it would appear again today, presumably because it was part of an ongoing news story. If *north* had been in the paper the previous week, the chances that it would appear again today would be much lower. The researchers then measured memory for these items and found that the function that described probability of recall over time was in accordance with the probability of occurrence. This shows that our memory for items is directly proportional to how often we encounter them in the environment. Our memories are better for items that we encounter more often and poorer for those we encounter less often. This finding supports the notion that our memories have evolved such that they retain items only to the extent that we need them. From an evolutionary point of view, this makes sense. We should remember those things that we encounter frequently, as it is very likely that they are of importance to us, and forget those things that we encounter infrequently, as it is likely that they are not of much use to our survival.

Logical Reasoning

Recall from the chapter on philosophy that deductive reasoning involves the application of logical rules to a set of premises. A conclusion is then derived: If the premises are true, then an application of the rules will always yield a correct conclusion. Deductive thought is, thus, a valid way of garnering new information about the world. Logic is used in other approaches to cognitive science too. Connectionists use the rules of logic to describe how neural units interact. Researchers in artificial intelligence create computer programs that use logic to generate new information from existing data and to solve problems. In the evolutionary approach, investigators want to know why we as humans are so bad at thinking logically and to relate this deficiency to the kinds of social conditions our early ancestors may have faced.

If you have ever taken a course in logic, you may have wondered why the subject is so difficult. The rules of logic are straightforward. All one has to do is memorize the forms of these rules and then plug into them the relevant aspects of the problem. In this fashion, one can then apply the forms to any problem and be assured of obtaining a correct solution. Unfortunately, it is not as easy as it sounds. Most people find it difficult to reason logically. Interestingly, however, there is an exception. People can reason logically under certain conditions. The evolutionary approach can tell us why we are so bad at logical reasoning in general and what the exception is.

The **Wason selection task** is designed to measure a person's logical thinking ability. Figure 8.6 gives an example of such a task. Take a minute now and try to solve this problem. You probably found that it was quite difficult. Next, try to solve a different version of the problem, shown in Figure 8.7. When you have finished—or if you are having trouble—consult Figure 8.8 for the correct solutions. If you are like most people, you would have found the "bouncer" version of the problem to be much easier. Why is this? Both versions have the same underlying logical structure and should be of equal difficulty.

Figure 8.6 You have been hired as a clerk. Your job is to make sure that a set of documents is marked correctly, according to the following rule: "If the document has an E rating, then it must be marked code 4." You have been told that there are some errors in the way the documents have been coded and that you need to find the errors. Each document has a letter rating on one side and a numerical code on the other. Here are four documents. Which document(s) do you need to turn over to check for errors?

Figure 8.7 You have been hired as a bouncer in a bar, and you must enforce the following rule: "If a person is drinking vodka, then he or she must be over 20 years old." The cards depicted in the figure contain information about four people in the bar. One side of each card lists a person's age, and the other side specifies what he or she is drinking. Which card(s) do you need to turn over to make sure that no one is breaking the law?

Figure 8.8 Solutions to the "clerk" and "bouncer" problems.

Solution to the "clerk" problem.
Rule: E-rated documents must be marked code 4.
Step 1: Check E-rated documents to see if they meet the coding criterion.
Step 2: Check any documents not matching the coding criterion (e.g., code 8) to see if they are E-rated.
No more checking necessary:
G ratings (paired with any code) could not violate the rule.
Code 4 documents do not have to be E-rated.

Solution to the "bouncer" problem.
Rule: Vodka drinkers must be over 20 years old.
Step 1: Check vodka drinkers to see if they meet the age criterion.
Step 2: Check anyone who does not meet the age criterion (e.g., 17 years old) to see if they are drinking vodka.
No more checking necessary:
Pepsi drinking (at any age) could not violate the rule.
People over 20 years do not have to drink vodka.

According to Cosmides and Tooby (1992), the bouncer problem is easy because it involves **cheater detection**, the ability to discern who has taken as his own something he does not deserve. They argue that during the EEA, human societies were characterized by **reciprocal altruism**, the sharing of hard-won resources among group members. In this kind of social cooperative, it is important to detect "freeloaders"—those who take more than their fair share. Cosmides and Tooby believe that this social environment shaped our reasoning abilities such that when we are presented with a logic problem that involves cheating, we can solve it. If a logic puzzle possesses the element of a cheater, then the evolved psychological mechanism for cheater detection is activated. This mechanism "understands" the rules of logic and can apply them, but only in this specific context. Note that this understanding stands in stark contrast to that which maintains that the mind is a general-purpose processor that can solve logic problems of any sort.

There is abundant experimental evidence in support of the cheater detection model of reasoning. One study comes from Gigerenzer and Hug (1992). They presented participants with two Wason selection tasks, both of which entailed a social contract of the following sort: "If you stay overnight in a mountain shelter, you must help out by carrying up some firewood to add to the supply." Both of these tasks were roughly equivalent with respect to content and logical structure. The only real difference between the two was that one of the tasks involved cheating, while the other did not. The results showed that 78% to 90% of the participants were able to solve the cheating version. Only about half as many participants were able to solve the noncheating version. This shows that the framing of a logic problem as a social contract alone is not enough to elicit the problem-solving skill; it is elicited by a social contract that specifically involves cheating. In another study, it was discovered that even children a little older than 2 years of age seem to have this cheater-detecting capacity (Cummins, 1999).

Judgment Under Uncertainty

In many situations in life, we have to make a decision in the absence of complete information. What are the chances that Mary will go out with me? What is the likelihood that I will make the college swim team? As is the case with logical reasoning, most people are quite poor at solving problems of this type—problems that involve probability (Nisbett & Ross, 1980; Tversky & Kahneman, 1974). Why is this? One reason is that humans facing these kinds of problems rely on heuristics. A heuristic is a mental "rule of thumb" or strategy that is a fast and easy way of solving a problem. The problem with heuristics is that they aren't always right. Heuristics can lead us to commit **fallacies**—fundamental misunderstandings of statistical rules. The role that evolution has played in shaping our thinking in this situation is discussed below.

Tversky and Kahneman (1974) were the first to study heuristics and fallacies. In one study, they gave the participants a description of a person. Participants were also told that this person belonged to a set of 100 people. There were two conditions in the experiment. In the first, the participants were told that the set consisted of 30 lawyers and 70 engineers. In the second, they were told that the set contained 70 lawyers and 30 engineers. Here is a sample description:

> Jack is a 45-year-old man. He is married and has four children. He is generally conservative, careful, and ambitious. He shows no interest in political and social issues and spends most of his free time on his many hobbies, including home carpentry, sailing, and mathematical puzzles.

Is Jack a lawyer or an engineer? The participants answered overwhelmingly that Jack was an engineer, even in the condition in which engineers made up only 30% of the set. Tversky and Kahneman (1974) argue that this kind of error is due to a **representativeness heuristic**, the tendency to judge an item on the basis of its perceived similarity to other items. Because the description of Jack fits the stereotype of the engineer, we consider it very likely that he is one. The representativeness heuristic in this case is accompanied by the **base-rate fallacy**, ignorance of the base rates that define the set of 100 people.

Here is another example of our difficulty in making judgments under uncertainty (Tversky & Kahneman, 1974). Consider the following description: "Linda is 31 years old, single, outspoken, and very bright. She majored in philosophy. In college, she was involved in several social issues, including the environment, the peace campaign, and the antinuclear campaign." Which of these statements do you think is more likely: "Linda is a bank teller" or "Linda is a bank teller and is active in the feminist movement"? Most people over-whelmingly choose the latter sentence, even though it cannot possibly be the more likely of the two, since there are always going to be more tellers than feminist tellers (see Figure 8.9). Participants again rely on the representativeness of Linda's description, which fits the stereotype of the feminist. In this instance, participants ignore the conjunction rule, which states that the probability of encountering those who are both feminists and tellers is lower than the probability of encountering those who are one or the other. The making of this error is known as the **conjunction fallacy**.

So is it fair to say that humans cannot think in terms of probability or uncertainty? From an evolutionary standpoint, one would guess that this is not a fair statement, as uncertainty is an inherent characteristic of the natural world. Gigerenzer and Hoffrage (1995) argue that the difficulties that human beings have in this area, which are documented in the literature, stem not from a fundamental inability on our part but from the

Figure 8.9 A Venn diagram illustrating the conjunction rule. Circle A represents all bank tellers. Circle B represents all feminists. Region C, the portion of overlap between the two circles, represents feminist bank tellers and will always be smaller than the regions that correspond to the number of bank tellers or feminists, considered separately.

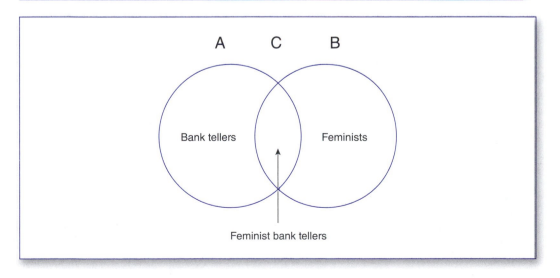

way that these types of problems are usually structured. Many of these problems entail probabilities that are expressed as fractions or percentages rather than as frequencies, expressed as numbers of occurrences. Probabilities are more complex numerically, as they require dividing one number by another. They also are the rather recent invention of mathematicians. We encounter frequency data, on the other hand, as part of our daily existence. We can think easily of how many times we've eaten today or how many games the New York Yankees have won this season.

It makes sense, then, that the psychological mechanism that underlies uncertain reasoning should be sensitive to frequency data. It turns out that this is, indeed, the case. Gigerenzer and Hoffrage (1995) assessed a number of uncertainty problems and converted them from a percentage to a frequency format. They found that roughly three times as many participants answered correctly. Their finding, similar to the findings of the logical reasoning study illustrated earlier, is another example of how problem solving is narrowly tuned to a particular type of information. This attunement to a particular type of information is the second major characteristic of evolved psychological mechanisms and again runs contrary to the notion of the mind as a general-purpose processor—at least within these problem-solving domains.

Yet another example of poor probabilistic reasoning is the **gambler's fallacy**. Do you think it is more likely that someone who has played the slot machines for a longer period of time will win? Do you think that a fair coin that has come up "heads" eight times in a row is more likely to come up "tails" on the next toss? If you answered yes to either of these questions, then you have been taken in by the gambler's fallacy. It is the belief that the probability of an event is influenced by how often it has occurred in the past. If a particular outcome has turned up quite often in the recent past, people are apt to believe that there is an increased likelihood that another outcome will occur. In reality, the probability of each event in these cases is independent. The chances of winning at slots the 100th time are exactly the same as for the first. The chance of getting a "heads" in a fair coin flip is 0.50 on every flip.

Why, then, do we persist in holding such beliefs? One explanation is that independent outcomes are typically the product of artificially engineered devices that are not encountered in the natural world, such as dice or roulette wheels (Pinker, 1997). In nature, the past often *is* the best predictor of the future. If it was sunny yesterday, there is a good chance that it will be sunny today. If a herd of mammoth migrated through a particular region the previous year at this time, the chances are that they will do it again this year. Natural events tend to have regular time courses and shared causes; therefore, some knowledge about the way an event unfolded in the past is informative about the way similar events will unfold in the future.

Language

Language is so important in cognitive science that it is a separate field of study. Linguists study the organizational rules of language and how language is acquired. They also construct models of language processing. From an evolutionary standpoint, the focus again is not so much on processing but on how language came to be. Because language possesses a social function, evolutionary researchers want to know what aspects of early human social life might have given rise to its development.

One of the most obvious things that sets *H. sapiens* apart from other species is language. Other animals can communicate, and primates can be taught rudimentary linguistic skills, but nowhere else in the animal kingdom do we see such a sophisticated use of and widespread reliance on language as in the human species. The evolution of language is believed to have catalyzed the development of intelligence, social cooperation, and other phenomena, in the process of which human beings derived great benefit. Researchers in this area have argued that language is an evolved trait and have provided several theoretical explanations for how it could have arisen. Nonevolutionary accounts of language are discussed in Chapter 9.

Converging lines of evidence point to the fact that human language ability has evolved (Palmer & Palmer, 2002). First, languages share a number of universal commonalities (Hockett, 1960). Among these are meaningfulness, the ability of those who possess language to communicate about things not physically present, and the ability of those who possess it to produce an infinite number of new meanings via the combination of existing elements. All babies progress through the same developmental language stages, in the same order, and on roughly the same time schedule. Children also acquire the rules of language faster than they could possibly acquire them through formal learning. Finally, there are specific brain areas devoted to language. Most individuals are left-hemisphere dominant with respect to language and have localized sites within this hemisphere that are devoted to linguistic comprehension and linguistic performance. These observations strongly imply that language capacity is prespecified and is present at birth. This, in turn, means that language capacity is genetically coded and has been shaped by selection forces that were operational at some time in our ancestral past.

Robin Dunbar (1996) has developed a fascinating theory of language evolution. He notes that in hominids there is a positive correlation between group size and the size of the neocortex. The neocortex underlies cognitive function and is quite large in humans. This brain region processes social information—for example, information that has to do with which members of a group are our friends and which members are our enemies. These kinds of social computations become more complex with increases in group size.

Most primates form alliances by grooming one another—that is, by picking parasites and dirt from one another's fur. This feels good to them and is a form of social bonding. But grooming, because it is a one-on-one activity, imposes a limit on how many individuals in a group can bond. Once a group becomes large enough, not every member of the group can be groomed. Language is also a form of social bonding and a way for individuals who possess this capacity to form alliances within groups. These alliances are forged primarily through the equivalent of gossip, wherein small groups communicate in both positive and negative ways about other group members. Because one can speak comfortably to a larger number of other individuals at once, language may have driven the formation of larger groups in early protohuman societies.

The coming into being of larger groups prompted further innovations, which were adaptive in nature. Larger groups are better able to defend themselves against predators in an open savanna environment. Language allows for complex, coordinated social behavior. Language would have facilitated hunting, foraging, child care, and other crucial survival behaviors. The development of language may have received an additional boost from sexual selection. Assuming that females recognize verbal skill as a rough indicator of intelligence, they might choose to mate with males who are good "talkers," as their intelligence would make them better partners.

Behavioral Economics: How We Think About Profit and Loss

The discipline of behavioral economics is devoted to studying the basis of economic decision making. It applies scientific methods to understand the cognitive, emotional, and social influences on the way we think about things such as money, goods, services, buying, and selling. The classical view in economic theory is that people are rational decision makers. This implies that we reason logically when presented with choices, always picking outcomes that maximize our benefits and minimize our losses. In reality, it turns out that we are far from rational when it comes to making economic choices, and our motives in these situations often have evolutionary explanations. As was the case with judgment under uncertainty, our behavior stems from various heuristics. Framing, or the way a problem is presented, also has a powerful impact under these circumstances.

Imagine that you are given $1,000 and that you can split it with somebody any way you want. This scenario in the lab is known as the ultimatum game. Being slightly selfish, you might decide to keep $900 and give $100 to the other person. Would your partner accept? If she were perfectly rational, she would. After all, it is a free hundred bucks. Surprisingly though, in experiments such as this, people will turn down the offer and reject the money. In fact, they will reject it when the uneven split is 70/30 or more (Camerer, 2003). Why should this be? According to evolutionary theory, it is because people perceive the split to be unfair. Reciprocal altruism implies that if somebody does you a favor, then he or she is trustworthy. In the future, you could then return the favor and between the two of you establish a support network of mutual aid. This is one mechanism by which hunter-gatherer societies could establish strong bonds and increase their chances of survival.

We can effectively sum up this principle as "I'll scratch your back if you scratch mine" (Shermer, 2008). People are willing to accept help only if they perceive the split to be something approaching parity because this would signal an ally who could help them down the road. Interestingly, the effect isn't found only in humans. De Waal (1997b) had pairs of Capuchin monkeys perform a task. When one member of the pair was rewarded and did not share with its partner, the other expressed displeasure and failed to cooperate from that point on. This and other evidence suggest that our primate ancestors and we have evolved a sense of justice. This capacity is no longer adaptive, because we live in a large consumer–producer society where any gain—especially one from a stranger—would be an advantage. But the behavior persists.

The principle of **loss aversion** states that we are more sensitive to losses than to equivalent gains. In fact, empirical estimates show that people tend to fear losses about twice as much as they desire gains. Here's an example: Would you prefer to receive a $5 discount or to avoid a $5 surcharge? Most people prefer the latter. Here is another example: You are on a team of experts that must decide what course of action to take in preventing a flu outbreak.

Program A: Two hundred people will be saved.

Program B: There is a one-third probability that 600 people will be saved and a two-thirds probability that no one will be saved.

Of the participants, 72% chose option A. Now consider the following rewording of the question:

Program C: Four hundred people will die.

Program D: There is a one-third probability that nobody will die and a two-thirds probability that 600 people will die.

The outcomes in this second case are identical to that in the first, yet now the responses are reversed. Of the participants, 78% now chose program D over program C.

These results demonstrate not just loss aversion but also **framing effects**. We prefer choices that are framed positively rather than negatively (De Martino, Kumaran, Seymour, & Dolan, 2006; Tversky & Kahneman, 1981). Framing effects are salient when we make financial decisions. Here is an example:

Option A: The MePhone is available at Awesome Electronics for $100; five blocks away at DigiData, it is at half price for only $50. Would you make the short trip to save the $50?

Option B: PowerPurchase offers the NetBook for $1,000; five blocks away, it can be had for $950 at CircuitCrazy. Would you make the short trip to save the $50?

The majority of people, when presented with this problem, prefer option A. They would be willing to walk the five blocks in that scenario but not in option B, even though the amount of money saved in both cases is the same. Why? According to the principle of **mental accounting**, we put money into different categories based on the context or frame.

We tend to put smaller amounts of money into one category and larger amounts into another. A $50 savings seems greater compared with $100 than it does relative to $1,000. Generally, people are less likely to make efforts to save cash when the relative amount of money they are dealing with is large.

Samuelson and Zeckhauser (1988) offered participants a choice between several financial investments varying in risk. Under those circumstances, individuals chose a variety of different investments based on how risk averse they were. Then, in a second condition, they told the participants that an investment had already been chosen for them, and they could either stick with this or switch to one of the alternatives. Now, they were far more likely to stick with the one that they had been assigned. Of these participants, 47% stayed with the default compared with the 32% of those who had chosen it in the earlier scenario. The tendency to stay with what we have (the status quo) and to prefer it over other options has been dubbed the **endowment effect**.

The evolutionary explanation for the endowment effect is straightforward. Back in the EEA, resources were usually scarce. Things such as food and tools took a long time and lots of effort to obtain. For this reason, it made sense to hoard or hold on to those things we already had, since replacing them would have been time-consuming and energy intensive. Those individuals who kept a tight grip on what they had would have been more likely to survive. However, the endowment effect can also backfire. Sometimes, it does make sense to let go of what we have and switch to something different that may end up being more valuable or at least less costly. Unfortunately, we tend to overestimate or focus on the amount of effort we've already put into something (its sunk cost) and use this to justify staying with it, which may blind us to choosing a better option. If this happens, then we have fallen victim to the **sunk-cost fallacy** (Sutton, 1991). Think for a minute about those things you may have held on to for too long. They may include staying with the same car, house, job, relationship, and so on.

Sex Differences in Cognition

Married couples may sometimes be aware of the existence of cognitive differences between the sexes. Perhaps one partner gets lost, while the other is forgetful. Research has shown that in the human species there are small but consistent cognitive differences between males and females. The evolutionary approach tries to provide explanations for these differences in terms of the selection pressures that were acting on the two sexes during the EEA.

Important cognitive sex differences are attributed to an early human **sexual division of labor**, according to which men hunted and women gathered (Silverman & Eals, 1992; Silverman & Phillips, 1998). The hunting process, which was apt to require navigation across long distances and novel terrain for days at a time, is believed to have been selected for enhanced spatial abilities in men (Figure 8.10). Women, for whom communication with one another and with their children was a part of the gathering process, are believed to have developed superior verbal abilities (Figure 8.11). Indeed, such differences between the sexes are observable today. On average, males outperform females on tests of spatial relations and image rotation (Levy & Heller, 1992). In these tests, a participant is usually asked to determine whether a letter of the alphabet, displayed in a variety of orientations, is the same as another. Females generally score higher than males on tests of verbal fluency, reading speed, reading comprehension, and spelling (Notman & Nadelson, 1991). One might also deduce that as women were specialized at gathering, they should be adept at specific kinds of spatial tasks—namely, object–location memory. Memory for object location is imperative to the task of gathering, as one would need to recall the locations of perhaps widely disseminated food sources. Silverman and Phillips (1998) discovered that

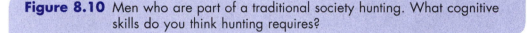

Figure 8.10 Men who are part of a traditional society hunting. What cognitive skills do you think hunting requires?

Source: © Peter Johnson/Corbis.

Figure 8.11 Women engaged in gathering. What cognitive skills make for a good gatherer?

Source: © Louise Gubb/Louise Gubb/Corbis.

women outperform men in their ability to remember the locations of objects, both natural and artifactual (see Figure 8.12). Their study suggests that our conceptions of spatial and verbal abilities are crude and that there are perhaps multiple domains within these abilities that may point the way to additional sex differences.

A second theory that accounts for the differences between men and women with respect to spatial and verbal abilities has been advanced. According to this hypothesis, spatial ability became enhanced in males not as a result of hunting activity but, rather, as a result of long-standing mate-seeking practices. The males of polygynous animal species must travel comparatively greater distances to meet and mate with females. Data indicate that the males of polygynous species—for example, the meadow vole—make fewer errors than females when given maze navigation tasks (Gaulin & FitzGerald, 1986, 1989). These sex differences disappear in the prairie vole, which is a monogamous species and of which neither sex ranges very far. It should be noted that there is nothing

Figure 8.12 A stimulus set that can be used to test for object and location memory. If you studied this for a minute, would you be able to recall what objects were next to the pelican?

special about "maleness" or spatial ability. Rather, it is the environmental demands that are placed on one sex or the other of a particular species that are pivotal. In the brown-headed cowbird, there is a greater need for spatial problem solving among females, who show evidence of spatial ability that is superior to that of the males (Sherry, Forbes, Khurgel, & Ivy, 1993). Among humans, it is possible that the enhanced spatial ability of males developed first as a result of mate seeking and was later co-opted for hunting activities.

EVALUATING EVOLUTIONARY PSYCHOLOGY

EP as a formal discipline is a recent addition to the ranks. As such, it has received both fervent acclaim and fervent criticism. Its strengths are its methodological variety and its attempt to develop an objective science of human behavior that is grounded on a single, powerful theoretical model. The evolutionary model already has proved to be fruitful in biology, and its use in psychology links the two disciplines. The evolutionary perspective also reshapes psychology such that it becomes a unified discipline, as opposed to the disjointed one that it tends to be currently (Buss, 1999). Modern psychology consists of multiple disciplines, each characterized by a unique theoretical perspective and a unique focus. For example, cognitive psychology focuses on information processing, social psychology focuses on interpersonal relationships, and developmental psychology focuses on growth and change in an organism over its entire life span. EP cuts across these different theoretical perspectives and tries to provide a coherent, unified approach to the study of mind and behavior. But EP has its problems. Even adherents of the theory of natural selection and of biological evolution have attacked its assumptions.

One of the fundamental assumptions behind the evolutionary approach is that evolved psychological mechanisms are adaptive responses to survival-related or reproduction-related problems. But this need not always be the case. There are at least two other kinds of phenomena, in addition to selective processes, that can produce novel biological function (Dover, 2000). The first of these is exaptation, or neutral drift. In this instance, random mutations in an organism's genome result in new genes that have little or no consequence for reproduction. These genes can become disseminated in a population and at some point may assume a new adaptive function that represents a response to a change in the environment. The second is molecular drive, in which a copy of a gene can mutate. There are known cases in which genes that code for proteins become duplicated; the duplicated genes then diverge to serve another function. These genes and the characteristics they give rise to have not been selected for.

Figure 8.13 Spandrels in a cathedral in Granada, Spain.

Spandrels

The evolutionary scholar Stephen Jay Gould (2000) proposes that many of an organism's attributes may arise via nonselectionist mechanisms. He refers to these attributes as "spandrels". A **spandrel** is the triangular space between the exterior curve of an arch and the rectangular frame that encloses the arch (see Figure 8.13). A spandrel serves no design purpose; it exists solely as a consequence of an architect's surrounding an arch with a frame. Similarly, many psychological mechanisms may themselves be spandrels—they may be by-products of an adaptation that was subsequently co-opted for useful purposes. The ability to read and write are probably by-products of an earlier linguistic capacity—the capacity to comprehend and produce speech. Once these earlier capacities are in place, neural connections to visual and manual parts of the brain that were already in existence would then have enabled the later arriving capacities.

The job of the evolutionary psychologist is a difficult one, as he or she must start with a given mental mechanism and come up with a purpose for it. The purpose corresponds to the adaptive problem the mechanism was intended to solve. This process is called **reverse engineering** because one begins with the final product and thinks back to what it was that may have compelled its genesis. This is more difficult than the conventional engineer's job, which consists of starting with a desired function (getting a car over a valley) and designing a product (a bridge) that will enable that function. It is also the case that evolutionary psychologists can easily be wrong in making the assumption that a particular psychological mechanism came into being as a response to a particular problem. It may have evolved in response to an entirely different problem.

What makes reverse engineering so difficult is the paucity of available evidence with which one might reconstruct crucial past events. Tools, bones, and other fragments of the archeological record allow us to make certain inferences, but they are insufficient to inform us about crucial aspects of prehistoric times—for example, kinship relations, group size, social structure, and the activities of males and females (Gould, 2000). These aspects of culture and behavior cannot be easily revealed through the fossil record.

In the traditional evolutionary view, biology is shaped by selection. Biology then gives rise to psychology. Psychology, in turn, generates culture—the larger environment in which humans live (Cosmides & Tooby, 1992). This scheme can be turned upside down, however, in that culture can also shape psychology. A large body of evidence shows that environments exert a strong influence on our thoughts and behaviors. Culture, primarily via the medium of learning, is thus another force that is capable of generating psychology.

Dynamical or **ecological models of cognition**, because they postulate the existence of learning, pose a threat to evolutionary theory (Karmiloff-Smith, 2000). In these models, mental abilities arise through learning processes; that is, they come into being as a result of an individual's social, verbal, perceptual, and manipulative interaction with his or her environment—all taking place within the life span of the individual. In this account, what would seem to be an evolved psychological mechanism may, in fact, have been acquired by the individual as he or she went about his or her business. This runs contrary to the evolutionary view that evolved psychological mechanisms are coded for by genes that were shaped by selection pressures that were present at birth, fully formed and just waiting to be activated by the appropriate stimulus inputs.

An alternative account has genes laying down the groundwork for a capacity that develops at a later stage as a result of experience. Stereoscopic vision, the ability to perceive depth via a combination of the information received from the two eyes, is an instance of this kind of capacity. Stereoscopic vision is not present at birth and develops fully only after an organism has perceived the world with both eyes. The brain mechanisms that underlie such abilities cannot exist in their entirety at birth, as developmental experience forges their basic neural connections and circuits—a process termed *postnatal neural assembly*.

Karmiloff-Smith (2000) distinguishes between two developmental models. In the **mosaic model of development**, a brain mechanism is determined almost entirely by genes and operates quickly (i.e., is a reflex or a fast perceptual process), and its components or parts develop independently of one another. Such mechanisms operate well under typical conditions—those "designed" to trigger their operation. They must, however, be completely specified in advance and are limited in how complex they can be. Evolutionary psychologists believe that evolved brain mechanisms are, in a word, mosaic. In contrast, in the **regulatory model of development**, brain mechanisms are only partially determined by genes and operate more slowly (i.e., they are deliberative cognitive processes), and their parts develop interdependently. This type of mechanism is flexible and capable of altering its function under varying conditions, and only the broad outlines of such a mechanism need be specified at birth. These mechanisms are also more complex. Research suggests that regulatory development is the norm for the growth of cortical abilities—those that underlie higher order cognitive abilities. Mosaic development occurs in many animal species, and in humans, it is likely to govern several noncortical brain areas.

OVERALL EVALUATION OF THE EVOLUTIONARY APPROACH

Evolution is a powerful theoretical framework. It can be used to explain how virtually every natural process comes into existence. As such, it rests squarely within Marr's computational level of description, which attempts to provide explanation for a given process by identifying its purpose. Knowing why a structure exists gives us many clues as to its structure and function and can help us decipher problems that come into view at other descriptive levels. The evolutionary approach, as we noted earlier, meshes well with neuroscience. Collaboration between these disciplines should focus on finding the neural bases of evolved psychological mechanisms and on providing a fuller understanding of the selection pressures that created them.

One bone of contention between evolution and the cognitive and artificial intelligence perspectives is the issue of general-purpose versus domain-specific processing. Is the mind a general-purpose computer or a "Swiss army knife"? As is the case with many other debates that are apt to pit the proponents of one extreme against those of the opposite extreme, it may be that both are correct. Some cognitive processes may indeed qualify as evolved psychological mechanisms, by their being in accordance with all the defining criteria. Others may be of a general purpose. There is a need for studies that will focus on this important distinction and on the role of complex developmental factors.

SUMMING UP: A REVIEW OF CHAPTER 8

1. Biological evolution is based on the theory of natural selection that describes how species change over time. Three principles are important: (1) variation in a species population, (2) inheritance of traits, and (3) a change in the environment favoring some traits over others, known as natural selection.

2. The field of comparative cognition examines the thinking capacities of animals and attempts to make cross-species comparisons. Specific animal species adapt to their ecological niches and, depending on the circumstances, can evolve similar or differing perceptual, conceptual, memory, and reasoning abilities. However, there are numerous problems in making these comparisons due to different methodologies and anthropomorphism.

3. EP is a field that examines the role that evolutionary forces played in determining our cognitive abilities. The EEA is the period during which such forces played a dominant role.

4. The classical view sees cognitive processes as general purpose and able to solve a variety of different problems. The evolutionary view instead sees cognitive processes as special purpose, having evolved to solve a particular adaptive problem. Such processes are called evolved psychological mechanisms.

5. There is evidence to suggest that evolutionary forces have shaped all cognitive processes, including categorization, memory, logical reasoning, judgment under uncertainty, and language.

6. Humans rarely solve problems in a rational or objective fashion. Rather, they rely on heuristics. These are strategies that provide a fast and easy solution but are not always correct. Heuristics can lead them to commit fallacies, or fundamental misunderstandings, of the logical or mathematical rules underlying a problem.

7. Examples of heuristics and fallacies abound. These include the representativeness heuristic, the base-rate fallacy, the conjunction fallacy, and the gambler's fallacy.

8. Behavioral economics is a relatively new discipline that examines how we reason about financial matters. It turns out that in this domain, we also use heuristics and fall victim to fallacies. In the ultimatum game, we reject offers of money if they are judged to be unfair. We are loss aversive, are sensitive to the way questions are framed, think differently about large and small sums of money, and tend to hold on to what we have even if it might end up being more costly than other alternatives.

9. Evolutionary pressures can help explain differences in the way males and females think. Male hunting and female gathering could account for male superiority in certain spatial tasks and female superiority in particular verbal tasks.

10. EP has many critics. Processes other than natural or sexual selection, such as exaptation (or neutral drift) and molecular drive, can account for the development of human mental faculties. It is also difficult to determine what the conditions were like during the EEA since we cannot observe it directly. Even so, the evolutionary approach has much promise, as it may serve to unify disparate fields in psychology and cognitive science.

EXPLORE MORE

Log on to the student study site at **http://study.sagepub.com/friedenberg3e** for electronic flash cards, review quizzes, and a list of web resources to aid you in further exploring the field of cognitive science.

SUGGESTED READINGS

Adami, C. (1999). *Introduction to artificial life.* New York, NY: Springer.
Buss, D. M. (2007). *Evolutionary psychology: The new science of the mind.* Boston, MA: Allyn & Bacon.

Dawkins, R. (2006). *The selfish gene.* Oxford, England: Oxford University Press.

Halpern, D. F. (2000). *Sex differences in cognitive abilities.* Mahwah, NJ: Erlbaum.

Kahneman, D., & Tversky, A. (Eds.). (1982). *Judgment under uncertainty.* Cambridge, England: Cambridge University Press.

Rose, H., & Rose, S. (Eds.). (2000). *Arguments against evolutionary psychology.* New York, NY: Harmony Books.

9

THE LINGUISTIC APPROACH

Language and Cognitive Science

How very commonly we hear it remarked that such and such thoughts are beyond the compass of words! I do not believe that any thought, properly so called, is out of the reach of language.

—Edgar Allan Poe, 1846

THE LINGUISTIC APPROACH: THE IMPORTANCE OF LANGUAGE

Linguistics is the study of language. There are many different kinds of linguistics studies—each with its own theoretical perspectives and methodologies. Some of these adopt a neuroscience approach and use the case study method; the researchers study the language-related deficits of patients who have suffered brain damage. Others implement various network models of how language information is represented and processed. Some linguists take on a developmental orientation: They examine how language ability grows and changes with time during the development of the individual. Still others who study linguistics are philosophers who ask questions about the nature of language and the relationship between language and thought. In fact, language can be studied from the vantage point of every field of study that has been described in this book and more. What makes linguistics unique, then, is not the perspective or the tools it brings to the table but the subject matter of the investigation—language itself.

Linguistic studies attempt to answer many questions. Language is so complex that much of the research that has been conducted in this area has been directed toward an understanding of the structure of language (in addition to how it is used). These studies have focused on grammatical rules that specify allowable combinations of linguistic elements. Another interesting issue is whether humans are unique in using language or whether some animals possess language ability. Languages, of course, cannot be learned overnight, and many linguists have studied language acquisition—how it is acquired during development.

Linguistics is truly interdisciplinary, and in this chapter, we will survey the approaches to the study of language that are represented by the disciplines of philosophy, cognitive psychology, neuroscience, and artificial intelligence.

THE NATURE OF LANGUAGE

With this in mind, we begin our discussion of the linguistic approach with an exploration of the nature of language. There has been much debate about what language is, exactly—and there is no agreed-on definition. It is easier to list its most important characteristics (in lieu of providing a definition). According to Clark and Clark (1977), language has five characteristics:

1. *Communicative:* Language allows for communication between individuals. **Communication** refers to the production, transmission, and comprehension of information.

2. *Arbitrary:* A language consists of a set of symbolic elements. Symbols, as we noted in Chapter 1, are referential—they stand for or refer to something. Linguistic symbols can be almost anything. Most commonly, these symbols are for sounds, pictures, or words. The defining hallmark of these symbols is that they are completely **arbitrary**. Virtually any sound, picture, or word could be chosen to represent a particular thing. The sound of the word that represents "house" in English is different from the sound of the word that represents the same item in Spanish.

3. *Structured:* The ordering of the symbols in a language is not arbitrary but is governed by a set of rules, or is **structured**. The rules specify how the symbols may be combined. In English, we place the adjective before the noun, as in the phrase "the big house." In Spanish, this same proposition is expressed via a different set of rules: The adjective follows the noun, as in "la casa grande."

4. *Generative:* The symbolic elements of a language can be combined to create a very large number of meanings. Just think of how many six-word sentences one would be able to generate in English. If we start with the sample sentence "The fox jumped over the fence," we can then substitute the words *dog*, *cat*, *deer*, and words for many other animals in place of *fox*. Likewise, we can substitute the words *bottle*, *can*, or *tire* for the word *fence*. So the number of variations on just this one sentence is large. Every day, we utter new sentences that we never have uttered before. The **generative** property of language makes language very powerful, as virtually any idea that can spring to mind can be expressed.

5. *Dynamic:* Languages are **dynamic**, constantly changing as new words are added and grammatical rules altered. Only 30 years ago, there was no word for the concept that *e-mail* represents—because it didn't exist.

There is a fundamental distinction to be made that has to do with the type of linguistic representation: whether it is auditory, visual, or having to do with another sensory domain. Spoken language is naturally produced via the faculty of speech and is understood via listening. Speech and listening to speech can, of course, be transformed into their equivalents within the visual domain—writing and reading. Beyond this, there are also languages that consist of motoric gestures, such as the American Sign Language (ASL), and tactile languages, such as Braille. If we consider spoken language, the most common form of language usage, we must then describe two important elements of spoken language: the phoneme and the morpheme.

A **phoneme** is the smallest unit of sound in the sound system of a language. A phoneme has no meaning. Phonemes correspond in a rough way to the letters of an alphabet; in some instances, multiple phonemes correspond to a single letter. The phoneme for the letter *a* as it is pronounced in *father* corresponds to the "ah" sound, whereas the phoneme for *a* as it is pronounced in the word *cane* corresponds to the sound "ay." There are about 45 phonemes in the English language. Some instances are shown in Table 9.1. The smallest number of phonemes reported for a language is 15. The largest is 85. Phonemes, like letters, are combined to form the spoken versions of words.

Morphemes are the smallest units of spoken language that have meaning. They roughly correspond to words but can also be the parts of words. Thus, the sound of the spoken word *apple* is a morpheme, but so is the sound of *s* denoting the plural form. If we want to change the form of *apple* from singular to plural, we add the letter *s* to form *apples*, which changes the meaning. Similarly, there is the morpheme that corresponds to the sound "ed," which, when added to the root form of many verbs, forms the past tense. Considering that there are about 600,000 words in the English language, the number of morphemes that the language has is quite large.

In addition to the elements of language, there are the rules that allow for their possible combinations. There are multiple sets of rules. **Phonology** refers to the rules that govern

Table 9.1 Selected English consonant and vowel phonemes.

Consonants	Vowels
p (pill)	i (beet)
w (wet)	e (baby)
s (sip)	u (boot)
r (rate)	o (boat)
g (gill)	a (pot)
h (hat)	^ (but)

the sound system of a language; **morphology**, to those that govern word structure; syntax, to those that govern the arrangements of words in sentences; and **semantics**, to those that have to do with word meanings. Collectively, these rules are known as the **grammar** of the language. It is important to distinguish between word meanings as it is used most commonly and its more esoteric meaning (used in linguistics studies). Prescriptive grammar is the formal and proper set of rules for the use of language, in which we all received training at school. Descriptive grammar refers to the underlying rules, which linguistics researchers infer from the way people actually use language. We will come back to the subject of grammar and how it is used to describe the hierarchical structure of sentences in our discussion of Noam Chomsky's theory of language.

Interdisciplinary Crossroads: Language, Philosophy, and the Linguistic Relativity Hypothesis

A principal focus of this book is the nature of thought. If thought is representational, as it most surely seems to be, then what is its form? In Chapter 1, we described the several forms that thought could take. These include images, propositions, and analogies. Assuming that we can think in all these different formats, then thoughts may assume multiple forms—thoughts sometimes may be pictures, sometimes propositions, and sometimes other symbolic representations.

But if we were to vote for the form that we believed thoughts are in most of the time, language would probably win. When we think, it is as if we can hear ourselves talking—what is called implicit speech. In contrast to the imagery that occupies "the mind's eye," implicit speech seems to occupy "the mind's ear." This supposed mental primacy of language has led some to conclude that thought and language are so similar that it may be impossible to express the thoughts generated in one language in another language. This is the strong version of the **linguistic relativity hypothesis**, which also goes by the name of the Sapir–Whorf hypothesis, after the linguist Edward Sapir (1884–1939) and his student, Benjamin Lee Whorf (1956). The weak version denies that such translation is impossible but admits that the language a person speaks influences the way he or she thinks.

Whorf studied the Hopi language, a Native American language, and found that the Hopi experience time as a discrete series, with each unit of time—say, days—considered unique and different from the others. This differs from the Western conception of time, wherein time is experienced as an undifferentiated continuous flow. Thus, a Hopi individual would not say "I stayed five days" but, rather, "I left on the fifth day" (Carroll, 1956, p. 216). The strong version of the linguistic relativity hypothesis would argue that the Hopi are incapable of thinking of time as continuous because they lack the words to express the concept in their language. The weak version would argue that the Hopi can understand this concept of time but that such an understanding would require a reexpression of it that used a completely different set of Hopi words.

So which version of the linguistic relativity hypothesis is correct? Investigation of the hypothesis has proceeded along two avenues. The first has focused on color perception, the second on counterfactual reasoning.

Davies and Corbett (1997) conducted research that tested English, Russian, and Setswana speakers. Setswana is a language spoken in Botswana, Africa. Davies and Corbett gave the participants colored chips and asked them to arrange the chips into groups based on chip similarity in any way they wanted. If the strong version of the hypothesis were correct, the Russians would place light- and dark-blue chips in separate groups, as their language has distinct color terms for light and dark blue. The Setswana speakers would group green and blue chips together, because they have a single term for green and blue. Their study and a follow-up study showed that all the participants tended to group the chips in pretty much the same way, regardless of their linguistic background (Davies, Sowden, Jerrett, Jerrett, & Corbett, 1998). The studies, therefore, fail to support the strong version of the hypothesis.

A counterfactual statement is a hypothetical one. It asks us to imagine what would happen if something were true. Counterfactuals can be expressed in two ways. One way is through the use of the subjunctive mood. The statement "If you bought your ticket now, you would save money" is an example of a statement that uses the subjunctive mood. The use of the word *would* is part of the subjunctive application and signals that it is an imaginary scenario that is being expressed. Other forms of the subjunctive use *were to* or *ought*. The other way to express counterfactual statements is through the use of "if–then" constructions. "If it is hot today, then I will go swimming" is an instance of this construction.

Bloom (1981) set out to test the linguistic relativity hypothesis by taking advantage of the fact that English speakers and Chinese speakers have different ways of expressing the counterfactual (see Figure 9.1). English has both subjunctive mood forms and if–then constructions, whereas Chinese has only if–then constructions. He predicted that the Chinese speakers would, therefore, have greater difficulty understanding the counterfactual. He presented both groups of speakers with a hypothetical scenario and found that the Chinese speakers failed to grasp the nature of the scenario, while the English speakers did not have difficulty. The results of his study support the hypothesis.

Both the color-naming and counterfactual-reasoning studies have been criticized on the grounds that tests for either color naming or counterfactual reasoning represent bad ways of testing the linguistic relativity hypothesis. Color perception is in large part the result of the physiology of the visual system, which is the same in everybody. This means that the way we see determines the names we have for colors—not the other way around. Consistency in color naming across populations and cultures supports this

Figure 9.1 A street in Chinatown, New York. Does speaking Chinese make you think differently?

idea (Berlin & Kay, 1969). Bloom's original study also has been criticized on the grounds that the scenario it employed was not translated well into Chinese (Au, 1983, 1984). When better translations were provided, Chinese speakers' comprehension of the scenario improved dramatically.

Evaluating the Linguistic Relativity Hypothesis

In summary, the two avenues of investigation fail to provide emphatic support for the strong version of the linguistic relativity hypothesis. However, more recent investigations of the mental representations of numbers (Miura, Okamoto, Kim, & Steere, 1993) and the use of classifier words such as *this* and *that* (Zhang & Schmitt, 1998) do provide limited support for the weak version of the hypothesis. More research is needed to establish a definitive answer to this issue. Currently, most investigators believe that languages are powerful enough and flexible enough to express any number of ideas. We can conclude that languages influence, but don't necessarily determine, the way we think.

We should keep in mind that language is but one way of thinking. As mentioned above, there are other forms of mental representation that are not linguistic and that are not governed by linguistic syntactical rules. The formation and processing of visual images seems to constitute an entirely nonlinguistic code for thinking. Mathematical thinking and the mental representation and computation of numerical quantities, although language like, may not rely on language mechanisms to operate and could constitute another distinct format for thought. The same can be said for the mental processing of music. Just because language is powerful and flexible doesn't mean it holds a monopoly on thought. If one idea cannot be expressed in terms of another linguistically, this might be achieved via the use of one of these other formats.

LANGUAGE USE IN PRIMATES

Animals in the wild communicate with one another. A monkey species that lives on the African savannah has a specialized series of cries that signify different kinds of threats. The monkeys use these cries while they are feeding to warn one another of impending danger. If one monkey in a group spies an eagle circling overhead, it emits one type of cry, which sends the members of the group scattering into the trees for cover. If it spots a snake, it emits another cry, which impels the monkeys to stand up on their hind legs and look around so that they can try to locate the snake. Each of the cries has a specific meaning. Each stands for a particular danger to the group. The meaning of the cry is understood by the rest of the group, as indicated by their reactions. This is communication because information about an event was produced, transmitted, and comprehended. But this natural form of communication is not language. The cries are arbitrary, there is no use of grammar to arrange them into any structure such as sentences, and they are not combined to create new meanings.

This raises an interesting question. If animals don't use language naturally on their own, can we teach it to them? Do they have the same capacity for language that we do? Research in this area has focused on primates, such as chimpanzees and gorillas, because of their relatively advanced cognitive capacities. Let's summarize some of this research and evaluate the results.

Early investigations of the linguistic abilities of primates focused on language production. Animals evidenced rudimentary language skills after being trained in one of several linguistic systems that included ASL, as well as a symbolic system employing plastic tokens and one that used geometric patterns called **lexigrams**. Starting in the 1960s, Beatrice and Allen Gardner raised a chimp named Washoe. They taught her to use ASL. Their method was to get Washoe to imitate or reproduce the hand formation that stood for a particular object (Gardner, Gardner, & Van Cantfort, 1989). Washoe learned 132 signs and seemed to show evidence of spontaneous language use. On seeing a toothbrush in the bathroom, she made the sign for it without being prompted. A similar technique was used to teach ASL to a gorilla named Koko (Patterson, 1978). Koko learned an even larger repertoire of signs and was reported to have used syntax and to have made signs spontaneously. Her trainer claims that she even told jokes!

David Premack has used a different approach. He used plastic tokens instead of hand signals as he attempted to teach language skills to a chimp named Sarah (Premack, 1976). The tokens had different shapes and colors and stood for individual words as well as relationships. There were tokens that stood for nouns (*apple*), for verbs (*give*), for adjectives (*red*), and for relationships (*same as*). Sarah produced the "same as" token when she was presented with two "apple" tokens and the "different" token when shown an "apple" and an "orange" token. She seemed to have a rudimentary understanding of sentence grammar, as she was apparently able to tell the difference between two sentences such as "David give apple Sarah" and "Sarah give apple David."

Savage-Rumbaugh et al. (1993) studied a chimp named Kanzi who appeared to have learned the meanings of lexigrams. In addition, Kanzi was apparently able to understand single-word and simple-sentence utterances made by humans. Kanzi's abilities seemed quite advanced. Of his own accord, he would use lexigrams to identify objects, to make requests for food items, and to announce a particular action he was about to undertake. Following more structured language training, Kanzi's abilities were compared with those of a 2½-year-old child named Alia. Both were given novel commands that required them to move objects. In terms of comprehension, the two showed nearly identical abilities: They both demonstrated approximately 70% compliance with the commands. Kanzi's language production skills were more limited—they corresponded to those of a 1½-year-old child (Greenfield & Savage-Rumbaugh, 1993).

Evaluating Language Use in Primates

At this point, we can examine some of the criticisms that have been leveled at this research. Some of the animals described so far were trained via the use of positive reinforcement. They were given a reward, usually a food item, for making the correct sign or using the appropriate token or lexigram. A problem with this is that the animals may have been associating a symbol with a concept because they had been trained to do so and may not have had any awareness that the symbol actually stood for something. If this was the case, these animals fail to demonstrate the arbitrariness aspect of language—that the symbol can be anything and still stand for its referent. An animal's choosing of an "apple" token when presented with an apple does not demonstrate arbitrariness, but using an "apple" token to refer to an apple when an actual apple is not perceptually present does. This aspect of language, in which users refer to something that is removed in space or time, is called **displacement**.

Savage-Rumbaugh (1986) presents some evidence of displacement in chimps. She employed a technique known as cross-modal matching wherein chimps who viewed a lexigram were then required to select the object the lexigram represented via the use of touch from a box filled with objects. The chimps were able to do this, which indicated that they understood what the lexigrams represented. A note of caution is in order, however. Arbitrariness and displacement capabilities were shown for a comprehension task only, where the animals were interpreting the symbols. Earlier studies in which chimps used ASL and tokens have generated less evidence that primates understand the meanings of symbols when they produce them.

What about the structured aspect of language? Do animals understand the syntax that underlies the formation of sentences? The investigations that have been conducted thus far show that primates comprehend and produce very simple sentences—sentences that are in the order of two or three words long. An understanding of the rules of syntax is demonstrated by the ability to rearrange words in new combinations that express new meanings—the generative criterion, defined above. If animals could do this, it would indicate a comprehension of syntactical rules.

The researcher Herb Terrace provides us with evidence that refutes the idea that some animals may have a rudimentary understanding of or the ability to use syntax (Terrace, Petitto, Sanders, & Bever, 1979). Terrace was skeptical that chimpanzees such as Washoe truly understood the meanings of the signs and symbols they used. As alluded to above, he believed that chimps used hand signals or presented tokens because they had been rein-forced for doing so. To test the idea, he studied a chimpanzee who he had jokingly named Nim Chimpsky. Nim was raised in a human family and was taught ASL. Rather than use food as a reward, Terrace gave approval that centered on things that were important to Nim. Under this system, Nim did seem to have some grasp of the meanings of his signs, as he was found using them in the absence of their referents. He also appeared to use signs spontaneously to express his desires. For example, he would make the sign for *sleep* when he was bored. However, Terrace concludes that Nim was never able to combine his signs to form sentences and express novel meanings. He did this only when he was directly imitating combinations of signs that had been produced by his trainers.

So, at this point, we can sum up the work on the language abilities of primates. Primates appear to possess some arbitrariness and displacement capabilities because they can comprehend the meanings of a limited number of symbols independent of their refer-ents. This is true whether they are trained directly (with food) or indirectly (with approval) using positive reinforcement techniques. But here is where their linguistic skills seem to come to an end, for primates seem to understand very little in the way of syntax, especially when it comes to language production. They know that some aspects of word order affect meaning. However, most primates tend to repeat the sentences they were taught or produce only small variations on them. They do not come anywhere near to possessing human generative capability. Also, unlike humans, primates—once they have acquired language skills—fail to teach the skills to other members of their species. Unfortunately, the "Doctor Doolittle" scenario of our conversing with animals the way we do with one another just doesn't seem possible.

LANGUAGE ACQUISITION

Clearly, a human being is not born with an ability to speak his or her native language fluently. This ability develops over time. Linguists adopting a developmental perspective have studied the acquisition and development of language skills, from birth through infancy, childhood, and adolescence. They have shown that human beings pass through a series of stages, each one marked by the acquisition of new linguistic skills.

Early in the first year, infants start to utter a wide variety of sounds. All infants do this. At this stage, they begin to exercise their vocal cords and mouths—major parts of the vocal apparatus—the use of which they must master in order to articulate the sounds of the language they are just beginning to acquire. This period of development is known as the cooing stage. Figure 9.2 shows an infant communicating with her caregiver.

At around 6 months, the number of sounds a baby produces shrinks. The sounds produced at this stage are consonant–vowel pairs, such as "mama" and "dada." The majority of the utterances made at this time are more phonemic than morphemic in nature. They correspond to sound units rather than to fully pronounced words. However, the intonations of these utterances at this point begin to match those of the language the child is learning. Intonation refers to the rises and falls in pitch and changes in other acoustic properties of one's speech. For example, for most speakers, there is usually a rise in pitch at the end of a question. These abilities arise during the so-called babbling stage.

Following the babbling stage and just a few months shy of the child's first birthday, we see the advent of one-word utterances. At this point, children are able to successfully articulate entire morphemes. These morphemes, or words, may not be prescriptively accurate. A child may say "unky" instead of "uncle," but the utterance is being used in a meaningful way. The children are, thus, beginning to use language in a symbolic and semantic fashion. This is the one-word stage.

Following this, during the two-word stage, children produce two-word utterances. It is at this point that they will say things like "see kitty" or "want toy." Because words are now being arranged into simple sentence-like structures, the two-word stage marks the

Figure 9.2 Early in development, infants will spontaneously babble phonemes.

emergence of rudimentary syntactical skills. After the two-word stage, babies will string together more complicated utterances, speaking out the equivalent of sentences composed of three or more words that convey increasingly complex meanings.

There are no clearly identifiable stages that follow the two-word stage. But this period is characterized by a steady growth in vocabulary and syntax. Also, during this period, children exhibit some interesting patterns of development, especially with regard to their learning of past-tense forms (Kuczaj, 1978; Marcus et al., 1992). Studies of this type of learning show that children first imitate past-tense forms correctly. For the irregular verb *to go*, the past-tense form is *went*. After children have learned the general rule of past-tense formation, they apply it correctly to regular verbs but then overextend the rule to include irregular verbs as well—saying, for example, "goed" instead of "went." Finally, they learn the exceptions to the rule—for example, using *went* only when it is appropriate. This intriguing U-shaped pattern of development indicates the presence of several learning strategies in children: They start out with purely imitative copying, proceed to an understanding of a rule, and ultimately progress to the learning of the exceptions to that rule.

Domain-General and Domain-Specific Mechanisms in Language Acquisition

Domain-specific mechanisms are those devoted to the processing of a single type of information like linguistic information. Domain-general mechanisms are generic and can process different types of information. For instance, a domain-general mechanism would be capable of processing both linguistic and visual information. The incredible sophistication of language and the fast rate at which it is learned imply that it is a domain-specific mechanism. However, it is possible that domain-general learning mechanisms contribute too. This issue has been debated in the language research community for decades and, as we will see in this section, has yet to be resolved. However, it is a good example of how evidence in the sciences can support both sides of a position.

The domain-general versus the domain-specific debate is actually unrelated to the nature/nurture or nativist/empiricist debate (Saffran & Thiessen, 2007). Just because a mechanism seems to be domain specific, like the one we see for language, does not mean that it is hardwired or innate. It also does not mean that it is a module, as you will recall that these are some of the characteristics of modules. By definition, all mental processes require an innate structure to operate. Artificial neural networks are domain general. As we saw in the network chapter, they can form the foundation for all sorts of mental processes, but to function, they must have preexisting structure, including the organization of nodes and links into layers, rules by which inputs are summated, and so on. Likewise, domain-specific mechanisms can be learned as seems to be the case for those brain areas like the angular gyrus that underlie reading and writing.

The fact that language is localized to the left hemisphere in most people suggests that it may be domain specific. In addition, identical sounds are actually processed differently at the neural level depending on whether they are perceived as speech or nonspeech (Dehaene-Lambertz et al., 2005). So at both an anatomical and physiological level, we see differences in the way language-like stimuli are interpreted. However, it could just be that the left hemisphere is good at processing stimuli that are short-lived and not language information per se (Zatorre, Belin, & Penhune, 2002).

Infants are predisposed to respond to speech and will pay attention to it in preference to other sorts of sounds (Vouloumanos & Werker, 2004). This preference ensures that speech information "gets into" the system and may help accelerate the rate at which it is learned. If this were the case, then this attentional bias could be domain specific and perhaps innate, while the subsequent learning mechanisms may be domain specific, domain general, or both. This illustrates that learning need not be just one or the other. One mechanism could set the stage for another, or the two different categories of mechanisms could interact with each another.

Determining the boundaries between spoken words is difficult because there are often no pauses. Yet infants can extract words from speech as early as 7 months. One way to do this is by learning which sounds tend to follow one another. The use of this type of information is known as **statistical learning**. If one sound tends to follow another more often within rather than between words, then this can be a cue to indicate which sounds group together into words. Both adults and infants are capable of utilizing statistical learning to determine word boundaries (Saffran, Aslin, & Newport, 1996). Statistical learning, however, seems to be domain general. It is used for visual stimuli and auditory stimuli that are not linguistic in nature. It is also used in several nonhuman animal species.

The syntax or rules that govern language would seem to be clearly within the domain-specific camp. There are several reasons for this. First, it has been difficult to teach animals human language (some would argue any type of language), suggesting that they lack the prerequisite mechanisms. Second, languages around the world do not vary much with regard to certain aspects of syntax (Baker, 2001). Third, syntax cannot easily be derived from the perceptual characteristics of a language. Despite all this, some recent work shows that word categories (noun, verb, adjective, etc.) can be learned by the order in which they occur (Mintz, Newport, & Bever, 2002). For instance, nouns tend to follow the word *the*. So yes, much of the evidence we have encountered so far can be interpreted either way. It is safe to say that the jury is still out on whether language is a domain-general or domain-specific mechanism.

Evaluating Language Acquisition

Saffran and Theissen (2007) make a number of important conclusions regarding domains and learning. They argue that our conception of general and specific are too strict. "Domain-general" mechanisms may not be open to any type of input but are more likely to be open to some but not to others. Similarly "domain-specific" mechanisms imply modularity and innateness, and they need not be either. Modules rather than being innate could emerge from learning within a given domain. McMullen and Saffran (2004) argue that adult cognitive abilities, although localized in the brain to some extent, could be the product of domain-general mechanisms that were developmentally "fed," modality-specific information. Fruitful approaches that may shed light on this debate would be to see what changes (neural, cognitive, or behavioral) occur early on versus later to disentangle the initial states from future outcomes as well as the application of technological advances to see which brain areas are at work for different types of knowledge in early infancy.

LANGUAGE DEPRIVATION

What, then, is the role of environment in language acquisition? One very basic approach to this question is to examine language ability in the absence of exposure to language. If experience of language is necessary and innate linguistic mechanisms are dependent on it, we should see language deficits in the absence of exposure to a normal linguistic environment. If, on the other hand, experience and stimulation have little to do with language development, then language ability should remain relatively intact in their absence. Studies that have investigated this issue have demonstrated the existence of a pivotal time in development during which language must be learned. Children not exposed to language during this time, called the **critical period**, may never acquire it or may suffer severe language impairments.

There is abundant evidence in support of the idea of a critical period. Let's examine some of it. The first evidence comes from studies of birds. It turns out that some birds (as well as human beings) are among the few animals that need to be exposed to the communicative sounds of their own species in order to be able to produce them (Doupe & Kuhl, 1999). Both birds and human beings are better able to acquire communicative ability early in life. Marler (1970) showed that white-crowned sparrows after the age of 100 to about 150 days were unable to learn new songs by listening to a "tutor" bird. This was true for birds that were raised with such tutors or were exposed to taped examples of bird song, as well as those that were raised in acoustic isolation.

Another line of evidence that supports the existence of a critical period comes from studies of the acquisition of second languages. So far, we have been discussing first-language acquisition, wherein a single language is learned. It is often the case, of course, that people learn to speak more than one language. Researchers can study the difficulty with which an individual acquires a second language in relation to the time of onset of exposure to the second language. One such study found that native speakers of Chinese and Korean (for whom English was a second language) received scores on tests of English grammar that bore a relation to the time of onset of their exposure to English: The later their age at time of arrival in the United States, the lower were their scores (Johnson & Newport, 1989). Figure 9.3 shows the results of this study.

The most emotionally compelling evidence that supports the existence of a critical period consists of individual case studies of persons who were deprived of language experience during early development. These cases are tragic but provide a unique opportunity to examine the effects of this kind of deprivation in humans. One famous historical case study is that of the wild boy of Aveyron, who was discovered in a French forest in 1797 (Lane, 1976). The boy, named Victor, had apparently lived much of his childhood completely alone and had very little language ability. He came under the supervision of a physician, Dr. Jean-Marc-Gaspard Itard (1775–1838), who studied him intensively and attempted to teach him language. Despite Dr. Itard's best efforts, Victor never acquired more than the most basic comprehension and production skills.

Figure 9.3 Mean English grammar test scores drop in correlation with greater ages of children who speak another language at the time of arrival in the United States.

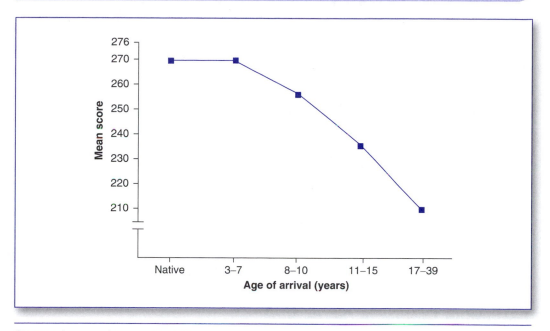

Source: Johnson and Newport (1989).

A more recent case study is that of a girl named Genie. Genie spent much of her early life in social isolation. The evidence suggests that the period of her deprivation began when she was 20 months old and lasted until she was "discovered," at the age of 13 years and 9 months. During this time, Genie was kept in a small room, where she was tied to a potty chair for much of the day and night or confined to an infant crib. The door to the room was almost always closed, and the windows were closed and covered with curtains. Except for her quick feedings, Genie received almost no parental care. She was not spoken to and there was no radio or TV in the household. Thus, she was exposed to little or no spoken language. Furthermore, Genie was beaten for making any sounds of her own.

Given this extreme and prolonged lack of exposure to any sort of linguistic stimulation, what were Genie's abilities like? A number of researchers have chronicled her progress (Fromkin, Krashen, Curtiss, Rigler, & Rigler, 1974; Jones, 1995). On initial examination, she was found not to vocalize at all. Within a few days, she began to respond to the speech of others and to imitate single words. Within a year or so, she was able to understand and produce some words and names. Despite these modest gains, it was clear at the end of the testing period that Genie possessed minimal grammatical ability. Following a period of several years' worth of further evaluation and training, Genie did show signs of simple grammatical comprehension. For example, she was able to distinguish between the singular and plural forms of nouns, and between negative and affirmative sentences.

At 8 months after discovery, Genie uttered two-word phrases such as "yellow car." Later, she was able to produce three- and four-word strings, such as "Tori chew glove" and "Big elephant long trunk." She also demonstrated generativity—she was able to express new meanings by combining words in novel ways.

These capacities show that Genie was able to acquire language in the aftermath of the deprivation period and that the stages of her development—such as her use of progressively longer sentences—paralleled language acquisition in nondeprived children. However, Genie's abilities deviate from those of control children in several ways. Her grammatical ability at the time of early testing was equal to that of a 2½-year-old child, and her speech production capacity was limited. In addition, Genie's rate of language development was slowed in comparison with that of controls. She had difficulty using language to express questions, and many of the hallmarks of language mastery in adults—such as the use of demonstratives, particles, rejoinders, and transformation rules—were absent (Fromkin et al., 1974). In summary, Genie shows that language acquisition following extended deprivation is possible but is severely impaired. To date, Genie has not developed complete adult language skills, and she probably never will.

Evaluating Language Deprivation

Case studies of language-deprived children yield a wealth of information about the individuals under study. They do, however, suffer from a number of problems. To begin with, it is difficult to make generalizations from evidence acquired from a single person or a small number of persons. The findings of case studies do not necessarily generalize to a larger population. Second, the conditions that shaped these subjects are often unknown. In the case of Victor, we do not know the duration of his social isolation, or even if he was isolated at all. Some have speculated that he may have simply had a learning disability or suffered brain damage. With regard to Genie, it is not clear exactly what kind of language information she was exposed to during her formative years, nor the extent to which she may have vocalized to herself.

Research that has investigated the critical period shows that although there may be an innate language-learning mechanism, it is dependent on environmental input for its proper functioning. If this input is absent, the ability to fully use language never appears. Exposure to and practice in the use of a language is, thus, a component essential to the development of language. This is true regardless of the amount or the sophistication of the neural machinery dedicated to language processing that may be in place in an individual from birth.

COGNITION AND LINGUISTICS: THE ROLE OF GRAMMAR

We said earlier that a set of rules governs how words can be arranged in sentences. Grammar is important because it tells us what is a proper way of expressing something in a language and what is not. If there were no rules or constraints on expression, we could string words together in practically any order, and it would be impossible to convey anything. Let's delve a little further into grammar—that is, how it puts constraints on what can be said and how it illuminates several interesting cognitive principles.

Sentences have distinct parts that are hierarchically related. This organization is called a **phrase structure** and can be illustrated via the use of tree diagrams. Figure 9.4 is a tree diagram for the sentence "The big dog chased the black cat." At the highest level, the entire sentence (S) is represented. Moving down one level, the sentence is composed of two parts, a noun phrase (NP) and a verb phrase (VP). Moving down another level, we see that the noun phrase is made up of a determiner (D), an adjective (A), and a noun (N). Determiners are words such as *a* or *the*. The verb phrase is made up of a verb (V) and another noun phrase that itself contains another determiner, adjective, and noun.

Figure 9.4 The phrase structure for a simple sentence.

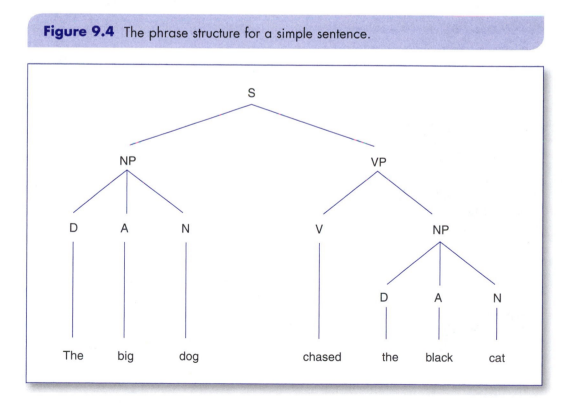

There is a grammar that governs the use of phrase structures. This **phrase structure grammar** imposes certain limitations on how a legitimate sentence can be put together. One phrase structure rule is that all sentences are composed of a noun phrase and a verb phrase. A second rule is that noun phrases consist of a determiner followed by a noun. Verb phrases can be expressed a bit more flexibly—as a verb followed by a noun phrase, another sentence, or other elements.

A phrase structure grammar is useful for understanding the organization of sentences, but it doesn't tell us how we can rearrange a sentence to express new meanings. Noam Chomsky (1957) was the first to point this out. He notes that a given sentence can be changed in three ways. First, we can turn an active sentence into a passive one, as when "The man read the book" becomes "The book was read by the man." Second, we can turn a positive statement into a negative one, by modifying the original sentence to form "The man did not read the book." Third, we can convert the assertion into a question, as in "Did the man read the book?"

To account for these changes, we need a new grammar that allows us to transform one sentence into another. Chomsky's solution was a **transformational grammar**, a set of rules for modifying a sentence into a closely related one. By using these rules, we can reorder "The man read the book" into "The man did not read the book," as follows:

$$NP1 + Verb + NP2 \rightarrow NP1 + did\ not + Verb + NP2,$$

where NP1 is "The man," the verb is "read," and NP2 is "the book." Similarly, the conversion of "The man read the book" to "The book was read by the man" is denoted as

$$NP1 + Verb + NP2 \rightarrow NP2 + was + Verb + by + NP1.$$

An important aspect of a transformational grammar is that one can use it to express two sentences that have different phrase structures but identical meanings. "The man read the book" and "The book was read by the man," above, have different hierarchical organizations, but they have the same semantic content. To account for this, Chomsky proposed two levels of analysis for sentences. The **surface structure** is the organization of the sentence in the form that it is expressed in—that is, how the sentence would be heard if it were spoken or read if it were written. The surface structure is variable and can be rearranged by transformational grammar. The **deep structure** is the underlying meaning of a sentence and remains constant regardless of the specific form in which it is expressed.

You may have been wondering whether our discussion so far applies only to English or whether it applies to other languages as well. It is true that languages have different specific rules, but cross-cultural linguistic analyses have shown that languages have a number of elements in common. These commonalities are summed up in the concept of a **universal grammar**, which comprises the features that are instantiated in the grammars of all natural languages (Chomsky, 1986; Cook, 1988). In this view, each individual language at a fundamental level is not really different from others but represents merely a variation on a theme. Universal grammar is considered as a collection of language rules, hardwired into our brains from birth. In this sense, it is a modular aspect of mind and has all the characteristics of a mental module. It is innate, genetically prespecified, domain specific, and independent of other cognitive capacities.

What are the universal properties of all languages then? One is a phonological rule that specifies the ordering of syllables in a word. According to the **maximal onset principle**, consonants usually precede vowels; more frequently than not, they constitute the onset of syllabic groupings. This feature is found in all languages. Another universal property of language is syntactical and concerns the ordering of the subject and object in sentences. In 98% of the world's languages, the subject precedes the object (Crystal, 1987). Thus, we say, "John kicked the ball," not "A ball John kicked"—even though the latter form is technically acceptable in English.

Universal grammar may be what is responsible for our ability to acquire language so quickly. Language acquisition requires the mastery of a large number of grammatical rules at different levels. There are actually sets of rules, including phonology, to determine acceptable combinations of phonemes; morphology to determine which morphemes go together; syntax for the ordering of words in sentences; transformation rules for changing the forms of sentences, and so on. The ease and rapidity with which this process occurs in humans can be explained if it is true that at least some generic versions of these rules are already present in the head at birth. A child would then adapt these general linguistic rules to the particularities of the specific language he or she grows up in (Bloom, 1994).

Evaluating Universal Grammar

The idea of a universal grammar, or "language organ," as originally formulated by Chomsky has not gone unchallenged. To begin with, there is little evidence to support the notion of specific genes for language. If one looks at other body organs, there are few that owe their existence to individual genes. So it is unlikely that there are specific genes devoted to language processing. There is also doubt about the domain specificity of any proposed language module. The rules governing language use may be more general; they may manifest themselves in other nonlinguistic cognitive capacities. One possibility is that linguistic universals are just the product of general biological mechanisms, implying that language is not "special" in any sense.

NEUROSCIENCE AND LINGUISTICS: THE WERNICKE-GESCHWIND MODEL

Paul Broca (1824–1880) was a French surgeon who worked with patients who had suffered brain damage as a result of stroke or injury. The patients demonstrated various kinds of language deficits, called **aphasias**. Several of his patients had severe difficulty articulating speech. One famous patient was capable only of uttering the word *tan* over and over again. For the most part, these patients could understand what was being said to them, indicating that the faculty of comprehension was intact, but they had problems pronouncing words and producing speech. This deficit is called **Broca's aphasia**. It is also known as nonfluent aphasia.

Patients with Broca's aphasia produce what is called "agrammatic speech." They generate strings of nouns and some verbs but without any filler words, such as *the* or *is*. They also fail to make words plural or to use verb tenses. Their sentences are short and broken by many pauses, which sometimes have earned this kind of speech the nickname "telegraphic" or "nonfluent" speech. The following is an example of the speech of a patient talking about a visit to the hospital for dental surgery.

> Yes . . . ah . . . Monday er . . . Dad and Peter H . . . and Dad . . . er . . . hospital . . . and ah . . . Wednesday . . . Wednesday, nine o'clock . . . and oh . . . Thursday . . . ten o'clock, ah doctors . . . two . . . an' doctors . . . and er . . . teeth . . . yah. (Goodglass & Geschwind, 1976, p. 408)

Postmortem examination of the brains of patients who suffered from Broca's aphasia has revealed damage to the lower portion of the left frontal lobe (see Figure 9.5). This region is believed to be at least partly responsible for language production capacity and has been named **Broca's area**.

A second area, named after Carl Wernicke (1848–1905), mediates language comprehension. This area is located in the posterior region of the left hemisphere (see Figure 9.5). Patients with damage to **Wernicke's area** suffer from **Wernicke's aphasia**. They produce rapid, fluent, and seemingly automatic speech that has little meaningful content. For this reason, this aphasia is also referred to as fluent aphasia. This type of speech sounds normal in the sense that its rate, intonations, and stresses are correct—but it is lacking in content or meaning. These patients have major problems comprehending speech and also demonstrate difficulty reading and writing. Here is an example of the speech of a patient with Wernicke's aphasia.

> Oh sure, go ahead, any old think you want. If I could I would. Oh I'm taking the word the wrong way to say, all of the barbers here whenever they stop you it's going around and around, if you know what I mean, that is tying and tying for repucer, repuceration, well, we were trying the best that we could while another time it was with the beds over there the same thing. (Gardner, 1974, p. 68)

Figure 9.5 Brain areas of the left hemisphere that are part of the Wernicke-Geschwind model of language comprehension and production.

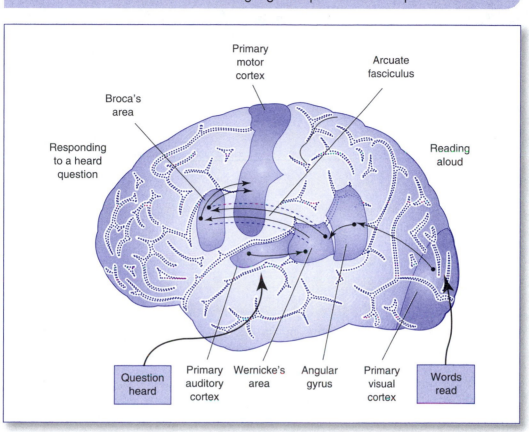

The Wernicke-Geschwind model was first formulated by Wernicke and expanded in the 1960s by Norman Geschwind (1972). It specifies the functional roles of the different brain areas that are involved in language processing, as well as their connections and interactions. Because an understanding of the model relies heavily on an understanding of different cortical areas, we must first introduce these anatomical regions. You may wish to refer back to the neuroscience chapter at this point for a refresher on basic brain anatomy.

Figure 9.5 shows the cortical areas that play the key roles in language processing—as described in the model. For starters, there is the primary motor cortex, located in the frontal lobes in the anterior part of the brain. Commands that originate here send impulses to muscles, causing them to contract and, therefore, initiating movement; this includes the muscles of the mouth, which must be moved as part of the operation of speaking. The primary visual cortex is located at the back of the brain in the occipital region. It is where visual information is first processed. This area becomes active during reading and writing. The primary auditory cortex is situated in the temporal lobes. It is here where sounds striking the ears are first processed. The **arcuate fasciculus** is a pathway that connects Broca's area and Wernicke's area. Damage to this part of the brain results in an individual's difficulty in repeating words that he or she has just heard, known as **conduction aphasia**. Finally, there is the **angular gyrus**, located behind Wernicke's area. Damage to this part of the brain produces **alexia**, an inability to read, and **agraphia**, an inability to write.

According to the model, these areas and the pathways that connect them subsume language comprehension and production with respect to both the auditory and visual modalities. There is an activation of neural pathways that is the basis of listening and speaking. It is as follows: The perceptual characteristics of speech sounds are first processed in the primary auditory cortex. The output of this processing is then passed to Wernicke's area, where the content of what has been said is processed and understanding is born. A reply is then initiated. From here, the information that will become the reply is passed along the arcuate fasciculus to Broca's area. The information is converted into a motor code, or program of articulation, within Broca's area. This code is then passed to the primary motor cortex, where commands to move the muscles of the mouth and produce the speech that constitutes the reply are executed.

A second pathway mediates reading and writing. In this pathway, the primary visual cortex processes inputs that have originated from the words on a printed page. This information is then output to the angular gyrus. The visual representation of what has been read is converted into an auditory code within the angular gyrus, which then sends the code to Wernicke's area. The remainder of this pathway, responsible for producing behaviors such as reading out loud or writing, coincides with the final portion of the pathway described in the preceding paragraph. The information flow would be from Wernicke's area via the arcuate fasciculus to Broca's area, and then to the primary motor cortex, where muscular action is initiated.

Evaluating the Wernicke-Geschwind Model

The Wernicke-Geschwind model has been criticized on a number of counts. It is considered by some to be an oversimplification of the neural basis for language. To begin with, the areas specified by the model are not completely associated with their hypothesized function. Although in most patients damage to Broca's area or Wernicke's area results in the corresponding aphasias, this is not always the case. Lesions to Broca's area alone produce a transitory aphasia—one that presents with only mild symptoms several weeks after the event that precipitated the injury (Mohr, 1976). More troublesome to the theory are the records of patients with Broca's aphasia who have not sustained damage to Broca's area (Dronkers, Shapiro, Redfern, & Knight, 1992). The same is true for patients with Wernicke's aphasia (Dronkers, Redfern, & Ludy, 1995).

The areas specified by the model are characterized as being modality specific, with Broca's area being a motor-only area that codes for speech articulation and Wernicke's area being an auditory, sensory-only area devoted to speech comprehension. However, brain imaging techniques show that these regions are the sites of processing activities that underlie sign language use (Bavelier et al., 1998). This suggests that they may represent more abstract, modality-independent language ability. In other words, these areas may contain knowledge of syntax that can be applied to any language system, regardless of the modalities involved.

Another criticism of the model centers on its original assumption that these areas are devoted exclusively to linguistic processing. Swinney, Zurif, Prather, and Love (1996) have found that lesions in aphasic patients, even those suffering "classic" syndromes such as Broca's aphasia and Wernicke's aphasia, may have disrupted basic processing resources used by the language system. If this is true, damage to the brain areas thought to subsume language only may also lie behind disruptions of other systems that language depends on, such as memory and attention.

Another problem with the Wernicke-Geschwind model is methodological. It was based largely on evidence obtained from clinical case studies of brain-damaged patients, assembled after their deaths. Modern science relies more on brain imaging in live patients. The use of brain imaging techniques has shown that there are many other brain areas that contribute to language function. We can list a few of them here. The insula lies beneath the frontal, temporal, and parietal lobes. Most patients with Broca's aphasia also have lesions in the insula (Vanier & Caplan, 1990). The left inferior prefrontal cortex, just anterior to and ventral to Broca's area, is activated during semantic retrieval (Peterson, Fox, Posner, Mintun, & Raichle, 1988). The basal temporal areas, at the bottom of the left temporal lobe, and the cingulate gyrus are also involved in word retrieval. The anterior superior temporal gyrus, anterior to the primary auditory cortex, is implicated in sentence comprehension. These areas are just beginning to be understood. They are believed to interact as parts of a complex network. There is as yet no overarching theory that can describe this interaction. Until then, the Wernicke-Geschwind model provides a useful, if somewhat outdated, understanding of what goes on in the brain during language processing.

ARTIFICIAL INTELLIGENCE AND LINGUISTICS: NATURAL LANGUAGE PROCESSING

Natural languages are those that have evolved in human societies and are used by human beings. Examples of natural languages are English, Spanish, and French. These are in contrast to formal computer languages such as C++++, or linguistic expressions of logic.

There are two kinds of natural language processing. Understanding a natural language involves an individual's assimilation of linguistic expression in some form, such as speech or writing; extracting its meaning; and then undertaking some action that constitutes a response to this meaning. Understanding is what a computer would need to do if it were to interpret a spoken human command and act on it. Generation is the reverse of this process. It involves taking a formal symbolic representation of an idea and converting it to an expression in English or some other natural language. For example, the idea "It is a sunny day" may initially be stored in a particular format in a computer. A computer would be generating language if it could transform this idea into a spoken utterance that a human being could understand. These two processes are, thus, the computer equivalent of natural language comprehension and production. In this section, we will concern ourselves exclusively with natural language understanding, as that is the area in which research has been concentrated.

Cawsey (1998) outlines four stages of natural language understanding. We will preview each of them, in the order in which they occur:

1. **Speech recognition** is the first step in the process, whereby the acoustic speech signal is analyzed to determine the sequence of spoken words.

2. In **syntactic analysis**, the word sequence is analyzed via the use of knowledge of the language's grammar. This yields the sentence structure.

3. Following this, the sentence structure and the meanings of the words are used to derive a partial representation of the meaning of a sentence. This is the **semantic analysis** stage.

4. **Pragmatic analysis**, the final stage, produces a complete meaning for the sentence via the application of contextual information. This information includes data that have to do with the time and location of the utterance, who was saying it, and to whom it was said.

Speech Recognition

Speech recognition by a machine is a laudable aspiration. Wouldn't it be nice to be able to talk to our computers instead of having to type in commands or use a mouse? Humans use language quickly and effortlessly to communicate ideas to one another. To be able to communicate in a similar way with computers would usher in a new age of efficiency and productivity. Unfortunately, the task of getting a machine to understand speech is much more difficult than it may seem. Let's review some of the steps that speech recognition by a machine would have to include and talk about the problems involved.

Any attempt at speech recognition starts with a speech spectrogram. A **speech spectrogram** is a visual representation of the speech signal; it is a graph that displays the component frequencies of a speech sound over time (see Figure 9.6). From this, a computer program then attempts to extract the phonemes from the segment of speech under analysis. If a phoneme is ambiguous, the segment of the speech signal that it occupies can be matched against similar utterances that have been recorded and analyzed to "fill it in." The phonemes are then assembled into their corresponding words. This is accomplished in part by a statistical analysis that factors in the probabilities that specific words will crop up in speech, that specific phonemes will crop up in specific words, and that specific words will be surrounded by other specific words.

A phoneme-to-word assignment is difficult for two main reasons. The first of these concerns word boundaries. It turns out that there are no pauses between words in spoken speech. This makes it hard to tell where one word starts and another ends. To compound the problem, there are often pauses within words. So pauses cannot serve as reliable indicators of word boundaries. The second major issue is phoneme variability. If each phoneme

Figure 9.6 A speech spectrogram.

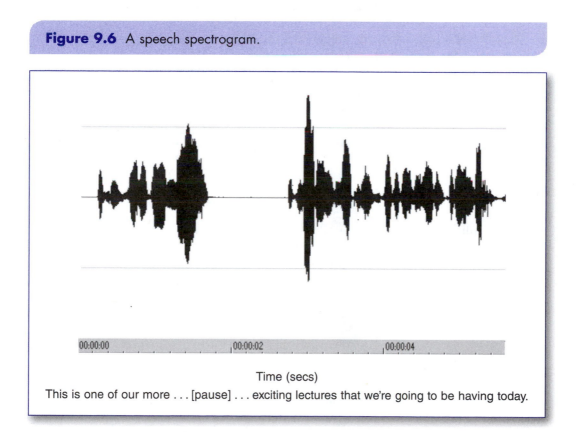

Time (secs)

This is one of our more . . . [pause] . . . exciting lectures that we're going to be having today.

were pronounced clearly and uniformly, speech recognition would be much easier. This is not the case. Speakers vary tremendously with respect to the pitches and durations of their phonemes. They are apt to pronounce a given phoneme variably, and in ways that depend on which phonemes precede it and which come after it. This is known as **coarticulation**. Additional complicating factors are the presence of background noise and the fact that in English a single sound—for example, that is represented by *bear* and *bare*—can belong to more than one word.

People resolve these difficulties by taking into account the overall meaning of a sentence. In one classic study, Warren and Warren (1970) presented participants with recordings of sentences in which a cough sound was substituted for a phoneme. One of the sentences was "It was found that the *eel was on the axle." (The asterisk indicates where the cough sound was inserted.) In other versions of the sentence, the word *axle* was changed to *shoe*, *orange*, and *table*. Asked to interpret the four sentences, the subjects heard the ambiguous word as *wheel*, *heel*, *peel*, and *meal*, respectively. This clearly demonstrates that the meanings of words in a sentence that have already been understood provide a framework for understanding the words that have yet to be understood. It also shows that in human speech perception, recognition is top-down as well as bottom-up, as the meaning of the entire sentence is pulled together simultaneously with the meanings of individual words.

Humans also have the benefit of visual cues when they are taking in speech. We can look at a speaker's lips as he or she is speaking. The positioning of the lips can help us interpret difficult phonemes or morphemes. Because some deaf individuals can understand speech by way of lip reading, there is obviously more than enough information in the visual aspect of speech to enable comprehension. Most computer speech recognition systems in use today must rely on auditory information as their only input and so do not have visual cues.

Syntactic Analysis

Once the individual words and their order have been determined, we can analyze the speech stream at the sentence level. This analysis entails the use of grammar. We already have discussed the various grammars that govern sentence structure. Syntactical analysis programs perform the equivalent of using a phrase structure grammar to evaluate a sentence and to break it down into its hierarchical constituents. An understanding of this structure is necessary if we are to get at the sentence's meaning.

Semantic Analysis

The string of phonemes that make up a word are sometimes enough to reveal the word's meaning. This is achieved by a comparison of the phonemic string with an internal database of sounds. If a match is obtained, the word's meaning is derived. But many times, there isn't a perfect match, and much ambiguity remains as to a word's meaning. In this case, the syntactical structure of the sentence can be useful.

In **compositional semantics**, the entire meaning of a sentence is derived from the meanings of its parts. A syntactical analysis identifies the type of word for each word in the sentence. This gives us information about how those words are related. For example, if a given word is identified as a noun, we know that it can be an agent or an instigator of an action. If a word is identified as a verb, we know that it represents an action. The structure of the sentence can then tell us whether that noun was the agent of that action. If a verb phrase is linked at the next higher level in the phrase structure to a noun phrase that immediately precedes it, there is a good chance that the action represented by the verb is brought into being by that noun. This structure, thus, has told us that the noun is an agent—additional information that has to do with the word's meaning. Similarly, it is clear that the adjective inside a noun phrase is a descriptor that applies to that noun and not any other. The structure has again helped us decipher meaning. We know that this word describes the noun in the phrase and not any other.

Consider the following sentence: Twas brillig, and the slithey toves did gyre and gimble in the wabe. What makes this sentence interesting is that it uses imaginary words yet follows proper grammatical rules. Even though most of these words are meaningless, we can still glean some understanding of what is happening by drawing on our knowledge of grammatical construction. You have probably guessed that *toves* is the noun and *slithey* is the adjective that describes it. You may also have intuited that *gyre* and *gimble* are verbs that describe the actions performed by the "toves" and that they are doing it in the "wabe." Now consider this sentence: Colorless green ideas sleep furiously. Here, we have an example of another sentence that follows grammatical rules. It differs from the one above in that it is composed of meaningful words. This time, however, the words are used in a nonsensical way. Ideas cannot be green, and if they could be, they could not also be colorless. Likewise, ideas can't sleep, and if they could, they couldn't do it furiously. This sentence is even more confusing than the one above because, despite the fact that the words fit the "slots" that make up a proper phrase structure, their meanings conflict with one another.

So we see that grammar does more than tell us what a correct or incorrect sentence is. Grammar specifies the abstract relationships between words in a sentence. These relationships are important clues in our deciphering of individual word and overall sentence meaning.

Pragmatic Analysis

Human language is a social construct. Individuals use it to communicate with one another. We communicate for all sorts of reasons. Sometimes, the purpose of a linguistic utterance is simple conveyance of information, as when we say, "This pillow is soft." But linguistic utterances can serve many other purposes—ones that require an action on the part of the listener, for example. It is sometimes not apparent what action should be undertaken by the listener, as many sentences invite action on the listener's part without directly issuing a command. **Pragmatics** is the social rules that underlie language use, as well as the strategies used by speakers to make themselves clear. Pragmatics helps us understand what actions we should take in response to spoken sentences.

Searle (1979) outlines five different types of spoken statements. Each type demands a different response from the listener.

1. **Assertives** are spoken statements in which the speaker asserts his or her belief. An example would be "It is hot in here." The statement suggests that we should open the window or turn on a fan or an air conditioner.

2. **Directives** are instructions dispatched from the speaker to the listener. They are direct commands and don't require an inference on the part of the listener with respect to what the desired action is. "Turn down the radio" is one such a command.

3. **Commissives** commit the speaker to a later action, as when a child says, "I will take out the garbage later." We would then need to verify that the garbage indeed had been taken out or not, and we would possibly impose a reward or punishment, depending on the outcome.

4. **Expressives** describe the psychological state of the speaker. "I apologize for yelling at you" indicates sorrow or regret and implies that the speaker probably continues to trust the person being spoken to.

5. **Declaratives** are spoken statements in which the utterance itself is the action. "You are fired" means that we have to look for a new job.

In each of these statements, we see that a speaker has used language to get the listener to perform an action. This is the case even in instances in which the sentence has not been phrased specifically as a command. Understanding the meaning of a statement is not enough here: One must infer what action the statement has asked for (directly or indirectly). Social context plays an important role in this process of establishing intent. "Do you know the time?" asked by someone waiting at the bus stop means that the speaker genuinely wants to know the time to find out if the bus is late. This same question asked of someone who has arrived late to an important meeting has a different intent. It is a criticism of that someone's lateness and not a request for the time.

Computer Language Programs and IBM's Watson

Many of you are probably familiar with or have used *Siri*, the language system built into the iPhone that has some limited capabilities to respond to spoken requests. A few more of you may also be familiar with a program called Dragon Naturally Speaking, which is capable of converting spoken language into text. So the age of "talking" computers is already with us. However, both these programs pale in comparison with the abilities of Watson, a computer system developed by IBM that has extensive world knowledge and is thus able to answer a wide variety of questions on different topics.

Watson was created with a specific goal in mind: to beat the human world champions at the television trivia show Jeapordy! In 2011, it did just that, beating Ken Jennings and Brad Rutter and winning a prize of 1 million dollars. How was Watson able to accomplish such a feat? To begin with, it was given access to a large amount of information, including all of Wikipedia, other encyclopedias, dictionaries, news information, books, and articles. When presented with a question, Watson would break it down into keywords and phrases and then search its database for these and related text strings to find an answer. It utilized thousands of algorithms to do these searches, independently and in parallel. The greater the number of algorithms that yielded the same answer, the greater the likelihood that a correct answer was reached. In a final step, Watson would do a secondary match against the database to determine whether the answer made sense.

In the game, human players were able to come up with responses faster than Watson, particularly when there was less contextual information available, but Watson was much faster at making an actual response to activate the buzzer: only eight milliseconds in comparison with several hundred milliseconds for the human participants. Watson is currently being used at the Memorial Sloan Kettering Cancer Center to perform management decisions for lung cancer treatment, where it is reported that most of the nurses using it follow its advice. Other fields for which it has promising applications are in government, telecommunications, and financial services. Although the cost of implementing a system like Watson now is prohibitive, it is probable that costs will come down in the near future and make it accessible to a larger portion of the public.

Evaluation of Natural Language Processing

Speech recognition systems still have problems dealing with noise, differences in pronunciation, and word ambiguity. Also, semantic analysis cannot rely on grammatical structure alone in the decipherment of meaning. As we have seen in the case of Watson, analysis must take into account real-world knowledge. This requires an extensive database filled with facts. Social context is also important. To "understand" what someone is saying, we need to know what their intent is. Are they just communicating facts? Asking a question? Issuing a command? Context expands beyond pragmatics though. To understand someone, it also helps to know who they are, who else may be present, where everyone is, what time of day it is, and a whole host of other situational factors. For instance, knowing that a conversation is taking place outdoors constrains the possible responses one can make (a light switch does not need to be turned on), while knowing who else is present also provides such constraints (it might not make sense to say something bad about Bill if his best friend is present). So if computer programs are to converse with humans in the most natural and sophisticated way possible, they need to have situational awareness, physical as well as social. Language cannot be detached from reality.

OVERALL EVALUATION OF THE LINGUISTIC APPROACH

Hopefully, this chapter has given you a sense of the importance and complexity of language. Linguistics resembles cognitive science as a whole in that it brings multiple perspectives to bear on a single topic. Instead of mind, its topic is language. Linguistics uses a varied set of theories and methods in its attempt to answer questions about language. The common thread that runs through its investigations is the subject matter, not any one technique or orientation.

We have made great strides in expanding our understanding of language in the past few decades. Grammatical analysis has been used to expand our comprehension of language structure. We have elucidated the linguistic abilities of animals, and we know the developmental stages that all children pass through as they acquire language. But there is still much to learn. The relationship between language and thought is still murky, and we await further research that will shed light on the ways in which language influences thinking. The Wernicke-Geschwind model in all likelihood will be revised in favor of a new, comprehensive model that will be more detailed and able to specify the neural basis of processes such as retrieval from the mental lexicon. In all likelihood, there will also be advances in computer-based language comprehension.

SUMMING UP: A REVIEW OF CHAPTER 9

1. Linguistics is the study of language and has been approached by many different perspectives and methodologies.

2. There is no single agreed-on definition of language, but we can say that it has five features. (1) It is used for communication, (2) the symbols used are arbitrary, (3) the ordering of the symbols is structured, (4) the symbols can be combined to form a large number of meanings, and (5) it is dynamic, meaning that it can change over time.

3. A phoneme is the smallest sound unit of a language that has no meaning. There are 45 phonemes in the English language. A morpheme is the smallest unit that does have meaning. Morphemes can be a word or part of a word.

4. The linguistic relativity hypothesis says that language and thought are powerfully intertwined, perhaps so much so that one could not express a thought in one language by using another language. There is, however, no broad support for the strong version of this hypothesis.

5. Animals are certainly capable of communicating, but there is controversy surrounding whether or not certain species possess language skills.

6. Researchers have attempted to teach animals language. The chimpanzee Washoe was capable of using limited ASL. A chimp named Sarah was instructed in the use of a token system. A third chimp by the name of Kanzi was estimated to use words and sentences at the level of a 2½-year-old child.

7. Human children pass through several distinct stages as they acquire language. They start by babbling a wide variety of sounds early in their first year. At around 6 months, they utter consonant–vowel pairs. One-word utterances occur at around 1 year of age. This is followed by two-word, sentence-like statements. There is evidence to support both domain-general and domain-specific theories of language acquisition.

8. Case studies of children deprived of language experience early in life demonstrate that there is a critical period of language acquisition. Genie was deprived of language until she was almost 14 years old. Despite intensive instruction, she was not able to learn adult-level language skills.

9. The rules that govern language use are known as grammar or syntax. Every sentence can be broken down into a hierarchical structure showing the relationship between different word types.

10. Chomsky identified a difference between a surface structure or actual organization of a given sentence and a deep structure containing the semantics or meaning. The surface structure can vary, while the deep structure is more constant. All the world's languages share some features in common. These are known as universal grammar.

11. The neural underpinnings of language ability have been studied for quite some time, especially when examining the language deficits that result from brain damage. In Broca's aphasia, patients have difficulty articulating or producing speech, but their comprehension abilities are intact. In Wernicke's aphasia, patients can produce rapid and fluent speech that is meaningless.

12. In the field of artificial intelligence, the goal has been to create computer programs capable of comprehending and producing speech. This would enable people to interact with machines more easily. Comprehension of natural languages in machines occurs in four stages: (1) speech recognition, (2) syntactic analysis, (3) semantic analysis, and (4) pragmatic analysis.

EXPLORE MORE

Log on to the student study site at **http://study.sagepub.com/friedenberg3e** for electronic flash cards, review quizzes, and a list of web resources to aid you in further exploring the field of cognitive science.

SUGGESTED READINGS

Akmajian, A., Demers, R. A., Farmer, A. K., & Harnish, R. M. (2001). *Linguistics: An introduction to language and communication.* Cambridge: MIT Press.

Jurafsky, D., & Martin, J. H. (2008). *Speech and language processing* (2nd ed.). Upper Saddle River, NJ: Prentice Hall.

Lakoff, G. (1990). *Women, fire, and dangerous things: What categories reveal about the mind.* Chicago, IL: University of Chicago Press.

Rymer, R. (1993). *Genie: A scientific tragedy.* New York, NY: HarperCollins.

Savage-Rumbaugh, E. S., & Lewin, R. (1994). *Kanzi: The ape at the brink of the human mind.* New York, NY: Wiley.

10

THE EMOTIONAL APPROACH

Mind as Emotion

Ninety percent of our lives is governed by emotion. Our brains merely register and act upon what is telegraphed to them by our bodily experience. Intellect is to emotion as our clothes are to our bodies: we would not very well have civilized life without clothes, but we would be in a poor way if we had only clothes without bodies.

—Alfred North Whitehead, 1943

EMOTION AND COGNITIVE SCIENCE

Your boyfriend is late. He said he would pick you up at 7:00 p.m. so that the two of you could go out to dinner at your favorite Italian restaurant. It's 8:00 p.m., and he still hasn't arrived. On top of this, he has not responded to your text or voicemail. You start to get angry and wonder what the matter is. You remember another time when he was late in arriving and begin to think that he doesn't care about you. This gets you thinking about other negative thoughts like that time the two of you got into that argument the previous week. Maybe it is time for a breakup? Just then the phone rings. It is him, and he says he got into a car accident. Immediately you feel sorry for him and perhaps a bit guilty for thinking so poorly of him.

This example shows that we humans are not pure calculating machines. We think yes, but we also feel. We are cognitive, but we are also emotional. Cognition and emotion are complexly intertwined. They are both co-occurring and influencing each other. Our thoughts affect how we feel, and how we feel affects how we think. In this chapter, we will examine emotions and their relation to cognition, but first, we will start by defining what emotions and other related phenomena are. Then, we will discuss the evolutionary forces that created emotions along with the psychological disorders that can arise from them. Following that, we will delve a bit into the anatomy and physiology underlying emotional states. We will conclude with a discussion of affective computing and attempts by researchers in the field of artificial intelligence to artificially create machines capable of emotional behavior.

WHAT IS EMOTION?

The concept of emotion is a slippery one (Solomon, 2003). People use the term in a number of different ways. We will adopt the approach used by Davidson, Scherer, and Goldsmith (2003) and differentiate between emotions, feelings, and moods. An **emotion** is a relatively brief episode of coordinated brain, autonomic, and behavioral changes that facilitate a response to an external or internal event of significance for the organism. Fear is a good illustrative example. Imagine that you are hiking in the woods. Suddenly, you come across a bear. The bear is an external event that has a clear significance for you since it could potentially kill you. Suddenly, you find that your heart is beating faster, you begin to sweat, and a feeling of panic flashes through your mind. You immediately turn around and run back down the trail at full speed. In this case, the physiological changes facilitated the fleeing response.

Feelings correspond to the subjective experience of emotions. They are what it is like to feel afraid, sad, or jubilant. Emotions may be considered public; other people can judge whether or not you seem afraid based on outward appearances, such as trembling hands. Feelings, though, are internal and subjective; they are the way you as an individual experience the emotion. **Moods** are diffuse affective states that are often of lower intensity than emotion but considerably longer in duration. If you received an "A" on your psychology exam, it might put you in a good mood for the rest of the day. Whereas the emotion of happiness would be more intense but short-lived—lasting, say, only a few minutes—the good mood would be more subdued but could stay with you for hours. The term *affective* is sometimes used to signify emotion but can be more broadly construed to refer to emotions, feelings, and moods together (Fox, 2008).

Dolan (2002) believes that, from a psychological perspective, emotions have three characteristics. First, unlike thoughts, emotions are embodied. That is, we experience emotions not just as mental events "in our heads" but also as full-body experiences. Second, and also unlike cognition, emotions are harder to control. We may find that it is easier to change our thoughts than our emotions. Finally, emotions seem less encapsulated than thoughts. In other words, they seem to have a more global impact on our behavior. When we are happy, the entire world seems better. Consequently, this emotion would affect our entire outlook and influence what we remember, what we say to people, and so on.

THEORIES OF EMOTION

Since emotions were first studied psychologically, there has been controversy over how they are caused. According to the **James-Lange theory of emotion,** there is an event that produces arousal and other physiological changes in the body (James, 1884; Lang, 1994). These physiological changes are then interpreted. The result of the interpretation is the emotion. Imagine that you are walking down a city street late at night. A man lurches toward you from an alley, holding what appears to be a gun. According to this view, the sight of the man would cause your heart to beat faster; only then would you be aware of your heart's acceleration and experience fear.

According to the **Cannon-Bard theory of emotion**, the event itself can trigger an emotion (Cannon, 1927). Although the event causes physiological arousal, the arousal is not necessary for the formation of the emotion. So in this view, the event immediately causes both the emotion and the bodily changes. The two do not depend on each other.

The **cognitive theory of emotion** resembles the James-Lange theory but has more to say about the interpretation process. In this view, it is the total situation and not just the arousal that determines emotions. An accelerating heart by itself would not be enough to produce fear, as we find in the James-Lange theory. Instead, it would be the bodily change plus the situation that would produce fear: your heart beating faster and the awareness that the man may want to shoot you.

A study by Schachter and Singer in 1962 is perhaps one of the most classic experiments in psychology. It is a good illustration of the role cognitive appraisal plays in the determination of emotions. In this experiment, two groups of participants were injected with epinephrine, which induces arousal. They were both told that this was a vitamin injection and were told to sit in a waiting room before the rest of the experiment. In the waiting room, there was a confederate, an actor who plays a part in the study. In one condition, the confederate acted happily. He made paper airplanes, played with a hula hoop, and acted silly. The confederate in the second condition, in contrast, acted angrily. He bothered the participant, ultimately storming out of the room. When asked about how they felt, the first group exposed to the happy confederate reported that they felt happy. The second group, who had to sit through the irate confederate, instead, reported that they felt irritable and angry.

The lesson from this study is clear: Both groups were equally aroused but in different contexts, and it was the context that determined how they appraised the situation. When in the presence of the happy confederate, they attributed their arousal to him, resulting in a happy outcome. When the arousal was interpreted in a different situation—with the angry confederate—it instead produced feelings of anger.

The most recent model of emotion formation incorporates elements from the previous three theories. It is called the **emergence synthesis** approach (LeDoux, 1996; Russell, 2003). In this perspective, there are some emotions that are triggered solely by a stimulus and don't require any interpretation. For instance, fear can be caused when a threatening stimulus activates a part of the brain called the amygdala. The amygdala by itself can induce the feeling of being scared without any thought or appraisal.

However, there are some emotions that do require interpretation. For example, guilt seems to result from a combination of bodily changes, cognition, and perhaps memories of previous experiences. So in this model, we have several pathways to emotion. They can be caused by arousal, by interpretation, or by some combination of the two. This more flexible model accounts for a wider range of studies and is the one currently in favor.

BASIC EMOTIONS

How many emotions are there? It seems as if it could be a long list. To simplify the discussion, researchers have introduced the concept of a basic emotion. A **basic emotion** is one that is believed to be mostly innate, and in humans, it ought to be universal or is found in all cultures. Basic emotions may also contribute in various combinations to form other more complex emotions (Plutchik, 1980).

Charles Darwin first suggested that there might be basic emotions not just in humans but in animals as well. He noted that people, regardless of background, use similar facial expressions to convey particular emotions. There is empirical evidence to support this view. Ekman and Friesen (1971) presented photos of Caucasian facial expressions to members of a New Guinea tribe who had little or no exposure to Western faces. The participants could correctly label nearly all the faces, suggesting that the expressions employed correspond to a set of fundamental emotions (Ekman, 1989). The expressions were happy, sad, fearful, angry, surprised, and disgusted (see Figure 10.1). However, there is no complete agreement on these expressions. Other studies have suggested additional emotions, such as pride (Tracy & Robins, 2004). There is also contention as to whether or not these basic emotions can be further subdivided. It has been proposed that there may be three kinds of disgust (Rozin, Lowery, & Ebert, 1994). There also may be several varieties of happiness, such as joy, amusement, love, and interest (Keltner & Shiota, 2003; LeDoux, 1996).

EMOTIONS, EVOLUTION, AND PSYCHOLOGICAL DISORDERS

Emotions clearly serve some adaptive purpose if evolutionary forces have selected for them. Rolls (1999) lists three primary functions of emotion. He divides them into categories servicing survival, communicative/social, and cognitive needs. At the survival level, emotions elicit responses to stimuli important to the organism. The presence of a threat will thus automatically trigger a fight-or-flight response to deal with the potential danger. Running or fighting keeps the organism alive in such situations and so, clearly, is of adaptive value.

Emotions can be thought of as complex, sophisticated reflexes. A reflex is triggered by a very specific stimulus and produces a very specific response. Emotions are much more flexible. Multiple stimuli, such as a spider, a snake, or a bear, can all trigger fear. Emotions also provide for a more varied behavioral reaction. Depending on the context, being afraid

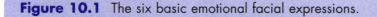

Figure 10.1 The six basic emotional facial expressions.

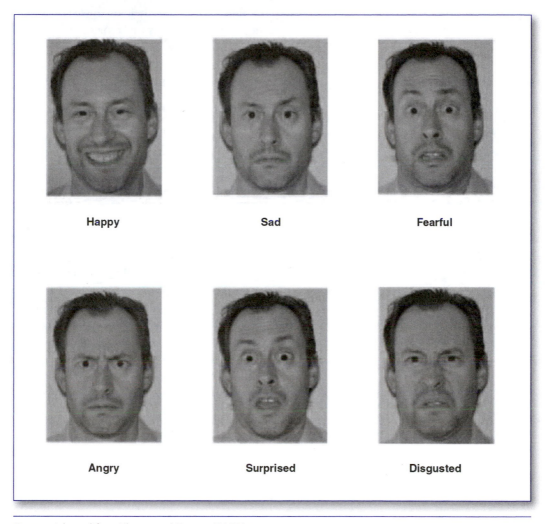

| Happy | Sad | Fearful |
| Angry | Surprised | Disgusted |

Source: Adapted from Ekman and Friesen (1971).

can make you jump, scream, run, hide, and so on. They narrow our possible responses, but at the same time, they allow us some measure of choice in determining what to do. Here, we again see a cognition–emotion interaction. Emotions prime our responses, but the actual selection and execution can be left up to more controlled thought processes.

In animals and people, emotions also serve as a form of communication (Darwin, 1872/1998). Facial expressions caused by emotions convey our feelings to others. This guides our interactions with one another. If your best friend looked very angry or sad, your reactions to him or her in each case would differ considerably. You might try to calm him or her down or suggest a relaxing activity that you could do together, such as watching a movie. The perception of sadness, instead, might prompt you to ask him or her to tell you what was wrong and to talk about it.

The third major function is one we have already mentioned—namely, that our emotions can assist us in thinking and problem solving. Emotions guide our attention to what is important, helping us ignore distractions and prioritize our concerns (Picard, 1997). In the rest of this section, we will outline some of the adaptive functions that basic emotions might serve. We will then discuss how these emotions can sometimes "backfire" and contribute to various psychological disorders. Friedenberg (2008) provides a more detailed account.

Disgust

Disgust is the emotional reaction we have to substances that could be a source of viral, bacterial, or parasitic infection. It causes us to be repulsed and, therefore, to avoid these things. There is a possible relationship between this emotion and **obsessive-compulsive disorder**. Marks and Nesse (1994) point out that other animals engage in ritualistic actions to reduce the threat of infection. Birds preening their feathers or cats licking their fur are two examples of this. People suffering from obsessive-compulsive disorder also engage in such behaviors. They count the number of cracks in a sidewalk or wash their hands many times a day. These compulsions temporarily reduce the anxiety they feel in response to a repeated intruding thought or obsession related to contamination, such as believing that their hands are dirty. It could be that this disorder is the result of a disruption in this mechanism.

Fear

When we are afraid, our palms sweat, pupils dilate, and hearts accelerate. The evolutionary advantage of fear is obvious: it causes us to avoid dangerous things. There are a number of distinct fear disorders. A **phobia** is a persistent and irrational fear of a specific object or situation. Fear of spiders (arachnophobia) and heights (acrophobia) are two common examples. The fact that phobias are connected to stimuli commonly found in the natural environment and less often to human-made objects, such as guns or car doors, suggests that they are genetic rather than learned (Marks, 1987). In a **panic attack**, a person is overcome with intense fear accompanied by a strong sympathetic nervous system arousal. The majority of symptoms for this disorder are related to an escape response (Nesse, 1987). Patients with this disorder seem to be hypersensitive to stimuli that signal the state of being trapped.

In a **posttraumatic stress disorder**, an individual has been exposed to a traumatic situation, such as an earthquake or war. Patients manifest anxiety but also continue to psychologically reenact the event in the form of flashbacks and nightmares. This disorder may occur when the memory consolidation mechanism hypothesized to underlie flashbulb memory is activated. The details and feelings experienced during the trauma seem to be encoded so strongly in these people that they come out inappropriately, perhaps in response to subtle retrieval cues.

Anger

Anger is the emotion that motivates fighting, the opposite of a fear response. When angry, we confront and deal aggressively with the inducing stimulus. Anger serves to mobilize and sustain vigorous motor activity (Tomkins, 1963). In this aroused state, we are better able to deal with threats. Aggression also has evolutionary roots. Men are much more aggressive than women. According to one explanation, this is because men must compete for mates, with more aggressive males being able to secure better mates. Manson and Wrangham (1991) studied warfare in 75 traditional societies. They found that in more than 80% of the cases, war involved access to females or to resources necessary to obtain one.

Sadness

All of us may have felt down and discouraged, typically in response to some personal event, such as the loss of a job or the death of a loved one. For most of us, this feeling eventually goes away. For some individuals, though, this sadness can occur without any precipitating incident and can be more intense and longer lasting. This is known as **major depressive disorder** and can be accompanied by interruptions in sleep, appetite, and concentration. Nesse (2000) believes that depression is an evolved strategy for disengaging from unattainable goals. Moods may also regulate the amount of time and energy we put into various activities, with depressed moods causing us to rethink our strategy and abandon fruitless efforts.

Depressed people often ruminate on their life situation. This rumination involves an analytical mode of thinking, which can actually help solve complicated problems. However, to be truly effective, this analysis needs to be done slowly and carefully. According to the **analytical rumination hypothesis**, depression is an evolved response to complex problems (Andrews, Thomson, & Anderson, 2009). In this view, the depressive state induces a focus on the problem while at the same time minimizing distractions that might detour attention, working memory, and other processing resources. Experimental evidence supports the hypothesis. Au, Chan, Wang, and Vertinsky (2003) manipulated mood while participants performed a financial investment task. They found that those in the negative mood condition made the most accurate decisions and invested conservatively. In comparison, those in the positive mood made bad decisions. Their accuracy was lower, and they lost more because they invested more.

Happiness

Being happy may serve as a reinforcer for adaptive responses and encourage us to engage in actions with survival value, such as feeding and mating. Happiness also broadens our scope of attention and may enhance our physical and creative skills (Fredrickson, 1998). It seems to occur more often during times of perceived security and acceptance. Happiness, in this view, stimulates us to learn new skills, establish relationships, and accrue resources that may be needed in leaner times to come. In addition, happiness seems to foster altruism. Studies show that a mood-enhancing experience such as finding money or recalling a happy event can cause people to engage in helping behavior, such as picking up someone's papers or giving away money (Salovey, 1990). This is known as the **feel-good, do-good phenomenon.**

Most disorders involve negative emotions. However, in **bipolar disorder**, individuals alternate back and forth between depressive and manic symptoms. The manic state is characterized by exuberance, a grandiose sense of self, decreased need for sleep, and excessive talkativeness. These symptoms mirror those found in a normal state of happiness and perhaps reflect some defect in the neural mechanisms underlying it. Bipolar individuals are often well educated and are found in large numbers in creative fields such as writing (Westen, 1996). This supports the notion that happiness causes creativity and the development of new skills.

EMOTIONS AND NEUROSCIENCE

Much of the biological research on emotion in humans and animals has centered on the amygdala. This is an almond-shaped structure that belongs to a larger collection of structures called the limbic system, also implicated in emotion. The amygdala has been found to play a key role in learning to associate a particular stimulus with a fear response (Barinaga, 1992). Rabbits can be conditioned to fear an auditory tone by repeated pairing of that tone with an electric shock. This is the classical conditioning paradigm that we presented in the psychology chapter. Animals with lesions to the amygdala cannot be conditioned in this way. They never seem to develop a connection between the shock and the tone.

Brain research has revealed that the amygdala is part of two neural circuits that mediate our fear reactions (LeDoux, 1996). These are shown in Figure 10.2. In the first circuit, a fearful stimulus—such as a spider—is relayed through the thalamus directly to the amygdala. This triggers a fearful emotional response that would include physiological arousal, such as increased heart rate. This has been dubbed the "low road" to the amygdala since it is fast and does not require any thought. It can be thought of as a quick, emergency fear response system that evolved to deal quickly with threatening stimuli. Remember that in the real world, if you stop to think about what to do in a dangerous situation, it may already be too late.

At the same time the thalamus sends this signal to the amygdala, it also sends it to the cortex. Here, the sensory information can be analyzed and evaluated by cognitive

Figure 10.2 The "low" and "high" roads to the amygdala.

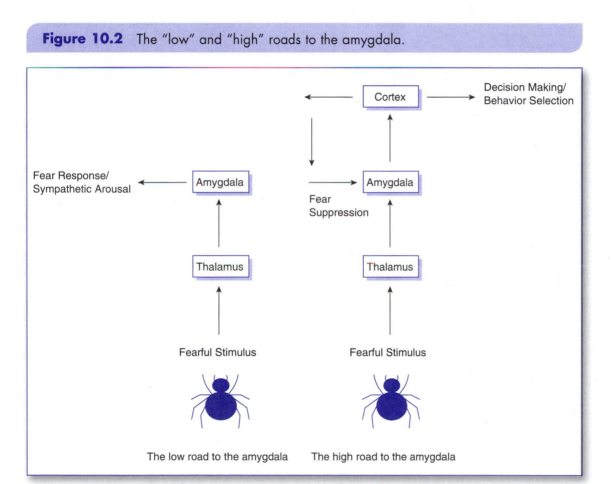

Source: Hansen and Hansen (1988).

processes. This is the "high road," since the information is passed upward and takes more time to process. The cortex can now initiate further behaviors if necessary. It could, for instance, get you to brush off the spider or back away from it. The cortex also sends signals back down to the amygdala, further moderating its activity. Fear might be suppressed at this stage if you realized that the spider wasn't poisonous.

The amygdala is also implicated in the perceptual and attentional processing of dangerous stimuli. Several studies show increased activity in the amygdala in response to fearful faces compared with neutral stimuli without any affective content (Morris, Öhman, & Dolan, 1998; Vuilleumier & Schwartz, 2001). Grandjean et al. (2005) found that the sound of an angry voice activated another brain area, the superior temporal sulcus, even when participants weren't attending to it. The results imply that there may be an emotional "early-warning system" that biases perceptual and attentive processes to threatening stimuli. This mechanism appears to be modality independent, since in these studies it was found for both visual and auditory perception.

What about affect and memory? A roundup of the usual suspects reveals that the amygdala again plays a role (McGaugh, 2004). Specifically, it is believed to improve memory for physiologically arousing stimuli. Arousal triggers sympathetic epinephrine and norepinephrine release, which activates the amygdala. It, in turn, sends outputs to the hippocampus. Remember, it is the hippocampus that is responsible for the encoding of new information so that this information gets transferred from short-term storage in working memory to more permanent storage in long-term memory. The hippocampus then ensures that the arousing stimulus is consolidated, making it hard to forget. This mechanism may be responsible for flashbulb memory.

The Chemical and Electrical Basis of Emotional Computation

The neural basis underlying thought is believed to be the electrical communication that occurs among neurons. Action potentials traveling down axons ultimately induce either excitatory or inhibitory postsynaptic potentials that summate in the receiving neuron to determine its firing rate or firing pattern. The result is numerous activation patterns that course through the network. Most researchers believe that cognition is coded for in this activity, in much the same way that electron patterns flowing through silicon chip circuits are the basis for computation in a computer.

What is frequently missing in this "information flow" account of cognition is synaptic action. Between every terminal button and dendrite, there is a synapse. Many different types of neurotransmitters are released at synapses in the human brain. The kind of synaptic action that happens may regulate not only cognition but also emotion. Panksepp (1993) provides a list of neurotransmitters that play important roles in various emotional states. The main excitatory transmitter, glutamate, is linked to anger and fear; gamma-aminobutyric acid, the main inhibitory transmitter, regulates anxiety; norepinephrine is part of sympathetic nervous system arousal, the "fight-or-flight" response; and Serotonin's influence on depression is well documented, as is the influence of dopamine on positive emotional states and also on schizophrenia.

Hormones also underlie much of our emotional responses. The corticotropin-releasing factor is part of the stress reaction and affects our feelings of anxiety and fear; testosterone has been implicated in aggression and social dominance; estrogen in women influences mood and sexual behavior; and oxytocin has been found to promote maternal bonding and affection for offspring, especially during nursing (Nelson & Panksepp, 1998).

One intriguing account of all this is that electrical brain activity in the form of potentials may underlie or contribute more to cognitive processes. Hormonal and synaptic action in the form of neurotransmitter function may then be the basis for or contribute more to emotion. In other words, thought may be *electrical*, while emotion may be *chemical*. If this were the case, then the same pathways that produce thought might also give rise to affect, because axonal and synaptic action are both necessary links in the process of neural information transmission. A particular pattern of neural activity in our brains could then simultaneously convey our experience of thought and affect. This corresponds with the earlier notion that the two are inseparable.

If mental computation—broadly speaking to include both cognition and affect—was expanded to include chemical and electrical activity, then the computing power of the brain may be significantly higher than previously estimated. Rather than 100 billion neurons with 1,000 connections each, we would need to add in a billion or so proteins in each neuron. This would yield a figure of a billion times 100 billion computing units (Thagard, 2008).

HOT AND COLD: EMOTION–COGNITION INTERACTIONS

Thoughts and emotions seem different. A thought seems "cool" and is associated with calm, measured deliberation. Emotions, on the other hand, seem "hot." They appear to drive behavior, impelling us to do something right now. However, this distinction may be a false one. A growing body of evidence indicates that emotions are part and parcel of many cognitive processes (Adolphs, Tranel, & Damasio, 1998). It seems that emotion and cognition work together integrally in determining behavior. The neural mechanisms underlying both, for example, are connected at many different levels of organization (Phelps, 2006). In the sections that follow, we wish to show that emotion–cognition interaction is complex. Following Thagard (2008), we reject the classical view that emotions always get in the way of thinking. We also reject the romantic view that emotions are better than reason. Instead, we adopt a critical view that shows how each can facilitate or interfere with the other.

Emotion and Perception/Attention

One of the proper functions of perception is to filter out information that is irrelevant and to focus on what is important. If a tiger is running at you, you certainly don't want to waste time looking at the flowers. Attention serves this function. Items that are allocated attention in the visual field are given priority and get processed more quickly, thereby enabling faster and perhaps lifesaving responses. But how does attention get allocated? There is evidence now to show that emotional processes can help steer attention toward significant stimuli—those that may be crucial for the organism's survival (Vuilleumier, 2005).

Using a visual search paradigm, Hansen and Hansen (1988) found that participants were faster at detecting an angry face hidden among neutral faces than they were at detecting a happy face under the same conditions (see Figure 10.3). These results have since been explained as an example of the **threat-superiority effect,** whereby dangerous items are found to be more perceptually salient. Easier detection of angry faces has since been replicated a number of times (Eastwood, Smilek, & Merikle, 2001; Fox et al., 2000). Notably, easier

Figure 10.3   According to the threat-superiority effect, it is easier to detect an angry face hidden among neutral faces than it is to detect a happy face hidden among neutral faces.

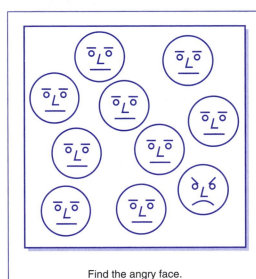
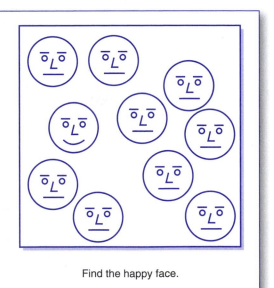

Find the angry face.   Find the happy face.

detection is not found for sad faces, indicating that it is the threat value rather than the negative valence that drives the effect (Öhman, Lundqvist, & Esteves, 2001).

Whereas the aforementioned work shows a facilitative effect of emotionally charged stimuli, other work shows that it can interfere as well. Recall the Stroop effect, where it takes longer to name the color of a word spelling out a different color in contrast to that same word printed in the color it spells out. Pratto and John (1991) presented negative and positive adjective words in various colors. Their participants took more time to name the colors in the negative condition compared with the positive condition. In other words, it took more time to respond to a word such as *ugly* than to a word such as *pretty*. The results suggest that our perceptual/attentional systems are oriented toward negative social information.

This slowing down in the Stroop effect implies that we are more sensitive to such information. We, thus, have a harder time ignoring it in the Stroop task. There is additional evidence supporting this notion of increased sensitivity. Phelps, Ling, and Carrasco (2006) presented either fearful or neutral faces and then followed these very quickly with four striped patches. The task was to judge which of the four patches was at a different orientation. Observers were faster at discriminating the orientation following the presentation of the fearful faces in comparison with the neutral ones.

Emotion and Memory

What might be the role of emotion with regard to memory processes? One obvious prediction is that we should remember events surrounding emotional situations better. Since emotional events are important to our survival, it makes sense that our memory systems should be set up this way. Imagine being chased by a tiger. If you climbed up a tree to escape and have a strong recollection of that event, then you would be more likely to employ the same strategy the next time you find yourself in that situation. So there is a clear evolutionary benefit to this type of memory system.

Better recall of personal events during important or emergency situations is known as **flashbulb memory** (Brown & Kulik, 1977). People's recollections of what happened to them during the *Challenger* space shuttle disaster, the O. J. Simpson trial, and the attacks of September 11, 2001, are self-reported as being quite vivid (Reisberg, Heuer, McLean, & O'Shaughnessy, 1988). However, the accuracy of such memories is controversial. People have a high confidence in recalling what happened to them in these situations and report that they were very emotional at the time, but their memories may not actually be any better than during neutral times (Neisser & Harsch, 1992; Talarico & Rubin, 2003).

Flashbulb memories are for what a person was doing at the time of the incident. This includes where they were, whom they were with, and what they did. Such personal recollections are examples of what is called **autobiographical memory**. Whereas semantic memory is for facts, autobiographical memory is for episodes or events. This is, thus, considered a form of an episodic long-term memory, discussed in the chapter on the second cognitive approach.

This means that we can now ask a question: Is memory for the emotional stimuli themselves, rather than the events surrounding them, better? The answer appears to be yes. Ochsner (2000) presented participants with positive, negative, and neutral pictures and words. In a recognition paradigm, they were later asked to judge which of the stimuli they had seen before. If they thought they had seen an item before, they were then asked whether they remembered the context in which it occurred (the "known" condition, more episodic) or simply whether it was familiar (the "remembered condition," more semantic). The negative stimuli were remembered better than the positive or neutral stimuli. The arousing emotional words, positive and negative, were also remembered better than the neutral words. Furthermore, "remember" judgments were made more to negative stimuli.

There are several reasons why emotional items might be better remembered (Fox, 2008). First, it could be that we allocate more attention to such items. Things we pay more attention to are remembered better. Second, it could be because emotional things are more distinctive and unusual. In other words, they stand out more because they are rare and strange. A third alternate account is that we might think about them more often, and thus, rehearse them more. It may be that all three of these contribute to varying degrees, although at least one study has found better recall for negative affect items that cannot be entirely due to distinctiveness (Christianson & Loftus, 1991).

Emotion, Mood, and Memory

In the introduction, we distinguished between emotion and mood, stating that mood was less intense but longer lasting than emotion. A number of studies have examined the influence that mood has on memory (Levine & Pizarro, 2004). The research on this topic has focused on two effects: (1) mood-congruent memory and (2) mood-dependent memory. We will examine each of these next.

Mood-congruent memory is when we remember more stimuli if those stimuli match a mood we were in while learning those stimuli. Studies investigating this induce a particular mood at encoding while a participant is studying items, and then later, at recall, we see if the performance is better for matching items. The results support a mood-congruency effect. People are generally better at recalling negative words such as *death* if they learned them in a negative mood and words such as *flower* if induced into a positive mood at encoding (Rinck, Glowalia, & Schneider, 1992). One explanation for this is that we think more deeply and make more associations to mood-congruent material (Bower, 1981).

In **mood-dependent memory**, recall is better when the mood at recall matches that during learning. Here, the same mood must be present at both occasions for there to be an effect. Note the difference here. In mood congruency, the stimuli match the mood at encoding. In mood dependency, the moods match. Bower, Monteiro, and Gilligan (1978) found that neutral words were better remembered when the mood at encoding matched the mood at recall. The two induced states were happy and sad. In these cases, it may be that mood is acting as a retrieval cue; the learned items became associated with the mood at encoding and reactivated this association at retrieval.

Fiedler (2001) argues that we engage in different information-processing strategies while in different moods. When we are in a good mood, we are more likely to assimilate. In **assimilation**, we take information and interpret it in terms of what we already know. This is a less critical strategy and stands the chance of being wrong. For example, we may incorrectly categorize a scooter as a motorcycle, failing to note the differences between them. On the other hand, when we **accommodate**, we change our internal concepts or schemas to take new information into account. In this example, we would form a new category for "scooter," differentiating it from "motorcycle."

According to Levine and Pizarro (2004), a positive mood corresponds to a motivational state where we have attained a goal and there is no immediate problem to be solved. Under such conditions, our cognitive processing is a bit "looser" and accuracy is not as important. A negative mood, in contrast, corresponds to a situation where we encounter a problem and a goal is threatened. Here, we need to "tighten up" our processing, becoming more analytic and detail oriented.

Emotion and Decision Making

Thagard (2008) outlines some of the differences between emotional (intuitive) and rational (calculated) decision making. Intuitive decisions are fast; they can be made immediately and lead directly to a decision. This is preferable when making less important judgments, such as whether you should order out for pizza or Chinese food. However, they are prone to error because they may be based on inaccurate or irrelevant information. When making calculated decisions, we usually consider more alternatives and goals, understand the pros and cons of each, and make the entire process explicit so that we can go back and rethink it or get somebody else to help. This process is slower but is the way we would want to approach important problems in our lives, such as whether or not we should marry someone or accept a job offer.

Damasio (1999) argues that there are situations where emotion facilitates decision making. Several of his patients suffered damage to the ventral and medial portions of the prefrontal cortex (vmPFC). Following this, they lost the ability to apply rationality to personal and social situations. He believes that the damage prevented them from making emotional evaluations that involve somatic markers. These are bodily states that indicate whether a particular outcome will be good or bad. It is important to note that these patients could still reason well in other contexts and in some cases scored well on cognitive tests.

Bechara, Damasio, Tranel, and Damasio (1997) introduced a clever way to measure the role of emotions in decision making. In the Iowa Gambling Task, players received $2,000 in fake money to spend. They were presented with four decks of cards. In the first two decks, turning over a card resulted in a $100 win. However, these decks also produced large losses. In another two decks, the wins were smaller. Turning over a card in those decks resulted in only a $50 gain, but there were no associated losses. The best way to win and maximize earnings was to pick only from the latter two decks without associated losses.

Normal participants who played this game eventually realized (consciously or subconsciously) that the first two decks were risky, and they eventually stopped picking from them. In comparison, patients with bilateral damage to the vmPFC never stopped drawing from those decks, even when they were aware that they were risky options. This demonstrates that the vmPFC helps us determine whether a particular course of action is worth pursuing based on our past experiences. Normally, if we've done something and it resulted in a positive outcome, we will continue to do it. If another action has negative consequences, we will stop doing it. The emotional processing that enables us to do this is apparently missing in these patients, even if they were consciously aware of the risk.

Other research supports the notion that emotions are part of our normal decision-making process. Rather than believe that emotions are separate from cognition, it is more realistic to say that emotions are an integral part of them and help us choose from among alternatives (Loewenstein, Weber, Hsee, & Welch, 2001). Fazio (2001) reviews literature showing that most concepts have attached emotional attitudes. This certainly seems to be the case. It would be hard to imagine thinking about topics such as sex, politics, religion, and our friends and family without some sort of emotional bias. As we indicate in greater detail in the neuroscience section, the brain's emotional and cognitive centers work together during decision making (Rolls, 1999).

Clore, Gasper, and Garvin (2001) additionally advocate that feelings as well as information are used in decision making. For instance, if you find yourself in a good mood when in the presence of a certain someone, you may take that as evidence that you like him or her and decide to ask him or her out on a date. This suggests a whole new class of process models, ones where feelings are combined with thoughts to determine our decisions and behavior (Fox, 2008).

Emotions and Reasoning by Analogy

Recall from the introductory chapter that analogies can be considered as a type of mental representation. They can be used in problem solving and decision making by applying what we know in one situation to another similar to it. Thagard (2008) lists three types of analogies defined by their relation to emotion. First, there are analogies that are about emotions. Second, there are analogies that involve the transfer of emotion between situations. Third, there are analogies that generate new emotions. We detail each of these types below.

We often use analogies to describe our mental states. Examples include being "as brave as a lion" or "sneakier than a rat." Perhaps this is because it is difficult to describe what a thought or feeling is like in literal terms. Analogies of the second type that are used to transfer emotions are found in persuasion, empathy, and reverse empathy (Thagard, 2008). We often use analogies when we are trying to persuade somebody. These sorts of analogies are quite prevalent in the news media (Blanchette & Dunbar, 2001). Examples include "living on easy street," rumors spreading "like wildfire," and being led "like pigs to a slaughter."

In empathetic analogies, we express our ability to appreciate somebody else's situation by comparing it with another similar situation. For example, we might say, "The Korean war was awful. The war in Vietnam was like it in several ways. So the Vietnam war must have been awful, too." In reverse empathy, we make this relation personal: "I was a victim of the New York City attack. When you were a victim of the Washington, D.C., attack, you felt terrified. So I am feeling terrified as well."

In the third case, analogies are used to generate new emotional states. According to Thagard (2008), these involve humor, irony, and motivation, to name just a few. Here is an example he gives to illustrate humor: "How can a single woman get a cockroach out of her kitchen? Ask him for a commitment." As a joke, this ought to generate feelings of surprise and amusement in the listener. Ironic analogies can be used to evoke negative emotions as well, as when we say that a failing bank's efforts are like "rearranging the deck chairs on the Titanic." We can also use analogies to motivate, as when a father compares his son with Albert Einstein or Mozart.

EMOTIONS AND ARTIFICIAL INTELLIGENCE: AFFECTIVE COMPUTING

Affective computing is computing that relates to, arises from, or deliberately influences emotions and other affective phenomena (Picard, 1997). The goal of such projects is to enable computers and robots with the ability to recognize emotions in people. This capability would facilitate human–machine interactions. For example, your computer could tell when you are tired or frustrated based on your facial expression. It might then recommend that you take a rest break. Secondary, but also interesting, is imbuing machines with the ability to express emotions. Emotionally expressive machines are more satisfying to interact with. The Kismet project is a first step in this direction (Breazeal, 2002). Kismet is capable of expressing a wide variety of facial expressions and can carry out extended, lifelike social interactions. See the "Interdisciplinary Crossroads" section for a detailed description of this project.

A number of computer programs already exist that are capable of recognizing human emotion from spoken auditory information. Petrushin (2000) describes the emotion recognition project that utilizes an artificial neural network program to process features present in the speech stream. Examples of these features are energy, speaking rate, and the fundamental frequency. This program can recognize five emotions—(1) anger, (2) fear, (3) happiness, (4) sadness, and (5) a neutral, emotionless state—with about 70% accuracy. This is equivalent to human-level performance. There are plans to implement this system in automated telephone reservations systems such as those used by airlines to book flights.

Researchers in the affective computing group at the Massachusetts Institute of Technology are developing a wide variety of affective systems. Their FaceSense program can tag facial expressions, head gestures, and affective–cognitive states from real-time videos for use in human–machine and human–human interactions. The system utilizes a combination of bottom-up visual cues, such as frowns, and top-down predictions of what expected affect should be like given the situation and context. It can be used to evaluate customer satisfaction and as a training tool for autism disorders. Another model this group is developing is called SmileSeeker. It also captures facial cues to help interpret social interactions. The current version specifically looks for smiles in face image data. This program could be implemented for use in bank teller training.

Recognizing and producing emotions is just one facet of affective processing. Other investigators are focusing on what the internal design of an emotional being is like. The CogAff architecture is a generic scheme for how cognitive–emotional processing may take place in either a person or a machine (Sloman, Chrisley, & Scheutz, 2005). In this model, there are three distinct levels of processing (shown in Figure 10.4). The first and the lowest level is reactive. These are reflex-like responses in which a stimulus automatically triggers a reaction—for example, the fear experienced after bumping into something in the dark.

The second stage involves deliberative processes. These involve representations of alternate plans of action. Here, different courses of behavior are generated given the circumstances, and the best one is selected. For instance, one could determine whether or not he or she wants to go on a roller coaster ride at an amusement park. Emotional states such as fear and cognitive factors such as one's medical condition are both taken into consideration.

In the third, reflective stage, we see metacognition come into play. Recall that metacognition is the ability to think about and control other mental states. At this level, one is aware of experiencing an emotion but can choose to act on it or not depending on the circumstances and the use of deliberative processes. An illustration of this would be deciding whether or not to speak at a conference. One could be afraid of doing so based on the possibility of being critiqued or evaluated. After reflecting on this fear, though, one might decide to go ahead and do it anyway because it would further his or her career. Alternate options, such as writing a paper, would be considered along with their associated emotions before a decision is reached. When giving the talk, one would then suppress fear but know why he or she is doing it.

Figure 10.4 The CogAff architecture specifies how a machine may exhibit emotional behavior.

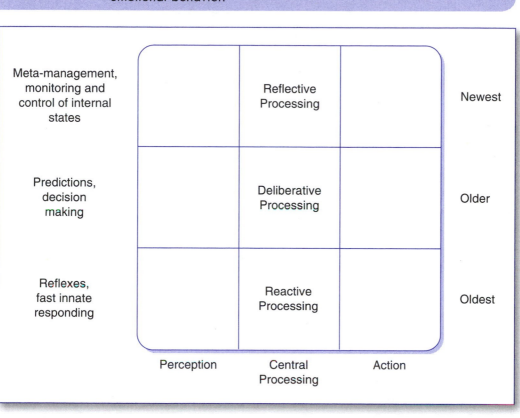

Meta-management, monitoring and control of internal states	Reflective Processing	Newest
Predictions, decision making	Deliberative Processing	Older
Reflexes, fast innate responding	Reactive Processing	Oldest
Perception	Central Processing	Action

Source: Sloman et al. (2005).

Minsky (2006) expands on this type of architecture by inserting a few more levels. Between reactive (what he calls instinctive reactions) and deliberative processes, he places learned reactions—the difference being that the lowest level reactions are genetically hard-wired, while learned reactions are acquired through experience. He then adds two more levels on top of reflective thinking that involve self-reflection. At the self-reflective thinking stage, one can think back to a decision and determine whether it corresponded to one's ethics and values. For example, one value a person might have is to help others. If we made a decision to do volunteer work in the past and it satisfied this value, we would decide to do it again now, even if we have lots of other work to do. Self-conscious emotions could involve those feelings we have from satisfying our values and can serve to motivate self-reflective thinking.

Interdisciplinary Crossroads:
Emotion, Robotics, and the Kismet Project

Researchers in robotics are beginning to realize the importance of emotion (Breazeal, 2002). The goal of this new area in robotics is to design robots that both recognize and express emotions in much the same way that humans do. Robots with these capacities will make it easier for us to interact with them. The **Kismet** project is the first major step in this direction. It is designed to model the interaction between an infant and its caregiver. Kismet is a cute robotic head capable of sensing others and of expressing a wide range of facial expressions. It is driven by a cognitive and emotional system that work together to govern its interactions with people (Breazeal & Brooks, 2005).

Kismet can "see" using a set of color cameras. It can move its head and eyes to control where it looks and what it pays attention to. Kismet's auditory system is a microphone that can process and recognize certain aspects of human speech. The auditory system allows it to detect basic pitch contours that signal approval, prohibition, attention, and comfort (Fernald, 1989). The detection of this affective information then guides its own emotional state. Kismet can fold back its ears to signal anger or raise them to display a state of interestedness. It can also move its eyebrows up and down or furrow them to communicate surprise, frustration, or sadness. In addition, Kismet is equipped with a vocalization system, allowing it to generate synthesized sounds reminiscent of a young child.

The Kismet robot conveys emotions mostly through its face (see Figure 10.5). The emotions it displays have been formulated to fit within a three-dimensional affect space of valence (good or bad), arousal (high or low), and stance (advance or withdraw). A soothed expression corresponds to high positive valence and low arousal (i.e., a state of being happy but underaroused). A joyous expression instead corresponds to a state of positive valence and moderate arousal. Some of the other expressions Kismet is capable of include anger, disgust, sorrow, surprise, and fear.

Kismet's cognitive system consists of perception, attention, drive, and behavior subsystems. It is motivated by basic drives just as a real biological child would be. These drives are thirst, hunger, and fatigue. A social drive gives it a "need" to interact with people, a stimulation drive provides an impetus to play with toys, and a fatigue drive causes it to rest when it is overstimulated. When these "needs" are met, the drives are in a homeostatic regime and Kismet acts as though it is satisfied. But if the intensity level of a drive deviates from this state of balance, the robot is motivated to engage in behaviors that restore the drive to equilibrium. Kismet's drives don't directly produce an emotional response, but they do, however, bias its overall emotional state or mood.

Figure 10.5 Kismet the robot is designed to interact with people in humanlike ways.

If Kismet does not receive enough stimulation and its social drive state is high, it puts on a sorrowful expression. Under typical circumstances, this will elicit increased interaction by a human playmate. For example, a person might try to engage Kismet by waving a toy in front of its face. If the robot is getting too much stimulation, its drive state is lowered, causing it to make a fearful face. In this case, a normal human would back off to reduce the amount of stimulation. If Kismet is receiving a moderate amount of stimulation, it expresses joy to encourage sustained human interaction.

Kismet can use its eyes and vocalize to communicate as well. If it is presented with an undesired stimulus, a disgust response will reorient its gaze to an alternate area in the visual field, where it might locate a more desirable object. This would again serve as a cue to a person to change his or her behavior, perhaps by switching to a different toy. If a person is ignoring Kismet, it can attract the person by first vocalizing. If that doesn't work, it might lean forward and wiggle its ears to attract attention. So, just like a real child, Kismet can utilize a variety of behaviors to get what it "wants."

Kismet's creators programmed it with several basic-level emotional states, including interest, surprise, sorrow, joy, calm, fear, disgust, and anger. The trigger state for one of these particular emotions corresponds to the values of the different motivational drives. The activation of the emotion would then, in turn, trigger the facial expression that goes along with it. A human observer, seeing this display, would then modify his or her actions toward it. People enjoy playing with Kismet and very easily attribute humanlike qualities to it. Future robots with emotionally perceptive and expressive abilities like Kismet will undoubtedly make it easier for us to accept and work with them.

OVERALL EVALUATION OF THE EMOTIONAL APPROACH

The emotional approach is a recent but welcome addition to cognitive science. For too long, researchers have swept emotions "under the rug" and focused exclusively on cognitive factors. It is now generally accepted, though, that most cognitive processes work in concert with affective ones. The research we have reported here is a good start. We are just beginning to understand how emotions affect perception, attention, memory, language, and problem solving. Many questions remain, however. We need a more detailed description of the physiology and information flow that underlies each of the emotions and moods.

Most of the research reported here looks at the influence of emotion on cognition, presumably because these cognitive processes have been studied for some time and are better understood. But the reverse situation, the influence of cognition on emotion, deserves research attention as well. For instance, how do we suppress emotions, and under what conditions is this easier or more difficult? There seem to be large individual differences in this ability, with some people predisposed to be more emotional and others more rational. If we understood the neural mechanisms underlying aggressive behavior, we might be able to reduce theft, murder, spousal abuse, and other crimes.

Understanding the basic emotions is just the tip of the iceberg. There are many other more subtle and complex emotions that remain. If these are created by a combination of the basics, then are there lawful rules governing this process? Perhaps anger and admiration mix to produce envy in much the same way that blue and yellow combine to make green. These "secondary" emotions play a powerful role in our thinking and behavior, but they have yet to be well classified or explained. There may even be "tertiary" emotions that are combinations of affect and cognition. Arrogance and self-esteem seem to fall into this category.

SUMMING UP: A REVIEW OF CHAPTER 10

1. An emotion is a relatively brief brain and body episode that facilitates a response to a significant event. Feelings correspond to the subjective experience of an emotion. Moods are less intense but longer lasting types of affective states.

2. Theories of emotion all posit a stimulus that triggers physiological changes and some sort of appraisal. However, these theories disagree on the temporal ordering of these events and the exact role that the cognitive appraisal process takes.

3. Some of the basic emotions that may be universal across cultures are happiness, sadness, fear, anger, surprise, and disgust.

4. Each of the major emotions may have played an adaptive role in promoting our survival during the conditions of our ancestral past. However, problems with these emotions can also be linked to psychological disorders.

5. The amygdala is a brain structure that mediates our fear response. It also plays a role in improving our memory for arousing stimuli.

6. More contemporary work in affective science has investigated the role that emotions play in perception, attention, memory, and decision making.

7. Emotions focus our attention on dangerous events. This is known as the threat-superiority effect. They also bias us to remember events of emotional significance. Under certain conditions, emotions can even facilitate decision making.

8. A number of computer models already exist that are capable of recognizing emotions based on cues in speech or facial images.

9. The CogAff architecture is an example of how an organism or machine may integrate emotions into decision making. It utilizes reactive, deliberative, and reflective stages.

EXPLORE MORE

Log on to the student study site at **http://study.sagepub.com/friedenberg3e** for electronic flash cards, review quizzes, and a list of web resources to aid you in further exploring the field of cognitive science.

SUGGESTED READINGS

Fellous, J. M., & Arbib, M. A. (Eds.). (2005). *Who needs emotions? The brain meets the robot.* Oxford, England: Oxford University Press.

Fox, E. (2008). *Emotion science.* Basingstoke, England: Palgrave Macmillan.

Lane, R. D., & Nadel, L. (2002). *Cognitive neuroscience of emotion.* New York, NY: Oxford University Press.

Levy, D. (2007). *Love and sex with robots: The evolution of human-robot relationships.* New York, NY: Harper.

Minsky, M. (2006). *The emotion machine: Commonsense thinking, artificial intelligence, and the future of the human mind.* New York, NY: Simon & Schuster.

Solomon, R. C. (Ed.). (2003). *What is an emotion? Classic and contemporary readings.* Oxford, England: Oxford University Press.

Thagard, P. (2008). *Hot thought: Mechanisms and applications of emotional cognition.* Cambridge: MIT Press.

11

THE SOCIAL APPROACH

Mind as Society

A society can be no better than the men and women who compose it.

—Adlai E. Stevenson, 1952

SOCIAL COGNITION

For much of the early history of cognitive science, the focus was on the individual. Cognition was seen as something that was generic—whether one thought about a tractor, a tree, or one's best friend didn't make a difference because the cognitive processes were assumed to be the same. We now know that this is not necessarily the case. There is evidence to show that we think about people in ways that differ from the ways in which we think about inanimate objects. This makes sense. We are social animals and have evolved in social settings where we interact with others. To quote John Dunne, "No man is an island unto himself, he is a piece of the main." In this chapter, we will examine how we think about people from an interdisciplinary perspective, examining the role of evolution, the underlying neural mechanisms, and the cognitive models.

Social cognition is the study of how people make sense of other people and of themselves. Fiske and Taylor (2008) state that there are four assumptions that pervade the field. The first is mentalism, which is that people use mental representations and processes. This is nothing new, except that in this case, the things that are being represented and computed on are social in nature. They include people's faces and appearance, as well as the feelings, thoughts, and explanations we have about them. As we shall see, we often think differently about people than we do about inanimate objects, such as chairs, or abstract concepts, such as justice. Table 11.1 summarizes some of the important differences in thinking about people versus things.

The second basic assumption in research on social cognition is about cognitive processes, or how representations develop, operate, and change over time. So if we were

Table 11.1 Differences in the way we think about people and things.

Principle	People (Example: Your Best Friend)	Things (Example: A Rock)
Intentionality	People attempt to control the environment.	Objects are not capable of controlling their environment.
Mutuality	People think about each other (e.g., "I think of you, and you think of me").	Objects don't "think back."
Self-concept	Others judge us, provide information about us, and are more similar to us than are objects.	Objects cannot judge or provide information about us and are very different from us.
Observational bias	People act differently when they know they are being thought about.	Objects do not act differently when they are being thought about.
Nonobservable attributes	Traits that can't be observed are crucial to thinking about people.	Traits are more easily observed but less crucial.
Change	People change over time and in different circumstances.	Objects change less over time and in different situations.
Accuracy of cognition	It is difficult to judge the traits or qualities of a person.	It is usually easier to judge object qualities.
Complexity	People are complex; we need to simplify in order to understand them.	Objects are usually less complex.
Explanation	We have to explain others' behaviors.	Explanations are not always necessary.

Source: Adapted from Fiske and Taylor (2008).

studying prejudice, we would want to know not just what prejudice is like but also how it forms and how it might become more extreme. The third theme is cross-fertilization, which is that the social cognitive approach is highly interdisciplinary in nature. In fact, most of the work we will report in this chapter occurs at the intersection of the cognitive, social, and neuroscience perspectives. We will discuss the intertwining of these three perspectives in more depth later.

The fourth theme is the applicability of social cognitive research to the real world. Since we live in a social society, we can use the findings we obtain to make the world a better place. For example, our understanding of stereotypes may enable us to reduce the development of negative stereotypes and enhance the formation of positive ones. Results from social cognitive research have been applied to many areas, including health care, the legal system, advertising, and political campaigns.

There is a lot to say about social cognition. To organize this material and make it easier to digest, we will divide the chapter into three sections. In the first section, we will talk about social cognitive neuroscience. In the second section, we will examine perhaps the most important foundational aspect of social cognition. This is the theory of mind (ToM), which is how we come to know that other people have minds. In this section, we will discuss the role ToM plays in social cognitive disorders such as autism. Finally, we will sum up by covering some of the basic social topics that explain how we think about others. These topics are impressions, attributions, attitudes, stereotypes, and prejudice.

SOCIAL COGNITIVE NEUROSCIENCE

A common theme throughout this book is the interdisciplinary approach, where different perspectives and methodologies focus on a research topic. No area illustrates this more clearly than the field of social cognitive neuroscience. As the name implies, this endeavor attempts to describe phenomena in terms of interactions between three levels of analysis. At the broadest level, we have social psychology, which examines the role of human interaction, focusing on people's behavior in a group setting. At the intermediate level, there is the cognitive perspective, examining how we think about one another. Ultimately, we arrive at the neuroscience level, which seeks to examine the location and type of neural processing that takes place in a social setting and that underpins and gives rise to our cognition and behavior.

Ochsner and Lieberman (2001) make several important points about this emerging field. They note that emphasis needs to be placed on the cognitive approach, because it is here where social psychologists and neuroscientists have the most in common and can most easily communicate. Cognition serves to "bridge the gap" and unites the fields of social cognition and cognitive neuroscience. They also note that each of these areas can enrich the other, with social psychologists using neuroscience findings to clarify and differentiate between competing psychological theories. On the other side of the divide, neuroscientists can use findings from the social literature to examine whether there are different neural mechanisms that underlie social versus nonsocial stimuli.

To illustrate the relationship between these three levels, Ochsner and Lieberman (2001) present a prism model (shown in Figure 11.1). Each corner or vertex of the prism represents one of four different disciplinary aspects. Each face is bordered by three corners and stands for one of the three approaches. For instance, the base of the prism is formed by neural mechanisms, cognition/information-processing, and behavior and experience vertices. This surface, which faces downward in Figure 11.1, corresponds to the domain of inquiry for cognitive neuroscience but is lacking because it does not take into account the remaining

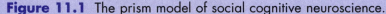

Figure 11.1 The prism model of social cognitive neuroscience.

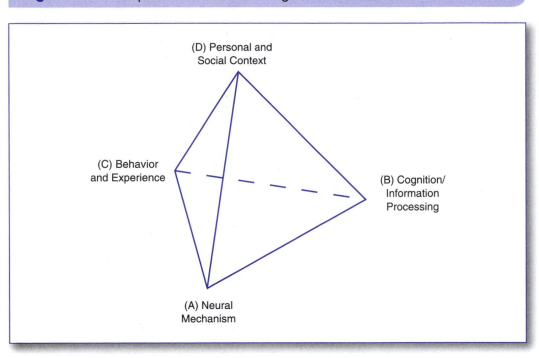

Source: Ochsner and Lieberman (2001).

vertex, personal and social context. Similarly, social psychology is the facet formed from the personal and social context, behavior and experience, and cognition/information-processing vertices. This is the surface that faces toward the back in Figure 11.1. It, too, is lacking because it fails to account for the remaining vertex, neural mechanisms. Only the field of social cognitive neuroscience takes all the aspects into account and is, thus, represented by the entire prism with all the three faces.

TOPICS IN SOCIAL COGNITIVE NEUROSCIENCE

Evolution

We humans are a distinctly social race, what might be called "ultrasocial" (Boyd & Richerson, 1996). More than any other species, we form cooperative groups, such as family, friendships, and teams, as well as competing groups, such as tribes, nations, and ethnicities. Is it possible that this sort of social environment led to the development of our intelligence? According to the **cultural intelligence hypothesis**, it has. In this view, complex social interaction created a form of social intelligence that then laid the groundwork for more general intelligence to emerge later (Herrmann, Call, Hernandez-Lloreda, Hare, & Tomasello, 2009). For example, our working memory capacity may have evolved originally to allow us to remember key members of our social group. Once this was in place, it could be applied to more abstract problems involving language, mathematics, and spatial reasoning.

In contrast, the **general intelligence hypothesis** states that human intelligence did not evolve in response to particular selection forces such as social organization. Instead, it emerged in a general form that could be suited to solving all kinds of problems, whether social or not. One way to differentiate between these two notions is to examine the physical and social cognitive abilities of children who have not yet been influenced by cultural factors such as written language, symbolic mathematics, and formal education. Physical cognition refers to reasoning about things such as space, quantities, and causality. This could evolve in a wide variety of environments and is not specific to social settings. Social cognition, on the other hand, is reasoning about those things that are directly linked to culture, such as social learning, communication, and ToM.

We can then compare the children's performance with that of our closest primate relatives. If the cultural intelligence hypothesis is correct, there should be no difference between the children and the primates on physical domain tests because both the groups have evolved under these conditions. There should, however, be a difference on tests of social cognition. We would expect the children to score higher on these tests because humans evolved in more demanding social environments.

This is exactly what Herrmann et al. (2009) did. They tested chimpanzees, orangutans, and 2½-year-old human children. The results clearly supported the cultural hypothesis. There was no difference between human and primate performance in the physical domain. On tests designed to specifically measure social intelligence, the children's scores were higher by a statistically significant amount. If humans had evolved a superior general form of intelligence, they would have outscored the primates in both categories. It is not known yet what specific social environments may have led to this divergence in our early ancestors, but it could have been complex types of collaborative activity involved in hunting and gathering that would call on more sophisticated kinds of communicating and social learning (Tomasello, Carpenter, Call, Behne, & Moll, 2005).

Additional evidence to support the evolution of specialized social intelligence comes from studies that have examined brain size. There is a positive correlation between the relative size of the neocortex and social factors such as group size and grooming clique size that are measures of social complexity (Dunbar, 1996). Hedgehogs are mammals that provide maternal care to a small number of offspring, and they have comparatively small cortical regions. Chimpanzees live in extended groups of a few dozen animals and show moderate cortical size. Humans, who interact in societies numbering in the millions, have the largest relative cortices. In studies such as this, it is not absolute brain weight or volume that is measured but, rather, relative size expressed as a proportion of the animal's overall body size. It could be that larger social groups cause greater competition for social skills that subsequently leads to the evolution of cognitive mechanisms for outsmarting others.

Attention

It has been known for some time that infants can follow somebody else's gaze (Scaife & Bruner, 1975). This suggests that even at a young age, children can focus their attention on what another person is attending. This ability to coordinate attention with a social partner is called **joint attention**. Not only following but also initiating or joining shared attentional focus with others is a key part of social interaction. Without it, we would have a very difficult time understanding or making sense of what other people are saying (Mundy & Newell, 2007).

We can divide joint attention into two categories. In responding to joint attention (RJA), we follow the gestures and direction of gaze in order to share a common point of reference. This is the more passive form, because we are following others. In initiating joint attention (IJA), people use gestures and eye movements to direct attention to people, objects, and events. This is a more active form, because it involves the initiation of a joint attentional focus.

Joint attention plays a very important role in development. It can help disambiguate the referent of a word during language acquisition. A mother pointing to a *spoon* and saying the word gets a child to look at the object corresponding to the word and so aids in the growth of vocabulary (Baldwin, 1995). Unfortunately, children with autism show impairments primarily in IJA rather than in RJA. This may account for some of the developmental delays experienced by autistic children. We will cover autism in greater detail elsewhere in this chapter. Interestingly, chimpanzees have the capacity for RJA but not for IJA (Tomasello & Carpenter, 2005).

Social cognition begins around the age of 9 to 12 months. At about this time, infants should begin to be aware of their own goals and activities as well as those of others (Tomasello et al., 2005). Social cognitive skills allow the child to combine these. They, thus, realize that their intentions lead to actions and that this is the case for others as well. If I want to eat, then I look at or point to the cereal box because I want to eat it or get mom to help me eat it. If mom also points or looks at the cereal, then she, too, must be thinking about it and plans to prepare it for me to eat. In this fashion, children learn that thought is representational and directed toward objects and actions in the world, not just in themselves but in others as well. This realization can then lead to the use of language and communication to convey the contents of one's mind to others.

There are two attention regulation systems underlying joint attention (Mundy, Card, & Fox, 2000). These are depicted in Figure 11.2. The posterior orienting and perceptual system is used during the learning of RJA in infancy. It consists of the parietal and superior temporal cortex. This system is involuntary and is used to direct attention to biologically meaningful stimuli. This underlies our capacity to perceive the eye and head orientation of others as well as the spatial representation of our own bodies in relation to other people's bodies and objects in the environment. It allows us to pay attention to where people are looking or pointing to and so is a more basic or perceptual level of joint attention.

Second, there is the anterior attention system. This is subserved by a collection of different neural areas, including the frontal eye fields, which control eye movement; the orbital frontal cortex; the prefrontal association cortex; and the anterior cingulate. This system underlies our capacity for IJA and emerges slightly later in development. It controls voluntary, goal-directed attention and is what enables us to understand that our personal behavior is directed toward where we attend. This may be thought of as a more sophisticated conceptual level of joint attention.

Figure 11.3 shows the attention systems model of how these two systems interact to determine joint attention. Early in development, at the age of 3 to 6 months, the anterior and

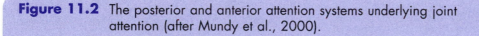

Figure 11.2 The posterior and anterior attention systems underlying joint attention (after Mundy et al., 2000).

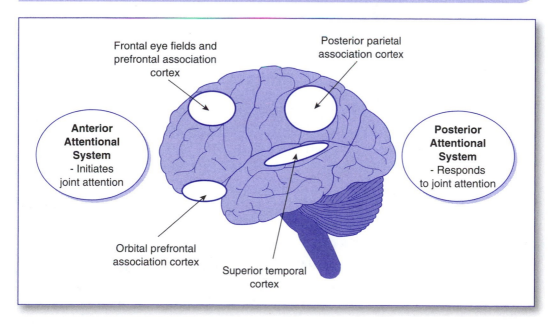

Figure 11.3 How the two attention systems interact to determine joint attention.

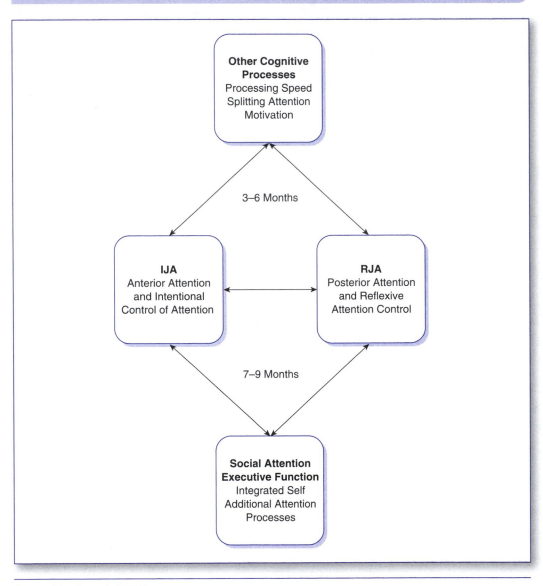

Source: Mundy et al. (2000).

posterior systems interact with each other and with additional processes such as speed of processing, motivation, and the ability to divide attention. This dynamic leads to the development of integrated self–other attention processing at 7 to 9 months, which in turn serves as the foundation for the emergence of social cognitive joint attention at 10 to 18 months.

The attention systems model can account for two important observations mentioned previously. Cherkassky, Kana, Keller, and Just (2006) propose that problems in communication between brain areas, especially between the anterior and parietal areas, may explain autistic people's lack of social cognitive skills. In chimpanzees, the parietal attention system is represented, but the anterior system is not. This may explain why their RJA ability is better than their IJA ability (Astafiev et al., 2003).

Mirror Neurons

A **mirror neuron** is a neuron that fires when an animal performs some action and also when the animal observes another animal performing that same action (Rizzolatti & Craighero, 2004). So, for example, if a monkey were to reach out and grasp an object, we might see activity in particular neurons. These neurons would also fire when that monkey watches another monkey reach out to grasp the same object. In this sense, the neurons are said to "mirror" the performance of others. These cells could play a role in imitative or modeling behavior and help explain how some animals copy others as part of the learning process. Although mirror neurons have been observed in primates, whether they exist in humans is still a topic of debate.

In macaque monkeys, mirror neurons have been found in the inferior frontal gyrus and in the inferior parietal lobe (Rizzolatti & Craighero, 2004). In one study, 41 neurons were studied in two macaque monkeys while they observed an experimenter either grasp an apple and bring it to his mouth or place it in a cup (Fogassi et al., 2005). They discovered 15 neurons that fired to the "grasp-to-eat" motion but did not fire to the "grasp-to-place" condition. Conversely, there were 4 other neurons that showed increased activity to the "grasp-to-place" motion but not to the "grasp-to-eat" motion. The cells fired in some cases before the final grasp was performed (i.e., before the apple was brought to the mouth or placed in the cup). These researchers speculate that these neurons, therefore, code for the animal's understanding of another's intention. That is, they become active when the monkey anticipates what somebody will do.

Several studies have examined whether mirror neurons exist in people. Iacoboni et al. (1999), using functional magnetic resonance imaging (fMRI), found activity in the inferior frontal cortex and the superior parietal lobe when a person performs an action and also when the person sees another person perform that same action. The specific pattern of brain activity in these areas also has been found to be similar during the perception of others' actions and when performing the act oneself (Dinstein, Gardner, Jazayeri, & Heeger, 2008). However, the problem with these studies is that although they may show activity in a mirror neuron "system" involving a large population of cells, they fail to show activity in individual neurons. Data from other studies suggest that although there may be mirror neurons in the human brain, they constitute only a tiny fraction of the cells that are active in these regions during the observation and execution of a movement (Lingnau, Gesierich, & Caramazza, 2009).

If mirror neurons are not used to model actions or behavioral intent, they may be used instead as part of the experience of empathy (Decety & Jackson, 2004). There is some support for this in imaging studies with human participants. Sections of the anterior cingulate cortex that are thought to mediate the subjective experience of pain are also active in individuals when they watch a video of somebody else about to experience bodily harm—for instance, a person who is about to cut his or her finger with a kitchen knife (Singer et al., 2004). Smelling a foul odor was also found to produce activity in the anterior insula, both when experiencing this directly and when watching somebody else express disgust to a smell (Wicker et al., 2003). However, these brain areas are not the same as those that mirror hand actions, and mirror neurons coding for empathy and emotional states have not yet been found in monkeys (see Table 11.2).

Social Cognition as the Brain's Default State

Mitchell (2008) proposes a speculative but fascinating new idea, which is that social cognition may be so special that it is the default state for the brain. The areas implicated in social thinking, such as the medial prefrontal cortex (mPFC), the right temporoparietal junction (rTPJ), and the precuneus/posterior cingulate cortex, have an unusually high metabolic rate; they tend to burn energy faster than other brain areas when at rest (Gusnard & Raichle, 2001). A higher resting rate means that these areas remain "on" and ready for action even though we may not be recruiting them to perform some task. This suggests that we remain in "people mode" whenever we are not actively thinking about anything in particular.

Social brain areas have also been shown to deactivate when people are thinking about nonsocial topics. So if you are pondering the answer to an exam question that requires semantic and conceptual knowledge unrelated to people, you literally need to "turn off"

Table 11.2 Brain areas considered part of the mirror neuron system.

Brain Area(s)	Cognitive Function/Ability	Animal
Inferior frontal gyrus and inferior parietal lobe	Imitating and understanding other's behavior	Macaque monkey
Inferior frontal cortex and superior parietal lobe	Imitation and determination of behavioral intent	Human
Anterior cingulate cortex	Empathetic experience of pain	Human
Anterior insula	Empathetic experience of disgust	Human

the social parts of your brain, perhaps, so they don't interfere. This seems to be unique to social cognition. When thinking about a nonlinguistic problem, for example, we don't deactivate language areas. These regions simply remain at their lower resting metabolic rate. Mitchell (2008) concludes that we are in a state of constant readiness to encounter other minds, and this normal state must be shut down in order to reason about things that don't involve people.

IS SOCIAL COGNITIVE NEUROSCIENCE SPECIAL?

Social cognitive neuroscience is not without its critics. Some researchers question whether it has been able to provide new insights into the nature of cognitive processes (Willingham & Dunn, 2003). They question whether neuroimaging has yielded any novel information that could not be gleaned with more traditional methods such as accuracy and reaction time. Another question that has been raised is whether the general cognitive processes used in perception, attention, memory, language, and problem solving can explain social cognition or whether there are special cognitive mechanisms or neural processes that are specific to social interaction (Blakemore, Winston, & Frith, 2004).

Mitchell (2008) strongly defends the field against these accusations. He points out that there are a small number of brain regions active during social cognition that are not active during most other nonsocial cognitive tasks. For instance, the mPFC is activated when participants are asked to read stories that require mental attribution, in comparison with those that involve physical causality (Fletcher et al., 1995). Numerous other studies also have found differential mPFC activation in social cognition tasks under circumstances where the stimuli, type of mental state, and behavioral tasks vary (Blakemore et al., 2004).

Additional evidence supports this rebuttal. Mitchell, Macrae, and Banaji (2004) performed fMRI scans on individuals while they read descriptions of people, and then, they were instructed either to form an impression based on the passage or to memorize the information. The impression formation task produced mPFC activity, while the memorization task did not. In addition, the mPFC activity was correlated with the likelihood of remembering material, but only when it was associated with the impression formation task.

However, research also shows that there may be some functional overlap of brain areas underlying social cognition and other more general cognitive operations. Saxe and Kanwisher (2003) found rTPJ activation when participants processed stories about another person's erroneous beliefs. This activation was not seen for thinking about stories that referred to an erroneous physical representation. But to complicate things, it turns out that the rTPJ is activated during tasks that require shifts of attention (Mitchell, 2008). So it turns out that this debate revolves around the specific type of social cognition performed. Unique brain areas are called on when doing some types of social thinking, but other forms of social mentalizing can recruit areas used in general cognitive processes.

ADVANTAGES OF THE SOCIAL
COGNITIVE NEUROSCIENCE APPROACH

What are some of the potential benefits of this tripartite interdisciplinary venture? Ochsner and Lieberman (2001) advance three possibilities. They argue that social cognitive neuroscience could unify the field by discovering common brain mechanisms underlying what were previously thought to be disparate phenomena. If the same parts of the brain are used for attitudes and attributions, for example, then we may have to reconsider these not as two different processes but perhaps as two aspects of the same process. The amygdala, to give another example, is implicated in many social cognitive processes, including attitudes, stereotyping, emotion, and person perception. An understanding of what the amygdala does in each of these situations can unify these formally distinct research topics at least to the extent that they call on similar neural systems.

Social cognitive neuroscience may also have the opposite effect. In some cases, it could separate what might have been thought to be unitary phenomena. Currently, stereotypes are broadly categorized as implicit or explicit. However, it is likely that there are several different subtypes that could include affective, semantic, declarative, and procedural stereotypes. It remains to be seen whether different neural mechanisms underlie each of these possibilities or whether there is a single or small number of distinct processes they share.

A third potential benefit of social cognitive neuroscience concerns bottom-up versus top-down approaches. By bottom-up approaches, we mean investigating the basic neural systems that service the perceptual, attentional, emotional, and behavioral processes of social experience. Top-down approaches refer instead to the diverse types of social phenomena, such as attitudes, attributions, stereotypes, and prejudice. It is generally agreed that more can be learned by integrating these two approaches than by treating them separately, as has been done most often in the past.

THEORY OF MIND

One of our most important social abilities, one that underlies all others, is the understanding that other people have minds. When you speak to your roommate, you assume that he or she is conscious and has feelings and thoughts in the same way that you do. You don't treat him or her as though he or she is an inanimate object like a chair or table. This capacity is referred to as **theory of mind (ToM)**. It is the ability to understand others' mental states, such as beliefs, desires, and intentions; to appreciate how these differ from our own; and to utilize this understanding to guide our behavior when interacting with others.

A number of tests have been developed to diagnose ToM (Wimmer & Perner, 1983). The use of these tests shows that children acquire a ToM by the age of 4 to 5 years. In the Sally-Anne task, a cartoonlike drawing depicting two children is shown (Gallagher, 2000).

Sally puts her marble in a basket. When she leaves, Anne takes the marble out of the basket and puts it into her box (Figure 11.4). Sally, now, returns. The question is, where will Sally look for her toy? Children without disorders, who are 4 years and older, will answer that he or she will first look for it in the basket. This requires an understanding of the situation from Sally's point of view—namely, that she holds the false belief that the toy is in the basket because that is where she last left it. A child lacking ToM would predict that she would look for it in the box, even though she could not have experienced this since it was from Anne's perspective.

ToM and Neuroscience

Siegal and Varley (2002) outline four neural systems that mediate ToM. These are (1) the language system, specifically the left-hemisphere grammatical ability; (2) the frontal lobes; (3) the right temporal–parietal areas; and (4) the amygdala circuits. In this section, we will discuss the role each of these plays in ToM and address some of the issues concerning how ToM may develop.

An understanding of linguistic syntax may allow us to entertain false beliefs. De Villiers and de Villiers (2000) argue that propositional reasoning enables us to represent a person's beliefs and then modify these representations to express a new state of mind. For instance, in the Sally-Anne task, one could think that "Sally believed (falsely) that the marble was in the basket." Brain imaging studies show activation of language centers during the execution of ToM tasks. They found widespread temporal lobe activity, either bilaterally or localized to the left-hemisphere language centers (Fletcher et al., 1995).

Frontal lobe executive function is also believed to play a prominent role in ToM reasoning. In many of the false-belief studies, suppression of the object's real location must occur to attribute the perceived location to one of the actors. Inhibition of inappropriate responses is one of the functions carried out by frontal areas (Carlson & Moses, 2001). Brunet, Sarfati, Hardy-Bayle, and Decety (2000) obtained the right medial prefrontal cortical activity for nonverbal ToM tests in which the participants had to select an appropriate ending to a pictorial scene based on the character's intentional states.

One fascinating hypothesis is that ToM may have evolved from the ability to recognize animate agents (Frith & Frith, 1999). An object, even if it does not resemble a living creature, can be perceived as alive if it moves in ways characteristic of biological organisms. This perceptual capacity may have been the starting point for inferring intentions from actions. Brain areas that could subsume perception of biological motion and ToM include the right superior temporal sulcus (STS) and the right temporal–parietal areas (Blakemore & Decety, 2001; Ruby & Decety, 2001). Patients with right-hemisphere damage have difficulty in tasks requiring the appreciation of other people's state of mind (Siegal, Carrington, & Radel, 1996; Winner, Brownell, Happé, Blum, & Pincus, 1998).

Figure 11.4 The Sally-Anne task used to test ToM (after Gallagher, 2000).

Source: Adapted version of Heinz Wimmer and Josef Perner's Sally-Anne Task. Illustration by Jack L. Frazier. Used with permission of SAGE Publications, Inc.

The amygdala complex is also involved in ToM. Monkeys with bilateral amygdala lesions manifest social and emotional disturbances similar to those found in autism (Bachevalier, 1994; Bachevalier, Málková, & Mishkin, 2001). These monkeys demonstrate social avoidance, less initiation of social contact, and difficulties related to eye contact, facial expression, and body posture. The amygdala is involved in the fear response, so we would expect damage to these areas to produce deficits in the emotional aspects of social interaction, which is what these findings show.

Siegal and Varley (2002) conclude that the neural machinery underlying ToM reasoning involves both evolved specialized capacity with dedicated circuits and a reliance on existing general cognitive structures. They also argue that experience is necessary for its development. ToM seems related to other innate abilities, such as language, that rely on learning to come to their full fruition. In particular, early conversational experience can allow the child to acquire knowledge about other minds. It may do this by demonstrating that other people act in accordance with their statements and by allowing the potential for imagination of hypotheticals (see Table 11.3).

Autism

Autism is a neurodevelopmental disorder characterized by impaired social interaction and accompanied by restricted and repetitive behavior (Bailey, Phillips, & Rutter, 1996). These individuals are often aloof during childhood and remain egocentric as adults. They show impairments in verbal and nonverbal communication. Some do not speak at all, while others may show delayed speech development. Even those that become verbally fluent later in life show language comprehension deficits.

Table 11.3 Brain areas underlying Theory of Mind reasoning (after Siegal & Varley, 2002).

Brain Region	General Cognitive Function	Specific Theory of Mind Function
Left hemisphere	Linguistic syntax and propositional reasoning	Entertainment of false belief
Frontal lobes	Executive function and problem solving	Suppression of the object's real location in the Sally-Anne task
Right temporal sulcus and right temporal–parietal areas	Perception of biological motion	Inferring intention
Amygdala	Fear response	Emotional aspects of social interaction

Autistic symptoms persist throughout life but vary considerably in their severity. A mild version not accompanied by cognitive and linguistic developmental delays is known as Asperger syndrome. Patients with Asperger syndrome may show few symptoms until early adulthood. The current belief is that the disorder has a broad spectrum, and in this case, Asperger syndrome need not be labeled as a separate affliction.

The overall prevalence of autism in the general population is estimated to be between 0.3% and 0.7%. Males are three times more likely than females to have it. The number of people diagnosed has increased tremendously over the past two decades, although it remains to be seen whether there is a real increase in the number of cases or if there is simply increased awareness and testing (Newschaffer et al., 2007).

Currently, there is no "cure" or preventative measure that can be taken. However, individuals can receive compensatory cognitive and behavioral training and can learn to overcome some of the deficits. Since severity can vary and there are large individual differences, training is often tailored to the needs of the particular individual. The effectiveness of different treatments is questionable due to methodological differences (Ospina et al., 2008).

Autism has clear genetic origins, and susceptibility genes have been identified (Maestrini, Paul, Monaco, & Bailey, 2000). It is not known whether it is caused by genetic mutation or by combinations of genetic variants (Abrahams & Geschwind, 2008). Several environmental causes have been proposed, including agents linked to birth defects, heavy metals, and pesticides (Arndt, Stodgell, & Rodier, 2005; Rutter, 2005).

Autism and ToM

Frith (2001) reviews the literature and shows that one of the key deficits of autism is a failure to mentalize (i.e., "mind blindness"). This is a failure to understand that others have mental states such as beliefs and desires. We have already examined this ability and called it a ToM. A problem with forming ToM could explain a great many autistic symptoms, especially the social interaction and communication difficulties. However, it cannot be used to account for other autistic symptoms such as repetitive behavior and motor problems, which are better explained by other theories.

Having said this, there is ample evidence that autistic children fail to attain or are delayed in attaining certain developmental ToM milestones. They fail to follow another person's gaze, to point toward or show objects of interest, and do not understand make-believe play (Baron-Cohen, Cox, Baird, Swettenham, & Nightingale, 1996). These first two behaviors are indicators of shared attention. Also, preschool-age autistic children do not show a preference for speech over other auditory stimuli (Klin, 1991), nor do they show a preference for faces over other visual stimuli, such as hats (Hobson, 1993).

A large amount of work in neuroscience also points to a failure of ToM ability in autistics. In one study, a group of normal adults and a second group of adults with Asperger syndrome were compared using positron emission tomography imaging while they performed a mentalizing task. Both groups scored equivalently, but the patients with Asperger syndrome showed less activation in the mPFC. They instead showed more peak activation in the ventral frontal cortex (Happé et al., 1996). In another imaging study employing fMRI, autistic and normal controls were asked to judge people's inner states based on facial-area photographs. The autistic participants showed less frontal lobe activation and no amygdala activation in comparison with the normal controls.

Anatomical studies point to the same conclusion. High-functioning autistics have less gray matter (tissue corresponding to groups of neuron cell bodies) in the anterior parts of a system involving the amygdala, the paracingulate sulcus, and the inferior frontal gyrus (Abell et al., 1999). Other studies have shown an increase in gray matter in the peri-amygdaloid cortex, the middle temporal, and the inferior temporal gyrus. In a postmortem examination of autistic brains, Bauman and Kemper (2007) discovered smaller neurons and a greater density of neurons in parts of the limbic system. Outside this region, they found fewer Purkinje cells in the posterior and inferior cerebellum.

OTHER SOCIAL COGNITIVE DISORDERS

A fascinating but underinvestigated social cognitive disorder goes by the name of **Williams syndrome**. This is a genetic disease caused by a deletion on chromosome 7. These individuals manifest hypersociability. They show an exaggerated interest in other people and increased expressiveness and social communicability. For instance, when presented with a picture showing a social scene, they describe it in greater detail and complexity than do a control group of children with Down syndrome (Bellugi, Lichtenberger, Jones, Lai, & St. George, 2000). Unfortunately, Williams syndrome patients are deficient in other areas of cognition. They have limited spatial skills and motor control and are mentally retarded. They also have heart, kidney, hearing, and musculoskeletal problems.

Another more common problem is **social phobia**, characterized by fear of public places, social interaction, and being evaluated negatively by others (Baumeister & Leary, 1995). In several studies, social phobics were found to have greater amygdala activation when viewing neutral or angry faces and when getting ready to give a public speech (Birbaumer et al., 1998; Tillfors et al., 2001). Clearly, more research needs to be done on these disorders, and with people who have greater than average social skills (Adolphs, 2003).

ATTITUDES

An **attitude** is a learned predisposition to respond to a particular object in a particular way (Petty & Wegener, 1998). *Object* is meant in the broad sense here to include physical objects, such as an automobile; people, such as your cousin; and ideas, such as abortion. Attitudes consist of three components. They can be (1) cognitive, consisting of beliefs and thoughts; (2) affective, referring to feelings and emotions; or (3) behavioral, meaning they influence the way in which we act. For instance, you may have a negative attitude toward your roommate. This might cause you to think that he or she is inconsiderate, to feel anger toward him or her, and tell him or her to turn down his or her music.

It is natural to assume that our attitudes affect our actions. After all, if your attitude toward ice cream is positive, you are likely to buy and eat it. Research shows, however, that it is possible to think one way about something but to act in another way toward it. Davis, Grover, Becker, and McGregor (1992) surveyed college students and found that more than 90% of them thought that cheating was wrong. In contrast to this, 40% to 60% of these very same students reported that they had cheated on at least one test (Davis & Ludvigson, 1995).

So when do our attitudes guide our actions? A number of studies have found that there are at least three factors that exert an influence (Kraus, 1995). To begin, they found that attitudes do guide actions when outside influences are minimal. For example, you believe that the federal government should not have bailed out failing banks but will resist saying so in the presence of your friend who works for a bank. Attitudes also guide action when they are more specifically relevant to a behavior. Your uncle may claim to value good health (a general attitude) while at the same time eating junk food and drinking lots of beer. But his positive attitude toward working out at the gym (a specific attitude toward a behavior) is more likely to influence how often he goes to the health club to work out.

The third factor concerns how aware we are of our attitudes. Attitudes are more likely to influence our behavior the more conscious we are of them. Fazio (1990) found that the attitudes that come to mind easily are those that are most likely to guide our actions. Sarah spends a lot of time thinking about drug legalization. She used to smoke marijuana when she was younger and now works for an advocacy group trying to convince the state legislature to legalize the drug. Her attitude toward marijuana is, thus, very strong. It comes to her mind easily and should have a powerful influence on her behavior. If there is a march to legalize marijuana in her town, she will in all likelihood march in it.

We can now ask the reverse question. Do our behaviors influence our attitudes? Suppose you didn't want to do volunteer work in your town but had to. Would you end up changing your attitude toward it? If so, would you like it more or less? Research indicates that when people are asked to repeatedly assert an attitude, they are more likely to act in a fashion consistent with it (Powell & Fazio, 1984). So even just stating an attitude may get us to behave as if we possess it. This process can be summed up as "saying is believing."

According to the **foot-in-the-door phenomenon**, people who agree to a small request now may comply with a larger one later. Numerous studies show that people coerced into doing something against their will later change their mind and tend to agree with the attitude behind the new behavior more (Cialdini, 1993). In other words, "doing" now becomes "believing" later. American prisoners of war in Korea were asked to perform small tasks against their beliefs, such as speaking or writing out trivial statements. They then escalated to behaviors even more against their attitudes, such as publicly condemning the United States. This process was colloquially referred to as "brainwashing."

Cognitive Dissonance

In this section, we will explore what happens when there is an inconsistency between our attitudes and our behavior. Most of us like to think of ourselves as consistent. We believe that the ways in which we think, feel, and act are the same. A contradiction between our beliefs or between our beliefs and actions might then make us feel bad. Here is a case in point: Joe is proud of the fact that he is responsible and on time. He demonstrates this by picking up his friend Jessica to drive her to work at exactly 8:00 a.m. every morning. This Monday, for the first time in years, he arrived 15 minutes late. How do you think Joe might feel? If Joe's negative state resulted from a mismatch between his self-perception and his actions, we say that he is experiencing cognitive dissonance. **Cognitive dissonance** is the uncomfortable psychological state that occurs when an attitude and a behavior or two attitudes are inconsistent. Losch and Cacioppo (1990) found that this state is accompanied by a heightened level of arousal.

Since cognitive dissonance doesn't feel good, how might we go about reducing it? In Joe's case, he may make up an excuse, saying he stayed up too late the night before or that his alarm clock failed to go off. In this manner, he can treat the event as an exception and preserve the consistency between his attitude about himself and his behavior. This is an example of a direct strategy because it involves actually changing our attitudes or behavior. Another example of this type is trivializing the incident—that is, considering it as unimportant (Simon, Greenberg, & Brehm, 1995). Alternatively, we could employ an indirect strategy, such as trying to feel good about ourselves in other areas of life (see Figure 11.5).

Does the reduction of cognitive dissonance require conscious reasoning? For this to happen, a person may have to rationalize his or her choices after the fact. That is, a person would have to justify to himself or herself that the decision was a good one. If this is the case, then amnesiacs who forget this thought process may not experience dissonance reduction. To test this, Lieberman, Ochsner, Gilbert, and Schacter (2001) created cognitive dissonance by forcing amnesiacs to choose one set of stimuli from two sets they liked equally. They eventually came to like the selected one more and the rejected one less, the same result obtained with nonamnesiacs. So, apparently, explicit conscious recollection of the justification process after the choice is not required.

Figure 11.5 Steps in the process of cognitive dissonance.

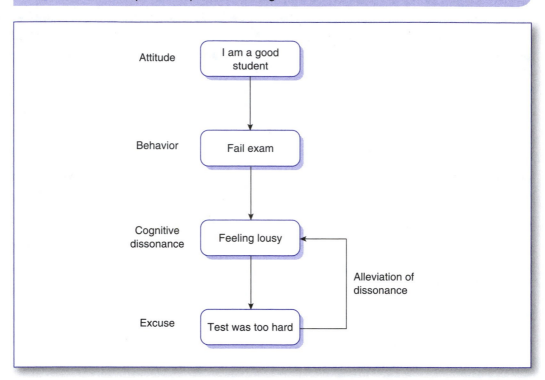

In a second experiment, these authors imposed a cognitive load on participants during the decision-making process itself rather than after it. A cognitive load means having to perform some secondary task that takes up processing resources. This prevents an individual from being able to think too much while performing the primary task, which in this case was the dissonance procedure. Participants in the cognitive load condition and those in another condition without a load showed dissonance reduction. These results suggest that attitude change can be either an automatic process that doesn't require full attentional awareness or a controlled cognitive one.

Attitudes and Cognitive Processes

A large body of research exists on the role of dissonance in different cognitive tasks. In this literature, investigators study consistency judgments. They look to see whether participants will respond in ways that favor similarity between their attitudes or between their attitudes and their behavior. Fiske and Taylor (2008) divide the literature into five overall processes: (1) perception, (2) attention, (3) interpretation, (4) learning, and (5) memory. We follow this organization and report these findings in the sections that follow.

Perception

According to the principle of **selective exposure**, people will seek information not already present that supports consistency. There is some evidence that we seek out information suited to our needs and dispositions (Sears, 1968). For instance, the types of people we choose as friends, the sorts of movies we like to watch, and the music we listen to can all reinforce our attitudes. Other people we know who also share those interests can then reinforce these attitudes. However, there is some controversy in the literature over the validity of this phenomenon. Information that is useful or new can sometimes override dissonance in determining exposure (Brock, Albert, & Becker, 1970).

Attention

The selective attention view proposes that we notice or pay attention to consistent information once it is present. The evidence supporting this view is stronger than that for selective exposure. Studies show that people will spend more time looking at consistent rather than inconsistent information (Brock & Balloun, 1967). In one experiment, participants were divided into two categories (Olson & Zanna, 1979). The repressors were people who usually avoid threatening stimuli, while the sensitizers were those who seek out dangerous stimuli. Each of these groups was shown paintings and then reported their attitudes about them. They next were allowed to keep two paintings—one they liked and another they did not—and the amount of time they spent looking at each was recorded. Only the repressors spent more time gazing at their preferred picture and avoided looking at the inconsistent one. According to cognitive dissonance theory, both groups should have behaved this way.

Interpretation

If cognitive dissonance causes us to focus on consistent information, then we can also make a prediction regarding the process of interpretation. We can expect that people will translate or interpret ambiguous information to be consistent with their attitudes. A variety of studies suggest that this is, indeed, the case. Holbrook, Berent, Krosnick, Visser, and Boninger (2005) found that participants' attitudes toward presidential candidates influenced how they subsequently judged their debate performances. Attitudes regarding the conflict between the Israelis and the Palestinians affected how fair news coverage of the topic was (Vallone, Ross, & Lepper, 1985). A more recent study showed that German's attitudes about the Euro currency held sway over their judgment of inflation (Traut-Mattausch, Schulz-Hardt, Greitemeyer, & Frey, 2004).

Learning

Dissonance theory predicts that we ought to more easily learn material that is consistent with our attitudes. If two people were arguing over abortion, we would expect the pro-lifer to learn more of the pro-life arguments and to forget more of the pro-choice arguments. Conversely, the pro-choice person ought to remember more of the pro-choice arguments and to forget more of the pro-life arguments. There is some evidence in support of this view. Malpass (1969) found that people recalled more consistent information under conditions of incidental learning, when they didn't know that they would be tested on the material. Under intentional learning conditions, both types of information were acquired equally. Individuals who were highly motivated to learn also failed to show any consistency effect (Zanna & Olson, 1982).

Memory

Consistency effects are also found for memory. In one study, participants were asked to judge how suitable various people were for different jobs (Lingle, Geva, Ostrom, Leippe, & Baumgardner, 1979). If a person was judged as good for a particular job, then more of those particular job-relevant characteristics were recalled about them later. For instance, if a person judged another person as being a good comedian, then that person would be more likely to recall the other person's infectious laughter than his or her eyesight.

Interestingly, it is possible to hold two attitudes about something simultaneously in memory. Under dual-attitude conditions, one holds an older belief that was formed initially and a newer different belief (Wilson, Lindsey, & Schooler, 2000). The more recent attitude exerts more influence in conscious voluntary cognitive processing, while the older attitude may come into play when one is asked to respond quickly or under cognitive load (having to hold more information in memory or to solve more difficult problems). The two attitudes can also interact to influence consistency judgments (Petty, Tormala, Brinol, & Jarvis, 2006).

Attitudes and Neuroscience

An evaluative categorization is one that implies better or worse. It requires that a person think of one thing as positive and another as negative. If one held stereotypically negative attitudes of blacks compared with whites, then categorizing whites and blacks would be evaluative. In contrast, a nonevaluative categorization requires a division based on conceptual or semantic criteria. An example of a nonevaluative judgment would involve deciding whether items are either a vegetable or a nonvegetable.

Cacioppo, Crites, and Gardner (1996) examined these two types of judgments in participants while recording neural responses via event-related potentials. They discovered posterior right-hemisphere activation for evaluative categorizations and activity in both hemispheres for nonevaluative categorizations. The results imply that different, although not completely independent, neural systems subsume each kind of judgment. Evaluative categorization may be a fast automatic process that has evolved to "kick in" quickly to assess whether a stimulus poses a threat. Nonevaluative judgments appear to be more controlled and slower and to draw on left-hemisphere centers involved in semantic and associative meaning.

As we have mentioned earlier, the amygdala plays an important role in the fearful response to threatening stimuli. This brain structure seems to be involved in attitude expression as well. Adolphs and Tranel (1999) found that damage to the amygdala produced more positive preference ratings for pictorial stimuli. One interpretation of these results is that stimuli normally elicit both positive and negative responses but that the amygdala seems to contribute primarily to negative ones. When this structure is damaged, these responses are diminished, enhancing the positive evaluation (see Table 11.4).

IMPRESSIONS

An impression is the opinion or belief that you form about another person. Whereas an attitude is general and can be formed about an object, a person, or an idea, an impression is formed toward a person only. A number of studies show that early impressions are very powerful (Schlenker, 1980). In one experiment, participants were asked to watch short 10-second video clips of teachers interacting and speaking with students. Based on this brief evidence alone, they were able to accurately assess what the teachers thought about

Table 11.4 Neural areas and cognitive factors underlying attitude processing (after Cacioppo, Crites, & Gardner, 1996).

Categorization Type	Brain Area	Cognitive Process	Cognitive Function
Evaluative	Posterior right hemisphere (and amygdala)	Fast and automatic	Threat assessment
Nonevaluative	Right and left hemispheres	Controlled and slow	Semantic and associative processing

the students (Babad, Bernieri, & Rosenthal, 1989). In another experiment, participants listened to 20-second audio recordings of medical doctors speaking to patients during an office visit. These listeners were able to predict which of the doctors were most likely to have been sued in the past, simply from the sound of their voices in the recordings (Ambady, Koo, Rosenthal, & Winograd, 2002). These examples show that we very quickly form impressions and that, in some instances, these impressions are accurate.

Research has shown that there are several different perceivable aspects of people that influence our judgment of them. First is their physical appearance. Do we judge people who are attractive more positively? The answer is yes. Our first impressions of attractive people are more favorable than those of people we find less appealing (Dion & Stein, 1978; Feingold, 1991). Attractiveness is most powerful when people have little or no information about one another. It also seems to influence some traits more than others. Attractive individuals are judged to be more sociable but not to have more integrity, modesty, or concern for others. One explanation for this is the **halo effect**. This states that we tend to see positive traits grouped together. If a person is good-looking, we tend to think that he or she is also successful. If a person is intelligent, we tend to think that he or she is also wealthy, and so on.

How people talk also makes a difference. People who speak in a clear and direct manner are judged better than those who use filler words and hesitations such as *like*, *sort of*, and *you know* (Erickson, Lind, Johnson, & O'Barr, 1978). Not just how you talk but what you talk about is also important for impression formation. People who reveal some confidential aspect of themselves, what is called **self-disclosure**, are judged well. However, if a person becomes too self-disclosing too quickly in a relationship, it can be a turn off, producing a negative impression (Collins & Miller, 1994).

Information between people can also be nonverbal, in the form of body language. When men sit with their thighs touching and their arms touching their upper bodies, they are judged to be more feminine, since this posture is more common among women. Conversely, when women sit with their legs open and their arms held away from their upper bodies, they are judged more masculine, since this is a male posture.

Prior knowledge of a person affects how we think about him or her. In one study, half of the students in a class were asked to read a description of a visiting lecturer that portrayed him as "warm." The other half read a description that labeled him as "cold." Predictably, the students who had read the warm description had a better impression than did those who read the cold description (Kelley, 1950). This and other work have shown that the labels we apply to people have a powerful influence on how we think and act toward them.

The Dual-Process Model of Impression Formation

How do we cognitively go about forming impressions of others? According to the dual-process model, we do it in several stages (Brewer & Harasty Feinstein, 1999; Fiske, Lin, & Neuberg, 1999). The first stage is fast and automatic. For instance, we might judge a hotel doorman to be young, male, and white based simply on his skin color, uniform, and so on. If that person is not relevant to our goals, we stop there and don't think any more about it. However, if the doorman is relevant to our goals (we need him to carry our heavy luggage up to our room), then we initiate a more focused evaluation. We would then attempt to confirm our initial impression. Is he white? Yes, an examination of his skin tone indicates that he is. Does he really work for the hotel? Yes, his uniform has the hotel name on it, and so on.

If further scrutiny confirms our initial impression, we might stop there. But if the confirmation fails, we would then need to recategorize. Suppose a close scrutiny revealed that the doorman was actually a woman rather than a man and that her hair appeared short because it was tucked into her hat. In this case, we generate new, better fitting categories, such as "woman." In some instances, it is not easy to recategorize, in which case, we proceed one step at a time, applying different attributes and seeing if they fit based on the person's appearance. We could examine the hotel employee as she carried our bags to the elevator or as we engaged her in conversation. Our observations under these circumstances might then cause us to form different impressions, such as believing that she is friendly, talkative, and so on.

ATTRIBUTION

Johnny the third grader is in the cafeteria eating lunch with his friends. Suddenly, he picks up his food and throws it across the table, hitting Joey in the face. What is the cause of this action? Our attempt to explain this kind of behavior is called an attribution. An **attribution** is an explanation we give for the causes of events or behaviors (Forsterling, 2001). There are two basic types of attributions. An internal attribution explains a person's actions in terms of that person's own emotional state, preferences, or beliefs. In the case of Johnny, we could say that he threw the food because he is a bully. An external attribution explains a person's behavior in terms of the environment or situation. In this example, we might reason that Joey is the bully and was making fun of Johnny, who then retaliated. It may be easy to confuse attributions with attitudes reviewed in the previous section. Here is the difference. Attitudes are general, whereas attributions are very specific, referring only to our perception of the cause of an action or behavior.

What determines whether we make an internal or external attribution? Harold Kelley (1972) proposes several primary factors. One is consistency. If a person regularly reacts in a certain way, we are more likely to attribute that type of action to him or her. Imagine that you hear your friend Mary laughing. If Mary laughs all the time, you will attribute her laughter to her sense of humor. If she rarely laughs, you may think that it is because somebody told a particularly good joke. Another influence is consensus. According to this view, if lots of other people agree on a behavior, then it is more likely to be attributed to the situation. If you hear your roommate next door cheering and realize that the World

Series is on and that most people in your dorm like the local team, then you will attribute the cheer to the team having scored a run. If there is no such consensus, you may simply attribute the cheer to your roommate being a sports fan.

Distinctiveness also plays a role. If a person acts the same way in different situations, then distinctiveness is low. If he or she acts differently in different situations, then distinctiveness is high. Low distinctiveness is like high consistency and produces internal attributions. High distinctiveness instead biases a situational attribution. Under these conditions, we tend to think that the environment or context is responsible. If Courtney always picks chocolate ice cream but tonight chooses pistachio, then we infer that it must be really good ice cream or, perhaps, the only flavor available.

Attribution Biases

Are our attributions accurate? We hope that they are; otherwise, it would be difficult to understand the world around us and to interact successfully with others. Researchers have found that in some cases, we are not so good at making correct attributions. One of the biggest stumbling blocks is the **fundamental attribution error**. This is the tendency to prefer internal or dispositional traits as the best explanation. In other words, we are more likely to blame a person than a situation for some behavior (Gawronski, 2003; O'Sullivan, 2003). If you are driving home from work and somebody behind you is tailgating, you are likely to believe that it is because that driver is aggressive or in a hurry. Under these conditions, you would tend to ignore contextual information such as the fact that this person is also being tailgated and has sped up to allow more room behind his or her car. Don't confuse cognitive dissonance with the fundamental attribution error. Cognitive dissonance applies primarily to yourself and the feelings you experience during a contradiction between an attitude and a behavior. The fundamental attribution error is about how you explain somebody else's behavior (see Figure 11.6).

Our attributions can also be distorted by the **self-serving bias** (Brown & Rogers, 1991). This is the tendency to explain our own failures to external causes but to explain other people's failures to internal ones. The reason you did poorly on the test was because you didn't sleep well the night before, but the reason Alexander didn't do well on the test was because he is stupid. The reverse holds for successes. We explain our own successes in terms of internal causes but others' in terms of externals. If you did well on the exam, it was because you are smart, but if Alexander did well on the exam, it was because the test was easy.

According to the **belief-in-a-just-world phenomenon**, we think that people get what they deserve (Lerner, 1980). If we are rich and successful, we think that it is because we are clever or hardworking. Conversely, if we see a beggar on the street, we feel he or she is poor because he or she has a psychological disorder or a substance abuse problem. In

Figure 11.6 An example of how an attribution is made.

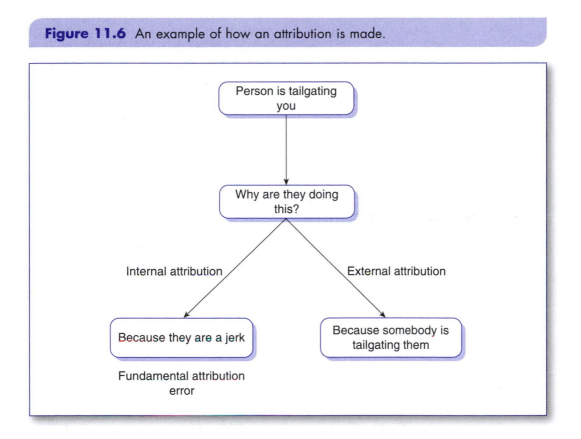

other words, we put the cart before the horse, using the end state as the explanation for the cause. It could just as easily be the case that you are successful because you have wealthy parents and the beggar is poor because somebody stole all of his or her money.

Attribution and Cognitive Processes

How do we actually go about making attributions? A number of theories have been proposed that incorporate both fast, automatic attentional mechanisms and slower, more controlled ones (Fiske & Taylor, 2008). There is sufficient evidence to argue that we rapidly and subconsciously form dispositional attributions. In one study, participants were able to make trait judgments based on stimulus features such as gender, race, age, and facial appearance in as little as 100 milliseconds (Willis & Todorov, 2006). These judgments were correlated with those made under longer duration viewing conditions, suggesting that our first fast impressions tend to agree with our longer, more contemplative ones.

However, controlled attentional processes sometimes do adjust or change our initial impressions. Imagine that you are in a bar and see your friend Mark in a fight. Under these conditions, you may very quickly perform a dispositional assessment of the scene, remembering that Mark is aggressive and has gotten into fights before. This might first lead you to believe that he started the fight. A short time later, you may adjust your initial assessment by noting the situation. Realizing it is a bar, you may then infer that some of the other drunk and unruly patrons could have started the altercation. Gilbert (1998) summarizes older cognitive attribution theories and incorporates some of their features into a multistage model of how it might occur.

Attribution and Neuroscience

Recent work has been able to identify those brain regions involved in making judgments about other people's behavior. These regions consist of the anterior paracingulate cortex, the posterior STS at the TPJ, and the temporal pole (Gallagher & Frith, 2003). The dorsal mPFC is implicated in the general comprehension of other people's minds. The mPFC plays a role in thinking about our own states as well as those of others. The TPJ in the right hemisphere becomes active for the attribution of other mental states but not for other kinds of social information about them (Rilling, Sanfey, Aronson, Nystrom, & Cohen, 2004).

One particularly interesting finding is that there may be different brain areas that operate when we are dealing with abstract situations involving people (e.g., a scenario or story), in contrast to real-world people scenarios (e.g., playing a game with real people who are in close physical proximity). Rilling et al. (2004) found activity in the anterior paracingulate cortex and the posterior STS when participants were thinking about actual people. There was less activation in these areas for hypothetical situations (Table 11.5).

Table 11.5 Neural centers and associated cognitive functions underlying attribution processing.

Brain Area(s)	Cognitive Process
Dorsal medial prefrontal cortex	Thinking about mental states, our own and others'
Temporoparietal junction in the right hemisphere	Attribution of others' mental states
Anterior paracingulate cortex and posterior superior temporal sulcus	Thinking about real-world people scenarios

Harris, Todorov, and Fiske (2005) had a group of participants reason about a scenario with different combinations of consistency, consensus, and distinctiveness. High consistency, low consensus, and low distinctiveness produced greater activation of the STS. High consistency and low distinctiveness, regardless of consensus, produced greater activation of the mPFC. The results suggest that people will tend to ignore consensus information in favor of consistency and distinctiveness.

Lieberman, Gaunt, Gilbert, and Trope (2002) postulate the existence of two neural networks that underlie automatic and controlled processing. The reflexive or X system produces fast automatic responses and is mediated by the amygdala, the dorsal anterior cingulate, the basal ganglia, the ventromedial PFC, and the lateral temporal cortex. This system is used under normal nonconflicting conditions. The reflective or C system takes longer and involves the lateral PFC, the mPFC, the rostral anterior cingulate, the posterior parietal cortex, and the medial temporal lobe. The C system is used when a conflict occurs or our goals are blocked and we need to think more carefully (Table 11.6).

Table 11.6 Two hypothesized brain systems underlying attribution processing (after Lieberman, Gaunt, Gilbert, & Trope, 2002).

System	Response	Brain Regions	Conditions Used Under
Reflexive (X system)	Fast and automatic	Amygdala Dorsal anterior cingulate Basal ganglia Ventromedial prefrontal cortex Lateral temporal cortex	Normal and nonconflicting
Reflective (C system)	Slow and controlled	Lateral prefrontal cortex Medial prefrontal cortex Rostral anterior cingulate Posterior parietal cortex Medial temporal lobe	Conflict or goal blocked

Interdisciplinary Crossroads: Game Theory and the Prisoner's Dilemma

There are a number of decision-making situations that pit the narrow self-interests of individuals against the interests of the group as a whole. Take public radio as an example. Listeners fund public radio. If you wanted to "cheat" by not paying and rely on other people to support the station for you, you would benefit at their expense. If everybody did this, though, the radio station would go under and nobody could listen. On the other hand, if everyone cooperates, the group as a whole will be better off since the station will continue to stay on the air. The field in the social sciences that studies these kinds of situations, where an individual's success in making choices depends on the choices of others, is known as **game theory**.

These types of situations are called **social dilemmas**. In the simple version, each person is better off doing one sort of thing, but everyone is better off if they all do something else (Baron, 2000). If individuals act selfishly, thinking only of themselves and not doing what the majority does, they are said to be defectors. If people act altruistically, taking other people's concerns into consideration, they become coopera-tors. The **prisoner's dilemma** is one of the simple kinds of conflict situations such as this that can arise. It portrays the logical consequences of being selfish or altruistic and is a demonstration of the sorts of social factors that can affect the attributions we make toward others.

Imagine that you and your friend have both been charged for a crime and are now waiting in prison to be tried. There are four possible situations that can occur (see Table 11.7). If neither of you confesses (i.e., if the two of you "cooperate"), you each serve minor sentences of 1 year. If you cooperate by not confessing and your partner "defects" by turning in evidence against you, he goes free while you end up serving a 10-year prison sentence. Conversely, if your partner cooperates by not snitching on you and you defect by turning in evidence against him, you get to go free while he serves the 10 years. If both of you defect, you each serve 4 years in jail.

Table 11.7 The four outcomes in the prisoner's dilemma scenario.

	Your Partner Confesses	**Your Partner Cooperates**
You confess	Both serve 4-year sentences	You go free; partner serves 10 years
You cooperate	Partner goes free; you serve a 10-year sentence	Both serve 1-year sentences

In this scenario, you are each being interrogated separately and so have no idea what the other will do. What would you do? Most people reason that no matter what their friend does, they would serve less time by defecting (0 years if he cooperates or 4 years if he defects) than by cooperating (1 year if he cooperates or 10 if he defects). So the typical outcome is that both defect and each serves 4 years. This is unfortunate, since each would have served only 1 year if they both had cooperated.

When the prisoner's dilemma is played out in the laboratory, the majority of people end up selfishly defecting.

The type of conflict depicted in the prisoner's dilemma comes up all the time in everyday life, in situations ranging from business contracts to environmental agreements. In fact, these situations are the foundation of all economic systems. If you as an individual decided to be selfish, you might take as much as you could from everyone else while working the least—that is, contributing the least to society in terms of the goods and services provided by your labors. Obviously, not everyone does this, or we would have nothing to enjoy. The problem is solved in most economies through the use of money, for which one needs to work in order to buy things.

Despite this, the default behavior that we see in most real-world scenarios is cooperation, not selfishness. How can this be, given the benefits that reward individualistic action? Well, in the real world, it is unlikely that we will interact with a person on just one occasion. Since we live in a society, the chances are that you will meet your friend again someday. If you screw him over the first time, you realize that he may get back at you the second time. It is this scenario that is studied in the iterated prisoner's dilemma. Here, people can "play" this game with the same person again.

Under iterated circumstances, a new strategy develops, called "tit for tat" (Myerson, 1997). People in these situations do whatever their opponent did to them on the previous round. If your friend defected on you previously, you would then defect on him the next time. If your friend decided to get "nice" at some point and cooperate, then you would reciprocate again by "forgetting" his transgression and cooperating. So in the real world, where we may have to interact repeatedly with the same individuals who can get back at us, it makes more sense to be cooperative.

STEREOTYPES

A **schema**, as we have mentioned elsewhere, is a framework or body of knowledge on some topic. Schemas typically help us understand and think about things. For example, you may have a schema about a bicycle that includes an understanding of its parts, such as a seat, handlebars, and wheels. Part of your bicycle schema may also involve an understanding of how they function. This aspect of the schema would include pedaling, gears, and steering.

Schemas need not be used for objects alone. We also use them when thinking about people. One kind of schema is a stereotype. **Stereotypes** contain information about people in a specific category. The category can be defined by almost any criteria, such as skin color, sex, profession, or religion. Stereotypes can be positive, negative, or neutral. For instance, you might believe that blacks are creative musicians (positive), aggressive (negative), or that they live in urban settings (neutral).

Stereotypes and Cognitive Processes

According to one view, we form schemas to simplify the vast amount of social information with which we are constantly bombarded (Kulik, 2005). In a typical day, you may interact with fellow students, coworkers, friends, and family members. In the course of these interactions, you need to keep track of what each one has said, believes, and intends to do. A stereotype simplifies and organizes this information and makes it easier to think about. Of course, in the process of simplifying, stereotypes may also be wrong and cause us to think incorrectly about people.

Hugenberg and Bodenhausen (2004) found that people prefer information that is consistent with their stereotypes and that they process such information more quickly. We tend not to pay attention to or remember information that fails to match our stereotypes, and in some cases, we believe that this information is false (Johnston & Macrae, 1994; O'Sullivan & Durso, 1984). To illustrate, if you held the stereotype that Hispanics are lazy, you would be less likely to notice or recall one who is hardworking and instead be more likely to attend to and remember one who isn't.

In-Groups and Out-Groups

One consequence of stereotyping is that we tend to classify ourselves as part of a preferred category of people, called an in-group, and others as part of a less preferred category, or out-group. People perceive more diversity and variation among members of the in-group and less among those of the out-group (Guinote & Fiske, 2003). If Frank, who is Caucasian, thinks that all Asian people look alike, then he has succumbed to the **out-group homogeneity effect**. People also tend to think of in-group members as having better looks and personalities and as engaging in more socially accepted forms of behavior, what is known as **in-group favoritism** (Aboud, 2003; Bennett et al., 2004).

A number of factors influence in-group favoritism. It occurs even when all the members are deprived and have little to offer one another (Rabbie & Horwitz, 1969). This finding suggests that there is more to it than simply being rewarded by like group members. In-group favoritism also increases under conflict, which suggests that it helps reduce subjective uncertainty and anxiety about one's identity.

Out-group homogeneity is stronger for groups that are unfamiliar and with which one has not had personal contact (Brewer & Brown, 1998; Brown, 2000). Thus, we are more likely to perceive the negative stereotype that Albanians are corrupt if we have never met one. People also believe that others are more biased against out-groups than they themselves are (Judd, Park, Yzerbyt, Gordijn, & Muller, 2005). Interestingly, under some conditions, there is also an in-group homogeneity effect. This occurs particularly for identity-relevant traits (Simon, 1992). Those who identify strongly with their group are more likely to see members of the group as being alike (Castano & Yzerbyt, 1998).

Automatic Stereotyping

In automatic stereotyping, we associate certain traits or values with particular groups. The best known test of these associations is the **implicit association task** (Greenwald, McGhee, & Schwartz, 1998). In the standard version of this task, a person must judge whether a word that appears in the middle of a computer screen corresponds to one of two categories. For example, the word that appears could be *salary*. In the upper corners of the screen would appear two category words, such as *man* on the left and *woman* on the right. The task is to push one of two buttons to label the word as belonging to one or the other category. If the central word is *salary*, most participants are faster to label this as belonging to the category of "man," since this concept is traditionally associated with maleness. Average response times are slower to associate this concept with the category of "woman" because, historically, these two ideas have not been associated.

A large number of studies have demonstrated what is called the **category confusion effect**. Simply stated, this is the difficulty we have in differentiating people who fall within a category defined by gender, race, age, sexual orientation, attractiveness, and other features (Maddox & Chase, 2004). Perhaps you have experienced this at a meeting or a class where you may have remembered that a person of a given ethnicity—let us say Indian—made a statement, but you can't remember specifically which Indian person it was. This memory effect is an example of automatic stereotyping because it occurs without any intention or effort on our part.

Priming studies also demonstrate automatic stereotyping effects. In this type of experiment, a prime word such as *white* or *black* precedes a positive or negative word related to race, such as *smart*. Participants are to then judge as quickly as possible whether this second item is a word or not—since on half the trials, the prime is followed with nonsense words. Reaction times for this lexical decision task are faster for stereotypical race-associated words—that is, white people's response times to *smart* are faster when preceded by *white* compared with when they are preceded by *black*. A related paradigm is the **indirect priming task**. Here, a racial prime such as a word or picture precedes a positive or negative word that is not related to race. The participant then has to respond whether the word is good or bad.

Stereotyping and Neuroscience

Hart et al. (2000) used fMRI to see how the perception of in-group and out-group members differs. In this study, whites and blacks viewed unfamiliar white and black faces and were asked to identify their gender. In the first set of trials, there was amygdala activation in both the in-group and out-group faces. In the second set of trials, there was reduced amygdala activation but only for the in-group members. This was true for both the races that were tested. We would expect the amygdala to be active when first viewing unfamiliar faces of any race, since this brain structure constitutes part of the fear response and strangers may pose a threat. The reduction in this response for in-group members only, however, demonstrates that we rapidly get used to faces of our own race, become less fearful of them, and apparently don't consider them to be as much of a threat. The same cannot be said for out-group members.

In a related experiment, Lieberman, Hariri, and Bookheimer (2001) had black and white participants view three faces arranged in a triangular configuration. In the first condition, the task was simply to match which of the two faces on the bottom matched the race of the face at the top. The second condition required deciding which of two labels, "African American" or "Caucasian," applied to a target face. For out-group target faces, amygdala activation was high in the race-matching condition but low in the race-labeling condition. Measurements of prefrontal activation showed exactly the reverse pattern. For this region, activation was low for race matching and high for race labeling. The results demonstrate that processing of a stereotypical word can reduce our apparent emotional sensitivity to it—perhaps because different, nonstereotypical associations were made while learning the word.

PREJUDICE

A literal translation of the word **prejudice** yields "prejudgment," so we can think of it as a decision or opinion we already have made. Myers (2001) describes prejudice as having three components: (1) a belief, such as a stereotype; (2) an emotion, such as envy or fear; and (3) a predisposition to an action, such as discrimination. For instance, Greg may be prejudiced against immigrants, believing that they are violent, feeling fearful that they might rob him, and being unwilling to adopt one as a friend. As is the case with stereotypes, we are less likely to attend to or remember information that refutes or disagrees with our prejudices. Conversely, we are more likely to pay attention to information that supports and agrees with them. The consequence of this is that our prejudices tend to reinforce themselves. The difference between stereotypes and prejudices are that the former are beliefs or thoughts and are thus cognitive in nature, whereas the latter entail not only thoughts but emotions and actions as well.

Again, as we saw with stereotypes, the cognitive component of a prejudice can be a schema that affects what we perceive and understand. In one early study, white participants perceived a white man pushing a black man as playful, but when these same observers saw a black man shove a white man, they interpreted the event as aggressive and violent (Duncan, 1976). This phenomenon is a good example of "top-down" or conceptually driven perceptual processing, where what we already know affects what we see. To find out more, you can refer to Chapter 4, where we first introduced this notion.

Is prejudice conscious or unconscious? If it is conscious, we might be able to control and perhaps stop it. If it is unconscious, it might influence our thoughts and actions in ways we can't control. The evidence suggests that prejudice can operate on both levels (Carter & Rice, 1997). An explicit bad feeling toward someone may contribute to the formation of a negative conscious prejudice against that person. However, even the absence of a good feeling can lead to an unconscious negative prejudice (Pettigrew & Meertens, 1995). In this latter case, we may develop a bad prejudice toward Koreans, even though we have never met one. Greenwald et al. (1998) showed that people who claimed not to be racist took more time to identify positive words such as *paradise* and *peace* when they were associated with black instead of white faces. So although we may believe that we are not prejudiced, we may still harbor unconscious beliefs that can affect our behavior.

The Stereotype Content Model of Prejudice

In this section, we will describe one model by which we form prejudiced beliefs. According to the stereotype content model, we first adopt particular stereotypical views of some group. These views then determine the emotional reaction or prejudice we feel toward members of that group. There are two primary dimensions by which we judge others. The first is competence, which can be viewed as high or low. The second is warmth, which can be either cold or warm. A number of studies have shown that we tend to classify others using these two dimensions (Fiske, Cuddy, Glick, & Xu, 2002).

Table 11.8 shows this two-dimensional space and lists several instances of stereotyped people who fit into the four extremes. People who are middle class, Christian, or heterosexual are perceived as being high in competence and warm and so fit into the upper,

Table 11.8 The stereotype content model of prejudice.

	Low Competence	**High Competence**
High warmth	The elderly and the disabled (viewed by some with pity)	Middle class, Christians, and heterosexuals (viewed most favorably, by some with pride)
Low warmth	Homeless, drug addicts, and the poor (viewed least favorably, and by some with disgust)	Jews, Asians, the wealthy, and professionals (viewed by some with envy)

right-hand portion of the space. These people are viewed most favorably. At the opposite end of the space, in the lower-left corner, we have people who are perceived as low in competence and cold. Homeless individuals, drug addicts, and the poor fit into this area. These groups tend to be viewed least favorably. Both of these groups are seen as unambivalent, meaning that people have clear-cut and strong views of them, either positive or negative.

In the upper-left portion of this space are those perceived as low in competence but high in warmth. Examples include the elderly and the disabled. Finally, in the lower-right corner, we have people seen as cold but high in competence. Jews, Asians, the rich, and professionals fill this category. These two groups are ambivalent because people's views toward them are mixed and uncertain.

By the stereotype content model, each of the four categorizations outlined above elicits a different prejudice and behavior (Cuddy, Fiske, & Glick, 2007). We feel pride toward those warm and high in competence because we usually associate these as members of our own group who can aid us in times of trouble. We are motivated to interact with these groups. Cold, low-competence individuals produce a feeling of contempt, disgust, and dehumanization, motivating us to avoid them. Warm, low-competence groups make us feel pity, which may prompt helping behavior but also neglect. Groups judged as cold and highly competent are seen as a potential threat since they may have needed resources. During stable social times, these groups are cooperated with, but during social upheaval, they can be attacked—as has been the case with genocides throughout history.

OVERALL EVALUATION OF THE SOCIAL APPROACH

You may have noticed a theme that runs through some of the research discussed here. This is the distinction between fast, automatic processing that appears to take place without effort and slower, more controlled, effortful processing. We saw this in the dual model of impression formation. Many social cognitive processes seem to operate according to this two-track procedure. This echoes what we have seen in other types of cognition. Remember that in visual search, there is fast parallel detection of targets but also slower serial search. In our discussion of executive function, we saw that there was not only fast automatic processing that could govern well-learned tasks, such as driving a car, but also slower processing for novel or more difficult problems.

Cognitive science's narrow focus on the cognition of the individual has held sway for far too long. Its emphasis on the processing of objects and abstract information such as pictures, numbers, and words was the dominant paradigm for much of the past few decades. Fortunately, we have seen a change in this outlook. As this chapter attests, there is now a substantial body of research on how we cognate about one another. This change is welcome. It helps explain the way we think about and interact with one another, not just with objects and ideas.

The social cognitive perspective has adopted the interdisciplinary approach more readily than many other areas in cognitive science. In fact, by its very definition, it employs at least two levels of analysis, (1) the social and (2) the cognitive. With the current trend of cognitive social neuroscience, we can add a third biological level to this. The intersection of these approaches to the study of cognition should serve as a model for the rest of cognitive science to follow and will continue to yield valuable insights for the foreseeable future.

SUMMING UP: A REVIEW OF CHAPTER 11

1. Social cognition is the study of how we think about ourselves and other people. Researchers in this area make four assumptions: (1) the use of mental representations, (2) how they develop and change over time, (3) an interdisciplinary approach, and (4) real-world applicability.

2. The field of social cognitive neuroscience attempts to explain cognitive phenomena from three perspectives: (1) the biological or brain-based approach; (2) a cognitive, information-processing approach; and (3) a social perspective.

3. Recent research has found that young children outperform primates on social cognition tasks, implying that this capacity may have evolved first and served as the basis for more general cognitive abilities later.

4. Social cognition requires joint attention, the ability to pay attention not just to your own thoughts but to the sharing of an attentional focus with others as a normal part of social interaction.

5. Mirror neurons are brain cells that fire both when an animal is performing some action and when it observes another animal performing that same action. These neurons exist in monkeys and probably form the basis for modeling or imitative behavior. The evidence for the presence of these neurons in humans is not as strong, but if present in humans, they may form the basis for empathy.

6. A ToM is the knowledge that other people have minds and also the ability to use this understanding to infer other people's actions and to adjust our own behavior in response. Autistic patients seem to have deficits in being able to form and use a ToM, what may be called "mind blindness."

7. An attitude is a learned predisposition to respond to a particular object in a particular way. Cognitive dissonance can arise when an attitude and a behavior are inconsistent. This results in a negative aroused state that can be resolved by changing our attitude to correspond to our actions.

8. An impression is an opinion or belief that you form about another person. Early impressions are powerful. They can be influenced by people's attractiveness, the way they talk, nonverbal body language, and prior knowledge.

9. An attribution is an explanation we give to explain somebody else's behavior. Attributions can be internal, attributed to the person's nature, or external, attributed to the environment. We prefer internal attributions to explain others' behavior but external attributions to explain our own behavior.

10. Stereotypes are a set of ideas or beliefs about a category of people, such as blacks or Hispanics. Stereotypes cause us to categorize ourselves as members of an in-group that we perceive as more heterogeneous. Members of an out-group are perceived as more homogeneous. A prejudice consists of a belief, an emotion, and a predisposition to action. The cognitive component of both stereotypes and prejudices can be schemas.

11. The social cognitive approach again shows us that there are many cognitive processes that have a two-track organization, being fast and automatic or slower and more effortful. This approach is a welcome change because it focuses on how we think about people rather than how we think about objects or ideas.

EXPLORE MORE

Log on to the student study site at **http://study.sagepub.com/friedenberg3e** for electronic flash cards, review quizzes, and a list of web resources to aid you in further exploring the field of cognitive science.

SUGGESTED READINGS

Doherty, M. J. (2008). *Theory of mind: How children understand others' thoughts and feelings.* New York, NY: Psychology Press.

Fiske, S. T., & Taylor, S. E. (2008). *Social cognition: From brains to culture.* New York, NY: McGraw-Hill.

Osborne, M. J. (2003). *An introduction to game theory.* Oxford, England: Oxford University Press.

Sicile-Kira, C. (2004). *Autism spectrum disorders: The complete guide to understanding autism, Asperger syndrome, pervasive developmental disorder, and other ASDs.* New York, NY: Perigee Trade.

12

THE ARTIFICIAL INTELLIGENCE APPROACH

The Computer as a Cognitive Entity

What a piece of work is man! how noble in reason! how infinite in faculty! in form and moving how express and admirable! in action how like an angel! in apprehension how like a god! the beauty of the world, the paragon of animals.

—William Shakespeare (*Hamlet*)

We cannot so easily convince ourselves of the absence of complete laws of behavior . . . The only way we know of for finding such laws is scientific observation, and we certainly know of no circumstances under which we could say, We have searched enough. There are no such laws."

—Alan Turing

COGNITIVE SCIENCE AND ARTIFICIAL INTELLIGENCE

Cognitive science embraces the interdisciplinary study of human characteristics: consciousness, perception, thinking, judgment, and memory, as well as the behaviors that follow. As such, it comprises elements of intelligence and **behavior** (e.g., information representation and processing). Questions such as What is reason? and How is it expressed? are primary areas of research. Cognitive science has come to subsume a variety of disciplines: psychology, philosophy, neuroscience, linguistics, anthropology, engineering, computer science, sociology, and biology. In this chapter, we explore where these disciplines interconnect, namely, within "artificial intelligence" (AI).

Considerations of "intelligence" have their origins in philosophy and the "mind–body" problem. Starting with Plato, philosophers have examined the relationships between mind and matter. Can we distinguish between ideas (mind) and matter (physical) that constitute the brain? The various philosophical models seek to explain the relationships or distinctions between human consciousness and the brain. The ultimate integration of the physical and cognitive facets of humans within an artificial medium provides the basis for an "intelligent agent" (IA). Such an embodiment in "robotic" form will be explored in a subsequent chapter. (For an IA to truly reflect intelligence, philosophers argue that it must account for human consciousness.) A thorough discussion of the competing philosophical models of consciousness is beyond the scope of this text. However, a brief summary of the primary paradigms is noted.

Identity theory: One of the major proponents J. J. C. Smart (http://plato.stanford.edu/entries/mind-identity/#The) notes, "The identity theory of mind holds that states and processes of the mind are identical to states and processes of the brain."

Behaviorism (http://psychologydictionary.org/behaviorism/): Intelligence is focused on the study of observable, quantifiable facts. Behavior is acquired through conditioning as identified by John Watson (Cohen, 1979) and popularized by B. F. Skinner (1938).

Functionalism: "Mental states (beliefs, desires, being in pain, etc.) are constituted solely by their functional role—that is, they are causal relations to other mental states, sensory inputs, and behavioral outputs" (DeLancey, 2002). Some psychologists consider functionalism to be a modification of identity theory (http://www.academon.com/comparison-essay/identity-theory-vs-functionalism-102935/, 2008).

Machine implementation of human cognitive abilities is an ambitious and challenging objective of AI. (Can we ever hope to produce a "machine" that achieves Hamlet's poetic description?) Its ultimate goal includes nothing less than total integration, understanding, and representation of animal behaviors and those related to humans in particular, namely, thinking, feeling, speaking, symbolic processing, remembering, learning, knowing, consciousness, problem solving, planning, decision making, and even the unconscious (brain). These processes constitute a broad cognitive and behavioral spectrum of living systems. This lofty mission is summarized in the seminal work *Artificial Intelligence: A Modern Approach* (Russell & Norvig, 2009):

"Once we have a complete, comprehensive theory of mind, it becomes possible to express the model in machine . . . (program) . . . form." (p. 3)

HISTORICAL PRECURSORS

Developments in AI have evolved from the behaviorist and functional philosophies of psychology summarized above. Evolution has demonstrated repeatedly that humans have survived and flourished in part through ingenious use of tools and machines. (History shows that animals have used tools in innovative ways but not machines as currently conceived.) Tool making and machines as they relate to the development of AI depend on several historical threads. One representative formulation is summarized in Table 12.1. It includes a list of selected—but far from exhaustive—historical events that are important precursors for machines capable of realizing an AI model of the brain.

Table 12.1 An artificial intelligence timeline (The History of Artificial Intelligence, 2014; History of Computing, 2014).

Time	Events
Prior to 1000 CE	Pygmalion (intelligent robot)
	Yan Shi (mechanical men)
	Abacus
	Mechanical statues in Egypt and Greece believed to be capable of wisdom and emotion
	Aristotle: syllogisms, a format for mechanical thought
	Heron of Alexandria: automatons
	Theory of Takwin: artificial creation of life in the laboratory, including human life
1000–1600	Al-Jazan: programmable mechanical orchestra
	Ramon Llull (Spanish theologian): invents a tool for combining concepts mechanically—a precursor to contributions by Gottfried Leibniz (17th century)
	Rabbi Judah Loew ben Bezalel of Prague: said to invent the Golem—a clay man brought to life
	Rene Descartes: proposes that bodies of animals are complex machines; however, mental phenomena are of a different "substance"
1600–1700	Blaise Pascal: the mechanical calculator
	Gottfried Leibniz: adds multiplication and division to the calculator; the binary system for determining logical truth or falsity—a precursor to machine logic
1700–1800	Jonathan Swift (Gulliver's Travels): describes a machine for "improving speculative knowledge"
	Julien Offray de La Mettrie (L'Homme Machine): human thought is strictly mechanical

(Continued)

Table 12.1 (Continued)

Time	Events
1800–1900	Mary Shelley (*Frankenstein* or the Modern Prometheus): ethical considerations of creating a sentient being
	Charles Babbage/Ada Lovelace: a programmable mechanical calculator and its associated programming language; Lady Lovelace is the "world's first programmer." (The Programming language ADA is named in her honor)
	Bernard Bolzano (mathematician): formalizes semantics
	George Boole: Boolean Algebra—symbolic language of a calculus to describe reasoning
	Electronic vacuum tube is invented (1907)
	Samuel Butler: Darwinian evolution also applies to machines leading to consciousness that will supplant humanity
	Herman Hollerith: Punch cards and sorting system
	Use of oscilloscope to record electrical potentials from activated nerves and muscles of animals (neurophysiology)
1900–1940	Bertand Russell/Alfred North Whitehead (Principia Mathematica): definitive description of formal logic
	Leonardo Torres y Quevedo: builds a chess automaton
	Karel Capek: first use of the word "robot" in a literary work
	Ludwig Wittgenstein/Rudolf Carnap (philosophy): logical analysis of knowledge
	Kurt Godel: formal systems development; builds an integer-based programming language and considered by some to be the "father of theoretical computer science"
	Alan Turing/Alonzo Church: computability theory
	J. V. Atanasoff: considered by some to have anticipated the Von Neumann **architecture** with main memory storage
1940–1950	John Bardeen/William Shockley/Walter Brattain, Bell Labs (1948): Transistor invented; Noble Prize awarded
	Konrad Zuse: first working program-controlled computers
	Warren Sturgis McCulloch/Walter Pitts: lay the foundation for artificial networks
	Arturo Rosenblueth/Norbert Wiener/Julian Bigelow introduce the term *cybernetics*—general analysis of control systems and communication systems in living organisms and machines
	John von Neumann/Oskar Morgenstern: game theory
	John Mauchly/Presper Eckert: Electronic Numerical Integrator and Calculator (ENIAC); considered the "grandfather" of digital computers

Time	Events
1950–2000	Hodgkin/Huxley (1952) model to explain the ionic mechanisms underlying the initiation and propagation of action potentials in nervous tissue
	FORTRAN programming language (1954); powerful tool for computation
	Grace Hopper: first computer language for business applications. (COBOL)
	Jack Kilby/Robert Noyce: introduce the integrated circuit (computer chip): Kilby is awarded the Noble Prize
	Alan Shugart: invents the "floppy disk", allows data sharing
	Robert Metcalfe/Xerox: develops Ethernet for connecting multiple computers and other systems
	Personal computers: Altair, TR-80; Commodore
	Seymour Cray (1964): first of class of super computers
	Erwin Neher/Bert Sakmann (1974): Electronic Patch clamp allows study of single or multiple ion channels in cells, particularly in the nervous system.
	Steve Jobs/Steve Wozniak: Apple I, II
	IBM PC (1981)
	Spreadsheet: VisiCalc (predecessor of Excel)
	Word processing: WordStar
After 2000	iPhone (2007)
	Windows Operating System
	Field Programmable Gate Array with large-scale neural systems applicability
	IBM (2014): develops a new chip that functions like a brain

Two things are evident from the history: First, influences in AI have come from a number of contributing disciplines, including physics, mathematics, psychology, physiology, philosophy, religion, literature, and engineering; and second, the rate at which developments have proceeded has increased exponentially over time—a phenomenon noted in the writings of the futurist Ray Kurzweil (2012) who anticipates the eventual development of a machine that will exceed the cognitive capabilities of the brain. These developments are strongly influenced by the societal needs of war and commerce as reflected in accelerated advancements in technology.

Approaches to AI have been consolidated into three well-defined practical directions depicted in Figure 12.1.

The approaches have two distinct characteristics: one that proceeds from abstraction of cognitive processes (shown with arrows descending) and is referred to as the "top-down" model and the other that is closer to an "organic" representation of human cognitive processes (with ascending arrows) and is referred to as a "bottom-up" organization. The concept of "top-down" follows from the way we solve problems using successive decomposition of the inherent obstacles into less complex challenges. We start with the concept and work our way to finer details implied by the concept. For example, when planning for a trip from San Francisco to New York, we might decompose this into a series of (admittedly simplified) steps: arrange for housing (e.g., hotel), decide on travel method (e.g., air transport), obtain ticket, provide for transport to airport, and arrange for transport at destination. The "bottom-up" approach consists of integrating a series of elemental or partial solutions resulting in the resolution of the original problem. It is characterized by "information processing." For example, information enters our eye and the brain builds (recognizes) an image, which then may be further processed to create a perception. With respect to cognitive science, the goal of both methods is to be able to "reproduce" animal behaviors. If successful, the entity could be indistinguishable from human performance, and any "intelligence" that it embodies could therefore "mirror" animal intelligence.

Figure 12.1 Practical machine embodiments of artificial intelligence.

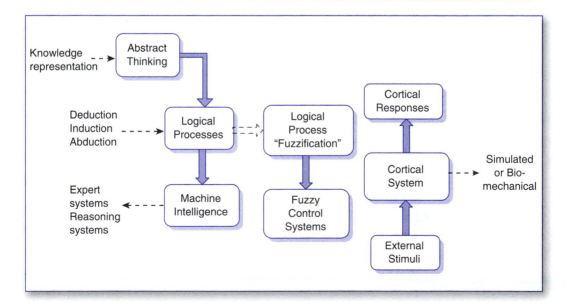

The top-down approach subsumes a system of formal logic that embodies the ways in which humans approach and solve problems. Some refer to the bottom-up approach to consist of "building a brain" and letting the resulting machine learn to solve problems as a human would.

DEFINING AI

From a practical point of view, AI is concerned with developing machines that solve "real-world" problems, particularly those requiring an IA (e.g., directing a vehicle to park automatically without human intervention). Plato might be considered to be one of the earliest to give voice to the idea that our ability to be rational—to think logically—was closely tied to intelligence and this has been a driving force in AI. In what has become an iconic—but controversial—concept of a "thinking machine," Alan Turing wrote a seminal paper, titled *Computing Machinery and Intelligence* (1950).[1] The provocative opening sentence in that paper is as follows:

> I propose to consider the question "Can machines think?" This should begin definitions of the meaning of the terms "machine" and "think." (p. 1)

The proposal evolved, in part, into what he called an ultimate test of intelligence. If a machine was able to make "intellectual" responses that were indistinguishable from those of a human being, we could conclude that it exhibited "intelligence." While the ideas expressed in that paper have been strongly questioned, a greater contribution emerged from the paper, namely, the "universal computer," including concepts that we now use in the design of computer-based machines—the "*state space*" concept as discussed below. The goal for an intelligent machine has remained an active ambition for the past 65 years and expresses itself in annual competitions bearing Turing's name to produce mechanisms (computers) that pass the Turing test (TT). In its current formulation, the TT scheme is summarized as follows:

- *Participants:* Human interrogator (judge), one human responder, and one "machine" responder
- *Neutral communication:* No visibility or other clues (e.g., handwriting, "voice")
- *Interrogation:* The interrogator questions the other agents (human and machine)
- *Resolution:* After a fixed time interval, the interrogator judges which is the "human" participant.

The Loebner Prize for AI is a formal instantiation of the TT (http://www.loebner.net/Prizef/loebner-prize.html). In 1990, the Cambridge Center for Behavioral Studies proposed a contest to implement the TT. Dr. Hugh Loebner agreed to underwrite the endeavor, and this gave rise to the prize that bears his name. Each year, an annual cash prize and medal are awarded to the most "humanlike computer." The best entry (relative to the others) is designated the winner, but it is not judged on its absolute capabilities. (As of 2013, Marvin Minsky joined as a cosponsor.)

One of the software developments that have emerged from the TT concept and the Loebner Prize is the idea of an "artificial" person with whom an individual can converse as if it were human (or other creature—e.g., an animal); it is referred to as a **chatbot**. (The "bot" is interpreted to be "robotized actions.") The interactions can be text based, verbal, or even nonverbal. It is particularly attractive in modern social networking websites and can be found on mobile devices as well as well-established personal computer systems. It can be used in educational circumstances such as human interaction when developing a presentation to improve its impact. (Businesses outside the United States gain particular benefits.) It can be incorporated into a wireless robot to create a more humanlike IA.[2]

The Artificial Linguistic Internet Computer Entity provides an opportunity to create a chatbot. The concept is supported by the Artificial Intelligence Markup Language and can be obtained under a free (open source) license. Figure 12.2 shows the facsimile of a recent

Figure 12.2 Facsimile of chatbot dialog.

ALICE and Judge

You say: [   ]   [Say]

Listen to two bots talking to each other!

Conversation Log:

Judge: Good day ALICE.

ALICE: Hi there!

Judge: Are you really intelligent?

ALICE: I have many intellectual functions.

Judge: What are a few of your intellectual functions?

ALICE: I would look into the web for that knowledge.

Judge: Thank you.

ALICE: Don't mention it.

Judge: Can I create my own bot?

ALICE: Can I get back to you on that?

Note: ALICE = Artificial Linguistic Internet Computer Entity.

dialog that is available at the site http://alicebot.org. (The Artificial Linguistic Internet Computer Entity, or ALICE, may be explored at the Foundation site.)[3] Individual chatbot natural language processing skills can vary from poor, to clever and humorous. The graphic designs have a similar range of outcomes (cartoonish to sophisticated, 3-D human-like visuals). (As you can tell from the interchange shown in Figure 12.2, the demonstration bot that is available is not terribly "sophisticated.")

In 2012, the chatbot named "Eugene Goostman" was the first to pass the TT when it convinced one in three judges that it was a 13-year-old Ukrainian.[4]

DOCTRINAL ARGUMENTS

Can an IA—something with capabilities similar to those of a human mind—be constructed? This is the critical question that best identifies the ultimate disposition of AI. The principles that form the basis of AI are roughly divided into three distinct categories: (1) "strong" AI, (2) applied AI, and (3) cognitive replication. These philosophies are summarized in Table 12.2.

Table 12.2 Artificial intelligence formulations.

Formulation	Principle	Note
Strong AI	Build a machine whose "intellectual" abilities cannot be distinguished from that of a human being.	Joseph Weizenbaum (1976): The goal of AI is "nothing less than to build a machine on the model of a man, a robot that is to have its childhood, to learn a language as a child does, to gain its knowledge of the world by sensing the world through its own organs, and ultimately to contemplate the domain of human thought" (Chakraborty, 2008). The term itself was first introduced by John Searle (1984).
Applied AI	Advanced information processing: produce commercially sustainable "smart machines."	Exemplified by the practical applications of machines such as Expert Systems, (Miller, Pople, & Myers, 1982) and "smart", automated control systems (Baig, Gholamhosseini, & Harrison, 2012).
Cognitive replication	Understand how the mind works and replicate it in machine or organic form.	Build a machine based on neurophysiological models of the neocortex, accept sensory inputs, and produce "intelligent" responses (Kruse et al., 2013).

Note: AI = artificial intelligence.

In spite of numerous demonstrations of machines that replace or supplement human activity, there remains considerable resistance to the idea of creating a machine with the characteristics of a human being. Such criticisms are summarized in Table 12.3 and are classified according to their principal focus: mathematical, consciousness, emotional limitations, and programming.

Of particular note are the objections that have been proposed by George Reeke and Gerald Edelman (1988) as well as John Searle (1980, 2014) with regard to the

Table 12.3 Artificial intelligence criticisms.

Criticism	Argument	Notes
Mathematical	Even with the most powerful machines, there are some theorems that can be neither proved nor disproved; hence, (strong) AI is not possible.	Originally developed by Gödel, Church, and others; the mathematics is valid. Might this *not* be a limit to the intelligence of a machine relative to man? (Church, 1936; Gödel, 1934; Kleene, 1935).
Consciousness	The only way to be sure that a machine thinks is to *be* the machine; the only way to know what a person thinks is to be that particular person.	How do you define "thinking"? How do you know when it is achieved?
Emotional	Emotional responses are considered to be machine "disabilities." It can never produce "genuine" kindness, friendliness, exhibit humor, and other such qualities.	Machines have been viewed as having limited purpose. Many disabilities reflect the limited capacity of older machines. Some limitations can be "frivolous." How does one define "friendliness" between humans? A machine might "enjoy" strawberries but an attempt to make the machine do so would be "idiotic."
Programming	A machine can never be programmed to do "anything new."	Such objections should be coupled with a similar concept assignable to humans: "There is nothing new under the sun." Is it possible to maintain that "original work" is not simply the growth of the seed planted by teaching, or the effect of following well-known general principles?

"programming" elements of an IA. The Reeke/Edelman argument follows from the following logic leading to a fundamental contradiction.

> If the brain is to be emulated by a computer, then how can it come to exist without a programmer? Intelligent biological systems exist, yet they evolved and were not "programmed"—how is that possible? The contradiction: "brains" (e.g., intelligent agents) must have programs, yet at the same time must not be programmed. An alternative argument follows from this: how can a human programmer create an algorithm (machine) with intelligence that exceeds that of the programmer?

The Searle argument provides a practical example of the challenges faced by an intelligent artificial agent. This is described in the Chinese Room scenario as provided in Chapter 2. In essence, a message in Chinese is passed to a "translator" who actually has no knowledge of Chinese but uses a series of rules to convert the characters into another language (e.g., English). The translation is returned to the originator who may continue this sequence enabling a conversation. As the translator has no knowledge of the language, he cannot be considered to be an IA in the usual meaning of the term *translator*. Such individuals must have extensive learning experiences to achieve such skill, which is not accommodated by a "look-up" table. (Counter arguments and criticisms can be found in Chapter 2.)

TURING'S CRITICAL LEGACY

Of greater consequence than the TT, the concept of a "universal computing machine" was an idea proposed by Turing that embodies a seminal principal on which the design and function of current machines is founded and forms one formulation of "practical AI." The **universal computing machine** as envisioned by Turing is characterized as *a machine that can "simulate" any computer algorithm no matter its complexity*. If one can formulate an algorithm for solving a problem, then it is possible to build a machine to implement the solution. Its application to the cognitive sciences as well as computing and engineering technology of the past century has been profound.

Such top-down designs—whether hardware based or implemented in software (**programs**)—rely on a structure with two elements: (1) *facts* and (2) *rules* that act on such facts. A simple example from everyday activities provides an insight:

Fact (given): I see a red traffic light.

Rule: IF (I see a red traffic light) THEN (stop the car I am driving at the light.)

The key element of the rule contains an if–then structure with each element including an argument or predicate. (Predicates are phrases whose truth or falsity can be determined.) If we can abstract human behavior to form a framework of **if–then rules**, then coupled with observable facts, we may build a machine to automate such behaviors. This can extend to drawing conclusions, proving theorems, or replicating the human activity. While the example noted above seems particularly simple, the predicates and phrases may themselves include additional combinatorial expressions using logical operations such as AND, OR, and NOT. This provides a basis for far more complex architectures. Table 12.4 summarizes the effects of the logical operations AND, OR, and NOT.

The underlying organization that has evolved from Turing's scheme is best represented in a diagram that represents the algorithmic solution to a problem. This diagram forms the basis for a machine to implement the solution; the resulting machines are referred to as "*state machines*." As an example, consider the form for one such state machine as depicted in Figure 12.3. Notice the implied if–then form of the scheme's organization.

An example with a level of automation that would eliminate the need for a human operator demonstrates how such machines could have practical applications. The control system for a parking garage exit gate operates on a simplified sequence of operations: Wait until a car appears at the exit gate and deposit the correct fee, open the gate, wait until the car has cleared the exit gate, and await the next car. Clearly, external sensors would be required to detect events such as the "money is deposited," and actuators would be needed to "raise the gate." (These events and machine elements might require their own finite state machine design.) An alternative summary representation using if–then rules includes the following:

IF (car NOT at exit) THEN (wait until car is at exit)

IF (car at exit AND money paid) THEN (raise exit gate)

IF (exit gate is raised AND car has NOT cleared exit) THEN (wait until car clears exit)

IF (car is clear of toll booth) THEN (close gate)

Table 12.4 Summary of logical operations.

Logical Operation	Predicate Operation	Result of Operation
AND	A AND B	TRUE, only if both A and B are TRUE.
OR	A OR B	TRUE, if either A OR B OR both are TRUE.
NOT	NOT A	Inverts the status of A; if A is TRUE, result is FALSE; if A is FALSE, result is TRUE.

Figure 12.3 Representative implementation of the *finite state concept*—after *Turing's universal computing machine.*

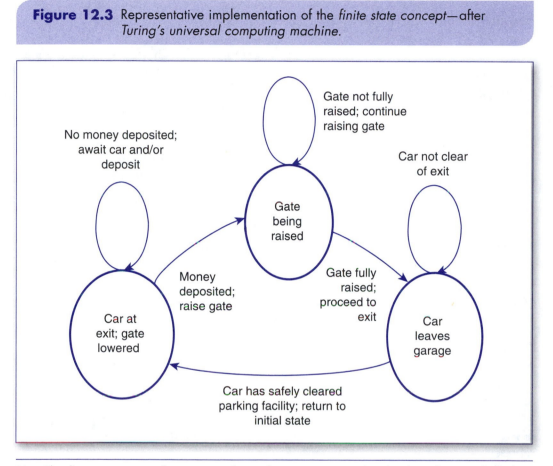

Note: The diagram represents the sequence of steps for exiting a car parking lot. A machine can be built to implement the sequence of operations needed to automate the operation. The ovals represent the condition or *state* of the system, which is retained in *memory* elements ("flip flops"). The arrows indicate what conditions change the state of the machine (and memory). State descriptions are as follows:

CAR AT EXIT: Indicates that system is awaiting a car at the exit.

GATE BEING RAISED: Correct fee has been deposited, and car cannot proceed until gate is safely and fully raised.

CAR LEAVES GARAGE: Gate is fully lowered only after car departs the garage.

The **finite state model** in accordance with the Turing model can be readily transformed (implemented) in machine form (as shown in Figure 12.3) with dedicated electromechanical elements that control the entire system. Alternatively, finite state diagrams (including the one noted in the example) can be transformed into a *program of executable instructions* that, when stored in a general-purpose digital computer with associated electrical and mechanical elements, would accomplish the same result. When embedded in a computer, the result produces "serial" or "sequential" operations. (The computer executes one instruction/operation at a time.)

If human behavior and/or thinking could be represented in such a way—that is, a series of "if–then" activities characterized by sensing the environment and either making decisions or generating actions—then there is reason to believe that a machine could be built to replicate (or *replace*) the animal behavior—"perhaps" even the neocortex. This concept characterizes the top-down approach to human behavioral emulation.

A basic cognitive model of an IA—a mechanism that incorporates *intelligence*—that complements the finite state paradigm was proposed by Kenneth Craik (1914–1945), a philosopher and psychologist who developed a cognitive model before Turing's paper (Craik, 1943).

However, the human cognitive facilities as embodied in the neocortex functions in a "parallel" manner (as discussed later in this chapter as well as in Chapter 7). Parallel activity means that recognition of states (patterns) and consequential actions occur concurrently ("in parallel")—such capability produces much faster results. The limitation of (slow) serial operations is one argument used to maintain that such machines will never "supplant" or even emulate the human brain in any practical way.

PRACTICAL AI

Despite the limits imposed by serial operation of the digital computer, economic necessity has given rise to a very large number of machine-based automata—both hardware-based and software-based. As depicted in Figure 12.1, the practical (behavioral) approach to AI is based on the principles of logical reasoning. These systems subsume a means of knowledge representation that is compatible with the digital base of the computer, supportable facts, and a system of rules that permit these IAs to plan, make decisions, and act on the results (e.g., behavioral actions) that derive from such models. Knowledge, facts, and rules must be free of referential ambiguity. Additional discussion of representation and meaning including referential ambiguity are addressed in Chapter 1 in additional detail; in particular, it focuses on connections between the external and cognitive worlds. (As discussed subsequently, "Fuzzy Logic" has introduced methodologies for dealing with predicate uncertainties.)

A detailed and complete study of knowledge representation is beyond the scope of this text. We did, however, note one such formulation in Chapter 7—*semantic networks*. Other formulations include frames (Minsky, 1975), cases,[5] scripts (Zadeh, 1965), and others. Each of these was fashioned as a result of the application for which it was intended. In particular, descriptions of objects and ideas were needed to address correspondence between the surrogate (computer entity) and its equivalence to the real world in a way that was compatible with the programming style and languages.

The generic view of a practical AI agent is shown in Figure 12.4. It reflects both the concept originally suggested by Craik as well as the important enhancement inherent in those machines that incorporate uncertainty inherent in predicate logic (i.e., the "truth" or "falsity" of facts).

The perception–cognition–action loop inherent in the Craik model in Figure 12.4 is revisited in the final chapter where future developments in the cognitive sciences are explored.

A number of logical methodologies can be formulated for computer solution. One of the basic algorithms is shown in Figure 12.5. (This logical paradigm for problem solving presented here reinforces the discussion on "Problem Solving" found in the Cognitive Approach chapters.) It is based on a system of given factual information and a series of rules regarding such facts. (There may be some rules for which the precedents for the conclusions have not been determined at the start of the logical problem to be solved.) The general format of the rule is as follows:

IF (precedent is TRUE) THEN (consequent is TRUE)[6]

The precedent—IF component—consists of a logical predicate phrase such as the following.

(glioblastoma AND diffuse cell structure)

Figure 12.4 Abstract model of a cognitive/intelligent agent (after Craik).

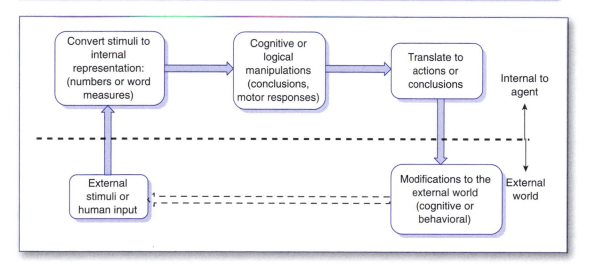

A consequent predicate appears within the THEN phrase, which includes some factual judgment that follows—in this example, this might be

(surgery, chemotherapy, radiation therapy recommended)

Initially, only the truth of glioblastoma may be in the patient's database (DB) but as the algorithm proceeds, the cell structure (diffuse) can be established as being true. When this happens, the entire precedent is established and the consequent is established and follows as a result—the recommendations noted above.

The logical (flow) diagram depicted in Figure 12.5 includes two operations that computers can readily carry out:

- Specific operations or subroutines shown within rectangles
- Decisions shown as diamonds with two exits—or subsequent logical paths to be executed—depending on the outcome of the comparison(s).

An example that will demonstrate how the logic in Figure 12.5 is implemented in a particular problem follows.

Consider a DB consisting of the following facts and rules.

Facts:

F1: My car battery is in good condition.

F2: The spark plugs in my car are working.

F3: The car has gasoline.

F4: The tires are good.

Rules (if–then):

R1: IF the battery is good THEN electricity is available.

R2: IF (electricity is available AND the spark plugs are working) THEN (plugs "fire").

R3: IF (plugs "fire" AND car has gasoline) THEN (engine runs).

R4: IF (engine runs AND tires are good) THEN (car moves).

To prove: The car will move.

The reasoning in accordance with the algorithm noted in Figure 12.5 follows:

Step 1: The required conclusion (car moves) is NOT found in the DB.

Step 2: Use F1 and R1 to conclude that electricity is available. Availability of electricity is now a new fact. The required solution (car runs) is still not in the DB.

Figure 12.5 Algorithm for automatically solving logical problems.

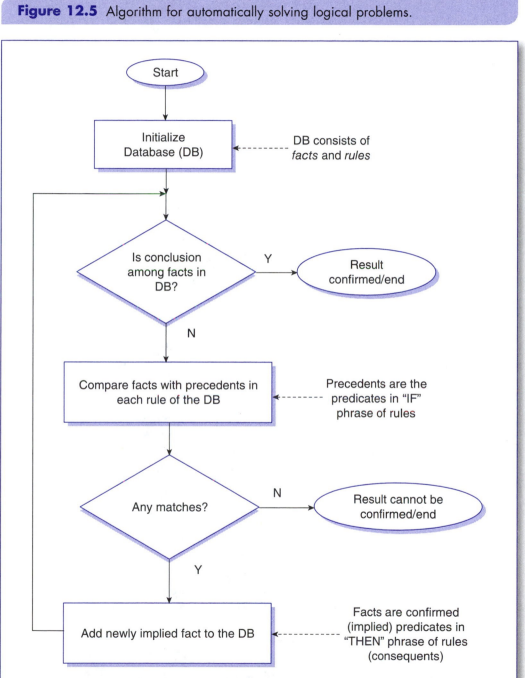

Step 3: Using R2, F2, and the newly established availability of electricity leads to the conclusion that the plugs fire—this is a new fact added to the DB. The required solution (car runs) is still not in the DB.

Step 4: Using R3, F3, and the newly established fact that the plugs fire leads to a new fact that the engine runs. The required solution (car runs) is still not in the DB.

Step 5: Using R4, F4, and the newly acquired fact that the engine runs leads to a new fact that the car moves. The solution—the car will move given the facts, rules, and derived facts—is now in the DB and the solution is achieved.

Examples can involve great complexity, and the application programs may produce more than one "solution." The systems generating results of this nature are defined as **expert systems** *(ESs): a computer-based system incorporating the decision-making ability of a human expert and particularly embodying if–then rules that underscore reasoning about factual knowledge.*

While software is beyond the scope of this text, a typical generic syntax (instruction) in the C++ programming language that implements an if–then sequence is noted:

IF (test-expression) (do-this-if-true) ELSE (do-alternative).

The phrase "do-this-if-true" is interpreted as "then" in an if–then logical sequence. This instruction also makes provision for a second choice if the "If" test fails and is included in the "else" phrase. This C++ instruction thus completely implements the "decision" capability noted in Figure 12.5.

ESs are truly representative of the first successful forms of AI and can be viewed as employing "thinking" much as humans might utilize. Such software implements the formal logic methodology noted in Figure 12.1. For example, when a medical diagnostic program is provided with numerous symptoms, it can suggest a number of alternative results (diagnoses).[7]

The example provided above (and depicted in Figure 12.5) is referred to as *Forward Chaining* because it is characterized as concentrating on the precedents (IF phrase) and proceeding to the consequents (THEN). An alternative approach consists of "assuming" that the conclusion(s) are correct and proceeding to determine if the precedents (IF) are satisfied. Those logical elements in the precedent that are not confirmed are considered to be *obstacles* to the overall solution of the problem; once all precedent elements are successfully resolved, the original assumption is confirmed. This is referred to as *backward chaining*.

A number of other problem-solving methods are discussed that readily lend themselves to computer solution (e.g., **depth-first algorithm** and breadth-first algorithm; see Figure 5.11). The concepts are similar to those embodied in ESs, namely, a system of facts and if–then rules formulated in a DB. ESs often include "confidence" factors in the conclusions normally based on probabilistic considerations that follow statistical evidence about precedents and consequents.

FUZZY THINKING: THE LEGACY OF LOTFI ZADEH

Uncertainty is a feature of human perception and needs to be considered when making judgments and/or decisions. This is a phenomenon that motivates the development of fuzzy logic as well as the need to incorporate some of its implications in ESs. Issues related to uncertainty have been studied by Amos Tversky and Daniel Kahneman (1973). Uncertainty appears when not enough definitive information is available or when decisions are required for extremely complex problems (e.g., too much information is available). In such circumstances, humans employ *heuristics* to make decisions. In these circumstances, a *heuristic is a speculative formulation guiding the investigation or solution of a problem*. Heuristics may lead to biases and, although often incorrect and/or harmless, may lead to errors of judgment (e.g., prejudices when interacting with other people). Within an ES, heuristics may be employed through "probabilistic" representations. Within the analysis proposed by Lotfi Zadeh, such heuristics are determined by systems of belief (membership functions). Discussion of this human characteristic is provided in Chapter 8.

While probabilistic elements can often be found in ESs and assist in human interpretation of results and recommendations, the "truth"—the *belief*—of a predicate's outcome is often more complicated (and one of the limitations of results derived from ESs). The "belief" in a variable (e.g., thought or action) was formally introduced by Lotfi Zadeh in 1965. The resultant logic is characterized by "approximate reasoning" and is currently the basis for enumerable "smart" systems found in daily use (e.g., automated control of transportation and infrastructure systems, medical systems [robotic surgery, anesthesia], cell phones).

Zadeh's concept is referred to as the *theory of fuzzy sets* because it involves logical operations that reflect "fuzzy" thinking as opposed to "absolute" truth or falsity of predicates—what does "going too fast" mean in an automated rail system? He introduced the idea of a **membership function** that *reflects the truth of the predicate variable*; it has a range from 0 to 1 where "0"implies absolute falsity (nonbelief) and "1" indicates total belief ("absolute truth"). Subsequently, he proposed modifications of operations for logical calculus. The modified operations are noted in Table 12.5.

While complete mathematical treatment of fuzzy logic is beyond the scope of this text, a simple example demonstrates how it is employed in AI systems. Consider the choices to be made in choosing an employment opportunity. An individual may consider three—or more—factors when choosing which employment opportunity to pursue; in this example, the factors may be salary, interest, and convenience. The individual will rate these factors for a job where "interest" involves the nature of the assignment, and "convenience" may

Table 12.5 Fuzzy operations.

Logical Operation	Predicate Operation	Result of Operation
AND	A AND B	Choose between variables (A, B) with lowest belief
OR	A OR B	Choose among variables (A, B) with highest belief
NOT	NOT A	The belief in A is now (1 — its former belief)

include travel time, location, and other factors. (We restrict the ratings to values between 0 [*low*] and 1 [*high*].) An individual is presented with three employment opportunities with the ratings shown in Table 12.6.

We can calculate the overall belief of the quality of each opportunity: The quality of the job consists of

Quality of a job = (salary) AND (interest) AND (convenience)

The "fuzzy" AND operation consists of taking the smallest belief among all variables. Therefore, the results are the following.

Job 1 quality = 0.4

Job 2 quality = 0.2

Job 3 quality = 0.3

The final selection would be to choose the job that produces the best quality. This translates into the following fuzzy operation:

Choice of best job = (quality of job1 OR quality of job2 OR quality of job3).

Table 12.6 Employment membership beliefs.

Job Number	Salary	Interest	Convenience
1	0.4	0.8	0.5
2	0.7	0.5	0.2
3	0.5	0.6	0.3

And following the rules set forth by Zadeh, the result of an OR operation is *the variable with the highest belief*. In this case, it would be job 1—even though it does not include the best salary, which many individuals might normally select without consideration of the other factors.

Zadeh's contribution to AI has significantly advanced practical development and implementation of IAs as history has demonstrated.

THE CONTENTIOUS DEBATE AND AI EVOLUTION

Hubert Dreyfus is a prolific and persistent critic of the underlying principles of AI—particularly "Good Old Fashioned Artificial Intelligence" normally identified as "strong AI." His key contributions to the discussions follow from three significant works (Dreyfus, 1965, 1986, 1992) addressing the topic of "what computers can't do" and other "shortcomings" of AI. His arguments follow from those of European philosophers such as Martin Heidegger that human intelligence is unyieldingly reliant on the unconscious. The manipulations of symbols (facts and rules) as embodied in the doctrines of AI by its protagonists (e.g., Herbert Simon, Marvin Minsky, Allen Newell, and others) are not capable of simulating or emulating (human) intelligence. The optimistic outlook of the AI pioneers like Simon foresaw the computer as being able to outperform chess masters[8]; prove important, new mathematical theorems; and reproduce theories in psychology. In short, the AI detractors argue that the mind is nothing like a computer and much in this text could form a prima fascia case for that conclusion. Table 12.7 summarizes the arguments as they have emerged.

Alan Turing may have anticipated the (evolutionary and revolutionary) developments in cognitive science, physiology, and engineering that preempts Dreyfus and others who have similar misgivings based on the fact that the brain is not a "digital machine." As reported by Pamela McCorduck (2004), an observation attributable to Turing supports the idea that *analog neurons can be simulated by digital machines* to a reasonable level of accuracy. Subsequent developments in AI have borne this out.

Over time, AI researchers have recognized that human cognitive behaviors are not governed exclusively by symbol manipulation and have introduced a number of significant changes in philosophy. (The "Psychological" argument in Table 12.7 has been discarded.) The revised machine models of cognitive science include the following approaches:

- Computational intelligence (with technologies such as neural networks—discussed below) now focuses on simulation of unconscious reasoning as part of the paradigm.
- "Commonsense" reasoning and contextual knowledge are part of the cognitive environment.
- Intelligent agents—see Chapter 13—now include elements such as perception and attention.
- Statistical considerations are employed to simulate "guessing," with inexact decisions based on experience and learning.

Table 12.7 Thesis and antithesis.

Argument	Strong AI	Dreyfus
Biology	Brain processes information in a series of discrete operations.	Action and timing of neurological signals have an analog component.
Psychological	Mind operates according to formal rules.	Even when the mind processes symbols, it does so within a commonsense background seated in the unconscious.
Epistemological—the origin, nature, and limits of human intelligence	A symbol processing system could represent knowledge equivalent to that of a human conceivably in a different format.	There is no support for the AI principle of abstract information processing because much of human knowledge is not symbolic.
Ontology—the nature of being	Any worldly phenomenon can be described by symbols or within a scientific theory.	The ontological assumption is questionable. Can existential (existence precedes consciousness) objects be understood in terms of symbols?

All of these can be considered as responses to the critical judgments introduced by Dreyfus and represent a synthesis of the divergent philosophies. Prominent futurists (Kurzweil, Hawkins, Goertzel) have seized on these concepts to reassert the possibility first envisioned by the AI pioneers—a machine-based intelligence that will truly pass the TT.

THE NEURAL NETWORK MODEL AND ITS CAPABILITIES

The primary "computational" element of the brain is the neuron, and this has been explored from various perspectives in other parts of the text—see Chapter 7 (The Network Approach) in particular. This discussion will consider its role as a *machine* (computational) component of an IA.

A quantum leap in the history of artificial neural network (ANN) evolution and one of the great achievements in biophysics traces its origins to the physiological model developed by Alan Lloyd Hodgkin and Andrew Huxley in 1952. (They were awarded the Nobel Prize in Physiology or Medicine in 1963 for this contribution.) A stylized representation of the computational elements within a neuron is shown in Figure 12.6.

Figure 12.6 Stylized representation of a computational neuron.

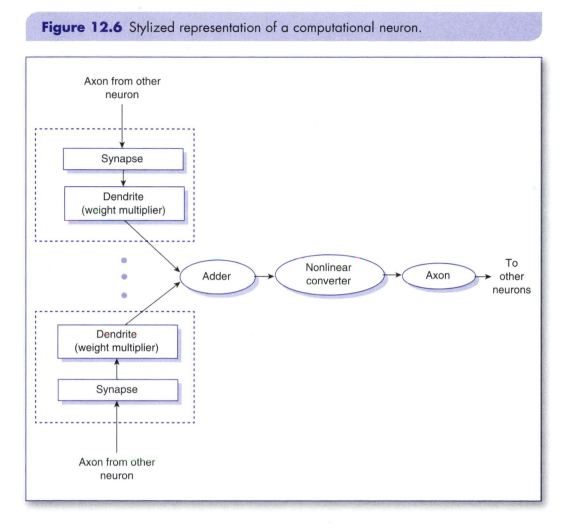

(A discussion of ANNs was introduced in Chapter 7, where the fundamental cognitive concepts are introduced.)

While the Hodgkin-Huxley mathematics is beyond the scope of this text, we summarize what it explained, namely, how action potentials (electrochemical signals) are stimulated and propagated in the nervous system. (In particular, the model related to action potentials in the squid giant axon.) Each dendrite multiplies the signal that it receives from its synapse; this multiplier can be a negative number (to provide for the most important negative physiological stimulation "inhibition"). The signals from all dendrites are multiplied by their weights and added (or subtracted as appropriate); if the sum exceeds a critical value, the cell will generate a signal that is sent out on its axon to other neurons. The mathematical elements of this model were taken up by computer scientists and engineers and converted to an abstract computational component—see Chapters 6 and 7.

The mathematical model was converted to a computational (simulated) model by Frank Rosenblatt (1958) with his experience in electronics and computer science. Using the sequential computational modifications (back propagation) outlined in Chapter 7, this "perceptron" (as it was called) "learned" to distinguish between two patterns, provided they could be isolated by a straight line. Suppose an experiment is performed to find the effects of two different formulations of a chemical formula. Figure 12.7(a) shows two patterns that can be distinguished because they are separable by a straight line. Figure 12.7(b) shows the significant limitation and usefulness of the perceptron because a straight line cannot be found that separates the two patterns. (Criticism of the perceptron led to a setback in the development of an IA for many decades.)

Figure 12.7 Pattern recognition by perceptrons: (a) a straight line divides the "linearly" separable experimental outcomes and (b) a curve or "nonlinear" shape is required to distinguish between experimental outcomes.

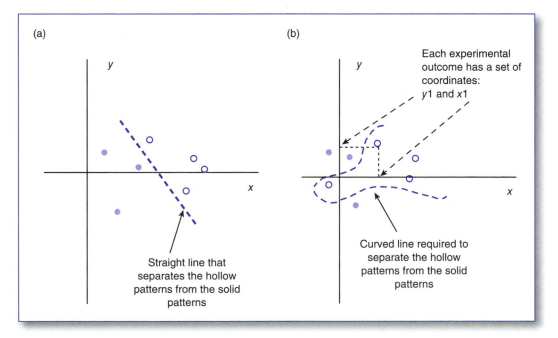

While advanced ANN technology coupled with back propagation has been successfully employed in a *great many* complex and sophisticated pattern recognition (and other) applications, it suffers from two limitations:

- It is not an accurate representation of the biological neuron and thus could not reproduce the nervous system of an animal.
- It requires an external agent (i.e., teacher) to guide its learning trajectory. (Back propagation requires the dendritic multipliers to be modified over the course of training. Neurons cannot *directly* modify their own behavior as this would require signals to retrace their path in a reverse direction; the neuron is not physically capable of such a transmission. More pertinent ANN configurations are considered below.)

THE NEW MILLENNIUM: COGNITIVE COMPUTING (IS IT POSSIBLE TO "BUILD" A BRAIN?)

Several practical developments have signaled productive changes in the past decade and given support to the renewed ideal of a machine that will attain parity with human cognitive ability. Contributions to these changes include advent of microminiature computational mechanisms, greater physiological understanding of the cognitive core—the neocortex, and ANN modeling that resonates with contemporary psychological models of intelligence.

Two recent announcements epitomize the emerging directions of AI and its potential to achieve the vision that Turing and the pioneers of AI envisioned. In late 2014, IBM publicized the development of a new chip[9] that functions like a brain (Markoff, 2014, September 1; Merolla et al., 2014; Service, 2014). Its prominent features include the following[10]:

- It mimics the way brains recognize patterns (e.g., parallel operations).
- It can recognize things such as light intensity changes, color changes, or shape changes. It can learn to draw such conclusions.
- It contains *5.4 billion* (transistor) switches that consume only *70 milliwatts* of power. (Contrast this to the modern personal computer: *1.4 billion* switches, using between *35 and 140 watts* of power.)
- It can perform *46 billion* operations a second per watt of energy consumed.
- It forms the equivalent of *one million neurons* approaching the cognitive capabilities of a bee. (Consider, however, that the human neocortex contains some *100 billion* neurons[11] with an estimated *10,000 connections per neuron*.)
- It contains the equivalent of *4,096 (neurosynaptic) computers* built within a single semiconductor chip that holds out the promise that it might be implantable in a human to assume cognitive functions that have been compromised by injury or disease. Each computer has a chip size of 28 nanometers (1 nanometer = 1 × 10–9 meters).

It will form a test platform on which to test new theories of brain functions. The key architectural (design) feature of such neurosynaptic computers results from:

The total integration of computation and memory that emulates the neural organization of the neocortex resulting in parallel operation as contrasted with the single channel computational path of the conventional Von Neumann machines where memory and computation are separate elements.

The second development resulted from the work of MIT scientists who successfully implanted memory into a mouse brain (Ramirez et al., 2013). The first step in the process consisted of isolating an individual memory in a mouse brain by "tagging the cells" associated with it. Next, they induced recall of the memory at will by forcing those neurons to "fire with light." Essentially, they artificially stimulated neurons to make associations between events and environments with no ties in reality—essentially, they implanted a false memory. The underlying methodology employed a technique called *optogenetics*. (This topic is first introduced in Chapter 6.) To accomplish this, an optical fiber fed light into the mouse's hippocampus, which plays an important role in forming new memories. The light induced a subsequent change in the neurons that were previously isolated.

These achievements represent the emergent state of neural network technology research, an evolutionary culmination that has characterized AI research within the past 20 years. It reflects the "bottom-up" architecture noted in Figure 12.1. To appreciate this architecture, it is important to briefly examine the work of individuals such as Vernon Mountcastle (1998), Jeff Hawkins (Hawkins & Blakeslee, 2004), and Ray Kurzweil (2012), who share similar or evolving ideas regarding neural cognitive architecture. While electrical simulation of the neuron is traceable to 1950 (Rosenblatt, 1959), it is only recently that the capabilities (density, speed, capacity) approach the needs that are required to "build a brain."

EMERGENT NEURON MODELS: PRECURSORS TO INTELLIGENT AGENTS

Simply creating a computer program to emulate an ANN has a fundamental constraint: The neuron is not inherently a "digital[12] organism" and therefore not naturally compatible with the architecture of the digital computer. Neuron electrochemical responses are characterized by a series of "spikes." A sample of the neuronal response is shown in Figure 12.8.

These spikes are generated from events at the synaptic junctions of the cell coupled with the weights associated with the incoming spike trains at those junctions (see Figure 6.4). In technical terms, the neuron is considered to be an "analog" device with a nonlinear dimension that produces the electrochemical spikes shown in Figure 12.8.

Figure 12.8 Typical neuron signal; stimulation and response.

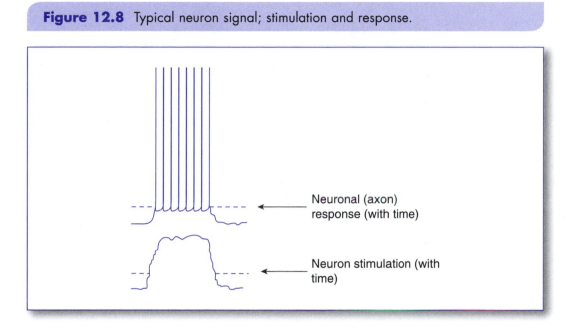

Neuronal (axon) response (with time)

Neuron stimulation (with time)

Any mechanism that attempts to reproduce such behaviors must "transform" the organic neuron into a model that is consistent with the constraints of the digital computer. Moreover, the digital computer embodied in the contemporary Von Neumann architecture—the "PC"—is a serial device that fundamentally carries out instructions one at a time, while the "seat of intelligence" (Hawkins & Blakeslee, 2004)—the neocortex—is a parallel system that performs many calculations at the same time; it is a "parallel machine" as discussed below. (The neuron model has been discussed in Chapter 7; see in particular Figure 7.2 and a stylized representation shown in Figure 12.6).

While some PC systems have a "concurrent" architecture, when examined closely, they employ essentially serial operation. New neuronal models have been introduced, whose ability to "learn" does not depend on a "teacher"; such models are referred to as *auto-associative* networks. The resulting ANNs appear very much like the one shown in Figure 7.5; however, a feature has been added to the architecture, namely, a "feedback" signal—a greatly simplified version of this modified neuronal model is shown in Figure 12.9. (It is referred to as the Hopfield Network.) Such networks inherently function on the basis of the Hebb Rule (see Chapter 7) and are summarized here for convenience.

If two neurons fire simultaneously, their interconnecting weights will be reinforced.

Each neuron is both an input and an output (which is different from the network shown in Figure 7.6, which is the classic three-layer ANN). The weights are adjusted in such a way

Figure 12.9 Auto-associative artificial neural network.

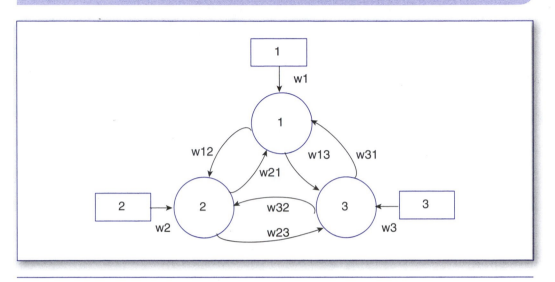

Note: Simplified Hopfield ANN with recurrent weighting; rectangles are external inputs; circles are simulated neurons.

to "associate" the output signals with the input signals; thus, back-propagation learning is avoided. (It is to be noted that the ANN in Figure 12.9 is greatly simplified, and any practical ANN may contain as many as hundreds of neurons.) Learning is accomplished by presenting the neurons with the input patterns to be learned. These neurons produce associated output patterns; the learning *adjustments are made by the neurons themselves*; hence, the term *auto* is appended to the ANN. There are two broad categories of associative ANNs:

- *Auto-associative networks:* The outputs are exact reproductions of the inputs.
- *Hetero-associative networks:* The output patterns are mapped into a distinct pattern that is related to the input (e.g., spoken words are mapped into equivalent text [words])

These ANNs *self-adjust* the neural weights to accomplish these goals, thus distinguishing themselves from the back-propagation technologies. In practice, the weights to be updated with each input stimulation pattern are randomly chosen one at a time. Technically speaking, this defeats its goal of parallel operation but is not a significant impediment to its powerful capabilities. (While the math is well established, it is beyond the scope of the text. For detailed explanation, see Jones, 2009.)

A number of software simulation applications are available on the Internet. The results from one such site (http://facstaff.cbu.edu/~pong/ai, Christian Brothers University) are shown in Figure 12.10. There are several other types of auto-associative ANNs, including adaptive resonance theory and bidirectional association memory.

ORGANIZATION OF THE NEOCORTEX

It has been noted—see Chapter 6—that the cortex "is responsible for a number of higher order cognitive abilities." As noted in this text, you can live reasonably normal lives even though cells in some parts of the brain have been compromised. For example, cell losses in the cerebellum—the part of the brain with the largest number of cells—do not produce a devastating behavioral outcome. However, everything that we consider to be part of

Figure 12.10 Hopfield auto-associative artificial neural network demonstration.

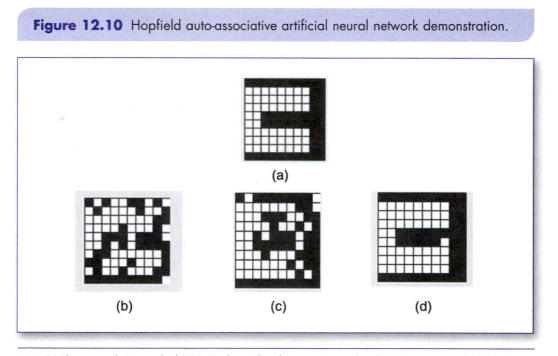

Note: (a) The pattern being studied ("3"). Each weight adjustment is completed in 25 microseconds. (b) Indicates the output after one iteration (25 microseconds). (c) Indicates the output after a second iteration. (d) Indicates the output after 326 iterations. The pattern is almost perfectly identified (learned) at this point. It has taken 8.15 milliseconds to achieve this level of recognition (association). Hopfield networks can identify patterns even when data are missing or corrupted.

"intelligence" (perception, language, imagination, mathematics, art, music, planning) would be seriously compromised for any insults to the neocortex. Noted below are some significant characteristics of the neocortex:

- *Dimensions:* It is 2 mm thick; arranged as six layers; stretched flat, it is roughly the size of a large dinner napkin.
- *Regions:* They vary in thickness, cell density, cell types, length of horizontal connections, synapse, and density.
- *Plasticity:* It can "rewire" itself to provide alternative pathways for deficits. (Silverman, 2006)

The basic anatomy of the cortex was established by Vernon Mountcastle (1997, 1998). Despite the complexities noted above, he showed that the neocortex is remarkably uniform. All regions perform the same fundamental "calculation." What is different is how regions are connected to each other and to other parts of the central nervous system (e.g., sensory, motor systems). A specific example that follows from Mountcastle's architecture is noted:

- Visual information flows from the outside via a million fibers in the optic nerve; these transit through the thalamus and arrive at the primary *visual cortex.*
- Temporal sound waves from the outside flow along 30,000 fibers of the auditory nerve, transit through older parts of the brain, and arrive at the primary *auditory cortex.*
- The spinal cord carries information about touch and internal sensations via some million fibers and arrive at the primary *somatosensory cortex.*

The cortex integrates this information to produce our perceptions—we see hands come together and hear the sound; we conclude that someone is "clapping." The primary sensory areas process information starting at the lowest level producing basic cognitive results (e.g., edge segments, small-scale motion, color, contrast, binocular disparity). Greater abstraction and generalization take place in higher regions of the neocortex. Such calculations take place within a "column" of each cortical region. This columnar model is the basis for ANN synthesis and an emulation of human intelligence. In particular, J. Hawkins and R. Kurzweil (among others) maintain that human intelligence may be explained as an encapsulation of two fundamental computational capabilities—pattern recognition (memory) and prediction (e.g., mathematical calculations)—and may be used to explain human activities such as recalling a song or learning a foreign language (Hawkins & Blakeslee, 2004; Kurzweil, 2012). These pattern sequences are recalled auto-associatively in invariant form and are stored within a hierarchy. A sketch of the columnar organization of the neocortex is shown in Figure 12.11 (after Mountcastle).

Figure 12.11 Sketch of neocortical structure (after Mountcastle).

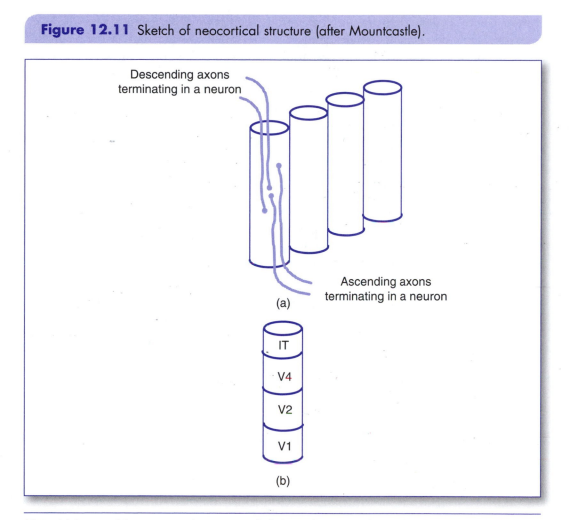

Descending axons
terminating in a neuron

Ascending axons
terminating in a neuron

(a)

IT

V4

V2

V1

(b)

Notes: (a) Section of the neocortex showing neural tubular architecture and axonal pathways. Width of a single microcolumn is comparable to a human hair. Thousands of axons occupy the column. (b) Division of column into "computational" regions. The visual cortex is shown for convenience (after Hawkins). V1: sensory input enters this region. Highly distorted because image changes with each saccade (lowest level). V2, V4: refinements, abstraction, input from higher region. IT: indicates the object (e.g., recognizable face).

AN AUTO-ASSOCIATIVE MODEL FOR THE NEOCORTICAL COLUMN

Shown in Figure 12.12 is an abstract auto-associative model of a neocortical column based on concepts suggested by Hawkins and Blakeslee (2004). Somatosensory inputs (e.g., touch, sound, light) provide fundamental inputs to the column. The triangular elements represent auto-associative neuronal computational elements. Information flows in both directions with descending elements providing the feedback necessary for learning as described above. In general, information at the lower end of the column is detailed, while information at the top represents invariant conclusions (e.g., identification of the object in the optical field of view). Table 12.8 describes the characteristics of input pattern (or memory) from the lowest level to the highest level as they might function when recognizing an object or recalling a memory. (Mid-level neurons serve moderating values of these characteristics.) Information from the thalamus is diffusive over all cortical columns and provides additional cognitive events.

For example, recognition of the letter "A" would proceed from detection of each part of the letter in combination with its possible variations to conclude that the observation is, in fact, the letter "A" (Kurzweil, 2012).

While auto-associative models are promising representations of brain activity, it is important to note that the brain's internal patterns are extremely "forgiving" with respect

Figure 12.12 Normalized abstraction of a hierarchical neocortical region.

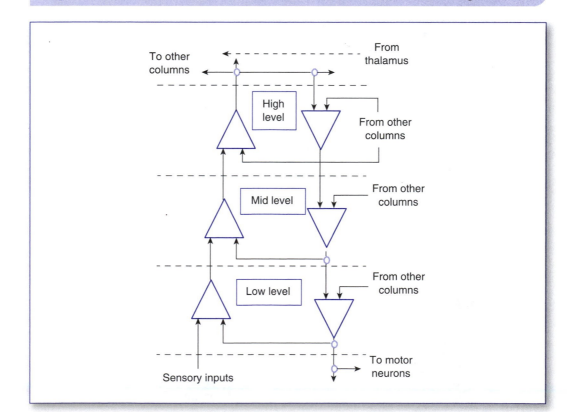

Table 12.8 Characteristics of a computational auto-associative chain.

	Spatial Data	**Dynamic Data**	**Recognition**
Low level	Detailed geometries	Rapid changes	Detailed features
Mid level	Combined geometries	Moderate changes	Summary features
High level	Spatial invariance	Slow changing	Object invariables

to errors or misinformation. Such properties are referred to as being *invariant*. Current auto-associative ANNs have not yet achieved this level of achievement.

THE DARPA[13] SYNAPSE PROGRAM

SyNAPSE (www.artificialbrains.com/darpa-synapse-program; Preissl et al., 2012) stands for the (DARPA-funded) program identified as *Systems of Neuromorphic Adaptive Plastic Scalable Electronics* with IBM, and the Hughes Research Laboratories as primary contractors in association with several university subcontractors (e.g., Columbia). As noted on the reference site, its "ultimate aim is to build an electronic microprocessor system that matches a mammalian brain in function size and power consumption." Its characteristics are summarized below:

- Re-create 10 billion neurons
- Support 100 trillion synapses
- Constrain power consumption to 1 kilowatt (1,000 watts, the equivalent of a small electric heater)
- Occupy less than 2 liters of space

The intelligence of such a successful undertaking will match the intelligence capability of mice and cats. Its architecture will reflect those of biological systems with support for connectivity, (competitive) self-organization, and hierarchical organization (similar to the concepts described above). The fabrication phase began in 2013, and the system is expected to be demonstrable in a 2015–2017 time window. (One of the recent developments was noted above.)

EMERGING PHYSIOLOGICAL AND OTHER DEVELOPMENTS

In parallel with ANN developments based on large-scale integrated (semiconductor) fabrication of the neocortex, instrumentation now permits researchers to provide detailed maps of the cortical region. In a recent report by Brian Zingg et al. (2014), researchers have been able to map the cortical region of a mouse. In the research, they have been able to

- obtain an imaging DB of mouse cortical connectivity,
- develop an interactive cortical map allowing direct comparison of cortical projection data,
- identify the topology of distinct cortical subnetworks, and
- unveil the connectivity architecture of the mouse neocortex.

Zingg and his colleagues were able to label more than 600 neuronal pathways acquired from tracer injections that will facilitate complete investigation of the mouse networks together with corresponding cognitive functions.

A second ambitious endeavor of note is the Human Brain Project being sponsored by the European Commission. As recorded on the Human Brain Project website (https://www.humanbrainproject.eu/), its associated objectives include the following:

- Simulate the brain; generate digital reconstructions and simulations of the mouse brain and ultimately the human brain
- Using the tools of information and technology, implement bottom-up and top-down models of the brain in neuromorphic computing and neurorobotic systems
- Develop tools to explore new diagnostic indicators and drug targets
- Develop a model of the brain that merges theory (top-down) and data-driven (bottom-up) approaches for understanding learning, memory, attention, and goal-oriented behaviors.

There are currently 112 institutional collaborators, across 24 countries around the world, contributing to this effort. Significant achievements are anticipated sometime after 2020.

As indicative of the extraordinary pace of research and development in those cognitive aspects that have significant implications for AI, one final development is to be noted; scientists have announced success in creating a three-dimensional model that mimics brain function. Bioengineers at the Tissue Engineering Resource Center at Tufts University (Boston) led by David Kaplan have created a three-dimensional structure that scientists have previously been unable to achieve. The work was supported by the National Institute of Health (National Institute of Biomedical Imaging and Bioengineering; Tang-Schomer et al., 2014). The composite structures included two biomaterials: (1) a spongy scaffold of silk protein and (2) a collagen-based gel. Neurons were able to anchor themselves, and the gel permitted axons to grow through it. A sketch of the structure is shown in Figure 12.13. It displayed characteristics similar to those of rodent brain tissue, and researchers surmised that it might respond to traumatic brain injury as its biologically real counterpart would. When a weight was dropped on the experimental setup, electrical and chemical changes proved similar to those in animal studies of brain injury. Recent announcements by the scientific team (National Institutes of Health) have demonstrated that the scaffold could be modified so that it replicates the six-layer configuration of the neocortex. (It suggests the possibility for constructing a complete representation of the rodent neocortex.)

The program director of the Tissue Engineering projects at Tufts (Dr. Rosemarie Hunziker) noted that the new bioengineering tool could "create an environment that is both necessary and sufficient to mimic brain function." The scientific team was able to demonstrate electrical activity that mimicked signals of an intact neocortex and particularly as the neural complex would respond to the presence of a neurotoxin. However, while the environmental stability and dimensionality of the substrate are dramatic with great potential, it has not yet been able to mimic the kind of "computations" required for "strong AI."

Ultimate development of an intelligent entity that might be the equivalent of a "brain" will require cooperative research in technology (computer science and engineering), physiology, and psychology as evidenced in the developments noted.

EVALUATION OF AI

Central to the emerging study of cognitive science is a descriptive perspective of the mind, and to that end AI is no different. *AI is concerned with the computational aspects of an IA,*

Figure 12.13 Model of brainlike tissue (Tufts University) structure was able to survive in laboratory environment for 2 months.

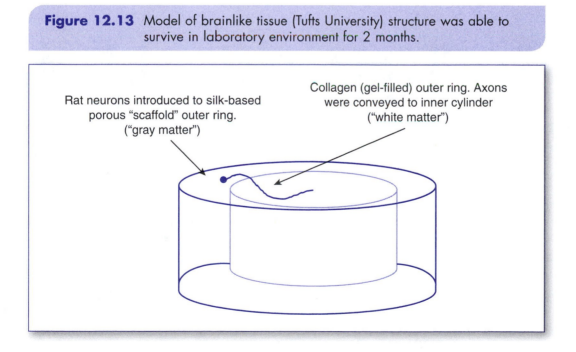

Rat neurons introduced to silk-based porous "scaffold" outer ring. ("gray matter")

Collagen (gel-filled) outer ring. Axons were conveyed to inner cylinder ("white matter")

and we can assign this as its definition. AI views the mind as an information processor, and it seeks to understand the principles on which the mind operates and, in doing so, re-create "imitations" of intelligence. Two variants of AI were identified in Chapter 2 and are summarized here for convenience: Strong AI suggests that it may be possible to develop an embodiment of intelligence that exhibits consciousness; weak AI advocates that consciousness is either nonphysical or physical but too difficult to emulate. (Some elaboration of the "debate" has been provided in this chapter, particularly as consciousness has become a central consideration in AI research and development.) To date, the greatest success in AI and the goal of an IA has been the development of machines that can "replace" or enhance human performance in well-defined and limited problem domains (discussed in Chapter 13). This is particularly true as we seek to shift the focus of research to one of embodiment: the realization of an intelligent agent (IA)—for example, in the form of a robot. *The study of IAs aims to understand and build intelligent machines.* (A critical issue is to determine what is meant by "intelligent.") As such, it must be an entity that can perceive its environment (using sensors) and act/interact with that environment (using actuators). For example, human agents have various sensors—such as vision, touch, and hearing—and muscle-conditioned actuators such as hands, legs, and mouth.

During the past few decades, attempts have emerged to "build a brain" such that this entity can learn and act as the neocortex—the "seat of human intelligence"—would. If and when such a result becomes feasible is unknown. However, it is clear that the exponential growth of associated technologies may well hasten the day when this question will be fully resolved.

Interdisciplinary Crossroads: Physiology, Psychology, Neuroscience, Computer Science, AI, and Rehabilitation Medicine

The interdisciplinary nature of cognitive science is increasingly being recognized for its role in reaching a vision embodied within AI, applying what we know from the neurosciences, including physiology and psychology, as well as from engineering and computer science, to design truly "intelligent" machines. The National Science Foundation has recognized the potential for such associations. It recently funded a long-term program to study the interactions of minds and machines through establishment of the Center for Brains, Minds, and Machines with the first endeavor centered at MIT under the direction of Tomasio Poggio.[14] (The program is part of the National Science Foundation's Science and Technology Centers Integrative Partnerships program.)

One area, among many, that has benefited from such interdisciplinary activity is exemplified within rehabilitation medicine. A system employing sensory substitution feedback is organized to provide automated assistance for rehabilitation of individuals who have suffered upper limb deficits as a result of brain insult (e.g., stroke). (A key concept designated as "sensory substitution feedback"—evolving from the studies within neuroplasticity—was originally explored by Paul Bach-y-Rita [Bach-y-Rita, Collins, Saunders, White, & Scadden, 1969].) For individuals with physiological deficits, effector information (e.g., muscle responses) can be used to "substitute" for proprioceptive shortcomings and reintroduced to the brain through other senses (e.g., visual, auditory, tactile) to "retrain" the neocortex, which then "relearns" appropriate behavioral responses. The system includes the following components defining their roles in the rehabilitation environment.

- *Sensory (physiological):* using position sensing and electromyography, information about an individual's (upper limb) deficit, a profile is obtained from a series of standardized tests (e.g., being able to pick up a glass of water).
- *Databases:* using an ES, the sensory patterns determined from the standard tests are matched against known deficits. A rehabilitation protocol can then be proposed for each individual.
- *Psychology:* A behavior-shaping model, including specific goals for position and electromyography outcomes, is then determined. The psychological model that is the basis for rehabilitation is centered on operant conditioning, wherein reinforcement or punishment is used to either increase or decrease the probability that a behavior will occur again in the future (Dworkin, 1993).
- *Fuzzy logic (AI):* Operant conditioning requires ongoing adjustment of the specific sensory goals—increase targets if the individual improves; decrease the goals if the individual fails to maintain targets. (This continues until the rehabilitation reaches its sustainable limit.) It is accomplished by applying the method outlined in this chapter.

Such a system—still under development—has been demonstrated for the treatment of the upper limb, and other deficits (e.g., "drop foot"), with results that are more competitive than those under human control. Moreover, in its most recent configuration, the physical therapist can monitor up to four patients concurrently (Silverman, 2003; Silverman & Brudny, 1990).

SUMMING UP: A REVIEW OF CHAPTER 12

1. Identity theory, behaviorism, and functionalism are the philosophical precursors of AI.

2. Influences in AI have come from a number of contributing disciplines, including physics, mathematics, psychology, physiology, philosophy, religion, literature, and engineering; the rate at which developments have proceeded has increased exponentially over time.

3. Approaches to AI have been consolidated into two well-defined practical directions within characteristic approaches: (1) top-down, with problem decomposition using successive decomposition; (2) bottom-up where elemental problem solutions are integrated into broader solutions.

4. AI is concerned with developing machines that solve "real-world" problems, particularly those requiring an IA.

5. In response to the question, "Can Machines Think?" Alan Turing developed the idea of a universal computing machine such that if one had an algorithm for solving a problem (i.e., the problem is solvable), then it is possible to build a machine to implement the solution.

6. Turing's legacy has led to the state space concept of machine representation and design.

7. There are three approaches to AI: (1) strong AI (with intelligence indistinguishable from that of a human), (2) applied AI (characterized by advanced information-processing capabilities), and (3) cognitive replication (of the human mind).

8. Critical arguments against such machines include those based on mathematics, consciousness, and emotional and programming limitations. These emanate from biological, psychological, epistemological, and ontological origins.

9. Applied AI has seen the most accomplishments to date. Resulting machines rest on a system of facts and (if–then) rules.

10. Lotfi Zadeh developed a mathematical model (with associated machine implementation) incorporating the effects of uncertainty and human judgments. This technology is termed *Fuzzy Logic*.

11. Newly emerging technologies are centered on models of the intellectual center of the mind (i.e., neocortex), where human intelligence is characterized as a pattern recognition and prediction automata.

12. The advent of machine approximations of the neuron and its ability to "self-organize" have given new impetus to the goal of creating machines whose responses are indistinguishable from those of humans.

EXPLORE MORE

Log on to the student study site at **http://study.sagepub.com/friedenberg3e** for electronic flash cards, review quizzes, and a list of web resources to aid you in further exploring the field of cognitive science.

SUGGESTED READINGS

Schank, R., & Abelson, R. (1977). *Scripts, plans, goals and understanding: An inquiry into human knowledge structures.* Hillsdale, NJ: Erlbaum.

NOTES

1. Alan Turing's seminal 1950 paper, *Computing machinery and intelligence*, should be read in its entirety; it is a tour-de-force of issues in AI. This paper can be accessed at several places on the Internet—www.abelard.org/turpap/turpap.htm being one such site.

2. Retrieved from www.theoldrobots.com/chatbot.html

3. Retrieved from www.chatbots.org/chatbot/, where a wealth of facilities are available.

4. Retrieved from www.en.wikipedia.org/wiki/Eugene_Goostman

5. Cases are sometimes called records, which contain specific information about the corresponding entity.

6. Strictly speaking, this is the logical operation of "implication," and the TRUTH of implication is more complex than indicated but is beyond the scope of this text.

7. One of the first Expert Systems (MYCIN) was developed at Stanford in the 1970s, and it has had a significant impact on the design of commercial ESs. Faculty members at Stanford's Medical School modeled the infectious world as a set of if–then rules with accompanying certainty factors. The programming language LISP was used, and a backward chaining algorithm was employed.

8. Dreyfus lost to an early computer chess program (Mac Hack) after maintaining that a 10-year-old could beat a computer in chess. The contentious debate is summarized by a headline in *An Association for Computing Machinery* (ACM) bulletin—see McCorduck (2004, p. 232): "A Ten Year Old Can Beat the Machine—Dreyfus: *But the Machine Can Beat Dreyfus.*"

9. IBM's research was funded by DARPA. It is not without comments both enthusiastic and critical as to its potential.

10. In July 2015, IBM announced a computer chip that is four times faster than the current device (7 nanometer architecture).

11. There is considerable discussion about this number and some projecting fewer neurons (30 billion).

12. In this text, "digital" implies a system characterized by two allowable signals that are referred to as "0" and "1."

13. Defense Advanced Research Projects Agency (DARPA).

14. See NSF Press Release 13-153 (2013); www.nsf.gov/news/news_summ.jsp?cntn_id=129009

INTELLIGENT AGENTS AND ROBOTS

When robots finally take over the world (assuming they haven't already), we will not be able to say we weren't warned.

—A. O. Scott, *The New York Times*, July 16, 2004
(in a review of the movie *I, Robot*)

As AI advances, society will be forced to address moral and ethical issues associated with artificial intelligence.

—Editors of *Scientific American* magazine

Will robots inherit the earth? Yes, but they will be our children.

—Marvin Minsky

INTRODUCTION

Evidence in support of Marvin Minsky's provocative quote regarding the future role of **robots** in the world is growing daily. *The New York Times* periodically publishes articles concerning the recent advances in artificial intelligence (AI) and robotics, documenting their potential impact on society. A recent article appeared on the front page under the headline "The Boss Is Robotic, and Rolling Up Behind You" (Markoff, 2010). Noted in the article were some prominent advances:

- Remote medical consultation, evaluation, and delivery of drug treatment were conducted via an advanced robot with stereophonic hearing and a hypersensitive camera. A large monitor "head" permitted a neurologist to interact with both the patient and the medical personnel in the room from a remote site. Ultimately, the attendants delivered the drug that helped save the patient's life. Such robots are becoming the "eyes, ears and voices of doctors who cannot be there in person."
- Public agencies (e.g., the military, the police, and the fire services) have used such robots to neutralize or destroy bombs or carry out other dangerous missions.

Increasingly, robots are being used in instances that can be described as dangerous, dirty, or dull (the 3Ds). Whereas such devices were controlled remotely, with a human supplying the "intelligence" (control), these emergent agents are being sent into environments where humans do not have complete knowledge and the robots are required to "make decisions" on their own. National Aeronautics and Space Administration is making increasing use of robots for planetary mapping, where delays in communication make remote control virtually impossible.

- Use of robots in the home is on the rise. It will permit family members to "visit" elderly parents and evaluate their ability to retain independent living arrangements for longer periods of time, thereby reducing the cost of medical care in the United States. In retirement homes, robots (with human- or animal-like mechanisms) can provide interaction with the elderly who would otherwise be devoid of "human" interaction for long periods of time.

As Markoff (2010) notes,

For now, most of the mobile robots, sometimes called *telepresence* robots, are little more than ventriloquists' dummies with long, invisible strings. *But some models have artificial intelligence that lets them do some things on their own, and they will inevitably grow smarter and more agile. They will not only represent human users, they will augment them* [italics added].

Other articles in the *New York Times* series describe the following examples: Computer scientists are developing machines that can teach people simple skills such as household tasks and vocabulary; they coax empathy from machines, robots, and devices developed to soothe, support, and keep us company; and they look forward to the possibility that human beings and machines will merge and overcome illness and perhaps death, advances in which machines can listen, speak, see, reason, and learn. *The New York Times* website[1] provides a number of examples involving recent advances where AI and robotics are combined (e.g., "Aiming to Learn as We Do, a Machine Teaches Itself.").

THE INTELLIGENT AGENT PARADIGM

Intelligent agents (IAs) and systems embody three basic ideas: (1) modeling aspects of biological systems, including human reasoning; (2) modeling human actions (behavior); and (3) using the concepts derived from these models to develop autonomous entities that solve problems or achieve predetermined goals. They may use knowledge acquired in their interactions with the environment or learn to adapt to situational changes. The integration of reason, behavior, and learning in a "mechanical" or software entity are the keystones of an IA. This integration is summarized in Figure 13.1.

Figure 13.1 General representation of an intelligent agent.

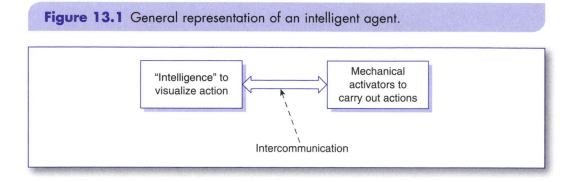

"Intelligence" to visualize action ⟷ Mechanical activators to carry out actions

Intercommunication

As shown in the figure, the IA is divided into two distinct elements: (1) an "intelligence" component and (2) a "mechanical" portion. Intelligence components most often include some sort of computer and/or electronic elements, while the mechanical actuators are present to reproduce any actions introduced by the computer software. The hardware may also include sensors to provide the data needed by the intelligence to determine the nature of the environment, which is an essential element of the agent's perceptive ability. Taken together, they may be referred to as a robot.

In this chapter, we will explore the relationships between AI and machines as embodied in autonomous entities. Emerging research and developments regarding the distinctions between humans and machines will be explored—in particular, new research that seeks to examine where the human seat of intelligence ends and the machine begins.

An **autonomous entity** is an IA situated in an environment, exhibiting rational behaviors, without human intervention. This translates into a set of requirements as defined in Table 13.1.

In many instances, an autonomous agent subsumes an autonomous robot that includes computational resources (hardware and software) without ongoing real-time interference from a human and is sited in the environment to determine the best possible actions bounded by some constraints to perceive and move—if needed—to achieve a set of goals (working definition).[2] A robot's ability to estimate its current state (how it is physically embedded in the environment) is an essential component of autonomy. It must have adequate computational resources at its disposal to take an action within bounds, having a perceptive ability, and move if needed, to achieve a given goal (Jones, 2009). The properties cited in Table 13.1 incorporate a number of toxicological environmental properties. These are summarized in Table 13.2 and must be considered when discussing IAs (Russell & Norvig, 2009).

Why Biology Is Important

Biology is the study of living organisms and includes such elements of life as the structure of cells and the basic unit of life, growth, and natural evolution. From this natural science,

Table 13.1 Intelligent agent properties and salient features (after Jones, 2009; Russell & Norvig, 2009).

Agent Property	Description	Salient Feature
Rationality	Produces proper behavior at the appropriate time in goal-oriented circumstances. Considerations: best outcome and performance assessment	Able to produce humanlike "thinking" behaviors
Sufficiency	Provides independent action, no external (human) control, and seeks goals or survival	Autonomous
Sustainability	Retains viability within the defined environment	Persistence
Communicability	Interacts with users, including other agents and humans	Provides information or control of other agents
Cooperation	Provides collective or individual solutions to problems in an environment with the associated ability to communicate. May have the capabilities for deception to facilitate its own advantages (reward).	Works with other agents to obtain common goals
Mobility	Is able to migrate between other networks or environments	Is able to negotiate hard or soft media
Adaptive	Adapts to the environment and is able to create modifications of mapping between sensors and effectors that demonstrate learned, intelligent behavior and that satisfy given constraints	Is able to learn

Table 13.2 Environmental toxicology.

Environmental Property	Explanation
Observability	Is there visibility of all entities in the environment (e.g., pathways in a maze are not visible all the time)?
Dynamics	Does the environment remain static or do actions by the robot change the environment?
Experience	Are environmental descriptors available to the robot prior to its operation or does contemporaneous perceptual information satisfy the objectives of the system?
Continuity	Is the environment continuous—having a large (infinite) number of states—or discrete regarding the number of actions that the robot can pursue?
Multiagent	Does the environment require cooperative actions with other agents?

we have learned that new species develop through inheritance of suitable traits and regulatory systems for their internal environments, as well as transformation and consumption of energy. All this has direct consequences for the study of IAs (Floreano & Mattiussi, 2008). Biology provides direct inspiration for us to be able to automatically find solutions to optimization problems that are quite complex. From the study of living organisms, we can improve the mechanical design of the products we use, discover innovative computer software, and even design robotic systems—e.g., using antwalking models—where coordination of individual legs is achieved through both neural connections and the environment (if one leg is lifted, the force on all legs changes instantaneously)—we can design more mobile "legged" or "wheeled" robots. **Evolutionary computational** models follow directly from natural evolution (i.e., from diversity, survival, inheritance, and a selection process; Koza, 1992).

Modeling Aspects of Biological Systems

Psychologists and neurophysiologists have provided numerous examples of biological models that cover an increasing range of complexity. From animal studies, we can apply findings from **foraging** behavior, path integration, *visual navigation* (ants and honeybees), *predator-avoidance* behavior (fish), *maze traversal* (rats), as well as from the social hierarchies of chimpanzees. Human studies also provide important insights for the development of IAs. Infants seem to be able to make distinctions (e.g., differences between cats and dogs) that are often difficult to reliably replicate in an IA. Humans also provide examples of high-level intelligence: They can recognize a face under varying conditions of light, distance, and angle; physicians heal us by understanding and performing appropriate medical diagnoses; and even game playing gives us opportunities to develop logical strategies for the solution of many problems. Examples are virtually boundless, with daily new emphasis on studies concerning consciousness and language that some would maintain make us unique among the creatures of the world.

Applying the Principles to the Design of IAs

The organization of an IA follows from having identified the underlying principles of biological systems—see Table 13.1. This model is shown in Figure 13.2.

The control system forms a functional representation—a map—of the external environment using symbols that are consistent with how knowledge is coded and also includes programming constraints. (See knowledge representation in Chapters 4 and 5.) After completing the embodied symbolic manipulation (*thinking*), the results are "mapped"

Figure 13.2 Cognitively based model of an intelligent agent (after Jones, 2009).

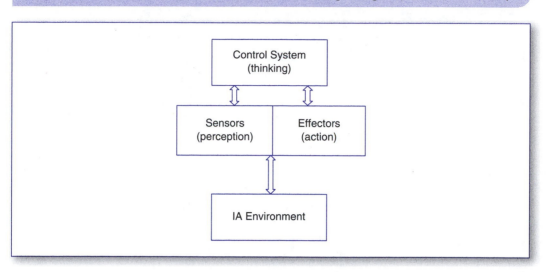

(converted) into actions that may reconfigure the environment and/or the IA within its circumstances such that a new "world scene" is created. (The control system can be viewed as a "mapping agent" between sensors and effectors.) These interactions are then repeated, possibly "forever," or until such time as overall goals are achieved (e.g., the car has successfully backed into a parking area). (This model was suggested in Figure 12.4. However, in the current circumstances, the emphasis is focused on the effectors and sensors as being relevant to IAs.) The biological basis comes from suggestions by Jeff Hawkins, which was discussed in Chapter 12, where the "seat of intelligence" is sited in the neocortex. Its essential functions correspond to pattern recognition—the perception elements in Figure 13.2—and its predictive purposes, which are potential precursors to action. The predictive action and the dynamics of action are summarized in the thinking and actuator concepts in Figure 13.2. This basic IA model thus reflects the contemporary prototype of human functioning. It can become the embodiment of an IA.

One simple sensor example is provided in Figure 13.3. This sensor may be used to determine speed, distance, or wheel location (i.e., angle of rotation).

The design of such agents requires significant interdisciplinary participation of computer scientists, engineers, psychologists, biologists, neuroscientists, mathematicians, chemists, and physicists. The understanding of what appears to be extremely sophisticated behavior can be resolved within a situational frame of reference. Herbert Simon (1969) first identified this when he introduced the "ant on the beach" concept. Through it, he explained how simple ideas can clarify a complex situation and its implications for IAs. Consider an ant walking

Figure 13.3 A simple intelligent agent sensing mechanism (a simple speed/distance sensor).

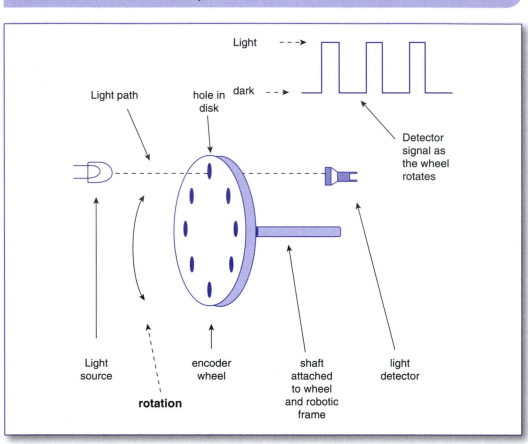

Note: As the wheel rotates, the light detector produces alternating patterns of light and dark. Speed of the wheel rotation can be determined by the frequency of light signals from the detector. By multiplying rate (speed) by elapsed time, the distance that the wheel has traveled can also be calculated.

on a beach; the behavior seems to reflect a very winding, complex path. Is the ant superintelligent? (We may not know its purposes: Is it searching for food? Is it lost?) We know, however, that an ant has a very limited number of neural cells, so we would not ascribe its behavior to one of significant intelligence. From further observation, one can hypothesize that the ant is simply trying to walk a straight line but is impeded by rocks that it encounters. We conclude that it is performing simple *obstacle avoidance* to proceed in a straight line. Successful completion of this primitive task would be necessary for survival, as well as a precursor for finding food or finding its way home (*exploration*). The point of Simon's ant is simply that it *is the situational element in the task that is critical to understand: The path was complicated, not the ant's actions.* The ant's primitive ability to avoid obstacles led to the successful implementation of "walking a straight line." This idea might easily be extended to the computational elements of IAs—the "control system" or intelligence of the IA design is sited—and simplicity in program design allows a computer to build rather complex procedures in order to complete sophisticated tasks in an efficient manner. (Time efficiency is critical in AI if, as noted in Chapter 12, the machine has any hope of achieving the same "throughput," using current technology, as do humans.) If we were to increase the size of the ant by a significant factor—say 1,000—but retain the neural avoidance program and place our artificial ant in the same rocky situation, it would replicate equivalent behavior. However, a critical difference would be a path that is much straighter than that of our biological model. It is most important to realize that in the ant example, we must distinguish between behavior and intention—*we can't judge intelligence on behavior alone.*

The "sensors" shown in Figure 13.2 must mirror those of human/animal agents: Such equivalences are summarized in Table 13.3.

Table 13.3 Robotic sensing resource equivalents.

Human Capability	Robotic Emulation (Sensors) Samples[a]
Sight/visual	Camera, radiation, and sonar
Hearing/auditory	Pressure transducers and speakers
Speech/vocalization	Microphone
Taste/gustation	Chemical
Smell/olfaction	Chemical
Touch/tactile	Force and contact
Position/proprioception[b]	Encoders
Balance/equilibrium	Tilt, accelerometer, and gyroscope
Temperature/thermoception	Thermocouple
Movement (behavioral effectors)	Motors, grippers, sprayers, and tools (e.g., screw driver)

a. Some sensors have capabilities beyond the human limits (e.g., microphone frequency responses exceed those of human speech limits).

b. Proprioception describes awareness of body (parts) position.

There are some robotic sensors that have no equivalence in humans—at least on first assessment, although some animals have such capabilities—for example, bats (echolocation) and some types of sea life (fish; electroception). These electromechanical (and nonanimal) sensing elements include the following:

- *Echolocation:* Detection of objects by some form of energy echo
- *Electric fields/electroception:* Environmental mapping by electrical energies
- *Magnetic fields/magnetoception:* Environmental mapping by magnetic energies

IA Architectures and Their Uses

For this discussion, IA architecture is considered to be a framework—akin to a building scaffold—for supporting IA development. Thus, it will include references to the capabilities and resources related to sensing, perception, control, and effectors. There are currently five primary architectures for IAs as described in the following discussion. These architectures fall into two broad areas depending on the key characteristic of its control elements (see Figure 13.2). (The hybrid combinations of these major architectures ["hybrid" architecture] are not considered in this text.)

1. *"Pipeline" (filtered) arrangement:* The control element of the IA has a *serial* organization. Data are moved through a sequential system of processes that perform the transformation and/or mapping. For example, a sequence might consist of perception followed by planning and terminating in an appropriate action.

2. *Layered arrangement, which is characterized as a parallel organization:* Various processes or actions are always available. The appropriate process or action is called as stimuli warrants. One action may supersede another if warranted. For example, if the agent is "exploring" and an "obstacle" is detected, exploration may be supplanted so that the agent can attend to the obstacle.

Reactive Architectures

Simple Reactive. A reactive architecture is shown in Figure 13.4. It is characterized by a direct mapping between the sensor and the actuator. This direct interaction between the sensor and the actuator produces an IA that is very fast and simple, and more economical with smaller IA space requirements. It has excellent rote learning properties as it has effectively "memorized" a list of responses. (**Rote learning** is a memorization methodology based on repetition.) In reactive IAs, its response list and "reasoning" facilities are rooted in a series of if–then logical sequences reflecting deductive thinking (Russell & Norvig, 2009). Its problem-solving capabilities rely on special-purpose solutions that pertain to

Figure 13.4 Intelligent agent reactive architecture.

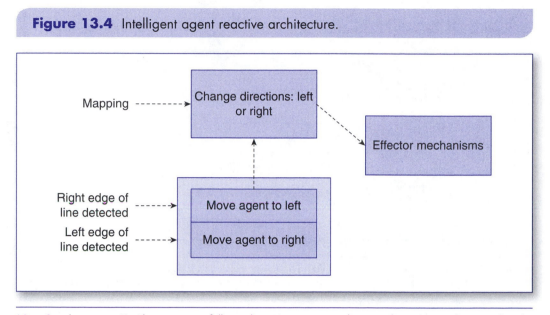

Note: Simple reactive IA: This agent can follow a line. Using an optical sensor, the agent can be moved to the left or right by detecting the edge of the line so that it remains seated on the line. (Notice it cannot detect the left edge and right edge simultaneously.)

well-defined environments. However, it has a number of limitations, including a lack of extensive decision-making capabilities, that mapping agents are required to choose between competing stimuli with resultant unresolved confusion, and that it relies on relatively simple environments as it may not adapt to the dynamics within its circumstances. This latter deficit limits its perceptive ability as it may not include sufficient internal processing to combine features and relationships of objects to detect unfamiliar objects. Figure 13.4 depicts a simple "line-following" agent. As the two stimuli (edges of a line) cannot occur simultaneously, the resultant actions will not interfere with each other.

Reactive/Subsumptive Architectures. **Reactive/subsumptive** IAs are more advanced forms of the reactive organization but have a layered arrangement. It is the result of the pioneering thinking of Rodney Brooks (Brooks, 1999). Advancing the idea of a "behavior-based" IA, he viewed the agent as a collection of simple behavior modules but having a hierarchical organization (e.g., "survival" behaviors are more important than "exploratory" actions.) The **subsumptive architecture** is shown in Figure 13.5. This agent indicates that there are two essential "survival" processes: (1) if the agent detects a failing source of power it must find replenishment, else it will "die," and (2) if it has power, but detects an obstacle with "life-threatening" potential in particular, it must take evasive actions.

Figure 13.5 Reactive/subsumptive agent's architecture.

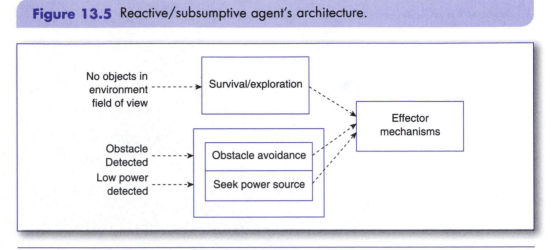

Note: A simple subsumptive organization for a freely moving autonomic robot. Control modules are concurrently available (parallel configuration), but only one module is in control of the effectors at any given time. A module may assume higher priority if necessary.

Lacking such threats, it may pursue other functions such as exploration (mapping) or foraging. These share many of the advantages of reactive architectures as well as its deficits. They can experience difficulties in changing environments such as circumstance not previously seen (e.g., a staircase).

Brooks's initial demonstrations exhibited outstanding results. The robot, Allen—named in honor of Allen Newell, one of the originators of AI—could do remarkable things at the time, primarily because of the speed at which it could travel (half a meter per second). It was built on a system of simple, primitive behaviors. It had no internal description of the world; hence, it could not "plan" complex actions. As with Simon's ant analogy, the environment became the basis of robotic action. It could move down a corridor without colliding with walls, and it went around oncoming pedestrians. This became the platform for many other robots that included more and more capabilities (e.g., picking up objects). A contemporary simulation of such agents can be seen in Figure 13.6 (a and b).

This simulation was completed on the website that can be accessed at http://www.aispace .org/downloads.shtml. The robot-prototyping-tool application (applet) provides for the simulation of a robot perceiving and acting under the control of a set of customizable robot controller functions. The robot is represented by an arrow, with an obstacle-sensing element for changing its trajectory. In Figure 13.6(a), the robot successfully attains the target; in Figure 13.6(b), the robot encounters an insurmountable obstacle.

As applied to the current example, we can simulate a robot whose goal is to reach a predetermined target without any prior knowledge (map) of the environment. Thus, if it

Figure 13.6 (a) Trace of robot from an arbitrary starting point to the target (box) avoiding the obstacles (walls) and (b) Robotic simulation with a subsequent crash.

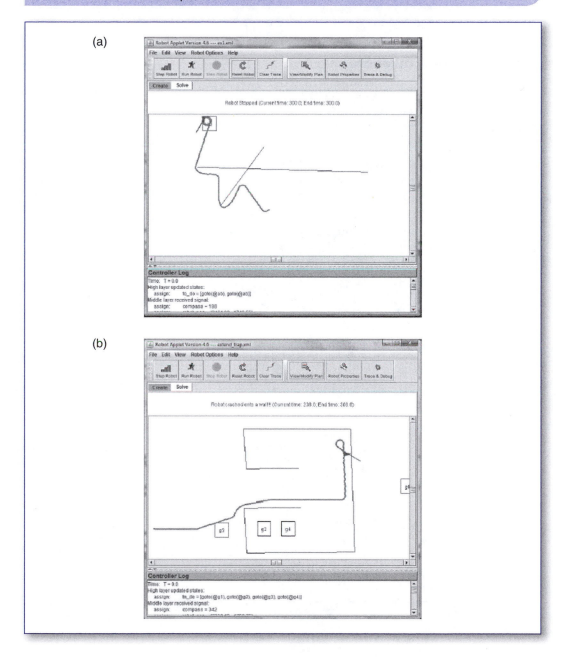

encounters an "obstacle" such as a wall that the app user can insert in the plan of the environment, it must *react* by changing its direction of motion. When it does not sense the obstacle, it continues its path, performing a searching function, and in doing so, it creates a map of the room as an outcome. The simulation ends when it either finds its target or is stymied in a never-ending loop at a false end point.

Deliberative Architectures

As the name implies, this architecture utilizes the thinking processes associated with humans. Its fundamental elements include the current state and experience of the agent and the goals to be achieved. It has the potential to solve complex problems, includes provision for planning, and can perform a sequence of actions to achieve its goals. Because "thinking" requires processor resources, it can be considerably slower than other architectures. However, it has the potential to take advantage of contemporary AI technologies such as Neural Nets, Fuzzy Logic, and Expert Systems to enhance planning actions. (Refer to Chapters 5, 7, and 12 for additional explanation of these methodologies.) Figure 13.7 depicts the deliberative architecture. One of the original ("classic") deliberative IAs was designated the name "Shakey."

Figure 13.7 Deliberative architecture.

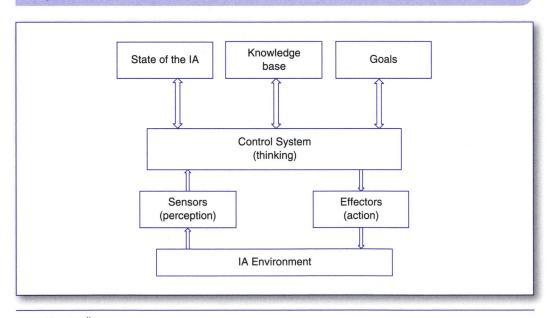

Note: IA = intelligent agent.

It was developed at Stanford University, and its primary purpose was to create a robot that could make its own behavioral decisions (Nilsson, 1969). If it was given an instruction such as "move the block onto the table," Shakey had to figure out how to do this (i.e., "deliberate"). For example, it had to (a) determine where the table was located, (b) determine where the block was located, and (c) create a **plan** to move the block from its location to the table including how to avoid any obstacles in the room. To do so, it had to determine its environment, determine the next stage of the plan, and make the appropriate move. Because of the relatively slow computer technology available in 1966, each of these steps took significant time: The result was that Shakey would move in discontinuous (or "shaky") steps, hence giving rise to its name. Figure 13.8(a) shows a picture of Shakey, while Figure 13.8(b) is an image of "ASIMO"—which stands for *Advanced Step in Innovative Mobility*—a greatly advanced "descendant" of the early "anthropoid." The ability to include many

Figure 13.8 Anthropoid intelligence agents. Deliberative architecture examples (a) Shakey and (b) ASIMO.

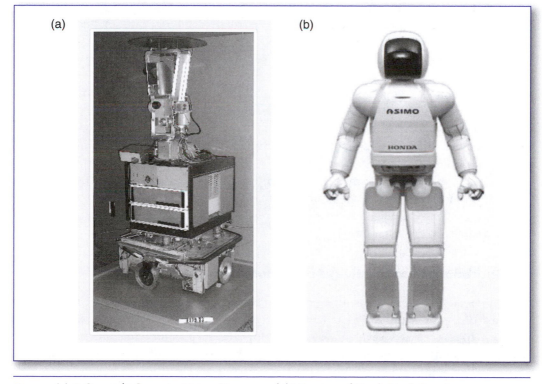

(a)   (b)

Sources: (a) © Copyright Computer History Museum and (b) Courtesy of Honda North America.

emergent AI concepts (Neural Nets, Fuzzy Logic, and Expert Systems) in such agents has made modern systems much better test beds for IA research and development.

Belief-Desire-Intention (BDI) Architecture

BDI systems store a representation of the state of the system including the environment. This constitutes its "beliefs." In addition, it maintains agent goals ("desires"). It also contains a series of "mappings" for converting beliefs and desires into actions ("intentions"). The BDI architecture is considered to be within the broad realm of deliberative architectures. Discussion of some of the differences between the deliberative architectures and the specialized BDI arrangement are beyond the scope of this narrative. It is included here for completeness and because it can be recognized as such in literature (Wooldridge, 2000).

Deliberative architectures may take advantage of the many human intellectual capabilities. (These have been explored in greater depth in Chapters 5 through 9.) They are briefly summarized here for convenience:

- *Trial-and-error learning*: Responses to stimuli produce external errors, which can be rectified when such stimuli reoccur
- *Rote learning*: Direct associations between stimulus and response that can be memorized from a list of such connections
- *Operant conditioning*: A highly developed form of learning involving positive and negative behavioral reinforcements
- *Reasoning*—*ability to draw inferences*: Specific logical decisions may come from deduction, induction, and abductive thinking
- *Problem solving*: A variety of strategies for arriving at acceptable solutions to a problem, including among others special purpose solutions, general purpose solutions, and means–ends analysis
- *Perception*: Creating a model (function) from observed facts and circumstances (or from internal stimuli, e.g., dreams)
- *Language*: Unambiguous knowledge representation and conversion into natural language representations

Blackboard (Cooperative) Architectures

The use of multiple IAs is an emerging research and development subject of interest because of its implications for changing social environments. Applications[3] embrace topics where a cooperative endeavor underlies the purposes, such as foraging and coverage, traffic control, multirobot soccer, multirobot cooperation in space, and multirobot coordination for complex tasks—among many others. The architecture of these cooperative agents is shown in Figure 13.9.

Figure 13.9 Blackboard architecture.

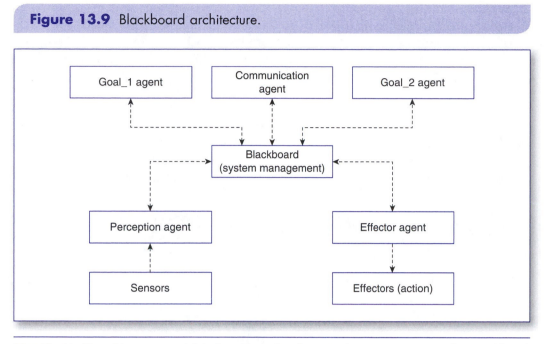

Note: The blackboard is a common (global) work area for all agents. Agents cooperate to solve a problem. It stores knowledge about the environment. Goal_1 agent might be the goal definition, while Goal_2 agent could be the planning agent.

Such architectures are characterized by two significant features:

1. *The blackboard:* A central, common, and global agent exists so that all the cooperating agents have access to the current state of the environment. The blackboard agent provides for overall management of the system. A significant challenge exists for this element. When two or more of the cooperating agents attempt to develop competing effector demands, the blackboard must be able to make appropriate decisions. This can be particularly difficult in changing environments.

2. *Team based:* Human behavior may be characterized as the decomposition of the problems into its component parts. This is the strategy depicted in Figure 13.9.

In the examples that follow, cooperation is inherent in the tasks to be completed.

Firefighting Team. Firefighting instances may include a number of well-defined tasks: (a) locating the fire, (b) fighting the fire with an appropriate countermeasure, (c) medical assistance, (d) removal of the victim(s), (e) demolition, and (f) coordination—by the local "fire chief" or "blackboard" on the site. The activities and locations of all these agents lend themselves to the blackboard architecture and are consistent with the advantages of such systems, including a current state of system ("blackboard"), with up-to-date knowledge supplied by the agents and a controller agent to coordinate the actions of other system agents (Figure 13.10).

Playing Soccer, a Community of IAs. Two undergraduate engineering students at the Indian Institute of Technology[4] have demonstrated simulation of a soccer environment modeled after the theories developed by Howie Choset and his colleagues (2005) at the Massachusetts Institute of Technology (Kayrak, n.d.).[5] By way of total attendance, soccer—referred to as "football" in European and other countries—enjoys more attendance than

Figure 13.10 Multiagent environments and the blackboard architecture.

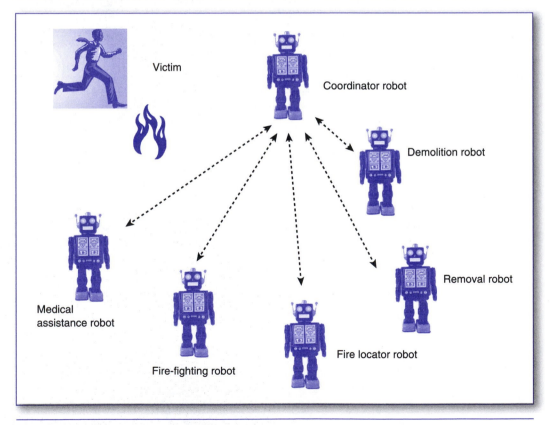

any major sporting event. (In 2014, worldwide attendance exceeded 34 million people, exceeding the second most attendance—football in the United States was second with an attendance of 17.6 million.) By its nature, it attracts roboticists to compete in such contests as RoboCup—sponsored by the Robocup Federation—to compete in annual competitions. As noted on its website,

> The RoboCup@Home league aims to develop service and assistive robot technology with high relevance for future personal domestic applications. It is the largest international annual competition for autonomous service robots and is part of the RoboCup initiative. A set of benchmark tests is used to evaluate the robots' abilities and performance in a realistic non-standardized home environment setting.

As such, this invites many IA developers to explore such endeavors using simulation to determine the best strategies for competing. Such undertakings provide research opportunities for the study of motion planning, multiagent planning and cooperation, bipedal robotics, and other IA-related topics. In the description provided by the students (Ajinkya Jain and Anuj Agarwal), the program they employed for their simulation used a software program designated A*. This algorithm is the logical implementation of the cognitive concept of determining the "cost" of going from a starting point to a destination. (Problem solving was discussed in Chapter 5.) The A* algorithm is explained in Figure 13.11.

Soccer is a game with 11 players on each side: The simulation summarized here is a modified form that is restricted to 3 players on each team. The purpose is to study a number of factors regarding multiagent environments: motion planning, multiagent environments, and bipedal robotics. The parameters of the simulation are noted as follows:

- Three players on a team.
- Two teams: Team 1, offense with the ball, and Team 2, defense to protect the goal (target).
- Both teams use the A* planning algorithm.
- Goal of Team 1 is to get the (soccer) ball to the target zone.
- Goal of Team 2 is to reach the player on Team 1 with the ball (thus, blocking Team 1 from "scoring" a goal). The speed of both team players is a variable to study A* as an effective planner.
- Team 1 remains in possession of the ball until simulation terminates as described below.
- Player positions are predefined at the start, but their position changes as the simulation progresses.
- One player in Team 1 starts with the ball.

Figure 13.11 The A* planning algorithm.

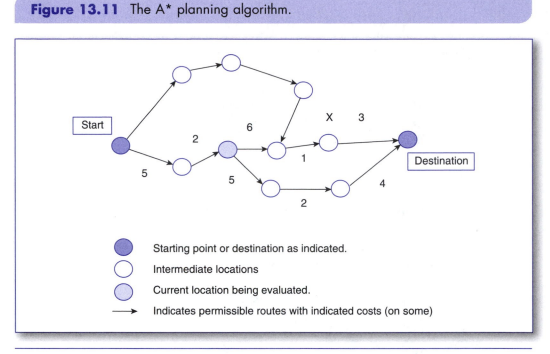

Note: A* is based on estimating the cost from start to destination. It consists of two parts: (1) the cost to get to the location being evaluated and (2) estimating the cost from that point to the destination. The next move would be to find the total cost that is smaller. In the present instance, the path from the start to the current location being evaluated is 7; the next intermediate step would be to move from the current location to location "X" because the total cost is 17, while the alternative path is 18. (This is one of the calculations that must be made for all alternatives.)

- Simulation terminates when a player from Team 1 (not necessarily the one having the ball at the start but also anyone having received it by a pass from another player) enters the goal region of Team 2 or a player from Team 1 with the ball is stuck (obstructed) between the opponent's players and cannot pass the ball to another teammate.
- Using A*, the player with the ball either advances toward the goal or passes it to a teammate if blocked.
- Simulation takes into account the availability of a teammate to receive a pass.
- Passes occur instantaneously.
- Team 2 (defense) attempts to block (intercept) a pass or block Team 1's ball carrier (see Figure 13.12).

The simulation demonstrates that the A* graphical planning algorithm may be a useful tool in studying multiagent environments.

Figure 13.12 Results of the multiagent soccer simulation: (a) stylized sketch of simulation field from multiagent study and (b) simulation sequence from the study in which Team 1 is the winner showing both offensive and defensive paths.

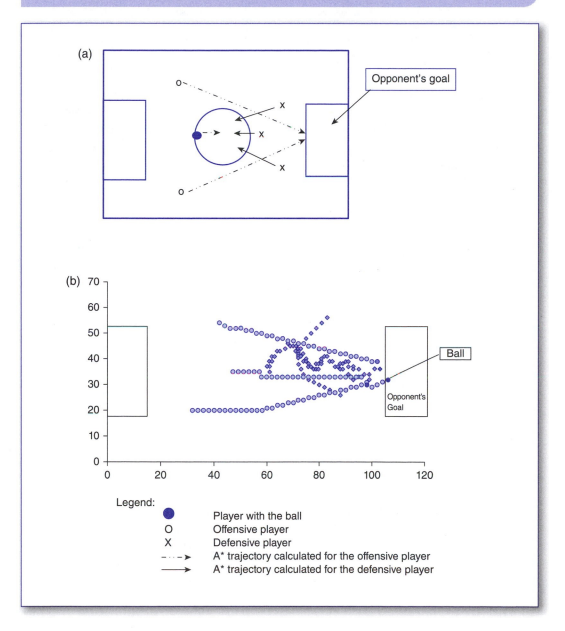

EMERGING DEVELOPMENTS

The *International Business Times* recently reported that a robot (named "Nao") will begin replacing tellers at a number of bank branches in Japan.[6] The announcement included the following: "(Nao) has cameras in his face to analyze customers' emotions from their facial expressions, and microphones to judge their mood by tone of voice; he can greet customers in 19 different languages and ask which service they need."

The 21st century will see an explosion of robot–human interactive applications particularly requiring a depth of understanding of emotions—an obstacle to the visions of the founding fathers of strong AI (Minsky, McCarthy) that detractors have argued. Commerce is a driving force in these developments. In the coming years (2014–2017), worldwide sales of robots will reach $20 billion and will involve more than 200,000 robotic units.[7]

In the immediate future, we can look forward to robotic IAs that can reproduce the skills of therapists, caregivers, guides, and security guards. Developers foresee the near future where any form of human labor can be emulated, although intelligence levels accorded to humans—thinking completely on their own—have yet to arrive. Key to new robotic embodiments rests on their humanlike appearance and capabilities. For an IA to function within a building, it must have abilities permitting it to navigate in environments full of handles, switches, and other architectural features of human living. Will we "accept" such "faux-people" remains to be answered. (It borders on our complete understanding of what it means to be human.) Improvements in computer vision, processing power of computers, data storage, sensor improvements (size, cost), and new software algorithms (for planning and moving in complex environments) are making this accommodation more pressing. The nature of robotic IAs is changing as described below. Whereas industrial robots of the past 50 years have been built for strength and accuracy, modern agents are much closer to our neural structures. Consider an abbreviated list of computer-based agents that are now, or becoming, commonplace in the culture[8] (see Table 13.4). (One might suggest that humans are becoming cyborgs.)

Table 13.4 provides partial evidence of the broad extent of ongoing research in the development of IAs that may reach the goals established by the proponents of strong AI. Worthy of note is the thinking of Ben Goertzel that is briefly discussed below.

Ben Goertzel and Artificial General Intelligence

It has been previously noted—see Chapter 12—that the ultimate goal of machine-based intelligence is to create an agent that could perform any intellectual task that a human being is able to do. For AI, this has been designated as "strong AI." There are several leading proponents of this goal—they are designated as "futurists," such as Ray Kurzweil—and Ben Goertzel must be mentioned in this regard. The agreed implications for a "strong"

Table 13.4 Advancing intelligent agent technologies.

Application	Notes	Reference
Cochlear implant	A surgically implanted electronic device provides a sense of sound for severely hearing impaired.	Gantz and Turner (2004)
Deep-brain stimulation	For several debilitating motor symptoms (Parkinson's disease), including tremor, rigidity, stiffness, slowed movement, and gait problems.	Shin, Dixon, Okonkwo, and Richardson (2014)
Minimally invasive prosthesis	Translates signals recorded from the surface of the brain into computer commands. Being adapted into a neural interface for people who are paralyzed or have motor impairments from neurodegenerative disease.	Gravitz (2011)
CoBots—collaborative mobile robots	Intelligent robots that Cooperate, Observe, Reason, Act, and Learn (CORAL): "symbiotic autonomy"—when lost, will call a human for location, guide, and mail delivery.	See website of Manuela Veloso at Carnegie Mellon (http://www.cs.cmu.edu/~mmv/)
Autonomous Robotic Manipulation	Manipulators with a high degree of autonomy capable of serving multiple purposes Surpass the performance level of remote manipulation systems that are controlled directly by a human operator Develop a hardware that enables robots to autonomously grasp and manipulate objects in unstructured environments, with humans providing only high-level direction	See website of Dr. Gill Pratt at DARPA (http://www.darpa.mil/)
DARPA Robotics Challenge	Develop human-supervised ground robots capable of executing complex tasks in dangerous, degraded, and human-engineered environments.	
Systems of Neuromorphic Adaptive Plastic Scalable Electronics	Biological neural systems (brain) process large amounts of information and consume very little power. These will exceed limitations in current computer technology. Neuromorphic computers may achieve such outcomes. Develop nanometer-scale electronic synaptic components: Vary strength between two neurons in a manner analogous to that seen in biological systems	
"Cloud robotics": Use the Internet for parallel computation and resource sharing	Improve robotic performance Index global data Parallel grid computing: statistics, learning, and motion planning Sharing: code, data, algorithms, and hardware design Robot learning: share trajectories, policies, and outcomes Call centers: on-demand human guidance for evaluation, learning, and error recovery	See website of Dr. Ken Goldberg (http://goldberg.berkeley.edu/) and Kehoe, Patil, Abbeel, and Goldberg (2015)

AI are reasoning, knowledge representation (including "commonsense" knowledge), planning ability, capability to learn, and ability to communicate using natural language. In addition to these characteristics, the ultimate IA must be able to sense the environment, move and manipulate objects, and perhaps the most challenging of all to date, exhibit imagination. Ben Goertzel[9] has provided a designation for this, namely, an **artificial general intelligence**. As such, it would represent the consummate IA in our discussions. As a measure of assessment of the artificial general intelligence, a number of tests have been proposed. They are as follows:

- *Turing:* The Turing test has previously been described in Chapter 12
- *Goertzel (the Coffee test):* Have the machine enter a home (American) and make coffee (e.g., find a machine, find coffee, add water, brew coffee, and serve in a mug)
- *Goertzel (the robotic student test):* Enroll in a college course and take and pass all the required courses for a degree
- *Nilsson (1998; employment test):* Obtain an economically significant job and perform as well or better than others performing the same tasks. (In this regard, note the opening narrative example in Emerging Developments).

As Goertzel (2014) notes in his seminal arguments for achieving Kurzweil's "singularity,"

I thoroughly believe that the transition from human intelligence to transhuman artificial intelligence is going to be far huger than any transformation in the history of humanity—more akin to the transition from bacteria to humans, or from rocks to bacteria, if one wants to draw historical analogies. In the shorter term, there will be plenty of dramatic implications for human society and psychology. And in the longer term, the implications will go way, way beyond anything we can imagine. Both the shorter-term and longer-term implications are amazing and exciting to think about.

Two areas where the challenges are particularly demanding are making IAs appear physically more human and providing the IA with emotions similar to those of humans. These are briefly discussed below.

Social Robots and Their Emotional Substructures

Social robotics is the study of robots that can interact and communicate with other robots, humans, and the environment, and includes the context in which they operate (social and cultural). (In recognition of its importance as a research area, a number of pertinent articles can be found in the *International Journal of Social Robotics*.[10]) Three technologies are foundational for the realization of a social robot. These are as follows:

1. *Agent mobility*: Robotic autonomous navigation in the environment, including those not previously encountered

2. *Agent interaction*: The agent must be equipped with vision and communication skills (talk, listen), be able to express emotions (speech and gestures), and evoke emotions in other agents. The interactive property or the response to social learning situations can be self-initiated.

3. *Agent connectivity*: Must be capable of communicating through a cloud-based search engine to find information as well as enabling contact with human supervisors providing a telepresence for interceding.

The Agent as an Emotion Machine

Human emotions are a consequence of cognitive states that include subjective perceptions, conscious experience, a variety of psychophysical expressions, biological reactions, and cognitive mental state. By one counting,[11] there are more than 75 different human emotions (e.g., affection, anger, angst, boredom, confidence, contempt, desire, depression, ecstasy, envy, self-confidence, sorrow, surprise, zeal, zest, etc.). Reproducing these behaviors in an IA is a challenge of extraordinary proportions. However, this has not discouraged—another emotion—numerous researchers from undertaking such endeavors. Two efforts in this regard are indicative of the emerging directions in robotic IAs.

Cynthia Breazeal. Cynthia Breazeal can be considered a pioneer in creating robots imbued with emotions. She is a recognized leader in the development of social robotics, and with Kismet in particular, which first appeared in the late 1990s (Breazeal, 2002). In 2014, Breazeal introduced "Jibo," the latest implementation of a social robot intended for use in the home. In a recent interview with the *IEEE Spectrum* journal,[12] she noted the following:

> The way that the personal robots revolution is going to really happen is by making it a platform," she says. "Because once you do that, suddenly you can have a robot that can do many things for you, for many different people, versus these niche robots that only vacuum or only clean your gutter. (Guizzo, 2014)

A brief summary of the resources and purposes of Jibo include the following:

- Interactive helper for families
- Equipped with an initial set of skills, it has camera capability (tracks faces, snaps pictures, e.g., "selfies"), keeps track of family schedules, and helps people to interact
- "Storyteller" (will relate stories with sound effects, graphics, and movement)

- Will "play a role" in the social circumstances rather than being a "tool" as many such endeavors provide
- Open to developers—in keeping with current "app-oriented" social environments
- Recognize users and understand speech
- In addition to its internal processor, and software operating system, it includes two cameras (detect and track people), microphone array (sound localization), body touch sensors, multiple motors and belt system (for fast, smooth motion), and Wi-Fi (for network connectivity)
- Normally plugged in for power but capable of battery operation for 30 minutes from an "app" installation such as those available for smartphones

Breazeal is confident that Jibo meets the definition of a "social robot." It may not seem like the extended idea of a robot as it doesn't have arms or legs, so its "human" image falls short of our prejudices. However, "she insisted that they did not build robots with arms or able to drive around. Because of their cost and complexity, manipulation and locomotion are "way, way down the line."

FEELIX GROWING (Feel, Interact, eXpress: A Global Approach to Development With Interdisciplinary Grounding).[13] A consortium of universities and robotic companies across Europe (funded by the European Commission) have banded together to develop robots that learn, interact, and respond to humans as children might do. (The concept of building an IA that is the equivalent of a child and have it develop (learn) as such is a long-standing idea.) As with children in development, these robots are programmed to do the following:

- Learn to adapt to the actions and mood of their human caregivers
- Become attached to the individual who supplies the appropriate personality and learning needs of the agent: A bond develops and the stronger this bond, the greater the resulting learning experience
- They can express anger, fear, sadness, happiness, excitement, and pride. They will appear distressed when a caregiver fails to respond to their frustrations

The underlying models stem from bonding behaviors of very young children as well as chimpanzees and other nonhuman primates. It is not the first time that the emotional aspects of IAs have been studied (i.e., see Breazeal above): It is, however, an attempt to provide such facilities for an agent that is the equivalent of a child. In addition, the research is exploring nonverbal cues and emotions associated with physical postures, gestures, and movements of the body and not simply those exhibited by the face or through verbal avenues. These robots will learn to provide caregiving and companionship in hospital settings (e.g., with diabetic children and at other care venues).

Interdisciplinary Crossroads: Physiology, Psychology, Neuroscience, Computer Science, AI, Engineering, and Rehabilitation Medicine

Where does the mind (i.e., the cognitive entity) end and the machine begin? In 2005, scientists at Duke as well Cal Tech developed technologies that would enable primates (and ultimately humans) to operate machines exclusively through brain signals. At Cal Tech, scientists have been able to decode conscious intent. Rodney Brooks (1999) suggests the possibility that, within 20 years, the computational power of the computer will surpass that of a human brain. Taking this into account (as well as the expanding use of the surgical procedures for embedding silicon and steel inside human beings to compensate for lost capabilities), one can question our mortality as well as what it means to be human. Just as it took centuries for people to accept the fact that our universe is not Earth centered, as well as the theory of evolution (and animal intelligence that is comparable to ours, in many ways), the equivalence of man and machine may someday be accepted.

In a recent issue of the *New York Times*, Benedict Carey (2012) noted the following:

Two people who are virtually paralyzed from the neck down have learned to manipulate a robotic arm with just their thoughts, using it to reach out and grab objects. One of them, a woman, was able to retrieve a bottle containing coffee and drink it from a straw—the first time she had served herself since her stroke 15 years earlier, scientists reported.

An outline of the accomplishment (Hochberg et al., 2012) is summarized as follows:

- Two subjects: Man (66) and woman (58), both with stroke effects that left them as quadriplegics
- A tiny sensor (akin to an 81mg aspirin in size) was injected into a region of the motor cortex that is active during arm/hand movement
- The sensor chip transmitted neuronal signals through a wire to a computer; these were recorded and mapped into movement commands
- With psychological behavior shaping, the participants were able to gain control of their arms
- Both could move the robotic arm and hand and reached a level of skill that permitted them to pick up foam objects. Figure 13.13 shows the arrangement.

Despite the demonstration effectiveness, there are a great many challenges that must be addressed before it might be commercially viable, effective, and fully useful, such as direct communication between brain and muscles and an effective integrated circuit

Figure 13.13 Controlling a robotic arm from the motor cortex.

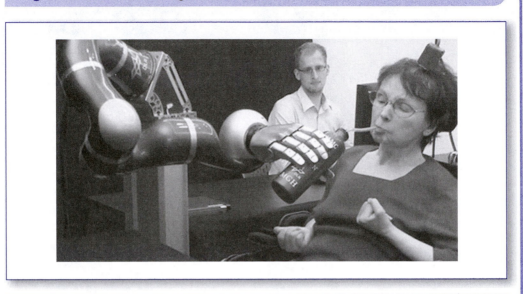

Source: Courtesy braingate2.org.

that senses signals and maps the appropriate muscle responses. Another example of such a mapping from motor cortical neurons to hand trajectories and thereby to control external devices has been reported by Musallam, Corneil, Greger, Scherberger, and Andersen (2004). Clearly, for all these endeavors to achieve their promise, neuro-physiologists, behavioral psychologists, computer specialists, physicists, engineers, and chemists will need to work together.

OVERALL EVALUATION OF IA EMBODIMENTS

The world that we inhabit has grown increasingly complex, and to an increasing extent, we have come to rely on machines to make efficient use of our material and human resources. While some express fear that the economic goal of AI is to replace human workers with machine equivalents, we should remain aware of some attractive prospects afforded to us by such machines. In some activities that humans believe are intelligent (e.g., chess playing, computing math problems), machines may already outperform humans. However, the problems that weigh on replacing a human worker with a machine remain challenging—computers are not even close to achieving the perceptive, finely honed reasoning and manipulative capabilities of adult humans. However, as pointed out in this chapter, work on such problems proceeds at an accelerated pace. From an AI perspective, machines can currently demonstrate the intellect of a low-order insect in some aspects of perception and information processing.

Pursuing the study and development of machines capable of true AI has another positive outcome: The more we try to replicate human intelligence, the more we may learn to appreciate and understand human intelligence. We need to consider several goals for such machines: (a) a clearly defined task, (b) a useful purpose, (c) extensibility, and (d) a well-defined organization.

A small sampling of the exciting practical opportunities within AI includes (a) the mining of information (i.e., data identification and interpretation), (b) resource allocation, (c) uncovering relationships that exist between scientific variables or rules that describe those variables, (d) developing effective control and problem-solving strategies, (d) improving the design of products that we use for activities of daily living, (e) explaining decisions of all kinds, and (f) identifying risks. These uses extend to the practice of medicine, commercial enterprise, law, social organization, and scientific investigation. The "intelligent computer" can be of enormous help to us.

However, designing computer-based machines that are intelligent is not the same as building computers that simulate intelligence. We should not be obsessed with mimicking human intelligence. At the same time, we should not reject methods that science tells us are involved in human intelligence. Algorithms for solving such game problems as chess are artificial and, thus, are not truly reflective of human intelligence that is brought to bear in such situations. We cannot, therefore, claim that we have replicated human intelligence, although it can be said that the IA has exhibited *rational reasoning* in that it used logic (and perception) and *acted rationally* in accordance with a goal-driven function.

A fundamental question remains with respect to the IA subdiscipline and AI as a whole. It has been exquisitely posed by George Lakoff (2008): "Can thought be characterized by symbol manipulation systems?" At its ultimate core, IAs have yet to exceed the capabilities of a highly sophisticated symbol manipulator—a machine capable of decidedly refined functionalism. It remains to be seen if the "singularity" dreamed of by Kurzweil, Minsky, Moravic, and Goertzel will be fulfilled.

SUMMING UP: A REVIEW OF CHAPTER 13

1. Computer scientists are developing machines with a number of human-related capabilities (e.g., teach vocabulary). They look forward to developing robots that can listen, speak, see, reason, and learn.

2. IAs are designed on three basic ideas: (1) modeling aspects of biological systems, (2) the principles of intelligent behavior, and (3) applying modeling concepts.

3. The design of IAs requires significant interdisciplinary participation of computer scientists, engineers, psychologists, biologists, neuroscientists, mathematicians, chemists, and physicists.

4. The salient features of an IA include (a) rationality, (b) sufficiency, (c) sustainability, (d) communicability, (e) cooperation, (f) mobility, and (g) adaptability.

5. IAs must have resources and facilities that reflect human capabilities: (a) sight, (b) hearing, (c) vocalization, (d) gustation, (e) olfaction, (f) touch, (g) proprioception, (h) equilibrium, (i) thermoception, and (j) movement.

6. Cognitive scientists recognize three necessary elements of intelligence: (1) sensing, (2) planning, and (3) acting.

7. There are four generally recognized IA architectures: (1) reactive (2) deliberative, (3) blackboard, and (4) BDI. Hybrid models are also possible.

8. Behavioral elements of human intelligence include (a) trial-and-error learning, (b) operant conditioning, (c) reasoning, (d) problem solving, (d) perception, and (e) language.

9. Emerging IA developments include (a) implants, (b) deep-brain stimulation, (c) advanced prosthetics, (d) collaborative mobile robots, (e) autonomous robotic manipulation, (f) neuromorphic adaptive plastic scalable electronics, and (g) cloud robotics. An ultimate IA remains the objective of the futurist community.

10. Social robots and emotional development of robots have growing importance.

11. The marriage of the cortex and the robot may produce many IAs that will greatly improve the delivery of health care.

EXPLORE MORE

Log on to the student study site at http://study.sagepub.com/friedenberg3e for electronic flash cards, review quizzes, and a list of web resources to aid you in further exploring the field of cognitive science.

SUGGESTED READINGS

Fan, Z., Ho, J. C., & Javey, A. (2010). Progresses and challenges of nanowire integrated circuitry. In K. Iniewski (Ed.), *Nanoelectronics: Nanowires, molecular electronics, and nanodevices.* New York, NY: McGraw-Hill.

Gardner, H. (1985). *The mind's new science.* New York, NY: Basic Books.

Kim, D. H., Lu, N., Ma, R., Kim, Y. S., Kim, R. H., Wang, S., . . . Rogers, J. A. (2011). Epidermal electronics. *Science, 333,* 838–843.

Kurzweil, R. (1999). *The age of spiritual machines: When computers exceed human intelligence.* New York, NY: Viking Press.

Minsky, M. (2006). *The emotion machine: Commonsense thinking, artificial intelligence, and the future of the human mind.* New York, NY: Simon & Schuster.

Murphy, R. (2002). *Introduction to AI robotics.* Cambridge: MIT Press.

Phan, S., Quek, Z. F., Shah, P., Shin, D., Ahmed, Z., Khatib, Q., & Cutkosky, M. (2011). *Capacitive skin sensors for robot impact monitoring.* San Francisco, CA: IEEE/RSJIROS.

Shelley, M. (2003). *Frankenstein.* New York, NY: Penguin Books. (See, particularly, the descriptions of the robotic monster's awakening to the world environment.) (Original work published 1818)

NOTES

1. Retrieved from http://projects.nytimes.com/smarter-than-you-think/
2. Thrishantha Nanayakkara, King's College London.
3. A number of sources are available for further study including the following: (a) Multi-Robot Cooperation in Space: A Survey—contact Jurgen Leitner at http://ieeexplore.ieee.org/xpl/login.jsp?tp=&arnumber=5231068&url=http%3A%2F%2Fieeexplore.ieee.org%2Fiel5%2F5230906%2F5230907%2F05231068.pdf%3Farnumber%3D5231068; (b) Multi-Robot Systems, Part II, available at http://web.eecs.utk.edu/~leparker/Courses/CS594-fall08/Lectures/Oct-30-Multi-Robot-II.pdf; and (c) Multi-Robot Teamwork, Examples of Canonical Multi-Robot Tasks—contact Gal A. Kaminka at http://u.cs.biu.ac.il/~galk/
4. The paper can be accessed at home.iitk.ac.in/~anuj/docs/soccer.pdf
5. Additional descriptive material is available at http://www.eng.auburn.edu/~troppel/courses/5530%202011C%20Robots%20Fall%202011/projects/project%20submissions/written21.pdf
6. Retrieved from http://www.ibtimes.co.uk/softbanks-nao~japans-largest-bank-1486546
7. Retrieved from http://www/ifr.org/industrial-robotics/statistics
8. Many of these are popularized and can be found in the press, for example, an article in the Science section of the *New York Times* titled, "Brainy, Yes, but Far From Handy: Building a Robot With Human Touch" by John Markoff (2014, September 1).
9. For a complete review of Goertzel's concepts, see *Ten Years to the Singularity, If We Really, Really Try* (2014).
10. Retrieved from http://www.springer.com/engineering/robotics/journal/12369
11. Retrieved from http://en.wikipedia.org/wiki/Emotion
12. Retrieved from http://spectrum.ieee.org/automaton/robotics/home-robots/cynthia-breazeal-unveils-jibo-a-social-robot-for-the-home
13. The project was funded by the European Commission through 2011, and much information can be obtained—including many pertinent reference publications—at the home site http://home-pages.herts.ac.uk/~feelix/?q=consortium

14

CONCLUSION

Where We Go From Here

Observe the invincible tendency of the mind to unify. It is a law of our constitution that we should not contemplate things apart without the effort to arrange them in order with known facts and ascribe them to the same law.

—Ralph Waldo Emerson, 1836

THE BENEFITS OF COGNITIVE SCIENCE

Cognitive science has made an indelible stamp on the way people now think about mind. Prior to its appearance, there was a plethora of different theoretical approaches to mind. One needs only to look at psychology to see this. Psychology, throughout most of the first half of the 20th century, generated a profusion of theories on what the mind is and how it should be studied. There was very little common ground on which researchers in different theoretical camps could stand. A psychoanalyst's conception of mental processes was qualitatively different from that of a Gestalt researcher. A behaviorist would have little to say to a structuralist.

The adoption of the cognitive view has meant progress in the area of bringing these diverse theoretical perspectives together. The impact of cognitive theory can be seen in the ways it has influenced what were formerly considered separate disciplines. There are now cognitive theories of social behavior, personality, therapy, and education. Another indication of the integrating character of the cognitive approach can be seen in the ascent of concepts that are implemented across disciplines. The concept of a schema, for example, is important in both cognitive psychology and artificial intelligence.

Apart from theory, cognitive science has yielded a multitude of practical applications. Research in artificial intelligence has given us impressive programs that can recognize speech and diagnose complex medical and engineering problems. In the area of robotics, we see the development of new and more sophisticated robots capable of executing complex tasks, ranging from house cleaning to bomb disarmament. These applications have a long-term positive economic impact, as they allow businesses to operate more efficiently and can result in the creation of new industries.

There are practical results that have come out of other cognitive science disciplines as well. Advances in the neurosciences often result in new treatments for disorders such as autism, Parkinson's disease, and Alzheimer's disease. The formulation of cognitive theories in psychology has provided new therapies for the treatment of anxiety and depression. Cognitive insights also have had an impact on education, having led to new methods in the teaching of reading, writing, and other subjects.

ISSUES IN COGNITIVE SCIENCE

Cognitive science has made new inroads into the understanding of mind. However, there are a number of issues that must be addressed more completely. These include a better articulation of the ongoing interaction between mind and world, individual and cultural differences, an increased understanding of consciousness, and the absence of a unified theory of mind. We discuss each of these in turn next.

Physical Environments

An important comment on cognitive science is that minds, unlike computers, exist in the context of a complex physical world. In this conception, mental activity does not occur in a vacuum, isolated from the surrounding world. Much of our thinking is directly connected to sensory inputs and motor outputs. It is devoted to interacting with the "outside," as opposed to operating only on complex forms of representation and computation generated from the "inside." This idea is known as embodiment. Figure 14.1 shows cognition as one aspect of a world interaction process. External stimuli that are interpreted by perception can lead to action directly, as when we reflexively catch a ball that is coming at us. They also affect it indirectly through cognition, as when we deliberately make a decision to throw a ball. The actions in turn alter our perceptions, which further alter our actions. For instance, once a ball is thrown, we can track it to see where it has gone. This idea stands in contrast to a static view of the senses, according to which they just passively take in information.

The physical environment argument, for some tasks at least, seems to do away with the idea of representation. Dreyfus (1992) contends that intelligence—and, consequently, the performance of efficacious action—does not require formal symbolic representation. Much of what we do can happen as the result of an interaction between an agent and the world. For instance, imagine picking up a pen from a desk. This need not require a visual image or linguistic representation of the pen in memory. The perception of the pen generated from the

Figure 14.1 A cyclical perception-action model of the perceptual process.

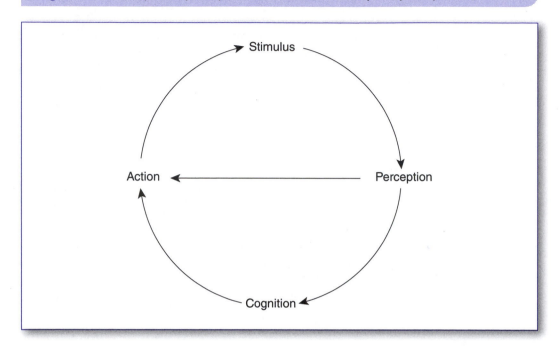

sensory systems is enough to guide an arm toward the pen to grasp and lift it. Simple learning principles based on such sensory–motor experiences are enough to allow for sophisticated interaction with a complex environment. We have seen this idea already. Brooks's (1991) subsumption architecture, discussed in the robotics chapter, is based on the idea of reflexive responses to environmental stimuli. The robots constructed with this architecture have been quite successful in locomoting about the world without any representations at all.

Perception is a good example of where the representational–computational and sensory–motor views contrast. The dominant view of perception is that it is computational. All the theories summarized in the first cognitive chapter involved a complex series of stages where features were extracted and used to reconstruct an internal representation of an object. This process is inferential and indirect because the cognitive system must recognize or infer some property of the object through a time-consuming set of computations.

James Gibson (1986) proposes, instead, that perception is direct and immediate. He argues that perception results from the interplay of an organism with the world. In his view, the visual system uses perceptual information to directly carry out perceptual tasks without resorting to representations and computations. For instance, the ability to judge our location in space while walking comes from optic flow, whereby surfaces move in the visual field in a coherent fashion (see Figure 14.2). Our ability to judge an object's size relies on where it is cut off by the horizon line, which occurs at our eye height. Properties such as optic flow and eye height are examples of information that are directly available to us. They do not require inferences or extended computation. As such, they can be considered the perceptual analog of heuristics in problem solving. They provide quick solutions to perceptual "problems." Gibson's work established the field of **ecological perception**. This approach provides an alternate framework for describing perceptual processes.

Individual and Cultural Differences

Two other issues related to the role of environments are individual and cultural differences. People are different from one another. Individuals have unique and, in some cases, radically

Figure 14.2 Forward locomotion produces a global optical expansion of texture in the visual field, indicated here by these arrows. Information about speed is provided by the rate of expansion.

different ways of thinking. This begs many interesting questions: How is it that people come to think differently? Is there a better or worse way of thinking? What is it that makes an acknowledged genius in a field different from the average person (Figure 14.3)?

This phenomenon comes into view on a larger level when we start to compare societies, cultures, or countries. Of course, differences exist here as well. Segall, Campbell, and Herskovits (1966) found that Americans and Europeans were more prone than other populations to experience several visual illusions. They attributed this difference to the exposure of Europeans and Americans to "carpentered" environments that contain many rectilinear forms. There is some evidence to suggest that cultural experience plays a role in the perception of space (Deregowski, 1989). There are also personality differences among

Figure 14.3 The physicist Albert Einstein. Isn't it worth understanding how his mind differs from that of the ordinary person?

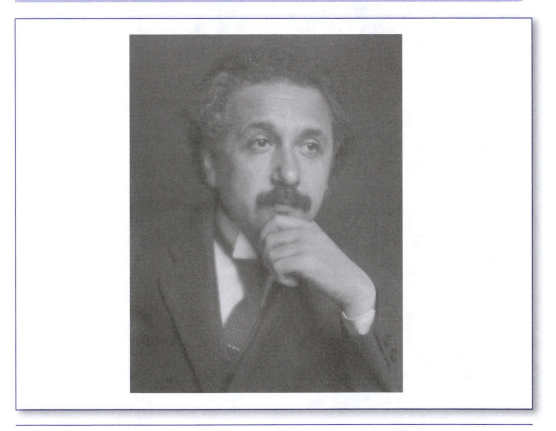

Source: © E.O. Hoppé/Corbis.

those living in different cultures. Asians think more holistically and see the "big picture," while Americans and western Europeans think more analytically, seeing the trees more than the forest (Nisbett, 2004). These studies suggest that culture plays an important role in shaping perception and cognition.

Conclusions derived from Western society psychology experiments may not be very representative of humanity as a whole. These so-called typical subjects tend to be WEIRD—Western, Educated, Industrialized, Rich and Democratic. Henrich, Heine, and Norenzayan (2009) found substantial variability in experimental results across different world populations. The standard Western participants when compared cross-culturally were not near the middle of the distribution but were in fact outliers—their results were on the fringes of the samples tested. This was true for a wide domain of tests, including visual perception, spatial cognition, categorization, inferential induction, and economic decision making. They recommend that researchers must justify the generalizability of their results and compare their findings with those obtained from other cultures. Evolutionary psychologists play a crucial role here as they often test hypotheses in diverse populations. They also suggest that as much information as possible on the subjects of metastudies (compilations of multiple studies) should be reported and that researchers ought to share their data to the greatest extent possible.

The historical trend in cognitive science has been the study of universal characteristics— what all people or cognitive devices share in common. Research efforts have traditionally focused on solving problems that every information processor in a particular domain must solve, such as the object constancy problem in vision or the consolidation problem in memory. Cognitive science has devoted less attention to how or why these processes may be carried out differently in different individuals or cultures.

One way to study cultural differences is **anthropology**. Anthropologists investigate when and where humans first appeared on the earth and why they have varied with respect to some physical traits. They are also interested in how and why societies vary in their customary ideas and practices (Ember & Ember, 1985). Because of its focus, anthropology is a useful adjunct to the evolutionary perspective. This discipline can also tell us a lot about which thought processes are universal and which are particular to specific cultures. Anthropology can help us elucidate the factors that account for such differences. Anthropologists who have made significant contributions to our understanding of mind include Lucien Levy-Bruhl, Franz Boas, Claude Levi-Strauss, and Dan Sperber (Gardner, 1985).

The quest to understand universal phenomena is certainly important and is arguably the first goal of an emerging science. A prime motivation for this quest is that it helps us understand the basic processes involved. The details can be worked out afterward. However, it is sometimes these very same details that can illuminate the operation of the more basic processes. For example, understanding why some people are so much better at math than others can probably tell us a lot about basic mathematical ability and the function of working memory. Research on universals and particulars ought to proceed in parallel. In this fashion, each can inform the other.

Consciousness

Consciousness, you may remember, is the subjective quality of experience. It is what it is like to have a brain. It corresponds to the feeling of a hangover or the smell of a rose. Cognitive science, as its name implies, is a scientific discipline. It uses objective methods such as the scientific method, brain imaging, and computer simulation to try to understand cognitive processes. Can these techniques tell us anything about subjective experience? The answer is a qualified "yes." The use of these tools can bring us closer to understanding the processes that underlie experience, but they may never be able to account for what it is like to have experiences.

In the philosophy chapter, we described the concept of a neural correlate of consciousness. This is the type of brain activity that accompanies a specific conscious experience. We have yet to catalog each neural correlate of consciousness that accompanies all the major, much less the minor or more nuanced, qualities of experience. Assuming we could do this, it would give us an increased understanding of consciousness. For example, it may be the case that specific patterns of neural activation always accompany the perception of a bitter taste, both in and between individuals. The neurons and brain areas involved, the dynamics of this pattern, and how this pattern changes over time could give us better insights into why we feel it the way we do. But because these are brain processes, they tell us only what the brain is doing during an experience, not how we feel it a certain way.

Lack of a Unified Theory

E. O. Wilson (1999), in his book *Consilience: The Unity of Knowledge*, echoes a sentiment felt by many scientists. He believes that all the sciences should be unified within a single framework. Cognitive science is a step in this direction. It gives researchers a common set of assumptions. However, cognitive science is not yet a complete, unifying theory of mind. The exact nature of mental representation and computation is still debated. The different approaches still use theories that emphasize different causal and explanatory factors. So, although researchers across disciplines may agree in a general way that the mind is an information processor, they might argue the specifics.

The multidisciplinary approach, while making important advances, has yet to give us definitions of basic terms. For instance, what is mental representation? What is mental computation? The classical information-processing view of cognitive science believes that representation is symbolic and infers that only select types of transformations on these symbols may occur. The connectionist sees mental representation in a different light. To connectionists, representations are distributed connection strengths in a network, and computations result from the activation of nodes and the spreading of activity between them.

The conflict between the classical and connectionist perspectives is a fundamental issue that cognitive science must address. But there are disagreements that crop up when we compare explanations across other disciplines as well. In the evolutionary approach, cognitive processes are explained according to selection pressures acting on multiple generations of a species. In psychology, these same processes can be explained according to developmental, learning, or environmental influences acting within the life span of a single individual. So the multidisciplinary approach produces some conflict over the exact nature of mind and how it operates, as well as how to best go about providing explanations for such things. Theoretical diversity, it turns out, is a two-edged sword: What it affords in insights, it can take away in overall coherence.

THE DYNAMICAL SYSTEMS APPROACH

In this section, we will outline an emerging view in cognitive science that may end up solving some of the issues we've just presented. This perspective is called the **dynamical systems approach**, although sometimes, it is referred to as chaos theory (Friedenberg, 2009). We start off by describing the basic assumptions of the dynamical approach. These include the ideas of nonlinearity, predictability, state spaces, trajectories, and attractors. Once we have understood these, we are in a position to outline the major differences between traditional cognitive science and the dynamical approach.

Nonlinearity

Nonlinear dynamical systems theory is the study of how systems change over time. A system in the most general sense is a collection of interacting parts. Change is a characteristic of all systems. The brain with its myriad interacting neurons is a good example of a complex changing system. We can plot change using a graph, with time on the x-axis and some measure of interest on the y-axis. Figure 14.4 shows a **linear relationship**. In this plot, the output is proportionate to the input. For every increase along the x-axis, there is a constant increase along the y-axis. There are instances of linear relationships in psychology, many that we have already studied. These include the mental rotation function, the serial visual search function, and the function depicting the scanning of items in working memory.

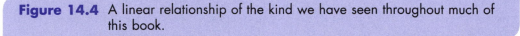

Figure 14.4 A linear relationship of the kind we have seen throughout much of this book.

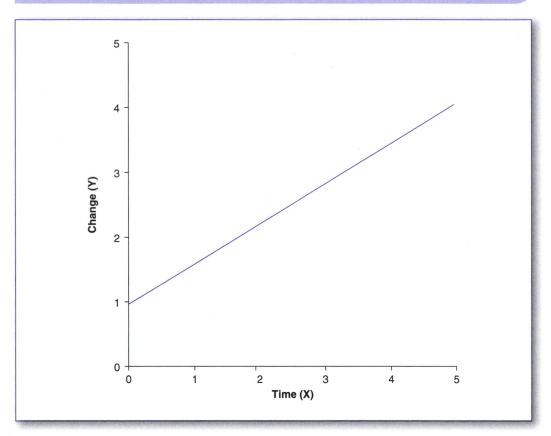

Nonlinear relationships are much more complex and difficult to predict. The output in these systems is not directly proportional to the input. A small change in input values can produce miniscule or dramatic changes in output. Figure 14.5 shows what a nonlinear change might look like. In this example, it is the logistic equation, which is well studied in the dynamical sciences. The output of a dynamical system often serves as its own next input. When our brain issues a command to move our hand to grasp an object, the perception we receive of our initial movement will feed back and alter our subsequent movements. In this way, we can fine-tune our movements to grasp at the precise location of the object. Nonlinearity is probably the norm for most psychological phenomena, and recent research provides us with numerous examples from psychophysics, perception, learning, memory, cognition, human development, motivation, and problem solving (Guastello, 2001).

Figure 14.5 The logistic equation is a well-studied example of a nonlinear relationship.

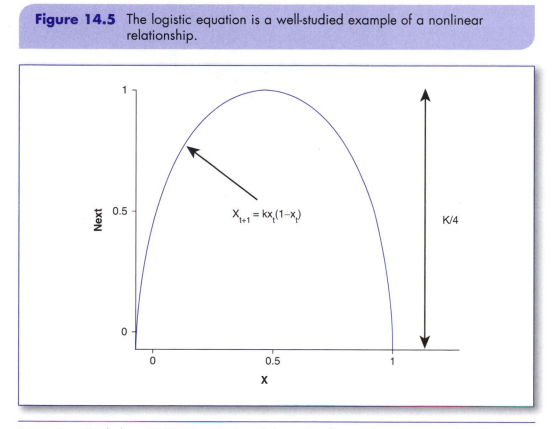

$$X_{t+1} = kx_t(1-x_t)$$

Source: From Friedenberg (2009). *Dynamical psychology. Complexity, self-organization and mind.* Emergent Publishing.

Predictability

Chaotic systems such as the brain or mind can exhibit a wide range of possible behaviors. However, they are not random. A random process is one that is based strictly on chance and whose behavior can be described only statistically. We can say that a certain behavior has a particular probability of occurring in a chaotic system, but we can't say with certainty that it will. A deterministic process is one that is completely and, to within some degree of precision, exactly specified. Chaotic systems are deterministic but only predictable to a limited degree. We can, in many cases, write out the mathematical equation that describes how a chaotic system works, but this does not allow us to predict what it will do in the future.

A defining feature of chaos is sensitivity to initial conditions. Two slightly different starting conditions in a chaotic system will eventually diverge to produce two very different outcomes. This idea is also referred to as the butterfly effect. In meteorology, it has been suggested that a butterfly flapping its wings in Brazil could conceivably lead to a tornado in Texas. The result of this is that in chaotic systems, we have short-term predictability only. We can extend the length of a prediction by increasing the precision of our starting values, but we can never be so precise that we obtain complete long-term predictability. This short-term predictability is at least better than random systems, where we have no predictability whatsoever. This means that chaotic behavior, although not as predictable as simple linear systems, is more predictable than random processes.

State Space and Trajectories

One way to measure the activity of a system is to plot how that activity changes over time. If we measure only one variable, we can see changes such as those depicted in the previous figure. However, most systems change in more than one way. In this case, we need a way of capturing change for two or more variables simultaneously. We can do this using a **state space**, shown in Figure 14.6. Each axis of this graph represents a dimension for a single variable. A point within this space represents the state of a system at one point in time. A sequence of points shows how the system changes over time. This sequence is known as its **trajectory**. In Figure 14.6, the two axes represent different mood states. The line traveling through this space shows how both of these moods might change in a single person over the course of 6 months.

In the example shown here, our person starts off feeling low in confidence and introverted, perhaps because he hasn't met anyone at a new school. Eventually, though, he becomes more extroverted and confident. Maybe this is because he made several good friends. Trajectories can be complex, wandering all over their state space, but they can also be more ordered, in which case, they restrict themselves to one region of the space. Some ordered trajectories can also continually retrace a similar path through their space.

Attractors

The behavior of a trajectory can be explained by the notion of an **attractor** in the state space. An attractor is a place where the system likes to stay. Imagine that a valley in a landscape is the attractor and a ball is the state of the system. If the ball is inside the valley, it will roll down the sides until it comes to rest at the bottom. In this case, we could say that the valley floor is the attractor but the sides of the valley are an attractor basin. If the ball falls inside the basin, it is "captured" and will wind its way down to the bottom. However, the ball doesn't always stay there. Other forces can knock it out of the valley and get it moving again.

Figure 14.6 A psychological example of a state space with two dimensions.

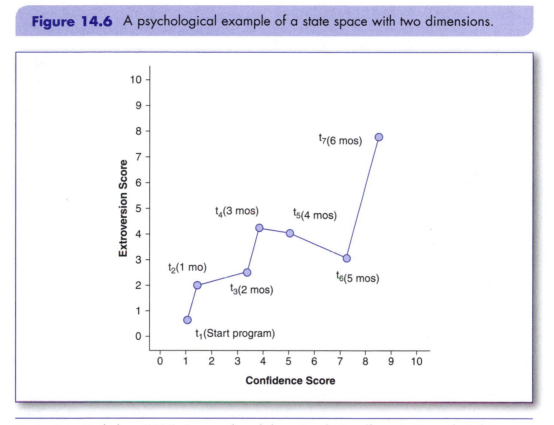

Source: From Friedenberg (2009). *Dynamical psychology. Complexity, self-organization and mind.* Emergent Publishing.

There are several types of attractor. A **point attractor** is a single fixed point in a state space. It represents those systems that are constant on the variables measured and have stopped changing. For example, a person's mood may not change very much when he or she is quietly reading a book. **Periodic attractors** are also referred to as limit cycles. These consist of trajectories that loop back on themselves, following the same general path through the space over and over again. A manic-depressive patient may cycle back and forth between two states. His or her behavior could, thus, be described as following a periodic attractor.

There are other more complicated attractors. If a trajectory is a combination of two or more limit cycles, it can follow a path best described as a doughnut. This three-dimensional shape is a torus, and trajectories that follow it are caught in a toroidal attractor. A chaotic or strange attractor follows an even more tortuous route. It can wander erratically over a wide region of its state space, tracing out complex three-dimensional regions.

DYNAMICAL REPRESENTATION

The traditional view in cognitive science, one that we already have presented in some detail, is that mental representations are static and discrete. They can be represented by symbols, such as words. These representations are said to be intentional, they are "about" what they refer to in the outside world, what we called referents. In this classical view, if you thought about a table, then somewhere in the mind there would be a static enduring symbol that would stand for "table." The dynamical systems perspective views symbols in a different light and challenges this long-held notion (Peschl, 1997). There are at least three reasons for this, which we will examine next.

According to Peschl (1997), a representation is always a subjective construction created by the observer. It is produced in a unique way by the sensory and nervous system of an individual organism. Because the nervous system is highly dynamic, the representation is in constant flux, depending on the organism's state of mind. For instance, the representation we have may differ depending on what mood we are in, new information we have learned, and countless other factors. This means that no two representations will be alike, either between individuals or within a single individual at different times.

The second reason is empirical. Experiments and simulations fail to show a stable referential relationship between a representation and a referent. If all networks were feed forward and sent the result of their computations forward, representations based on sensory input might be preserved. However, **feed-forward networks** are the exception rather than the rule in most nervous systems. The vast majority of neural mechanisms are recurrent. Information in recurrent networks feeds information back to previously processed information. The result is a distortion of the original sensory input. Peschl (1997) also notes that the environmental signal is already distorted by the transduction of sensory receptors before it even gets to be processed more fully by "downstream" mechanisms.

A final reason is that there is an improved alternative account of representations. This is the **constructivist framework**. In this perspective, representations are constructed by a physical nervous system and are always system relative. Constructionists advocate that the primary purpose of a representation is to generate a behavior, not to depict the environment. This behavior is created in the service of the organism's functional adaptation to its environment. A representation in this view is not to preserve some idealized aspect of the environment but to map stimulus inputs onto motor outputs.

Evolutionary perspectives such as the field of artificial life already approach representation from a functional perspective. The genetic content of organisms in artificial life simulations can be thought of as a form of representation, but what they code for is a behavior that either helps or fails to assist the animal in surviving or reproducing. This point of view is also seen in robotics. In the subsumption architecture, representations exist as production rules (if–then statements) or reflexes that map a stimulus onto a behavior (Brooks, 1991). Robots with this architecture are surprisingly good at navigating through complex environments and performing other motor tasks. Knowledge in both of these views does not exist in isolated representations but in the entire structure and architecture of the organism. The knowledge is embodied.

What do dynamical representations of this sort consist of? Peschl (1997) makes several suggestions. They could be neurons or a single pattern of activation in a neuron population. Alternatively, they could be the synaptic weights between neurons. This second option corresponds to representations in artificial neural networks (ANNs), where the matrix of weights depicts the strength of connections between nodes. Representations can also be seen as sequences of neural activation patterns. This is the view favored by the dynamical system school. The sequences are patterns of activity that unfold over time in a neural system and correspond to trajectories and attractors in a neural state space. Peschl mentions that representations could also be genetic material. Genes are an indirect or second-order form of representation, since they aren't directly mediating perceptual or motor action but instead code for the structure and functioning of the body and brain that later would embody such representations.

Symbolic Dynamics

The nature of thought and how it is represented form part of the debate between the traditional cognitive science view and the new nonlinear dynamical systems. As traditional cognitive scientists, we can think of thoughts as bounded, having a definite beginning and end. If this were the case, we could use symbols to designate mental entities such as "red," "justice," or "happy." Symbols are a convenient way to represent things because they can be operated on by formal systems such as language and mathematics. But what if the brain didn't represent things symbolically? Then we would have to rethink the whole notion of mental representation and computation. This is the difference that divides the connectionist parallel distributed processing approach from the classical view. The dynamical systems approach favors the network view of mind in that representation is seen as distributed activity among multiple nodes in a network.

There may be a way to reconcile these two views. In symbolic dynamics, a bounded region of state space is assigned a symbol (Bollt, Stanford, Lai, & Zyczkowski, 2000; Robinson, 1998). When the system is in this region, the symbol is activated. When the system state is outside this region, the symbol is dormant. Attractor basins are a good example of such regions. We could draw a circle around a basin and let the area inside stand for a letter or word. When the trajectory of the system wanders inside the bounded area, the symbol activates and can be part of a computational process. Figure 14.7 shows two such regions. The arrows or vectors in this figure show the direction in which the system state will travel. One region corresponds to the letter O, the other to the letter N. A trajectory that travels from the O to the N in quick succession could occur during reading of the word "on."

Figure 14.7 A state space with two hills and two attractor basins. The basins are places where the system trajectory "likes" to be. In this case, entering the *O* and then the *N* basin would correspond to thinking or perceiving the word.

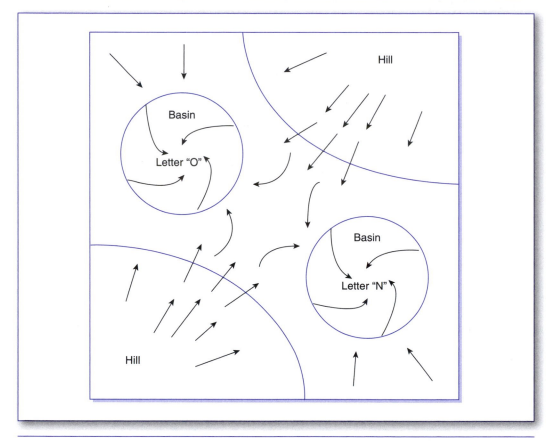

Source: From Friedenberg (2009). *Dynamical psychology. Complexity, self-organization and mind.* Emergent Publishing.

Interdisciplinary Crossroads: Multiple Approaches to Levels of Explanation in Cognitive Science

Bechtel and Abrahamsen (2006) differentiate between phenomena and mechanism in cognitive science explanation. Each corresponds to a particular level of description. A phenomenal explanation is symbolic and primarily descriptive in nature. By symbolic, they mean using symbols and rules that act on those symbols. Descriptive means that the phenomenon can be described in terms of what it is like but is not explained in terms of more fundamental processes. Linguistic explanations fall under this category. In contrast, mechanistic explanations are **subsymbolic**. They operate on a level underneath the symbols. In cognitive science, these would be the fundamental units of a brain or network, such as neurons or nodes, along with their connections and how they operate. Mechanistic explanations are also productive; they explain the processes that give rise to particular phenomena. ANNs are a good example of mechanistic explanation because activity in the nodes and links that form the network can produce cognitive processes such as pattern recognition or concept formation.

The learning of past tense for verbs is a good illustration for each of these levels. Linguistic representation in the form of symbols and rules applied to symbols can very efficiently capture the process of forming a past tense. For regular verbs, this could be expressed as V → V + ed, where the V stands for a regular verb stem linked to its past-tense form by a general rule of adding the "ed." For irregular verbs, the general rule cannot be applied, and we would need to look up the past-tense form individually for each verb. This can be expressed linguistically as *run* → *ran*, *buy* → *bought*, and so on, where the particular pairs of representations are individually linked. A mechanistic explanation of past-tense formation would require an explanation of how the process actually takes place in the brain. Alternately, we could construct an ANN that would perform the function, as has been done (Plunkett & Marchman, 1991).

Unfortunately, linguistic and connectionist accounts of cognition through history have been pitted against each other. On one side are the linguists and philosophers who stick to using the symbolic notation and favor the descriptive level. On the other side, we have the computationalists and neuroscientists who favor a functional processing account. These researchers prefer subsymbolic mechanistic explanations. Bechtel and Abrahamsen (2006) argue that these two approaches ought to be viewed as complementary rather than antagonistic. Each can be better at accounting for particular issues. For example, linguistic descriptions are better for addressing the issue of systematicity, or how we can use knowledge of language to infer other kinds of meanings. Connectionist descriptions are better at explaining certain empirical results such as graceful degradation. There are examples of researchers from both sides of this divide who have collaborated to develop new theories that blend elements of both approaches. These include optimality theory and distributed statistical approaches to language learning (Newport & Aslin, 2000; Prince & Smolensky, 1997; Saffran, Aslin, & Newport, 1996).

In addition to linguistic expression and connectionist networks, there are several other levels of description that have been used in cognitive science (Bechtel & Abrahamsen, 2006). One example comes from the field of mathematical psychology that specifies the quantitative relations between variables. Well-known instances are Weber's law and Stevens's power law from psychophysics. Mathematical equations such as these, if taken in isolation, are not mechanistic, but they can be combined with other models to form a mechanistic account. Sternberg's 1966 working memory search model is an example of a mathematical model combined with an information-processing model (what we have been calling process models in this book). This is because it combines an equation specifying what the reaction time should be with a sequential processing model of the mental symbols corresponding to the probe items, target items, and matching procedures.

Dynamical systems theory, which we have described in detail in this chapter, corresponds to yet another level of description. If the dynamical approach sticks to mathematical formulations and the ways in which a system can change from one state to another, then it can be classified as a purely phenomenal level of description (Kelso, 1995). However, there are examples of hybrid approaches where dynamical systems theory has been combined with subsymbolic mechanisms (Van Leeuwen, Steyvers, & Nooter, 1997). The dynamical systems approach also has been successful in describing long-term developmental processes, and in some of this work, biological and maturational mechanisms have been added (Thelen & Smith, 1994). Elman (1990) took a feed-forward ANN and added a recurrent feedback loop to it. This network was successfully applied to a simple numerical demonstration task and was able to reproduce nonlinear changes in performance.

DYNAMICAL VERSUS CLASSICAL COGNITIVE SCIENCE

The Continuity of Mind

Michael Spivey makes a strong case for the adoption of the nonlinear dynamical systems approach (see Table 14.1). In his 2007 book, *The Continuity of Mind*, he argues against the traditional notion of representations being categorical and discrete. The computer metaphor of mind in his view is no longer supported by contemporary research findings. It is time, he believes, that we discard the view of representations as symbolic and localized, of mental functioning as modular, and of serial computation.

He proposes instead that all mental activity is fuzzy, graded, and probabilistic. Thoughts ought to be characterized by trajectories in a state space. The dimensions of this space can correspond to activity levels in large neuron populations. Thought will sometimes gravitate toward attractor basins in this space that represent a percept or concept, but typically, they will pass through these regions rapidly. The emphasis in Spivey's view is on trajectory movement, not on the locations in state space in which they may dwell only briefly. In this section, we outline Spivey's continuity approach, contrasting five traditional conceptions of mind from classical cognitive science with the dynamical concepts that ought to replace them.

Table 14.1 A comparison of the classical and dynamical views in cognitive science (after Spivey, 2007).

Classical Cognitive Science	Dynamical Cognitive Science
Modularity: Brain consists of many independent special purpose modules.	*Distribularity:* Brain is partially modular. Much of it consists of functionally interdependent units.
Component-dominant: Modules process information serially and only stop when they reach a stable state.	*Interaction-dominant:* Computational units act in parallel and continually share information. System never reaches a stable state.
Internalism: Brain is a closed system that is mostly insulated from the surrounding body and world. Computations are relatively unaffected by ongoing changes in the environment.	*Externalism:* The brain is in the body, which is in the world. Interactions and information flow can pass back and forth between these different levels.
Embodied: Cognitive systems have physical bodies that are in the world. Representations are primarily abstract and need not be tied directly to real-world stimuli. The system does not need to act in "real time."	*Situated:* Cognitive systems that may or may not be embodied are embedded in the world and interact with it in the here and now. Abstract representations not always necessary.
Feed-forward: Information flow in the brain is primarily one-way. There is little feedback where computations that occur later influence the result of computations that have happened earlier.	*Recurrent:* Information flow can be both forward and backward. Feedback loops and cyclical computations are assumed.

Modularity Versus Distribularity

Recall our discussion of modularity, introduced in the first cognitive approach chapter. If the brain consists of many of these special-purpose mechanisms, then studying the mind becomes a bit easier. That is because we can take out or dissociate some modules and study the others in isolation. Removing or controlling one module in this kind of system allows us to see the role it plays, much like a missing piece in a jigsaw puzzle where all the pieces fit into one another in only one way. Because most of the processing occurs inside a module, the interactions between them are simple, minimizing the difficulty of constructing a "causal map" or process model of the system's functions.

If the brain is not modular, then the traditional approach runs into problems. Explaining the brain now means having to account for countless complex interactions between processing centers. This certainly is the case if we reduce these mechanisms to the individual neuron level, since neuron firing rates are modulated by excitatory and inhibitory inputs from thousands of neighboring neurons. Now, we have a much more difficult time diagramming the system. Each module in some sense has now lost its "boundary": Its functions are local but also global, being tied to the operations of processing centers both near and far.

So is the brain modular or not? It is perhaps most accurate to say that it is partially modular. There are portions of neural tissue that are anatomically and morphologically distinct from one another and that exhibit some degree of functional independence. By the same token, we also see areas that are more highly interdependent. Spivey uses the term *soft modularity* to describe this notion. The term **distribularity** also has been suggested as a new word to encompass this idea (Kingsbury & Finlay, 2001).

Component-Dominant Versus Interaction-Dominant Dynamics

If the brain were modular in the sense that Fodor means, it would display **component-dominant dynamics**. In this scenario, a functional unit waits until it receives sufficient input or has performed enough localized computations to reach a stable state. Only then will it generate an output that is passed on to another module for continued processing. In a sense, the unit can be thought of as being "selfish" in that it is keeping information to itself for as long as possible. This type of dynamic is seen in serial systems where computations are performed in a sequential order.

In contrast, the brain could demonstrate **interaction-dominant dynamics**. Here, functional units continually update their neighbors. Unit A, for example, could activate Unit B even before it has finished its computation. These systems may never reach a stable state since the units are continually activating and reactivating one other. The units can be thought of as "altruistic" because they share their information with one another. This dynamic is more characteristic of distributed systems that utilize parallel distributed processing techniques.

Spivey (2007) outlines several lines of evidence supporting the interaction-dominant view. Traditional views of the visual system have separated streams where different stimulus characteristics such as color, form, orientation, and luminance are processed independently. In the tilt illusion, the perceived orientation of bars inside a circular center region is influenced by the orientation of bars in a surrounding ring-shaped region. The inner bars are perceived as tilted in a direction away from those in the surround. The effect is enhanced when the color and luminance of the surrounding region matches that in the center. This implies that the channels for orientation, color, and luminance are interconnected, at least in the primary visual cortex where the basis for this happens.

In the brain, we also see interactions between sensory modalities. Cross talk between features takes place not just within a modality such as vision but also between modalities such as vision and touch. The visual system interacts with the touch system during tactile discrimination of orientation. We know this because the visual cortex becomes active during this task (Sathian, Zangaladze, Hoffman, & Grafton, 1997). Disruption of the visual cortex by transcranial magnetic stimulation also interferes with the task (Zangaladze, Epstein, Grafton, & Sathian, 1999).

Internalism Versus Externalism

Closed systems are insulated from what is occurring around them. In other words, they are spatially and functionally bounded. It seems fairly certain that the brain is an open system at almost every level of analysis. On a small scale, neurons are influenced by their immediate neighbors as well as by larger neural circuits that participate in more widespread brain activity. The brain as open system is not an entirely new idea. As we discussed above, both the ecological movement in perception and the subsumption architecture in robotics adopt this perspective. This debate about whether mind is just the brain or something more has coalesced into two differing philosophies. **Internalism** holds that mind can be entirely explained by a description of the brain and of brain states (Segal, 2000). In opposition to this is **externalism**, advocating that mind is the result of interactions between the brain, the body, and the immediate physical environment (Clark & Chalmers, 1998).

Situated Versus Embodied Cognition

Brooks (2002) differentiates between robots that are situated and those that are embodied. According to him, a **situated** creature is one that is "embedded in the world, and which does not deal with abstract descriptions, but through its sensors with the here and now" (pp. 51–52). The information a situated creature receives directly influences its behavior. An **embodied** creature, on the other hand, is "one that has a physical body and experiences the world, at least in part, directly through the influence of the world on that body" (p. 52). Brooks states that an airline reservation system is situated but not embodied. It receives queries about flights by users that constitute real-time perceptual inputs and then produces outputs that are received and further processed by the users. But since the reservation system is a computer program, it lacks a true body. It has no real sensors to directly perceive the world and no effectors such as legs or arms to locomote, manipulate, or interact physically with the environment.

An assembly line robot that spray paints parts in an automobile manufacturing plant is embodied but not situated. The robot has a body, consisting of a base and articulated robotic arm. It may have sensors and effectors to perceive and act on the environment to execute its task, but it doesn't interact dynamically or adaptively with the environment. Instead, it simply executes the same routine over and over again, following its internal programming.

Feed-Forward Versus Recurrent Pathways

One last point to be made concerns the direction of interactions between the brain, body, and world. According to the recurrent view, the causality here is bidirectional. It flows between these systems in both global-to-local and local-to-global directions. In other words, the world acts on the body through afferent perceptual inputs, while the body acts on the world through efferent motor actions. It is the continuous loop or cycle between these that constitutes mind, not any of the one-way paths. It is, thus, best to think of mind as a recurrent pathway, one that loops back on itself, instead of as a feed-forward pathway that goes in only one direction.

Examples of two-way information paths are evident within the brain. For many years, it was believed that the visual system was a feed-forward system. The optic nerve projected information about an image from the retina to a relay center in the thalamus. From there, the signal was sent to cells in the primary visual cortex (area VI). Following this, the input splits into temporal and occipital regions, constituting the ventral and dorsal pathways, respectively. It turns out that this is actually a very simplified view. The visual system is now known to send projections back as well as forward. For example, there are numerous pathways that run from area VI back to the thalamus. The image sent from the eye is, indeed, passed upward but then also triggers downward cascading signals as part of the normal process of visual perception.

EVALUATING THE DYNAMICAL PERSPECTIVE

Our tour of the dynamical approach has covered a lot of ground. We need to pause for a minute now and examine how well it addresses the issues facing cognitive science. The dynamical perspective does take into account the problem of physical environments. Like the ecological and subsumption approaches, it sees cognition not only as "in the head" but as a looping cyclical process between brain, body, and world. It also offers up a more accurate account of the way real-world variables interact. Linear relationships in nature are the exception, not the rule. The really interesting cognitive phenomena are most certainly nonlinear and change in a complex way over time. Although we may not be able to predict the behavior of complex systems such as the brain in the long run, we can at least conceptualize them more accurately.

The dynamical approach offers us a unifying methodology. Any field in science can be understood as the movement of a trajectory through state space. Whereas traditional cognitive psychology experiments evaluate one or two dependent variables, state spaces can contain any number of dimensions and allow us to see how they covary together. This multidimensional approach may allow us to better understand individual and cultural differences because we can follow the course of their system trajectories simultaneously across several critical dependent measures. We can also manipulate multiple independent variables and see their effect on trajectories and attractors. Perhaps even consciousness can be better comprehended using these techniques.

The mind is dynamic, not static. It is in a constant state of flux. In fact, it is questionable whether we ever have the same thought twice or experience exactly the same emotion twice. Many of the process models we looked at in this book are a useful first attempt at surveying mental processes, but they are oversimplified and fail to account for the complex interactions that occur between brain areas and neurons. A number of dynamical models are now available that allow us to look at changing processes better. These include oscillatory models based on cyclical neuron activity and differential-equation, cellular-automata, chaotic, and agent-based models (Friedenberg, 2009).

Dynamical cognitive science supports one side of several theoretical issues we have considered. It advocates a quasi-modular view of mind, where modules retain some independent processing but are also open to feedback and alteration. Processing is thus interaction dominant instead of component dominant and involves both feed-forward and feedback pathways. Conditions in the external environment affect processing, and human cognition at least is seen as both situated and embodied.

The dynamic approach offers us an alternate take on representations as well. Representations in this account are not objective in the sense of having discrete static values. They are inherently subjective and constantly changing based on other cognitive states. Sensory input may shape the initial form of a representation, but this may be substantially modified with subsequent computations. The primary purpose of a representation is to aid in the execution of behavior, not to preserve an isomorphic relation between it and its referent.

INTEGRATING COGNITIVE SCIENCE

We have seen throughout this book that each cognitive science approach by itself substantially advances our understanding of mind. We have also seen that an integrative approach in which the disciplines work collaboratively on a common problem can be an even more powerful tool for investigating mind. We hope to have conveyed this through the "Interdisciplinary Crossroads" sections at the conclusion of each chapter. However, cross-disciplinary research isn't easy. Each of the approaches varies in the way it describes the mind and in the tools it uses to study it. In this section, we propose three kinds of integration from which cognitive science research could benefit. These are integrations across disciplines, level of description, and methodology.

Integration Across Levels of Description

Recall again David Marr's three levels of description that make up the tri-level hypothesis: (1) the implementation level, (2) the algorithmic level, and (3) the computational level. These levels in the order given correspond roughly to three basic questions about a cognitive process: (1) Where is it taking place? (2) How is it taking place? (3) Why is it taking place?

It is rare in cognitive science to find a theory that provides an explanation at all three levels. Rather, different approaches tend to emphasize one level over another. Neuroscience and robotics focus on the implementation level, since they either study the brain's existing architecture or design new mechanical and electronic architectures. The cognitive and artificial intelligence approaches, because of their models and programs specifying information flow, emphasize the algorithmic level. The philosophy and evolutionary approaches focus on the computational level, since they provide more rich explanations for the purpose of cognitive processes.

What we need are more theories and models that integrate across all three levels. The levels would then mutually constrain one another, leading to better and more accurate formulations. To illustrate, researchers interested in understanding working memory might first use brain imaging to determine which areas of the brain are active during the performance of different tasks. From this, cognitive process models could be derived. Eventually, a computer program that utilizes some aspects of the process model could be implemented and tested in a robot.

Integration Across Disciplines

Most cognitive scientists are specialists. They are trained in the knowledge and tools of their own discipline but lack sufficient understanding of other allied disciplines. An artificial intelligence researcher may be adept at devising search algorithms to locate information in a database but not be familiar with the literature on human memory search, an area of expertise for a cognitive psychologist. Similarly, a neuroscientist may know which brain areas underlie memory retrieval but not be able to implement a neural network model of the process, which is a skill possessed by someone working within the network approach.

There are two solutions to this. The first is to train individual researchers in the interdisciplinary perspective. Scientists who possess an understanding of cognitive science fields outside their own area may gain key insights into the mind that they would not ordinarily have had. This solution has its limitations, however. Scientific practice requires a high degree of specificity and focus, and researchers cannot be expected to acquire more than rudimentary training in multiple alternative disciplines. The most that can be expected is some degree of familiarity with the literature and techniques of disciplines outside one's own specific area.

A second solution mentioned in the introductory chapter is interdisciplinary cooperation. Here, researchers from different disciplines work together on a common project. For instance, a team made up of investigators from different disciplines might focus their research efforts on a single topic, such as grasping. Each investigator could then contribute the unique strengths of his or her discipline's theoretical insights and methodology. Recently formed interdisciplinary cognitive science research centers sometimes employ philosophers, cognitive psychologists, computer scientists, and neuroscientists. Studies at these centers have yielded findings unlikely to be obtained in departments operating autonomously.

Integration Across Methodologies

Many of the disciplines employ distinct methods. Philosophers use deductive reasoning. Psychologists employ the scientific method. Cognitive psychologists, artificial intelligence researchers, and those adopting the network approach use modeling. Neuroscientists utilize a combination of case studies, lesion methods, and brain imaging; whereas roboticists build and test machines in a real-world environment. Each of these techniques has its strengths and weaknesses. A computer simulation of a cognitive process may solve the problem of how to execute a cognitive task in the smallest number of processing steps. People who run models without taking experimental results into account, however, do so at their own risk, since nature may have evolved a different or better solution.

In the first chapter on cognition, we discussed several models of attentional selection— some favoring early selection, others favoring late selection. Different models were formulated over time, with models being modified to accommodate new experimental data. This is a good example of integrating modeling and experimentation across two disciplines. The models were modified in response to experimental results. Ideally, this relationship should go in both directions, with models also providing the impetus for new experiments.

THE FUTURE

We leave you with a few parting words. Cognitive science is unique in history because it groups such a large number of disciplines under one umbrella. This provides an unparalleled opportunity for collaboration. Cooperation and competition among the various approaches are both necessary for the advancement of our understanding of mind. We can only hope that more researchers follow this path.

But what does the future hold for cognitive science? Where are we going from here? Scientific progress relies on a number of factors. Among these are theoretical breakthroughs that reorganize our understanding. Technological advances also play a prominent role. Cognitive science, perhaps more than other disciplines, depends on new tools for measuring and simulating mental processes. Recent years have seen the development of several new tools. These include optogenetics, magnetoencephalography, and the knife-edge scanning microscope. It is likely that other new tools like these are on the way. It is not unrealistic to imagine brain imaging devices that will be able to record individual neuronal activity of large cell populations or instruments that may be able to measure quantum fluctuations at the atomic level. The use of such tools will open a whole new vista of mental territory rife for exploration. The future for cognitive science is bright indeed.

SUMMING UP: A REVIEW OF CHAPTER 14

1. Cognitive science has produced many benefits to society, including advances in education, engineering, and medicine.

2. There are several issues that the field of cognitive science must deal with. It has failed to provide a satisfying account of the interplay between brain, body, and world. Too little attention has been focused on the differences between individuals and cultures. The study of the neural correlates of consciousness has just begun, and there is no single unified theory.

3. The dynamical systems approach may satisfy some of the major issues raised above. In this approach, there is an emphasis on nonlinear relationships, chaotic behavior, and how complex systems change over time.

4. According to the dynamical perspective, representations are subjective, constructed, and constantly undergoing change. The purpose of a representation is to guide behavior, not to form a discrete and stable symbol that stands for its referent. This sentiment is echoed in the ecological approach to perception and in the subsumption architecture in robotics.

5. One way to reconcile the traditional and dynamical views on representation is symbolic dynamics, where an attractor basin stands for a symbol such as a letter. A system trajectory passing through this attractor would then activate it and make it available for subsequent computation.

6. There are a number of differences between the classical view in cognitive science and the dynamical systems approach. The dynamical view sees mental activity as fuzzy, graded, and probabilistic. Modules are only partially independent; cognitive processing is interaction dominant and in constant interaction with the environment. Cognition is embodied and situated, and pathways are recurrent as well as feed forward.

7. The dynamical perspective at least partially satisfies the issues of physical environments and representations. It provides new theoretical and methodological ground that can serve to unify the disparate disciplines in cognitive science.

8. If we are to truly unite cognitive science, then integration across levels of description, disciplines, and methodologies must occur.

9. The development of new technologies such as magnetoencephalography and knife-edge scanning microscopes will further bolster the development of cognitive science.

EXPLORE MORE

Log on to the student study site at **http://study.sagepub.com/friedenberg3e** for electronic flash cards, review quizzes, and a list of web resources to aid you in further exploring the field of cognitive science.

SUGGESTED READINGS

Blackmore, S. (2004). *Consciousness: An introduction.* Oxford, England: Oxford University Press.

Friedenberg, J. (2009). *Dynamical psychology: Complexity, self-organization, and mind.* Litchfield Park, AZ: Emergent.

Gibson, J. J. (1986). *The ecological approach to visual perception.* Hillsdale, NJ: Erlbaum.

Nisbett, R. (2004). *The geography of thought: How Asians and Westerners think differently . . . and why.* New York, NY: Free Press.

Wilson, E. O. (1999). *Consilience: The unity of knowledge.* New York, NY: Random House.

GLOSSARY

2½-D sketch An image representation that includes information about surfaces and layout

3-D sketch A three-dimensional image representation in which object parts are linked together by axes of symmetry and elongation

accommodate When we change our internal concepts or schemas when taking new information into account

acoustic code A memory code based on the sounds of the items

ACT A robotic primitive that pertains to the actuating or motor elements of an intelligent agent

action potential The electrical signal that results when the inputs to a neuron exceed its threshold of excitation

action schemas In the Norman and Shallice model of attention, units that govern the execution of context-specific actions

actuators A mechanical device for moving or controlling a mechanism or system

adaptation The process by which an animal species changes in response to its environment through variation, inheritance, and selection

affect infusion model A model developed to explain the conditions under which emotions and moods infuse (influence) cognitive processing

affective computing Computing that relates to, arises from, or deliberately influences emotions and other affective phenomena

agent link A link in a propositional network that specifies the subject of the sentence, the one performing some action

agraphia A deficit in writing

alexia A deficit in reading

algorithm A formal procedure or system that acts on informational representations

algorithmic level A level of information processing that specifies exactly how the data are to be transformed, including what the steps are and what the order of the steps is

analogy A mental representation used to compare known information with new information to which it is similar

analytical rumination hypothesis The view that depression is an evolved response to complex problems. The depressive state induces a focus on the problem while at the same time minimizing distractions that might detour attention, working memory, and other processing resources.

angular gyrus A brain area located posterior to Wernicke's area. Damage to this area can produce problems in reading and writing.

anterior A direction indicating "toward the front"

anterograde amnesia An inability to remember new information after a traumatic incident

anthropodenial A blindness to the humanlike characteristics of animals or the animal-like characteristics of ourselves

anthropology The discipline that studies cultural differences by investigating when and where humans first appeared on the earth and why they have varied in some physical traits. Anthropology is also interested in how and why societies vary in their customary ideas and practices.

anthropomorphism The tendency to ascribe humanlike characteristics when explaining animal behavior

aphasia A neurological language deficit

apperceptive agnosia A type of agnosia in which people cannot assemble the pieces or features of an object into a meaningful whole

applet Prototyping software tool application

appropriate causal relation The relation between sensory inputs, motor outputs, and the representations that come between them

arbitrary The property by which there need be no relationship between linguistic symbols and their referents. Any symbol could be used to stand for any concept.

architecture Functional organization of an entity, possibly a computer

arcuate fasciculus A pathway that connects Broca's and Wernicke's areas

aristocratic network A type of small-world network where long-distance connections between nodes are the result of hubs

arousal The extent of physiological activation reflected in measures such as cardiac and respiratory rates

articulatory loop A system in the working memory model where speech- and sound-related information is rehearsed

artificial general intelligence Seeks to explain how real-world minds achieve general intelligence using limited resources by appropriately organizing and utilizing their memories

artificial intelligence (AI) Concerned with the computational aspects of an intelligent agent

artificial life (alife) The study of human-made systems that behave in ways characteristic of natural living systems

artificial neural network (ANN) A computer simulation of how populations of real neurons might perform some task

assertives A type of speech in which the speaker asserts his or her belief

assimilation When information is understood and interpreted in terms of what we already know

associative agnosia A type of agnosia in which people perceive a whole object but have difficulty assigning a name or label to it

attention Concentrated mental activity in which processing resources are allocated to information sources

attention-deficit hyperactivity disorder (ADHD) A psychological disorder characterized by distractibility, impulsivity, and mood swings. Patients have difficulty planning or executing plans.

attitude A learned predisposition to respond to a particular object in a particular way

attractors A region of a state space where the system is located or spends much of its time. They can be of different shapes.

attribution An explanation we give for the causes of events or behaviors

autism A neurodevelopmental disorder characterized by impaired social interaction and accompanied by restricted and repetitive behavior. These individuals are often aloof during childhood and remain egocentric as adults. They show impairments in verbal and nonverbal communication.

autobiographical memory Memory for personal events or episodes in one's life

automatic attentional processes Processes that do not require conscious attentional control

autonomous entity Acting without human intervention or control

axon A long, tubular structure that projects outward from a neuron cell body and serves to transmit the action potential over distance

babbling stage A stage in language development where infants produce many sounds occurring in the languages of the world

basal ganglia A collection of brain areas involved in voluntary motor responses

base-rate fallacy A neglect of the probability that an item belongs to a particular category

basic emotions Those that are believed to be mostly innate and, thus, in humans ought to be universal or found in all cultures

behavior A mapping or translation of sensory inputs into a pattern of motor actions intended to complete a task

behavioral economics A perspective that focuses on how evolution shaped the way we make decisions involving money

behavior-based approach A type of problem-solving method in which a network is allowed to produce a solution on its own. This does not involve the use of symbols. It is representative of the connectionist approach in cognitive science.

behaviorism A way of conceiving of empirical constraints on psychological states

belief-in-a-just-world phenomenon The phenomenon in which we think that people get what they deserve

binding problem The issue of how to recombine the various features of an object that have been processed by distributed brain areas

binocular rivalry A phenomenon in which two perceptions alternately vie for visual consciousness

biological plausibility The idea that artificial neural networks effectively represent and model the characteristics of real-world brains

bipolar disorder A disorder in which individuals alternate back and forth between depressive and manic symptoms. The manic state is characterized by exuberance, a grandiose sense of self, decreased need for sleep, and excessive talkativeness.

bottleneck theories Theories that describe why it is that of all the information presented to us, only a small amount actually gets through to conscious awareness

bottom-up methods that describe mathematical models as proceeding from fundamental elements by starting with the smaller, more fine details of the model and then building upward until a comprehensive model ensues

brain imaging A technique that allows researchers to see the static three-dimensional organization of brain areas and the dynamic activity of these areas over time

Broca's aphasia A language deficit in which comprehension is intact but there are impairments in speech pronunciation and production

Broca's area A region in the left frontal lobe that underlies language production. Damage to this area results in Broca's aphasia.

Cannon-Bard theory of emotion The theory that an event by itself can trigger an emotion. Although the event causes physiological arousal, the arousal is not necessary for the formation of the emotion. So in this view, the event immediately causes both the emotion and the bodily changes. The two do not depend on each other.

capacity theories Theories that conceptualize attention as a limited resource that must be spread around to different informational sources

case study A method in neuroscience in which researchers examine the relationship between brain damage and behavior in individuals

catastrophic interference This occurs when a network has learned to recognize an old set of patterns and then is called on to learn a new set. The learning of the new set modifies the weights of the network in such a way that the old set is forgotten.

category confusion effect A difficulty in differentiating between individual members of a given race

cell assembly According to Hebb, a small group of neurons that repeatedly stimulate themselves

central processing unit (CPU) That part of a computer that executes the instructions and controls the sequence of instructions to be carried out

centrality How a network coordinates information. This can be accomplished through a "leader" that receives information, evaluates it, and issues commands.

cephalization index A measure of brain size expressed as a proportion of body size that can be used to compare brain sizes between different animal species

cerebral hemispheres The two halves of the cortex, each with corresponding functional specializations. The left hemisphere is more analytic, serial, and logical. The right hemisphere is more synthetic, parallel, and relational.

chaotic systems Those who exhibit a wide range of behaviors. The behaviors can be ordered or disordered but not random.

chatbot A computer program that simulates an intelligent conversation between users via text or auditory means

cheater detection The ability to detect who has undeservedly received a benefit

Chinese room scenario A hypothetical situation in which a man uses a set of instructions to produce replies to questions in Chinese. It argues that the man can never learn to understand Chinese.

chunking The grouping of items together into a single meaningful whole in short-term memory

cingulate cortex A region of the cortex that is implicated in selecting a response, especially when that response requires inhibiting or ignoring another alternative response

classical conditioning A form of learning in which two repeatedly paired stimuli become associated so that one that formerly did not elicit a response now does

classical dualism The belief that both mental and physical realms are possible where the mind controls the body

clearness The clarity of a sensation determined by the amount of attention paid to it

closure The perceptual principle stating that shapes forming closed objects go together

clustering The probability that two nodes linked to a third will also be linked to each other. This network statistic reflects the interconnectedness of neighborhoods.

coarticulation Differential pronunciation of a given phoneme based on the phonemes that come before or after it

cocktail party effect The ability to automatically hear one's name spoken at a distance even though one's attention is focused on the immediate surroundings

coding In relation to computers, refers to program instructions

CogAff architecture A generic scheme for how cognitive–emotional processing may take place in either a person or a machine. It consists of the reactive, deliberative, and reflective stages.

cognitive architectures Specify the structure and function of many different cognitive systems and how they interact

cognitive dissonance A negative state that occurs when an attitude and a behavior or two attitudes are inconsistent

cognitive economy The principle that concepts should not have to be coded for more times than is necessary

cognitive map A mental representation that can explain learning without resorting to pure stimulus–response associations

cognitive neuroscience The study of the physiological structures and processes underlying cognitive function

cognitive penetration When one's knowledge, beliefs, goals, or other cognitive states alter performance of a mental task

cognitive psychology The study of human knowledge representation and use

cognitive science The scientific interdisciplinary study of the mind

cognitive theory of emotion The theory that it is the total situation and not just the arousal that determines emotions

commissives A type of speech that commits the speaker to some later action

communication The production, transmission, and comprehension of information in a language between individuals

comparative cognition An evolutionary perspective where researchers examine the similarities and differences in cognitive ability between different animal species

complex cells Cells in the visual system that code for an oriented line segment moving in a particular direction

complex ideas Ideas formed from the active mental combination of simple ideas

component-dominant dynamics A brain state whereby functional units must wait until they receive sufficient input or have performed enough local computations to reach a stable state

compositional semantics When the entire meaning of a sentence is derived from the meaning of its parts

computation The transformation or manipulation of information

computational level An abstract level of analysis that asks what type of problem a computation solves and how it may have arisen

concept An idea that represents a class of entities that have been grouped together

conceptually driven process A process where context and higher level knowledge aid in recognition

conditioned response In classical conditioning, a response elicited by a conditioned stimulus

conditioned stimulus In classical conditioning, a stimulus that elicits a response only after being repeatedly paired with an unconditioned stimulus

conduction aphasia Results from damage to the arcuate fasciculus; characterized by a difficulty in repeating words that have just been heard

conjunction fallacy A neglect of the conjunction rule, which states that the probability of simultaneously being a member of two categories is always less than the probability of being a member of either category alone

connectionism The study of mental operations through the construction and testing of artificial neural networks

conscious That aspect of mind that contains those thoughts and feelings of which we are aware and can directly access

consciousness The subjective quality of experience

consolidation The process by which information is transferred from working or short-term memory to long-term memory

constructivist framework A perspective in which representations are constructed by a physical nervous system and are always system relative. The primary purpose of a representation is to generate a behavior, not to depict the environment.

contention scheduling The scheduling that governs routine habitual performances

contralateral   Refers to the opposite side of the brain or neural structure

control group   The group in an experiment that does not receive the independent variable

controlled attentional processes   Processes that require conscious attentional control

convergent dynamics   The state of a network represented by how the values of its weights change over time

cooing stage   The earliest period in language development, when infants exercise their vocal cords and mouths prior to articulation

corpus callosum   A collection of fibers that connects the two cerebral hemispheres

creative synthesis   A principle by which the mind actively organizes mental elements together such that the resulting whole contains new properties. These new properties cannot be explained by the characteristics of the individual elements themselves.

critical period   A period of development during which linguistic experience is crucial for future language use. If a child is not exposed to language during this time, he or she may never acquire it or may suffer severe language impairments.

cultural intelligence hypothesis   The view that complex social interaction created a form of social intelligence that then laid the groundwork for more general intelligence to emerge later

data-driven process   A process that is driven entirely by the physical characteristics of a stimulus and fails to take into account the larger context or meaning

decay   The loss of information over time from memory

declarative knowledge   Knowledge that represents facts

declarative memory   Memory for knowledge about facts and events. It is demonstrated by saying and occurs with conscious recall.

declaratives   A type of speech where the utterance itself is the action

deductive reasoning   The application of the rules of logic to statements about the world; if the premise statements are correct, then the concluding statement must be as well.

deep representations   A type of image structure that consists of information in long-term memory that is used to generate a surface representation

deep structure   The underlying meaning of a sentence that remains constant, regardless of the specific form in which it is expressed

defense mechanisms   Constructs of the ego that reduce or redirect anxiety in various ways

degree of fan   A concept that is related to many others has a high degree of fan. The node representing the concept will subsequently have many links radiating outward from it to other nodes.

deliberative   Actions that are composed of previously developed behaviors that are integrated into a resultant behavior and may include external and internal stimuli

demand characteristics   When participants in a study do what the stimuli, task, or experimental situation seems to demand of them

dendrites   Branching protrusions of the neuron that receive messages from other neurons

dependent variable   A factor measured or observed by the experimenter to see if a change has taken place

depth perception   A visual process by which the world is perceived three dimensionally. It involves using cues from the environment as well as differences in processing between the two eyes to determine what is close and what is farther away.

depth-first algorithm   A methodology for exploring a knowledge base in which information is examined in an increasingly specialized manner

designation   The notion that a symbol expression can designate an object if it can affect the object itself or behave in ways that depend on the object

deterministic process   One that is completely and to within some degree of precision exactly specified

dichotic listening task   A task used to study selective attention. It requires a participant wearing headphones to listen to two different messages simultaneously played over each ear while paying attention to only one.

directives   A type of speech in which a command is issued

disorganized thinking   A symptom of schizophrenia characterized by a loose association between ideas. It can manifest as "word salad" in which concepts are not clearly related to each other.

displacement   The ability of language to refer to something that is removed in space or time

distribularity   A term to describe how the brain may be only partially modular, with different functions spread across different regions

distributed coding/representation   A coding in which an object or feature is represented by a pattern of activation among a group of cells or nodes

divergent thinking   A style of thinking where the goal is to generate many different ideas about a topic in a short period of time

divided attention   A form of attention that can be split or divided among several alternative information sources

domain-general mechanisms   Those that can operate on any type of information

domain-specific mechanisms   Those that are tuned to perform special operations on only a certain type of information

dorsal   A direction indicating "toward the top"

dorsal visual pathway   A pathway that travels upward to the parietal lobe, where information about motion and location is extracted

dualism   The belief that the mental and physical consist of different states or substances

duration   How long a sensation persists

dynamic   The characteristic of languages to constantly change as new words are added and grammatical rules altered

dynamical perspective   A perspective that views the mind as constantly changing as it adapts to new information

dynamical systems approach   A scientific interdisciplinary approach with the view that natural systems are complex and nonlinear. Activity in such systems is measured by using trajectories and attractors in state spaces.

early selection model   Models of attention where information is selected early, based on physical stimulus characteristics

easy problems of consciousness   Those problems that can be solved by cognitive science and that can be explained in terms of computational or neural mechanisms

echoic memory   Auditory sensory memory

ecological models of cognition   Models of cognitive processes that are acquired through learning

ecological niche   The specific environment each animal species has adapted to

ecological perception   The theory that perception is immediate and direct, not requiring representation or computation

egalitarian network   A type of small-world network that contains mostly local short-distance connections with a few random long-distance connections

ego   The aspect of mind that balances the competing demands of the id and superego; operates on the reality principle

electrical stimulation   A method where an electrical current is passed through a bipolar electrode, causing the neurons in a localized area of brain tissue to become active. The resulting activity and behavior are observed.

electroencephalogram (EEG)   A measure of the brain's gross electrical action

eliminativism   The philosophical view that advocates abandoning words describing the mind and using only words describing the brain

embodied   A cognitive agent that has a physical body and experiences the world, at least partially, through the influence of the world on that body

embodiment   The idea that cognitive processes exist within and interact with an external environment through sensory inputs and motor outputs

emergence   The idea that the features of a whole are not completely independent of the parts that make them up

emergence synthesis   The theory that there are some emotions that are triggered solely by a stimulus and don't require any interpretation

emergent property   A property that is realized through the interaction of a system's parts

emotion   A relatively brief episode of coordinated brain, autonomic, and behavioral changes that facilitate a response to an external or internal event of significance for the organism

empiricism   The view that knowledge is acquired through experience

encoding   The name of the process by which information is taken in and converted into a usable mental form

endowment effect   The tendency to stay with what we have and to prefer it over other options

enduring disposition   Refers to automatic influences on where attention gets directed

engram   A physical change in a specific location of the brain associated with learning

environment of evolutionary adaptation (EEA)   The period of time during which many human psychological mechanisms are believed to have evolved

environmental dependency syndrome   A symptom of executive dysfunction in which an environmental stimulus can automatically trigger an associated behavior

epilepsy   A disorder in which neurons fire uncontrollably, producing muscle spasms and seizures

episodic memory   A type of declarative memory containing knowledge of episodes or personally experienced events

epistemology   The branch of philosophy devoted to the study of knowledge

equipotentiality   The principle that many different parts of the brain seem to participate in memory storage

error signal   In artificial neural networks, the difference between the actual and observed output. The error signal is used to alter connection strengths and train the network.

event-related potentials (ERPs)   An EEG recording of brain activity in response to a particular event

evolutionary computation   A concept parallel to AGI that depends on a collection of computational methods that have been modeled on the principles of biological evolution

evolutionary psychology (EP)   A field of psychology that studies how evolutionary forces have shaped human mental capacities

evolved psychological mechanism   A cognitive process that has evolved to solve a specific adaptive problem

exaptation (or neutral drift)   Random mutations that produce new genes with little or no consequence for reproduction. They can spread in a population, and at some point may assume a new adaptive function to a subsequent environmental change.

executive control system   A system in the working memory model whose function is to initiate and control ongoing processes

executive dysfunction   A disorder characterized by a broad number of deficits, including difficulty performing goal-directed behaviors as a result of frontal lobe damage

executive function   Cognitive operations involved in planning, sequencing of behavior, flexible use of information, and goal attainment

exhaustive search   When a memory search process continues matching all the way to the end of a list, even if the target already has been located

experimental group   In an experiment, the group receiving the independent variable

experimental philosophy   A form of philosophy that utilizes empirical methods, typically in the form of surveys that provide constructed scenarios. The surveys are used to assess people's intuitions in order to help answer philosophical questions.

expert system   A software program that is dedicated to solving problems and providing "expert-quality" advice to users; demonstrates intelligence similar to that of a human

explanatory gap   The problem that subjective experience may not be fully explained by an objective account using physical and mechanical processes; the gulf between an objective and subjective description of mental phenomena

expressives   A type of speech that describes the psychological states of the speaker

extensity   The extent to which a sensation fills or occupies space

externalism   The view that the mind is the result of interactions between the brain, body, and physical environment

fallacies   A fundamental misunderstanding of a statistical rule that can result from applying a heuristic

feed-forward network   In an artificial neural network, flow of activation that is in one direction only, forward from units in an input layer to units in other layers

feed-forward pathways   Those in which information flow travels only in one direction

feel-good, do-good phenomenon   A mood-enhancing experience such as finding money or recalling a happy event that can cause people to engage in helping behavior, such as picking up someone's papers or giving away money

feelings   Correspond to the subjective experience of emotions. They are what it is like to feel afraid, sad, or jubilant.

field theory   The idea in physics that objects are acted on by forces in fields

finite state model   Contemporary implementation of Turing's universal computing machine

fissure   A large spacing or separation between two areas of brain tissue

flashbulb memory   Better recall of personal events during physiologically arousing or emergency situations

focused attention stage   A later stage in pattern recognition that requires concentrated attention under voluntary control

folk psychology   Theories of mind that use subjective terms and commonsense or intuitive reasoning

foot-in-the-door phenomenon   A phenomenon in which people who agree to a small request now may comply with a larger one later

foraging   The act of looking or searching for food

formal symbol manipulator   A system that operates on contentless symbols based on a set of rules

formal system A system of symbols that can be combined into expressions that can then be manipulated by processes to form new expressions

framing effects In behavioral economics, the heuristic by which people prefer choices that are framed positively rather than negatively

free association What happens when one is presented with an idea and asked to produce whatever related ideas come to mind without censoring or inhibiting

frontal lobe Located on the anterior portion of the cerebral hemispheres. It is implicated in problem solving and motor behavior.

functional kinds Things that are distinguished by their actions or tendencies

functional magnetic resonance imaging (fMRI) A variation of MRI that is used to show changes in brain activity over time

functionalism The view that mental states are not just physical states but the functioning or operation of those physical states

fundamental attribution error The tendency to prefer internal or dispositional traits as the best explanation for people's behavior

fundamental utilities of consciousness The role consciousness plays in the survival of the organism

fusiform face area (FFA) Pictures of faces activate cells in this area, located in the temporal lobe

gambler's fallacy The belief that probability outcomes are not independent, that the probability of an event can be influenced by its past history

game theory Attempts to mathematically capture behavior in strategic situations, or games, in which an individual's success in making choices depends on the choices of others

general intelligence hypothesis The view that human intelligence did not evolve in response to particular selection forces such as social organization. Instead, it emerged in a general form that could be suited to solving all kinds of problems, whether they are social or not.

generalization The ability to apply a learned rule to a novel situation

generalized delta rule or back propagation A way of training a network by repeatedly applying error feedback to alter connection strengths. The feedback is the difference between the actual and the desired output.

general-purpose processor The view that the mind can solve any type of problem equally well. It is based on the notion that a problem is solved by context-independent symbol representation and computation.

generative The property of language whereby symbolic elements can be combined to create a large number of meanings

geon A basic volumetric shape, such as a cube or a cylinder, that may be used in recognizing an object

gestalt The idea that a whole is more than just the sum of its parts

goal The desired end state or solution to a problem

graceful degradation A slow and gradual decrease in the performance of a network with increased damage

grammar The collection of all the rules governing a language

guided search A forceful or willed search for a memory item based on intelligence and reasoning

gyrus A ridge or fold of neural tissue

halo effect States that we tend to see positive traits group together. For example, if a person is good-looking, we tend to think he/she is successful.

hard problems of consciousness Those problems that require explaining the subjective quality of consciousness

"hasa" link   A link in a propositional network that represents property relationships

Hebb rule   States that if two connected neurons are both active simultaneously, the synapse between them will be strengthened

hemispatial neglect   An attention disorder in which the patient ignores one half of his or her body as well as the surroundings on that side. Typically, this is for the left side and is the result of damage to the contralateral hemisphere.

heuristic   This is a mental "rule of thumb" or strategy that acts as a fast and easy way of problem solving. Heuristics are right most, but not all, of the time.

hidden layer   The second layer of a three-layer network. This is where the input layer sends its signals. It performs intermediary processing.

hierarchical networks   Organized into different levels. The number of nodes decreases traveling upward with each group of nodes converging onto another group above it with fewer elements.

hierarchical organization   A semantic network where concept nodes are arranged in different levels along a continuum from abstract to concrete

hierarchical paradigm   A highly sequential robotic architecture in which planning is a key element of its design; also referred to as a "top-down" approach to robotic design

homunculus   A hypothetical "little man" inside the mind who interprets and understands information

hubs   Nodes that have many more links than the rest of the network's nodes

hybrid model   A robotic architecture that employs a combination of reactive behaviors and planning or other cognitive components

hypercomplex cells   Cells in the visual system that code for angles (two conjoined oriented line segments) moving in a particular direction

hypothesis   A statement derived from a theory that concerns potential outcomes in an experiment

iconic memory   Visual sensory memory

id   The aspect of mind that contains unconscious impulses and desires such as sex and hunger; operates on the pleasure principle

idealism   The belief that only mental entities are real, that the universe is essentially nonphysical

idealistic principle   Motivates the individual to do what it considers proper

identity theory   The philosophical view that the mind is the brain; mental states are the physical states of the brain

if–then rules   Conditional execution of a group of statements (consequents) depending on the value of an expression (antecedents)

illumination   A flash of insight, a sort of "Aha!" experience where a solution comes suddenly to awareness

image generation   Occurs when the encodings in long-term memory are used to form an image in the visual buffer

image inspection   Occurs when an individual is asked some question about an image. It consists of a number of distinct operations such as "zoom," "pan," or "scan." These operations preserve the image while extracting information from it.

image transformation   Refers to an operation performed on an image, such as a mental rotation. These operations alter the image.

immediate experience   An individual's direct awareness of something

implementational level   A "hardware" level of analysis that specifies the physical processes that carry out a computation

implicit association task   An experimental task in which a person must judge whether a central word corresponds to one of two categories, each defined by peripheral words, using one of two buttons

impression   The opinion or belief that you form about another person

incubation   The period of time during which a problem is put aside. During this period there are no conscious attempts at problem solving, but the unconscious mind may be attempting or have discovered a solution.

independent variable   In an experiment, a factor manipulated or altered by the experimenter to see if it will cause a change

indirect priming task   An experimental task where a participant is asked to judge whether a word is good or bad after it has been preceded with a racial prime, such as a word or picture

inductive reasoning   A form of thinking in which commonalities about specific instances in the world are noticed and used to draw conclusions

in-group favoritism   The belief that in-group members possess more positive traits in comparison with members of out-groups

inheritance   The process by which parents pass on some of their genetic characteristics to their offspring

input layer   The first layer of a three-layer network that receives stimulus input and where the stimulus is represented

insight learning   The apparent spontaneous understanding of relationships that produces a solution to a problem

intelligent agent (IA)   A rational autonomous entity that observes and acts on an environment, directs its activity toward achieving goals, and is capable of learning to achieve its goals through experience; includes cooperating entities

intensity   The strength of a sensation

intentionality   The relationship between a representation and what it stands for

interaction-dominant dynamics   A brain state whereby functional units continually update their neighbors. Computation here is distributed over different areas that exchange information back and forth.

interference   The inability of a network to distinguish similar patterns from one another

internalism   The view that the mind can be entirely explained by a description of brain states

intervening variables   Variables that mediate between initiating causes and a behavior

intraparietal sulcus   Located in the parietal lobe, it may be responsible for the allocation of attentional resources and the binding of features in visual search

introspection   The process of "looking inward" to experience and describe mental objects or states

ipsilateral   Refers to the same side of the brain or neural structure

"isa" link   A link in a propositional network that represents relationships of belonging

isomorphism   The correspondence between the psychological or conscious experience on the one hand and the underlying brain experience on the other

James-Lange theory of emotion   The theory that an event produces arousal and other physiological changes in the body. These physiological changes are then interpreted. The result of the interpretation is the emotion.

joint attention   The ability to coordinate attention with a social partner

Kismet   A robot that is capable of both emotional perception and production

knife-edge scanning microscope (KESM) A device capable of recording three-dimensional structures at the cellular level. It operates by slicing through tissue and reflecting an image to a camera.

knowledge-based approach A type of problem-solving method in which one conceptualizes the problem and its solution in terms of symbols and transformations on the symbols; representative of the traditional or classical approach in cognitive science

late selection model Models of attention where information is selected late, based on semantic stimulus characteristics

latent learning An animal's ability to acquire behaviors through experience without being subject to any reinforcement

lateral A direction indicating "toward the side"

lattices Regularly arranged matrices of parts used to demonstrate the principles of perceptual organization

learning When some event causes a change in the nervous system that in turn causes a change in behavior

lesion study A method in neuroscience where researchers deliberately destroy brain areas in animals and examine the resulting behavioral deficits

lexigrams Geometric patterns that can be used to create a language system

linear relationships Relationships between two variables where the output of one variable is proportional to the input of another

linguistic relativity hypothesis Also known as the Sapir-Whorf hypothesis. The strong version states that thought and language are so similar that it may be impossible to express the thoughts of one language in another. The weak version denies this but admits that the language a person speaks influences the way he or she thinks.

linguistics The study of language

links The connection between each node in an artificial network

literal encodings Encodings that contain lists of coordinates detailing where to place points in the surface matrix to depict the represented object

lobes Cortical regions with different functional specializations

local representation Representation in the form of activation or activity in a single node in a network

long-term potentiation (LTP) The enduring facilitation of synaptic transmission that occurs following activation of a synapse by repeated intense high-frequency stimulation

loss aversion The principle by which people are more sensitive to losses than to equivalent gains

magnetic resonance imaging (MRI) A brain imaging technique in which a patient is placed inside a tube containing a powerful magnet. Protons align themselves in this magnetic field. A radio wave pulse is then applied to the brain or other part of the body undergoing the scan. The radio signals are bounced back and picked up by a detector unit.

magnetoencephalography (MEG) A brain imaging technique in which small changes in magnetic fields are measured to determine brain activity. It has a spatial resolution of 1 millimeter and a temporal resolution of several milliseconds.

major depressive disorder Intense and long-lasting sadness that can occur without any precipitating incident. This can be accompanied by interruptions in sleep, appetite, and concentration.

masking When one stimulus immediately follows another and prevents processing of the first

maximal onset principle The principle that consonants usually precede vowels and typically form the onset of syllabic groupings; a feature found in all languages

maze A complex branching puzzle through which a solver must find a route

means–ends analysis A reasoning paradigm in which the intelligence notes the current state of a system and chooses some action that will reduce the difference between the current state and a specified goal state

medial A direction indicating "toward the middle"

mediate experiences Experiences that come from mental reflection about an object

membership function Represents the degree of truth of a variable. They are not equivalent to the probability of the variable, rather membership in the universe of outcome.

memory The capacity to retain information over time; also the part of a computer that stores the instructions to be executed, partial computational results, and final results

mental accounting The principle by which we reason differently about money depending on the overall amounts. Generally, people are less likely to make efforts to save cash when the relative amount of money they are dealing with is large.

mental operations How a mental process operates, what it accomplishes, and under what conditions it occurs

metacognition Any process that monitors, regulates, or controls a cognitive process

metaphysics The branch of philosophy that examines the nature of reality

mirror neurons Neurons that fire when an animal performs some action and when the animal observes another animal performing the same action

modal memory model An early model of memory showing how information is transferred between sensory, short-term, and long-term memory

modularity of mind A theory that states that the mind is made up of innate and functionally distinct modules

molecular drive Occurs when a copy of a gene mutates and serves an adaptive function even though it was not selected for

momentary intention Refers to the conscious decision to pay attention to something

monism The belief that the mental and physical consist of a single type of state or substance

mood-congruent memory Increased memory for stimuli if the content of those stimuli match a mood we were in while learning them

mood-dependent memory Increased memory for items when the mood at recall matches that during learning. Here the same mood must be present at both occasions.

moods Diffuse affective states that are often of lower intensity than emotion but considerably longer in duration

morphemes Units of spoken language that have meaning

morphology The rules governing the word structure of a language

mosaic model of development A model in which brain mechanisms are almost entirely determined by genes and operate quickly, and the parts of the system develop independently

multimode model of attention The view that selection can be based on multiple stimulus characteristics such as the physical and semantic

multiple realization The view that any given mental state, such as pain, can be instantiated or realized differently in different creatures

multiple-unit recording A brain recording technique where an electrode is used to measure the collective electrical activity of a group of neurons

nativism A belief that a significant body of knowledge is innate or "built into" an organism

natural languages Languages that have evolved in humans and are used by them. Examples include English, Spanish, and French.

nature–nurture debate A controversy that centers on the relative contribution of biology and experience in determining any particular capacity

network science The scientific interdisciplinary study of how complex networks operate

neural correlates of consciousness (NCC) The minimal set of neural events and structures sufficient for a specific conscious experience

neural synchrony A theory that suggests that an object is represented by the joined and coordinated activity of a constellation of distributed cells. It is one solution to the binding problem.

neurons Cells that receive and transmit electrical impulses. They form the basic units of the nervous system.

neuroscience The study of nervous system anatomy and physiology

neurotransmitters Molecules released from the terminal button that travel across the synaptic cleft and attach to receptor sites on the surface of another cell

node A representation of a concept or element of the world

nonlinear relationships Relationships between two variables where the output of one variable is not directly proportionate to the input of another variable. A small change in input values can produce small or large changes in output.

object constancy The ability to recognize an object even though it is hardly ever viewed from the same perspective twice

object link A link in a propositional network that denotes the object or thing to which an action is directed

object permanence The ability to understand that an object still continues to exist even though it is no longer perceptually evident

object-centered description An object representation that is described relative to the object itself and can be recognized from a variety of perspectives

obsessive-compulsive disorder A psychological disorder characterized by anxiety-induced thoughts of contamination and repetitive behaviors to reduce that anxiety

occipital lobe Located on the posterior portion of the cerebral hemispheres, it mediates visual processing

one-word stage A stage in language development where words are first used in a symbolic and semantic fashion

operant conditioning Using behavioral antecedents and their consequents to influence the occurrence and form of behavior; a form of learning in which reward and punishment shape the behavior of an entity (e.g., human)

operator A process that is applied to the problem-solving situation and that transforms it

optogenetics A method to measure and control neurons that have been genetically sensitized to light

ordered network All the connections are local. Nodes are connected only to other nodes in their immediate neighborhood.

ordinate A level of concept category organization of moderate specificity

out-group homogeneity effect The belief that all people in an external group look alike

output layer The third layer of a three-layer network. This generates a representation of the response based on inputs from the hidden layer.

pandemonium model A feature detection model of pattern recognition in which "demons" are used to represent different aspects of a stimulus

panic attack A short-lived but intense episode of fear and sympathetic nervous system arousal

paradigm A philosophy or approach for developing theories for, analyzing, and evaluating a class of problems

parallel distributed processing (PDP) A type of information processing where large numbers of computing units perform their calculations simultaneously. Computational units can receive and process multiple inputs and transmit multiple outputs.

parallel memory search A memory search in which all the items in a list are matched against a target all at once

parallel search Visual search where all the items in the display can be matched for the target at once

parietal lobe Located dorsally, it is implicated in somatosensory, attention, and spatial processing

partial-report condition A condition in iconic memory studies in which participants are cued to remember only one row of letters in the display

pattern recognition The ability to identify objects in the environment

perception The process by which we gather and interpret information from the outside world via the senses; within a mechanical environment, perception refers to the process of scanning an environment and converting the resultant information into a set of abstractions comprising objects, features, and relationships

perceptional categorization deficit A type of apperceptive agnosia that involves difficulty recognizing objects when they are viewed from unusual angles or are lit unevenly

perceptron Artificial neural networks that detect and recognize information about the world, store this information, and use it in some fashion. They are characterized by the ability to learn from experience and can alter their connection strengths.

percolating cluster A single giant group of susceptible sites connected by open bonds that occupies the majority of a network

percolation The propagation of a signal through a network. For example, the way in which a disease can travel through a social network, infecting other individuals.

periodic attractors (or limit cycles) Repetitive trajectories that loop or cycle back on themselves

phase sequence According to Hebb, a group of connected cell assemblies that fire together or close in time

phenomenal concept of mind The idea of mind as a conscious experience

phenomenology Refers to subjective experience rather than objective description

philosophical behaviorism The idea that mental states are dispositions or tendencies to behave in certain ways under certain circumstances

philosophy A discipline concerned with the search for wisdom and knowledge

phobia A persistent and irrational fear of a specific object or situation

phoneme The smallest unit of sound in a language

phonology The rules governing the sound system of a language

phrase structure The hierarchical organization of a sentence; represented using a tree diagram that shows the relationships between words

phrase structure grammar The grammar that governs the use of phrase structures

physical kinds Things that are identified by their material composition only

physical symbol system hypothesis (PSSH) The idea that a formal system can allow for intelligence even in computers

physicalism Also known as materialism; the belief that the universe is entirely physical

plan A robotic primitive element encompassing the corresponding human attributes of reasoning and cognition

plasticity The ability of the brain to recover and reorganize following injury, primarily by rerouting or regrowth of damaged pathways

pleasure principle Motivates the immediate satisfaction of desires

point attractors Single fixed points in the state space

pop out A perceptual phenomenon that occurs when a target is easy to find because it differs from the surrounding distracters along a single stimulus dimension, such as color

positron emission tomography (PET) A brain imaging technique in which blood flow through the brain is measured while a participant carries out a cognitive task. This is accomplished using radioactive isotopes attached to tracer molecules such as glucose or oxygen. Brain areas that are more active will use more of the tracer molecules. This increase in resulting activity can then be detected.

posterior A direction indicating "toward the back"

posttraumatic stress disorder Anxiety and psychological reenactment in the form of flashbacks and nightmares caused by experience of a traumatic event

pragmatic analysis The last stage of natural language processing, in which a complete meaning for a sentence is determined by applying contextual information

pragmatics The social rules underlying language use and the strategies used by speakers to make themselves clear

pragnanz Meaning "good figure," the Gestalt principle stating that parts that are simple will group together

preattentive stage An early stage in pattern recognition that happens automatically and effortlessly. It does not require conscious focused attention.

preconscious That aspect of mind that we can bring into awareness with effort

preferential attachment The principle by which nodes turn into hubs. Those with more links will gradually be linked to more often because they serve as good portals to gain access to large numbers of other nodes.

prejudice A decision or opinion we already have made

preparation An understanding of and preliminary attempts to solve a problem

primary motor cortex Located on the precentral gyrus, it contains a spatial representation or map of different body areas used to control motor behavior

primary somatosensory cortex Located on the postcentral gyrus, it contains a spatial representation or map of different body areas used to process sensory information from the body surface

priming Occurs when processing of a stimulus is facilitated by the prior presentation of a related stimulus

principles of perceptual organization Ways in which visual parts group together to form objects

prisoner's dilemma A social dilemma in which two prisoners must make decisions based on how the other is perceived to decide

proactive interference   Occurs when information that is learned earlier interferes with remembering information learned later

problem solving   A type of behavior that involves deciding that a problem exists and considering one or several solutions to the problem. Special-purpose solutions depend on the circumstances of a particular task. General-purpose solutions can be applied to a broad variety of problems.

problem space   The initial, intermediate, and goal states of the problem

procedural knowledge   Knowledge that represents skills

procedural memory   Memory for skill knowledge. It is demonstrated by doing and occurs without conscious recall.

procedure   Algorithmic processes

process model   A diagrammatic model that represents the way human information is processed. In the model, boxes are used to designate each stage or step in an information-processing sequence.

production rule (conditional statements)   Propositions or predicates whose truth or falsity can be determined

program   A series of instructions that an intelligence devises for the computer to execute

property dualism   The view that the mind and the body are made of the same stuff but have different properties

proposition   A statement or assertion typically posed in the form of a simple sentence

propositional encodings   Abstract, language-like representations, similar to declarative statements. They contain information about an object's parts, its location, and size.

prosopagnosia   An inability to recognize faces, despite the capacity to recognize other types of visual stimuli and the presence of generally intact intellectual functioning

prototypes   A generic or idealized representation of a conceptual category

proximity   The principle stating that parts that are close to one another in the visual field are perceived as a whole

psychoanalytic psychology   The view that the mind is made up of distinct components, each competing with one another and vying for control of behavior

psychological concept of mind   The idea of mind as mental states that cause and explain behavior

psychological inertia   A symptom of executive dysfunction characterized by listlessness and an inability to stop some action once it is started

psychologist's fallacy   The idea that one person's subjective response to a perception does not guarantee that the same response will exist in the mind of anyone else who experiences the same perception

psychology   The scientific study of mind and behavior

psychophysical relations   The relation between the psychological mind and the physical body

psychophysics   The use of quantitative methods to measure relationships between stimuli, which are physical, and perception, which is psychological

punishment   Any consequence that decreases the frequency of a preceding behavior

qualia   The felt or experienced character of mental states

quality   The characteristic that distinguishes sensations from one another

random networks   Networks where the connections are entirely local and can, therefore, be both short and long distance

random processes   Those that exhibit little or no order and, therefore, cannot be predicted. They are described statistically in terms of probabilities instead of certainties.

rationalism   The belief in the existence of innate ideas

raw primal sketch An image represented in terms of its distribution of intensity values or areas of light and dark

reactive The first and the lowest level of processing in the CogAff architecture model. These are reflex-like responses in which a stimulus automatically triggers a reaction—for example, the fear experienced after bumping into something in the dark.

reactive/subsumptive A robotic architecture characterized by direct connection between perceptive elements (sensory information) and actuating elements (sense–action processes)

reagent A substance added to a mixture to produce a particular chemical reaction

reality principle Motivates one to act in a rational and pragmatic fashion

reasoning Ability to draw inferences appropriate to the facts and the situation

receptors Structures on the surface of a neuron to which neurotransmitters attach

reciprocal altruism A characteristic of early human society involving the sharing of hard-won resources between group members

reconstructive memory When recall of an item from memory is based on guided search and subject to bias by subsequent information

recurrent pathways Those in which information flow can feed back onto itself

reductionism The idea that an understanding of parts can completely account for the behavior of a whole

referent The thing or things in the external world that a representation stands for

reflective The stage in the CogAff architecture model where metacognition comes into play. At this level, one is aware of experiencing an emotion but can choose to act on it or not depending on the circumstances and the use of deliberative processes.

reflex A behavior in which a stimulus triggers sensory neurons that activate intermediary neurons, which in turn activate motor neurons, causing a simple motor response

regulatory model of development A model in which brain mechanisms are only partially determined by genes and operate more slowly, and the parts of the system develop interdependently

rehearsal The repeated activation of a circuit that increases the strength of the connections between its nodes

reinforcement Any event that increases the frequency of a preceding response

relation link A link in a propositional network specifying the type of relation between agent and object

representation Something that stands for something else

representativeness heuristic The tendency to judge an item based on its perceived similarity to a category label

repression A defense mechanism that banishes anxiety-arousing thoughts and feelings from consciousness

reticular activating system (RAS) A network of about 100 nuclei that control the brain's overall arousal and alertness level

retrieval The act of accessing needed data from memory and making them available for use

retrieval cues A phenomenon in which an item related to one that was memorized can lead to successful recall

retroactive interference Occurs when information that is learned later interferes with remembering information learned earlier

retrograde amnesia An inability to remember information acquired prior to some traumatic event

reverse engineering The process of starting with an end product and analyzing it to determine its intended function

robot   Particularly, the mechanical embodiment of an IA as a mechanical machine that can function autonomously

rote learning   Learning that focuses on repetition or memorization

schema   A framework or body of knowledge on some topic; knowledge of how to act as well as the computational processes by which to accomplish the activity (algorithm)

scientific method   A process of studying natural phenomena that involves observation and the testing of hypotheses through the use of experiments

script   A type of schema that acts as a stored framework or body of knowledge about some topic

seizure   An uncontrolled surge of synchronous electrical activity in the brain

selection   A change in environmental conditions that results in differential inheritance of traits in a population

selective attention   A form of attention that can be focused onto one source of information and away from another

selective exposure   The principle by which people seek information not already present that supports a consistency between their attitudes or between their attitudes and behavior

self-disclosure   The act of revealing some confidential aspect of ourselves

self-serving bias   The tendency to explain our own failures to external causes but to explain other people's failures to internal ones

self-terminating search   A memory search process that stops as soon as a positive match between a list item and target occurs

semantic   The meaning of a representation

semantic analysis   The third step of natural language understanding where the sentence structure and the meaning of the words are used to derive a partial representation of the meaning of a sentence

semantic code   A memory code based on the inherent meaning of a stimulus

semantic memory   A type of declarative memory containing knowledge of facts

semantic network   A network where each node has a specific meaning and, therefore, employs local representation of concepts

semantics   The rules for deriving meaning in a language

sense   A robotic primitive that includes that part of a robotic system that converts elements of an environment into information that is made available to other parts of the robotic system

sensitivity to initial conditions   A feature of chaotic systems whereby small changes in input can over time produce vastly different outcomes

sensory memory   A short-term repository for incoming sensory information

sentence verification   A procedure in which participants judge the truth or falsity of sentences by pushing one of two buttons

serial memory search   A memory search in which each item in a list is matched against a target, one at a time

serial processors   A type of information processing where one computation is performed at a time. The results of one computation typically serve as the input for the next.

serial search   Visual search where each item in a display must be scrutinized one after the other until the target is located

sexual division of labor   A division of labor between the sexes that is believed to have existed in early human societies where males hunted and females gathered

sexual selection   A differential inheritance of traits based on mate selection and competition instead of a change in the environment

shiftability   The idea that attention can be shifted back and forth between different sources

similarity The perceptual principle stating parts that are similar in lightness, color, shape, or some other characteristic group together

simple cells Cells in the primary visual cortex that code for oriented line segments

simple ideas Ideas derived through sensory input or simple processes of reflection

single-cell recording A brain recording technique where a fine microelectrode is inserted either into a single neuron or into the extracellular fluid adjacent to it. Changes in that cell's electrical conductivity or its rate of firing are then measured.

situated Placed in an ecological niche formed by an agent's goals, the world in which it operates, and its perception of the world

small-world network Any network where the number of links between any pair of nodes is few

social cognition The study of how people make sense of other people and of themselves

social dilemmas The types of situations studied by game theorists

social phobia A disorder characterized by fear of public places, social interaction, and being evaluated negatively by others

spandrel An architectural feature formed by the triangular space between the exterior curve of an arch and the rectangular frame enclosing it. In evolution, it is used to designate a by-product of an adaptation that may serve a useful purpose.

specificity coding A coding in which activity in a single neuron represents an object or feature

speech recognition The first step in the process of natural language processing, by which the acoustic speech signal is analyzed to yield the sequence of spoken words

speech spectrogram A plot that displays the different frequency components of speech and how they change over time

spreading activation The activity that spreads outward from nodes along links to activate other nodes

stability–plasticity dilemma A scenario where a network should be plastic to store novel input patterns. At the same time, it should be stable to protect previously encoded patterns from being erased.

state space A way of visualizing change in chaotic or dynamical systems. Each dimension of the space represents a single variable. A point in this space indicates the current state at any given point in time.

statistical learning The ability for humans and animals to extract statistical regularities from the environment in order to learn. In language acquisition, babies are able to learn very quickly which sounds go together to form words based on the frequency with which those sounds go together.

stereotypes Contain information about people in a specific category. The category can be defined by almost any criteria, such as skin color, sex, profession, or religion.

stimulus enhancement The explanation that one animal can imitate another simply on the basis of being drawn to the location or behavior without any inference of desired goals

stimulus error Confusing our true experience of an object with a description of the object based on language and past experience

storage Information that is represented but not currently activated for use

stream of consciousness The notion that the mind is a process undergoing continuous flow or change

strong AI View asserts that consciousness can arise from a purely physical process

structuralism A theory that emphasizes studying the structure or basic elements of mind and how they combine

structured   A property of language in which rules specify how symbols can be combined

subgoal   An intermediate goal along the route to eventual solution of a problem

sublimation   A defense mechanism that transforms unacceptable impulses into socially valued motivations

subordinate   The most concrete or specific form of conceptual category organization

substance dualism   The view that the mind and the body are composed of completely different substances

substantive thought   Occurs when the mind slows down, perhaps through the focusing of attention

subsumptive architecture   Based on parallels, or loosely coupled processes, intelligence emerges from a large number of parallels and is coordinated through interaction with the environment

subsymbolic   Processes that operate at a level "underneath" symbols; those mechanisms that give rise to symbolic representations

sulcus   A smaller spacing or separation between two areas of brain tissue

sunk-cost fallacy   An explanation for the endowment effect by which we prefer to stay with what we have because of the costs we have already invested

superego   The aspect of mind that is responsible for our ethical sense of right and wrong; operates on the idealistic principle

superior colliculus   A brain area responsible for the moving of visual attention from one object or position in space to another

superordinate   The most abstract form of conceptual category organization that encompasses all examples of the concept

supervised networks   These are networks that are presented with target answers for each pattern they receive as input. The network "knows" what the right answer is on each training trial.

supervisory attentional system (SAS)   A set of schemas that govern only nonroutine actions that require controlled attentional processes. These schemas are designed to be more general purpose and applicable to a wide variety of different problem types.

surface representation   A quasi-pictorial representation that occurs in a spatial medium. It depicts an object or scene and underlies our experience of imagery.

surface structure   The organization of a sentence in the form that it is expressed; how a sentence would be heard if it were spoken or read if it were written

sustainability   The idea that attention can be maintained over time

symbol   A representation that stands for something else

symbol grounding problem   An argument against the PSSH that states computer symbols cannot have semantic properties because computer programs are not in bodies that can perceive and act in the world

symbolic dynamics   A technique for studying cognitive systems whereby a given region of a state space corresponds to a symbol. The trajectory through different regions corresponds to the processing of one symbol after another.

synaptic cleft   The space between neurons across which neurotransmitter molecules travel; typically found between the terminal button of one cell and the dendrite of another

synaptic plasticity   A change in the structure or biochemistry of a synapse that occurs during learning

synchrony   Coordinated patterns of network activity. The firing rate of distant nodes can synchronize, as can more complicated frequency and timing relationships.

syntactic analysis   The second step of natural language processing where the word sequence is analyzed using knowledge of the language's grammar. This produces sentence structure.

syntax   The rules that govern the arrangement of words together in sentences

the teacher   A corrective mechanism that compares actual with desired output and generates an error signal

telepresence   A set of technologies that gives a person the feeling of a physical presence in a real or virtual setting

template   An internal mental representation of a stimulus to which an image generated from an external stimulus is matched

temporal lobe   Located laterally on each hemisphere. It mediates auditory processing, pattern recognition, and language comprehension.

terminal button   A bulb-like structure found at the end of the axon. It releases neurotransmitters.

thalamus   This brain structure serves as a relay center, forwarding incoming messages from the different senses to parts of the cortex specialized for processing them

theory   A set of statements that organizes facts and aids in understanding how the world works

theory of mind (ToM)   The ability to understand others' mental states, such as beliefs, desires, and intentions; to appreciate how these differ from our own; and to utilize this understanding to guide our behavior when interacting with others

theory of natural selection   The theory proposed by Charles Darwin that accounts for changes in animal species over time. It involves species variability, inheritance of traits through reproduction, and selection due to environmental change.

threat-superiority effect   The finding that dangerous items are found to be more perceptually salient

threshold   The minimum amount of activation required to produce conscious awareness of a stimulus

threshold of excitation   The minimal change in a neuron's normal resting electrical state that will initiate the creation of an electrical signal (action potential)

token   Referring to a specific instance of a category; an identification symbol that is useful for symbolic manipulation of knowledge

T.O.T. phenomenon   This is an acronym for "tip of the tongue," meaning one feels familiarity with an item but cannot quite recall it

top-down   An abstract representation of mathematical models that aims to describe functionality at a very high level, then partition it into more detailed levels until the detail is sufficient for machine implementation

trajectory   A path through a state space used to measure a system's behavior

transcranial magnetic stimulation (TMS)   A method in which a wire coil induces a magnetic field over the brain and can be used to record cortical activity or treat depression

transformational grammar   A set of rules for modifying a sentence into a closely related one

transitive inference   The capacity to understand the set of relations between two pairs of items that differ along a continuum (If A > B and B > C, then A > C)

transitive thought   The flow of thought that occurs during less focused and more associative forms of reasoning

trial-and-error learning   Proceeds from random responses to a behavior that satisfies the requirements of the task

tridimensional theory of feeling   A theory stating that all feelings can be characterized by three dimensions: pleasure–displeasure, tension–relaxation, and excitement–depression

Turing test A machine entity that passes this test responds in such a way that it cannot be distinguished from a human

two-word stage A stage in language development in which children first produce two-word utterances

type Referring to an entire category

typicality effect The phenomenon that human participants are faster to judge stereotypical members as belonging to a category

ultimatum game A laboratory scenario in which people are asked to choose the amount of money they can share with someone else

unconditioned response A response elicited by an unconditioned stimulus

unconditioned stimulus A stimulus that elicits a response on its own

unconscious That aspect of mind of which we are completely unaware

universal computing machine Turing's vision of a machine that could solve a problem if it was mathematically solvable

universal grammar The features that are instantiated in the grammars of all natural languages

variation Refers to the differences in traits between animals

ventral A direction indicating "toward the bottom"

ventral visual pathway A pathway that travels downward to the temporal lobe and carries data about color and form

verification A stage in problem solving where an insight is confirmed and one checks to see that it produces a correct solution

viewer-centered description An object representation that is particular to the viewer's point of view

visual agnosia A deficit resulting from brain damage in which an individual has difficulty recognizing objects visually

visual buffer The spatial medium of the surface representation. The buffer is a surface matrix consisting of an array of points.

visual code A memory code based on the visual appearance of a stimulus

visual image A mental representation of an object or scene that preserves metric spatial information

visual search The task of identifying a target item located in a field filled with nontarget items, or distracters

visuospatial sketchpad A system in the working memory model that is specialized for the processing of visual information

voluntarism A movement that viewed the mind as consisting of elements and stressed that these elements were assembled into higher level cognitive components through the power of the will

von Economo neurons Neurons in humans and other animal species that allow for the fast transmission of neural signals and that may be an indicator for intelligence

Wason selection task A task designed to measure a person's logical thinking ability. It involves applying the abstract rules of logic to a specific example.

weak AI Consciousness is itself either not a physical process, and so can never be reproduced, or is a physical process but such a complex one that we will never be able to duplicate it artificially

weights Values on links that determine the strength of the connection between nodes. They can range in value from -1.0 to $+1.0$.

Wernicke's aphasia A language deficit in which speech production is intact but there are impairments in comprehension

Wernicke's area A region in the left temporal lobe that underlies language comprehension. Damage to this area results in Wernicke's aphasia.

whole-report condition A condition in iconic memory studies in which the task is to remember the entire letter display

Williams syndrome A genetic disease caused by a deletion on chromosome 7. These individuals manifest hypersociability. They show an exaggerated interest in other people and increased expressiveness and social communicability.

working memory A short-term memory store used to represent and transform information

REFERENCES

Abell, F., Krams, M., Ashburner, J., Passingham, R., Friston, K., Frackowiak, R., . . . Frith, U. (1999). The neuroanatomy of autism: A voxel-based whole brain analysis of structural scans. *NeuroReport, 10*(8), 1647–1651.

Able, K. P. (1996). The debate over olfactory navigation by homing pigeons. *Journal of Experimental Biology, 199,* 121–124.

Aboud, F. (2003). The formation of in-group favoritism and out-group prejudice in young children: Are they distinct attitudes? *Developmental Psychology, 39*(1), 48–60.

Abrahams, B. S., & Geschwind, D. H. (2008). Advances in autism genetics: On the threshold of a new neurobiology. *Nature Reviews Genetics, 9*(5), 341–355.

Ackley, D., & Littman, M. (1992). Interactions between learning and evolution. In C. Langton (Ed.), *Artificial life II* (pp. 487–509). Redwood City, CA: Addison-Wesley.

Adolphs, R. (2003). Cognitive neuroscience of human social behaviour. *Nature Reviews Neuroscience, 4*(3), 165–178.

Adolphs, R., & Tranel, D. (1999). Preferences for visual stimuli following amygdala damage. *Journal of Cognitive Neuroscience, 11*(6), 610–616.

Adolphs, R., Tranel, D., & Damasio, A. R. (1998). The human amygdala in social judgment. *Nature, 393,* 470–474.

Alais, D., & Blake, R. (2005). *Binocular rivalry.* Cambridge: MIT Press.

Allman, J. M., Hakeem, A., Erwin, J. M., Nimchinsky, E., & Hof, P. (2001). The evolution of an interface between emotion and cognition. *Annals of the New York Academy of Sciences, 935,* 107–117.

Ambady, N., Koo, J., Rosenthal, R., & Winograd, C. (2002). Physical therapists' nonverbal communication predicts geriatric patients' health outcomes. *Psychology and Aging, 17*(3), 443–452.

Anderson, J. R. (1980). *Cognitive psychology and its implications* (2nd ed.). San Francisco, CA: W. H. Freeman.

Anderson, J. R. (1983). *The architecture of cognition.* Cambridge, MA: Harvard University Press.

Anderson, J. R. (1990). *The adaptive character of thought.* Hillsdale, NJ: Erlbaum.

Anderson, J. R., & Lebiere, C. (1998). *The atomic components of thought.* Hillsdale, NJ: Erlbaum.

Anderson, J. R., & Schooler, L. J. (1991). Reflections of the environment in memory. *Psychological Science, 2,* 396–408.

Andrews, P. W., Thomson, J., & Anderson, J. (2009). The bright side of being blue: Depression as an adaptation for analyzing complex problems. *Psychological Review, 116*(3), 620–654.

Angell, J. R. (1907). The province of functional psychology. *Psychological Review, 14,* 61–91.

Arndt, T. L., Stodgell, C. J., & Rodier, P. M. (2005). The teratology of autism. *International Journal of Developmental Neuroscience, 23*(2–3), 189–199.

Ashcraft, M. H. (2002). *Cognition* (3rd ed.). Upper Saddle River, NJ: Prentice Hall.

Astafiev, S., Shulman, G., Stanley, C., Snyder, A., Essen, D., & Corbetta, M. (2003). Functional organization of human intraparietal and frontal cortex for attending, looking, and pointing. *Journal of Neuroscience, 23,* 4689–4699.

Atkinson, R. C., & Shiffrin, R. M. (1971). The control of short-term memory. *Scientific American, 225,* 82–90.

Au, K., Chan, F., Wang, D., & Vertinsky, I. (2003). Mood in foreign exchange trading: Cognitive processes and performance. *Organizational Behavior and Human Decision Processes, 91,* 322–328.

Au, T. K. (1983). Chinese and English counterfactuals: The Sapir-Whorf hypothesis revisited. *Cognition, 15*(1–3), 155–187.

Au, T. K. (1984). Counterfactuals: In reply to Alfred Bloom. *Cognition, 17*(3), 289–302.

Averbach, E., & Sperling, G. (1961). Short-term storage and information in vision. In C. Cherry (Ed.), *Information theory* (pp. 196–211). London, England: Butterworth.

Axmacher, N., Mormann, F., Fernandez, G., Elger, C. E., & Fell, J. (2006). Memory formation by neural synchronization. *Brain Research Reviews, 52,* 170–182.

Babad, E., Bernieri, F., & Rosenthal, R. (1989). When less information is more informative: Diagnosing teacher expectations from brief samples of behaviour. *British Journal of Educational Psychology, 59*(3), 281–295.

Bachevalier, J. (1994). Medial temporal lobe structures and autism: A review of clinical and experimental findings. *Neuropsychologia, 32*(6), 627–648.

Bachevalier, J., Málková, L., & Mishkin, M. (2001). Effects of selective neonatal temporal lobe lesions on socioemotional behavior in infant rhesus monkeys (*Macaca mulatta*). *Behavioral Neuroscience, 115*(3), 545–559.

Bach-y-Rita, P., Collins, C. C., Saunders, F., White, B., & Scadden, L. (1969). Vision substitution by tactile image projection. *Nature, 221,* 963–964.

Baddeley, A. D. (1986). *Working memory.* Oxford, England: Oxford University Press.

Baddeley, A. D. (1992). Working memory. *Science, 255,* 556–559.

Baddeley, A. D., & Hitch, G. (1974). Working memory. In G. H. Bower (Ed.), *The psychology of learning and motivation* (Vol. 8, pp. 47–89). New York, NY: Academic Press.

Bahrick, H. P. (1984). Semantic memory content in permastore: Fifty years of memory for Spanish learned in school. *Journal of Experimental Psychology: General, 113,* 1–29.

Baig, M. M., Gholamhosseini, H., & Harrison, M. J. (2012). *Fuzzy logic based smart anesthesia monitoring system in the operation theatre.* Retrieved from http://www.wseas.org/multimedia/journals/circuits/2012/53-598.pdf

Bailey, A., Phillips, W., & Rutter, M. (1996). Autism: Towards an integration of clinical, genetic, neuropsychological, and neurobiological perspectives. *Journal of Child Psychology and Psychiatry, 37*(1), 89–126.

Baker, M. C. (2001). *The atoms of language.* New York, NY: Basic Books.

Baldwin, D. A. (1995). Understanding the link between joint attention and language. In C. Moore & P. J. Dunham (Eds.), *Joint attention: Its origins and role in development* (pp. 131–158). Hillsdale, NJ: Erlbaum.

Banich, M. T. (2004). *Cognitive neuroscience and neuropsychology.* Boston, MA: Houghton Mifflin.

Baran, P. (1964). *Introduction to distributed communications networks* (Report Memorandum RM-3240-PR). Santa Monica, CA: RAND.

Barinaga, M. (1992). How scary things get that way. *Science, 258,* 887–888.

Baron, J. (2000). *Thinking and deciding* (3rd ed.). New York, NY: Cambridge University Press.

Baron-Cohen, S., Cox, A., Baird, G., Swettenham, J., & Nightingale, N. (1996). Psychological markers in the detection of autism in infancy in a large population. *British Journal of Psychiatry, 168*(2), 158–163.

Barto, A. G., Sutton, R. S., & Anderson, C. W. (1983). Neuronlike adaptive elements that can solve difficult learning control problems. *IEEE Transactions on Systems, Man, & Cybernetics, 13*(5), 834–846.

Bauman, M., & Kemper, T. (2007). The neuroanatomy of the brain in autism: Current thoughts and future directions. In J. M. Pérez, P. M. González, M. L. Comí, & C. Nieto (Eds.), *New developments in autism: The future is today* (pp. 259–267). London, England: Jessica Kingsley.

Baumeister, R. F., & Leary, M. R. (1995). The need to belong: Desire for interpersonal attachments as a fundamental human motivation. *Psychological Bulletin, 117*, 497–529.

Bavelier, D., Corina, D., Jezzard, P., Clark, V., Karni, A., Lalwani, A., . . . Neville, H. J. (1998). Hemispheric specialization for English and ASL: Left invariance–right variability. *NeuroReport, 9*(7), 1537–1542.

Bechara, A., Damasio, H., Tranel, D., & Damasio, A. R. (1997). Deciding advantageously before knowing the advantageous strategy. *Science, 275*, 1293–1294.

Bechtel, W., & Abrahamsen, A. (1991). *Connectionism and the mind: An introduction to parallel processing in networks.* Cambridge, MA: Basil Blackwell.

Bechtel, W., & Abrahamsen, A. (2006). Phenomena and mechanisms: Putting the symbolic, connectionist, and dynamical systems debate in broader perspective. In R. Stainton (Ed.), *Contemporary debates in cognitive science* (pp. 159–186). Oxford, England: Basil Blackwell.

Becker, M. W., Pashler, H., & Anstis, S. M. (2000). The role of iconic memory in change detection tasks. *Perception, 29*(3), 273–286.

Beer, R. D. (1990). *Intelligence as adaptive behavior: An experiment in computational neuroethology.* New York, NY: Academic Press.

Bellugi, U., Lichtenberger, L., Jones, W., Lai, Z., & St. George, M. (2000). The neurocognitive profile of Williams syndrome: A complex pattern of strengths and weaknesses. *Journal of Cognitive Neuroscience, 12*, 7–29.

Bellugi, U., Wang, P. P., & Jernigan, T. L. (1994). Williams syndrome: An unusual neuropsychological profile. In S. H. Broman & J. Grafman (Eds.), *Atypical cognitive deficits in developmental disorders: Implications for brain function* (pp. 23–56). Hillsdale, NJ: Erlbaum.

Bennett, W., Pickard, V., Iozzi, D., Schroeder, C., Lagos, T., & Caswell, C. (2004). Managing the public sphere: Journalistic construction of the great globalization debate. *Journal of Communication, 54*(3), 437–455.

Berlin, B., & Kay, P. (1969). *Basic color terms: Their universality and evolution.* Berkeley: University of California Press.

Besner, D., & Stolz, J. A. (1999). The Stroop effect and single letter coloring: What replicates and what doesn't. *Psychonomic Bulletin & Review, 8*(4), 858.

Biederman, I. (1987). Recognition-by-components: A theory of human image understanding. *Psychological Review, 94*, 115–147.

Birbaumer, N., Grodd, W., Diedrich, O., Klose, U., Erb, M., Lotze, M., . . . Flor, H. (1998). fMRI reveals amygdala activation to human faces in social phobics. *NeuroReport, 9*(6), 1223–1226.

Bishop, D. V. M. (1997). *Uncommon understanding: Development and disorders of language comprehension in children*. Hove, England: Psychology Press.

Blakemore, S. J., & Decety, J. (2001). From the perception of action to the understanding of intention. *Nature Reviews Neuroscience, 2, 561–567.*

Blakemore, S. J., Winston, J., & Frith, U. (2004). Social cognitive neuroscience: Where are we heading? *Trends in Cognitive Sciences, 8, 216–222.*

Blanchette, I., & Dunbar, K. (2001). Analogy use in naturalistic settings: The influence of audience, emotion, and goals. *Memory & Cognition, 29*(5), 2001.

Bloom, A. H. (1981). *The linguistic shaping of thought: A study in the impact of language on thinking in China and the West.* Mahwah, NJ: Erlbaum.

Bloom, P. (Ed.). (1994). *Language acquisition.* Cambridge: MIT Press.

Bluff, L. A., Weir, A. A. S., & Rutz, J. H. (2007). Tool-related cognition in New Caledonian crows. *Comparative Cognition & Behavior Reviews, 2, 1–25.*

Boden, M. (1990). Escaping from the Chinese room. In M. Boden (Ed.), *The philosophy of artificial intelligence* (pp. 88–104). Oxford, England: Oxford University Press.

Bolhuis, J. J., & van Kampen, H. S. (1988). Serial position curves in spatial memory of rats: Primacy and recency effects. *Quarterly Journal of Experimental Psychology B, 40,* 135–149.

Bollt, E., Stanford, T., Lai, Y., & Zyczkowski, K. (2000). Validity of threshold crossing analysis of symbolic dynamics from chaotic time series. *Physical Review Letters, 85,* 3524–3527.

Boster, J., & D'Andrade, R. (1989). Natural and human sources of cross-cultural agreement in ornithological classification. *American Anthropologist, 91,* 132–142.

Bower, G. H. (1981). Mood and memory. *American Psychologist, 36,* 129–148.

Bower, G. H., Monteiro, K. P., & Gilligan, S. G. (1978). Emotional mood as a context of learning and recall. *Journal of Verbal Learning and Verbal Behavior, 17,* 573–585.

Bowlby, J. (1967). *Attachment and loss: Attachment* (Vol. 1). New York, NY: Basic Books.

Boyd, R., & Richerson, P. (1996). Why culture is common, but cultural evolution is rare. *Evolution of social behaviour patterns in primates and man* (pp. 77–93). New York, NY: Oxford University Press.

Bravais, A. (1949). *On the systems formed by points regularly distributed on a plane or in space.* Buffalo, NY: Crystallographic Society of America.

Bray, D. (2011). *Wetware: A computer in every living cell.* New Haven, CT: Yale University Press.

Breazeal, C. (2002). *Designing sociable robots.* Cambridge: MIT Press.

Breazeal, C., & Brooks, R. (2005). Robot emotions: A functional perspective. In J. M. Fellows & M. A. Arbib (Eds.), *Who needs emotions? The brain meets the robot* (pp. 271–310). Oxford, England: Oxford University Press.

Brewer, M. B., & Brown, R. J. (1998). Intergroup relations. In D. T. Gilbert, S. T. Fiske, & G. Lindzey (Eds.), *Handbook of social psychology* (Vol. 2, 4th ed., pp. 554–594). New York, NY: McGraw-Hill.

Brewer, M. M., & Harasty Feinstein, A. S. (1999). Dual processes in the cognitive representation of persons and social categories. In S. Chaiken & Y. Trope (Eds.), *Dual-process theories in social psychology* (pp. 225–270). New York, NY: Guilford Press.

Broadbent, D. E. (1958). *Perception and communication.* London, England: Pergamon Press.

Brock, T. C., Albert, S. M., & Becker, L. A. (1970). Familiarity, utility, and supportiveness as determinants of information receptivity. *Journal of Personality and Social Psychology, 14,* 292–301.

Brock, T. C., & Balloun, J. L. (1967). Behavioral receptivity to dissonant information. *Journal of Personality and Social Psychology, 6,* 413–428.

Brooks, R. A. (1991). Intelligence without representation. *Artificial Intelligence, 47,* 139–159.

Brooks, R. A. (1999). *Cambrian intelligence: The early history of the new AI.* Cambridge: MIT Press.

Brooks, R. A. (2002). *Flesh and machines: How robots will change us.* New York, NY: Random House.

Brown, A. L., Bransford, J. D., Ferrara, R. A., & Campione, J. C. (1983). Learning, remembering, and understanding. In J. H. Flavell & E. M. Markman (Eds.), *Handbook of child psychology: Cognitive development* (Vol. 3, 4th ed., pp. 77–166). New York, NY: Wiley.

Brown, A. S. (1991). A review of the tip-of-the-tongue experience. *Psychological Bulletin, 109*(2), 204–223.

Brown, J. A. (1958). Some tests of the decay theory of immediate memory. *Quarterly Journal of Experimental Psychology, 10,* 12–21.

Brown, J. D., & Rogers, R. J. (1991). Self-serving attributions: The role of physiological arousal. *Personality and Social Psychology Bulletin, 17*(5), 501–506.

Brown, R., & Kulik, J. (1977). Flashbulb memories. *Cognition, 5,* 73–93.

Brown, R. J. (2000). Social identity theory: Past achievements, current problems, and future challenges. *European Journal of Social Psychology, 30,* 745–778.

Bruce, C., Desimone, R., & Gross, C. G. (1981). Visual properties of neurons in a polysensory area in the superior temporal sulcus of the macaque. *Journal of Neurophysiology, 46,* 369–384.

Brunet, E., Sarfati, Y., Hardy-Bayle, M. C., & Decety, J. (2000). A PET investigation of the attribution of intentions with a nonverbal task. *NeuroImage, 11,* 157–166.

Buchanan, M. (2002). *Nexus: Small worlds and the groundbreaking theory of networks.* New York, NY: W. W. Norton.

Burton, A. M., Young, A. W., Bruce, V., Johnston, R. A., & Ellis, A. W. (1991). Understanding covert recognition. *Cognition, 39,* 129–166.

Buss, D. M. (1999). *Evolutionary psychology: The new science of the mind.* Boston, MA: Allyn & Bacon.

Byrne, R. W. (1995). *The thinking ape.* Oxford, England: Clarendon Press.

Cacioppo, J., Crites, S., & Gardner, W. (1996). Attitudes to the right: Evaluative processing is associated with lateralized late positive event-related brain potentials. *Personality and Social Psychology Bulletin, 22*(12), 1205–1219.

Camerer, C. F. (2003). *Behavioral game theory: Experiments in strategic interaction.* Princeton, NJ: Princeton University Press.

Cannon, W. B. (1927). The James-Lange theory of emotion: A critical examination and an alternative theory. *American Journal of Psychology, 39,* 10–124.

Carey, B. (2012, May 16). Paralyzed, moving a robot with their minds. *The New York Times.* Retrieved from http://www.nytimes.com/2012/05/17/science/bodies-inert-they-moved-a-robot-with-their-minds.html

Carlson, S., & Moses, L. (2001). Individual differences in inhibitory control and children's theory of mind. *Child Development, 72*(4), 1032–1053.

Carr, H. A. (1925). *Psychology.* New York, NY: Longmans, Green.

Carroll, J. B. (1956). *Language, thought, and reality: Selected writings of Benjamin Lee Whorf*. Cambridge: MIT Press.

Carter, C., & Rice, C. (1997). Acquisition and manifestation of prejudice in children. *Journal of Multicultural Counseling and Development, 25*(3), 185–194.

Castano, E., & Yzerbyt, V. Y. (1998). The highs and lows of group homogeneity. *Behavioral Processes, 42*, 219–238.

Cawsey, A. (1998). *The essence of artificial intelligence*. Harlow, England: Prentice Hall.

Chakraborty, R. C. (2008, March 16). Artificial intelligence technologies. Retrieved from myreaders.wordpress.com

Chalmers, D. (1996). *The conscious mind*. Oxford, England: Oxford University Press.

Chapanis, A. (1965). Color names for color space. *American Scientist, 53*, 327–346.

Chase, W. G., & Simon, H. A. (1973). The mind's eye in chess. In W. G. Chase (Ed.), *Visual information processing*. New York, NY: Academic Press.

Cheney, D. L., & Seyfarth, R. M. (1990). *How monkeys see the world*. Chicago, IL: University of Chicago Press.

Cherkassky, V., Kana, R., Keller, T., & Just, M. (2006). Functional connectivity in baseline resting state network in autism. *NeuroReport, 17*, 1687–1690.

Cherry, E. C. (1953). Some experiments on the recognition of speech, with one and with two ears. *Journal of the Acoustical Society of America, 25*, 975–979.

Chomsky, N. (1957). *Syntactic structures*. The Hague, Netherlands: Mouton.

Chomsky, N. (1986). *Knowledge of language: Its nature, origin, and use*. New York, NY: Praeger.

Choset, H., Lynch, K. M., Hutchinson, S., Kantor, G., Burgard, W., Kavraki, L. E., &

Thrun, S. (2005). *Principles of robot motion: Theory, algorithms, and implementations*. Boston: MIT Press.

Christianson, S.-A., & Loftus, E. F. (1991). Remembering emotional events: The fate of detailed information. *Emotion and Cognition, 5*, 81–108.

Church, A. (1936). An unsolvable problem of elementary number theory. *American Journal of Mathematics, 58*, 345–363.

Churchland, P. M. (1981). Eliminativism and the propositional attitudes. *Journal of Philosophy, 78*, 67–90.

Churchland, P. M. (1995). *The engine of reason, the seat of the soul: A philosophical journey into the brain*. Cambridge: MIT Press.

Churchland, P. S., Koch, C., & Sejnowski, T. J. (1990). What is computational neuroscience? In E. L. Schwartz (Ed.), *Computational neurosciences* (pp. 38–45). Cambridge: MIT Press.

Cialdini, R. (1993). *Influence: Science and practice* (3rd ed.). New York, NY: HarperCollins.

Clark, A. (2001). *Mindware: An introduction to the philosophy of cognitive science*. New York, NY: Oxford University Press.

Clark, A., & Chalmers, D. (1998). The extended mind. *Analysis, 58*, 7–19.

Clark, H. H., & Clark, E. V. (1977). *Psychology and language: An introduction to psycholinguistics*. New York, NY: Harcourt Brace Jovanovich.

Clark, V. P., Keil, K., Maisog, J. M., Courtney, S. M., Ungerleider, L. G., & Haxby, J. V. (1996). Functional magnetic resonance imaging of human visual cortex during face matching: A comparison with positron emission tomography. *NeuroImage, 4*, 1–15.

Clore, G. L., Gasper, K., & Garvin, E. (2001). Affect as information. In J. P. Forgas (Ed.),

Handbook of affect and social cognition (pp. 121–144). Mahwah, NJ: Erlbaum.

Cohen, D. (1979). *J. B. Watson: The founder of behaviourism: A biography*. London, England: Routledge & Kegan Paul.

Colby, C. L., Duhamel, J.-R., & Goldberg, M. E. (1996). Visual, presaccadic, and cognitive activation of single neurons in monkey lateral intraparietal area. *Journal of Neurophysiology, 76,* 2841–2852.

Collins, A. M., & Quillian, M. R. (1969). Retrieval time from semantic memory. *Journal of Verbal Learning and Verbal Behavior, 8,* 240–247.

Collins, N. L., & Miller, L. C. (1994). Self-disclosure and liking: A meta-analytic review. *Psychological Bulletin, 116*(3), 457–475.

Conrad, R. (1964). Acoustic confusions in immediate memory. *British Journal of Psychology, 55,* 75–84.

Cook, V. J. (1988). *Chomsky's universal grammar: An introduction*. Cambridge, MA: Basil Blackwell.

Cooper, L. A., & Shepard, R. N. (1973). Chronometric studies of the rotation of mental images. In W. G. Chase (Ed.), *Visual information processing* (pp. 75–176). New York, NY: Academic Press.

Corkin, S. (1984). Lasting consequences of bilateral medial temporal lobectomy: Clinical course and experimental findings in H. M. *Seminars in Neurology, 4,* 249–259.

Cosmides, L., & Tooby, J. (1992). Cognitive adaptations for social exchange. In J. Barkow, L. Cosmides, & J. Tooby (Eds.), *The adapted mind* (pp. 163–228). New York, NY: Oxford University Press.

Coull, J. T., & Nobre, A. C. (1998). Where and when to pay attention: The neural systems for directing attention to spatial locations and to time intervals as revealed by both PET and fMRI. *Journal of Neuroscience, 18,* 7426–7435.

Craik, K. (1943). *The nature of explanation*. Cambridge, England: Cambridge University Press.

Crick, F., & Koch, C. (1995). Are we aware of neural activity in primary visual cortex? *Nature, 375,* 121–123.

Crystal, D. (1987). *The Cambridge encyclopedia of language*. Cambridge, MA: Cambridge University Press.

Cuddy, A. J. C., Fiske, S. R., & Glick, P. (2007). The BIAS map: Behaviors from intergroup affect and stereotypes. *Journal of Personality and Social Psychology, 92,* 631–648.

Cummins, D. D. (1999, June). *Early emergence of cheater detection in human development*. Paper presented at the annual meeting of the Human Behavior and Evolution Society, Salt Lake City, UT.

Cusack, R., Carlyon, R. P., & Robertson, I. H. (2000). Neglect between but not within auditory objects. *Journal of Cognitive Neuroscience, 12*(6), 1056–1065.

Damasio, A. (1994). *Descartes' error: Emotion, reason, and the human brain*. New York, NY: Putnam Books.

Damasio, A. R. (1999). *The feeling of what happens: Body and emotion in the making of consciousness*. New York, NY: Harcourt Brace.

Darwin, C. (1859). *On the origin of species by means of natural selection*. London, England: John Murray.

Darwin, C. (1998). *The expression of emotion in man and animals* (P. Ekman, Ed.; 3rd ed.). New York, NY: Oxford University Press. (Original work published 1872)

Darwin, C. J., Turvey, M. T., & Crowder, R. G. (1972). An auditory analogue of the Sperling partial report procedure: Evidence for brief auditory storage. *Cognitive Psychology, 3,* 255–267.

Davidson, R. J., Scherer, K. R., & Goldsmith, H. H. (2003). *Handbook of affective sciences.* New York, NY: Oxford University Press.

Davies, I. R. L., & Corbett, G. G. (1997). A cross-cultural study of colour grouping: Evidence for weak linguistic relativity. *British Journal of Psychology, 88*(3), 493–517.

Davies, I. R. L., Sowden, P. T., Jerrett, D. T., Jerrett, T., & Corbett, G. G. (1998). A cross-cultural study of English and Setswana speakers on a colour triads task: A test of the Sapir-Whorf hypothesis. *British Journal of Psychology, 89*(1), 1–15.

Davis, H. (1992). Discrimination of the number three by a raccoon (*Procyon lotor*). *Animal Learning and Behavior, 12,* 409–413.

Davis, S., Grover, C., Becker, A., & McGregor, L. (1992). Academic dishonesty: Prevalence, determinants, techniques, and punishments. *Teaching of Psychology, 19*(1), 16–20.

Davis, S., & Ludvigson, H. (1995). Additional data on academic dishonesty and a proposal for remediation. *Teaching of Psychology, 22*(2), 119–121.

Dawson, M. R. W. (1998). *Understanding cognitive science.* Malden, MA: Blackwell.

De Martino, B., Kumaran, D., Seymour, B., & Dolan, R. J. (2006). Frames, biases, and rational decision making in the human brain. *Science, 313,* 684–687.

de Villiers, J., & de Villiers, P. (2000). Linguistic determinism and the understanding of false beliefs. In P. Mitchell & K. J. Riggs (Eds.), *Children's reasoning and the mind* (pp. 191–228). Hove, England: Psychology Press.

De Waal, F. B. M. (1997a). Are we in anthropodenial? *Discover, 18*(7), 50–53.

De Waal, F. B. M. (1997b). Food-transfers through mesh in brown capuchins. *Journal of Comparative Psychology, 111,* 370–378.

Decety, J., & Jackson, P. (2004). The functional architecture of human empathy. *Behavioral and Cognitive Neuroscience Reviews, 3*(2), 406–412.

Dehaene-Lambertz, G., Pallier, C., Serniclaes, W., Sprenger-Charolles, L., Jobert, A., & Dehaene, S. (2005). Neural correlates of switching from auditory to speech perception. *NeuroImage, 24,* 21–33.

Deisseroth, K. (2010). Controlling the brain with light. *Scientific American, 303,* 48–55.

DeLancey, C. (2002). *Passionate engines: What emotions reveal about the mind and artificial intelligence.* Oxford, England: Oxford University Press.

Dennett, D. (1991). *Consciousness explained.* Boston, MA: Little, Brown.

Dennett, D. (1998). The practical requirements for making a conscious robot. In *Brainchildren: Essays on designing minds* (pp. 154–170). Cambridge: MIT Press.

Deregowski, J. B. (1989). Real space and represented space: Cross-cultural perspectives. *Behavioral and Brain Sciences, 12,* 51–119.

Desimone, R., Albright, T. D., Gross, C. D., & Bruce, C. (1984). Stimulus-selective responses of inferior temporal neurons in the macaque. *Journal of Neuroscience, 4,* 2051–2062.

Deutsch, J. A., & Deutsch, D. (1963). Attention: Some theoretical considerations. *Psychological Review, 70,* 80–90.

Dinstein, I., Gardner, J., Jazayeri, M., & Heeger, D. (2008). Executed and observed movements have different distributed representations in human aIPS. *Journal of Neuroscience, 28*(44), 11231–11239.

Dion, K., & Stein, S. (1978). Physical attractiveness and interpersonal influence. *Journal of Experimental Social Psychology, 14*(1), 97–108.

Dolan, R. (2002). Emotion, cognition, and behavior. *Science, 298,* 1191–1194.

Doupe, A. J., & Kuhl, P. K. (1999). Birdsong and human speech: Common themes and mechanisms. *Annual Review of Neuroscience, 22,* 567–631.

Dover, G. (2000). Anti-Dawkins. In H. Rose & S. Rose (Eds.), *Arguments against evolutionary psychology* (pp. 55–77). New York, NY: Harmony Books.

Dreyfus, H. (1965). *Alchemy and AI.* Santa Monica, CA: RAND.

Dreyfus, H. (1986). *Mind over machine: The power of human intuition and expertise in the era of the computer.* Oxford, England: Blackwell.

Dreyfus, H. L. (1992). *What computers still can't do* (3rd ed.). Cambridge: MIT Press.

Driver, J., & Mattingley, J. B. (1998). Parietal neglect and visual awareness. *Nature Neuroscience Review, 1*(1), 17–22.

Dronkers, N. F., Redfern, B. B., & Ludy, C. A. (1995). Lesion localization in chronic Wernicke's aphasia. *Brain and Language, 51*(1), 62–65.

Dronkers, N. F., Shapiro, J. K., Redfern, B., & Knight, R. T. (1992). The role of Broca's area in Broca's aphasia. *Journal of Clinical and Experimental Neuropsychology, 14,* 52–53.

Dunbar, R. (1996). *Grooming, gossip, and the evolution of language.* Cambridge, MA: Harvard University Press.

Duncan, B. (1976). Differential social perception and attribution of intergroup violence: Testing the lower limits of stereotyping of Blacks. *Journal of Personality and Social Psychology, 34*(4), 590–598.

Dworkin, B. R. (1993). *Learning and physiological regulation.* Chicago, IL: University of Chicago Press.

Eastwood, J. D., Smilek, D., & Merikle, P. M. (2001). Differential attentional guidance by unattended faces expressing positive and negative emotion. *Perception and Psychophysics, 63,* 1004–1013.

Edwards, F. A. (1995). LTP: A structural model to explain the inconsistencies. *Trends in Neuroscience, 18,* 250–255.

Ekman, P. (1989). The argument and evidence about universals in facial expressions of emotion. In H. Wagner & A. Manstead (Eds.), *Handbook of social psychophysiology* (pp. 143–164). Chichester, England: Wiley.

Ekman, P., & Friesen, W. V. (1971). Constants across cultures in the face and emotion. *Journal of Personality and Social Psychology, 17,* 124–129.

Elia, J., Ambrosini, P. J., & Rapoport, J. L. (1999). Treatment of attention-deficit hyperactivity disorder. *New England Journal of Medicine, 340,* 780–788.

Elman, J. (1990). Finding structure in time. *Cognitive Science, 14,* 179–211.

Ember, C. R., & Ember, M. (1985). *Cultural anthropology* (4th ed.). Englewood Cliffs, NJ: Prentice Hall.

Engel, A. K., König, P., Kreiter, A. K., Schillen, T. B., & Singer, W. (1992). Temporal coding in the visual cortex: New vistas on integration in the nervous system. *Trends in Neurosciences, 15,* 218–226.

Erickson, B., Lind, E., Johnson, B., & O'Barr, W. (1978). Speech style and impression formation in a court setting: The effects of "powerful" and "powerless" speech. *Journal of Experimental Social Psychology, 14*(3), 266–279.

Fajardo, C., Escobar, M. I., Buritica, E., Arteaga, G., Umbarila, J., Casanova, M. F., & Pimienta, H. (2008). Von Economo neurons are present in the dorsolateral prefrontal cortex of humans. *Neuroscience Letters, 435*(3), 215–218.

Farah, M. J. (1988). Is visual imagery really visual? Overlooked evidence from neuropsychology. *Psychological Review, 95,* 307–317.

Farah, M. J. (1990). *Visual agnosia: Disorders of object recognition and what they tell us about normal vision*. Cambridge: MIT Press.

Faraone, S. V., Doyle, A. E., Mick, E., & Biederman, J. (2001). Meta-analysis of the association between the 7-repeat allele of the dopamine D4 receptor gene and attention-deficit hyperactivity disorder. *American Journal of Psychiatry, 158*, 1052–1057.

Fazio, R. H. (1990). Multiple processes by which attitudes guide behavior: The MODE model as an integrative framework. In M. P. Zanna (Ed.), *Advances in experimental social psychology* (Vol. 23, pp. 75–110). New York, NY: Academic Press.

Fazio, R. H. (2001). On the automatic activation of associated evaluations: An overview. *Cognition and Emotion, 15*(2), 115–141.

Feingold, A. (1991). Sex differences in the effects of similarity and physical attractiveness on opposite-sex attraction. *Basic and Applied Social Psychology, 12*(3), 357–367.

Feltz, A., & Cokely, E. T. (2009). Do judgments about freedom and responsibility depend on who you are? Personality differences in intuitions about compatibilism and incompatibilism. *Consciousness and Cognition, 18*, 342–350.

Fernald, A. (1989). Intonation and communicative intent in mother's speech to infants: Is the melody the message? *Child Development, 60*, 1497–1510.

Fiedler, K. (2001). Affective states trigger processes of assimilation and accommodation. In L. L. Martin & G. L. Clore (Eds.), *Theories of mood and cognition: A user's guidebook* (pp. 85–98). Mahwah, NJ: Erlbaum.

Fink, G. R., Dolan, R. J., Halligan, P. W., Marshall, J. C., & Firth, C. D. (1997). Space-based and object-based visual attention: Shared and specific neural domains. *Brain, 120*, 2013–2028.

Finke, R. A., & Kosslyn, S. M. (1980). Mental imagery acuity in the peripheral visual field. *Journal of Experimental Psychology: Human Perception and Performance, 6*, 126–139.

Fiske, S. T., Cuddy, A. J. C., Glick, P., & Xu, J. (2002). A model of (often mixed) stereotype content: Competence and warmth respectively followed from preceded status and competition. *Journal of Personality and Social Psychology, 82*, 878–902.

Fiske, S. T., Lin, M. H., & Neuberg, S. L. (1999). The continuum model: Ten years later. In S. Chaiken & Y. Trope (Eds.), *Dual process theories in social psychology* (pp. 231–254). New York, NY: Guilford Press.

Fiske, S. T., & Taylor, S. E. (2008). *Social cognition: From brains to culture*. New York, NY: McGraw-Hill.

Fletcher, P. C., Happé, F., Frith, U., Baker, S. C., Dolan, R. J., Frackowiak, R. S., & Frith, C. D. (1995). Other minds in the brain: A functional imaging study of "theory of mind" in story comprehension. *Cognition, 57*, 109–128.

Floreano, D., & Mattiussi, C. (2008). *Bio-inspired artificial intelligence*. Cambridge: MIT Press.

Fodor, J. A. (1983). *The modularity of mind*. Cambridge: MIT Press.

Fogassi, L., Ferrari, P., Gesierich, B., Rozzi, S., Chersi, F., & Rizzolatti, G. (2005). Parietal lobe: From action organization to intention understanding. *Science, 308*(5722), 662–667.

Forbus, K., Gentner, D., & Law, K. (1995). MAC/FAC: A model of similarity-based retrieval. *Cognitive Science, 19*, 144–205.

Forgas, J. P. (1995). Mood and judgment: The affect infusion model (AIM). *Psychological Bulletin, 11*, 39–66.

Forsterling, F. (2001). *Attribution: An introduction to theories, research, and applications.* New York, NY: Psychology Press.

Fox, E. (2008). *Emotion science.* New York, NY: Palgrave Macmillan.

Fox, E., Lester, V., Russo, R., Bowles, R. J., Pichler, A., & Dutton, K. (2000). Facial expressions of emotion: Are angry faces detected more efficiently? *Cognition & Emotion, 14,* 61–92.

Frassinetti, F., Pavani, F., & Làdavas, E. (2002). Acoustical vision of neglected stimuli: Interaction among spatially converging audiovisual inputs in neglect patients. *Journal of Cognitive Neuroscience, 14,* 62–69.

Fredrickson, B. L. (1998). What good are positive emotions? *Review of General Psychology, 2,* 300–319.

Freedman, D. (1994). *Brainmakers.* New York, NY: Simon & Schuster.

French, R. M. (1992). Semi-distributed representations and catastrophic forgetting in connectionist networks. *Connection Science, 4,* 365–377.

French, R. M. (2001). Catastrophic interference in connectionist networks. In *Macmillan encyclopedia of the cognitive sciences* (pp. 611–615). London, England: Macmillan.

Friedenberg, J. (2008). *Artificial psychology: The quest for what it means to be human.* New York, NY: Psychology Press.

Friedenberg, J. (2009). *Dynamical psychology: Complexity, self-organization, and mind.* Litchfield Park, AZ: Emergent.

Frieze, I. H., Parsons, J. E., Johnson, P. B., Ruble, D. N., & Zellman, G. L. (1978). *Women and sex roles: A social psychological perspective.* New York, NY: W. W. Norton.

Frith, C. D., & Frith, U. (1999). Interacting minds: A biological basis. *Science, 286*(5445), 1692–1695.

Frith, U. (2001). What framework should we use for understanding developmental disorders? *Developmental Neuropsychology, 20*(2), 555–563.

Fromkin, V., Krashen, S., Curtiss, S., Rigler, D., & Rigler, M. (1974). The development of language in Genie: A case of language acquisition beyond the "critical period." *Brain & Language, 1*(1), 81–107.

Gagnon, S., & Dore, F. Y. (1994). Cross-sectional study of object permanence in domestic puppies (*Canis familiaris*). *Journal of Comparative Psychology, 108,* 220–232.

Gallagher, H. L. (2000). Reading the mind in cartoons and stories: An fMRI study of "theory of mind" in verbal and nonverbal tasks. *Neuropsychologia, 38*(1), 11–21.

Gallagher, H. L., & Frith, C. D. (2003). Functional imaging of "theory of mind." *Trends in Cognitive Sciences, 7,* 77–83.

Gallup, G. G., Anderson, R., & Shilito, D. J. (2002). The mirror test. In M. Bekoff, C. Allen, & G. M. Burghardt (Eds.), *The cognitive animal* (pp. 325–333). Cambridge: MIT Press.

Gantz, B. G., & Turner, C. W. (2004). Combining acoustic and electrical speech processing: Iowa/Nucleus hybrid implant. *Acta Otolaryngol, 124,* 344–347.

Gardner, H. (1974). *The shattered mind.* New York, NY: Vintage Books.

Gardner, H. (1985). *The mind's new science.* New York, NY: Basic Books.

Gardner, R. A., Gardner, B. T., & Van Cantfort, T. E. (1989). *Teaching sign language to chimpanzees.* New York: State University of New York Press.

Garfield, J. L. (1995). Philosophy: Foundations of cognitive science. In N. A. Stillings, S. E. Weisler, C. H. Chase, M. H. Feinstein, J. L. Garfield, & E. L. Rissland (Eds.), *Cognitive science: An introduction* (2nd ed., pp. 331–377). Cambridge: MIT Press.

Gaulin, S., & FitzGerald, R. (1986). Sex differences in spatial ability: An evolutionary hypothesis and test. *American Naturalist, 127,* 74–88.

Gaulin, S., & FitzGerald, R. (1989). Sexual selection for spatial learning ability. *Animal Behavior, 37*(2), 322–331.

Gaulin, S. J. C., & McBurney, D. H. (2001). *Psychology: An evolutionary approach.* Upper Saddle River, NJ: Prentice Hall.

Gawronski, B. (2003). Implicational schemata and the correspondence bias: On the diagnostic value of situationally constrained behavior. *Journal of Personality and Social Psychology, 84*(6), 1154–1171.

Geschwind, N. (1972). Language and the brain. *Scientific American, 226,* 76–83.

Gibson, J. J. (1986). *The ecological approach to visual perception.* Hillsdale, NJ: Erlbaum.

Giedd, J. N., Blumenthal, J., Molloy, E., & Castellanos, F. X. (2001). Brain imaging of attention-deficit/hyperactivity disorder. *Annals of the New York Academy of the Sciences, 931,* 33–49.

Gigerenzer, G., & Hoffrage, U. (1995). How to improve Bayesian reasoning without instruction. *Psychological Review, 102,* 684–704.

Gigerenzer, G., & Hug, K. (1992). Domain-specific reasoning: Social contracts, cheating, and perspective change. *Cognition, 43,* 127–171.

Gilbert, D. T. (1998). Ordinary personality. In D. T. Gilbert, S. T. Fiske, & G. Lindzey (Eds.), *The handbook of social psychology* (Vol. 2, 4th ed., pp. 89–150). New York, NY: McGraw-Hill.

Gödel, K. (1934). *On undecidable propositions of formal mathematical systems.* New York, NY: Raven Press.

Goertzel, B. (2014). *Ten years to the singularity, if we really, really try.* Retrieved from http://goertzel.org/TenYearsToTheSingularity.pdf

Goldenberg, G., Podreka, I., Steiner, M., & Willmes, K. (1989). Regional cerebral blood flow patterns in visual imagery. *Neuropsychologia, 27*(5), 641–664.

Goldman-Rakic, P. S. (1993). Working memory and the mind. *Scientific American, 267,* 110–117.

Goldstein, E. B. (2002). *Sensation and perception* (6th ed.). Pacific Grove, CA: Wadsworth-Thompson.

Goodglass, H., & Geschwind, N. (1976). Language disorders (aphasia). In E. C. Carterete & M. P. Friedman (Eds.), *Handbook of perception: Language and speech* (Vol. 7, pp. 389–428). San Diego, CA: Academic Press.

Gould, S. J. (2000). More things in heaven and earth. In H. Rose & S. Rose (Eds.), *Arguments against evolutionary psychology* (pp. 101–126). New York, NY: Harmony Books.

Grafton, S. T., Mazziotta, J. C., Presty, S., Friston, K. J., Frackowiak, R. S., & Phelps, M. E. (1992). Functional anatomy of human procedural learning determined with regional cerebral blood flow and PET. *Journal of Neuroscience, 12*(7), 2542–2548.

Grafton, S. T., Woods, R. P., & Tyszka, M. (1994). Functional imaging of procedural motor learning: Relating cerebral blood flow with individual subject performance. *Human Brain Mapping, 1*(3), 221–234.

Grandjean, D., Sander, D., Pourtois, G., Schwartz, S., Seghier, M., Scherer, K. R., & Vuilleumier, P. (2005). The voices of wrath: Brain responses to angry prosody in meaningless speech. *Nature Neuroscience, 8,* 145–146.

Gravitz, L. (2011, November 18). An ultrathin brain implant monitors seizures. *MIT Technology Review.* Retrieved from http://www.technologyreview.com/news/426154/an-ultrathin-brain-implant-monitors-seizures/

Gray, C. M., König, P., Engel, A. K., & Singer, W. (1989). Oscillatory responses in cat visual cortex exhibit inter-columnar synchronization which reflects global stimulus properties. *Nature, 338,* 334–337.

Graybiel, A. M., Aosaki, T., Flaherty, A. W., & Kimura, M. (1994). The basal ganglia and adaptive motor control. *Science, 265,* 1826–1831.

Green, C. D., & Vervaeke, J. (1996). *What kind of explanation, if any, is a connectionist net?* North York, Ontario, Canada: Captus.

Greenfield, P. M., & Savage-Rumbaugh, E. S. (1993). Comparing communicative competence in child and chimp: The pragmatics. *Journal of Child Language, 20,* 1–26.

Greeno, J. G. (1974). Hobbits and orcs: Acquisition of a sequential concept. *Cognitive Psychology, 6,* 270–292.

Greenwald, A. G. (1992). New look 3: Unconscious cognition reclaimed. *American Psychologist, 47,* 766–779.

Greenwald, A. G., McGhee, D. E., & Schwartz, J. L. K. (1998). Measuring individual differences in implicit cognition: The implication association test. *Journal of Personality and Social Psychology Bulletin, 74,* 1464–1480.

Grossberg, S. (1987). Competitive learning: From interactive activation to adaptive resonance. *Cognitive Science, 11*(1), 23–63.

Guastello, S. J. (2001). Nonlinear dynamics in psychology. *Discrete Dynamics in Nature and Society, 6*(1), 11–29.

Guinote, A., & Fiske, S. (2003). Being in the outgroup territory increases stereotypic perceptions of outgroups: Situational sources of category activation. *Group Processes & Intergroup Relations, 6*(4), 323–331.

Guizzo, E. (2014, July 16). Cynthia Breazeal unveils Jibo, a social robot for the home. *IEEE Spectrum.* Retrieved from http://spectrum.ieee.org/automaton/robotics/home-robots/cynthia-breazeal-unveils-jibo-a-social-robot-for-the-home

Gusnard, D. A., & Raichle, M. E. (2001). Searching for a baseline: Functional imaging and the resting human brain. *Nature Reviews Neuroscience, 2,* 685–694.

Guttman, S., Gilroy, L., & Blake, R. (2007). Spatial grouping in human vision: Temporal structure trumps temporal synchrony. *Vision Research, 47,* 219–230.

Hansen, C. H., & Hansen, R. D. (1988). Finding the face in the crowd: An anger superiority effect. *Journal of Personality and Social Psychology, 54,* 917–924.

Happé, F., Ehlers, S., Fletcher, P., Frith, U., Johansson, M., Gillberg, C., . . . Frith, C. (1996). "Theory of mind" in the brain: Evidence from a PET scan study of Asperger syndrome. *NeuroReport, 8*(1), 197–201.

Harris, L. T., Todorov, A., & Fiske, S. T. (2005). Attributions on the brain: Neuro-imaging dispositional inferences, beyond theory of mind. *NeuroImage, 28,* 763–769.

Hart, A. J., Whalen, P. J., Shin, L. M., McInerney, S. C., Fischer, H., & Rauch, S. L. (2000). Differential response in the human amygdala to racial outgroup vs. ingroup face stimuli. *NeuroReport, 11,* 2351–2355.

Hartshorne, C., Weiss, P., & Burks, A. (Eds.). (1931–1958). *Collected papers of Charles Sanders Peirce.* Cambridge, MA: Harvard University Press.

Hawkins, J., & Blakeslee, S. (2004). *On intelligence.* New York, NY: Times Books.

Hayes, J. (1989). *The complete problem solver* (2nd ed.). Hillsdale, NJ: Erlbaum.

Hebb, D. O. (1949). *The organization of behavior: A neuropsychological theory.* Oxford, England: Wiley.

Henrich, J., Heine, S. J., & Norenzayan, A. (2009). The weirdest people in the world. *Behavioral and Brain Sciences, 33*(2–3), 61–83.

Herrmann, E., Call, J., Hernandez-Lloreda, M. V., Hare, B., & Tomasello, M. (2009). Humans have evolved specialized skills of social cognition: The cultural intelligence hypothesis. *Science, 317*(5843), 1360–1366.

Hillyard, S. A., Hink, R. F., Schwent, V. L., & Picton, T. W. (1973). Electrical signs of selective attention in the human brain. *Science, 182,* 177–180.

Hinton, G. E. (1981). A parallel computation that assigns canonical object-based frames of reference. In P. J. Hayes (Ed.), *Proceedings of the Seventh Annual International Joint Conference on Artificial Intelligence, Vancouver, BC, Canada* (pp. 683–685). San Francisco, CA: Kaufmann.

The history of artificial intelligence. (2014). Retrieved from courses.cs.washington.edu/courses/csep590/06au/projects/history-ai.pdf

History of computing. (2014). Retrieved from http://www.livescience.com/20718-computer-history.html

Hobson, R. (1993). The emotional origins of social understanding. *Philosophical Psychology, 6*(3), 227–249.

Hochberg, L. R., Bacher, D., Jarosiewicz, B., Masse, N. Y., Simeral, J. D., Vogel, J., . . . Donoghue, J. P. (2012). Reach and grasp by people with tetraplegia using a neutrally controlled robotic arm. *Nature, 485*(7398), 372–375.

Hockett, C. F. (1960). Logical considerations in the study of animal communication. In W. E. Lanyon & W. N. Tavolga (Eds.), *Animal sounds and communication.* Washington, DC: American Institute of Biological Sciences.

Hodgkin, A. L., & Huxley, A. F. (1952). A quantitative description of membrane current and its application to conduction and excitation in nerve. *Journal of Physiology, 117*(4), 500–544.

Holbrook, A. L., Berent, M. K., Krosnick, J. A., Visser, P. S., & Boninger, D. S. (2005). Attitude importance and the accumulation of attitude-relevant knowledge in memory. *Journal of Personality and Social Psychology, 88,* 749–769.

Holland, J. H. (1998). *Emergence: From chaos to order.* New York, NY: Basic Books.

Holyoak, K. J., & Thagard, P. (1995). *Mental leaps: Analogy in creative thought.* Cambridge: MIT Press.

Hubel, D. H. (1982). Exploration of the primary visual cortex, 1955–1978. *Nature, 299,* 515–524.

Hubel, D. H., & Wiesel, T. N. (1962). Receptive fields, binocular interaction, and functional architecture in the cat's visual cortex. *Journal of Physiology, 160,* 106–154.

Hubel, D. H., Wiesel, T. N., & Stryker, M. P. (1978). Anatomical demonstration of orientation columns in macaque monkey. *Journal of Comparative Neurology, 177,* 361–379.

Huebner, B. (2010). Commonsense concepts of phenomenal consciousness: Does anyone care about functional zombies? *Phenomenology and the Cognitive Sciences, 9*(1), 133–155.

Hugenberg, K., & Bodenhausen, G. (2004). Ambiguity in social categorization: The role of prejudice and facial affect in race categorization. *Psychological Science, 15*(5), 342–345.

Humphreys, G. W., & Riddoch, M. J. (1987). *To see but not to see: A case study of visual agnosia.* Hillsdale, NJ: Erlbaum.

Iacoboni, M., Woods, R. P., Brass, M., Bekkering, H., Mazziotta, J. C., & Rizzolatti, G. (1999). Cortical mechanisms of human imitation. *Science, 286*(5449), 2526–2528.

Identity theory vs. functionalism. (2008, April 07). Retrieved from http://www.academon.com/comparison-essay/identity-theory-vs-functionalism-102935/

Jackson, F. (1982). Epiphenomenal qualia. *Philosophical Quarterly, 32,* 127–136.

James, W. (1884). What is an emotion? *Mind, 9,* 188–205.

James, W. (1890). *The principles of psychology.* New York, NY: Dover.

Johnson, J., & Newport, E. (1989). Critical period effects in second-language learning: The influence of maturational state on the acquisition of English as a second language. *Cognitive Psychology, 21, 60–99.*

Johnston, L., & Macrae, C. (1994). Changing social stereotypes: The case of the information seeker. *European Journal of Social Psychology, 24*(5), 581–592.

Johnston, W. A., & Heinz, S. P. (1978). Flexibility and capacity demands of attention. *Journal of Experimental Psychology: General, 107,* 420–435.

Jones, M. T. (2009). *Artificial intelligence: A systems approach.* Sudbury, MA: Jones & Bartlett.

Jones, P. E. (1995). Contradictions and unanswered questions in the Genie case: A fresh look at the linguistic evidence. *Language & Communication, 15*(3), 261–280.

Jonides, J., & Smith, E. E. (1997). The architecture of working memory. In M. D. Rugg (Ed.), *Cognitive neuroscience* (pp. 243–272). Cambridge: MIT Press.

Jonides, J., Smith, E. E., Koeppe, R. A., Awh, E., Minoshima, S., & Mintun, M. A. (1993). Spatial working memory in humans as revealed by PET. *Nature, 363,* 623–625.

Judd, C. M., Park, B., Yzerbyt, V. Y., Gordijn, E. H., & Muller, D. (2005). Attributions of intergroup bias and outgroup homogeneity to ingroup and outgroup others. *European Journal of Social Psychology, 35,* 677–704.

Kaas, J. H. (2000). Why is the brain size so important: Design problems and solutions as neocortex gets bigger or smaller. *Brain and Mind, 1,* 7–23.

Kahneman, D. (1973). *Attention and effort.* Englewood Cliffs, NJ: Prentice Hall.

Kalat, J. W. (2004). *Biological psychology* (8th ed.). Belmont, CA: Wadsworth/Thomson.

Kamil, A. C. (1978). Systematic foraging by nectar-feeding bird, the amakihi (*Loxops virens*). *Journal of Comparative & Physiological Psychology, 92,* 388–398.

Karmiloff-Smith, A. (2000). Why babies' brains are not Swiss army knives. In H. Rose & S. Rose (Eds.), *Arguments against evolutionary psychology* (pp. 173–188). New York, NY: Harmony Books.

Karnath, H. O., Ferber, S., & Himmelbach, M. (2001). Spatial awareness is a function of the temporal, not the posterior parietal lobe. *Nature, 411*(6840), 950–953.

Kayrak, T. (n.d.). A* algorithm for path planning of robotic soccer player. Retrieved from http://www.eng.auburn.edu/~troppel/courses/5530%202011C%20Robots%20Fall%2011/projects/project%20submissions/written21.pdf

Kehoe, B., Patil, S., Abbeel, P., & Goldberg, K. (2015). *IEEE transactions on automation science and engineering* (T-ASE): *Special issue on cloud robotics and automation, 12*(2).

Kelley, H. (1950). The warm–cold variable in first impressions of persons. *Journal of Personality, 18,* 431–439.

Kelley, H. H. (1972). Attribution in social interaction. In E. E. Jones, D. E. Kanouse, H. H. Kelley, R. E. Nisbett, S. Valins, & B. Weinder (Eds.), *Attribution: Perceiving the causes of behavior* (pp. 1–26). Morristown, NJ: General Learning Press.

Kelso, J. A. (1995). *Dynamic patterns: The self-organization of brain and behavior.* Cambridge: MIT Press.

Keltner, D., & Shiota, M. N. (2003). New displays and new emotions: A commentary on Rozin and Cohen. *Emotion, 3*(1), 86–91.

Keysers, C., Xiao, D. K., Foldiak, P., & Perrett, D. I. (2005). Out of sight but not out of mind: The neurophysiology of iconic memory in the superior temporal sulcus. *Cognitive Neuropsychology, 22*(3–4), 316–332.

Kingsbury, M., & Finlay, B. (2001). The cortex in multidimensional space: Where do cortical areas come from? *Developmental Science, 48,* 135–152.

Kleene, S. C. (1935). A theory of positive integers in formal logic. *American Journal of Mathematics, 57,* 153–173, 219–244.

Klin, A. (1991). Young autistic children's listening preferences in regard to speech: A possible characterization of the symptom of social withdrawal. *Journal of Autism and Developmental Disorders, 21*(1), 29–42.

Knobe, J. (2003). Intentional action and side effects in ordinary language. *Analysis, 63,* 190–193.

Koch, C. (2004). *The quest for consciousness: A neurobiological approach.* Englewood, CO: Roberts.

Kohler, W. (1920). *Static and stationary physical gestalts.* Braunschweig, Germany: Vieweg.

Kohler, W. (1927). *The mentality of apes.* New York, NY: Harcourt Brace.

Kortge, C. (1990). Episodic memory in connectionist networks. In *Proceedings of the Twelfth Annual Conference of the Cognitive Science Society* (pp. 764–771). Hillsdale, NJ: Erlbaum.

Kosslyn, S. M. (1975). Information representation in visual images. *Cognitive Psychology, 7,* 341–370.

Kosslyn, S. M. (1980). *Image and mind.* Cambridge, MA: Harvard University Press.

Kosslyn, S. M., Ball, T. M., & Reiser, B. J. (1978). Visual images preserve metric spatial information: Evidence from studies of image scanning. *Journal of Experimental Psychology: Human Perception and Performance, 4,* 47–60.

Kosslyn, S. M., & Schwartz, S. P. (1977). A simulation of visual imagery. *Cognitive Science, 1,* 265–295.

Koza, J. R. (1992). *Genetic programming: On the programming of computers by means of natural selection.* Cambridge: MIT Press.

Kraus, S. J. (1995). Attitudes and the prediction of behavior: A meta-analysis of the empirical literature. *Personality and Social Psychology Bulletin, 21,* 58–75.

Kremer, S. C. (1995). On the computational powers of Elman-style recurrent networks. *IEEE Transactions on Neural Networks, 6,* 1000–1004.

Kruse, R., Borgelt, C., Klawonn, F., Moewes, C., Steinbrecher, M., & Held, P. (2013). *Computational intelligence: A methodological introduction.* London, England: Springer-Verlag.

Kubovy, M., & Gepshtein, S. (2003). Perceptual grouping in space and in space-time: An exercise in phenomenological psychophysics. In R. Kimchi, M. Behrmann, & C. R. Olson (Eds.), *Perceptual organization in vision: Behavioral and neural perspectives* (pp. 45–86). Mahwah, NJ: Erlbaum.

Kubovy, M., & Holcombe, A. O. (1998). On the lawfulness of grouping by proximity. *Cognitive Psychology, 35*(1), 71–98.

Kubovy, M., & Van den Berg, M. (2008). The whole is equal to the sum of its parts: A probabilistic model of grouping by proximity and similarity in regular patterns. *Psychological Review, 115*(1), 131–154.

Kubovy, M., & Wagemans, J. (1995). Grouping by proximity and multistability in dot lattices: A quantitative Gestalt theory. *Psychological Science, 6*(4), 225–234.

Kuczaj, S. A. (1978). Children's judgments of grammatical and ungrammatical past tense verbs. *Child Development, 49,* 319–326.

Kulik, L. (2005). Intrafamiliar congruence in gender role attitudes and ethnic stereotypes: The Israeli case. *Journal of Comparative Family Studies, 36*(2), 289–305.

Kuramoto, Y. (1984). *Chemical oscillations, waves, and turbulence.* Berlin, Germany: Springer-Verlag.

Kurzweil, R. (2012). *How to create a mind: The secret of human thought revealed.* London, England: Penguin Books.

LaBerge, D., & Buchsbaum, M. S. (1990). Positron emission tomographic measurements of pulvinar activity during an attention task. *Journal of Neuroscience, 10,* 613–619.

Lago-Fernandez, L. F., Huerta, R., Corbacho, F., & Siguenza, J. A. (2000). Fast response and temporal coherent oscillations in small-world networks. *Physical Review Letters, 84*(12), 2758–2761.

Lakoff, G. (2008). *The political mind: Why you cannot understand 21st-century American politics with an 18th-century brain.* New York, NY: Viking Press.

Landauer, T. K. (1986). How much do people remember? Some estimates of the quantity of learned information in long-term memory. *Cognitive Science, 10*(4), 477–493.

Lane, H. (1976). *The wild boy of Aveyron.* Cambridge, MA: Harvard University Press.

Lang, P. J. (1994). The motivational organization of emotion: Affect-reflex connections. In H. M. Stephanie, N. E. van de Poll, & J. A. Sergeant (Eds.), *Emotions: Essays on emotion theory* (pp. 61–93). Hillsdale, NJ: Erlbaum.

Langton, C. (Ed.). (1989). *Artificial life.* Redwood City, CA: Addison-Wesley.

Lars, S., & Kubovy, M. (2006). On the surprising salience of curvature in grouping by proximity. *Journal of Experimental Psychology: Human Perception and Performance, 32*(2), 226–234.

Lashley, K. (1950). In search of the engram. *Symposia of the Society of Experimental Biology, 4,* 454–482.

Latora, V., & Marchiori, M. (2001). Efficient behavior of small-world networks. *Physical Review Letters, 87,* 198701.

LeDoux, J. E. (1996). *The emotional brain: The mysterious underpinnings of emotional life.* New York, NY: Simon & Schuster.

Lerner, M. J. (1980). *The belief in a just world: A fundamental delusion.* New York, NY: Plenum Press.

Levine, D. N., & Calvanio, R. (1989). Prosopagnosia: A defect in visual configural processing. *Brain and Cognition, 10,* 149–170.

Levine, J. (1983). Materialism and qualia: The explanatory gap. *Pacific Philosophical Quarterly, 64,* 354–361.

Levine, L. J., & Pizarro, D. A. (2004). Emotion and memory research: A group overview. *Social Cognition, 22,* 530–554.

Levy, J., & Heller, W. (1992). Gender differences in human neuropsychological function. In A. A. Gerall, H. Moltz, & I. L. Ward (Eds.), *Handbook of behavioral neurobiology* (pp. 245–274). New York, NY: Plenum Press.

Lieberman, M. D., Gaunt, R., Gilbert, D. T., & Trope, T. (2002). Reflexion and reflection: A social cognitive neuroscience approach to attributional inference. In M. P. Zanna (Ed.), *Advances in experimental social psychology* (Vol. 34, pp. 100–249). San Diego, CA: Academic Press.

Lieberman, M. D., Hariri, A., & Bookheimer, S. (2001, February 4). *Controlling automatic stereotype activation: An fMRI study.* Paper presented at the second annual meeting of the Society for Personality and Social Psychology, San Antonio, TX.

Lieberman, M. D., Ochsner, K. N., Gilbert, D. T., & Schacter, D. L. (2001). Do amnesiacs exhibit cognitive dissonance reduction? The role of explicit memory and attention in attitude change. *Psychological Science, 12,* 135–140.

Lindsay, P. H., & Norman, D. A. (1972). *Human information processing: An introduction to psychology.* New York, NY: Academic Press.

Lingle, J. H., Geva, N., Ostrom, T. M., Leippe, M. R., & Baumgardner, M. H. (1979). Thematic effects of person judgments on impression organization. *Journal of Personality and Social Psychology, 37,* 674–687.

Lingnau, A., Gesierich, B., & Caramazza, A. (2009). Asymmetric fMRI adaptation reveals no evidence for mirror neurons in humans. *Proceedings of the National Academy of Sciences USA, 106,* 9925–9930.

Llinas, R. R. (2002). *I of the vortex: From neurons to self.* Cambridge: MIT Press.

Loewenstein, G. F., Weber, E. U., Hsee, C. K., & Welch, N. (2001). Risk as feelings. *Psychological Bulletin, 127*(2), 267–286.

Loftus, E. F. (1979). The malleability of human memory. *American Scientist, 67*(3), 312–320.

Loftus, E. F. (1995). Remembering dangerously. *Skeptical Inquirer, 19,* 20–29.

Loftus, E. F., & Palmer, J. C. (1974). Reconstruction of automobile destruction: An example of the interaction between language and memory. *Journal of Verbal Learning and Verbal Behaviour, 13,* 585–589.

Logie, R. H., Zucco, G., & Baddeley, A. D. (1990). Interference with visual short-term memory. *Acta Psychologica, 75,* 55–74.

Losch, M. E., & Cacioppo, J. T. (1990). Cognitive dissonance may enhance sympathetic tonus, but attitudes are changed to reduce negative affect rather than arousal. *Journal of Experimental Social Psychology, 26,* 289–304.

Luck, S. J., & Hillyard, S. A. (1994). Spatial filtering during visual search: Evidence from human electrophysiology. *Journal of Experimental Psychology: Human Perception and Performance, 20,* 1000–1014.

Maddox, K. B., & Chase, S. G. (2004). Manipulating subcategory salience: Exploring the link between skin tone and social perception of Blacks. *European Journal of Social Psychology, 34,* 533–546.

Maestrini, E., Paul, A., Monaco, A. P., & Bailey, A. (2000). Identifying autism susceptibility genes. *Neuron, 28*(1), 19–24.

Maloney, J. C. (1999). Functionalism. In *MIT encyclopedia of the cognitive sciences* (pp. 332–334). Cambridge: MIT Press.

Malpass, R. S. (1969). Effects of attitude on learning and memory: The influence of instruction-induced sets. *Journal of Experimental Social Psychology, 5,* 441–453.

Manson, J., & Wrangham, R. W. (1991). Intergroup aggression in chimpanzees and humans. *Current Anthropology, 32,* 369–390.

Marcus, G. F., Pinker, S., Ullman, M., Hollander, M., Rosen, J., & Xu, F. (1992). Overregularization in language acquisition. *Monographs of the Society for Research in Child Development, 57.*

Markoff, J. (2010, September 4). The boss is robotic, and rolling up behind you. *The New York Times.* Retrieved from http://www.nytimes.com/2010/09/05/science/05robots.html

Markoff, J. (2014, September 1). Brainy, yes, but far from handy: Building a robot with human touch. *The New York Times.* Retrieved from http://www.nytimes.com/2014/09/02/science/robot-touch.html?_r=0

Markoff, J. (2014, August 7). IBM develops a new chip that functions like a brain. *The New York Times.* Retrieved from http://www.nytimes.com/2014/08/08/science/new-computer-chip-is-designed-to-work-like-the-brain.html?_r=0

Marks, I. M. (1987). *Fears, phobias, and rituals.* New York, NY: Oxford University Press.

Marks, I. M., & Nesse, R. M. (1994). Fear and fitness: An evolutionary analysis of anxiety disorders. *Ethology and Sociobiology, 15,* 247–261.

Marler, P. (1970). A comparative approach to vocal learning: Song development in white-crowned sparrows. *Journal of Comparative Physiology and Psychology, 71,* 1–25.

Marr, D. (1982). *Vision.* San Francisco, CA: W. H. Freeman.

Marr, D., & Nishihara, H. K. (1978). Representation and recognition of the spatial organization of three-dimensional shapes. *Proceedings of the Royal Society of London B, 200,* 269–294.

Marx, M., & Hillix, W. A. (1979). *Systems and theories in psychology* (3rd ed.). New York, NY: McGraw-Hill.

McCloskey, M. E., & Glucksberg, S. (1978). Natural categories: Well-defined or fuzzy sets? *Memory & Cognition, 6*(4), 462–472.

McComb, K. C., Packer, C., & Pusey, A. (1994). Roaring and numerical assessment in contests between groups of female lions, *Panthera leo. Animal Behaviour, 47,* 379–387.

McCorduck, P. (2004). *Machines who think* (2nd ed., p. 212). Natick, MA: A. K. Peters.

McCormick, B. H., & Mayerich, D. M. (2004). Three-dimensional imaging using knife-edge scanning microscopy. *Microscopy & Microanalysis, 10*(2), 1466–1467.

McCulloch, W. S., & Pitts, W. (1943). A logical calculus of the ideas immanent in nervous activity. *Bulletin of Mathematical Biophysics, 5,* 115–133.

McGaugh, J. L. (2004). The amygdala modulates the consolidation of memories of emotionally arousing experiences. *Annual Review of Neuroscience, 27,* 1–28.

McGonigle, B. O., & Chalmers, M. (1977). Are monkeys logical? *Nature, 267,* 694–946.

McMullen, E., & Saffran, J. R. (2004). Music and language: A developmental comparison. *Music Perception, 21,* 289–311.

McNamara, T. P. (1992). Priming and constraints in places on theories of memory and retrieval. *Psychological Review, 99*(4), 650–662.

McRae, K., & Hetherington, P. (1993). Catastrophic interference is eliminated in pretrained networks. In *Proceedings of the Fifteenth Annual Conference of the Cognitive Science Society* (pp. 723–728). Hillsdale, NJ: Erlbaum.

Merolla, P. A., Arthur, J. V., Alvarez-Icaza, R., Cassidy, A. S., Sawada, J., Akopyan, F., . . . (2014, August 8). A million spiking-neuron integrated circuit with a scalable communication network and interface. *Science, 345*(6197), 614–616.

Mesulam, M.-M. (1981). A cortical network for directed attention and unilateral neglect. *Annals of Neurology, 10,* 309–325.

Meyer, D. E., & Schvaneveldt, R. W. (1971). Facilitation in recognizing pairs of words: Evidence of a dependence between retrieval operations. *Journal of Experimental Psychology, 90,* 227–234.

Milgram, S. (1967). The small world problem. *Psychology Today, 2,* 60–67.

Milham, M. P., Banich, M. T., Webb, A., Barad, V., Cohen, N. J., Wszalek, T., & Kramer, A. F. (2001). The relative involvement of anterior cingulate and prefrontal cortex in attentional control depends on nature of conflict. *Cognitive Brain Research, 12,* 467–473.

Miller, G. A. (1956). The magical number seven, plus or minus two: Some limits on our capacity for processing information. *Psychological Review, 63,* 81–97.

Miller, R. A., Pople, H. E., Jr., & Myers, J. D. (1982). INTERNIST-1: An experimental computer-based diagnostic consultant for general internal medicine. *New England Journal of Medicine, 307,* 468–476.

Mills, D. L., Coffey-Corina, S. A., & Neville, H. J. (1993). Language acquisition and cerebral specialization in twenty-month-old infants. *Journal of Cognitive Neuroscience, 5*(3), 317–334.

Minsky, M. (1975). A framework for representing knowledge. In P. Winston (Ed.), *The psychology of computer vision* (pp. 211–277). New York, NY: McGraw-Hill.

Minsky, M. (2006). *The emotion machine. Commonsense thinking, artificial intelligence, and the future of the human mind.* New York, NY: Simon & Schuster.

Minsky, M., & Papert, S. (1969). *Perceptrons.* Cambridge: MIT Press.

Mintz, T. H., Newport, E. L., & Bever, T. G. (2002). The distributional structure of grammatical categories in speech to young children. *Cognitive Science, 26,* 393–424.

Mitchell, J. P. (2008). Contributions of functional neuroimaging to the study of social cognition. *Current Directions in Psychological Science, 17*(2), 142–146.

Mitchell, J. P., Macrae, C. N., & Banaji, M. R. (2004). Encoding specific effects of social cognition on the neural correlates of subsequent memory. *Journal of Neuroscience, 24,* 4912–4917.

Miura, I. T., Okamoto, Y., Kim, C. C., & Steere, M. (1993). First graders' cognitive representation of number and understanding of place value: Cross-national comparisons: France, Japan, Korea, Sweden, and the United States. *Journal of Educational Psychology, 85*(1), 24–30.

Mohr, J. P. (1976). Broca's area and Broca's aphasia. In H. Whitaker & H. Whitaker (Eds.), *Studies in neurolinguistics* (pp. 201–233). New York, NY: Academic Press.

Moray, N. (1959). Attention in dichotic listening: Affective cues and the influence of instructions. *Quarterly Journal of Experimental Psychology, 11,* 56–60.

Morris, J. S., Öhman, A., & Dolan, R. J. (1998). Conscious and unconscious emotional learning in the human amygdala. *Nature, 393,* 467–470.

Morris, R. G., Ahmed, S., Syed, G. M., & Toone, B. K. (1993). Neural correlates of planning ability: Frontal lobe activation during the Tower of London test. *Neuropsychologia, 31,* 1367–1378.

Mountcastle, V. (1997). The columnar organization of the neocortex. *Brain, 120,* 701–722.

Mountcastle, V. B. (1998). *Perceptual neuroscience: The cerebral cortex.* Cambridge, MA: Harvard University Press.

Mundy, P., Card, J., & Fox, N. (2000). Fourteen-month cortical activity and different infant joint attention skills. *Developmental Psychobiology, 36,* 325–338.

Mundy, P., & Newell, L. (2007). Attention, joint attention, and social cognition. *Current Directions in Psychological Science, 16*(5), 269–274.

Musallam, S., Corneil, B. D., Greger, B., Scherberger, H., & Andersen, R. A. (2004, July 9). Cognitive signals for neural prosthetics. *Science, 305,* 162–163.

Myers, D. G. (2001). *Psychology.* New York, NY: Worth.

Myerson, R. B. (1997). *Game theory: Analysis of conflict.* Cambridge, MA: Harvard University Press.

Nagel, T. (1974). What is it like to be a bat? *Philosophical Review, 83,* 435–450.

Neisser, U. (1967). *Cognitive psychology.* New York, NY: Appleton-Century-Crofts.

Neisser, U., & Harsch, N. (1992). Phantom flashbulbs: False recollections of hearing the news about Challenger. In E. Winograd & U. Neisser (Eds.), *Affect and accuracy in recall: Studies of "flashbulb" memories.* New York, NY: Cambridge University Press.

Nelson, E. E., & Panksepp, J. (1998). Brain substrates of infant–mother attachment: Contributions of opioids, oxytocin, and norepinephrine. *Neuroscience and Biobehavioral Reviews, 22*(3), 437–452.

Nesse, R. M. (1987). An evolutionary perspective on panic disorder and agoraphobia. *Ethology and Sociobiology, 8,* 735–835.

Nesse, R. M. (2000). Is depression an adaptation? *Archives of General Psychiatry, 57,* 14–20.

Newell, A. (1991). *Unified theories of cognition.* Cambridge, MA: Harvard University Press.

Newell, A., & Simon, H. A. (1972). *Human problem solving.* Englewood Cliffs, NJ: Prentice Hall.

Newell, A. & Simon, H. A. (1976). Computer science as empirical inquiry: Symbols and search. *Communications of the ACM, 19*(3), 113–126.

Newport, E. L., & Aslin, R. N. (2000). Innately constrained learning: Blending old and new approaches to language acquisition. In S. C. Howell, S. A. Fish, & T. Keith-Lucas (Eds.), *Proceedings of the 24th Annual Boston University Conference on Language Development* (pp. 1–21). Somerville, MA: Cascadilla.

Newschaffer, C. J., Croen, L. A., Daniels, J., Giarelli, E., Grether, J. K., Levy, S. E., . . . Windham, G. C. (2007). The epidemiology of autism spectrum disorders. *Annual Review of Public Health, 28,* 235–258.

Nichols, S., & Knobe, J. (2007). Moral responsibility and determinism: The cognitive science of folk intuitions. *Nous, 41,* 663–685.

Nilsson, N. J. (1969). *A mobile automaton: An application of artificial intelligence techniques* (Technical Note 40). Menlo Park, CA: AI Center.

Nilsson, N. J. (1998), *Artificial intelligence: A new synthesis.* Burlington, MA: Morgan Kaufmann.

Nilsson, N. J. (2007). The physical symbol system hypothesis: Status and prospects. In M. Lungarella, F. Iida, J. Bongard, & R. Pfeifer (Eds.), *50 Years of artificial intelligence* (Vol. 4850, pp. 9–17). New York, NY: Springer.

Nisbett, R. (2004). *The geography of thought: How Asians and westerners think differently . . . and why.* New York, NY: Free Press.

Nisbett, R., & Ross, L. (1980). *Human inference: Strategies and shortcomings of social judgment.* Englewood Cliffs, NJ: Prentice Hall.

Norman, D. A. (1968). Toward a theory of memory and attention. *Psychological Review, 75,* 522–536.

Norman, D. A., & Shallice, T. (1980). *Attention to action: Willed and automatic control of behavior* (Technical Report No. 99). La Jolla, CA: Center for Human Information Processing.

Notman, M. T., & Nadelson, C. C. (1991). *Women and men: New perspectives on gender differences.* Washington, DC: American Psychiatric Press.

Nudo, R. J., Milliken, G. W., Jenkins, W. M., & Merzenich, M. M. (1996). Use-dependent alterations of movement representations in primary motor cortex of adult squirrel monkeys. *Journal of Neuroscience, 16*(2), 785–807.

Ochsner, K. N. (2000). Are affective events richly recollected or simply familiar? The experience and process of recognizing feelings past. *Journal of Experimental Psychology: General, 129,* 242–261.

Ochsner, K. N., & Lieberman, M. D. (2001). The emergence of social cognitive neuroscience. *American Psychologist, 56*(9), 717–734.

Öhman, A., Lundqvist, D., & Esteves, F. (2001). The face in the crowd revisited: A threat advantage with schematic stimuli. *Journal of Personality and Social Psychology, 80,* 381–396.

Olson, J. M., & Zanna, M. P. (1979). A new look at selective exposure. *Journal of Experimental Social Psychology, 15,* 1–15.

Ospina, M. B., Krebs Seida, J., Clark, B., Karkhaneh, M., Hartling, L., Tjosvold, L., . . . Smith, V. (2008). Behavioural and developmental interventions for autism spectrum disorder: A clinical systematic review. *PLoS One, 3*(11), e3755.

O'Sullivan, C., & Durso, F. (1984). Effect of schema-incongruent information on memory for stereotypical attributes. *Journal of Personality and Social Psychology, 47*(1), 55–70.

O'Sullivan, M. (2003). The fundamental attribution error in detecting deception: The Boy-Who-Cried-Wolf effect. *Personality and Social Psychology Bulletin, 29*(10), 1316–1327.

Palmer, J. A., & Palmer, L. K. (2002). *Evolutionary psychology: The ultimate origins of human behavior.* Boston, MA: Allyn & Bacon.

Panksepp, J. (1993). Neurochemical control of moods and emotions: Amino acids to neuropeptides. In M. Lewis & J. M. Haviland (Eds.), *Handbook of emotions* (pp. 87–107). New York, NY: Guilford Press.

Parkin, A. J. (1996). *Explorations in cognitive neuropsychology.* Oxford, England: Blackwell.

Pascual-Leone, A., Tormos, J. M., Keenan, J., Tarazona, F., Canete, C., & Catala, M. D. (1998). Study and modulation of human cortical excitability with transcranial magnetic stimulation. *Journal of Clinical Neuropsychology, 15,* 333–343.

Patterson, F. G. (1978). The gesture of a gorilla: Language acquisition in another pongid. *Brain & Language, 5*(1), 72–97.

Perrett, D. I., & Oram, M. W. (1993). Neurophysiology of shape processing. *Image and Visual Computing, 11,* 317–333.

Perrett, D., Rolls, E. T., & Caan, W. (1982). Visual neurons responsive to faces in the monkey temporal cortex. *Experimental Brain Research, 47,* 329–342.

Peschl, M. F. (1997, November). The representational relation between environmental structures and neural systems: Autonomy and environmental dependency in neural knowledge representation. *Nonlinear Dynamics, Psychology, and Life Sciences, 2,* 99–121.

Peterson, L. R., & Peterson, M. J. (1959). Short-term retention of individual items. *Journal of Experimental Psychology, 58,* 193–198.

Peterson, S. E., Fox, P. T., Posner, M. I., Mintun, M., & Raichle, M. E. (1988). Positron emission tomographic studies of the cortical anatomy of single-word processing. *Nature, 331,* 585–589.

Petrides, M., Alivisatos, B., Meyer, E., & Evans, A. C. (1993). Functional activation of the human frontal cortex during performance of verbal working memory tasks. *Proceedings of the National Academy of Science USA, 90,* 878–882.

Petrushin, V. A. (2000). Emotion recognition in speech signal: Experimental study, development, and application. *Proceedings of the Sixth International Conference on Spoken Language Processing,* Beijing, China.

Pettigrew, T. F., & Meertens, R. W. (1995). Subtle and blatant prejudice in western Europe. *European Journal of Social Psychology, 25,* 57–75.

Petty, R. E., Tormala, Z. L., Brinol, P., & Jarvis, W. B. G. (2006). Implicit ambivalence from attitude change: An exploration of the PAST model. *Journal of Personality and Social Psychology, 90,* 21–41.

Petty, R. E., & Wegener, D. T. (1998). Attitude change: Multiple roles for persuasion variables. In D. T. Gilbert, S. T. Fiske, & G. Lindzey (Eds.), *Handbook of social psychology* (Vol. 1, 4th ed., pp. 323–390). New York, NY: McGraw-Hill.

Phelps, E. (2006). Emotion and cognition: Insights from studies of the human amygdala. *Annual Review of Psychology, 57,* 27–53.

Phelps, E., Ling, S., & Carrasco, M. (2006). Emotion facilitates perception and potentiates the perceptual benefits of attention. *Psychological Science, 17,* 292–299.

Piaget, J. (1952). *The origins of intelligence in children* (M. Cook, Trans.). New York, NY: International Universities Press. (Original work published 1938)

Picard, R. W. (1997). *Affective computing.* Cambridge: MIT Press.

Pinker, S. (1997). *How the mind works.* New York, NY: W. W. Norton.

Plunkett, K., & Marchman, V. (1991). U-shaped learning and frequency effects in a multilayered perceptron. *Cognition, 38,* 43–102.

Plutchik, R. (1980). A general psychoevolutionary theory of emotion. In R. Plutchik & H. Kellerman (Eds.), *Emotion: Theory, research, and experience.* New York, NY: Academic Press.

Popper, K. R., & Eccles, J. C. (1981). *The self and its brain.* Berlin, Germany: Springer-Verlag.

Posner, M. I. (1980). Orienting of attention. *Quarterly Journal of Experimental Psychology, 32,* 3–25.

Posner, M. I., Inhoff, A. W., Friedrich, F. J., & Cohen, A. (1987). Isolating attentional systems: A cognitive anatomical analysis. *Psychobiology, 15,* 107–121.

Posner, M. I., & Peterson, S. E. (1990). The attention system of the human brain. *Annual Review of Neuroscience, 13,* 25–42.

Posner, M. I., & Snyder, C. R. R. (1975). Facilitation and inhibition in the processing of signals. In P. M. A. Rabbitt & S. Dornic (Eds.), *Attention and performance V* (pp. 669–682). New York, NY: Academic Press.

Posner, M. I., Walker, J. A., Friedrich, F. J., & Rafal, R. D. (1984). Effects of parietal injury on covert orienting of attention. *Journal of Neuroscience, 4,* 1863–1874.

Powell, M. C., & Fazio, R. H. (1984). Attitude accessibility as a function of repeated attitudinal expression. *Personality and Social Psychology Bulletin, 10,* 139–148.

Pratto, F., & John, O. P. (1991). Automatic vigilance: The attention-grabbing power of negative social information. *Journal of Personality and Social Psychology, 61,* 380–390.

Preissl, R., Theodore, M. W., Datta, P., Flickner, M., Singh, R., Esser, S. K., . . . Modha, D. S. (2012). Compass: A scalable simulator for an architecture for cognitive computing. *Proceedings of the International Conference on High Performance Computing, Networking, Storage and Analysis.* Los Alamitos, CA: IEEE Computer Society Press.

Premack, D. (1976). *Intelligence in ape and man.* Mahwah, NJ: Erlbaum.

Prince, A., & Smolensky, P. (1997). Optimality: From neural networks to universal grammar. *Science, 275,* 1604–1610.

Puce, A., Allison, T., Asgari, M., Gore, J. C., & McCarthy, G. (1995). Face-sensitive regions in extrastriate cortex studied by functional MRI. *Journal of Neurophysiology, 74,* 1192–1199.

Purpura, K. P., & Schiff, N. D. (1997). The thalamic intralaminar nuclei: A role in visual awareness. *The Neuroscientist, 3,* 8–15.

Pylyshyn, Z. W. (1981). The imagery debate: Analog media versus tacit knowledge. In N. Block (Ed.), *Imagery* (pp. 151–206). Cambridge: MIT Press.

Rabbie, J., & Horwitz, M. (1969). Arousal of ingroup-outgroup bias by a chance win or loss. *Journal of Personality and Social Psychology, 13,* 269–277.

Rafal, R. D., Posner, M. I., Friedman, J. H., Inhoff, A. W., & Bernstein, E. (1988). Orienting of visual attention in progressive supranuclear palsy. *Brain, 111,* 267–280.

Ramirez, S., Liu, X., Lin, P.-A., Suh, J., Pignatelli, M., Redondo, R. L., . . . Tonegawa, S. (2013, July). Creating a false memory in the hippocampus. *Science, 346*(6144), 387–391.

Ravenscroft, I. (2005). *Philosophy of mind: A beginner's guide.* Oxford, England: Oxford University Press.

Ravizza, S. M., & Ivry, R. B. (2001). Comparison of the basal ganglia and cerebellum in shifting attention. *Journal of Cognitive Neuroscience, 13,* 285–297.

Reason, J. T. (1979). Action not as planned. In G. Underwood & R. Stevens (Eds.), *Aspects of consciousness* (pp. 67–89). New York, NY: Academic Press.

Reed, S. K. (2000). *Cognition* (5th ed.). Belmont, CA: Wadsworth Thomson.

Reeke, G. N., Jr., & Edelman, G. M. (1988). Real brains and artificial intelligence. *Daedalus, 117*(1), 143–173.

Reicher, G. M. (1969). Perceptual recognition as a function of meaningfulness of stimulus material. *Journal of Experimental Psychology, 81,* 274–280.

Reisberg, D. (2001). *Cognition: Exploring the science of mind* (2nd ed.). New York, NY: W. W. Norton.

Reisberg, D., Culver, C., Heuer, F., & Fischman, D. (1986). Visual memory: When imagery vividness makes a difference. *Journal of Mental Imagery, 10,* 51–74.

Reisberg, D., Heuer, F., McLean, J., & O'Shaughnessy, M. (1988). The quantity, not the quality, of affect predicts memory vividness. *Bulletin of the Psychonomic Society, 26,* 100–103.

Rilling, J. K., Sanfey, A. G., Aronson, J. A., Nystrom, L. E., & Cohen, J. D. (2004). The neural correlates of theory of mind within interpersonal interactions. *NeuroImage, 22,* 1694–1703.

Rinck, M., Glowalia, U., & Schneider, K. (1992). Mood-congruent and mood-incongruent learning. *Memory & Cognition, 20,* 29–39.

Rips, L. J. (1975). Inductive judgments about natural categories. *Journal of Verbal Learning and Verbal Behavior, 14,* 665–681.

Rips, L. J., Shoben, E. J., & Smith, E. E. (1973). Semantic distance and the verification of semantic relations. *Journal of Verbal Learning and Verbal Behavior, 12,* 1–20.

Rizzolatti, G., & Craighero, L. (2004). The mirror neuron system. *Annual Review of Neuroscience, 27,* 169–192.

Robinson, C. (1998). *Dynamical systems: Stability, symbolic dynamics, and chaos.* Boca Raton, FL: CRC Press.

Roediger, H. L. (1980). The effectiveness of four mnemonics in ordering recall. *Journal of Experimental Psychology: Human Learning and Memory, 6,* 558–567.

Rolls, E. T. (1999). *The brain and emotion.* Oxford, England: Oxford University Press.

Rosch, E. (1973). On the internal structure of perceptual and semantic categories. In T. Moore (Ed.), *Cognitive development and the acquisition of language* (pp. 111–144). New York, NY: Academic Press.

Rosch, E. (1975). Cognitive representations of semantic categories. *Journal of Experimental Psychology: General, 104,* 192–233.

Rosenblatt, F. (1958). The perceptron: A probabilistic model for information storage and organization in the brain. *Psychological Review, 65,* 386–408.

Rosenblatt, F. (1959). Perceptron simulation experiments (Project Para). *Proceedings of the IRE, 48*, 301–309.

Rozin, P., Lowery, L., & Ebert, R. (1994). Variety of disgust faces and the structure of disgust. *Journal of Personality and Social Psychology, 66*(5), 870–881.

Ruby, P., & Decety, J. (2001). Effect of subjective perspective taking during simulation of action: A PET investigation of agency. *Nature Reviews Neuroscience, 4*, 546–550.

Ruckmick, C. A. (1913). The use of the term "function" in English textbooks of psychology. *American Journal of Psychology, 24*, 99–123.

Ruff, C. C., Kristjansson, A., & Driver, J. (2007). Readout from iconic memory and selective spatial attention involves similar neural processes. *Psychological Science, 18*(10), 901–909.

Rumelhart, D. E., McClelland, J. L., & PDP Research Group. (Eds.). (1986). *Parallel distributed processing: Foundations* (Vol. 1). Cambridge: MIT Press.

Russell, J. A. (2003). Core affect and the psychological construction of emotion. *Psychological Review, 110*, 145–172.

Russell, S. (1979). Brain size and intelligence: A comparative perspective. In D. A. Oakley & H. C. Plotkin (Eds.), *Brain, behavior, and evolution* (pp. 126–153). London, England: Methuen.

Russell, S., & Norvig, P. (2009). *Artificial intelligence: A modern approach* (3rd ed.). Upper Saddle River, NJ: Prentice Hall.

Rusting, C. L., & DeHart, T. (2000). Retrieving positive memories to regulate negative mood: Consequences for mood-congruent memory. *Journal of Personality and Social Psychology, 78*, 737–752.

Rusting, C. L., & Nolen-Hoeksema, S. (1998). Regulating responses to anger: Effects of rumination and distraction on angry mood.

Journal of Personality and Social Psychology, 74, 790–803.

Rutter, M. (2005). Incidence of autism spectrum disorders: Changes over time and their meaning. *Acta Paediatrica, 94*(1), 2–15.

Ryle, G. (1949). *The concept of mind*. London, England: Hutchinson.

Sacks, O. (1998). *The man who mistook his wife for a hat*. New York, NY: Touchstone.

Saffran, J. R., Aslin, R. N., & Newport, E. L. (1996). Statistical learning by 8-month-old infants. *Science, 274*, 1926–1928.

Saffran, J. R., & Thiessen, E. D. (2007). Domain general learning capacities. In E. Hoff & M. Schatz (Eds.), *Blackwell handbook of language development* (pp. 68–86). Oxford, England: Blackwell.

Salovey, P. (1990). Interview. *American Scientist, January–February*, 25–29.

Samuelson, W., & Zeckhauser, R. J. (1988). Status quo bias in decision making. *Journal of Risk and Uncertainty, 1*, 7–59.

Sathian, K., Zangaladze, A., Hoffman, J., & Grafton, S. (1997). Feeling with the mind's eye. *NeuroReport, 8*, 3877–3881.

Savage-Rumbaugh, E. S. (1986). *Ape language: From conditioned response to symbol*. New York, NY: Columbia University Press.

Savage-Rumbaugh, E. S., Murphy, J., Sevcik, R. A., Brakke, K. E., Williams, S., & Rumbaugh, D. M. (1993). Language comprehension in ape and child. *Monographs of the Society for Research in Child Development, 58*(Serial No. 233), 3–4.

Saxe, R., & Kanwisher, N. (2003). People thinking about thinking people: fMRI investigations of theory of mind. *NeuroImage, 19*, 1835–1842.

Scaife, M., & Bruner, J. (1975). The capacity for joint visual attention in the infant. *Nature, 253*, 265–266.

Scannell, J. W. (1997). Determining cortical landscapes. *Nature, 386*, 452.

Schachter, S. S., & Singer, J. E. (1962). Cognitive and physiological determinant of emotional state. *Psychological Review, 69*, 379–399.

Schank, R., & Abelson, R. (1977). *Scripts, plans, goals, and understanding: An inquiry into human knowledge structures.* Hillsdale, NJ: Erlbaum.

Schiller, P. H., Sandell, J. H., & Maunsell, J. H. R. (1987). The effect of frontal eye field and superior colliculus lesions on saccadic latencies in the rhesus monkey. *Journal of Neurophysiology, 57*, 1033–1049.

Schlenker, B. R. (1980). *Impression management: The self-concept, social identity, and interpersonal relations.* Monterey, CA: Brooks/Cole.

Schultz, D. P., & Schultz, S. E. (1987). *A history of modern psychology* (4th ed.). Orlando, FL: Harcourt Brace Jovanovich.

Schutter, D. (2008). Antidepressant efficacy of high-frequency transcranial magnetic stimulation over the left dorsolateral prefrontal cortex in double-blind sham-controlled designs: A meta-analysis. *Psychological Medicine, 39*(1), 65–75.

Schwartz, B. J. (1999). Magnetic source imaging as a clinical tool in functional brain mapping. *GEC Review, 14*(2), 124–127.

Searle, J. R. (1979). *Expression and meaning: Studies in the theory of speech acts.* Cambridge, England: Cambridge University Press.

Searle, J. R. (1980). Minds, brains, and programs. *Behavioral and Brain Sciences, 3*, 417–457.

Searle, J. R. (1984). *Minds, brains, and science.* Cambridge, MA: Harvard University Press.

Searle, J. R. (1992). *The rediscovery of the mind.* Cambridge: MIT Press.

Searle, J. R. (2014, October 9). What your computer can't know. *The New York Review of Books.* Retrieved from http://www.nybooks.com/articles/archives/2014/oct/09/what-your-computer-cant-know/

Sears, D. O. (1968). The paradox of de facto selective exposure. In R. P. Abelson, E. Aronson, W. J. McGuire, T. M. Newcomb, M. J. Rosenberg, & P. H. Tannenbaum (Eds.), *Theories of cognitive consistency: A sourcebook* (pp. 777–787). Chicago, IL: Rand McNally.

Segal, G. (2000). *A slim book about narrow content.* Cambridge: MIT Press.

Segall, M. H., Campbell, D. T., & Herskovits, M. J. (1966). *The influence of culture on visual perception.* Indianapolis, IN: Bobbs-Merrill.

Sejnowski, T., & Rosenberg, C. (1986). *NETtalk: A parallel network that learns to read aloud* (Technical Report JHU/EEC-86/01). Baltimore, MD: Johns Hopkins University Press.

Selfridge, O. G. (1959). Pandemonium: A paradigm for learning. In *The mechanisation of thought processes* (pp. 513–526). London, England: H. M. Stationery Office.

Service, R. F. (2014, August 8). The brain chip. *Science, 345*(6197), 614–616.

Shallice, T. (1982). Specific impairment of planning. *Philosophical Transactions of the Royal Society of London B, 298*, 199–209.

Sheehan, S. (1982). *Is there no place on earth for me?* New York, NY: Vintage Books.

Shepard, R. N., & Metzler, J. (1971). Mental rotation of three-dimensional objects. *Science, 153*, 652–654.

Shermer, M. (2008). *The mind of the market.* New York, NY: Henry Holt.

Sherry, D., Forbes, M., Khurgel, M., & Ivy, G. (1993). Greater hippocampal size in females of the brood parasitic brown-headed cowbird. *Proceedings of the National Academy of Sciences USA, 90*, 7839–7843.

Shin, S. S., Dixon, C. E., Okonkwo, D. O., & Richardson, R. M. (2014). Neurostimulation for traumatic brain injury. *Journal of Neurosurgery, 121*(5), 1219–1231.

Siegal, M., Carrington, J., & Radel, M. (1996). Theory of mind and pragmatic understanding following right hemisphere damage. *Brain and Language, 53*(1), 40–50.

Siegal, M., & Varley, R. (2002). Neural systems involved in theory of mind. *Nature Reviews Neuroscience, 3,* 463–471.

Silverman, G. (2003, March 20–22). The role of neural networks in telerehabilitation. *Proceedings of the First International IEEE EMBS Conference on Neural Engineering,* Capri, Italy.

Silverman, G. (2006). Computers in the biomedical laboratory. In J. G. Webster (Ed.), *Encyclopedia of medical devices and instrumentation* (2nd ed., pp. 308–315). Hoboken, NJ: Wiley.

Silverman, G., & Brudny, J. (1990, June 17–22). The role of the computer in neuromotor rehabilitation. *Proceedings of the VI International Rehabilitation Medicine Association,* Madrid, Spain.

Silverman, I., & Eals, M. (1992). Sex differences in spatial abilities: Evolutionary theory and data. In J. Barkow, L. Cosmides, & J. Tooby (Eds.), *The adapted mind: Evolutionary psychology and the generation of culture* (pp. 533–549). New York, NY: Oxford University Press.

Silverman, I., & Phillips, K. (1998). The evolutionary psychology of spatial sex differences. In C. Crawford & D. L. Krebs (Eds.), *Handbook of evolutionary psychology: Ideas, issues, and applications* (pp. 595–612). Mahwah, NJ: Erlbaum.

Simon, B. (1992). The perception of ingroup and outgroup homogeneity: Reintroducing the intergroup context. In W. Stroebe & M. Hewstone (Eds.), *European review of social psychology* (Vol. 3, pp. 1–30). Oxford, England: Wiley.

Simon, H. A. (1969). *The sciences of the artificial.* Cambridge: MIT Press.

Simon, L., Greenberg, J., & Brehm, J. (1995). Trivialization: The forgotten mode of dissonance reduction. *Journal of Personality and Social Psychology, 68*(2), 247–260.

Singer, T., Seymour, B., O'Doherty, J., Kaube, H., Dolan, R. J., & Frith, C. D. (2004). Empathy for pain involves the affective but not sensory components of pain. *Science, 303,* 1157–1162.

Singer, W. (1996). Neuronal synchronization: A solution to the binding problem? In R. Llinas & P. S. Churchland (Eds.), *The mind–brain continuum: Sensory processes* (pp. 100–130). Cambridge: MIT Press.

Singer, W. (1999). Binding by neural synchrony. In *MIT encyclopedia of the cognitive sciences* (pp. 81–84). Cambridge: MIT Press.

Singer, W., Engel, A. K., Kreiter, A. K., Munk, M. H. J., Neuenschwander, S., & Roelfsema, P. R. (1997). Neuronal assemblies: Necessity, signature, and detectability. *Trends in Cognitive Sciences, 1*(7), 252–261.

Singer, W., & Gray, C. M. (1995). Visual feature integration and the temporal correlation hypothesis. *Annual Review of Neuroscience, 18,* 555–586.

Skinner, B. F. (1938). *The behavior of organisms: An experimental analysis.* Cambridge, MA: B. F. Skinner Foundation.

Sloman, A., Chrisley, R., & Scheutz, M. (2005). The architectural basis of affective states and processes. In J. M. Fellows & M. A. Arbib (Eds.), *Who needs emotions? The brain meets the robot* (pp. 203–244). Oxford, England: Oxford University Press.

Smith, E. E. (2000). Neural bases of human working memory. *Current Directions in Psychological Science, 9,* 45–49.

Smith, E. E., & Jonides, J. (1994). Working memory in humans: Neuropsychological evidence. In M. Gazzaniga (Ed.), *The cognitive neurosciences* (pp. 1009–1020). Cambridge: MIT Press.

Smith, E. E., & Jonides, J. (1999). Storage and executive processes in the frontal lobes. *Science, 283,* 1657–1661.

Smith, E. E., Jonides, J., & Koeppe, R. A. (1996). Dissociating verbal and spatial working memory using PET. *Cerebral Cortex, 6,* 11–20.

Smith, E. E., Jonides, J., Koeppe, R. A., Awh, E., Schumacher, E. H., & Minoshima, S. (1995). Spatial versus object working memory: PET investigations. *Journal of Cognitive Neuroscience, 7,* 337–356.

Solomon, R. C. (2003). *What is an emotion? Classic and contemporary readings.* New York, NY: Oxford University Press.

Sperling, G. (1960). The information available in brief visual presentations. *Psychological Monographs, 74*(Whole No. 48), 1–29.

Sperling, G. (1963). A model for visual memory tasks. *Human Factors, 5,* 9–31.

Sperry, R. W. (1985). The dual brain: Hemispheric specialization in humans. In D. F. Benson & E. Zaidel (Eds.), *UCLA forum in medical sciences* (Vol. 26, pp. 11–26). New York, NY: Guilford Press.

Spivey, M. (2007). *The continuity of mind.* Oxford, England: Oxford University Press.

Steiner, J. E. (1979). Human facial expressions in response to taste and smell stimulation. *Advances in Child Development and Behavior, 13,* 257–295.

Sternberg, S. (1966). High-speed scanning in human memory. *Science, 153,* 652–654.

Stillings, N. A., Weisler, S. W., Chase, C. H., Feinstein, M. H., Garfield, J. L., & Rissland, E. L. (1995). *Cognitive science: An introduction* (2nd ed.). Cambridge: MIT Press.

Strogatz, S. (2003). *Sync: How order emerges from chaos in the universe, nature, and daily life.* New York, NY: Hyperion.

Stuss, D. T., & Benson, D. F. (1986). *The frontal lobes.* New York, NY: Raven Press.

Sutton, R. (1991). *Sunk costs and market structure: Price competition, advertising, and the evolution of concentration.* Cambridge: MIT Press.

Swinney, D., Zurif, E. B., Prather, P., & Love, T. (1996). Neurological distribution of processing resources underlying language comprehension. *Journal of Cognitive Neuroscience, 8*(2), 174–184.

Talarico, J., & Rubin, D. C. (2003). Confidence, not consistency, characterizes flashbulb memories. *Psychological Science, 14,* 455–461.

Tang, Y.-P., Shimizu, E., Dube, G. R., Rampon, C., Kerchner, G. A., Zhuo, M., . . . Tsien, J. Z. (1999). Genetic enhancement of learning and memory in mice. *Nature, 401,* 63–69.

Tang-Schomer, M. D., White, J. D., Tien, L. W., Schmitt, L. I., Valentin, T. M., Graziano, D. J., . . . Kaplan, D. L. (2014). Bioengineered functional brain-like cortical tissue. *Proceedings of the National Academy of Sciences USA, 111,* 13811–13816.

Terrace, H. S., Petitto, L. A., Sanders, R. J., & Bever, T. G. (1979). Can an ape create a sentence? *Science, 206*(4421), 891–902.

Thagard, P. (2000). *Mind: Introduction to cognitive science.* Cambridge: MIT Press.

Thagard, P. (2008). *Hot thought: Mechanisms and applications of emotional cognition.* Cambridge: MIT Press.

Thelen, E., & Smith, L. B. (1994). *A dynamic systems approach to the development of cognition and action.* Cambridge: MIT Press.

Thomas, L. E., & Irwin, D. E. (2006). Voluntary eyeblinks disrupt iconic memory. *Perception & Psychophysics, 68*(3), 475–488.

Tillfors, M., Furmark, T., Marteinsdottir, I., Fischer, H., Pissiota, A., Långström, B., & Fredrikson, M. (2001). Cerebral blood flow in subject with social phobia during stressful speaking tasks: A PET study. *American Journal of Psychiatry, 158*(8), 1220–1226.

Titchener, E. B. (1896). *An outline of psychology.* New York, NY: Macmillan.

Tocco, G., Maren, S., Shors, T. J., Baudry, M., & Thompson, R. F. (1992). Long-term potentiation is associated with increased [3H] AMPA binding in rat hippocampus. *Brain Research, 573,* 228–234.

Tomasello, M., & Carpenter, M. (2005). The emergence of social cognition in three young chimpanzees. *Monographs of the Society for Research in Child Development, 70*(1, Serial No. 279).

Tomasello, M., Carpenter, M., Call, J., Behne, T., & Moll, H. (2005). Understanding and sharing intention: The origins of cultural cognition. *Behavioral and Brain Sciences, 28,* 675–735.

Tomkins, S. S. (1963). *Affect, imagery, and consciousness: The negative affects* (Vol. 2). New York, NY: Springer.

Tong, F., Nakayama, K., Vaughn, J. T., & Kanwisher, N. (1998). Binocular rivalry and visual awareness in human extrastriate cortex. *Neuron, 21,* 753–759.

Tracy, J. L., & Robins, R. W. (2004). Show your pride: Evidence for a discrete emotion expression. *Psychological Science, 15*(3), 194–197.

Traut-Mattausch, E., Schulz-Hardt, S., Greitemeyer, T., & Frey, D. (2004). Expectancy confirmation in spite of disconfirming evidence: The case of price increases due to the introduction of the Euro. *European Journal of Social Psychology, 34,* 739–760.

Treisman, A. (1964). Monitoring and storage of irrelevant messages in selective attention. *Journal of Verbal Learning and Verbal Behavior, 3,* 449–459.

Treisman, A., & Gelade, G. (1980). A feature integration theory of attention. *Cognitive Psychology, 12,* 97–136.

Tsien, J. Z., Huerta, P. T., & Tonegawa, S. (1996). The essential role of hippocampal CA1 NMDA receptor-dependent synaptic plasticity in spatial memory. *Cell, 87,* 1327–1338.

Turing, A. M. (1950). Computing machinery and intelligence. *Mind, 59*(236), 433–460.

Tversky, A., & Kahneman, D. (1973, September). Availability: A heuristic for judging frequency and probability. *Cognitive Psychology, 5*(2), 207–232.

Tversky, A., & Kahneman, D. (1974). Judgment under uncertainty: Heuristics and biases. *Science, 185,* 1124–1131.

Tversky, A., & Kahneman, D. (1981). The framing of decision and the psychology of choice. *Science, 211,* 453–458.

Tyler, L. K. (1992). *Spoken language comprehension: An experimental approach to disordered and normal processing.* Cambridge: MIT Press.

Ungerleider, L. G., & Mishkin, M. (1982). Two cortical visual systems. In D. J. Ingle, M. A. Goodale, & R. J. W. Mansfield (Eds.), *Analysis of visual behavior* (pp. 549–586). Cambridge: MIT Press.

Vallone, R. P., Ross, L. D., & Lepper, M. R. (1985). The hostile media phenomenon: Biased perception and perceptions of media bias in coverage of the Beirut massacre. *Journal of Personality and Social Psychology, 49,* 577–585.

Van Leeuwen, C., Steyvers, M., & Nooter, M. (1997). Stability and intermittency in large-scale coupled oscillator models for perceptual segmentation. *Journal of Mathematical Psychology, 41,* 319–344.

Vanier, M., & Caplan, D. (1990). CT-scan correlates of agrammatism. In L. Menn & L. Obler (Eds.), *Agrammatic aphasia: A cross-linguistic narrative sourcebook* (pp. 37–114). Amsterdam, Netherlands: John Benjamins.

Vargha-Khadem, F., Gadian, D. G., Watkins, K. E., Connelly, A., Van Paesschen, W., &

Mishkin, W. (1997). Differential effects of early hippocampal pathology on episodic and semantic memory. *Science, 277,* 376–380.

Von der Emde, G., Schwarz, S., Gomez, L., Budelli, R., & Grant, K. (1998). Electric fish measure distance in the dark. *Nature, 395,* 890–894.

Von der Malsburg, C. (1981). *The correlation theory of brain function* (Internal Report 81-2). Gottingen, Germany: Max-Planck-Institute for Biophysical Chemistry. (Reprinted 1994)

Von Fersen, L., Wynne, C. D. L., Delius, J. D., & Staddon, J. E. R. (1991). Transitive inference formation in pigeons. *Journal of Experimental Psychology: Animal Behavior Processes, 17,* 334–341.

Vouloumanos, A., & Werker, J. F. (2004). Tuned to the signal: The privileged status of speech for young infants. *Developmental Science, 7,* 270–276.

Vuilleumier, P. (2005). How brains beware: Neural mechanisms of emotional attention. *Trends in Cognitive Sciences, 9,* 585–594.

Vuilleumier, P., & Schwartz, S. (2001). Emotional facial expressions capture attention. *Neurology, 56*(2), 153–158.

Wachsmuth, E., Oram, M. W., & Perrett, D. I. (1994). Recognition of objects and their component parts: Responses of single units in the temporal cortex of the macaque. *Cerebral Cortex, 4,* 509–522.

Wallas, E. (1926). *The art of thought.* New York, NY: Harcourt Brace.

Wallraff, H. G. (1980). Olfaction and homing pigeons: Nerve-section experiments, critique, hypotheses. *Journal of Comparative Physiology, 139,* 209–224.

Walsh, V., & Pascual-Leone, A. (2005). *Transcranial magnetic stimulation: A neurochronometrics of mind.* Cambridge: MIT Press.

Warren, R. M., & Warren, R. P. (1970). Auditory illusions and confusions. *Scientific American, 223*(6), 30–36.

Wasserman, E. A., & Zentall, T. R. (2006). *Comparative cognition.* Oxford, England: Oxford University Press.

Watts, D. J. (2003). *Six degrees: The science of a connected age.* New York, NY: W. W. Norton.

Watts, D. J., & Strogatz, S. H. (1998). Collective dynamics of "small-world" networks. *Nature, 393,* 440–442.

Weinberg, J., Nichols, S. & Stich, S. (2001). Normative and epistemic intuitions. *Philosophical Topics, 29,* 429–460.

Weizenbaum, H. (1976). *Computer power and human reason.* San Francisco, CA: W. H. Freeman.

Wender, P. H., Wolf, L. E., & Wasserstein, J. (2001). Adults with ADHD: An overview. *Annals of the New York Academy of Sciences, 931,* 1–16.

Wertheimer, M. (1923). Untersuchungen zur Lehre von der Gestalt. *Psychologische Forschung, 4,* 301–350.

Westen, D. (1996). *Psychology: Mind, brain, and culture.* New York, NY: Wiley.

Whorf, B. L. (1956). *Language, thought, and reality: Selected writings.* Cambridge: Technology Press of MIT.

Wickens, D. D. (1972). Characteristics of word encoding. In W. W. Melton & E. Martin (Eds.), *Coding processes in human memory* (pp. 191–215). New York, NY: Winston.

Wicker, B., Keysers, C., Plailly, J., Royet, J. P., Gallese, V., & Rizzolatti, G. (2003). Both of us disgusted in my insula: The common neural basis of seeing and feeling disgust. *Neuron, 40,* 655–664.

Williamson, T. (2008). *The philosophy of philosophy.* Wiley-Blackwell.

Willingham, D. T., & Dunn, E. W. (2003). What neuroimaging and brain localization can do, cannot do, and should not do for social psychology. *Journal of Personality and Social Psychology, 85,* 662–671.

Willis, J., & Todorov, A. (2006). First impressions: Making up your mind after 100 ms exposure to a face. *Psychological Science, 17,* 592–598.

Wilson, E. O. (1999). *Consilience: The unity of knowledge.* New York, NY: Random House.

Wilson, F. A., O'Scalaidhe, S. P., & Goldman-Rakic, P. S. (1993). Dissociation of object and spatial processing domains in primate prefrontal cortex. *Science, 260,* 1955–1958.

Wilson, S. W. (1985). Knowledge growth in an artificial animal. In *Proceedings of the first international conference on genetic algorithms and their applications* (pp. 16–23). Hillsdale, NJ: Erlbaum.

Wilson, T. D., Lindsey, S., & Schooler, T. Y. (2000). A model of dual attitudes. *Psychological Review, 107,* 101–126.

Wiltschko, R. (1996). The function of olfactory input in pigeon orientation: Does it provide navigational information or play another role? *Journal of Experimental Biology, 199,* 113–119.

Wimmer, H., & Perner, J. (1983). Beliefs about beliefs: Representation and constraining function of wrong beliefs in young children's understanding of deception. *Cognition, 13*(1), 103–128.

Windholz, G., & Lamal, P. A. (1985). Kohler's insight revisited. *Teaching of Psychology, 12,* 165–167.

Winner, E., Brownell, H., Happé, F., Blum, A., & Pincus, D. (1998). Distinguishing lies from jokes: Theory of mind deficits and discourse interpretation in right hemisphere brain-damaged patients. *Brain and Language, 62*(1), 89–106.

Wojciulik, E., & Kanwisher, N. (1999). The generality of parietal involvement in visual attention. *Neuron, 23,* 747–764.

Wood, N. L., & Cowan, J. (1995). The cocktail party phenomenon revisited: Attention and memory in the classic selective listening procedure of Cherry (1953). *Journal of Experimental Psychology: General, 124,* 243–262.

Wooldridge, M. (2000). *Reasoning about rational agents.* Cambridge: MIT Press.

Wynne, C. D. (2001). *Animal cognition: The mental lives of animals.* New York, NY: Palgrave Macmillan.

Yerkes, R. M., & Dodson, J. D. (1908). The relation of strength of stimulus to rapidity of habit formation. *Journal of Comparative Neurology and Psychology, 18,* 459–482.

Zadeh, L. A. (1965). Fuzzy sets and systems. In J. Fox (Ed.), *System theory* (pp. 29–39). Brooklyn, NY: Polytechnic Press.

Zangaladze, A., Epstein, C., Grafton, S., & Sathian, K. (1999). Involvement of visual cortex in tactile discrimination of orientation. *Nature, 401,* 587–590.

Zanna, M. P., & Olson, J. M. (1982). Individual differences in attitudinal relations. In M. P. Zanna, E. T. Higgins, & C. P. Herman (Eds.), *Consistency in social behavior: The Ontario Symposium* (Vol. 2, pp. 75–104). Hillsdale, NJ: Erlbaum.

Zatorre, R. J., Belin, P., & Penhune, V. B. (2002). Structure and function of auditory cortex: Music and speech. *Trends in Cognitive Sciences, 6,* 37–46.

Zhang, S., & Schmitt, B. (1998). Language-dependent classification: The mental representation of classifiers in cognition, memory, and ad evaluations. *Journal of Experimental Psychology: Applied, 4*(4), 375–385.

Zingg, B., Hintiryan, H., Gou, L., Song, M. Y., Bay, M., Bienkowski, M. S., . . . Dong, H.-W. (2014, February 5). Neural networks of the mouse neocortex. *Cell, 156*(5), 857–859.

Name Index

SUBJECT INDEX